ANXIOUS DECADES

ANXIOUS DECADES

America in Prosperity and
Depression

1920 ⌁ 1941

MICHAEL E. PARRISH

W·W·NORTON & COMPANY·NEW YORK·LONDON

First published as a Norton paperback 1994

The text of this book is composed in Linotype Walbaum with the display set in
Walbaum.
Composition and manufacturing by The Maple-Vail Book Manufacturing Group.

Library of Congress Cataloging-in-Publication Data
Parrish, Michael E.
Anxious decades: America in prosperity and depression, 1920–1941
 / Michael E. Parrish.
p.   cm.
Includes bibliographical references and index.
1. United States—History—1919–1933.   2. United States—
History—1933–1945.   3. Depressions—1929—United States.   4. New
Deal, 1933–1939.   I. Title.
E784.P37   1992
973.91—dc20   92-3735

ISBN 0-393-31134-1

W. W. Norton & Company, Inc.
500 Fifth Avenue, New York, N.Y. 10110
www.wwnorton.com

W. W. Norton & Company Ltd.
Castle House, 75/76 Wells Street, London W1T 3QT

        7 8 9 0

for Scott and Stephanie

Contents

Introduction

From historians to poets, opinions abound concerning when to date the beginning of the modern era, that moment in time when many of the institutions, ideas, preoccupations, and problems of our own age first took shape. For American historians, it is possible to point to the Civil War and Reconstruction years that saw the destruction of slavery, propelled the country toward a future of industrialization and large cities, and forced it to confront seriously its heritage of racial oppression. Others single out the war with Spain in 1898 or the days of World War I, when America's destiny became indissolubly linked to events happening far away in Europe and Asia.

The novelist Virginia Woolf said that "in or about December 1910, human character changed." She picked the date of the famous Postimpressionist exhibition in London. According to Willa Cather, "the world broke in two in 1922 or thereabouts," the year which saw the publication of T. S. Eliot's poem *The Waste Land*, James Joyce's novel *Ulysses*, and Ludwig Wittgenstein's philosophical masterwork the *Tractatus Logico-philosophicus*. Gertrude Stein also opted for a date following World War I. After that catastrophic event, she declared, "we had the twentieth century."

While persuasive arguments can be made for all these choices, there are also good reasons to focus upon the years covered by this volume when looking back from the last decade of the twentieth century for the sources of our contemporary world. Hardly a dimension of that world, from the institutions of popular culture to those of government, does not trace its roots to this era of talking motion pictures, nationwide radio networks, the mass ownership of automobiles, the spread of chain stores, the first battle for an equal rights amendment, and the dominating political influence of Franklin D. Roosevelt, who was called

by more than one American "the commander in chief of my generation."

In these years, Americans had to cope both with unprecedented economic prosperity and the worst depression in their history. Which condition produced the greater collective anxiety remains an open question.
The decades between our two great wars saw the maturation and temporary collapse of a full-blown, consumer-oriented economy that profoundly affected the physical welfare and moral sensibilities of men,
women, and children from all walks of life in every region of the United
States. Both the new affluence of the 1920s and the deprivations of the
1930s left no facet of American society—productive relations, race
relations, or gender relations—untouched.

We began to experience in these years the virtues and vices of a consumer society, in which the production, marketing, and individual
accumulation of a seemingly endless stream of goods and services
threatened to become for many the chief preoccupation of daily life, a
virtual secular religion. And although the roots of consumerism reached
back to the creation of a continental market and the rise of big business
in the last third of the nineteenth century, the years after World War I
witnessed its ultimate triumph with wide ownership of automobiles
and other consumer durable goods, the spread of installment credit
plans, extensive use of national advertising, and the persuasive powers
of radio and motion pictures.

In their first sustained experience with consumer culture, Americans
learned the truth of the ancient poet Juvenal's observation that "luxury
is more ruthless than war." A consumer society that sanctioned perpetual technological change, the generation of new fashions and desires,
and the ultimate sovereignty of the market did not respect inherited
values or the social status quo. It produced as much social conflict as
consensus. Traditional American cultures, anchored to particular ethnic communities, religious traditions, and geographic places, faced
absorption or dilution in a sea of standardized products and homoge-
nized attitudes spread by manufacturers, advertisers, the airwaves, and
the silver screen. The nationalizing influence of the Civil War or World
War I seemed insignificant when compared to the cultural integration
(some said degeneration) produced by the Model T Ford, A&P grocery
stores, Twentieth Century–Fox, and WXYZ's weekly *Lone Ranger*.

A consumer culture that condoned hedonism and challenged even
the primacy of the work ethic heightened for many the old questions
about personal identity and spiritual integrity in a society where the
market appeared to structure and dominate human relationships. Did

individual consumption constitute both the means and ends of existence? A consumer culture that daily put affluence on display in magazines, radio, and motion pictures also raised to a new level of intensity old questions about economic equality and fairness, both staples of American political debate since the eighteenth century.

The American people had to decide during these years what would be the relationship of the state, particularly the federal government in Washington, to their new consumer-oriented economy. Would the state remain a mere umpire of private bargains struck in the marketplace? Should it seek to foment greater economic activity by providing incentives such as tax breaks, easy credit, and subsidies? Did it have both a moral and practical interest in the ultimate distribution of economic rewards and final responsibility for guaranteeing a minimum level of consumption to all citizens? Under Harding and Coolidge, the nation opted for a minimalist state that monitored the economic game with a light hand and largely ignored issues of distribution. The collapse of prosperity forced Hoover, Roosevelt, and the nation to rethink these fundamental questions and conceive new solutions.

A consumer-oriented economy, staffed increasingly by blue-collar and white-collar employees, transformed decisively the meaning of opportunity and success in American society, which for generations had stressed the importance of independent proprietorship. Most late-nineteenth- and early-twentieth-century reformers from the Populists to Woodrow Wilson had put the fight against monopoly and the restoration of competition at the top of their political agendas. They envisioned America as basically a nation of producers, each battling for a share of the market. Between the wars and especially when prosperity collapsed after 1929, the debate about opportunity in America shifted to questions of consumption and the restoration of purchasing power. FDR's New Deal was the first American reform movement shaped largely by the consumer culture.

Try as they might during these years, Americans could not escape from the problems of a larger world they increasingly influenced by their economic power and example. In the wake of the most devastating general war in a century, a war in which American intervention had tipped the military balance decisively against Germany, how should the United States now relate to other nations, especially those in Europe, Latin America, and Asia?

Memories of the European bloodbath shadowed virtually every decision made by American leaders abroad after 1920. Had World War I been simply a horrible diplomatic blunder, a gigantic aberration of

human nature unlikely to be repeated? Or, on the contrary, was that
conflict the ghastly opening act of a much longer and even more violent drama about the restructuring of international relations throughout the world? Americans reached no consensus on this issue even as
bombs fell at Pearl Harbor. If the first, then perhaps intervention in
1917 had been a terrible error and the United States Senate had been
correct to reject the Versailles Treaty and American membership in the
League of Nations, which threatened to involve the country perpetu-
ally in foreign conflicts. If the second, then sooner or later one of the
largest and richest nations on earth could not escape from the world's
turmoil while it profited from its trade and resources.

Many of the political and moral dilemmas that Americans faced in
these years resemble ones they still confront today. How does one find
personal meaning in a consumer society? What is the nature of community? Can government both promote economic growth and guarantee economic justice? What should be our role in the world? What
follows is an effort to understand how Americans of an earlier generation answered these fundamental questions and why they answered
them the way they did.

Acknowledgments

Anyone who writes a work of broad historical interpretation accumulates along the way a considerable intellectual debt to many people. At the threshold, I wish to thank the many scholars whose books and articles are noted all too briefly in the bibliographical comments at the end of this book. It is impossible to pay them proper tribute. But without their imagination and hard work, I could not have attempted this volume.

John Blum and Edwin Barber first suggested that I participate in the Norton series on twentieth-century America. To them I therefore owe the ensuing years of frustration and creative joy. John remains a source of both inspiration and discouragement to his former students and all who labor to make sense out of modern America. We shall never know as much as he does about these matters; and we shall never write about them with such eloquence. Ed is a peerless editor, whose skill with the pen is matched only by his patience with authors who miss deadlines and still nag him for more money.

A number of my colleagues at the University of California, San Diego, shared their rich knowledge and insight into a number of the issues discussed in this volume. I thank especially Michael Bernstein, Stephanie McCurry, Steve Hahn, and John Galbraith.

Alan Brinkley, Nelson Lichtenstein, and David Kennedy read the entire manuscript, offered valuable suggestions, and spared me from the embarrassment of many errors. This would have been a better book had I the energy and wit to incorporate all the sound advice they offered. As it stands, they are absolved from the remaining defects of interpretation and organization.

I owe special thanks to Robin Mendelson, Ted Johnson, and Amy Loyd for unstinting editorial assistance, and to Ruth Mandel for her wise choice of many photographs and cartoons.

Finally, I thank Susan, who suffered through the author's many moments of mental distraction with unfailing good cheer and encouragement.

San Diego, California
1991

PART ONE

1

Republican Restoration

> *Of the vaguer assumptions, liberty and the love of human-*
> *ity remain in the cocked hat where they landed between*
> *1914 and 1919. No one believes that these apotheoses are*
> *final, or even important. They are convenient and melo-*
> *dramatic excuses for not bothering anymore about knowl-*
> *edge, politics, economics, and good works.*
> —Gilbert Seldes in the *New Republic*

> *The only man, woman or child*
> *who wrote a simple declarative sentence*
> *with seven grammatical errors.*
> —e. e. cummings on Warren G. Harding

WILSON AND THE PROGRESSIVE LEGACY

Americans have elected a new president every four years since 1789. In this quadrennial ritual of national politics, they make a statement about themselves—define who they think they are and what they hope to become. In the fall of 1920, sixteen million Americans, slightly more than 60 percent of those who went to the polls, voted for Warren Gamaliel Harding, a dapper, silver-haired United States senator from Ohio. In terms of the popular vote, Harding's margin of victory over his Democratic opponent, his fellow Ohioan Governor James N. Cox, was the most decisive since Theodore Roosevelt's in 1904. In choosing Harding, however, millions of Americans rejected both the tone and substance of the political movement Roosevelt had galvanized two decades earlier. They declared themselves weary of crusades and of charismatic leaders who constantly demanded that they live a political life of great deeds and heroic sacrifice at home and abroad.

Harding's election rang down the curtain on the progressive movement. That extraordinary burst of late-nineteenth-century Protestant evangelism saw millions of middle-class citizens take up the cause of social regeneration under the leadership of Roosevelt, Woodrow Wilson, Robert La Follette, Hiram Johnson, Jane Addams, Frances Willard, and others. These progressives stood often, as TR declared in 1912, "at Armageddon and we battle for the Lord." Infusing each campaign against the political, economic, and social disruptions of post–Civil War America with a moral stridency, they laced their speeches and writings with words such as "sinful," "wicked," "obligation," and "duty." As their predecessors had summoned the nation to eradicate the curse of slavery, so turn-of-the-century progressives urged all right-thinking citizens to fight against predatory monopolies, foul tenements, corrupt political organizations, intemperance, and child labor. Wilson, called the Protestant Pope, Archangel Woodrow, and a "bombastic pedagogue" by those who disliked his political sermonizing, roused the progressives to their final and most idealistic crusade—to fight "the war to end all wars," one that would create "a universal dominion of right . . . as shall bring peace and safety to all nations and make the world itself at last free."

Given the perfectionist rhetoric employed during most progressive campaigns, it is not surprising that what these reformers actually achieved proved ambiguous, contradictory, often disappointing. A few trusts were busted, but a smaller number of giant companies continued to dominate the principal sectors of the American economy in 1917. The war accelerated this trend toward economic concentration. By statute and the pressure of organized labor, the hours of daily toil were reduced for many workers, but legal barriers continued to block the right to unionize, minimum wage legislation, and attempts to abolish child labor. Progressive political innovations—the referendum, initiative, and primary election—were intended to curb the power of party bosses and machines but increased the influence of wealth and the mass media in campaigns. Progressives fashioned the modern regulatory state, designed through administrative agencies to protect the public from tainted food and drugs, unfair utility rates, and the sharp practices of businessmen. So doing, they endowed a new class of bureaucrats and highly organized interest groups with unusual control over the nation's economic welfare, while diminishing the participation and influence of average citizens.

Abroad, progressives also left a mixed legacy of high ideals, opportunism, and exploitation. Isolationism, long the rhetorical cornerstone of the nation's foreign relations, gained new recruits in the face of Europe's carnage, while for a smaller number the war confirmed the futility of such a policy. Even before 1914, many progressives who encouraged the use of the state to ameliorate domestic social conditions seldom hesitated to project American power abroad, especially when confronting weaker adversaries. As he helped to dismember the Colombian nation in order to build a canal in Central America, Roosevelt invoked honor, patriotism, and progress. President Taft claimed to be defending property rights and restoring order when he sent a "legation guard" of Marines to Nicaragua in 1912 to secure the regime of Adolfo Díaz. Wilson, appalled by the murderous course of the revolution south of the Rio Grande, announced that he would "teach the Mexicans to elect good men" as he dispatched troops to Veracruz. But changing the course of history in Cuba, Colombia, or Nicaragua proved somewhat easier than in Mexico or, a few years later, Western Europe.

America's experience during the Great War continued to reflect these contradictions by both fulfilling and defeating progressive goals. War temporarily brought government protection to union members in key industries. For women it hastened the right to vote. From Wilson came a perfect progressive blueprint for reconstructing the postwar world. As the Federal Reserve Board or the Federal Trade Commission managed the conflicts of domestic economic competition, so would the League of Nations adjust competition among the nations of the earth.

But nineteen months of frantic economic and ideological mobilization during the war also generated a steep rise in the cost of living, new income tax burdens on the middle class and corporations, and a far-reaching campaign by the federal government to forge a patriotic consensus through propaganda, censorship, and prison terms for dissenters. "Woe be to the man or group of men that seeks to stand in our way in this day of high resolution," declared the president. A draconian Sedition Act, passed by Congress in 1918, made it a crime to speak or print "any disloyal, profane, scurrilous or abusive language" about America's form of government, Constitution, or flag. In the struggle to make the world itself at last free, Wilson's Justice Department secured indictments against antiwar protesters who declared that "I am for the people and the government is for the profiteers" or who dared to suggest that "men conscripted to Europe are virtually condemned to death and everyone knows it."

There followed a strange interlude, two years of "peace" and "readjustment" between the Armistice of 1918 and Harding's election. The country suffered unusual political turmoil, economic disruption, and

social disorder. Once again, the blame fell on Wilson and the Democrats, and by implication on anything or anyone associated with progressivism or the war. The president was now a pale shadow of the
vibrant leader who had entered the White House in 1913. Felled politically by the off-year elections that returned Republican majorities to
Congress, he had also been weakened both physically and mentally by
two strokes. Declaring at one moment that the Russian people should
decide their own destiny, at the next he dispatched fourteen thousand
American soldiers to Siberia, where they kept an eye on the Japanese
and ultimately fought against the Bolsheviks. Bedridden and irascible,
Wilson in 1919–20 all but abdicated control of the executive branch to
subordinates who were either too ambitious or too timid. Unfortunately, he continued to direct personally the struggle to ratify the Versailles Treaty, and with it American membership in the League of
Nations.

For many Americans and their political representatives in Congress,
both that treaty and the League had become potent symbols of all the
country's woes, especially its enthrallment to distant, alien forces. "Shall
we entangle and embarrass the efforts of a powerful and independent
people," asked Senator William Borah of Idaho, ". . . or shall we yoke
our deliberations to forces we cannot control and leave our people to
the mercy of powers which may be wholly at variance with our conception of duty?" Those political leaders who supported the treaty or the
League of Nations nonetheless despised the architect of both. Wilson's
opponents, noted former secretary of state Robert Lansing, "are simply
saturated with hatred of the man rather than the treaty. It is something
like the feeling against Andrew Jackson." Wilson lacked the votes to
push the treaty through the Senate unmodified. Yet he remained stubborn enough to kill his own progeny when opponents refused to ratify
without concessions. And while president and Congress remained tied
in knots over this issue, other important postwar policies unraveled.
The Army released soldiers indiscriminately into a slack labor market.
Government controls came off business, labor, and agriculture. Prices
shot up briefly, then plummeted along with wages into a deep recession that stirred social conflict.

From Seattle to Boston, four million Americans marched on picket
lines in 1919. Even Boston's policemen, symbols of law and order,
joined shipyard workers, meat-packers, and steelworkers from across
the country to protest wage cuts, discrimination against union members, and layoffs. Many confrontations turned violent once employers
secured court injunctions, hired strikebreakers, and demanded protec-

tion from state or federal troops. Rejecting the recommendation of a citizen's committee that favored arbitration, Governor Calvin Coolidge of Massachusetts endorsed the firing of striking policemen and backed up his decision with the state guard. Declaring that "there is no right to strike against the public safety by anybody, anywhere, anytime," Coolidge became an instant hero to millions of frightened citizens. Even President Wilson sent congratulations "to the man who defied Bolshevism and won."

On Wall Street, an anarchist's bomb killed thirty-eight people. Swollen with discharged veterans and unemployed workers both black and white, cities such as Chicago and St. Louis erupted into violence between the races, struggles there left hundreds dead or injured and thousands without shelter. In Chicago alone the reign of terror against black residents and their property lasted thirteen days, despite the presence of state militia. Attempts at controlling these disturbances and explaining their causes were led by Attorney General A. Mitchell Palmer and J. Edgar Hoover, the aggressive new chief of the Justice Department's Bureau of Investigation. They fueled a hysterical press by blaming the disorders on communist agents and propaganda from Lenin and the Bolsheviks. The federal government arrested thousands of alleged subversives in 1919–20 and eventually deported more than five hundred of them. "Wherein do the police of the New England metropolis differ from the mad minority which overthrew Kerensky and ruined Russia?" asked the Philadelphia *Evening Public Ledger.* To the misery Americans inflicted upon each other in 1919–20, nature added more: an outbreak of Spanish influenza left several hundred thousand dead, a figure greater than the nation's battlefield losses in the Great War.

HARDING AND "NORMALCY"

By the fall of 1920, a huge bloc of American voters, many of whom had supported Wilson in 1912 and 1916, had had enough—they longed for stability and order. They were tired of war and wrangling about peace; weary of sacrifice; fearful of radicalism and frightened by class and racial strife. Above all, they wanted to be left alone—by their own government, by foreign nations, by striking workers. For a generation, they had been urged by the prophets of reform to change the world and help others. In 1920 they were terrified of more change and most eager to help themselves.

These feelings ran deep among members of the educated profes-

sional classes, a key part of the progressive coalition, who now resented
wartime taxes and feared the violence associated with striking workers
and political radicals. Union members, courted by progressives during
the war, felt betrayed by their former patrons, who greeted strikes not
with sympathy but with injunctions and soldiers. Ethnic Americans,
especially the Irish, Germans, Italians, and Eastern Europeans, nursed
assorted grievances against Wilson and the peace settlement he had
helped to negotiate. They regarded it as too pro-British, too anti-Ger-
man, or not sufficiently favorable to the interests of Serbs, Poles, or
Italians. While it is probably true that virtually any Republican (save
perhaps a military leader identified with the war) could have defeated
the Democratic ticket in 1920, Harding proved especially strong precisely because he was not identified with any of the grand progressive
designs to make over America or the world.

Warren Harding was a joiner, not a prophet or a crusader. During
his long career in public life, first as a newspaper editor in Marion,
Ohio, and later in the state legislature and United States Senate, he
rarely staked his reputation or future on the promotion of a controversial issue. He bore a striking resemblance to Sinclair Lewis's fictional
real estate salesman of 1922, George Babbitt. Like Babbitt, Warren
Harding always tried to fit in. He was a swell guy. At the Elks Lodge
or Rotary Club in Marion, the state capitol in Columbus, or the Senate
cloakroom in Washington, Harding spent his time cultivating friendships, not making enemies. He had slapped many a back, played innumerable games of stud poker, and hoisted his share of cocktails. Along
the way, he had not written a single piece of important legislation,
been hanged in effigy, or been raked by opponents on either the left or
right of the political spectrum. He was handsome, charming, convivial,
and given to the type of florid oratory—he called it "bloviating"—heard
throughout the Midwest on the Fourth of July.

Unlike other potential Republican presidential candidates in 1920—
Hiram Johnson, General Leonard Wood, Governor Frank Lowden of
Illinois, or Senator Robert La Follette—Harding had not committed
himself on the issue of reviving the defeated Versailles Treaty and the
League of Nations; his views on this were as hazily defined as on most
public controversies. Aware of the candidate's garrulousness, Senator
Boise Penrose of Pennsylvania advised Harding's managers: "Keep
Warren at home. Don't let him make any speeches. If he goes out on
a tour, somebody's sure to ask him questions, and Warren's just the
sort of damn fool to try to answer them." Since both members of the
Democratic ticket, Cox and Assistant Secretary of the Navy Franklin

President Warren G. Harding (left) and Vice President Calvin Coolidge.

Roosevelt, clearly supported American membership in the League, Harding stood to gain votes simply by remaining mute. In fact, he made more than a dozen pronouncements about the League from his front porch in Marion during the campaign, but these only darkened the mystery. Finally, savoring his victory on election night, he told a crowd of supporters that American membership in the League was a dead issue. In a rare appearance outside Marion, he forever entered the nation's political folklore when he told a Boston audience that "America's present need is not heroics but healing; not nostrums but normalcy." By "normalcy," he told reporters later, he did not mean reaction or the old order, "but a regular steady order of things. I mean normal procedures, the natural way, without excess."

Most Americans, like the new president, regarded the ordeal of war and reconversion through which the country had passed as unnatural, a terrible aberration. But maintaining "a regular steady order of things" in a dynamic, market-oriented society such as the United States seemed almost a contradiction in terms. Women now voted, while others practiced law or flew airplanes. The vast experiment of prohibition had begun to modify people's drinking habits. The automobile transformed the nation's physical and social landscape. Advertising, radio, and motion pictures were likewise rearranging the landscape of the mind by creating a new world of fantasy and desires to be satisfied through consumption and self-indulgence. While some American values remained fixed or moved at a glacierlike pace after 1920, others, especially those shaped by new technology and the economy, surged forward without much respect for tradition or a presidential candidate's aphorisms.

During the almost three and a half years of his presidency, Warren Harding enjoyed the affection of the American people. And when he died suddenly in San Francisco on August 2, 1923, their shock and grief were genuine. Harding has fared less well, however, in the hands of historians, especially those who equate excellence in presidential leadership with a certain degree of intellectual sophistication, vigorous administration of the affairs of the executive branch, and a commitment to government policies that help the weak and restrain the powerful. On such criteria, Harding does not measure up to Jefferson, Lincoln, Wilson, or either Roosevelt. In the opinion of these critics, his presidency constituted a flat repudiation of the nation's best political ideals as those were embodied in the prewar progressive tradition. Some have suggested that he ranks at or near the bottom of all our presidents in that special purgatory reserved for the likes of Fillmore, Grant, and Arthur. "Save for the Washington arms conference and the creation of the Bureau of the Budget," declare the authors of one textbook, "Harding's administration was barren of accomplishment and tarnished by scandal." Others conclude that the president had "only average talents, no will power, and a striking inability to discriminate between right and wrong. . . . There is also strong evidence that [he] was adulterous." Considerable evidence supports these negative assessments, yet it should be noted that Harding had not secured the White House because his party or the electorate expected him to extend or perpetuate the progressive tradition. Even had he been so inclined, the Ohioan had no mandate to be a president in the mold of Roosevelt or Wilson or to complete their unfinished agenda of social reforms. Lacking TR's vision, Taft's tenacity, and Wilson's rhetorical skills, Harding earned a failing grade on the progressive report card. But even the most inspired and talented reformer would have faced daunting obstacles in the climate of disillusionment and apathy that spread over the country in the early twenties.

Harding had few intellectual pretensions. His chief diversions outside of politics consisted of poker, golf, highballs, and other men's wives. His speeches often lacked substance. William McAdoo, the former

Treasury secretary and leader of the Democratic Party, once described a Harding speech as "an army of pompous phrases moving over the landscape in search of an idea." The poet e. e. cummings observed that Harding was "The only man, woman or child / who wrote a simple declarative sentence / with seven grammatical errors." During the heated debate over tax reform in 1921 the president admitted, "I can't make a damn thing out of this tax problem. I listen to one side and they seem right, and then—God!—I talk to the other side, and they seem just as right." According to the influential journalist William Allen White, Harding confided to another friend, "My God, this is a hell of a place for a man like me to be!" Even so, Harding's historical reputation might have survived intellectual mediocrity, but not faithless subordinates.

"My Damn Friends"

Four years after Harding's death, a half-dozen members of the administration, including two cabinet officers, had been forced to resign and indicted for crimes ranging from defrauding the government to bribery and conspiracy. Charles Forbes, for example, director of the Veterans' Bureau, went to prison for accepting "loans" from a construction firm bidding on government contracts and for selling medical supplies to another friendly purchaser at ridiculously low prices. Forbes's chief legal adviser in the bureau, Charles Cramer, committed suicide before he could be charged with similar improprieties. Jess Smith, personal secretary to Attorney General Harry Daugherty, conspired with Thomas W. Miller, the custodian of alien property, to uphold the dubious claims of a German banking family to recover $7 billion in securities confiscated during the war. From the grateful Germans, Miller received $50,000 and Smith over $224,000 "for expediting the claim through [an] acquaintance in Washington." Smith killed himself when it was discovered that he had deposited $50,000 of the money in an Ohio bank account used jointly with Attorney General Daugherty. A jury convicted Miller, who served over a year in prison. The attorney general, fired by Coolidge after Harding's death, twice went to trial, but was found not guilty on both occasions.

The biggest scandal of all brought down the secretary of the interior, Albert Fall, whose lavish expenditures on his New Mexico ranch began to stir the curiosity of reporters and United States senators. They wanted to know how it was possible for a cabinet officer earning $12,000 a year to finance such improvements. They also wanted to know about

Fall's relationship with two buccaneers of the oil industry, Edward L. Doheney of the Pan American Petroleum Company and Harry F. Sinclair of the Continental Trading Company. Their companies had received valuable leases from Fall's department to drill for oil at Elk Hills in California and Teapot Dome in Wyoming, both federal petroleum reserves held in trust for the Navy. Through the tenacious investigation of Senator Thomas J. Walsh of Montana, the curious finally learned that Fall had placed extraordinary pressure on the Navy Department to transfer administration of the reserves to the Interior Department. Following execution of the leases, Doheney "loaned" Fall $100,000 in cash, delivered by the oilman's son to the secretary in a little black bag; Fall and his son-in-law had also received in excess of $200,000 in Liberty Bonds from the Continental Trading Company. In court, Fall claimed that he had always acted in the public interest to promote oil conservation and to safeguard the national interest by reducing the amount of petroleum drained from the reserves by adjacent operators. The jury believed otherwise. Convicted of taking a bribe, the former secretary was fined $100,000 and sentenced to a year in jail. Voiding the leases in a later civil case, the Supreme Court of the United States found them to be tainted with "fraud and corruption." A few months before his death, a harried Harding complained, "I have no trouble with my enemies. I can take care of my enemies all right. But my damn friends . . . my God-damn friends . . . they're the ones that keep me walking the floor nights."

Not since the years of Ulysses S. Grant had Washington been rocked by so many examples of easy virtue in the executive branch. Not until the presidencies of Richard Nixon and Ronald Reagan would high officials, including cabinet members, again face indictment and trial for breaking the nation's laws. Unlike President Nixon, named by a federal grand jury as an unindicted co-conspirator in the Watergate scandal, Harding did not encourage or condone these violations of public trust. Unlike the presidential advisers in Watergate or the Iran-Contra affair of the Reagan era, Harding's subordinates were motivated by simple greed, not a desire to destroy their political opponents or subvert the Constitution. At worst, Harding can be convicted of lax administration and of incredible naiveté in selecting people like Daugherty and Fall to run key departments. He was not the last occupant of the White House to suffer from the financial misdeeds of close friends. Harry Truman, Dwight Eisenhower, Lyndon Johnson, and Jimmy Carter made similar blunders and endured like political embarrassment as a result of misplaced personal loyalty. Combined with Harding's intellectual limitations and his sexual peccadilloes, however, the scandals have cast a long historical shadow by encouraging scholars to dismiss the administration as simply corrupt, mediocre, and reactionary. In truth, its record was somewhat more mixed.

"THE BEST MINDS" ABROAD: CHARLES EVANS HUGHES

Harding did not name to high office only crooks, political hacks, and intellectual lightweights. The president said that he would appoint "the best minds" to his regime. If those called to duty did not measure up to the standards of the first Washington administration, they were on the whole much superior to Woodrow Wilson's. As secretary of state, Harding tapped Charles Evans Hughes, the former governor of New York and associate justice of the Supreme Court. Hughes had built a lucrative legal practice servicing giant corporations, and his appointment dismayed many old progressives, but his record as New York's chief executive and on the bench had displayed much sympathy for social reform. No enemy of capitalism, Hughes did insist that business function with a modicum of social compassion and honesty. Utility companies and insurance firms had both benefited from his legal advice and suffered from his wrath when they ignored the interests of consumers and shareholders. On the nation's highest court, Hughes had voted to uphold maximum-hours laws, to curb the use of labor injunctions, to prohibit debt peonage, and to extend the reviewing authority of federal courts over state criminal trials. As Harding's expert on foreign affairs, he displayed boldness and tenacity in promoting the reorganization of the foreign service through the Rogers Act and in the immediate postwar negotiations to reduce naval armaments.

There are few better examples of the persistence of progressive thinking in the Harding era than the Rogers Act of 1924, regarded as the "basic charter of the modern diplomatic service." That law owed its existence to Hughes's belief that appointment and promotion in the foreign service should not be monopolized by what he called "young men of wealthy families who are willing and able to . . . pay their own way." Through the use of standardized written examinations, the Rogers Act sought to temper social class with a meritocracy. Himself an example of how far a bright young man from a modestly endowed family might travel, Hughes argued that brains, not wealth, should determine the distribution of diplomatic posts. "The notion that a wide-awake, average American can do anything is flattering to the American pride," he said, "but costs the Government dearly. . . . You cannot obtain the necessary technical equipment through mere general experience or by reading instructions. . . . It is a very shortsighted and foolish view which would confuse routine and expert knowledge."

The full impact of the Rogers Act on State Department personnel procedures would not be felt for several years, but under Hughes's masterful direction the Washington Conference of 1921–22 brought immediate benefits. One was the Five-Power Treaty, which froze the battleship and carrier strength of England, the United States, Japan, France, and Italy at immediate postwar levels. In his greatest feat of diplomacy, assisted by American code-breakers, Hughes persuaded the Japanese to accept less tonnage than the British or Americans over a twenty-year period and the French to accept the same ratios as the Italians. In addition to limiting naval armaments, the delegates at the Washington Conference signed a series of agreements in which they pledged to respect one another's interests in East Asia and to uphold the principles of the Open Door in China. The Japanese also vowed to remove their troops from Shantung, to give the United States cable rights on the island of Yap, and to cease their occupation of Soviet territory in Siberia and the island of Sakhalin. The Americans agreed in turn not to reinforce Guam.

At the Washington Conference Hughes clearly provided the energy and brains in the American delegation, but Harding made two important contributions to the success of the meeting: first, he named both Republicans and Democrats to the delegation; and second, he delivered a thoughtful speech before the Senate urging ratification. His bipartisan approach contrasted sharply with Wilson's handling of the Paris Peace Conference and made ratification of the naval treaty much easier in the Senate.

Some critics have condemned the Washington Conference as another instance of American naiveté, similar to the Kellog-Briand Party that outlawed war five years later. The naval treaty, they note, contained many loopholes that were not closed until too late in the 1930s. A general reduction of land forces did not follow. The Far Eastern agreements rested largely on the sufferance of the Japanese, who ignored them when it became expedient to do so. Hindsight is always superior to foresight, however. The Five-Power Treaty marked the first time in modern history that great nations agreed to curb their military arsenals. Harding and Hughes can hardly be blamed for the failed efforts of their successors or for not predicting how a worldwide economic collapse might influence geopolitical developments after 1929. America's sphere of influence in Asia, principally the Philippines, had always rested on Japan's acceptance of a U.S. presence. The agreements reached at the Washington Conference cannot be regarded as the greatest diplomatic victories in American history, but they rested on a careful calculation of the balance of power and largely ratified it. This was not a trifling achievement in the wake of the more grandiose and failed ambitions of the Wilson era.

The Harding-Hughes approach to foreign relations spurned internationalism in the Wilsonian sense of full-fledged membership in the League of Nations or support for collective security. But neither did it endorse isolationism. The American minister in Switzerland took pains to avoid the building in Geneva where the League met regularly, and the Department of State often ignored official communications from the international assembly, but on the eve of Harding's death U.S. representatives had begun to cooperate informally with the League's efforts to stem the trade in opium and arms. And to the chagrin of strict isolationists, Harding called on the Senate to endorse American membership on the League's World Court, also known as the Permanent Court of International Justice. Although the court's charter sharply limited its jurisdiction over all sovereign nations, a fearful Senate refused to ratify the protocol without embarrassing reservations that blocked America's membership.

The Harding administration supported efforts to defend American shores from an anticipated flood of foreign people and goods with immigration quotas and high tariffs, but it made little effort to curb the flow of U.S. capital and products into the four corners of the globe. Every Singer sewing machine sold in Argentina, every dollar invested by New York banks in German chemical plants or Peruvian railroads, however, spread American values and interests abroad, with the result of deepening the influence of the United States in foreign nations and linking its economic destiny to the fate of other regimes.

Perhaps the sharpest contrast between the behavior of the Harding administration and its progressive predecessors abroad came in the Western Hemisphere. When the Ohioan entered the White House in 1921, American troops remained stationed in Nicaragua, where Taft had sent them a decade earlier. The United States Navy ran affairs in Haiti and the Dominican Republic. Having failed through bluster and military force to stop the course of the Mexican Revolution, the United States still had not officially recognized the government in Mexico City. During the 1920 campaign, the Democrat's vice presidential candidate boasted that the United States could control the votes of over a half-

dozen Central American and Caribbean nations in the League of
Nations. "Until last week, I had two of these votes in my pocket,"
Franklin Roosevelt told one audience. "One of them was Haiti. I know,
for I wrote Haiti's Constitution myself, and if I do say it, I think it was
a pretty good little Constitution." Candidate Harding pointed out that
Roosevelt's exercise in constitution-writing had cost the loss of Haitian
and American lives "to establish laws drafted by the Assistant Secretary of the Navy, to secure a vote in the League."

Although U.S. troops did not depart from other countries in the
hemisphere until after his death, President Harding began slowly to
dismantle the crude interventionist policies that had clouded American
relations in Latin America from Theodore Roosevelt to Wilson. The
United States recognized the government of General Álvaro Obregón
in return for Mexico's pledge to compensate Americans whose property had been seized during the revolution. They established a joint
American-Mexican commission to arbitrate these claims. And in a
gesture that would have made Teddy Roosevelt furious, the administration persuaded the Senate to ratify a new treaty with Colombia that
included $25 million to indemnify that country for our participation in
the Panamanian revolt of 1903.

"THE BEST MINDS" AT HOME: MELLON, WALLACE, AND HOOVER

For the Treasury Department, Harding chose one of America's richest men, Andrew William Mellon, whose fortune rested on control of
the Pittsburgh National Bank, the Alcoa Aluminum Company, and the
Gulf Oil Corporation. Dark-suited, frail of body, and pale in complexion, Mellon resembled the village undertaker. His fondness for che-
roots and French Impressionist paintings constituted the extent of his
enthusiasm for social experiments, artistic or otherwise. Like most men
of his social background and economic influence, Mellon believed
devoutly that the health and security of the republic reposed in those
who managed the institutions of commerce, industry, and finance and
in the capacity of public officials to meet their needs. Low tax rates,
low interest rates, sound money, a balanced federal budget, and a minimum of government regulation—these were Mellon's definition of good
government.

Since the late nineteenth century, the federal income tax had been
a litmus test of political identification that often separated progressives

Andrew Mellon, secretary of the treasury.

from conservatives. But only the unprecedented fiscal demands of World War I made it a major instrument of government policy and brought its implications home to most Americans. In the landmark revenue laws of 1917 and 1918, the Democrat-controlled Congress attempted to finance about one-third of the war or $10 billion directly through taxation rather than borrowing. These laws cut the exemption for both married and single taxpayers and increased the normal income tax to 6 percent on all incomes up to $4,000 and to 12 percent on those above that figure. On the highest incomes, the maximum surtax hit 65 percent. Congress imposed an excess profits tax on corporations in an effort to recover some of the windfall from cost-plus government contracts. Congress also raised the estate tax to a maximum of 25 percent. The principal architect of these revenue laws, Congressman Claude Kitchen of North Carolina, was the son of a Populist and a devout believer in progressive taxation. By war's end, "Kitchenism" and high federal taxes had turned many middle-class voters against Wilson and the Democrats.

If Harding's pledge to restore "normalcy" meant anything, therefore, it meant relief from what most Americans regarded as the
unprecedented and burdensome taxes of the war years. In Andrew
Mellon the president had a cabinet member quite friendly to such a
policy. Mellon loathed progressive taxes generally. He regarded high
surcharges as a moral and economic abomination, because they penal-
ized those who were rich, discouraged enterprise, and held back economic growth. When the wealthy kept a larger portion of what they
produced, Mellon argued, the average worker and consumer would
benefit through reinvestment, higher productivity, more jobs, and lower
prices. His critics called it the "trickle-down" theory or feeding the
sparrows by stuffing the horses.

In 1921 the secretary presented to the House Ways and Means
Committee a package of tax reductions that totaled $800 million,
including abolition of wartime luxury taxes and the excess profits tax,
and a sharp cut in the maximum surtax on personal incomes to 33
percent. To sweeten the offer and secure the votes of Western and
Southern congressmen, Mellon recommended a modest increase in
the standard exemption for families, a new federal tax on luxury automobiles, and a 2 percent hike in the corporate income tax. Much to his
chagrin, Congress ratified these suggestions, but deferred action on
the excess profits tax, and trimmed the maximum surtax only to 50
percent. Undaunted, Mellon returned to the attack in 1923, several
months after Harding's death. He now asked Congress to slash the
maximum surtax to 25 percent and to abolish entirely the federal estate
tax, a source of great unhappiness among the wealthy. Even the
Republican majority in Congress found these ideas too radical. They
trimmed the maximum surtax to 40 percent, but kept the estate tax
intact, and added a new federal gift tax. The ideal of progressive taxation remained, but Mellon had established an important beachhead
for later reductions by a more compliant legislature.

By 1920, farmers who raised staple crops such as wheat and cotton
formed a vociferous and well-organized interest group demanding
government intervention to protect their living standards and way of
life from the gouging of railroads, commodity brokers, and bankers.
Because of the expansion of federal programs to assist agriculture during the Wilson years, the secretary of agriculture had become a powerful symbol of agrarian interests and an important broker of the farmers'
political fate. To fill this key cabinet post, Harding tapped the thinking
man's farmer, Henry C. Wallace, who had graduated from the state

agricultural college in Iowa and later taught there as an assistant professor of dairy farming.

As a spokesman for the rural producers, the publisher of *Wallace's Farmer* remained generally in the progressive mold. Three decades of agricultural expansion, consolidation, and periodic collapse had left the American countryside stratified between large-scale commercial operators at the very top and armies of tenant farmers, sharecroppers, and landless laborers at the bottom. Wallace eloquently and persistently represented those farmers who were more interested in crop rotation than in social revolution, those who hoped to emulate big business by harnessing the plow to the miracles of science and technology.

Harding's most controversial cabinet selection proved to be Herbert Hoover as secretary of commerce. A figure straight out of American folklore, Hoover had been orphaned and left almost penniless by his parents only to become a world-famous mining engineer and multi-

Henry Wallace, secretary of agriculture, demonstrates his technique with a Holstein.

millionaire before the age of forty. The Wilson administration had called him to public service, first as director of relief efforts for war-ravaged Belgium and later as chief of the domestic Food Administration. Against the hostility of the belligerent nations, he distributed food and medical supplies to the victims of war. Hoover's passion for efficiency guaranteed that almost every dime of the millions raised for relief found its way to the needy, not into the pockets of administrators. Without the authority to impose domestic rationing, he kept food prices in the U.S. reasonably stable by persuading consumers to eat less wheat and meat and spurring farmers to produce more food and fiber for the American and Allied armies. A member of Wilson's official entourage at the peace conference, he spoke out against a punitive treaty and the reparations inflicted on Germany. John Maynard Keynes, the youthful British economist whose scathing critique of the Versailles settlement made him a hero to American progressives, called Hoover "the biggest man" in the American delegation. Justice Louis Brandeis and Franklin Roosevelt both thought Hoover a superb candidate for president on the Democratic ticket, until the latter announced his preference for the GOP.

The very qualities that made Hoover attractive to Keynes, Brandeis, and FDR—his humanitarianism, internationalism, and penchant for scientific management—made him highly suspect among professional politicians in the Republican Party and among the traditional business and financial elites who usually supported it. Party professionals, hungry for patronage after eight years of Democratic rule, wanted a free hand in appointments without interference from a Boy Scout of clean government such as Hoover. Businessmen, eager to dismantle many government regulations of the progressive era, remained uncertain where Hoover stood on these matters. He did not hide the fact that he idolized Wilson, supported American membership in the League, and believed government to be more than a necessary evil. He praised free enterprise, but also urged businessmen to pursue their goals through "voluntary cooperation" or "associative individualism," both of which sounded dangerous to orthodox conservatives.

When the brief postwar recession of 1921 threw five million people out of work, Hoover urged an accelerated program of federal public works to combat the problem. Harding rejected the idea, but it confirmed for many Republican leaders Hoover's subversive tendencies. As commerce secretary during the next eight years, Hoover expended enormous energy attempting to persuade manufacturers and distributors to form trade associations. By promoting the standardization of

Herbert Hoover, center, headed the Commerce Department.

products and sharing other information, Hoover believed, these voluntary organizations would eliminate waste, reduce costs, and improve the competitiveness of American capitalism. Many businessmen saw them as a wonderful tool for fixing prices, allocating markets, and engaging in other practices forbidden by the antitrust laws—all with the official imprimatur of Hoover's department. When the secretary turned thumbs down on such illegal collusion and gave businessmen a sermon on the benefits of free competition and voluntary cooperation, they again shook their heads in disbelief.

RESHAPING THE COURT

While his cabinet had a progressive tinge that alarmed many hard-boiled Republicans, they could not complain about the president's judicial appointments. In 1920 the Supreme Court's writ ran less far and wide than even a decade later, but the decisions of its nine justices had enormous consequences for individual litigants and the whole community, because they drew the boundary between personal liberty and government authority. For many conservatives and progressives, the Court under Chief Justice Edward White had tilted the balance too far in favor of the state during the wartime emergency. To the chagrin of businessmen, the White Court upheld the power of Congress to impose an eight-hour day on the nation's railroads and rent controls in the District of Columbia. The justices also let stand an Oregon law that required employers to pay time and a half for all labor in excess of ten hours. These rulings, grumbled conservatives, trampled on economic liberty and property rights by restricting freedom of contract. Supporters of civil liberties denounced the Court when it upheld conscription, censorship, and long jail terms for all the antiwar protesters convicted under the Espionage or Sedition Act. These decisions, they cried, made a mockery of the Bill of Rights, especially freedom of speech and press.

Because the justices had been divided on many of these cases, more than ordinary interest surrounded each death and resignation that gave Harding four appointments to the Supreme Court—including a new chief justice—between 1921 and 1923. No president since Taft had a greater opportunity to reshape the nation's jurisprudence by selecting "the best minds" for its highest court. Harding's choices—William Howard Taft, George Sutherland, Pierce Butler, and Edward Sanford—were not greeted with acclaim by most progressives. The corpulent Taft, chosen to replace White as chief justice, seemed likely to replicate the conservatism of the man he had placed in the center chair a decade earlier. The former president had long harbored ambitions to lead the Court, and cynical observers believed that Taft picked White for the job in 1911 rather than the more youthful Charles Evans Hughes with these thoughts in mind. Without a trace of irony, Taft once observed that judges "typify on earth what we shall meet hereafter in heaven under a just God." He had vehemently opposed Brandeis's appointment to the Court in 1916 and regarded Justice Oliver Wendell Holmes as wholly unreliable on issues of government regulation of business.

Sutherland, a former congressman and United States senator from Utah, studied law at the University of Michigan under Thomas M. Cooley, the famous theoretician of constitutional limitations. Cooley had preached that most forms of government regulation were unwise and illegal. At the American Bar Association convention in 1917 Sutherland expressed total sympathy for businessmen "beset and bedeviled with vexatious statutes, prying commissions, and government intermeddling of all sorts." He denounced the Wilson administration for creating "an army of official agents . . . to smell out our shortcomings and tell us what we may and what we may not do."

Butler had practiced law briefly in Minnesota with the son of the

Populist intellectual Ignatius Donnelly, but he was certainly no radical. As the senior partner in a prosperous St. Paul law firm, the Minnesotan normally represented railroads against state regulatory agencies. A millionaire's son and a graduate of the Harvard Law School, Sanford owed his appointment to Chief Justice Taft's influence and seldom failed to follow the latter's views.

The Harding-Taft Court pleased those who believed that government economic regulation had gone too far during the progressive era. But while sanctioning entrepreneurial liberty, the justices let stand a variety of laws designed to repress political subversives whose ideas threatened the status quo. Over biting dissents by Brandeis and Holmes, for instance, the justices told the federal government and the states that they could not fix minimum wages or standard weights for bread, limit the fees charged by employment agencies, or control the resale price of theater tickets. If government did these things, the majority declared, economic freedom would perish. Yet the justices permitted New York and California to imprison political radicals who advocated revolution or joined organizations that preached such notions. The federal government, the Taft majority ruled, could employ wiretapping without violating the search and seizure provisions of the Fourth Amendment. And Congress might bar from citizenship an alien pacifist who refused to bear arms for the country, although the alien in this particular case was female and unlikely to be called to military service.

Although the Harding-Taft Court seldom resisted government encroachments on civil liberties and civil rights, there were a few notable exceptions to this trend. With Holmes writing for the majority, the justices in 1923 overturned the convictions and death sentences of five Arkansas Negroes whose trial had been disrupted by an armed mob of white vigilantes. Where a state criminal proceeding became a mere sham and local courts failed to protect the accused, Holmes declared, the federal judiciary must guarantee due process of law. For the first time in history, the justices reversed a state criminal conviction on these grounds. At about the same time, the Taft Court also struck down as unconstitutional an Iowa law that sought to prevent the teaching of languages other than English in the public schools and an Oregon statute, backed by the Ku Klux Klan, that attempted to shut down all parochial schools. These measures trampled on economic liberty by restricting freedom of contract, the majority ruled, and also violated other fundamental rights, such as a parent's right to have choice about where and how to educate a child.

Harding's judicial appointments, like his cabinet selections, did not produce a complete purge of progressive ideals from the federal government. Except for cronies such as Fall and Daugherty, the Ohioan opted for well-known Republicans who could lend an aura of competence and stability to his regime. This formula favored conservatives such as Taft and Sutherland, but it also dictated the elevation of Hughes and Hoover, too. Political pragmatism and expediency drove Harding's choices, not ideological purity. A similar pattern came to characterize the important public policies of his short administration. "Normalcy," in other words, did not mean a bold expansion of the progressive tradition, but neither did it repudiate that tradition entirely.

CONTINUITY AND CHANGE

As shaped by Teddy Roosevelt and Wilson, the progressive movement emphasized strong presidential leadership to mold the country's domestic and foreign policies. In style and substance, Harding proved to be closer to this new ideal of the presidency than to its pre-Roosevelt alternative. Two decades of reform and energy in the White House had transformed everybody's expectations about the office, including Warren Harding's. Candidate Harding had vowed to restore balance between the executive and Congress, which in his view had been twisted out of shape by the war and years of presidential aggrandizement under his predecessors. The pledge proved easier to make than to implement. The landmark Budget Act of 1921, for example, required the president to submit an estimate of receipts and expenditures for all departments of the government to each regular session of Congress. This law automatically thrust the White House ever more deeply into the legislative process and the fixing of domestic priorities. A provision of the Fordney-McCumber Act gave to the president, upon the recommendation of the Tariff Commission, authority to reduce or lower duties by as much as 50 percent. It too enhanced presidential power at the expense of the legislature. Wilson had often broken precedent by addressing a joint session of Congress on important legislative items. Harding carried this a step further during a special session of the 67th Congress in 1921, when the Senate voted on a veterans' bonus that he opposed. The president came in person to the chamber and delivered a stinging rebuke to its members. Before his death, Harding addressed Congress five more times, behavior which generated cries of executive tyranny for opposing the bonus and supporting other pet measures, such as federal subsidies for the nation's merchant fleet.

Any expectation that the Harding administration would actually roll back the Roosevelt-Wilson reforms was quickly dashed by a president who pardoned the socialist antiwar leader Eugene Debs (something a vindictive Wilson refused to do) and pressured the giant U.S. Steel Corporation into adopting the basic eight-hour day for many employees, an achievement that had eluded labor during the war. Sending his first legislative program to Congress, Harding called for the federal government to play a larger, not smaller, role in the country's social and economic life. He urged Congress to pass a host of new laws to aid farmers, raise tariffs, punish lynching, enforce prohibition, curb immigration, and reduce taxes. In the case of the tariff and taxes, it can be said that the Harding administration retreated from the progressive agenda. But in another area, federal grant-in-aid programs, it forged ahead dramatically.

These aid programs, requiring states to follow federal guidelines if they accepted funds for specific activities, traced their origin to the famous Morrill Act of 1862. Then Congress made federal land available to the states when they built agricultural colleges. Cash replaced land when a major expansion in this form of federal assistance and regulation occurred during the progressive era. By 1917, federal grant-in-aid programs provided money for fighting fires, vocational and agricultural education, building highways, and rehabilitating veterans. In 1921, Harding and the Republican-controlled Congress approved the last important federal grant-in-aid effort before the Great Depression. It touched off a fierce debate. The Sheppard-Towner Maternity Aid Act made federal money available to states that operated infant and maternity health care programs in local hospitals. Some militant feminists and birth control advocates denounced the measure for subsidizing procreation. Moral fundamentalists, Catholics as well as Protestants, critized it as a dangerous intrusion by government into the affairs of the family. The state of Massachusetts and local taxpayers sought to have the law declared unconstitutional with claims that it exceeded the authority of Congress, coerced the states, and destroyed their sovereignty. Without dissent, the Supreme Court threw out the lawsuit on jurisdictional grounds, but the justices also indicated that they were unimpressed with these efforts to curb the spending powers of the national government.

It is difficult to imagine a clearer example of the persistence of progressivism than Sheppard-Towner. An often forgotten product of the Harding era, the law provided a notable precedent for the even broader social welfare programs of the New Deal, including social security.

Sheppard-Towner succumbed to the Republican budget ax later in the decade, but other grant-in-aid programs continued to flourish. Under Wilson, federal grants to the states for specific programs had totaled about $11 million annually. By 1925, despite Andrew Mellon's efforts to cut federal expenditures, such grants had climbed to over $93 million. They had become permanent fixtures of the American political landscape along with other innovations of the progressive era: the Federal Reserve System, the Food and Drug Administration, and the Federal Trade Commission.

President and Race

Harding did little to resist the nativist members of Congress who demanded strict curbs on foreign immigration, but he did make a token effort to revive his party's long-dormant commitment to civil rights for African-Americans. Theodore Roosevelt invited Booker T. Washington to the White House, but never challenged the South's racial caste system. When black soldiers were charged with fomenting a riot in Brownsville, Texas, he cashiered them all from the Army without proof of individual guilt. Woodrow Wilson sanctioned racial segregation in the offices of the federal government. Warren Harding became the first president in this century to criticize it publicly before a white audience in the South. Invited to Birmingham, Alabama, in 1921 for that city's fiftieth birthday celebration, the president declared that "we cannot go on, as we have gone on for more than half a century, with one great section of our population . . . set off from real contributions to solving national issues, because of a division on race lines." Southern racists picked up his meaning. Senator Pat Harrison of Mississippi called the speech "unfortunate indeed." Alabama's arch-segregationist, Tom Heflin, reminded the president that "God Almighty has fix'd limits and boundary lines between the races, and no Republican living can improve upon His handiwork."

Since Southern laws barred blacks from elections by various discriminatory methods, Harding's critics noted that the president hoped merely to gather in more black votes from that traditional Republican constituency in the North. But he soon followed the speech with a specific legislative proposal by urging passage of a law giving federal courts jurisdiction over the crime of lynching, an idea only slightly less revolting to the white South than ending segregation itself. The Harding-endorsed bill passed the House in 1922, but fell victim to a Southern filibuster in the Senate. Fearing that a long, angry debate would side-track other projects, the president and his legislative allies finally cast the bill adrift. Black leaders expressed bitterness at Harding's capitulation, which seemed to turn away from the sentiments of the Birmingham speech and to place ship subsidies above human rights. Until Harry Truman sat in the White House, however, no president took a stronger legislative stand against lynching.

A DEATH IN SAN FRANCISCO

Despite achievements that included a historic disarmament treaty, normalization of relations with Mexico, tax reduction, and aid to agriculture, Harding and the Republicans suffered a sharp rebuff at the polls in the 1922 congressional elections. With the economy still sluggish, the GOP lost seven seats in the Senate, including the leader of the protectionist forces, Porter McCumber, and seventy seats in the House. This gave the balance of power in the lower chamber to those who opposed the administration on taxation and ship subsidies, but wanted more federal aid to agriculture and veterans. It would be a mistake, however, to regard the 1922 elections as a repudiation of the Harding administration or its works. Incumbent presidents had generally suffered setbacks in the midterm elections. Several of Harding's decisions, notably his veto of a veterans' bonus and intervention against striking railroad workers, prompted loud outcries from the injured groups, but the outcome of most Senate and House races in 1922 depended as ever on a host of local issues and personalities. In an attempt to mend his political fences and gain new momentum for the next two years, Harding embarked on a fatal political tour in the summer of 1923. Almost duplicating Wilson's strenuous journey on behalf of the League, Harding delivered fourteen speeches in two weeks. Near the end of the trip, traveling from Alaska to San Francisco, he suffered a heart attack. Three days later at the Palace Hotel, the president died from a cerebral hemorrhage. At the time of his death, the scandals that would soon rock the party remained hidden. Whether he could have regained the initiative in the wake of those exposures and against a more unruly Congress is very doubtful.

Warren Harding was not the political Neanderthal of historical legend. While no progressive, he did not dismantle institutions of the progressive era or turn his back entirely on its legacies. The regulatory apparatus created under Roosevelt, Taft, and Wilson, although weakened by new appointments, remained in place, even augmented by new programs for commercial farmers and an expansion of federal grant-in-aid efforts, especially Sheppard-Towner. If not all of his appointments were as good as Hughes or Hoover, neither were they as poor as Harry Daugherty or Pierce Butler. Clearly, Harding lacked the intellectual acumen of TR or Wilson, but he may have killed himself in an attempt to master the details of his job. The accusation that he abdicated executive leadership would have astonished most congress-men of the time, who complained about his vetoes and what they regarded as excessive meddling by the White House in legislative affairs. And by criticizing segregation and abandoning the policy of interven-tion in the hemisphere, Harding challenged traditions of the progres-sive era that were little credit to the nation or its leaders.

2

The Great Boom

Oh, it was Tin, Tin Tin!
Though I constantly degrade you
By the Henry Ford who made you.
You're better than Packard,
Hunk o' Tin!
—Anonymous

The successful business man among us . . . enjoys the pub-
lic respect and adulation that elsewhere bathe only bishops
and generals of artillery.
—H. L. Mencken

CONSUMER SOCIETY

For many of the nation's founders, a rising standard of living was not judged to be an unmixed blessing. Too much wealth, they feared, menaced republican institutions and public virtue no less than grinding poverty. To be sure, poverty sowed resentment and fear. Abundance, however, would infect all classes with a taste for luxury, certain to siphon off more and more human energy into private accumulation and extravagance.

After learning from Benjamin Franklin in 1786 that "the consumption of goods was never greater, as appears by the dress, furniture, and manner of living, of all ranks of the people," Thomas Jefferson lamented that "all my letters are filled with details of our extravagance." He looked back to the days of the Revolutionary War "as a time of happiness and enjoyment, when admidst the privation of many things not essential to happiness, we could not run into debt, because nobody would trust us." Jefferson's friend the gifted scientist David Ritten-house hoped devoutly that "our harbours, our doors, our hearts be shut against luxury," an opinion shared by Tom Paine and others, who regarded great wealth as the harbinger of social degeneration.

Had Jefferson and Rittenhouse lived to view the American condition in the decade after Versailles, the sight would have alarmed them greatly, for this was a time of both bustling new wealth and dismal poverty. In these years, with notable exceptions, the American people enjoyed a rising standard of living and luxury unknown on their continent or to the human race generally. Between 1919 and 1929, most Americans worked fewer hours than their parents or grandparents, produced more even so, and took home ever fatter paychecks. They ate better, enjoyed improved medical care, and as a result lived longer, healthier lives. Spending less on the daily necessities of food, clothing, and shelter, they lavished a rising fraction of their personal incomes on self-improvement and recreation. Leisure activities, spectator sports, and entertainment tapped huge audiences and became big business. Warren Harding and the Republicans had promised the American people "normalcy"—stability, a respite from the unsettling changes of war—not an unprecedented economic boom that rattled the social order. Shortly after Harding's death, however, the country entered a new world of high mass consumption and affluence that produced optimism and anxiety in about equal measure.

One test of a modern economic system is surely its capacity to provide steady work, a rising output of goods and service, higher real wages, and low prices. The American economy during the Republican restoration passed that test with flying colors. Based on aggregate figures, its performance may have been the most successful in the history of the United States, earlier or later. Following the short postwar recession of 1920–21, the output of goods and services—the gross national product—grew at a steady rate of 2 percent per year. Annual average unemployment rates never rose above 3.7 percent from 1922 to 1929, and the annual average increase in prices was less than 1 percent for the same period. In other words, Americans in this decade experienced something that eluded virtually all later generations: full employment and low inflation. As per capita hours worked in factories fell more than 1 percent a year, per capita income jumped from $517 in the years 1909 to 1918 to $612 between 1919 and 1928. The first two decades of the century had been good for Americans as the real income of the average employee had grown by 25 percent. But that was only a prelude. From Harding's inauguration in 1921 to Hoover's in 1929, annual income increased on average a whopping 30 percent.

With more money in their pockets and in the banks, Americans went on a decade-long buying spree that kept factory orders and profits high. In 1922, for example, American producers turned out slightly more than 100,000 radios. Seven years later that figure had climbed to 350,000, and twelve million families owned at least one. Companies making refrigerators saw their volume jump 150 percent during the decade. The number of passenger cars produced in a single year rose from 1.5 million to 4.7 million. The profits of the 300,000 largest corporations increased a staggering 62 percent between 1923 and 1929. General Motors, which ranked thirtieth on the eve of World War I, was the third largest enterprise in the land by 1929; its revenues swelled from $173 million in a single year to $1.5 billion. In the summer of 1927, Americans paid $2.6 million in Philadelphia to watch heavyweight champion Gene Tunney defend his title against Jack Dempsey. A year earlier, they had spent ten times that sum at box offices across the country to watch a single motion picture, *The Big Parade*, and one studio, Metro-Goldwyn-Mayer, paid actress Greta Garbo $5,000 a week to perform before its cameras. When he left the White House in 1929, Calvin Coolidge became a newspaper columnist who earned $1 for every word he wrote, or about $200,000 a year, three times his salary as president of the United States.

TECHNOLOGICAL REVOLUTION

Describing the economic boom of the 1920s is easier than explaining why it took place or what cultural and material consequences it held for the American people. Republicans, of course, argued then and later that their efforts to curb government regulation and reduce taxes played the key roles in stimulating the economy. But of equal importance, business corporations eagerly seized the extraordinary achievements of the nation's scientific and technical laboratories.

The decade spawned a profusion of new inventions and processes of great commercial importance. Newly discovered properties in quartz crystals made it possible to stabilize radio signals and thereby allocate broadcast frequencies with greater precision. Under government contract, Dr. Frank Conrad of the Westinghouse Electric and Manufacturing Company conducted experiments with radio transmissions during the war. His twice-weekly broadcasts, which included music, baseball scores, and news, became the foundation of the nation's first commercial radio station. When area department stores and mail-order companies offered crystal sets for sale, Conrad's audience swelled. In time to broadcast the 1920 election returns, Westinghouse secured a federal license to operate station 8ZZ in Pittsburgh, later renamed KDKA. People as far away as Boston and Atlanta learned over KDKA of Harding's victory. Within two years, twenty-two radio stations operated around the country. Montgomery Ward, offering receiving sets for $49.50, which included headphones, A and B batteries, and a 125-foot antenna, promised buyers entertainment and education: "not only concerts, sports, sermons and lectures but also Board of Trade reports, news items and weather forecasts." The Radio Corporation of America broadcast the Dempsey-Carpentier heavyweight title fight in 1921 from its Hoboken station.

Not be be outdone, Westinghouse brought its listeners the World

By the mid-twenties, RCA marketed a portable radio.

Series that fall. Manufacturers and their advertising advisers soon realized the potential of using the airwaves to sell Americans everything from cooking oil to chewing gum. In 1922, station WEAF in New York City, an affiliate of American Telephone and Telegraph, sent out over the airwaves the first commercial advertisement. Fueled by this new and potentially unlimited source of revenue, radio stations multiplied across the country. By 1927, hundreds of them had been welded together in two gigantic chains controlled by the National Broadcasting Company and the Columbia Broadcasting System.

The mechanical telephone switchboard, first installed in New York City and Philadelphia in 1922, facilitated business transactions. Mixing latex with liquid soap, the Dunlop Rubber Company produced foam rubber. Building on discoveries in the United States and abroad, scientists at E. I. du Pont de Nemours and Company marketed cellophane and rayon. By the end of the decade, du Pont made hundreds of chemistry-based products in addition to explosives, dyes, and paints. Kimberly Clark, which had already created a disposable handkerchief, Kleenex, and pioneered the development of bandages made from wood cellulose during the war, began marketing sanitary napkins from the same fiber in 1921. The company called its new product Kotex. At about the same time, Clarence Birdseye began spraying fresh fish with a brine solution, freezing them at very low temperatures, and selling them throughout New York City.

Arthur D. Little, the founding genius of one of the country's leading research firms, actually made a silk purse out of a sow's ear, something the proverb said couldn't be done, even in America. Little ordered from a meat-packing plant ten pounds of gelatin produced wholly from sow's ears. Using a new synthetic process, he spun the gelatin into artificial silk threads and had a purse "of the sort which ladies of great estate carried in medieval days" woven from these fibers. Americans produced more and earned more between 1919 and 1929 not because they worked harder or longer, but because they worked smarter. The explosive growth in GNP, real wages, and profits rested on the simple fact that each hour of labor and each dollar of capital was used more productively than in the past.

KING OF KILOWATTS

The waterwheel and steam engine powered America's first industrial revolution, beginning in the eighteenth century. New sources of cheap energy—petroleum and electricity—drove the second one after World War I. Progressives regarded their successful antitrust suit against John D. Rockefeller's Standard Oil Company in 1911 as a landmark victory for free enterprise and consumers over monopoly when the courts split the giant oil firm into four regional companies. What brought more competition to the petroleum business and reduced fuel costs, however, was not antitrust lawyers, but swarms of wildcat drillers who sank thousands of new wells across a broad swath of Louisiana, Texas, and Oklahoma after 1920. Oil rigs became almost as ubiquitous in the Lone Star State as longhorn cattle—and far more profitable. Although a few big firms such as Texaco soon gobbled up the prime fields and state regulation sought to curb the glut of new oil, a considerable number of shoestring operators became very rich. The center of wealth and power within the industry shifted decisively from the old Midwest to the Southwest and West. While older centers of oil production and refining such as Cleveland struggled to keep pace, newer ones like Houston, Dallas, Tulsa, and Long Beach, California, bustled with activity.

Much of the new oil gushing out of the ground in Texas, Oklahoma, and California fueled huge generators, high-voltage transmission lines, and electric motors that brought cheap, efficient power to factories, office buildings, and private homes. The spread of electricity cut production costs and created new markets for electric appliances. By 1929, close to half of the nation's manufacturing plants used electricity and over sixteen million homes, sheltering about 63 percent of the population, had been wired. Some 50 percent of Americans owned an electric iron and 15 percent either a washing machine, a fan, or a toaster.

Electrification brought mass-production techniques to new levels of sophistication. Because of it, the petroleum industry could install a continuous cracking process that increased the efficiency of refining by 42 percent over the decade. From electric power flowed similar gains to the manufacturers of paper products, glass, chemicals, rubber tires, steel, and automobiles. Electricity powered America in the twenties, and the king of kilowatts was Chicago's Samuel Insull. One of eight children born to an English temperance leader, Insull began his extraordinary business career in 1880 when he answered an advertisement for a secretary placed in the London *Times* by a man who turned out to be Thomas A. Edison's chief European representative. By the time he moved to America two years later, Insull had become the indispensable private secretary to the genius who invented the light bulb, the phonograph, motion pictures, and the electric power station. He ran Edison's office, bought his clothes, kept him fed. Recognizing the young man's talent for figures and negotiating, Edison put Insull in charge of his construction company that sold and built electric stations throughout the United States. Together they created the General Electric Company, which finally caught the eye of the biggest financial fish in the pond, J. P. Morgan, who bought out Edison for $5 million cash and offered his personal secretary the presidency of the firm. Insull declined. He wanted to be a big fish in his own pond.

With Edison's blessing and a large loan from Marshall Field, Insull acquired control of the Chicago Edison Company in 1892. The city then had about five thousand users of electricity. Fifteen years later, when he combined this company with Commonwealth Electric to form a monopoly throughout the city and its suburbs, the number of customers had grown to fifty thousand. Insull's philosophy was simple: adopt the best technology available, keep costs down, and expand the market with low rates. He installed the nation's first steam-electric turbines, a wonder for their time, employed cost accounting methods to pare overhead, hired the best managers and paid them well. "We will make electric light so cheap," he boasted, "that only the rich will burn candles." By World War I, thanks largely to Insull's example, electricity had ousted gas as the primary source of energy for industrial and residential purposes. And having electrified Chicago and its environs, he set out to conquer the rest of America's heartland as well.

With his ample white mustache, spats, and expensive walking cane, Insull looked like a capitalist straight from the novels of Theodore Dreiser. There was nothing old-fashioned about his business methods. The foundation of Insull's utility empire had been technological daring: bigger generators, more powerful transmission lines. Financial innovation became the basis for its expansion. Insull did not invent the holding company, a legal device that permitted one corporation to own others, but he raised this corporate form to a high art, one undreamed of even in the imagination of J. P. Morgan or John D. Rockefeller. Insull discovered that with a small investment (often using borrowed funds) he could purchase a controlling interest in hundreds of local utility companies scattered around the country. And once in control of these individual operating companies, his parent firm, Middle West Utilities, could provide them with the technology and management sophistication that had turned Chicago Edison and Commonwealth Electric into models of efficiency and growth.

From the point of view of the companies he absorbed, however, there were several drawbacks to Insull's strategy. Middle West Utilities charged

Samuel Insull, titan of the utilities industry.

substantial consulting, management, and engineering fees for all the assistance rendered to its new corporate subsidiaries. These charges were in turn passed along to consumers in the form of higher rates. Insull also discovered that he could sell the securities of his holding companies directly to the public through his own employees, avoiding the expense of outside investment bankers and raising millions of dollars with which to acquire ever more operating companies. By 1928, Edison's former secretary controlled over two hundred operating utilities and twenty-seven pure holding companies that delivered electricity and gas to more than a million customers in five hundred communities in thirty-two states. Middle West Utilities, the main holding company, had 111 subsidiaries. Insull's empire also included the street railway systems of Chicago and Minneapolis—St. Paul. His utilities alone were valued at $3 billion. And by one estimate, a million people had purchased Insull's securities, which included a bewildering variety of common stock, preferred stock, and bonds. "It is like the Hanging Gardens of Babylon," one critic observed, "a pyramidal structure, built in weird design, worthy of a Nebuchadnezzar. The luxurious vegetation in this ethereal garden, the many and varied types of securities that have germinated there, has grown with rare rapidity."

More than any other single figure, Samuel Insull introduced cheap electricity and stock ownership to ordinary, middle-class Americans. Long before his competitors and the New Deal, he pioneered in rural electrification by bringing power to some of the nation's farmers. While not sympathetic to unions, he was a model employer who not only hired blacks, but gave his workers an education allowance, medical care, pensions, and stock ownership. He gave generously to charity and the arts in Chicago, underwriting, for example, the construction of a new home for the city's opera company. To the millions who used his electricity, owned his stock, and enjoyed his patronage, Insull symbolized the epitome of enlightened capitalism, the merger of technology, high finance, and benevolence. "In the hero-worshiping postwar decade," wrote his admiring biographer, "Insull became the Babe Ruth, the Jack Dempsey, the Red Grange of the business world. . . . He measured up to America's image of itself: a rich, powerful, self-made giant, ruthless in smashing enemies, generous and soft-hearted in dealing with the weak."

But even in the warm glow of prosperity, Insull did not lack for critics, who pointed out a few cracks in his imperial business structure. By gobbling up hundreds of local operating companies, Middle West Utilities ignited a bidding war for these properties with other holding companies and drove up the purchase price for many far beyond their present or future earning capacity. In order to finance these expensive takeovers, Insull and other holding company leaders sold large blocks of securities, hefty amounts in the form of fixed-interest obligations, that represented nothing but these inflated values and the distant expectation of anticipated income—what skeptics called, uncharitably, "water."

By 1929, a mere sixteen holding companies controlled over 90 percent of America's electric power production. Major holding companies such as Middle West, Electric Bond and Share, Associated Gas and Electric, and American Power and Light owned operating companies in dozens of states, their organizational charts a crazy quilt worthy of a legislative gerrymander. Even in Insull's case, economies of scale had been reached, exceeded, and turned into chaos. Not even the king of kilowatts himself knew how all of the more than two hundred pieces of his empire fit together. Physical interconnection among many of the operating companies did not, in fact, exist, which meant that savings existed largely on paper. Holding companies milked many of their subsidiaries by charging exorbitant fees for physical equipment and services, inflated costs ultimately imposed on consumers. And because holding companies were seldom chartered in states where most of their subsidiaries operated, they remained wholly beyond the regulatory authority of local public utilities commissions. In short, the only check on the ambition, avarice, and incompetence of the industry was the marketplace itself, which did not begin to impose its discipline until stock prices crashed in 1929.

THE WIZARD OF DETROIT

At the turn of the century, three million horses still inhabited American cities, and their excrement constituted one of the nation's greatest health problems. By the mid-twenties, that menace had abated, only to be replaced by the more lethal pollution from horseless carriages. Social paradox often rode with progress. With automobiles, innovations in technology, organization, and finance created the premier growth industry of the decade, one that rivaled the railroads of the nineteenth century as catalysts of change. And no one businessman better symbolized the economic and cultural contradictions of the boom than the former mechanic's apprentice Henry Ford. In his Model T automobile, mass production and mass consumption reached their apotheosis.

Beginning in 1909, Ford transformed an industry that produced expensive, luxury vehicles for the rich into one that provided cheap, reliable transportation for the masses. "I will build a motor car for the great multitude," Ford told his incredulous salesmen. "It will be large enough for the family but small enough for the individual to run and care for. It will be constructed of the best materials, by the best men to be hired, after the simplest designs that modern engineering can devise." His car, Ford added, "will be so low in price that no man making a good salary will be unable to own one." To the astonishment of bankers and other economic pundits who predicted failure, Ford realized his dream. In a tiny factory of less than a third of an acre that employed about 350 workers, he produced 1,708 cars in his first year and sold them for $950 apiece.

A vehicle of splendid simplicity, the Model T contained only four basic units—the power plant, the frame, the front axle, and the rear axle. It was not, however, a handsome piece of machinery. Why was the Model T like a bathtub? Because, went the joke of the time, you hated to be seen in one. Easy to maintain and repair, it could be driven on almost any surface, which was a good thing given the primitive state of the nation's mostly dirt roads. This made the Model T especially attractive to farmers and traveling salesmen. According to legend, one farmer told his relatives to bury his Model T with him when he died:

"I've never been in a hole yet where my Ford didn't get me out." Instead of filing for bankruptcy, Ford struggled to keep up with demand.

By 1911, the factory space of the Ford Motor Company had grown a hundredfold. Ford now employed over four thousand workers who produced nearly 35,000 cars a year. The price of the Model T, called affectionately the Tin Lizzie or the flivver, had fallen to under $700. That was only the beginning. Three years later with the introduction of the moving assembly line, "taking the work to the men instead of the men to the work," the Ford Motor Company could turn out a Model T every ninety-three minutes, sell it for less than $500, and pay some of its production workers the astronomical wage of $5 per day. "The first men fasten four mud guard brackets to the chassis frame," rhapsodized Mr. Ford, "the motor arrives on the tenth operation and so on in detail. Some men do only one or two small operations, others do more. The man who places a part does not fasten it. . . . The man who puts in a bolt does not put on the nut; the man who puts on the nut does not tighten it. On operation number thirty-four the budding motor gets its gasoline. . . . and on operation number forty-five the car drives out onto John R. Street."

In the year of Harding's election, Ford produced 1,250,000 automobiles, one every sixty seconds, priced from $335 to $440. With over nine million cars registered that year, economic experts predicted that the American market for automobiles had become saturated. "The use in the near future of anything like twice the present number of cars," said the *New York Times*, "seems most unlikely." On a single day, five years later, however, Ford turned out one Model T every ten seconds. From coal and iron ore deposits to lumber and machines tools, the Ford Motor Company controlled every aspect of production. Noting that Mr. Ford earned $264,000 a day, the Associated Press pronounced him a billionaire. People sought his opinions on subjects ranging from war debts to the latest dance craze, and Ford usually obliged in the pages of his own newspaper, the *Dearborn Independent*. A Ford for President campaign flourished briefly in 1924. College students ranked him behind Jesus Christ and Napoleon as the greatest person in history. A bit more modestly, the labor leader Samuel M. Vaudain asserted that Ford had "saved America from a social crisis. . . . When alcohol was taken [away] . . . the flivver was needed to replace it." But the shrewdest appraisal came from Will Rogers: "So good luck, Mr. Ford. It will take a hundred years to tell whether you have helped us or hurt us, but you certainly didn't leave us like you found us."

By mid-decade, Ford's Model T and the automobiles produced by

Henry Ford poses with his first Model T and number ten million.

his competitors—General Motors, Chrysler, Studebaker, Packard, and Hudson—played a crucial role in the nation's new economic order. By 1929, the industry employed directly over 7 percent of all manufacturing workers and paid almost 9 percent of all manufacturing wages. In addition, it stimulated employment, production, and investment in a wide range of other basic industries that kept Detroit's assembly lines moving—steel, glass, rubber, paints and varnishes, and machine tools. Ford boasted that his flivvers were "always going" whatever the road conditions, but owners of the 26 million registered vehicles in 1929 came to expect better highways paved with concrete and asphalt and construction firms stood ready to meet this demand at taxpayers' expense. The petroleum industry reaped a bonanza from both road construction and the service stations that sprouted up everywhere to sell gasoline and lubricants. As auto traffic increased, so did the accidents that left drivers, passengers, pedestrians, and animals maimed and killed. The traffic court, meting out fines to careless and reckless operators, became an important new source of revenue for local government. The horseless carriage replaced the railroad as the major source of tort litigation, gave the insurance industry a boost, and spawned a new breed of enterprising lawyers, known pejoratively as "ambulance chasers."

In addition to stimulating established sectors of the economy, the automobile generated a host of new activities. Ford hoped to design a car "so completely simple that no one could fail to understand it," but owners soon discovered that the more complex vehicles required a skilled mechanic to diagnose and repair their high-compression engines and four-wheel braking systems. Specialized shops opened to fix dented fenders, shattered glass, and bent frames. Uncle Fred and Aunt Maude sold off a part of the old family homestead along Route 1 to developers who erected tourist camps and motels catering to weary motorists. Because not every American could afford a new Ford, Chevy, or Chrysler, a thriving market sprang up in used autos. And for those determined to have a new vehicle but short on cash, the manufacturers made it easy. As early as 1919, General Motors offered installment purchase plans that soon attracted fierce competition from banks and finance companies.

Although a man of stupendous wealth, Ford's homespun ways and lack of sophistication endeared him to the nation's villagers, who also shared most of his prejudices. He loathed tobacco and alcohol and loved square dancing. A farmer's son, steeped in the morality of rural Protestantism and McGuffey readers, he had only eight years of formal schooling. Put on the witness stand when he sued the *Chicago Tribune* for libel, Ford could not identify Benedict Arnold or distinguish between the Revolutionary War and the War of 1812. He never read books. He did not want his son, Edsel, to attend college. But he spent huge sums of money to build replicas of an America that was disappearing or that existed long ago—Greenfield Village in Dearborn; Sudbury in Massachusetts. He blamed Jews for causing World War I, for all the ills of capitalism, and for spearheading communism, too. Ford's *Dearborn Independent* ran articles entitled "The Gentle Art of Changing Jewish Names" and the "All-Jewish Mark of Red Russia." Sued for libel in 1927 by Aaron Shapiro, a prominent Jewish lawyer, Ford settled out of court and made a public apology for past anti-Semitic slurs, but in private his paranoia continued. "It is a sad commentary on humanity," observed newspaper editor William Allen White, "that Ford's great wealth has concealed his mental sloth and his incapacity to think."

Ford took it for granted that his automobile would strengthen traditional American values of self-reliance, hard work, and frugality. He would pay good wages to workers who built an affordable, dependable, no-frills vehicle that placed new power and opportunity in the hands of average men and women in Kalamazoo or Wichita Falls. By permitting millions of Americans to own and operate a machine capable of traveling at speeds of up to twenty-five miles per hour, Ford saw himself as one of America's greatest liberators: a modern equivalent to the patriots who secured national independence or who fought slavery. The Model T would strike another blow for personal freedom by permitting the American worker to travel farther, faster, and more cheaply in search of economic opportunity and self-fulfillment or, as Ford put it more poetically, to "enjoy with his family the blessings of pleasure in God's great open spaces." He expected, too, that this revolution in production and consumption could be fulfilled without upsetting the social arrangements and values of his own youth.

Ford was very much mistaken. He had in fact unleashed a whirlwind on the country. Even as Ford set forth his vision of a traditional America, his Model T helped destroy it. While he deplored the cities as places of congestion, crime, and moral debauchery, the automobile helped swell the population of cities across the continent, gave criminals new mobility, and provided an inexpensive, migratory place for making love. The *Dearborn Independent* regularly denounced the Charleston, jazz, smoking, and drinking, but Ford helped to put sex, booze, and music on wheels.

There were other ironies in Ford's world. An apostle of rugged individualism and the pioneer spirit, he made certain that these values did

A sea of autos at Nantasket Beach, Massachusetts, in the early 1920s.

not interfere with his iron-fisted management of the company. Ford's employees were not free to join a labor union. "Unions are organized by Jewish financiers," he once told a magazine editor. "They are a scheme to interrupt work. A union is a neat trick for a Jew to have in hand when he wants to get a clutch on industry." The repetitive operations of his assembly line stifled creativity and turned workers into automatons. "Ford employees are not really alive," remarked a labor leader, "they are half dead."

Ford's personnel department kept a close eye on his employees' private lives, too. Because Ford believed that tobacco and alcohol led inevitably to a life of crime, his workers were told: "It will cost a man his job to have the odor of beer, wine or liquor on his breath or have any of these intoxicants in his home." He hired ten thousand blacks and people with serious physical disabilities to work on the assembly line, but treated others with ruthlessness and cruelty. Executives who displeased the boss might find their offices in a shambles or their desk hacked to pieces by an ax. "What children and adults need is a chance to breathe God's fresh air and to stretch their legs and have a little garden in the soil," Ford declared. By decade's end, God's fresh air contained a rising amount of noxious hydrocarbons. In order to enjoy God's great open spaces, even country drivers endured traffic jams.

Traditional middle-class ideals of thrift, frugality, and self-restraint fared little better in the new automobile-dominated consumer culture. Cheap and dependable, Ford's Model T gave people basic transportation. Available in one color—black—and in a single open-body design, it was also ugly and very uncomfortable in foul weather. Having introduced the common man and woman to a product once enjoyed only by the wealthy, Ford did not expect that the common man and woman would soon expect something better: a car of greater luxury and a bigger price tag in which they could emulate the rich.

THE TRIUMPH OF FASHION

Ford's competitors understood before he did that the auto market was being rapidly transformed by rising incomes, installment selling, a huge used-car inventory, closed-body styles, and annual model changes. "Thousands of men," declared a Packard advertisement in 1924, "are denying their wives Packard Six cars." With less hyperbole, Alfred P. Sloan, the head of General Motors, observed that when first-time car buyers returned to the market for a second time, usually with

Unlike Henry Ford, some car manufacturers empha-
sized power, prestige, and luxury in catering to the
classes not the masses.

their old auto as a down payment, "they were . . . demanding something more. . . . Middle-income buyers, assisted by the trade-in and
installment financing, created the demand, not for basic transportation, but for progress in new cars, for comfort, convenience, power, and
style. This was the actual trend of American life and those who adapted
to it prospered."

Sloan and the giant company he led after 1923 represented the
industry's new face. Unlike the lightly educated Ford, whose cracker-
barrel philosophy and populist prejudices made him a folk hero in
small-town America, Sloan held an engineering degree from the Massachusetts Institute of Technology. He became the beau ideal of a new
generation of corporate managers and technicians, most of them college-educated, some with advanced degrees in law, business administration, and engineering. Henry Ford, one of the last patriarchal

capitalists, achieved success through intuitive genius, hard work, and luck. Sloan, one of the first managerial capitalists, triumphed through his ability to generate and process information, to know what kinds of data should be provided by his many subordinates and how to utilize it. Methodical, civilized, and urbane, he did not curry favor with the masses by flailing Wall Street, baiting Jews, and holding forth on the evils of tobacco and drink. Rather, he mastered cost accounting, budgeting, and marketing, the tools of modern scientific management, and with these he turned what had been a haphazard collection of auto-parts firms into one of the world's largest and most profitable industrial corporations.

In 1925, General Motors unveiled its sleek K Model Chevrolet with a closed, longer body line, more legroom, a Duco finish, a one-piece windshield with automatic wipers, a dome light, an improved clutch, and a Klaxon horn. At about the same time, Hudson began to sell its sporty closed-body Essex coach for $895. In 1925, Ford's share of new car sales plummeted from 54 percent of the market to 45 percent. Two years later, the Tin Lizzie became history. Ford shut down his gigantic River Rouge factory for twelve months, laying off ten thousand workers, in order to retool for production of his new car—the Model A. And when it appeared, shortly before Christmas in 1927, heralded by a $1.3 million advertising campaign, it marked a victory for the product philosophy of Ford's competitors. Customers could buy the more glamorous Model A on the installment plan, in various body styles, and in a riot of colors that ranged from Niagara Blue to Arabian Sand. The Model A enabled Ford to regain sales leadership in 1929 and twice again during the Great Depression, but on terms set by the real industry leader, General Motors.

Ford's initial strategy had been to sell an increasing volume of similar vehicles at decreasing prices. He assumed this market would continue to grow. He also aspired to build a car that would last a long time. His was the ultimate dream of a production-oriented capitalist, who sought more efficient methods of reducing production costs in order to compete through lower prices. But Ford's desire for a durable product ultimately doomed his first goal. Sales could not continue to increase, because his old Model Ts eroded the market for new ones. The Sloan / General Motors strategy, the more radical vision of consumption-oriented capitalists, assumed that auto production could be sustained over the long run only by persuading buyers that each new style change represented a decisive improvement over the old one and that higher prices arose inevitably from such "progress." This approach to producing and selling cars required a huge investment in research and development to generate frequent changes in design. It also required massive outlays for advertising to convince car buyers that they should mortgage more of their future earnings to buy an expensive new car every three or four years on the installment plan.

Numerous improvements such as the self-starter, four-wheel brakes, and higher-compression engines arose initially from this strategy, but by the end of the twenties, revolutionary changes largely vanished from the industry. So did price competition. With many of their costs for research, development, production, and advertising fixed from year to year, the big three automakers—GM, Ford, and Chrysler—sold vehicles almost identical in quality for about the same price. Advertising and salesmanship replaced engineering and organizational efficiency as the critical variables of competition. The sums allocated to these marketing activities grew each year, as automakers bombarded the public with a barrage of inducements to buy the latest model and pay for it later. Customers did not purchase transportation. As Sloan predicted, Americans bought status, power, sex appeal, peace of mind. After all, what decent, successful husband wished to deny his wife a Packard Six? It worked. The head of the Federal Reserve Board observed in 1925 that "people will have an automobile and sacrifice paying their doctor bill, the grocery bill and the clothing bill." One Midwestern housewife told interviewers at the end of the decade, "We'd rather go without clothes than give up the car."

In Henry Ford and the automobile many Americans sought to have their cake and eat it too. They could race furiously into the future, enjoy the fruits of the great economic boom, but still pay lip service to old-fashioned values. They found a similar combination in the politician who sat in the White House after Harding's death.

3

Puritan in Babylon

Charles Hopkinson: *Mr. Coolidge, what was the first thought that came into your mind when you were told that Mr. Harding was dead and the presidency was yours?*
Coolidge: *I thought I could swing it.*

CONSERVATISM, UNVARNISHED

With the Harding administration about to be engulfed by assorted scandals, the Republican Party could not have hoped for a greater stroke of good fortune than the elevation to the presidency of Calvin Coolidge. Born on the Fourth of July, 1872, in the tiny Vermont hamlet of Plymouth Notch, Coolidge climbed slowly and steadily up the long ladder of American political life. His father had taught school and operated a local dry goods store, and had been deputy sheriff, constable, tax collector, and selectman of Plymouth before serving three terms in the Vermont house of representatives and one in the state senate.

Calvin followed an almost identical political path after graduating from Amherst College. He read law in the offices of a small Northampton firm and was admitted to the Massachusetts bar in 1897. That same year he launched his political career in Northampton's second ward as a delegate to the Republican state convention. Either through election or appointment, Coolidge subsequently held the post of city councilman, city solicitor, clerk of the courts, state representative, mayor, president of the state senate, lieutenant governor, and finally, governor of Massachusetts. Along the way, he married the astute and vivacious Grace Goodhue, a Phi Beta Kappa graduate from the University of

Vermont, and acquired the backing of two powerful patrons, Frank Stearns, a wealthy Boston merchant, and Dwight Morrow, an Amherst classmate and partner at J. P. Morgan. His unyielding opposition to the Boston police strike made Coolidge a national hero and catapulted him to the vice presidency, despite the doubts of many party chieftains, who hoped to balance the Republican national ticket in 1920 with a more liberal candidate.

The fortieth president of the United States, Ronald Reagan, admired the thirtieth, Calvin Coolidge. They were alike in many ways. Both served as governors and achieved national fame as advocates of law and order who stood firm against radicals during periods of social unrest and protest. Governor Reagan used force against college students who demonstrated against the Vietnam War. Governor Coolidge crushed the policeman's union and refused to rehire those officers who had walked the picket line. President Reagan did the same when the nation's air traffic controllers went out on strike in 1981. Coolidge was more seasoned and sophisticated in matters of politics and government than Reagan, a professional actor for most of his adult life, but both men were ideologues whose approach to public problems rested on the application of a few broad, simple homilies: the American social and economic order was basically sound; those who criticized it or attempted to alter it were therefore misguided and / or dangerous radicals; private enterprise was the backbone of the society; the role of government should be kept small, especially with respect to regulating business or redistributing the rewards handed out by the market; among the nations of the earth, the United States held an exceptional place by virtue of its superior institutions and enlightened moral sense.

Reagan's glamorous Hollywood past and his taste for luxury fit well with the rampant consumerism of the 1980s. Coolidge, on the contrary, was an authentic small-town Yankee, in William Allen White's immortal phrase a "Puritan in Babylon," whose parsimony, restraint, and laconic behavior contrasted sharply with the raucous hedonism permeating much of the culture of the 1920s. In a nation of bustling, chaotic cities, he symbolized the traditional order of the New England village; to a nation rocked by scandals, he brought rectitude; in the midst of political cynicism, a renewed emphasis on fundamentals; in an era of spiritual doubt, piety. In short, Coolidge was an ideal leader for many Americans who wished to explore the new land of materialism and self-indulgence, but who also feared the loss of traditional values. Coolidge's supporters "think . . . they are stern, ascetic and devoted to plain living because they vote for a man who is," observed journalist Walter Lippmann. "Thus we have attained a Puritanism de luxe in which it is possible to praise the classic virtues, while continuing to enjoy all the modern conveniences."

Experts in public relations could not have planned better the circumstances of Coolidge's ascension to the White House. Newspaper readers learned that John Coolidge, a notary, administered the official oath to his son at 2:45 A.M. on August 3 in the kitchen of the family homestead at Plymouth Notch. Two kerosene lamps lit the solemn ceremony. Only later was it noted that this rustic drama need not have been performed. As a local official, John Coolidge lacked authority to swear in his son as president of the United States. The oath he gave was probably superfluous in any event. Under the Constitution, Calvin Coolidge became president the moment Warren Harding died a continent away.

In an age of material excess, the new president's frugality (some called it stinginess) was legendary. In Northampton, the Coolidges' telephone had been a party line. They lived in half of a rented two-family home. Calvin stoked his own furnace. The Coolidges did not own an automobile until he became vice president. At a large 1919 reception for returning veterans in Dorchester, Massachusetts, the organizers were astonished to find Governor Coolidge standing alone in the hotel lobby. "Why, Governor, when did you get here?" asked the chairman. "We didn't see your car or any of your aides." "No, I haven't any automobile and there aren't any aides with me," replied Coolidge. "Thought I'd take the night off, so I came out in the streetcar."

In the White House, Coolidge expected small change from servants sent out to buy newspapers. He inspected the White House iceboxes, criticized the menus, and once objected when the housekeeper prepared six hams for one dinner of sixty persons. His bodyguard, Colonel Edmund Starling, recalled that Coolidge prepared sandwiches for them both in the pantry after their afternoon walk. "I'll bet no other president ever made cheese sandwiches for you," Coolidge had said. "No indeed," Starling replied. "It is a great honor, Mr. President." Responded Coolidge, grimly, "And I have to furnish the cheese, too."

President Coolidge, said a critic, "can be silent in five languages." When the ex-president's death was announced in 1933, the writer Dorothy Parker quipped, "How can they tell?" However, transcripts of his press conferences and testimony from cabinet members and congressmen suggest that this reputation for taciturnity has been greatly exaggerated. Coolidge delivered more formal speeches and met with reporters more frequently than any previous president. During these

President Coolidge and sons.

sessions he could be quite garrulous on a wide range of topics. What he wrote was often brief, but it impressed no less an expert than H. L. Mencken, who declared without irony, "He has a natural talent for the incomparable English language." In public, his reticence proved to be a valuable political weapon. "If you don't say anything," he advised Herbert Hoover, "you won't be called on to repeat it."

Coolidge's dry wit, his penchant for practical jokes, his boorishness, and his frequent cruelties were not exaggerated, however. He told a press conference that he planned to attend a county fair and when asked if he would speak there, replied: "No, I'm going as an exhibit." He pressed the alarm button on the front porch of the White House, then hid behind the living-room curtains and watched bewildered security guards search for the elusive intruder. Much to Grace Coolidge's chagrin, her husband devoured his dessert at state dinners and promptly left the table before the guests had finished theirs. Coolidge ridiculed his wife's education, told her not to wear culottes (even on vacation), and refused to give her a copy of his daily schedule. In 1928, when he announced his decision not to run for a second full term, Grace Coolidge read about it in the newspapers. A Secret Service agent, asked to bait the president's fishing hook, swore that Coolidge deliberately snagged him with it.

The Business of Government

Coolidge's impassive countenance and quirks of behavior made him an easy target for critics. William Allen White observed that he always had the appearance of someone "looking down his nose to locate that evil smell which seemed forever to affront him." Humorist Will Rogers, noting both the president's fondness for dogs and his parsimonious habits, brought down theater audiences by remarking that he only got a square meal at the White House when on all fours. But this president, who took pleasure in having his head rubbed with Vaseline while eating breakfast in bed, was no buffoon. Coolidge was an astute political professional who pursued his policy goals with ruthless consistency. Those on the political left came quickly to the realization that with his rigid devotion to an unfettered capitalist economy, he presented a far greater threat to the progressive legacy than Harding and all his corrupt minions. The *New York Call* denounced him as "probably the man of smallest caliber who has ever been made President of the United States." With such a leader in the White House, said the *Nation*, "every reactionary may today rejoice; in Calvin Coolidge he realizes his ideal; and every liberal may be correspondingly downcast." Harding pardoned Eugene Debs. In 1927, Coolidge deported the black nationalist leader Marcus Garvey.

The new president moved swiftly to distance himself from the Harding administration. Coolidge, the public soon learned, did not drink, smoke, play cards, or chase women. When the citizens of Marion, Ohio, staged a memorial service for their deceased favorite son, Coolidge found pressing presidential business elsewhere. Harding's ablest cabinet members—Hoover, Hughes, Mellon—were asked to stay. Those tarred with scandal such as Attorney General Harry Daugherty were soon axed. To head the demoralized Justice Department, Coolidge turned to his old Amherst classmate Harlan Fiske Stone, dean of the Columbia Law School, whose brains and integrity were unquestioned.

Stone, in turn, fired William Burns, chief of the Bureau of Investigation, who was widely believed to have conspired with Daugherty to block an investigation of the Teapot Dome affair. To fill Burns's post, the attorney general followed the recommendation of Herbert Hoover and selected John Edgar Hoover (no relation), the youthful and zealous head of the bureau's general intelligence division, a man whose distaste for political radicals was exceeded only by his passion for bureaucratic efficiency and order. The new leader of the G-men, whose sanctimonious manner resembled the president's, began to transform the bureau from a second-rate private detective agency into a modern investigative force. He upgraded the educational standards of agents and utilized scientific methods of crime detection such as fingerprint files. In an organizational sense, although not in terms of political philosophy, J. Edgar Hoover brought a progressive spirit to the nation's chief institution of law enforcement.

Elsewhere in the government, Coolidge and his appointees chloroformed the remnants of the progressive movement. For one whose entire adult life had been spent on the public payroll, the president had a remarkably limited view of the national government's capabilities and responsibilities. On a theoretical level, Coolidge articulated laissez-faire doctrine as pure as Grover Cleveland's. Because it could never create wealth, but could only drain it from the private, wealth-producing sector, government should remain small and frugal. The national government, Coolidge believed, should avoid military conflict and promote American trade abroad, while encouraging economic expansion at home through policies that allowed businessmen to earn a profit. It was not the function of government to impose unnecessary regulatory burdens on capital or interfere with the bargains struck by employers, workers, and consumers in the free market. The fact that some players, notably corporations, had greater power in the market than others did not concern him in the least, because these inequalities would be corrected by the market itself in due course. "Economic effort ought not to partake of privilege," he told the New York State Chamber of Commerce, "and business should be unhampered and free." The country already had too many laws, Coolidge observed on another occasion, "and we would be better off if we did not have any more. . . . The greatest duty and opportunity of government is not to embark on any new ventures. . . . It does not at all follow that because abuses exist . . . it is the concern of the federal government to attempt their reform."

On the level of practice, however, the administration normally acted in ways that promoted and protected the privileges of business. With

the approval of the president, for example, the Tariff Commission continued to raise the duties on foreign manufactured goods, pricing them
out of the American market, enriching their American competitors (some
of whom served on the commission), and forcing American consumers
to subsidize inefficiency. When he resigned in protest from the commission in 1928, Edward P. Costigan noted that Coolidge had approved
tariff *reductions* for only a handful of products, all of them insignificant, including bobwhite quail and paintbrush handles.

THE NADIR OF REGULATION

The Coolidge administration commenced more antitrust suits—over
seventy—than any of its predecessors, but the results did not pose a
serious threat to economic concentration. The three biggest cases—
against Standard Oil of Indiana, cement manufacturers, and maple
flooring firms—were all lost by the government on appeal. In nearly a
third of the cases, the Justice Department entered into a consent decree
with the offending company before trial. This procedure, one critic
lamented, promoted lax enforcement, because "the parties meet informally behind closed doors; the negotiations leave no public record. . . .
The instrument is useful to a sympathetic administration in building
up a paper record of accomplishment." Conviction seldom brought stiff
penalties. The largest fine—$2,000—was levied against an official of
the National Cash Register Company for price-fixing, but an appeals
court reduced the amount to $50 and the administration never col-
lected even that trifling sum. When Attorney General Stone threatened
to take action against a genuine monopoly, the Alcoa Aluminum Company, the president promoted him to the Supreme Court. Stone's successor never filed suit against the firm controlled by Coolidge's secretary
of the treasury.

To the Federal Trade Commission, the other agency charged with
rooting out "unfair methods of competition," Coolidge named people
such as William E. Humphrey, a former attorney for the lumber industry, who prior to his appointment had denounced the FTC as "an
instrument of oppression and disturbance and injury instead of help to
business." During the Coolidge era, the FTC's investigators prepared
enough reports on the milk, meat-packing, appliance, and radio industries to fill a small library, but they had little impact on the structure of
actual competition. Humphrey and his fellow commissioners adopted
a series of new regulations that significantly reduced the agency's sur-

veillance over business practices. The commission kept complaints against offending companies secret until a final decision had been reached. Instead of filling formal cease-and-desist orders against violators, the FTC promoted private settlements and trade practice conferences, where business groups adopted their own rules of competition that the agency soon ratified. In those few situations where the FTC sought information that a firm believed too sensitive, it fought the agency in court for years.

The conservative fiscal policies of Coolidge, Treasury Secretary Mellon, and budget director Herbert M. Lord eviscerated other regulatory agencies not subject to direct capture by probusiness appointees, such as the FTC and the Federal Power Commission. Their philosophy of balanced budgets and tax reductions meant fewer investigators for the Department of Agriculture's meat inspection service and the Food and Drug Administration. The Interior Department, with extensive responsibilities for policing the public lands, saw its budget decline from $48 million in 1921 to $32 million seven years later. The president ordered fewer towels in lavatories of the executive branch and asked White House reporters to buy their own pencils for press conferences. Lord decreed that federal agencies mimeograph on both sides of the paper. Except for expenditures on the presidential yacht *Mayflower*, even the budgets of the War and Navy Departments were trimmed. Federal receipts exceeded expenditures in each of the Coolidge years, reaching a surplus of $677 million in 1925 and $607 million in 1927.

LOOPHOLES AND EASY MONEY

By slashing federal outlays, of course, the Coolidge administration further justified Mellon's crusade to cut federal taxes. With some grumbling from the Democrats, Congress approved additional tax reductions in 1924, 1926, and 1928. Mellon claimed that these changes benefited some of the nation's least fortunate members by exempting from taxation those whose net annual income fell below $5,000, but various loopholes gave an even greater windfall to those whose incomes exceeded $100,000. Some paid no federal income tax at all between 1924 and 1929. At Mellon's request, the commissioner of internal revenue sent him a memorandum on various ways to avoid paying federal income tax and provided an expert to help prepare the secretary's own return. Senator George Norris observed, "Mr. Mellon himself gets a larger personal reduction than the aggregate of practically all the tax-

"The Cash Register Chorus." Businessmen celebrated Coolidge's program of low taxes, easy money, and light regulation.

payers in the state of Nebraska." Behind closed doors, it was discovered later, Secretary Mellon over eight years handed out cash refunds, credits, and abatements to wealthy individuals and corporations that amounted to $3.5 billion.

Not to be outdone by the Treasury Department, the U.S. Shipping Board, packed with Coolidge loyalists, sold 104 of its vessels built during the war to private companies and individuals at less than one-tenth of their actual cost. Only adroit parliamentary maneuvering by Senator Norris prevented government-built power dams, steam plants, and nitrate plants at Muscle Shoals from also falling into the hands of Henry Ford, the Alabama Power Company, American Cyanamid, or Union Carbide. When the Nebraskan finally pushed legislation through Congress in 1928 that permitted the federal government to operate an experimental fertilizer plant at Muscle Shoals and sell surplus power to municipal utilities, Coolidge allowed it to die without his signature. Norris's bill was very dangerous, he told congressional Republicans, "the opening wedge for socialism."

As an ex officio member of the Federal Reserve Board, Secretary
Mellon also resisted unorthodox ideas with respect to monetary policy,
although the ones he finally implemented proved highly dangerous to
the nation's long-term economic welfare. Working in tandem with
Benjamin Strong, the president of the powerful New York district bank,
the Treasury secretary easily dominated a board composed largely of
second-rate political appointees, who were stupendously ignorant of
central banking methods and their long-range economic consequences. In the judgment of Mellon and Strong, a sound monetary
policy for the United States had to rest on two principles: low interest
rates at home and restoration of the gold standard as the basis for
international financial transactions. The first would fuel economic
growth by providing ample funds for private investment. The second
would inspire confidence among those with money to lend by protecting against inflation and guaranteeing the conversion of major national
currencies at fixed exchange rates.

This was a businessman's monetary policy (more properly, a banker's monetary policy) whose two pillars seemed perfectly compatible.
By keeping American interest rates down, for example, wealthy Europeans would be encouraged to keep their gold at home, thus permitting the prewar gold standard to function once again. In 1924 and
1925, Mellon and Strong forced a reduction in the rediscount rate
charged by the Federal Reserve System to its member banks and flooded
the New York district with cash in an attempt to slash American interest rates and thereby stimulate the export of gold to England and the
continent.

With discount rates hovering between 3.5 and even 3 percent, the
Coolidge years represented a paradise for domestic borrowers, but many
of the costs and contradictions of this easy-money policy remained hidden from view. Despite low interest rates, foreigners continued to send
their funds to the United States because of the unsettled economic
conditions elsewhere. As a result, the European gold drain could be
halted only sporadically and the gold standard maintained only through
massive loans from American banks. Moreover, the United States bore
considerable responsibility for the disordered economic conditions that
plagued Europe in the mid-twenties. According to the World War Foreign Debt Commission, created by Congress in 1922, England, France,
and Italy owed the United States $22 billion in principal and interest
for money borrowed to fight the war. Coolidge may not have said, "Wal,
they hired the money, didn't they?" but he did say, "Unless money that
is borrowed is repaid, credit cannot be secured in time of necessity,"

and he made it clear that the United States expected every dollar to be paid back. He turned down the bold proposal of two Wall Street bankers, Norman Davis and Thomas Lamont, that the war debts be forgiven as a gesture of goodwill among former allies and in the interest of world economic stability.

Given the rigidity of Coolidge on the debt issue, the Allies were not disposed to modify Article 231 of the Versailles Treaty, which imposed reparations of $33 billion, plus interest, on Germany. Since America had not signed the treaty or sought reparations, Coolidge and his advisers insisted that the two issues remain separate, but they were, of course, indissolubly linked in terms of international trade and finance. The administration's passion for high tariffs also prevented both the Allies and the Germans from earning enough dollars in the American market to meet these obligations without impoverishing their own citizens with heavier taxes. To meet their reparations payments, the German government simply printed more money, which created hyperinflation and economic chaos. When Germany finally stopped payment altogether in 1923, the French sent troops to occupy the Ruhr and Europe tottered again on the edge of war.

Now the United States had to act. With only modest encouragement from the State Department, American bankers and businessmen led by Charles Dawes and Owen D. Young took the initiative to shore up the faltering international financial structure. Dawes and Young negotiated settlements in 1924 and 1929 that trimmed German reparations to $26 billion, put them on a regular payment schedule over fifty-nine years, and provided new loans to underwrite the plans and stabilize the German currency. Germany paid reparations to the Allies, the Allies in turn paid back the Americans—all with money borrowed from the United States. The easy-money policies of Mellon and Strong permitted Dawes and Young to carry out an exquisite piece of international financial legerdemain. However, the same low interest rates that underwrote these schemes to promote world monetary stability also began to encourage reckless speculation in America during the Coolidge years.

FRUGALITY AND FOREIGN POLICY

As the case of Europe demonstrated, Republicans hoped to reap the benefits of America's new economic muscle with minimum cost to the nation's budget, military resources, or emotional capital. Under Coolidge, therefore, the United States led new efforts to curb government spending on armaments, especially naval forces, and to secure its interests in Asia and Latin America through commercial penetration and dependency, not brute force. In consequence, a somewhat schizophrenic foreign policy grew up, one emphasizing formal legal documents defining rights, duties, and methods of resolving conflicts, while eschewing mutual security arrangements like the League of Nations that might compromise America's freedom of action or lead to actual military engagement.

The landmark Five-Power Treaty of the Washington Conference had capped the great-power naval race in battleships and aircraft carriers by limiting new construction and fixing their size and armaments. This treaty did nothing, however, to put a lid on spending for other fighting ships, especially submarines and cruisers, which the United States at the end of World War I had far fewer of than either England or Japan. As those two countries continued their building programs between 1922 and 1924, the United States faced an unpleasant choice—to accept permanent inferiority or launch a costly crash program. Congress chose the latter, authorizing the Coolidge administration in 1924 to begin building eight ten-thousand-ton cruisers; this course was coupled with a plea for another international conference on arms limitations. The parsimonious Coolidge quickly took the hint, and at the urging of the United States a new, three-power naval conference opened at Geneva in the summer of 1927.

Unfortunately, Coolidge's desire for naval economy was not matched by his grasp of technical military details or diplomatic skills. And his secretary of state, Frank Kellogg, a former United States senator from Minnesota and ambassador to Great Britain, lacked the brains and guile of Charles Evans Hughes. Subordinates in Foggy Bottom found their new chief "wildly inaccurate, intolerably rude, unwilling to read memoranda or to listen to an oral argument." Although the Americans had few actual cruisers to put on the negotiating table, they insisted on a formula that authorized some big ships with large guns. The British, on the other hand, demanded many smaller vessels with less firepower. France, still smarting over its reduced naval allocation at the Washington Conference, refused to send delegates to Geneva; the Italians stayed home, too. Even before the European press began to ridicule Coolidge's "insufficient preparation," the much-heralded Geneva conference failed.

The Kellogg-Briand Pact

A year after the Geneva debacle, Kellogg did secure a diplomatic triumph, but one now regarded as the most illusory and meaningless of the era—the Treaty of Paris, which renounced war as an instrument of national policy. In its assumption that war, like drinking, gambling, prostitution, and other social evils, could be eliminated through the force of law and public opinion, the Kellogg-Briand Pact expressed a deep American idealism and legalism that survived even the disillusionment of the war.

The Kellogg-Briand Pact also embodied the fading hopes of old Wilsonians such as Professor James T. Shotwell of Columbia; they saw the treaty as a tiny but significant step toward genuine collective security arrangements and closer ties with the League. But Kellogg-Briand would never have come about without the French government's badgering of the Americans throughout the twenties for a bilateral security treaty. When French foreign minister Aristide Briand raised that possibility again in 1927 on the tenth anniversary of American interven-

Frank Kellogg, secretary of state.

tion into World War I, weary State Department officials proposed to scotch the idea permanently with a new twist: a multilateral agreement in which all the signatories renounced war. To his credit, Secretary of State Kellogg did not take much interest in the idea at first, but hounded by subordinates and criticized by Senator Borah for failing to seize the initiative for peace, the secretary soon became a rabid convert.

The fifteen nations, led by the United States, France, England, Germany, Japan, and Italy, that signed the Kellogg-Briand Pact in the summer of 1929 pledged not to wage war, except in situations of self-defense, and to resolve their disputes by peaceful means. To the regret of many, the concept of self-defense was ill-defined and the agreement contained no mechanism for consultation among the parties in the event of a violation. Even with these glaring omissions, the hard-core isolationists in the United States Senate declined to approve it without a long-winded appendix from the Foreign Relations Committee that proclaimed the right of the country to fight if attacked or to enforce the Monroe Doctrine. At the same time, the Senate report noted that the proposed pact did not sanction the use of force or require the United States to use coercive measures of any kind against another country. Senator Carter Glass of Virginia said he would vote for the measure, but hoped his constituents would not take it too seriously. Declaring his reluctant support, Hiram Johnson quoted the poet François Villon:

> To Messur Noel, named the neat
> By those who love him, I bequeath
> A helmless ship, a houseless street,
> A wordless book, a swordless sheath,
> An hourless clock, a leafless wreath,
> A bell sans tongue, a saw sans teeth,
> A bed sans sheet, a board sans meat,
> To make his nothingness complete.

Within five years, sixty-four countries had signed the Kellogg-Briand Pact; even so, as the use of force in international affairs escalated after 1929, the verdict passed by Senator Johnson seemed prescient. Others denounced the treaty as "an international kiss," "absurdly impractical," or "worthless, but harmless." An aging Henry Cabot Lodge declared that it "only thickens the haze, deepens the pitfalls, and once again postpones the day when some really clear thinking is done." The pact, according to these critics, lulled the country into a false sense of security; by helping to defer military expenditures it made the coming of war in the 1930s all that more disillusioning and tragic for the people of the United States. But were there viable alternatives? Stronger measures, such as a genuine mutual security treaty or closer cooperation with the League of Nations, lacked support in the executive branch and Congress. When the United States entered numerous mutual security pacts after World War II, they proved to be a very mixed blessing, especially in Southeast Asia. Whatever its simplicities, the Kellogg-Briand Pact did spotlight culprits when armies organized by its signers began to march across national boundaries in the thirties.

The Kellogg agreement bore other wholesome fruit in the late twenties, when the Coolidge and Hoover administrations renegotiated arbitration agreements with over two dozen nations. To be sure, these treaties, most dating back to the era of Elihu Root and William Jennings Bryan, contained important escape clauses exempting certain issues from arbitration (such as the Monroe Doctrine and those deemed within "domestic jurisdiction"). Even so, they displayed a bona fide repugnance toward the use of force in international affairs. As always, the acid test of this policy for the United States came in relations with its neighbors in the Western Hemisphere. Under Coolidge those results remained mixed.

The Good Neighbor

Apart from Nicaragua, the Coolidge administration continued the policy begun by Harding: more American troops left the soil of Latin America than arrived. Several factors spurred this abandonment of direct military intervention. First, budget-conscious Republicans such as Coolidge and Mellon hoped to avoid the large expenses associated with such endeavors. Second, the use of force had proved futile in large, complex nations such as Mexico. Third, it was simply bad public relations to deploy American troops to protect the profits of a handful of American companies. The Coolidge administration therefore pioneered more subtle methods for promoting and defending the nation's strategic and economic interests in the hemisphere; these it gave a trial run in the Dominican Republic and Haiti.

In both these impoverished Caribbean nations, the United States ended its official protectorate policy and withdrew its military force, but not before concluding sweetheart treaties. The agreements gave Uncle Sam's financial representatives a dominant voice in managing the revenues of Haiti and the Dominican Republic, spending their funds, and paying off their outstanding public debts. All of these debts, not incidentally, were owed to American banks. Even more critically, the Coolidge and later the Hoover administrations began to organize and arm local military and police forces in both countries, cadres that could serve as surrogates for the departed American soldiers. Trained by United States Marines, these low-cost indigenous forces quickly became a new social elite, devoted to law and order. They enjoyed a higher standard of living than other groups, and they defended the local status quo with gusto and ruthlessness against disgruntled peasants and workers. In 1930, the chief of the Dominican model army, tutored by the Americans, General Rafael Leónidas Trujillo, overthrew the elected Dominican government and installed himself as president. For the next thirty years, this "Benefactor of the Fatherland," the son of a poor mulatto family, erected one of the most efficient and murderous dictatorships in the hemisphere. He lined his own pockets while at the same time protecting American investors.

It required a bit more effort and bloodshed to accomplish the same results in Nicaragua, where a violent civil war erupted in 1925 after Coolidge pulled the last Marines out of Managua, the nation's capital. By the summer of 1926, much to the chagrin of Congress and other critics, Coolidge sent the Marines back. He also sent along Henry Stimson, veteran diplomat and former secretary of war, to bring the warring Nicaraguans together and stop the killing. Backed by American arms, Stimson forced two of the combatants, Adolfo Díaz and José Moncado, to lay down their guns, organize a coalition government, hold American-style elections, and create a new security force, the Guardia Nacional. Stimson claimed he had quelled "the bloodiest and cruelest revolution in modern times," but one of Moncado's generals, the charismatic Augusto César Sandino, repudiated the so-called Peace of Tipitapa. Sandino had an enthusiastic following among the poorest farmers, and they continued to fight on against both his Nicaraguan rivals and the American Marines.

The Nicaraguan elections of 1928 and 1932 restored what American partisans called "orderly democracy and self-government" although forty-two Marines and three thousand local citizens had been killed before they were held. Critics such as Senator Borah claimed that Stimson had "totally misjudged the Nicaraguan people," many of whom followed Sandino in rejecting the agreements reached at Tipitapa. A deceptive calm settled over Managua when Juan Bautista Sacasa, a so-called liberal, took office as president in 1932. The Marines went home again. The new American-trained Guardia Nacional, led by Sacasa's

*Augusto Sandino (center, checkered shirt), leader of the Nicaraguan resis-
tance to U.S. intervention.*

nephew, Anastasio "Tacho" Somoza, ensured "orderly democracy and
self-government" by torturing, killing, and jailing the regime's opponents, variously labeled as bandits, communists, and agitators. After
dining with Sandino at a heralded peace conference in 1934, Sacasa
and Somoza had the rebel leader murdered, thereby sowing the seeds
of more civil strive and anti-Americanism in the years to come.

Despite heightened tensions, Mexico and the United States avoided
a repetition of the open warfare of the Wilson era. The thaw in their
relations begun under Harding rested on a series of delicate compromises over the Mexican debt owed to U.S. bankers and the interpretation of Article 27 of the Mexican constitution of 1917, which
nationalized lands and subsoil rights held by foreigners. In the so-called
Bucareli agreements of 1923, the government of Álvaro Obregón pledged
not to expropriate foreign subsoil holdings acquired and developed prior
to 1917. At about the same time, a Wall Street syndicate reached a
settlement with the government providing that oil export taxes would

be used to pay off those who held Mexican bonds. American financiers, oil companies, and mining firms breathed a bit easier. A grateful Coolidge later permitted Obregón to buy American weapons and even traverse American soil to crush an attempted coup by disaffected members of the Mexican army.

However, Obregón's hand-picked successor, Plutarco Elias Calles, a former schoolteacher and bartender, stunned American leaders in 1925 when he pushed through the Mexican congress a major revision of the Bucareli agreements. It limited to fifteen years the ownership of all subsoil rights acquired even before 1917. The new president also lashed out at American policy in Nicaragua. Secretary Kellogg proclaimed that the Mexican government had been taken over by communists; Mexico, he said, was "now on trial before the world." American oil companies and land syndicates beat the drums for military action. They were joined by Catholic leaders in the United States, who accused the Calles regime of waging a vendetta against the church. Veterans of Pershing's punitive expeditions oiled their service revolvers in anticipation of another march south of the Rio Grande.

Cooler heads prevailed. Led by Borah and the Foreign Relations Committee, the Senate voted 79–0 in early 1926 for arbitration of all disputed American property claims in Mexico. Lacking support in Congress for more coercive measures, Coolidge reined in his secretary of state and Mexican ambassador, James R. Sheffield, who had also called for tough measures against Calles. Within six months, Coolidge had scrubbed this old diplomatic team by sending to Mexico his Amherst classmate Dwight Morrow.

Morrow remained in Mexico for a year after Coolidge left the White House, but when he departed in 1930, the oil controversy had been diffused, Calles had toned down his attacks on the Catholic Church, and the Mexicans had softened their criticism of U.S. policy in Nicaragua. Morrow disarmed Calles and other leaders with his sincere desire for peace and his avid interest in their country. Goodwill visits by Will Rogers and the dashing Charles Lindbergh helped, too. But the biggest factor in the settlement was Calles's own desire to move his political base back to the center of the Mexican political spectrum. The Calles-Morrow compromise, ratified by the Mexican congress in 1928, let American firms retain property bought before Article 27 took effect, but required leases for that acquired after 1917. It remained in force for a decade, until Mexico's reform-minded new president, Lázaro Cárdenas, sponsored its abolition and nationalized all foreign oil holdings.

A peaceful resolution of Mexico's dispute with the United States did not mollify most Latin American nations while American troops still patrolled the streets of Managua. At the triennial conference of Western Hemisphere republics held in Havana in 1928, El Salvador's representative, backed by delegates from Argentina and Mexico, offered a sharp anti-American resolution denouncing the right of any state "to intervene in the internal affairs of another." The U.S. delegation, led by Coolidge himself, managed to sidetrack this motion, but a speech by former secretary of state Hughes defending America's quest for "peace, order and stability and the recognition of honest rights properly acquired" was greeted with cynicism and open contempt. Fearing that the Havana debacle presaged a new burst of anti-Americanism in the hemisphere, Kellogg put the department's chief legal adviser, J. Reuben Clark, to work on a solution.

Clark's now-famous 1928 memorandum to Kellogg—not officially published until 1930—has long been regarded as a major milestone in U.S. foreign relations and the intellectual foundation of the so-called Good Neighbor Policy later articulated by Franklin Roosevelt. It was, however, less radical than commonly assumed. Clark argued that Theodore Roosevelt had been wrong in 1904 when he invoked the Monroe Doctrine as the legal basis for the right of the United States to intervene in the internal affairs of other hemispheric nations. The Monroe Doctrine, Clark pointed out, focused on the behavior of European nations, not that of the United States' neighbors. Clark demonstrated that Roosevelt's corollary had little foundation in past history or international law; but he did not say (nor did Hoover or FDR later) that the United States lacked other justifications for meddling in Latin American affairs. And the methods, already tested in the Dominican Republic, Haiti, Nicaragua, and Mexico, were at hand: training and arming military surrogates; squeezing nations with economic sanctions. Instead of gunboat diplomacy, the United States under Coolidge had devised more subtle means to maintain its hegemony in the hemisphere.

The Business of America

A minimum of government regulation, tax cuts, balanced budgets, low interest rates, and cheap foreign policy—these constituted the core of Coolidge's unwavering pro-business philosophy at home and abroad. But lest the electorate come to regard him solely as a spokesman for

Mammon, the president always took pains to describe his mission and the nation's in more lofty, idealistic terms. In an age of unabashed materialism, the man from Plymouth Notch won the hearts and minds of the American people by emphasizing spiritual values:

—"Business rests squarely on the law of service, reliance on truth, faith and justice."
—"In all our economic discussions we must remember that we cannot stop with the mere acquisition of wealth. The ultimate result to be desired is not the making of money, but the making of people. Industry, thrift, and self-control are not sought because they create wealth, but because they create character."
—"The things of the spirit come first. Unless we cling to that, all our material prosperity, overwhelming though it may appear, will turn to a barren scepter in our grasp."
—"After all, the chief business of the American people is business. They are profoundly concerned with producing, buying, selling, investing, and prospering in the world. . . . We make no conceal-ment of the fact that we want wealth, but there are many other things that we want very much more. . . . The chief ideal of the American people is idealism. I cannot repeat too often that America is a nation of idealists."

THE LAST PROGRESSIVE

Lincoln Steffens, the aging journalist whose writings had often stirred the social conscience of an earlier generation, observed wryly that Cal-vin Coolidge had put to rest the idea that the federal government was simply the mistress of business. Under Coolidge, he said, they got mar-ried. Most Americans who went to the polls in the 1924 election put their stamp of approval on the wedding. With the Harding scandals receding into the past, the economy about to move into high gear, and no foreign policy crisis on or near the horizon, Coolidge easily secured the Republican nomination in Cleveland and swept to a decisive vic-tory in November over John W. Davis, the Democratic candidate, and Robert M. La Follette, "Fighting Bob," the sixty-nine-year-old United States senator from Wisconsin, who carried the banner of the Progres-sive Party. Probably no opponent living could have overcome Cool-idge's many advantages in 1924, which included incumbency, prosperity, peace, and a very fat campaign treasury. When Coolidge's youngest son, sixteen-year-old Calvin, Jr., died suddenly in August 1924 from an infected toe, the tragedy produced a huge outpouring of sympathy for the president and his wife.

The Democrats did their best to ensure Coolidge's victory by the quality of their candidate and the circumstances of his selection. First, they held a tumultuous national convention in New York City, carried live over the radio, where the party's ethnic, religious, and cultural divisions burst forth in all their intensity and rancor. Delegates from the West and South, overwhelmingly sympathetic to prohibition, supported the candidacy of William Gibbs McAdoo, the former treasury secretary and President Wilson's son-in-law, who was a more sophisticated version of William Jennings Bryan. Those from the big cities, heavily Catholic, immigrant, and opposed to prohibition, rallied to Alfred E. Smith, the governor of New York, called "the Happy Warrior" by the man who nominated him, Franklin Roosevelt. The voting for a presidential candidate began on June 30 and did not end until July 9. For 102 ballots in the sticky heat of Madison Square Garden, the McAdoo and Smith camps fought to a standstill, neither side able to command the two-thirds majority needed for the nomination. Finally, on the 103rd ballot the groggy delegates accepted a compromise worked out by James M. Cox and other party leaders: Davis would head the ticket with Bryan's brother, Governor Charles W. Bryan of Nebraska, as his running mate.

Davis, a West Virginia native, was a man of sterling character with an impressive résumé. He had been Wilson's solicitor general and ambassador to Great Britain. Unfortunately, at the time of his nomination he was also a senior partner in one of Wall Street's biggest law firms, whose principal client was J. P. Morgan and Company. In terms of symbol and substance, John W. Davis was unsuited to run a campaign against wealth and privilege. The keynote of all Democratic policies, he told the convention, should be "to keep the road open for private enterprise and personal initiative," a position that sounded strikingly similar to Coolidge's. Very soon political wits observed that the only difference between the two major parties in 1924 was "whether the entrance to the office of J. P. Morgan and Company should be on Wall or Broad Street."

The lone voice of genuine opposition came, therefore, from La Follette, one of the founding fathers of progressive reform, who had grown accustomed to the role of dissenter in a political career spanning four decades. There was hardly a cause in the progressive movement—the income tax, workmen's compensation, railroad regulation, antitrust

John W. Davis (left), the Democrats' choice in 1924.

legislation, women's rights—that had not been touched by his intelligence and passion. The titans of business and finance despised La Follette because of his stands on regulation and his sympathy for the working man. Patriots hated him because he had opposed the arming of American merchant ships during the neutrality crisis of 1917 and voted against war with Germany. But to the six hundred delegates who came to the Cleveland convention of the Committee for Progressive Political Action on July 4—grizzled Populists, pacifists, union members, former Bull Moosers, socialists, feminists, and farmers—he was the David of reform who would slay the Goliaths of reaction and return the nation to its true, progressive course.

Fearing defeat for progressives in Congress, La Follette vetoed a full-blown third party effort, but he willingly accepted the CPPA nomination for president and vowed an all-out campaign against Coolidge and Davis with the support of his running mate, Senator Burton K. Wheeler of Montana, who had helped expose malfeasance in Harry Daugherty's justice department. La Follette and Wheeler welcomed support from the American Federation of Labor (which broke a longstanding tradition of not endorsing third-party candidates), the railroad brotherhoods, the Farmer-Labor Party, and the Socialist Party, but they spurned assistance from William Z. Foster and the Communist Party, which La Follette called "absolutely repugnant to democratic ideals and to all American aspirations." The communists, in turn, labeled the La Follette–Wheeler ticket more backward than the Republicans, largely because of its militant anti-monopoly stand.

From the perspective of Marxists and others, who believed that capitalism progressed inevitably to higher and higher levels of financial concentration before its collapse, the Progressive platform seemed an exercise in nostalgia. Although La Follette endorsed government ownership of public utilities, especially hydroelectric power and railroads, the heart of his campaign became a pledge to destroy "the combined power of private monopoly over the political and economic life of the American people." According to the party's platform, the great issue before the electorate in 1924 was "the control of government and industry by private monopoly," a process that had "crushed competition, stifled private initiative and independent enterprise."

Except for more vigorous enforcement of the existing antitrust laws, however, La Follette and Wheeler remained painfully vague about how the power of monopolies might be broken. They were not at all vague about other issues. The Progressive Party vowed to abolish the use of injunctions in labor disputes, to guarantee the right of workers to collective bargaining, and to support constitutional amendments restricting federal judicial power, including the election of federal judges for ten-year terms. For good measure, they denounced American military intervention abroad, opposed conscription, and called for a popular referendum before the country went to war again.

Old progressives such as Justice Brandeis and Jane Addams, who had long opposed the curse of bigness and the scourge of war, could not have been more pleased with the platform and with La Follette's campaign. Predictably, Davis and Coolidge spent more time attacking La Follette than each other. Davis was especially horrified by the senator's proposals for restructuring the federal judiciary. A large number of voters, however, simply yawned their way through the campaign. A pro–La Follette editorial in the *New Republic*, written by Harvard law professor Felix Frankfurter, argued that a "great inequality of property" was "the most significant characteristic of our social-economic life" and that only "Fighting Bob" and the Progressive Party addressed this issue, but in the fall of 1924 more Americans probably contemplated the fate of Alvin "Shipwreck" Kelly, sitting atop a flagpole for thirteen hours, than the distribution of wealth. On election day, with barely half of the eligible voters going to the polls, Coolidge secured 15 million popular votes to Davis's 8 million and La Follette's 4.8 million. The incumbent president swept to victory in thirty-five states with 382 electoral votes, and this landslide also returned big Republican majorities to both houses of Congress. Davis carried only the eleven states of the Old Confederacy plus Oklahoma. La Follette won only Wisconsin's thirteen electoral votes. The Socialist Party, which had attracted nearly a million votes for Eugene Debs in 1912 but now endorsed La Follette, virtually disappeared from the political landscape.

At first glance, the Republican victory in 1924 seemed devastating and complete, a total repudiation of reform and progressivism. Beneath the surface, however, the results could be read differently. Outside their traditional bastion in the white South, the Democrats had been the big losers. La Follette and Wheeler, drawing support chiefly from strapped farmers and workers who had not tasted Republican prosperity, ran ahead of the Democrats in eleven states, including California. And if an aging progressive candidate on a third-party ticket with a total campaign budget of little more than $200,000 had been able to tap so much discontent in a year of fair economic winds, imagine what might happen if the economic climate went bad! Davis's defeat and La Follette's efforts also convinced some Democratic leaders, especially Franklin Roosevelt, that their party could never hope to beat the Republicans with appeals to conservatism that ignored its own tradition as "the party of progress and liberal thought." For the moment, however, the skies showed Republican, progressivism had been routed, the Democratic Party was in disarray, and Roosevelt, recently recovered from a near-fatal bout with polio, remained only a former vice presidential candidate and a promising New York politician who quoted Wordsworth.

4

Winners and Losers

*I don't care if it doesn't make a nickel, I just want every
man, woman, and child to see it.*
—Samuel Goldwyn

*Yes, sir; the girls work 10 hours a day, and then on Satur-
day you cannot eat a bite of lunch from the time you get in
the plant until you get out Saturday, and when you think
about working until 11:30 through the week and getting a
lunch at 11:30 and then have to work until 1 o'clock on
Saturday before you get anything to eat, you are
exhausted.*
—Margaret Bowen, Elizabethton textile worker

DREAM FACTORIES

While Coolidge's popularity indicated that most Americans gave the
Vermonter and his party credit for their newfound prosperity after 1924,
the pockets of discontent tapped by La Follette suggested the existence
of another side to the country's economic coinage. Production provided one measure of the economy's health, the allocation of its rewards
still another. The great Indian chief Sitting Bull once observed that the
white men of North America knew how to make many things, "but
they do not know how to distribute them properly." The economy of
the twenties confirmed the truth of that statement. There were big winners, as radio, petroleum, electric power, and automobiles demonstrated. But there were also many losers, whose numbers mounted as
the decade wore on.

"Flagstaff no good for our purpose. Have proceeded to California.

Want authority to rent barn in place called Hollywood for $75 a month. Regards to Sam." Thus wrote writer-director Cecil B. De Mille to his financial backers Jesse Lasky and Samuel Goldwyn on the eve of World War I. European governments consulted Insull about running their electric power systems. Lenin and the Bolsheviks admired the efficiency of Ford's auto plants. But the industry that was truly American and best symbolized the new economic order of the twenties took shape on the outskirts of Los Angeles: motion pictures.

While some heralded the film industry as a revolutionary art form and others marveled at its technical innovations, those who built empires out of celluloid knew that their fortunes rested on the exploitation of capitalism's newest mass commodity—leisure—and the supplying of this market with fantasies of heroism, comedy, tragedy, power, wealth, sex, and violence. In a culture long saturated with the work ethic, the business of entertainment was almost a contradiction in terms, which is why "respectable" capitalists shunned the motion picture industry in the twenties as they did bootlegging until the profits became too tempting to resist. Like bootlegging, the motion picture industry thrived on the ambition, cunning, and imagination of first- and second-generation immigrants: Goldwyn (Poland), Louis B. Mayer (Lithuania), William Fox (Hungary), the Warner brothers (Poland), Lewis Selznick (Russia). The most indigenous of all American businesses had a distinctive foreign cast in an era that slammed the door against other foreigners.

The genius of Edison made the motion picture camera and projector possible, but it took the daring and business acumen of former glove salesmen, furriers, jewelers, and nickelodeon operators to turn an inventor's toy into big business. And because the paths to power and riches in this industry were so various, it remained in a condition of competitive anarchy long after others had succumbed to oligopoly. Penny arcade and peep show promoters like Marcus Loew and William Fox began at the distribution end, with the logical belief that those who controlled where movies were shown would ultimately dominate the industry. Loew, for example, once purchased a burlesque house in Brooklyn that the police had closed down, allowed a legitimate acting troupe to use it for a few months, and then opened it as a respectable movie theater.

Loew's onetime partner Adolph Zukor, who made a fortune in the fur business before branching out into penny arcades, thought film production, not distribution, the key to success. Seeking to corner the market on talent, he signed up many of the best actors, actresses, and directors to long-term contracts, turned out feature-length films, and forced the theater chains to accept his inferior products if they wanted to exhibit his quality ones, a practice called block-booking. Zukor's aggressive tactics forced the exhibitors, in turn, to form a production combine, First National Pictures, in order to develop their own films. Fearing that his competitors would now exclude him from their theatres, Zukor finally began to acquire his own movie houses.

The furious scramble for theaters ensued throughout the twenties, often resembling the competitive warfare of the infant petroleum industry. Independent theater operators were told to sign up with one chain or watch a new movie house built nearby. At the start of the decade, Zukor's Paramount Pictures company controlled over three hundred theaters, a figure that rose to sixteen hundred (roughly one-tenth of all American movie houses) ten years later. His most glamorous was the Paramount in New York City, where at intermission the bands of Paul Whiteman or John Philip Sousa played and bathing beauties paddled around in a huge tank. Its only rival, New York's Roxy, called the Cathedral of the Motion Pictures, boasted three organs, a prodigious chandelier in a gargantuan lobby, and a red carpet that cost $100,000.

Zukor's chief rivals in the twenties proved to be the former glove salesman Goldwyn and the three Warner brothers, Harry, Sam, and

First nighters outside Warners' Theatre, 1926.

Abe, who parlayed the income from a traveling exhibit of *The Great Train Robbery* into a nickelodeon and then into a profitable movie exchange. Both Goldwyn and the Warners at first eschewed the scramble for theaters and concentrated instead on making quality feature-length films. Since Zukor sought to monopolize acting talent, Goldwyn signed up writers. Although far from learned (he once told a group of producers, "Include me out"; informed that a particular play was caustic, he retorted, "I don't care what it costs, buy it!"), Goldwyn's hunch about the importance of writing paid off once dialogue became important with the advent of sound. Metro-Goldwyn-Mayer and later Samuel Goldwyn, Inc., set artistic standards that few in the industry could match.

Edison had put sound and motion pictures together before the turn of the century. President Coolidge and Governor Al Smith had both appeared in talking campaign films in 1924. William Fox had wired many of his theaters for sound by 1925 and was busy showing newsreels that utilized the Movietone system developed by Theodore Case and Earl Sponable. Most of the leading studios held back, however, fearful of undermining their current investments in expensive stars and losing lucrative foreign markets in silent films. The Warner brothers broke ranks. Backed by the financial resources of Wall Street's Goldman, Sachs and the technical ingenuity of the Western Electric laboratories of Bell Telephone, they realized the dream in a feature-length film when Al Jolson belted out "Kol Nidre" and "Mammy" in the October 1927 debut of *The Jazz Singer*. Enriched and emboldened by this success, the Warners acquired their own chain of theaters and began to finance all their activities from production to distribution by marketing securities without the help of Wall Street. The dreams now spoke. The managers of the dream factories had moved from the periphery of the consumer society to its very center.

CAPTAINS OF CONSCIOUSNESS

As automobiles and motion pictures went, so did the rest of the country's commerce. A torrent of novel products and their attendant advertising flooded American consumers in the twenties: the Milky Way candy bar, Welch's grape jelly, Popsicles, Wheaties, the permanent wave, Scotch Tape, flavored yogurt, the wall-mounted can opener, clock radios, Rice Krispies, mobile home trailers, aluminum furniture, and hair color rinse in ten shades. Through newspapers, magazines, billboards, radio, and the motion pictures, leading manufacturers and their advertising advisers attempted to execute a momentous dual revolution in American economic life, one structural, the other in people's values and habits.

Of the two, the structural revolution was perhaps the more important, because it transferred economic power over basic consumption patterns from wholesalers and myriad retailers who had historically controlled the distribution of products to the large-scale manufacturers who made them. Through saturation advertising, the manufacturers of products such as soap, breakfast cereals, cooking oil, packaged meats, and canned vegetables could directly influence the choices consumers made at the corner market or the general store. By equating their particular brand names—Ivory Soap, Kellogg's Corn Flakes, Crisco, Old Dutch Cleanser, Campbell's Soup—with quality, convenience, and status, the manufacturers sought to cement consumer loyalties and steady profits by reducing the marketing influence of independent businessmen. The retail merchant who failed to carry Quaker Oats, Heinz pickles, Gillette safety razors, or Kodak cameras might find himself losing business to those down the street who did.

Independent retailers in big-city neighborhoods and small country towns, the symbolic backbone of the American free enterprise system, sensed their new dependence on Madison Avenue and the giant manufacturers, who, one complained, "want to make of him [the retail grocer] a mere automaton for the vending of their wares." Traditional wholesale merchants and their retail allies found themselves under mounting attack from other sources as well—the huge mail-order houses such as Sears, Roebuck and Montgomery Ward, and the spreading chain stores such as A&P, Woolworth's, and S. S. Kresge, which often sold brand names at substantial discounts.

The independent merchants fought back in a series of political campaigns that dotted most states for the next two decades. Raising high the banners of local autonomy and antimonopoly, they secured zoning regulations and tax laws designed to thwart the march of the chain stores. They even made peace with some giant manufacturers by supporting retail price maintenance laws to curb the discounting of major brand-name products. But even before the Great Depression squeezed them further, the independent retailers managed to hang on largely by becoming "mere automatons" to the large-scale manufacturers and their ad agencies.

In addition to the key role they played in reorganizing the distribution of products, experts of advertising, called by one scholar "captains of consciousness," sought to create new desires and discontents. They stigmatized last year's model, brand, or fashion as obsolete, outdated, a badge of social inferiority. "If I wear a certain brand of underwear," noted a critic of the times, "I have the satisfaction of knowing that my fellow-men not so fortunately clad are undoubtedly fouled swine." Spending money was encouraged, thrift ignored or impugned. Consumption, not hard work and self-restraint, became the path to fortune and personal happiness. In an increasingly urban and bureaucratic society, when the presentation of the self and effective interpersonal relationships became key ingredients to success, one could not hope to move ahead in business, consummate a good marriage, or run a decent home without certain commodities that enhanced one's appearance and personality. According to one of advertising's leading theorists, J. Walter Thompson, the typical consumer had the mental sophistication of a "fourteen-year-old human animal." His firm and others prospered on this assumption.

—The Post cereal company warned that "faulty elimination" was "the greatest enemy that beauty knows," because "it plays havoc with the complexion, brings sallow skin, dull and listless eyes." But Post's Bran Flakes, eaten every day, provided "an ounce of prevention."
—"Often a bridesmaid, but never a bride? For halitosis, use Listerine."
—"The virile chaps who send their deals over with a snap that takes your breath away. . . . These are healthy chaps. . . . Fleischmann's Yeast is tuning up a lot of good fellows to concert pitch and making them stick. Lots of fellows are taking the Fleischmann's Yeast road to 100% Health and Success."
—"He changed his stance. He should have changed his underwear. He couldn't relax. He was muscle bound. . . . Have you ever worn the Lewis Gold Suit?"
—"Why drown your soul in a greasy dishpan? The greatest gift of electricity to the modern housewife is the Conover Electric Dishwasher."

In a land whose chief business was business, advertising assumed a commanding role. "It is," said President Coolidge, "the most potent influence in adopting and changing the habits and modes of life, affecting what we eat, what we wear, and the work and play of the whole nation." Less sanguinely, economist Stuart Chase estimated that in 1925, $1 was spent "to educate consumers in what they may or may not want to buy" for every 70 cents spent on all other forms of education from primary grades through the university. Advertising, he wrote, fashioned a "dream world" of "smiling faces, shining teeth, school girl

*Milton Feasley's classic advertisement for Listerine
mouthwash linked consumption with success in love
and marriage.*

complexions, cornless feet, perfect fitting union suits, distinguished
collars, wrinkleless pants, odorless breaths, regularized bowels, happy
homes in New Jersey . . . perfect busts, shimmering shanks, self-wash-
ing dishes—backs behind which the moon was meant to rise."

The railroad, the telegraph, the automobile, and the telephone had
forged a continental commercial empire, but advertising sought nothing less than a continental marketplace of nearly uniform emotions,
desires, tastes, and fantasies. This is not to say that manufacturers and
their advertising agencies ignored the extraordinary regional, ethnic,
and class diversity among American consumers. Procter & Gamble
marketed kosher Crisco to grocers who catered to a largely Jewish
clientele. Wrigley's sold its chewing gum around the world, but tar-

geted certain brands—Juicy Fruit and Sweet 16—for the Southern states. The manufacturer of Yuban coffee and its advertising agency, J. Walter Thompson, did not expect to sell that expensive label in the hollows of West Virginia or the Texas panhandle. But despite such product segmentation, the overriding goal was to shape one market where people of all regions, social classes, and ethnic groups belonged to a single, transcendent community of brand names dedicated to consuming more. "Do I understand you to say that you do not believe in advertising?" wrote a contemporary observer. "Indeed! Soon you will be telling me that you do not believe in God."

HIGH PRIEST

It was no coincidence that the advertising industry's most influential voice in these formative years was Bruce Barton, the son of a prominent Congregational minister, who looked upon his activities as essentially sacerdotal. He led a new class of secular priests conveying the gospel of consumption to the nation's anxious flock of consumers. After graduating from Amherst College and the University of Wisconsin with a Phi Beta Kappa key, Barton became a free-lance writer and magazine editor; his early articles included glowing portraits of famous preachers such as Billy Sunday and A. C. Dixon. Shortly after the war, he joined Roy S. Durstine to create the firm that soon became synonymous with the advertising industry in America—Batten, Barton, Durstine & Osborne. He wrote copy there for Lucky Strikes, Bankers Trust Company, Oakland Motors, and other leading brand names, but Barton's fame rested less on his success at marketing specific products than on his attempt to reshape traditional Protestant morality to the dictates of a consumer society.

Orthodox Protestantism stressed hard work, the sinfulness of man, and salvation in the world beyond, while denouncing idleness and self-indulgence. It hardly sanctioned an economic world where leisure activities and conspicuous personal consumption played ever more prominent roles. The Jesus Christ who drove money changers from the temple and delivered the Sermon on the Mount could not be invoked to defend an economic system that encouraged brutal competition and promoted inequalities of wealth. In a series of books and articles written over the course of the decade—*It's a Good Old World, The Man Nobody Knows,* and *What Can a Man Believe*—Barton turned this world upside down. The greatest sin was repression, the failure of the indi-

Bruce Barton, prophet of advertising.

vidual to find and enjoy happiness and self-fulfillment in the everyday
world. Barton ridiculed "the old-fashioned notion that the chief end in
life is a steadily growing savings account, and that one must eliminate
all pleasures from his vigorous years."

Life, according to Barton, was "meant to live and enjoy as you go
along." The chief obstacles to happiness and fulfillment were not original sin or human depravity, but negative thoughts and bad habits that
could be changed through willpower, a positive mental attitude, and a
better appearance. "The devils which Jesus expelled from sick folk,"
according to Barton, "were the devils of shattered nerves and divided
minds, what we term 'complexes.' " In Barton's hands, Jesus became
a psychologist, a Rotarian, a master of business organization and public relations; in fact, the first genius of advertising. In *A Young Man's
Jesus* (1914), Barton had portrayed the Prince of Peace as an up-and-
coming executive, well-adjusted, who shared "our bounding pulses,
our hot desires." Barton's Jesus had "perfect teeth" and fit in well with
crowds of people. "If there were a world championship series in town,"
Barton opined, "we might look for Him there."

Twelve years later in a sequel, *The Man Nobody Knows*, Barton's Christ was the most-sought-after dinner guest in Jerusalem because of his vibrant personality. His parables were "the most powerful advertisements of all time." He "spread health wherever he went." And He "picked up twelve men from the bottom ranks of business and forged them into an organization that conquered the world." In his private life Barton may have expressed reservations about the new era of high mass consumption, but the public Barton, whose books became best-sellers, had reconciled Christianity and consumption.

The mass consumer market of the twenties with its installment plans, incessant advertising, and Barton-like priesthood did not lack for critics such as Chase, Justice Brandeis, and others, who blamed these developments for destroying independent businessmen, creating more powerful monopolies, encouraging waste and extravagance, eroding local autonomy, and compounding economic inequalities. Americans, it was said, had sold their economic independence for a precarious claim upon a flow of consumer goods controlled and manipulated by a few giant companies.

Brandeis, the old progressive, spurned the telephone and refused to own or drive an automobile, until the volume of traffic in Washington made his horse-drawn buggy a menace to public safety. According to one of his law clerks, the justice became furious over advertisements for automobile tires that read: "Ride Now, Pay Later." The automobile, he declared, diverted public expenditures away from education and health care into less useful projects such as highway construction. He applauded anti-chain-store legislation in the states and price maintenance laws to protect the small retailers and grocers. Like Jefferson, his intellectual ancestor, he feared that public virtue and individual liberty would be snuffed out by concentrations of wealth and the pursuit of luxury.

There was much truth in these complaints. Clearly, the growing power of manufacturers and advertisers had rendered problematic the "laws" of supply and demand touted in classical economic theory. New products came forth each year, not in response to unfulfilled consumer demand, but because companies sought more profitable utilization of existing technologies and resources. They created markets where none had existed before. Listerine was simply an all-purpose antiseptic until George Lambert invented something called "halitosis," derived from the Latin word for "breath." The massive advertising campaign for Lambert's product, similar to those mounted by other manufacturers, devoured millions of dollars, ultimately subsidized by the consumers of mouthwash.

On the other hand, the "captains of consciousness" and their manufacturing allies did not sweep all before them. Individual retailers and grocers continued to hold their own in many working-class neighborhoods and small towns, aided by ethnic loyalties and liberal credit policies. Many consumers eschewed fancy brand names and continued to buy their products from oatmeal to peanut butter in bulk form. Not ever aspiring white-collar professional bought a Gillette Safety Razor with disposable blades, Gillette Shaving Brush, or Gillette Shaving Stick. Some still patronized barber shops or honed their straight-edged razor at home each morning as their grandfathers had done.

By advertising a world of ceaseless consumption, the managers of big business and mass persuasion fashioned ideas with both conservative and radical social consequences. For some, the endless parade of new goods simply confirmed a belief in progress and ratified the existing order of things. For the many others who remained on the outskirts of affluence, however, the inevitable question became why they, too, should not be allowed a place at such a bountiful table.

THE OTHER AMERICA: DOWN ON THE FARM

Like the economic boom it helped to nourish during the twenties, advertising raised expectations and fostered a belief that Americans were entitled as a matter of right and destiny to an ever-rising standard of living. The Republican Party and its allies in the business community reaped the benefits of this optimism until 1929; thereafter, they harvested the wrath of disappointed and disillusioned consumers. However great its powers of persuasion, not even the god of advertising could mask the serious ailments that sapped the economy's long-term vitality.

In simplest terms, the vaunted prosperity of the decade fell to some more than others and did not touch the lives of millions. Radiant statistics about per capita income and wage growth cloaked numerous cases of economic catastrophe, and the distribution of the nation's income grew progressively worse each year. By 1929, according to the Bureau of Labor Statistics, it required an income of $2,500 a year to maintain what was called a "decent standard of living" for a family of two adults and two children in the United States. But 12 million of the

27 million families who filed income tax returns that year earned $1,500 or less, and another 6 million families received below $1,000, figures that placed well over half of the country's households in a condition of economic hardship. At the same time, the richest tenth of the population received nearly 40 percent of the national income, before taxes, while the poorest tenth survived on a paltry 1.8 percent. The nation's staple-crop farmers who raised grains, livestock, and cotton from the Dakotas to the Carolinas were a prominent example of the affluence that never arrived.

The 1920 census reported that a majority of the nation's people lived in "urban" areas of 2,500 residents or more for the first time and that nearly three-quarters of the country's labor force worked in nonfarm occupations, but agriculture accounted for almost $10 billion of the gross national product and the value of all farm property in the United States approached $80 billion. Farmers did not dominate the American economy as they once had, but if their fortunes took a turn for the worse, it could spell disaster far beyond the plains of Kansas or the hills of Georgia.

World War I had been good to farmers. It brought to a climax one of the great agricultural booms in American history, one which began in the late 1890s and peaked in the five years between 1914 and 1919 when the war-induced demand for food and munitions seemed insatiable. From 1913 to 1917, raw farm prices, already healthy, rose almost 82 percent. Within a year, they had shot up another 25 percent. Inspired by patriotic rhetoric ("Food Will Win the War"), government purchases, and the prospect of becoming very rich, many farmers borrowed heavily in order to buy more cropland and machinery. Net farm income more than doubled during the war years from $4 billion to $10 billion. For those who owned their farms, real income grew by 30 percent. The number of farmers who earned at least $2,000 a year rose from 140,000 to over 1,800,000.

The bubble burst in 1920. Once the United States government and the Allies stopped buying wheat, its price plunged from $2.50 a bushel to less than $1. Wool fell from 60 cents a pound to 19 cents. Corn producers were rocked with a 75 percent drop in price. While farm prices recovered somewhat after 1922, those who had known almost two decades of prosperity now entered an almost identical period of economic decline. An advertisement for Cream of Wheat in the March 1926 issue of the *Saturday Evening Post* captured unintentionally the grim situation. A citizen farmer of the new age of high mass consumption, attired in worn overalls, holds up a box of the hot cereal and declares, "Empty, by Heck."

The farmer's economic fall in the twenties was as sudden and as simple to explain as his rise. The end of the Great War cut demand sharply, and the recovery of European agriculture after 1922 reduced it even further. Middle-class consumers ate more fruits, vegetables, and meat after the war, but far less cereals. Prohibition took its toll by forcing breweries and distilleries underground. Synthetics narrowed the market for natural fibers such as cotton. At the same time, farmers in America and elsewhere produced more as a consequence of technical and scientific innovations. Encouraged by the government-financed Agricultural Extension Service, a creation of the last Wilson years, many commercial farmers took advantage of fertilizers, pesticides, hybrid seeds, and improved breeding techniques that doubled and in some cases tripled the production of grains, cotton, and livestock. Five percent fewer workers earned their living on American farms in 1929 than a decade earlier. Farmers took thirteen million acres of land out of production during the twenties. Yet farm output actually grew by 9 percent as the productivity of the remaining agricultural workers rose an extraordinary 15 percent.

Mechanization and its efficiencies cursed the countryside with overproduction. The cheap, gasoline-powered tractor, for example, proved to be as revolutionary as the Model T. It reduced dramatically the time required to plow, plant, and harvest an acre of land. Substituting the tractor for horse and mule power also released about one-quarter of the pre-1914 acreage for the production of foodstuffs rather than animal feed. In short, staple-crop farmers raised more for smaller markets, while their expenses—especially the long-term debts incurred during the war—remained fixed. Catastrophe followed. Over the course of the twenties, both the net income and the real purchasing power of farmers declined by 25 percent from the war years and the total value of farm products fell by one half. Except during 1925 and 1929, according to one estimate, perhaps as many as two-thirds of the nation's farms actually operated at a net capital loss.

While economic devastation covered the Great Plains and the South, it fell with special force on the most vulnerable groups in agriculture: wage laborers, tenants, and sharecroppers. Many of them were already victimized by debt peonage or trapped in the toils of the crop-lien system. To the afflictions of the marketplace, nature added others during the decade: drought, the boll weevil, the Mexican bean beetle, and the

Technology, symbolized by the electric milker, brought progress and overproduction to the nation's farmers.

European corn borer, all of which cut production temporarily, but at great cost to the individual farmers whose crops they ravaged from Georgia to Michigan. From the perspective of many farmers, their economic predicament arose in large measure from policies pursued by the national government during the war, when bureaucrats in Washington urged farmers to produce more. Now left holding the bag of farm surpluses, falling prices, and crushing debts, they wanted the same federal government to make them solvent again. "Under the policy of protection we have built up a great industrial nation," said one of their leading spokesmen, Senator Arthur Capper of Kansas, "and the same protection cannot now be withheld from agriculture."

Such demands for government aid continued a long tradition of rural protest against the inequities of the industrial order. Through their organization the National Grange, farmers played a key role in forcing rate regulation on railroads and grain elevator companies in the late nineteenth century. The People's Party, a coalition of wheat and cotton growers, terrified Democrats and Republicans in the 1890s with its success at the polls and radical demands for currency inflation, public ownership of interstate railroads, and a government-operated warehouse system. On the eve of World War I, angry wheat producers in North Dakota spearheaded the formation and growth of the Farmers' Nonpartisan League. The league's platform called for state-owned grain elevators and packing plants, subsidized hail insurance, and low-interest bank loans. Branded as unpatriotic and socialistic during the war, the league fell victim to rising wheat prices and a government campaign to jail its leaders for sedition—but not before electing a governor in North Dakota and claiming over 200,000 members in thirteen states. Despite these setbacks, the league continued to limp along throughout the decade and experienced a renaissance when the farm depression deepened after 1929.

On the whole, however, the fires of rural radicalism burned lower after 1920. Many of the poorest farmers who had rallied to the Populist standard and the Nonpartisan League had not survived economically. The most influential organizations among farmers in the twenties were the Farm Bureau Federation, a creature of the U.S. government Agricultural Extension Service, and the Farmer-Labor Party, a less-militant successor to the Nonpartisan League. These new pressure groups attracted mostly prosperous, commercial producers who sought immediate benefits from the system, not a frontal assault on capitalism. They also enjoyed support from powerful industrial-commercial interests that profited from the farmer's patronage—farm-equipment manufacturers, rural banks, mail-order companies—and from a considerable group of senators and congressmen who represented agricultural districts. Because of malapportionment, farmers enjoyed substantial political influence in Congress during the twenties. They used it, but sometimes not wisely.

Farmer grievances traditionally included high interests rates and the availability of credit. The farm bloc in Congress with strong backing from Secretary Wallace tackled this matter early in the decade by passing legislation that increased the capital resources of the Federal Farm Loan Bank system, established during the Wilson years. The new law permitted the agency to refinance at lower rates privately held farm mortgages and thereby reduced the interest burdens of many rural producers.

In addition, the Agricultural Credits Act of 1923 authorized twelve so-called Intermediate Credit Banks, also funded by the federal government, to make low-interest loans for up to three years to cooperatives that marketed a wide range of farm products. The Capper-Volstead

Act of that same year then gave farm cooperatives broad legal immunity from antitrust prosecutions when they attempted to fix prices. Since the Federal Reserve System already made loans to rural banks on the basis of their short-term agricultural paper, virtually all of the farmer's credit needs had been met, often with direct subsidies from the American taxpayer. Critics pointed out, however, that only well-to-do producers with collateral could take full advantage of these new credit opportunities, that cooperatives seldom helped farmers with perishable crops, and further that expanding the borrowing capacity of farmers already struggling under a mountain of debt did not address the more critical issue of overproduction and low prices.

The farm bloc, departing sharply from past agrarian demands, also pursued the nostrum of tariff protection in the Harding years. In the South and West among agricultural producers, low tariffs and free trade had often served as a litmus test of progressivism. Protectionism invited retaliation by foreign nations against American farm products. It protected American manufacturers from competition and gouged consumers. But the collapse of farm prices immediately after the war turned many free traders into rabid protectionists. In tandem with manufacturers and union leaders who argued that cheap foreign products destroyed American firms and jobs, the farm bloc secured a sharp upward revision of rates in the Emergency Agricultural Tariff Act of 1921 and again in the more permanent Fordney-McCumber Act a year later.

The emergency tariff measure placed heavy duties on twenty-eight foreign agricultural products, including wheat, corn, beef, wool, and sugar. The Fordney-McCumber Act, boosting tariff rates back to late-nineteenth-century levels, retained these prohibitive rates for foreign farm products. But in the long run it probably took more money out of the pockets of farmers than it returned. The new duties all but barred foreign raw wool from the American market, for example, but the rates on both woolen and cotton textiles were high enough to price all but the cheapest of these foreign goods out of the country, too. Farmers and other consumers paid the bill. By erecting an impenetrable wall around the domestic market, the Fordney-McCumber tariff gave windfall profits to American chemical, dye, steel, and aluminum producers. Except for farmers who raised very special crops such as almonds, olives, dates, and citrus fruits, the measure proved to be an empty victory for agriculture. By making it more difficult for foreigners to earn dollars in the American market, moreover, it lessened the demand for the farmers' products. Like the barrage of new credit legislation, it did nothing to address the central problem of overproduction.

Managing surpluses became the major goal of the commercial farmers and their political allies during the decade. The most direct remedy for reducing output and boosting prices, of course, was to cut annual production to the anticipated American demand and reduce or eliminate export surpluses. American farmers, however, regarded it as their God-given right to raise as much wheat or corn as possible and sell it everywhere in the world. Thus, voluntary restrictions were not likely to garner much support and mandatory controls were equated with socialism.

A second approach focused on raising the domestic price without production controls and dumping the surplus abroad at whatever price it could command. George N. Peek and General Hugh Johnson, two executives of the Moline Plow Company, had worked under Bernard Baruch at the War Industries Board. They put this idea into more concrete detail and sold it to the Farm Bureau Federation and key members of Congress. "You can't sell a plow to a busted customer," observed the voluble Peek, who argued that economic justice for the farmer meant boosting the price of farm commodities until a bushel of wheat in 1923 purchased the same nonfarm commodities that a similar bushel had purchased before the war. Supporters dubbed this concept "parity" for farmers.

Some economists and farm leaders had urged "parity" for agriculture in the past, but Peek and Johnson were the first to realize the vision in national legislation. Their plan, introduced initially in Congress in 1924 by Senator Charles McNary of Oregon and Representative Gilbert Haugen of Iowa, authorized a federally created Agricultural Export Corporation to buy on the American market eight basic farm commodities—wheat, flour, corn, cotton, wool, cattle, sheep, and hogs—at a price that would restore the farmer's purchasing power to pre-1914 levels. The corporation could dispose of the exportable surplus on the world market at the prevailing lower price. Those farmers who participated in the program would be charged an "equalization fee" on each unit sold (the difference between the higher "parity" price and the lower world price) to cover the corporation's anticipated deficit from foreign dumping. Since this fee per unit would be less than the farmer's income derived from higher domestic prices, it was anticipated that most major farm producers would eagerly sign up.

They never got the chance. After almost two more years of legislative maneuvering that expanded the list of eligible farm commodities and shifted the "equalization fee" off farmers onto transportation and processing companies, the McNary-Haugen bill passed Congress twice, but failed to survive two scathing vetoes by Coolidge. He denounced it as unconstitutional, a fiscal calamity, and a bureaucratic nightmare.

Supporters of McNary-Haugen, of course, excoriated the president for his insensitivity to the economic plight of the farmer. Even some of the plan's backers, however, had to concede that the measure contained several lethal defects. Constitutional questions to one side, McNary-Haugen failed to impose any restraints on production and thereby virtually guaranteed bigger farm surpluses. With a subsidized high domestic price, farmers would produce more, not less. The Agricultural Export Corporation would be condemned to purchase endless tons of wheat and corn at the "parity" price. McNary-Haugen struck many people as a naked raid on the U.S. Treasury by a special-interest group.

Dumping the growing farm surplus overseas at rock-bottom prices would seriously complicate the nation's foreign relations, especially in Europe. Nor was the strategy certain to succeed. "George, this is the last heat I trot," one supporter told Peek after Coolidge's second veto. "We can't dump surpluses over the sort of tariff walls they're rearing over the water now." His zeal for McNary-Haugen exceeded only by his bellicose nationalism, Peek thundered, "The hell we can't!" In providing more incentives for higher production, finally, the measure promised to enrich the wealthiest and most efficient commercial farmers, while providing limited assistance to poorer family farms. By refusing to surrender any of their economic freedom or income, the agricultural elite guaranteed a presidential veto.

On the other hand, the Coolidge administration offered farmers little beyond the president's vetoes. It had twice killed a flawed attempt to assist the farmers, but never offered an alternative plan. The farmer's share of the national income continued to slide, with dire consequences for all who depended on his bounty. When the Depression hit, the political failure to address the curse of overproduction guaranteed even more tragedy in the countryside.

THE OTHER AMERICA: LABOR

In the economy of the twenties, one man's loss proved to be another's gain. The country's low inflation and the rise in real income experienced by many industrial workers rested in part on the economic misfortune of the farmers. Overproduction and falling commodity prices translated into lower food prices at the corner market. The decade also saw an expansion of corporate welfare programs, as the leading firms, flush with profits, strove to secure the loyalty of their employees and to raise morale. Under the banner of "welfare capitalism," a few of the largest corporations sought to dampen enthusiasm for autonomous labor unions with grievance committees, group life insurance, old-age pensions, and stock ownership plans. "We must find ways and means to help our workers get their worries out of their minds, so they can get on the job rarin' to go," said E. K. Hall, president of the gigantic American Telephone and Telegraph Company. He recommended that others follow AT&T's example of providing accident, health, and life insurance to employees in addition to common stock. Charles Schwab, praising his own efforts at Bethlehem Steel, declared that American workers deserved steady employment, a voice in determining their working conditions, the possibility of owning stock in their company, and some guarantee of economic security in old age. "A sense of proprietorship affords a powerful incentive to . . . performance in work," he concluded.

Corporate welfare programs and rising real wages disguised the fact that the income of most industrial workers did not keep pace with their soaring productivity. The gap between what they produced and what they could buy therefore widened over the course of the decade. The spread of "scientific management" techniques, pioneered by Frederick W. Taylor before the war, encouraged this growing deficit. Contemptuous of unions, regarding unskilled laborers as little more than dumb brutes and skilled craftsmen as obstacles to efficiency, Taylor hoped to place total control of the work routine in the hands of engineers and managers equipped with stopwatches and time sheets. If individual workers could be made to perform each task more efficiently, Taylor argued, productivity, profits, and wages could rise in harmony for the benefit of all. After Taylor's death in 1915, many of his disciples in the business world stressed anti-unionism, efficiency, and profits, but ignored wages. As practiced by Ford and others, scientific management and Taylorism became little more than a euphemism for unchecked managerial power, breaking the influence of craft workers, and speeding up the assembly line.

The impotence of organized labor contributed in a major way to the productivity-wage gap as well. During the war, the federal government had protected the right of workers to join labor unions. Membership had jumped to over four million and included many mass-production industries such as meat-packing and steel that had long resisted union organization. Once government controls were lifted, however, employers reverted to what became known as "the American Plan," a slogan for crushing workers' organizations with injunctions and strikebreakers and returning to the nonunion open shop.

By 1929, union membership had declined by nearly a million workers, an indication that the movement had failed to keep pace with the growth of the labor force. The federal government, so lately the unions' ally, actively aided employers' efforts to eradicate them. Attorney General Daugherty broke the railroad shopmen's strike in 1922 by securing a sweeping injunction from a sympathetic federal judge. Between 1921 and 1925, four decisions by the Supreme Court of the United States hammered the labor movement further. Despite rather explicit language to the contrary, a majority of the justices ruled that the anti-trust laws did not prohibit employers from securing injunctions against secondary boycotts organized by unions. The Court also ruled that states could not deny injunctive relief to employers who faced union picketing; that the federal government could not abolish child labor through prohibitive taxes; and that minimum wage laws denied freedom of contract.

The labor movement was weakened further by the bigotry and caution of those who led the American Federation of Labor (AFL). This nation-wide confederation of craft unions, which traced its history back to the 1880s, emerged from the war with its organization nearly intact. Dominated for almost half a century by Samuel Gompers, a former cigar maker, the AFL strengthened the bargaining power of skilled workers in the building trades and elsewhere, but generally ignored the plight of the unskilled, except in coal mining and the garment industry. While recruiting a few black workers, the AFL relegated them to segregated affiliates. It also scorned most forms of government assistance to working people, fearing that such aid would weaken their allegiance to the unions.

Gompers's death in 1924 and the elevation of William Green from the United Mine Workers to the presidency of the federation did not alter the AFL's basic philosophy or tactics. A member of the Odd Fellows and the Elks who sported a diamond ring and a gold watch, Green's perspective on the struggle between labor and capital remained profoundly cautious. "So, my friends," he told the AFL national convention in 1928, "we have the two extremes attacking and opposing [us] . . . the Manufacturers Association . . . and the Communists. . . . I think we must be pretty decent, respectable citizens when we are able to invite the opposition and the antagonism of these two extremes."

Devoted to the strike as the most effective weapon in labor's arsenal, the AFL watched as the number of workers who went on strike fell each year between 1923 and 1929. Using its treasury to support already powerful craft unions, it did little to promote organization in mass-production industries—steel, rubber, textiles, automobiles, chemicals. When it did send money and organizers into strike-torn textile towns like Gastonia and Marion, North Carolina, in 1929, the federation's efforts proved too little and too late in the face of corporate power backed by local and state law enforcement agencies.

Even in the bustling, generally prosperous industrial sector, the bloom of affluence did not touch many communities during the decade. Business titans such as Hall and Schwab might trumpet that "welfare capitalism" could provide economic security for the American worker. In truth, the spread was thin. Corporate life insurance plans covered barely six million workers in 1928 and stock-ownership plans gave only one million employees a real stake in American capitalism. Steady employment, a voice in working conditions, and paid-up life insurance may have been available at AT&T, Procter & Gamble, General Electric, and a few other large firms, but such was not the reality for the vast majority of American workers. A social worker at Chicago's Hull House reported on the plight of one worker, Alex Pavlowski, in 1927. Laid off from the coal mines in Pennsylvania, he brought his wife and four children to Chicago in search of work. Unable to read or write, Pavlowski found only part-time jobs loading ammonia trucks or shoveling snow. "The little money that had come in had been spent on food and this had been of poor quality. . . . There was no coal and the house was cold and damp . . . the gas had been shut off. The children were all ill with heavy colds. Added to this, they were soon to be evicted and there was no money to pay the old rent or the new." The Pavlowskis were not unique in an economy where machines displaced some three million workers; one-third of them could not find new jobs.

Conditions in a number of industries remained depressed throughout the twenties. Style changes, imports, and the automobile sent the boot and shoe manufacturers into a decline along with the entire leather products industry. Despite a postwar construction boom, lumber companies from Washington to Georgia showed only modest gains as builders turned to substitute materials such as concrete. Competition from silk and rayon and excess capacity made cotton and woolen textiles among the sickest industries of the decade, with dire consequences for hundreds of towns from New Hampshire to North Carolina. Output in these cutthroat industries remained high, and prices tumbled between 1923 and 1929. Wages, of course, remained depressed, and because this industry employed more workers than any other sector of the industrial economy, the drag on purchasing power was enormous.

High mass consumption never arrived in Elizabethton, Tennessee, for instance, where in 1929 teenage girls worked fifty-six hours per week in the cotton mills for 16 to 18 cents an hour. "I ain't afeared of hell," went the saying in Gastonia. "I've spent twenty summers in the mills." The strike erupted there, led initially by communist organizers, when the companies insisted that harried workers tend ninety looms instead of the customary forty. Before the violent Gastonia strike ended, the poet laureate of the union, Ella May Wiggins, mother of five, had been shot to death and seven strike leaders had been convicted by a fear-ridden jury of the murder of the town's sheriff.

For sheer futility and exploitation, however, nothing approached conditions in the coal mining communities that stretched from western Colorado to northern Alabama. Like textiles, the coal mining industry provided a grim illustration of the evils of unregulated competition. Abundant coal deposits and minimal capital requirements made entry into the industry easy. Despite the presence of a few large companies, including steel producers and railroads who owned "captive mines," thousands of medium-sized and small operators who tended to raise their output the moment prices moved upward dominated the industry. In the company-owned mining towns that dotted Logan and Mingo counties, West Virginia, miners enjoyed neither regular work nor basic civil liberties, such as freedom of speech. "We work in *his* mine," one complained. "We live in *his* house. Our children go to *his* school. On Sunday we're preached at by *his* preacher. When we die we're buried in *his* cemetery."

Neither the large companies nor the United Mine Workers, strong in a few states, could exercise enough control to restrict production. The UMW followed John L. Lewis, a man of imposing countenance and oratorical powers, who had devoted his life to fighting management and crushing all opposition to his control of the union. By mid-decade in the wake of several disastrous strikes and internecine conflict, especially with the communists, the UMW's membership had fallen sharply. Lewis, a lifelong Republican, abandoned attempts to organize the numerous nonunion fields and remained content to preside as an absolute despot over his shrinking union empire. "He killed more than the leaders of our union," remarked one UMW dissident. "He killed its very soul." As a result, the industry remained plagued by huge coal inventories, falling prices, low wages, and frequent bouts of high unemployment. Competition from heating oil ravaged jobs in the anthracite mines. Mechanical cutting machines and loading devices raised production and simultaneously threw men out of work in the bituminous fields. In this environment of ruthless competition, safety and conservation received scant attention. The only thing cheaper than coal in places like Harlan County, Kentucky, was human life.

Indeed, human life, at least the quality of human life, was at risk all over America during this affluent decade. The ordeal of industries such as textiles and coal, the depressionlike conditions in agriculture, the bumpy performance of even automobiles and construction, and the growing volume of consumer debt led some observers to doubt the solidity of economic progress and to predict that a day of reckoning would arrive soon. "I can't understand where all this . . . money comes from," Justice Brandeis lamented to his brother. "We are certainly not earning it as a nation. I think we must be exploiting about 80 percent of Americans, for the benefit of the other 20 percent." Brandeis remained a true conservative, however, in an era of radical change and sham conservatism. The worsening distribution of the fruits of prosperity troubled him on both moral and practical grounds. Few shared the Justice's forebodings. For most Americans in the twenties the cry was full speed ahead into what seemed surely an ever more prosperous new world. And so it was—for a time—until Jefferson's old fears about the dangers of too much wealth came true.

5

Wets, Drys, and Immigrants

The speed at which we run our motor cars, operate our machinery, and generally live, would be impossible with liquor.
—Henry Ford

These immigrants adopt the language of the native American, they wear his clothes, they steal his name and they are beginning to take his women, but they seldom adopt his religion or understand his ideals.
—Madison Grant, *The Passing of the Great Race*

THE NOBLE EXPERIMENT

Karl Marx, the intellectual founder of communism, once observed that "men make their own history, but they do not always make it under circumstances of their own choosing." Many Americans did not accept this idea easily. Blessed by natural abundance, technological prowess, secure borders, and relative political stability, they often believed that their destiny unfolded outside the historical forces that restrained and limited other nations. Millions of Americans who voted for Warren Harding's "normalcy" or Calvin Coolidge believed that through this simple act of political will they could restore America to an imagined social equilibrium that prevailed before the Great War. The size and scope of government, bloated by the unnatural demands of that conflict, would be reduced; family structures, disrupted by the draft and mobilization, would return to normal; ethnic relations, long predicated on the domination of white Protestants and the subordination of people of color, would be maintained; the values of their grandparents' era—hard work, thrift, self-restraint—would remain infallible guides to personal conduct; the farm and the small town would continue to be the center of the nation's moral universe.

It was not to be. Americans of the Harding-Coolidge era discovered what others had before: in a dynamic capitalist society, where economic development, individualism, and social change were widely sanctioned values, the locomotive of history surged ever forward and would not turn back. Americans raised the jeremiad to an art form, because they worshiped innovation, but remained forever anxious about its consequences. They waxed eloquent about "the good old days" as they plunged eagerly into the future. Harding and Coolidge applied the brakes to the progressive movement by seeking to reduce the role of government in certain areas of social life, but they could not restore the past. On one front—prohibition—they even took on the task of implementing one of the last reforms of the progressive era. Republicans spoke often during the decade about curbing the powers of government over individuals and unleashing private initiative. Prohibition, governmental regulation to the hilt, became a crashing exception to this rule.

The prohibition movement, which finally achieved national political success during World War I with the adoption of the Eighteenth Amendment and the Volstead Act, was one of the most durable social crusades in the country's history. Beginning in the colonial period, upper- and middle-class citizens attempted to limit the consumption of spirituous drink to what they called "responsible and respectable persons." They condemned drunkards to the stocks or required them to wear the stigma of the letter D. Despite frequent legislation, however, the American nation remained, in one historian's memorable phrase, "the alcoholic republic"—a country notorious for its heavy consumption of hard cider, rum, and corn whiskey.

The Revolution ousted King George, not Demon Rum. Between 1792 and 1832, according to one estimate, Americans raised their intake of intoxicating beverages from a little over two gallons per person per year to over seven gallons. During the antebellum period, reformers regarded slavery and intoxicating drink as the two forms of oppression that most threatened progress and liberty. The enslavement of Africans undermined free labor and free land. Demon rum encouraged vice, idleness, and poverty. In this period, too, the prohibition crusade became linked to nativism and ethnic conflict as old-stock Yankees led the effort to banish the saloons and beer gardens patronized by Irishmen and Germans.

Even before America went to war in 1917, eighteen states in the South, the Midwest, and the West had passed total prohibition or local option laws that made hard drink illegal for almost 65 percent of the adult population. At the federal level, a titanic political struggle pitted the antiprohibition forces (led by urban political machines and the leading manufacturers of beer and distilled liquors) against the "drys," a broad coalition whose main shock troops included the small-town, churchgoing Protestants of the Women's Christian Temperance Union and the Anti-Saloon League. The drys also drew on the considerable financial resources of business tycoons such as Rockefeller, Wana-maker, Heinz, and Kresge as well as from the leaders of the scientific management movement, who regarded drink as a leading cause of industrial inefficiency.

Before the war, President Taft vetoed the Webb-Kenyon bill, which made it a federal crime to ship intoxicating beverages across state lines in violation of local law, but the bill's supporters rounded up enough votes in Congress to override him. When Wilson and his southern Democrats arrived in Washington, the prohibition forces gained new momentum. Secretary of State Bryan served only grape juice at diplo-matic functions. Navy Secretary Daniels banned alcohol from the offi-cers' mess shortly before the Germans marched into Belgium.

In addition to its nativism, the prohibition crusade fit neatly into the ameliorative schemes of many progressive reformers who wished to eliminate poverty, protect the family, promote social efficiency, and curb big business. Many feminists saw liquor as a contributing cause of unemployment and the leading source of physical attacks by men against women and children. Those who hoped to purify urban politics regarded the corner saloon as a breeding ground for corrupt bargains struck between ward bosses and their ethnic constituents. For leaders of the new corporate elite and disciples of Frederick Taylor, sobriety in the workplace had become an urgent issue as technology and busi-ness organizations grew more complex. A drunken shoemaker alone at his bench or a tipsy farmer behind his horse-drawn plow did not present the same danger to other employees or profits as an intoxicated worker on the assembly line. Progressives preoccupied with the issue of big business and the shady nexus between money and politics also found a ready example of both abuses in the liquor industry.

War finally tipped the balance decisively in favor of the WCTU and the Anti-Saloon League. How could a government that called for max-imum agricultural production, cried the prohibitionists, justify the wasteful use of grains for intoxicants? Like the brothel, the saloon was said to undermine military discipline and the virtue of young soldiers. Prohibitionists noted that the great brewers—Ruppert, Pabst, Lieber, Schmidt—were German and that their trade association, the United States Brewers' Association, helped finance the National German-American Alliance, a potent source of propaganda for the Kaiser.

After less than three days' debate, the Eighteenth Amendment, banning the manufacture, sale, or transportation of intoxicants throughout the United States and giving both the states and the federal government authority to pass enforcement laws, swept through Congress. By early 1919, the required thirty-six states had ratified it, five without a dissenting vote. A year later, over Wilson's veto, Congress passed the Volstead Act, which defined as "intoxicating" any liquor having as much as 0.5 percent alcohol. It gave enforcement responsibilities to the Department of the Treasury. On the statute books, at least, America was dry.

Given the distribution of votes in Congress that favored rural districts over urban ones, the Eighteenth Amendment and the Volstead Act symbolized the political and cultural victory of the small towns over the big cities; of evangelical and pietistic Protestants over Roman Catholics, Lutherans, and Jews; of old-stock Anglo-Saxons over newer immigrants; and finally, of rich over poor. The dry forces, of course, counted in their ranks some Protestants from New York City, San Francisco, and other cities; not every working-class Irishman was a wet, but the prohibition battle divided the nation along sharp geographic, religious, and ethnic boundaries that defined much of America's political landscape in the postwar years.

Supporters of the Volstead Act usually lived south of the Mason-Dixon Line and west of the Mississippi on farms and in small towns. They were likely to belong to a Methodist or Baptist church, to vote Republican (except in the South), and to be self-employed—farmers or professionals. Aside from Protestant clergymen, the most zealous leaders of the dry crusade were female and married. The typical wet, on the other hand, was a single man who lived in an ethnic neighborhood in a large metropolitan area, attended mass at least on Christmas and Easter, worked in a factory, and voted for the Democratic Party.

For the drys, passage of the Volstead Act began the millennium. They expected the measure to elevate the nation's moral tone, increase its productivity, reduce crime and political corruption, and protect the hearth. Secretary Daniels declared the saloon "as dead as slavery." Bryan said "the man who peddles liquor, like the man who sells habit-forming drugs, is an outlaw." As "the virtue of the country asserts itself,"

the Great Commoner predicted, the number of citizens with a fondness for beer and hard drink would "constantly decrease."

Few anticipated massive resistance to the law and the Constitution.
The first chief of the enforcement division in the Treasury Department,
John F. Kramer, vowed that "this law will be obeyed in cities, large
and small, and in villages, and where it is not obeyed it will be enforced.
. . . We shall see that it [liquor] is not manufactured . . . sold, nor given
away, nor hauled in anything on the surface of the earth or under the
earth or in the air." Congress, however, gave Kramer only $2 million
to achieve his goals. What Herbert Hoover once called "a great social
and economic experiment, noble in motive and far-reaching in purpose" started on a wave of utopian rhetoric and expectations. It soon
ran aground, however, on the shoals of fiscal conservatism, rugged
individualism, self-indulgence, and American federalism, when national
policy collided with deeply entrenched local customs, mores, and
interests. Sensing an all-out attack on their liberties, social status, profits, and institutions, many immigrants fought back in the cities to defend
their neighborhoods, saloons, political clubs, and police forces from
outside control by moral vigilantes. They were joined by enterprising
criminals, often excluded from legitimate occupations, who hoped to
cash in on the country's continuing thirst for liquor, and by many young
war veterans and college-age men and women from "better families,"
who defied prohibition in order to assert their generation's cultural
independence.

THE FUTILITY OF ENFORCEMENT

Despite the optimism of Daniels and Bryan, the virtue of the country
failed to assert itself over the next thirteen years. Federal officers charged
with implementing Kramer's pledge soon discovered that it was no easier
to enforce the Volstead Act in New York City, Chicago, or New Orleans
in 1925 than it had been to collect a federal tax on whiskey in western
Pennsylvania in 1794, to return a fugitive slave from Boston to
Charleston in 1854, or to close the nation's borders to Mexican immigrants in the 1980s. Unless the national government secured the active
support of important local elites for its programs or was prepared to
employ to the fullest its own fiscal and coercive resources, it could never
hope to prevail against united local resistance. The bitter struggle to
dismantle racial segregation in the South during the 1950s and 1960s

demonstrated this proposition just as did the failure to enforce prohibition between 1920 and 1933.

At its peak strength near the end of the decade, the Treasury Department fielded about three thousand prohibition agents. They were paid on average $2,500 a year to close down an illegal industry whose income probably reached $2 billion annually. In a pinch, these prohibiton sleuths could call on the Coast Guard, customs, and immigration officials for assistance, but even if every one of them had been a model of zeal and integrity (10 percent were fired for corruption between 1920 and 1930), they faced the staggering task of damming the flow of intoxicating drink that reached thirsty consumers through smuggling, diversion, and illicit stills. From the perspective of rumrunners and bootleggers, America had been blessed with twelve thousand miles of coastline and borders; alcohol was readily available in hundreds of legal products ranging from perfume to antifreeze; breweries continued to manufacture gallons of "near beer" that awaited enrichment; and home-brewing gear could be purchased at most local hardware stores for less than $10. When it came to defying the Volstead Act, the imagination and ingenuity of those breaking the law knew few bounds; the resources allocated to enforcement remained pathetically small.

By all accounts, diversion and redistillation of alcohol intended for industrial and commercial purposes constituted the single largest source of illegal liquor sold to Americans between 1920 and 1933. Illicit distilling ran a close second. Even when the federal government tightened its licensing system after 1930, an estimated ten to fifteen million gallons of alcohol, once destined for hair tonics, cosmetics, and paint, turned up in the bootleggers' inventory each year. Sometimes it was called Scotch whisky, sometimes "Kentucky Tavern" or "Pebble Ford," which prohibition agents in Detroit discovered had been concocted from "Parisienne Solution for Perspiring Feet, 90 Per Cent Alcohol." Although not widespread, wood-alcohol poisoning from liquor made by incompetent or greedy bootleggers became a grim reality. Thirty-four people died from such poisoning in New York City during a brief four-day period in 1928. Throughout the decade, doctors and coroners saw cases of impoverished drinkers felled by Sterno, while the more affluent succumbed to crudely distilled corn mash, squash, and potatoes. According to legend, one skeptical buyer took his bootlegged purchase to a chemist, who reported to him after analysis: "Dear sir, your horse has diabetes."

Whether operated by amateurs for home consumption or by professional criminals for a wider market, the illicit still that produced pure grain alcohol became another ubiquitous source of cheer. In some Northern cities, entire neighborhoods were major centers of production; the mash vat and the three-spout copper still replaced sewing machines as the basic tools of sweated labor. A single such operation on Chicago's South Side or in the Great Dismal Swamp could turn out two hundred gallons of alcohol a day. Cut with a little California or New York grape juice, water, juniper drops, and glycerine, it could bring from 2 to 4 cents an ounce, depending on the market. Manufacturers of corn sugar did a booming business in the twenties as their output rose in some cases sixfold to meet the demand of moonshiners, home brewers, and the mob.

Smuggling by land and sea, although it did not account for the bulk of the nation's illegal liquor, became the most romantic form of entrepreneurship. Caravans of trucks laden with Canadian whiskey roared down the back roads of Vermont, New York, Minnesota, and Washington to bring shipments of liquid contraband to patrons in speakeasies from Boston to Seattle. Similar traffic, specializing in tequila and mescal, poured across the U.S.–Mexico border from Texas to California.

Loaded to the gunwales with liquor from Cuba, Belize, and St. Pierre and Miquelon, many vessels rocked gently off the coasts of New Jersey and Florida in Rum Row for an opportunity to bring their lucrative cargoes ashore in speedy launches whose horsepower and numbers placed them beyond the reach of the Coast Guard. By one estimate, two thousand cases of liquor a day entered the coves and bays of Long Island Sound alone. In 1925, the assistant secretary of the Treasury in charge of enforcement confessed that his agents probably seized about 5 percent of all the liquor smuggled into the United States that year. Samuel Bronfman, a titan of the Canadian distilling industry, thought that a generous estimate. "I never went to the other side of the border to count the empty Seagram's bottles," he quipped.

The forces of law and order recorded a few notable victories during the decade. In the first two years of enforcement, the federal government initiated 3,500 civil and 65,000 criminal actions under the Volstead Act and won about 60 percent of these cases. Prohibition agents smashed 172,000 illegal stills in 1925 alone. Two agents, Izzy Einstein and Moe Smith, became celebrities because of their innovative methods. When the roly-poly Izzy nearly froze to death outside a notorious speakeasy while waiting for an illegal shipment to arrive, his sidekick carried him into the place, pounded the bar, and demanded: "Give this

*Federal prohibition agents display their disguises prior
to raid on speakeasy.*

man a drink! He's just been bitten by a frost." When the kindly bartender obliged, they arrested him and closed down his establishment.
The team of Izzy and Moe made four thousand arrests in five years and
seized five million bottles of illegal liquor worth $15 million. But for
every illicit still they destroyed, probably nine continued to operate.
Four out of every five shipments from Canada, Mexico, or the West
Indies eluded federal agents. At the conclusion of Izzy and Moe's crime-
busting campaign, any thirsty citizen could still buy a drink in most
major American cities about one minute after stepping off the train.

Some states, notably New York and Wisconsin, showed their defiance by repealing all local laws that supplemented the Volstead Act.

Others simply left the entire fiscal and administrative burden of enforcement on Washington. Inefficiency and bribery added still more loopholes. Every prohibition agent and federal prosecutor carried back to headquarters tales of local juries who refused to convict popular bootleggers, and of mayors, police chiefs, and district attorneys who patronized speakeasies regularly. "Conditions in most important cities very bad," reported one agent from Indiana in 1929. "Lax and corrupt public officials great handicap . . . prevalence of drinking among minor boys and the . . . middle or better class of adults."

The chief of police in Leavenworth, Kansas, was indicted for violating the Volstead Act. In neighboring Wichita, a federal prosecutor noted, the police tried to crack down on the bootleggers, but the county attorney and sheriff had been bought off by the criminals. Leavenworth and Wichita were relatively small cities in a state with a long tradition of support for prohibition. In larger cities, where the ties among bootleggers, the police, judges, and politicians were more extensive and lucrative, enforcement proved impossible.

Chicago's colorful Mayor William Hale "Big Bill the Builder" Thompson announced proudly that he was "as wet as the middle of the Atlantic Ocean," a description that probably fit most of his constituents as well as the city's police force. Big Bill declined to stand for reelection in 1923 when it was revealed that some of his closest political allies had stolen nearly $1 million in school funds. Chicagoans chose William E. Dever, a judge with a spotless reputation, who pledged to enforce prohibition and break the hold of the underworld on city hall. The bootleggers merely shifted their headquarters to the city's suburbs and waited for the reign of righteousness to pass away. In four years they were back, when Thompson trounced Dever at the polls and restored Chicago's reputation as "the wickedest city in the world."

Disgusted with the extent of bootleggers' influence in the City of Brotherly Love, Philadelphia's leaders appointed Smedley D. Butler, a Marine Corps brigadier general, director of public safety in 1924. "Treat 'Em Rough" Butler had won the Medal of Honor in 1917 for crushing a revolt in Haiti during which more than two hundred unarmed or poorly armed natives had been killed. He vowed a similar slash-and-burn campaign against those in Philadelphia who defied the Volstead Act. The general discovered, however, that it was much easier to impress Haitians into road-building service under bayonets than to locate and destroy Philadelphia's illegal stills and the networks of distributors who marketed their output. "Treat 'Em Rough" Butler marched smartly into the city one year and right out twelve months later in defeat. He

blamed politicians, police, the courts, and defiant civilians for his failure to root out the bootleggers and their allies.

Supporters of prohibition deplored the many gaps in enforcement
and thundered against those like Mayor Thompson who thumbed their
noses at the law. Civil libertarians, on the other hand, noted with concern that enforcement, although haphazard and improvised, often
brought with it questionable legal behavior by the police and a disre-
gard for basic constitutional rights. Federal agents and local police,
usually acting on tips supplied by informants, broke into homes, garages,
offices, and warehouses without valid search warrants. In 1925, the
Supreme Court sharply limited the Fourth Amendment's ban on
unreasonable searches and seizures when it held that federal officers
did not need a warrant to search an automobile if they had probable
cause to believe the vehicle contained illegal liquor. Draconian provisions of Indiana's enforcement law included a mandatory sentence of
thirty days to six months in jail for the first offense of either selling,

Putting bootleggers out of business.

possessing, or giving away contraband liquor. Even possession of empty bottles that contained the aroma of alcohol could be used as evidence in that state's courts. Police used physical coercion to wring confessions from suspected bootleggers and shot to death two hundred alleged violators of the Volstead Act between 1920 and 1929.

A distinguished panel of experts, led by former attorney general George Wickersham and including Harvard professor Zechariah Chafee, reported to President Hoover in 1931 that the social and political costs of prohibition outweighed the benefits. The Volstead Act, they argued, promoted disrespect for law on the part of ordinary citizens, lawlessness by the police, and demoralized the federal judiciary. Although its eleven members could not agree about what to do, the negative verdict of the Wickersham Commission gave further ammunition to those who advocated repeal of the Eighteenth Amendment.

BARONS OF BOOZE

The deepest irony of prohibition arose not from the desire to impose virtue through repression, but from the success and power that flowed to many ethnic Americans who became the beneficiaries of the very laws intended to limit their cultural influence. German-Americans had long dominated the American beer market. The Irish had operated saloons and pubs from San Francisco to Boston. Prohibition now delivered a $2 billion illegal industry into the hands of an underworld dominated by second-generation Italians, Jews, and Irish, who faced far less discrimination in this line of work than in the more reputable middle-class professions of law, medicine, accounting, and teaching. The mortality rate might be high and job security low, but the opportunities for quick riches proved very attractive.

Crime became a highly organized big business in these years when the local purveyors of prostitution and gambling discovered they could reap huge profits by controlling on a regional basis the manufacture and distribution of illegal alcohol, too. The ingredients for entrepreneurial success were very simple: a dependable source of supply and a steady, predictable number of brothels, restaurants, and speakeasies where customers consumed it. The police could not be counted on to protect the means of production and no civil court would enforce these business contracts, so professional criminals devised their own methods for defending markets and safeguarding profits. Like the businessmen of an earlier era who struggled to bring order to the fledgling railroad, petroleum, and meat-packing industries, the barons of booze hated competition and cherished monopoly, even when the latter could be imposed only through the muzzle of a submachine gun.

The Torrio-Capone gang of Chicago emerged as the prototype of the new criminal organization specializing in the business opportunities created by the Volstead Act. A few months after prohibition became the law of the land in 1920, one of Chicago's leading mobsters, James "Big Jim" Colosimo, was shot to death by a gun-toting hoodlum from Brooklyn, Frankie Yale. It is likely that Yale had been hired by Colosimo's own partner in crime, Johnny Torrio, who wished to overrule the boss's decision not to expand from brothels and gaming into bootlegging. The flowers had barely wilted on Big Jim's casket when Torrio took charge of the operations, imported additional firepower from New York, and began lining up new clients for his growing business.

Torrio's ambitions infuriated the city's other gangs, especially those run by the Irish, but Johnny had struck it rich with one of his Brooklyn imports—a heavyset twenty-three-year-old Italian with a love of opera, a taste for good cigars, and a real flair for mayhem and murder. On his business cards, Alphonse "Al" Capone listed his occupation as "secondhand furniture dealer," but as Torrio's lieutenant and later his partner, he specialized in protecting the organization's Canadian pipeline and making certain that Chicago's hotels, brothels, and speakeasies gave their product a fair deal with the competition. When other gangs failed to respect the Torrio-Capone territory, they faced swift retaliation—beatings, a hail of bullets, bombings.

In the first four years of prohibiton, until the Italian-dominated Torrio-Capone mob consolidated its control over Chicago, the city witnessed over two hundred gang-related killings, an average of almost one a week. In November 1924 the Capone forces eliminated Dion O'Banion, an archrival with good political connections, who had made the fatal mistake of having Torrio picked up by the police on bogus charges. The Irish boss was gunned down outside his flower shop. The fallen gang leader's grieving widow described O'Banion as an ordinary family man who was never late for dinner and loved to tinker with the radio. Along with thousands of other mourners, Capone sent a huge wreath of flowers for the casket, but he was very blunt when speaking to reporters about how O'Banion had failed to respect the bootleggers' code of fair competition. "His head got away from his hat," Al told them. "Johnny Torrio taught O'Banion all he knew and then O'Banion grabbed some of the best guys we had and decided to be boss of the booze racket in Chicago. . . . It was his funeral."

Two years later, the remnants of the O'Banion Irish gang struck back. Eight heavily armored touring cars opened fire on Capone's headquarters at the Hawthorne Hotel in the suburb of Cicero. The machine-gun-and-pistol barrage lasted ten minutes, turning the streets and buildings nearby into a shooting gallery, but Capone escaped without a scratch. The gruesome conclusion to Chicago's prohibition wars came on St. Valentine's Day 1929, when seven O'Banions, waiting for a shipment of stolen liquor in the garage of the S.M.C. Cartage Company, surrendered calmly to five men dressed in police uniforms. Standing against a wall, unarmed and their hands raised, the unsuspecting hoodlums were riddled by machine-gun fire from the "officers of the law" who then walked out of the garage and sped away.

The St. Valentine's Day Massacre ended Chicago's bloody "beer wars" and established the Torrio-Capone gang as the dominant power in Chicago's underworld. Capone was clearly the firm's senior partner. From his suite at the Hawthorne, the man known variously as "the Big Fellow" or "Scarface" presided over a vast empire of legitimate and illegitimate enterprises that included the city government of Cicero. By the end of the decade, federal investigators who finally sent him to jail for income tax evasion estimated that the organization's annual income from illegal booze, prostitution, slot machines, bookmaking, loan-sharking, and highway construction exceeded $70 million. Al Capone had become the General Motors of the underworld, a man who prospered through diversification.

Befitting a wealthy Italian businessman who found himself often locked in combat with the city's older Irish power structure, Capone voted Republican, and his soldiers made certain that the party of Coolidge and Hoover swept Cicero on election day. The irony of this situation was no doubt lost on the stalwart Republicans downstate in Illinois, who fervently supported prohibition. If Cicero's mayor strayed too far from the Capone interests, however, he risked being kicked down the steps of city hall. Unreliable council members and newspaper editors were bought off, beaten up, and run out of town.

Despite his unsavory reputation for violence and corruption, Capone became something of a folk hero to many who resented prohibition and felt themselves to be social outcasts. Like heavyweight champ Jack Dempsey, "the Manassa Mauler," Capone came from the wrong side of the tracks, a scrapper, who had battled his way to the top of the booze business. Now he lived as well as the upper-class big shots who had gone to Princeton, ran the brokerage houses on LaSalle Street, and looked down on ethnic minorities. Capone could afford to dine where they did, buy his clothes from the same tailors, and drive a Cadillac—bulletproof, of course.

Reporters covered the details of Capone's public and private life with the same zeal accorded movie stars. They hung on his words as if he were a candidate for governor. In Chicago, Capone usually received as much press as Mayor Thompson and only a bit less than the elusive running back for the University of Illinois, Harold E. "Red" Grange. Although Calvin Coolidge might wince at the idea, Al Capone embodied the spirit of free enterprise and the power of the market; he was a perverse symbol and parody of America's business culture. "If people didn't want beer and wouldn't drink it," he once observed, "a fellow would be crazy for going around trying to sell it. I've seen gambling houses, too . . . and I never saw anyone point a gun at a man and make him go in . . . . I've always regarded it as a public benefaction if people were given decent liquor and square games."

Al Capone (left), king of the Chicago mob.

THE BALANCE SHEET

The epidemics of gangland violence generated by prohibition brought forth new demands for the modification or repeal of the Eighteenth Amendment. The Reverend Billy Sunday had called liquor "God's worst enemy . . . Hell's best friend," but from the perspective of others, the efforts to eradicate its use had created even more terrifying allies of the devil. At decade's end, especially as the nation slid into economic depression, a great many Americans questioned whether the costs of the "noble experiment" did not exceed the benefits. Was the open saloon really a greater menace to society than the Capone mob? Had the old liquor monopolies not been replaced by new, criminal ones? Were urban politics less or more venal as a result? Were the social problems attributed to hard drink—unemployment, poverty, family violence—now under control?

As the answers to these and other questions became increasingly problematic, popular support for national prohibition eroded. Herbert Hoover, whose political career in the twenties had included support for the Volstead Act, signaled the change in public mood. In the wake of the negative findings of the Wickersham Commission, he promised more efficient enforcement by placing the Prohibition Bureau under the supervision of the Justice Department and raising the civil service requirements for its agents. A year later, as the nation's economic fortunes worsened, Hoover, a Quaker who loathed alcohol and the saloon, endorsed repeal.

More than half a century after its demise, scholars continue to debate the costs and benefits of the "noble experiment." Congress, some point out, never appropriated sufficient money to ensure effective enforcement. It preferred a symbolic crusade to a real one by choosing to pay lip service to the forces of righteousness while maintaining a flow of liquor to the unrepentant. But more than fiscal conservatism, a lack of political will, or hypocrisy explains this gap between congressional rhetoric and resources. In both monetary and legal terms, the true costs of effective national enforcement would have been astronomically high, including a large increase in police and judicial personnel along with perilous consequences for constitutional rights. The nation would face this dilemma again in the 1980s, when engaged with the far greater social menace of heroin and cocaine.

In the short run, prohibition proved a boon to boat operators, firearms manufacturers, auto dealers, ethnic mobility, and undertakers. But the workingman's corner saloon shut its door for a decade, to be replaced by the elegant speakeasy that catered especially to a middle-class and upper-class clientele. Except in rural areas where high-grade moonshine or "white lightning" had always been available, the quality of liquor available to the lower classes, never high to begin with, deteriorated further. Like the impact of many other Republican policies during the decade, the burdens of prohibition fell heavily on economic and racial minorities.

For all their defects and contradictions, some students argue, the Eighteenth Amendment and the Volstead Act changed for the better the nation's drinking habits. We became, according to this theory, a more sober society after prohibition when per capita consumption of hard liquor declined significantly in favor of beer and wines. But it is not altogether clear that these changes arose solely because of prohibition and the legal stigma attached to drinking. As before, the American public officially denounced drunkenness and alcoholism in the twenties, but the press still reported mirthfully on intoxicated celebrities riding through the streets of New York atop taxis and taking a 3:00-A.M. dip in one of the city's public fountains. Americans probably drank less hard liquor after prohibition for a variety of reasons unrelated to the Volstead Act—greater affluence following World War II, changing status expectations, the spread of medical knowledge, and new dietary habits.

The historical and sociological connection between organized crime and prohibition is far less problematic. Without the considerable economic resources and managerial experience generated by the traffic in illegal alcohol, the mob could not have developed its nationwide network of influence or branched out into other lucrative activities. Shortly before his problems with the Internal Revenue Service began, Capone almost realized his ambition to create a national crime cartel and his organization had begun to invest in reputable enterprises of all kinds, including banks and real estate firms. The expansion of vice and the bureaucratization of crime flourished long after the Anti-Saloon League had passed from the scene.

Closing the Door

The acrimonious battle over prohibition constituted one skirmish on a much larger cultural battlefield during the 1920s. Millions of Americans, many of them native-stock Protestants living in small towns and the countryside or recent migrants from such communities, attempted to defend their vision of the nation against the manners and mores of the cities with their diverse ethnic groups, relaxed ethical codes, easy political virtue, and newfangled economic ways. During these years, the automobile, motion pictures, radio, chain stores, and mass advertising fashioned a national consumer culture that began its pervasive conquest of America by catering first to the educated, urban middle class. But these secular, standardized messages of progress, consumption, and self-indulgence frequently clashed with older, more traditional values rooted in particular geographic regions, in religious sentiments, and in ethnic traditions. A protracted struggle erupted over America's cultural soul that often pitted urban dwellers against country folks, college-educated sophisticates against believers in old-time religion, white Protestants against ethnic and racial minorities.

Ethnic, racial, and religious differences had from the beginning played a formative and often divisive role in American society. Throughout the nineteenth century, the nation's passion for economic growth encouraged a broad welcome mat for strangers, a generous conception of citizenship, and a relaxed immigration policy. At the same time, economic rivalries and fearfulness about cultural cohesion led to periodic outbursts of nativism directed against foreigners and immigrants. The passage of the Chinese Exclusion Act in 1882 and the almost simultaneous unveiling of the Statue of Liberty four years later spoke volumes about the ambivalence of the American people on this subject. Strangers were welcome, so long as they didn't flaunt their alien ways and resist becoming Americans like everybody else. At the same time, they shouldn't forge ahead too quickly.

Until World War I, the country remained officially open to most foreigners, although Congress had tightened up on immigration by banning contract laborers, paupers, and anarchists, and by giving federal courts exclusive jurisdiction over citizenship. The foreign-born never constituted more than 15 percent of the American population even at the peak of migration in 1911. But the heavy concentration of new arrivals in urban areas after 1880 and the prominence of Eastern and Southern Europeans among them provoked rising demands for restriction based on crude notions of racial inferiority and hereditary determinism.

Intellectuals such as John R. Commons, Edward Ross, and William Z. Ripley propagated the idea that the human race could be divided up neatly into fixed hereditary types, with Teutons leading the march of civilization while Mediterranean, Oriental, and African peoples brought up the rear. The Dillingham Commission, appointed by Congress in 1907 to study immigration and recommend legislation, called for a restrictive literacy test based on the assumption that "new" immigrants from Eastern and Southern Europe were fundamentally different from and inferior to the "old" immigrants from Northern Europe and Great Britain. On the eve of World War I, a wealthy New Yorker who dabbled in eugenics, Madison Grant, wove these cultural anxieties and pseudo-scientific ideas into a best-selling book, *The Passing of the Great Race*. Unless the country excluded all inferior racial and ethnic groups, Grant warned, the superior Nordic strain, the source of "rulers, organizers, and aristocrats" would be swamped by "the weak, the broken and the mentally crippled."

Despite mounting intellectual and political pressures to restrict immigration and defend racial purity, both Taft and Wilson vetoed efforts to impose a literacy test on newcomers. Two months before America entered the war, however, Congress overrode Wilson's veto and passed the Immigration Act of 1917, which excluded from the country aliens unable to read English or some other language. America's intervention then unleashed a torrent of antiforeign sentiment against "hyphenated Americans," especially Germans. An Army manpower policy in 1917–18 reinforced the widespread notion that hordes of undesirable ethnic minorities were about to swamp the nation's social structure, destroying cultural purity and intellectual standards. At the suggestion of the American Psychological Association, the Army began to administer Stanford-Binet intelligence tests to new recruits in an attempt to identify potential officers, assign soldiers to appropriate jobs, and exclude the mentally defective.

Many critics of the Stanford-Binet tests pointed out that most questions could not be answered without a basic knowledge of American history and geography, which gave a heavy advantage to native-born recruits from middle-class backgrounds, especially young people who had attended high school. Given this cultural bias, it is hardly surprising that "new" immigrants (Italians, Poles, Russians) and Southern blacks achieved inferior scores. To the average American who read about these reports, however, the authority of more experts and the government of the United States had now been added to the arguments of Madison Grant and other proponents of restriction.

The wave of postwar strikes, many in industries with large numbers of "hyphenated Americans," racial conflict in the cities, and the equation of aliens with political radicalism during the Red Scare intensified the drive to shut out all foreigners in 1919–20. "America will be saved," declared Columbia University President Nicholas Murray Butler, "not by those who have only contempt and despite for her founders and history, but by those who look with respect and reverence upon the great series of happenings extending from the voyage of the *Mayflower.*" To the long-standing calls for restriction shouted by Anglo-Saxon aristocrats and conservative trade unionists since the 1880s were now added the voices of influential businessmen, middle-class professionals, and veterans' groups. Shaken by domestic strife and the specter of revolution abroad, they, too, had begun to lose faith in the nation's capacity to absorb more immigrants.

Congress began to pull up the drawbridge with an emergency immigration law in 1921. For the first time, it fixed a ceiling on annual immigration from any European country, limiting it to 3 percent of the number of nationals who resided in the United States a decade earlier. The more permanent Johnson-Reed Immigration Act of 1924 slammed the door with a vengeance against Eastern and Southern Europeans and the Japanese.

Congressman Albert Johnson of Washington, chairman of the House Committee on Immigration, led the crusade for the permanent 1924 law. An open admirer of Madison Grant, Johnson built his political career in the Northwest on blatant appeals to the antiradical and anti-Japanese prejudices of his constituents. He hired two militant eugenicists as consultants to the committee, John B. Trevor, a New York lawyer with a penchant for baiting Jews, and Harry L. Laughlin, cofounder of the Eugenics Record Office, who believed that the fundamental purpose of the nation's immigration laws should be the defense of racial purity. Johnson and Laughlin proposed a simple scheme to tighten further the restrictions contained in the 1921 law: quotas should be based on the census of 1890, not 1910, giving an even greater advantage to Northern Europeans and Scandinavians. Each quota should be cut from 3 percent to 2. Under this formula, for example, the Italian quota would have been slashed form 42,000 persons to 4,000, the Polish from 31,000 to 6,000. Immigration from Japan would be barred entirely.

The Johnson bill, however, proved too blatantly discriminatory for the Senate, which backed a modified plan devised by Trevor and Senator David Reed. It fixed an absolute ceiling of 150,000 on all transatlantic immigration and apportioned this figure according to the "national origins" of the present white population, not the number of foreign-born in an earlier census year. But because the calculation of "national origins" would take some time, the Senate agreed to use the 1890 census for three years.

On close analysis, the differences between the House and the Senate on immigration restriction were negligble. Both approaches rested on the racist objective of maintaining an ethnic status quo and defending the cultural hegemony of what crackpot eugenicists called the Nordic or Teutonic peoples. Under either formula, immigrants from England, Germany, Ireland, and Scandinavia received favored treatment, while those from Eastern and Southern Europe and Asia faced impenetrable barriers to reaching the land of the free. Only with respect to migrants from Mexico, the Caribbean, Latin America, and French-speaking Canada did the law make any concessions to dark-skinned people or those from predominantly Catholic lands. In deference to the economic needs of American farmers, especially in California and in the Southwest, the quotas did not apply to immigrants from south of the border in order to guarantee a cheap, dependable supply of field labor.

Although the forces that shaped the Johnson-Reed Act had gathered momentum over many decades, its passage in the early twenties finally marked a watershed in the nation's history. Confidence about the nation's capacity to absorb a steady stream of people from diverse ethnic, religious, and cultural backgrounds had now given way to a new pessimism about assimilation and the resilience of the social order. Few white Americans ever questioned the idea that Providence had reserved the territory of the United States exclusively for their use and enjoyment. The immigration statutes of the 1920s wrote this awful assumption into federal law and even added a preference for white Northern Europeans.

When Americans turned their backs on the League of Nations and the World Court, they said two things: we are superior and the rest of the human race can fend for itself. These themes resounded through the decade's debates about tariffs, war debts, and immigration. In an era of rapid demographic and economic change, when new fortunes often unsettled the established hierarchies of status and power, old-stock Americans could not always defend their neighborhoods, clubs, and professions against invasion by second-generation Irish, Jews, and Italians. But the nation's fundamental immigration law gave them symbolic supremacy atop the social pyramid at the same time that the Eighteenth Amendment and the Volstead Act were intended to affirm their cultural hegemony as well.

6

One Nation, Divisible

Not for self but for others.
—Ku Klux Klan motto

The Bible states it.
It must be so.
—William Jennings Bryan

THE INVISIBLE EMPIRE

From the perspective of many native-born white Protestants, adoption of national prohibition and the Johnson Act offered only partial solutions to the daily problems generated by America's ethnic and cultural diversity during the postwar economic boom. Feeling themselves besieged in local communities by alien forces that ranged from political radicals, Italian mobsters, and car-crazed young adults to chain-store operators and salacious motion pictures, they also perceived little relief from the election of Harding or Coolidge. The man in the White House, preoccupied with national and international issues such as tariffs, taxes, and treaties, could not control the behavior of those in Mobile, Columbus, or Denver who did not always accept a subordinate social status, who drank too much, who scorned religion, or who defied other traditional social norms.

Some of these beleaguered Americans found an answer in an organization founded shortly before the country went to war by William J. Simmons, a former Methodist circuit preacher and history instructor at Lanier University in Atlanta. In 1915, Simmons led a small band of followers to the top of Stone Mountain outside the city once burned by

General Sherman. There they set fire to a large cross. As it burned, Simmons and his followers pledged to save America's white, Christian civilization by re-creating the Ku Klux Klan, a secret white-supremacist organization that had once terrorized Southern blacks and Northern carpetbaggers during Reconstruction.

Simmons had probably read Thomas Dixon's racist polemic *The Clansman*, and perhaps sat in a darkened Atlanta theater to see D. W. Griffith's *Birth of a Nation*, a 1915 motion picture epic that portrayed blacks during Reconstruction as ignorant and depraved savages, bent on the political and sexual conquest of the white South. Within a decade, the organization re-created by Simmons claimed a membership of over four million. The old Reconstruction-era Klan had concentrated its attention on destroying black political power in the South. By World War I, that goal had been accomplished through a combination of terror, economic reprisals, poll taxes, and literacy tests. While the reborn Klan still remained a hotbed of antiblack sentiment, now focused on returning war veterans, its list of enemies broadened after the war to include Jews, Catholics, bootleggers, adulterers, atheists, and others who offended against the Klan's vision of a racially and morally pure America. By 1925, it had also become a potent political force in states as remote from the Old Confederacy as Oregon and Colorado.

The new Klan emphasized what its leaders called old-fashioned values, but the organization utilized up-to-date techniques for recruitment and persuasion that mirrored other institutions in the consumer society. Simmons gave the reborn Klan a regalia and ritual that drew on his own experience as a recruiter for the Woodmen of the World, one of the innumerable prewar fraternal societies that offered its members cheap life insurance, a place to go on Saturday night, and the security of belonging to a community in which everyone thought alike. Minus its hooded white robes, open bigotry, and taste for violence, the Klan resembled other bastions of male fellowship that flourished during the decade—the Elks, the Moose, the Lions, the Kiwanis, and the Rotary. The Knights of the Ku Klux Klan met in a local Klavern, under the leadership of a Kleagle, and received the invocation from the Kludd. A gathering of several Klaverns became a Klonklave, presided over by a Grand Dragon, Grand Goblin, and Exalted Cyclops. Simmons took the title Imperial Wizard.

The crusade against the Hun and alien communists plus the fear sparked in the South by the return of black veterans kept Simmons's organization afloat financially from 1917 to 1920. Thereafter it would not have gained a nationwide following had the Imperial Wizard not

joined forces with Edgar Young Clark, another recruiter for the Woodmen of the World, and his mistress, Elizabeth Tyler. Founders of the
Southern Publicity Association, Clark and Tyler were among the more
brazen public relations entrepreneurs created by wartime programs
designed to sell patriotism and Liberty Bonds to the American people.
After raising funds for the Red Cross and the YMCA, the pair marketed the Klan across the nation with the same zeal and ballyhoo used
to sell real estate in Florida, bars of Ivory Soap, and Kellogg's Corn
Flakes.

Clark and Tyler broadened the Klan's menu of intolerance by stress-
ing its defense of traditional moral values and Biblical fundamentalism. They founded the Kemellia, a women's auxiliary, and launched a
vigorous recruitment drive that included one thousand Kleagles who
were promised $4 out of each $10 initiation fee paid by a new member.
Clark and Tyler told the Kleagles "to play upon whatever prejudices
were most acute in the particular area," a piece of marketing advice
that J. Walter Thompson might have endorsed. A congressional inquiry
and sensational articles in the Hearst papers that documented Klan-
inspired floggings and lynchings stunned civil libertarians, but probably boosted the organization's membership.

By the time Tyler died in 1924, the Klan's enrollments hit almost
four million and its Atlanta headquarters raked in $40,000 a month in
initiation fees and dues. Clark and Tyler had proved that bigotry could
be big business. With large sums of money at stake, a power struggle
erupted among the defenders of white Protestant civilization. Clark
and Tyler ousted Simmons from day-to-day control of the organization, but their regime collapsed when the former Woodman went to
jail for mail fraud and violating the Mann Act. The task of refurbishing
the Klan's tarnished image fell to the Exalted Cyclops of the Dallas
Klan and the Great Titan of the Texas Province, a college graduate
and dentist by the name of Hiram Wesley Evans. Self-described as
"the most average man in America," Evans proved equal to the job as
the new Imperial Wizard. As Klan membership grew, the Invisible
Empire spread its tentacles as far north as Maine and Oregon.

RISE AND FALL

Although both critics and supporters tended to exaggerate the Klan's
power, it did become an important force in local and national politics.
By 1924, according to its own figures, 40 percent of the organization's

members came from three states—Indiana, Ohio, and Illinois. Another 25 percent were found in the Southwest from Louisiana to Arizona; the Old Confederacy accounted for 16 percent, the wheat-growing Midwest 8 percent, the Pacific Coast 6 percent, and the North Atlantic–New England region 3 percent. Even within New England, however, the Klan's presence could be felt, as Maine attorney general W. R. Pattangall discovered when he denounced the Invisible Empire at the Democratic Party's 1924 national convention. The Maine Klaverns helped to defeat Pattangall in the next election by igniting hatred in the state against Irish and French-Canadian Catholics. Those groups, they alleged, backed the attorney general and hoped to use Maine as a beachhead for the pope's conquest of America. Although the courts struck them down, the Klan pushed through laws and referenda in several states designed to close parochial schools. Georgia's two United States senators probably belonged to the Invisible Empire, in addition to the governor of Alabama and one senator from Texas. The Klan claimed the governor's mansion in Colorado and a majority in the lower house of the state legislature. In Jefferson County, Alabama, and its major city, Birmingham, the Klan controlled judges, sheriffs, and prosecutors. When the local bar association there sponsored a resolution to "wage unrelenting war on the . . . mystic organization," almost half of its members voted against the proposal.

The Invisible Empire savored its greatest victories in Oklahoma and Indiana and at the Democratic Party's 1924 convention. With its new wealth, fluid social structure, heavy migration from the South, and abundance of bootleggers and prostitutes, Oklahoma proved to be a fertile recruiting ground for Evans's organization. The Klan faced a formidable opponent, however, in the mayor of Oklahoma City, John Calloway "Jack" Walton, who hired blacks on the police force and regularly denounced his hooded opponents. When Klan-led violence reached a near epidemic in Tulsa, Walton, who had been elected governor in 1923, placed the city and later the entire state under martial law. The Klan retaliated by encouraging the legislature to oust Walton through impeachment, and they later thwarted his attempt to win election to the United States Senate.

Headquartered in Indianapolis and boasting the most local Klaverns in the nation, Indiana's Invisible Empire gained enormous influence within the national organization through its flamboyant Grand Dragon, David Curtis Stephenson. He presided over recruitment efforts in twenty-three other states, published the *Fiery Cross*, and defended traditional American values from his office suite, equipped with a bank of eight

Women of the Klan lead march up Pennsylvania Avenue.

telephones, atop the Kresge Building. Weekends, as befitted any head of a wealthy corporate organization, Stephenson sailed a ninety-eight-foot yacht on Lake Huron. "I am the law," declared the Grand Dragon, and the 1924 elections bore him out. Klan-endorsed candidates won the Indiana governorship and a majority in the state legislature. The new mayor of Indianapolis vowed not to appoint anyone to city government without Stephenson's approval.

That same year the Klan flexed its muscles inside the national Democratic Party. With large Catholic, Jewish, and black constituencies, many big-city party leaders wanted the New York convention to condemn the Klan in its platform. Delegates from the South and West would accept only an innocuous statement that affirmed the party's support for civil liberties and civil rights. "My friends," intoned William Jennings Bryan, speaking for the weaker plank, "it requires more courage to fight the Republican Party than it does to fight the Ku Klux Klan." As the Oklahoma and Indiana cases illustrated, fighting the Klan and fighting the Republicans were not mutually exclusive, but with Bryan leading the opposition, the strong anti-Klan resolution went down to defeat, an indication of how powerful the organization had become in regions outside the urban Northeast.

The reborn Klan did not flourish solely by exploiting ethnic and religious hatreds. Appeals to white supremacy and attacks on Jews and Catholics played a significant role in the organization's ideology, but such prejudice flourished before the Klan's resurgence and continued to live after its demise. The Invisible Empire grew because it tapped other inchoate anxieties as well. Many of its members saw the organization as an instrument for expressing white-working-class grievances against big business and economic exploitation. Its greatest success, for example, came in "boom" cities such as Indianapolis, Denver, Portland, Dallas, Detroit, Tulsa, and Atlanta, where explosive economic and population growth brought people of varying social backgrounds into sudden proximity and unsettled old patterns of deference and authority.

In addition to economic tensions, recent migrants from smaller towns and villages to these cities felt acutely the absence of widely shared community norms with respect to gender roles, sexual decorum, drinking, and gambling. Longtime residents, accustomed to running local affairs, found themselves thrown on the defensive by waves of newcomers who strained public services and demanded their share of political power. By attempting to create an exclusive tribal community based on race, religion, and moral consensus, the Klan offered its members shared meanings and values usually missing from their daily lives. Klan-led beatings and lynchings reflected not just the sado-masochistic tendencies of many members, but also the pathetic effort by the tribe to impose its values by force on the broader community.

Whether they joined a Klavern in Portland or Atlanta, Klan members shared other social characteristics apart from white skin and the Protestant religion. Usually they arrived as new recruits to the industrial working class—displaced farmers, tenants, and sharecroppers—suddenly thrown together in factories and mills. Or they were petty businessmen and professionals who maintained a precarious foothold on the status ladder above the working class. Those who advertised regularly in Klan publications such as the *Fiery Cross* included tailors, dry cleaners, grocers, druggists, dentists, accountants, and chiropractors. In short, the Klan served as a haven for "the little people" of America, many of them uneducated and unsophisticated, who felt mocked and exploited by the country's distant social and economic elite. On that account, the Klan sometimes combined appeals to racial and religious solidarity with calls for social reform. In Birmingham, for instance, the local Klavern echoed some of the old Populist platform of the 1890s when it attacked banks, insurance companies, and public utilities as well as blacks, Jews, and bootleggers.

Often the source of brutality, the Klan had no monopoly on vigilantism and terrorism. Sometimes Klansmen found themselves on the receiving end of mob violence. When Ohio's Klan attempted to meet and parade in the tiny town of Niles on November 1, 1924, they met angry members of the Knights of the Flaming Circle, mostly Catholics, who broke up the Klonklave with stones, bricks, clubs, and fists. In Carnegie, Pennsylvania, opponents stopped another Klan parade from taking place when they shot to death one hooded member and seriously injured others. A mob estimated at five thousand by New Jersey police surrounded the Perth Amboy Odd Fellows Hall, where the Klan was holding a meeting, and pelted the Knights with debris, smashed their automobiles, and held them prisoner until morning.

After 1925 the Klan fell almost as quickly as it had risen, although it succumbed largely to self-inflicted wounds, not vigilantism or the wrath of public opinion. The most serious setback took place in Indianapolis, where a jury convicted Stephenson of the rape and murder of a twenty-eight-year-old secretary who took poison after the Grand Dragon attacked her on an overnight train ride to Hammond. When the judge sentenced Stephenson to twenty-five years to life in prison, the Klan's reputation for defending the purity of Christian womanhood suffered a heavy blow. A federal courtroom in Pennsylvania also rang with charges of Klan-led violence and financial misconduct when warring factions battled fruitlessly to gain control of the organization's treasury. Other political scandals, including indictments for bribery and election fraud, claimed the careers of Klan-supported officials in a half-dozen states between 1925 and 1929. In a futile effort to clean the organization's soiled robes, Evans banned the wearing of masks or visors in public and attempted to restore some of the Boy Scout atmosphere associated with the Woodmen of the World. But despite these efforts, membership in the organization plummeted to about 200,000 by 1929. The Stephenson scandal drove out many true believers. Others spurned Evans's strategy of turning the Klan into a respectable social club similar to the Odd Fellows. Preferring their bigotry loud and undiluted, many of these ex-Klansmen drifted into paramilitary hate groups such as the Silver Shirts.

The triumph of immigration restriction in 1924 took considerable steam out of the Klan's efforts to mobilize white Protestants against the alien hordes who no longer flooded the nation's shores. The economic collapse after 1929 and the onset of the Depression did not eradicate ethnic and religious intolerance, but encouraged greater solidarity among workers and saw the creation of new institutions such as the CIO-led industrial unions, which attempted to forge class alliances across ethnocultural lines. Finally, the rise and fall of the Invisible Empire proved the near-impossibility of recreating tribal communities within a dynamic capitalist society. It had become difficult in a consumer-oriented regime to sustain people's attention and allegiance in competition with other mass spectacles and amusements.

THE SHAME OF BIRMINGHAM

The social anxieties and primitive emotions that fed the growth of the Invisible Empire also eroded the ideals of liberty and equal justice under law in a Klan stronghold such as Birmingham. On a steamy August afternoon in 1921, Father James E. Coyle, pastor of St. Paul's Cathedral and one of the city's leading Catholics, was shot to death on the front porch of his rectory. Within a half hour, Coyle's assailant walked into police headquarters and confessed. Edwin R. Stephenson, an ordained Methodist minister without a regular congregation, told authorities he went to St. Paul's in search of his daughter, Ruth, a convert to Catholicism, who had earlier that day married a Puerto Rican paperhanger in a ceremony performed by Father Coyle. Stephenson admitted that he called Coyle names. When Coyle struck him, Stephenson claimed, he fired his gun in self-defense. His month-long trial for second-degree murder became a tragic example of the depths of religious and racial bigotry in the citadel of the New South.

Ruth Stephenson testified that her father had never accepted her religious conversion and had threatened to kill Father Coyle unless she stopped going to mass. The priest's sister swore she did not hear a scuffle on the front porch before the gunshot. The location of the fatal bullet suggested that Father Coyle had been seated at the moment of the attack. In the face of this evidence, the preacher's lawyers pleaded "not guilty" and "not guilty by reason of insanity." They were led by a young former prosecutor, Hugo Lafayette Black, a future United States senator and justice of the United States Supreme Court. He pandered shamelessly to the anti-Catholic and anti-black phobias of the all-white Birmingham jury. Black ridiculed the murdered priest and suggested that he had provoked the incident by seducing Ruth Stephenson into the Catholic faith. "I would write [a] verdict in words that cannot be misunderstood," Black told the jury, "that the homes of Birmingham cannot be touched." He waved a photograph of Ruth's husband, Pedro Gussman, around the courtroom. "I just wanted the jury to see this picture taken before [he] had his hair worked on," Black said, pointing to the dark-skinned witness. "You've had the curls rubbed from your hair since you had that picture taken." The jury found Stephenson not guilty, a result commended by the judge. But former Alabama governor Emmet O'Neal, hearing the verdict, expressed grief for the state's legal system and honor. "We have not advanced far from barbarism," he said, "if murder is to be justified on account of the religious creed of the victim."

BLACK MESSIAH

Faced with an Anglo-Saxon Protestant crusade to draw the line everywhere between insiders and outsiders, to slam the door on immigrants, and to keep racial and religious minorities in their place, some on the receiving end of intolerance responded with a fierce tribalism of their own. Fraternal societies such as the Knights of Columbus, the Sons of Italy, and the Knights of the Flaming Circle, usually based on ethnic and religious affiliations, gathered new members and momentum. In those economic niches where the foreign-born and their children had established a foothold—some trade unions, police departments, state and local governments—they fought vigorously to prevent the intrusion of other clans. Among the most powerful examples of ethnic self-consciousness was the black nationalist movement led by a charismatic West Indian immigrant, Marcus Garvey, who attracted a huge following among poor and middle-class migrants to cities like New York.

Harlem on New York's Upper West Side became the mecca of black intellectual and cultural life during the postwar years. Jazz and blues, migrating from the South along with people, floated from its clubs and speakeasies. W.E.B. Du Bois, a founder of the National Association for the Advancement of Colored People and the leading black historian, there published Crisis magazine as a forum for poets, essayists, and novelists who formed the vanguard of what soon came to be called the Harlem Renaissance. Du Bois encouraged Langston Hughes, Countee Cullen, Claude McKay, and countless other young black artists, who, lionized by wealthy white patrons, were said to represent the spirit of "the New Negro," a somewhat condescending phrase which suggested

W.E.B. Du Bois, NAACP leader.

that African-Americans had never before displayed intellectual distinction. Garvey and Du Bois, battling for the soul of the urban black movement, became implacable enemies during the postwar decade. In retrospect, they shared much in common.

Garvey, a dark-skinned West Indian, openly preached black pride, solidarity, and self-determination. He found a responsive audience among many American Negroes at a time when white liberals and mulattoes like Du Bois ran the NAACP and preached the gospel of nondiscrimination. The NAACP's ideal seemed tame in the face of a dominant white society that practiced segregation and attended plays entitled *The Coon at the Door* and *The Coon and the Chink*. Garvey told his audiences to glory in their blackness and African heritage. He advocated the necessity for racial purity among Negroes with the same vehemence that Hiram Evans thundered about the virtues of white supremacy.

American blacks would achieve power and dignity, Garvey said, when they had reclaimed Africa from the white man. The best way to hasten that day, he added, was for American blacks to build a strong, inde-

pendent economic base in the United States. On the eve of World War
I, he founded in Harlem the Universal Negro Improvement Association (UNIA). By 1919 one of the UNIA's major subsidiaries, the Negro
Factories Corporation, operated a chain of cooperative grocery stores,
a laundry, a publishing house, and a restaurant.

The UNIA also underwrote the *Negro World*, by the early 1920s the
most widely read black newspaper in America. The capstone of Garvey's economic empire, however, was the Black Star steamship line, a
venture designed to promote trade among Africans and their descendants throughout the world. By 1920, Garvey's Universal Negro
Improvement Association claimed upward of two million members in
eight hundred chapters on four continents.

In return for monthly dues, UNIA members received modest health
insurance and death benefits, plus the emotional satisfaction of promoting racial solidarity. A derisive popular song of the time claimed
that "Every Race Has a Flag but the 'Coon.' " Garvey gave his followers a flag—red ("the color of the blood men must shed for their liberty"), black ("the color of the noble race to which we belong"), and
green ("for the luxuriant vegetation of our Motherland"). At the conclusion of the 1924 International Convention of Negro Peoples of the
World, the Garveyites canonized Jesus Christ as the "Black Man of
Sorrows" and the Virgin Mary as the "Black Madonna." Sporting military uniforms and insignia, UNIA chapters created a sensation when
they marched through black neighborhoods. J. Saunders Redding
recalled that his father took him to a UNIA parade in Wilmington's
black ghetto in the early 1920s: "They came with much shouting and
blare of bugles and a forest of flags—a black star centered in a red
field. They made speeches in the vacant lot where carnivals used to
spread their tents. They had a huge, colorful parade, and young women,
tensely sober of mien and plain even in their uniforms, distributed millions of streamers bearing the slogan 'Back to Africa.' "

Redding also noted that his father, still an active member of the
NAACP, spotted among the UNIA paraders a number of "advancers,"
a term he used to describe ambitious members of the black middle
class. "They were not people of the slums. They were men with . . .
clothes-pressing shops and restaurants, personal servants, and . . . 'black
yeomen,' unlearned but percipient. They had been . . . somewhat awed
members of the NAACP. Some of them my father had personally
recruited, and low groans of dismay escaped him when he saw them
in the line of march."

Fearing that Garvey's UNIA posed a threat to their organization,

*Marcus Garvey, leader of the Universal Negro Improve-
ment Association.*

NAACP leaders denounced the Jamaican leader with a vehemence
usually reserved for the Klan. Noted poet James Weldon Johnson
declared that Africans should be allowed to wage their own struggles
without interference from American Negroes. W. E. B. Du Bois, while
sympathetic to Pan-African ideas, called Garvey "either a lunatic or a
traitor." He began a "Garvey Must Go" campaign among blacks and
encouraged government officials to investigate the UNIA. Garvey, who
had once discussed with Klansmen the virtues of racial separation for
both blacks and whites, hit back at his opponents. Denouncing the
NAACP's leadership, he declared that integration represented "the
greatest enemy of the Negro" because it retarded self-reliance and
nationalism.

Garvey's nationalist and separatist crusade attracted the attention of
another formidable opponent—J. Edgar Hoover, director of the Justice
Department's general intelligence division and soon to be crowned chief
of the FBI. Hoover perceived Garvey's UNIA as a dangerous source of
unity among urban blacks and as great a menace to the social order as
communists or anarchists. His antiradical division produced and circulated a pamphlet in 1920 entitled *Radicalism and Sedition Among*

the Negroes as Reflected in Their Publications. He told his superiors in the Justice Department that "unfortunately" Garvey had not broken any federal laws, but he urged a thorough investigation of the UNIA's business activities with an eye to later criminal prosecution.

For two years, Hoover's eager agents infiltrated the UNIA and combed through its records in an effort to gather incriminating evidence. Chaotic record-keeping by the Black Star Steamship Company made an indictment rather easy, and in 1923 Garvey was convicted of mail fraud. The judge who presided at Garvey's trial, himself a member of the NAACP, imposed the maximum fine of $1,000 and a five-year prison sentence. After the black nationalist leader left federal prison in 1927, he faced immediate deportation as an undesirable alien. The American branch of the UNIA lay in ruins.

Government harassment dealt a heavy blow to Garvey's black nationalist movement. Hoover and FBI devoted far greater manpower to toppling the UNIA than to investigating the Klan. Yet Garvey faced other obstacles to building a durable black organization based on principles of racial separatism. The vast majority of the black population, still impoverished tenant farmers and sharecroppers in the South, did not have the resources to sustain his dream. Many middle-class "advancers" joined UNIA chapters and listened to rousing speeches on black separatism, but still others remained devoted to the goal of non-discrimination and eventual integration taught by the NAACP. The Klan's vision of an all-white Protestant community of perfect moral harmony sprang in large part from the anomie of modern urban life. So, too, did Garveyism thrive on the pain, anger, and frustration that attended the uprooting of traditional black communities as they made the long march from the rural South to the cities.

THAT OLD-TIME RELIGION

Deeply rooted religious values colored the struggle over prohibition and immigration and shaped the outlook of the Klan. They also lay at the heart of other cultural conflicts, such as that symbolized by the 1925 trial of John Scopes in the tiny Tennessee hamlet of Dayton. There, two aging lions of the political culture, William Jennings Bryan and Clarence Darrow, battled over a state law that made it a crime to teach evolution in the public schools. For most scientists and a fair number of theologians, too, Charles Darwin's theories about natural selection and the evolution of species laid the foundations of modern biology and offered a coherent explanation of man's place in God's universe. For Christian fundamentalists like Bryan, who believed literally in the Bible, the idea that human beings descended from amphibians and primates contradicted the Book of Genesis. Evolution, in their view, threatened to erode the whole fabric of moral order contained in the Good Book. If Darwin triumphed, Bryan also reasoned, ideas about the survival of the fittest would come to dominate American social life as well. What then would restrain the rich as they crushed the poor?

Having already written their beliefs about alcohol into the Constitution of the United States, the defenders of Biblical literalism did not hesitate to support state laws that banned interpretations of human creation other than their own. With the support of the Klan, the Tennessee legislature passed the Butler Act, which declared it unlawful "to teach any theory that denies the story of the Divine Creation of man as taught in the Bible." Conviction carried a fine of up to $500.

Progressive theologians and civil libertarians regarded the Butler Act and similar anti-evolution measures passed by other states as a serious threat to academic freedom and the First Amendment. In Dayton they found a local high school science teacher and football coach willing to break the law in order to test its constitutionality. John Thomas Scopes was indicted and put on trial, ironically, after reading to his class passages on evolution contained in a volume approved for use in the Dayton schools by the Tennessee textbook commission. Taking time off from his lecture tour and selling real estate in Florida, Bryan volunteered to assist God and the prosecution. Darrow, smelling another opportunity to swell his reputation as America's foremost defender of justice and leading enemy of closed minds, joined the American Civil Liberties Union in defense of Scopes's right to teach Darwin.

In a decade of many staged gladiatorial contests—Jack Dempsey versus Gene Tunney, Notre Dame versus Army—the "monkey trial" that pitted Bryan against Darrow transformed Dayton briefly into the news capital of America. Bryan was no longer the dashing boy orator from the Platte. His stomach now fell over his belt; his once-vibrant voice often cracked. But he came to Dayton to fight again on behalf of the nation's embattled Protestant villagers. As a three-time presidential candidate for the Democrats, he had often taken up the cause of the sunbaked farmers and the little shopkeepers who believed they had been gouged for decades by railroads and other monopolists; during

The antagonists: Clarence Darrow (left) and William Jennings Bryan.

the Wilson years he spoke out for those who didn't want their sons sent to France to save the bankers' loans. Now he fought for those who believed their religion ridiculed by professors and intellectuals.

Darrow of Chicago, avowed atheist, foe of prohibition, defender of labor radicals and salacious books, represented the cultural and political enemy. A year before Dayton, he had successfully defended in Chicago two wealthy college whiz kids, Nathan Leopold and Richard Loeb, who believed they had committed "the perfect crime" in bludgeoning to death a fourteen-year-old boy, Bobby Frank, and then disfiguring his body with acid. For this heinous crime, prosecutors demanded the death penalty. In an impassioned argument that lasted nearly two days, Darrow persuaded the judge that his two clients were insane and should be sent to prison for life. Darrow's supporters called his defense brilliant, humane, just. But critics saw in Leopold and Loeb the moral wasteland created by families with too much money, young men with too much education and not enough simple morality grounded in religion. If Darrow won at Dayton and Darwin entered the schools, would it not inevitably produce more monstrous young men and women who lacked a conscience?

By the time the Scopes trial formally began in July's scorching Tennessee heat, Dayton resembled a carnival. Over a hundred newspaper, magazine, and radio reporters, some from as far away as London and Paris, jammed the tiny courthouse. Outside, vendors of soda pop, hot dogs, fans, and Bibles hawked their goods. Beginning each day at dawn, a steady stream of Model T Fords and horse-drawn wagons clogged the streets as country people for miles around came to town to watch the struggle between God and Satan. Some carried signs proclaiming, "Read Your Bible," and "Be Sure Your Sins Will Find You Out." The results of the trial, however, were never in doubt. John T. Raulston, who called himself "jist a reg'lar mountain'eer jedge," opened the first session with a prayer and told the defense lawyers that he would not permit testimony by scientific experts. Facing certain defeat in Raulston's court, Darrow could only hope for a later victory on appeal and in the court of public opinion. He tried to win the latter by putting Bryan on the stand as an expert witness on the Bible.

With the extraordinary session moved outdoors to accommodate the crowds, Darrow asked Bryan a series of questions that he hoped would "show up Fundamentalism [and] prevent bigots and ignoramuses from controlling the educational system of the United States." Before the judge mercifully halted the relentless cross-examination, the Great Commoner affirmed his belief that Eve had come from Adam's rib, that a whale swallowed Jonah, and that Joshua had stopped the sun. Sophisticated readers of the urban press roared with laughter. Fundamentalists, however, believed that Bryan had defended the word of God against "the greatest atheist and agnostic in the United States." The jury took only nine minutes to find Scopes guilty of violating the Butler Act. Raulston fined him $100. Five days later, after leading a prayer meeting at a local Methodist church and eating a large meal, Bryan died of heart attack. His tearful supporters eulogized him as a true Christian martyr, fallen in defense of the faith.

As cultural theater, the Scopes trial degenerated at times into a parody of the social and intellectual tensions that strained America's social fabric. College-educated intellectuals and literati poked fun at the Biblical literalism of Bryan and those who thought like him. The journalist H. L. Mencken called them "bigots," "yokels," and "hookworm carriers." But such ridicule seldom provided an emotional road map to help individual souls navigate the darker passages of modern life. Ironies abounded. The farmers, steeped in fundamentalism, denounced atheism at the state university, but still received advice from trained agronomists and biologists, many of whom worshiped Darwin.

Anti-evolutionists do a lively business in Dayton, Tennessee, on eve of Scopes trial.

And John Scopes never paid his fine. In 1927, the Tennessee supreme court, no doubt embarrassed by the trial, upheld the Butler Act, but reversed Scopes's conviction on a legal technicality: Judge Raulston had imposed a larger fine than the state constitution permitted without the recommendation of the jury. With this decision, the Tennessee supreme court prevented Scopes and the ACLU from carrying an appeal to the federal courts. A few other states, notably Arkansas, took heart from the Tennessee example and passed their own version of the Butler Act, which remained in force until the 1970s. What kept full-throated Darwinism out of American high schools for decades after the Scopes trial, however, was not legislation, but the economic decisions of frightened textbook publishers who catered to the sentiments of Bryan and his followers by expunging evolution from their volumes. The Great Commoner won his last battle from the grave.

BILLY AND AIMEE

The gravest challenge to fundamentalism, however, came not from John Scopes or Clarence Darrow, but from other Protestant denominations, from competition with other forms of popular entertainment, and from those who undermined religion by reducing theology to a theatrical extravaganza in order to meet this competition. When Bryan affirmed at Dayton that Eve came from Adam's rib and that God had punished the serpent by forcing it to crawl on its belly, his supporters nodded their assent. In many big-city Protestant churches and theological seminaries, however, ministers, parishioners, and students shook their heads in disbelief.

For decades, the more liberal branches of the Protestant faith, especially the Episcopalians, Presbyterians, Congregationalists, and Unitarians, had attempted to demonstrate the compatibility of science and religion and to turn the spiritual energies of their churches toward the alleviation of social problems. Incorporating historical and archaeological evidence about the ancient Near East and its civilizations into religious education, they subjected Biblical texts to rigorous criticism and cast doubt on many cherished tenets of fundamentalism. Darwin's ideas, some argued, were perfectly consistent with an orderly universe created by a rational God. "Science is but the deciphering of God's thought as revealed in the structure of this world," declared one of their leaders. "It is merely a translation of God's primitive revelation." And while striving for salvation in the hereafter, good Christians were admonished to make this world better by fighting poverty, racism, and war.

Without such intellectual accommodation, urban Protestantism could not have hoped to retain its hold on an increasingly prosperous, secular, educated middle class. But each step taken along this road to modernism tended to dampen the fires of religious enthusiasm and bring thunderous denunciations from fundamentalists, who preached the old-time religion. A cerebral Protestantism did not always nourish the soul, and it had difficulty competing with baseball, football, the motion pictures, and Sunday drives in the family automobile. "My people seem to sit through the sermon in a kind of dazed, comatose state," complained one minister. "They don't seem to be wrestling with my thought." What passed for reasonable doctrine at Union Theological Seminary or in the Congregationalist pulpits of New England seemed outlandish heresy in the Baptist and Methodist strongholds of the rural South and West or among their urban congregations populated by recent migrants from the countryside. Church membership kept on rising in the 1920s as it had from the beginning of the century, reaching about one-half of the adult population by 1930, but the fundamentalists, not the modernists, and preachers of the social gospel, reaped the largest gains, even in the booming cities.

For the millions of Protestants who still thought theologically as Bryan

Billy Sunday, evangelist.

did, who believed in the virgin birth, the divinity of Christ, and the fires of hell, the Reverend Billy Sunday assured them that their beliefs remained America's beliefs. He carried the banner of fundamentalism into Satan's own territory by holding mammoth revival meetings in cities such as Chicago and Philadelphia. "The Untired Businessman of Theology," Sunday turned evangelism into a consumer product like any other by utilizing up-to-date management and mass marketing techniques. His sermons, loud and repetitious, blended political, theological, and cultural conservatism:

—On radicals: "If I had my way with these ornery wildeyed Socialists and IWWs, I would stand them up before a firing squad and save space on our ships."

—On freedom of speech: "America is not a country for a dissenter to live in."

—On the social gospel: "The fatherhood of God and the brotherhood of Man is the worst rot that ever was dug out of hell and every minister who preaches it is a liar."

—On women and Christianity: "If some of you women would spend less on dope and cold cream and get down on your knees and pray, God would make you prettier."

—On the Savior: "Jesus was no dough-faced lick-spittle proposition. Jesus was the greatest scrapper that ever lived."

Sunday's two-fisted, bare-knuckled fundamentalism appealed to many of the same people who flocked to the Klan and who believed that only a restoration of pure religious faith could halt the nation's slide into immorality and social chaos. A similar message, but somewhat softer in tone and wrapped in a more glamorous package, was delivered by "the world's most pulchritudinous evangelist," Aimee Semple McPherson.

McPherson fused fundamentalism with Hollywood glamour and sex appeal. Converted at seventeen by an itinerant preacher whom she later married, the redheaded McPherson parlayed faith healing, good looks, and a flair for the dramatic into a formidable religious and business empire on the West Coast that included by the end of the decade a college, overseas missions, a publishing house, and a radio station. Her

Aimee Semple McPherson.

radio transmitter was so powerful that it regularly jumped across the wave band and disrupted other programs. Reprimanded by Commerce Secretary Hoover, who was charged with policing such matters, McPherson replied: "Please order your minions of Satan to leave my station alone. You cannot expect the Almighty to abide by your wavelength nonsense. When I offer my prayers to Him, I must fit into His wavelength reception." Southern California, populated largely by fundamentalists from somewhere else who hungered for community, proved fertile ground for McPherson's brand of religion, known as the "foursquare gospel"—Regeneration, Divine Healing, the Second Coming, and the Baptism of the Holy Ghost.

Once word spread that Aimee had cured the lame and the sick, people packed her $1.5 million Pentecostal Temple in Los Angeles, a facility complete with a huge illuminated cross, visible for miles, and a "miracle room" where the formerly afflicted discarded their wheelchairs and crutches. Believers huddled around radios to hear McPherson denounce the many vices of modern America. She offered the soothing balm of love as an antidote. Although she regularly condemned the wicked ways of Hollywood, her religious services, complete with orchestra, chorus, and elaborate sets, rivaled the motion picture pageants produced a few miles away. In a mock battle between God and the devil, heroic Christians fired holy artillery at Satan, who floated across the battlefield in a hot-air balloon while a giant scoreboard kept tally. Clad in a flowing white gown, McPherson opened another service by riding a motorcycle down the temple's center aisle.

Only a love affair with the married manager of her radio station, rumors of a Mexican abortion, several dubious disappearances, and reckless financial transactions cooled the enthusiasm of McPherson's parishioners, who had kept the seats and the collection plate at the Pentecostal Temple filled. Billy Sunday turned fundamentalism into big business by selling salvation in a consumer society the way General Motors sold Chevrolets. Aimee Semple McPherson made it show business, a spectacle capable of competing for the entertainment dollar with marathon dancing, King Vidor, and Cecil B. De Mille.

7

Fortunes of Feminism

*The real hope of the world lies in putting as painstaking
thought into the business of mating as we do into other big
businesses.*
—Margaret Sanger

*At thirty every woman reaches a crossroads. Will she
develop—or merely age?*
—Boncilla Beautifier, *The Clasmic Clay*

THE WOMEN'S MOVEMENT

In the big cities of America during the postwar decade, especially New
York and Chicago, the emergence of the "New Negro," who wrote
poetry, composed music, practiced medicine, and taught philosophy,
stirred awe, confusion, and anxiety among many whites. Seeking to
explain the dazzling dramatic and singing talents of Paul Robeson, an
honors student at Rutgers, football star, and Columbia Law School
graduate, the critic George Jean Nathan could only conclude that
Negroes seemed to be "natural-born" actors. Whether in the metropolis or the small towns of the era, the presence of the "New Woman"
who challenged traditional gender boundaries generated a similar
mixture of feelings.

Many male religious leaders and social critics, for example, denounced
Aimee Semple McPherson as a theological charlatan who made money
by exploiting the social insecurities of her gullible parishioners. When
Billy Sunday or another man preached, however, it was more often
said that he filled the longing for intense religious emotion in a culture
preoccupied with material progress. As the first woman to found a major

religious denomination, the first to control a powerful radio station, and the first to preach over the airwaves, McPherson symbolized the changing status of women and their continuing battle for full equality. Like other crusades shaped by the prewar progressive movement, the one for women's rights, too, underwent dramatic changes when the emphasis on the public good faded before a new ethic of private self-fulfillment.

War hastened the triumph of women's suffrage as it did prohibiton. When he first entered the White House in 1913, Woodrow Wilson rejected a constitutional amendment to enfranchise women. The individual states controlled voting rights, he said, not the federal government. His was the message of a traditional states' rights Democrat and Southerner, who believed women should tend the hearth, not the ballot box. Five years later, all had changed. With American soldiers dying at the Meuse River in 1918, Wilson made an unprecedented appearance before the Senate to urge a favorable vote on the proposed Nineteenth Amendment, which banned sex discrimination in voting.

Since America entered the conflict, Wilson told the senators, her women had become full partners in a war to further democracy, but "shall we admit them only to a partnership of suffering and not to a partnership of privilege and right?" A year later, with the Treaty of Versailles on the table in Europe, the Senate finally passed the Nineteenth Amendment by the necessary two-thirds vote and sent it on to the states for ratification. With the approval of Tennessee in August 1920, American women had achieved national suffrage. According to legend, the vote that put Tennessee in the pro-suffrage camp and the Nineteenth Amendment into the Constitution was cast by its youngest state legislator, twenty-four-year-old Harry Burn, who had received a message from his mother before the final tally: "Vote for suffrage and don't keep them in doubt. . . . Don't forget to be a good boy and help Mrs. Catt put 'Rat' in Ratification." Assuming that Mrs. Burn invoked maternal affection to secure adoption of the suffrage amendment, the event symbolized the potency of conservative ideals that helped to shape the women's rights movement by the 1920s and fixed much of its course for many years thereafter.

FROM SENECA TO SUFFRAGE

Equal suffrage had been only one among many goals of the middle-class women who gathered at Seneca Falls in 1848 to issue their celebrated "Declaration of Rights and Sentiments." Written principally by Elizabeth Stanton, this manifesto boldly proclaimed that "the history of mankind is a history of the repeated usurpations on the part of man toward woman, having in direct object the establishment of an absolute tyranny over her." Stanton and her followers demanded full political, social, and economic equality for women, the overthrow of patriarchy, and a fundamental transformation in gender relations from the ballot box to the family. Many of them rejected the notion that men and women had inherently different natures that fixed their appropriate areas of activity; the concept of "separate spheres" restricted women to the supporting roles of wife and mother, while men pursued careers in business and politics. "How rebellious it makes me feel," wrote Stanton, "when I see Henry [Stanton] going about where and when he pleases. . . . While I have been compelled to be a household drudge."

Progress came slowly for women's rights advocates during the remainder of the century. The Fifteenth Amendment sought to end racial barriers to voting, but did not mention sex discrimination. While women could sue to enforce contracts and bring personal injury suits, most areas of family law continued to favor men; coeducation at colleges and universities had not become a reality; high-status professions remained closed to women; states made abortions criminal. A gender-blind society seemed almost as remote in 1900 as in 1848.

Male domination of the legal and political system accounted in large measure for the persistence of sex discrimination. But reformers also faced apathy and hostility from members of their own sex, especially from the many immigrant women who entered American society in the late nineteenth century. Reared in preindustrial peasant societies where patriarchy often reigned supreme and where the family functioned as a potent social and economic institution, they did not easily identify with the spirited individualism and egalitarian rhetoric of white middle-class Protestants who carried the banner of the women's movement. The sisters from Seneca Falls often condemned traditional family arrangements and aspired to professional careers outside the home; most immigrant and minority women battled to keep their families intact in a hostile economic world. They favored the solidarity of a trade union and sought special legislation to protect the health and income of working women.

Confronted with these formidable political, ideological, and cultural obstacles, the advocates of women's rights during the progressive era made a number of important tactical innovations, each designed to

broaden support and quiet their critics. Instead of attacking the concept of sex-based differences and separate spheres, many movement
leaders sought to exploit these ideas for their own ends. A woman's
higher spiritual nature would be corrupted by exposure to politics, ran
the traditional argument. Reformers answered that feminine virtue,
honesty, and morality would reduce graft and corruption in public life.

Motherhood and child-rearing served as weapons in many wars of
progressive reform. If women were to fulfill these traditional roles in
the home, they needed to fight in the public arena to protect their special sphere from the many social evils that menaced family life and
children: slum housing, poor sanitation, tainted food and drink, low
wages, and unsafe working conditions that might kill or maim the
breadwinner. "Running New York," declared a publication from the
Henry Street Settlement, where college-educated reformers ministered to the urban poor, "is just a big housekeeping job, just like your
own home, only on a larger scale. Therefore you should be interested
in city-wide affairs." Even socialists found arguments based on home
and hearth appealing. Running for Congress in 1910, Kate Richards
O'Hara declared, "I long for domestic life, home and children with
every fiber of my being. . . . Socialism is needed to restore the home."

Reformers also turned biological arguments against opponents.
Because of their unique maternal functions and responsibility for propagation of the race, women had to be given special legal protection in
situations that would be unconstitutional when applied to men. "The
two sexes differ in structure of body, in the functions to be performed
by each," declared the justices of the Untied States Supreme Court in
1908, as they upheld a law restricting the hours women might labor in
certain occupations. "This difference justifies a difference in legislation . . . to compensate for some of the burdens which rest upon her. . . ."

Some feminists such as Charlotte Perkins Gilman continued to
emphasize the broader struggle against patriarchy and the necessity for
a basic reorganization of power within the household. The most visible
leaders and organizations, however, placed the suffrage issue above all
others. It was the most simple and direct manifestation of discrimination, and it could be attacked without a frontal assault on orthodox
gender relations and stereotypes. Women's suffrage, they noted, would
not destroy the traditional family, but strengthen it by permitting mothers
to defend their historical domain. The enfranchisement of women would
protect the nation as well from the rising menace of foreign-born males,
whose propensity for radicalism threatened the conventional political
balance. "There is but one way to avert the danger," said Carrie Catt

Women's suffrage and the politics of virtue.

of the National American Woman Suffrage Association (NAWSA), "cut off the vote of the slums and give to woman . . . the power of protecting herself . . . the ballot."

With its single-minded emphasis on the ballot box and conservative ideals, the suffrage campaign therefore did much to blunt the edge of the women's movement even before the Nineteenth Amendment became a part of the nation's fundamental law. The broader feminist vision of Seneca Falls was kept alive by women's colleges, the birth control movement, and the unique economic opportunities created by the war. Before the twenties had well begun, however, the radical potential of these efforts had been tamed, too.

WOMAN'S WORK

The pending suffrage victory raised feminist hopes high during the war years, but so did the sight of American women working in foundries, machine shops, armament factories, steel mills, railway yards, and printing plants. These were jobs reserved historically for men. Never in such numbers had American women tended lathes, stoked furnaces, operated trolleys, welded ship hulls, and sold Liberty Bonds. With over one million men called to military duty by the first draft in 1917, employers in industry, agriculture, and government had little choice but to recruit women for these traditional male tasks. "When men go a-waring," wrote Harriot Stanton Blatch in her 1918 book *Mobilizing Woman-Power*, "women go to work." Through service to their nation in time of crisis she added, American women might secure "that economic freedom which will change a political possession into a political power."

On the surface the war seemed to bring an occupational revolution for women. Their sweat, skill, and devotion kept the economy from falling apart between 1917 and 1919. Their labor truly ensured the triumph of Allied armies in France. Over 100,000 women put on overalls and manned munitions plants. The Woman's Land Army recruited 15,000 sisters to milk cows, feed chickens, pick fruit, and run tractors. In the lumber mills of Idaho, Oregon, and Washington, women cut the pine and spruce to build military barracks and airplane frames. The United States Public Health Service recruited female doctors for the first time. Wells Fargo hired women as cashiers, accountants, and auditors. Below the surface of statistics, however, gender relations changed at a glacierlike pace.

The discussion of an employment revolution often ignored one palpable fact: the war years did not bring a huge surge of new women into the labor force. According to one estimate, probably 95 percent of the women who went to work outside the home from 1917 to 1919 had already been employed there before the war. And by 1920, fewer women worked outside the home than a decade earlier. This could hardly be counted as progress by those who viewed such employment as the litmus test of gender equality.

When women entered traditionally male occupations for the first time during the war years, they faced stiff resistance, and in certain areas they made almost no progress. Some federal agencies such as the National War Labor Board and the Women's Bureau in the Labor Department fought valiantly to secure women shorter hours, decent working conditions, and equal pay for equal work. But other government entities such as the Council of National Defense recognized women's interests grudgingly, and others continued to discriminate openly. As one wartime bureaucrat put it, the "strain" of particular jobs made women unfit for "certain positions in the public service."

The War Labor Board protected the right of women as well as men to join trade unions during the conflict, but Samuel Gompers and the leaders of the American Federation of Labor displayed little interest in recruiting more feminine members. Why lavish the organization's time, they reasoned, on those whose role in industry was only temporary? The AFL complained instead that women diluted the standards in many trades and expressed hope that they would go back to homemaking as soon as possible, a view expressed by some women, too. "The same patriotism which induced women to enter industry during the war should induce them to vacate their positions after the war," declared the AFL's Central Federated Union in New York.

Wartime employment gains for women proved to be very short-lived, as figures from the 1920s demonstrated. Between 1920 and 1930, two million females joined the labor force, but the number of women actually employed grew only a single percentage point, from 23 to 24 percent. Instead of becoming producers, most white middle-class women took on the role of chief of consumption in the postwar household. The 1930 census listed American women in an extraordinary number of occupations from lawyers to steeplejacks, but the vast majority of those women who worked outside the home remained segregated in five low-paying, low-status jobs, as before—nursing, teaching, domestic service, clerical, and sales.

Nearly 700,000 women, mostly racial minorities and the daughters of immigrants, became domestic servants during the flush times of Harding and Coolidge, but by 1930 the country could count only 151 women who practiced dentistry and less than half that number who worked as accountants. The percentage of women compared to men who attended colleges and universities during the decade actually fell by 5 percent. And while women received about one-third of all advanced graduate degrees, they filled less than 8 percent of the academic posts in institutions of higher learning. Even in the occupational niches that they dominated, women seldom held managerial or supervisory positions. They taught first grade, but did not become school principals or superintendents. They manned cosmetic counters at Macy's, but did not run its departments. Women who worked next to men at the same job still earned a lower wage, on the theory that they required only "pin money," not income to support a family.

POLITICS AS USUAL

Instead of being a springboard to further victories as some feminists predicted, the war proved to be a short coda to a movement that lost much of its dynamism and coherence in the next decade. Those who believed the Nineteenth Amendment would transform the nation's politics felt special disillusionment. With new power at the ballot box, some assumed, women would revise the stale agendas of the parties, elevate the tone of debate, elect members of their own sex to office, and secure other feminist goals.

In the twenties, however, a distinct "women's vote" never materialized. On the whole, women showed less inclination to vote than men at all levels of balloting. When they did vote, they cast their ballots much as their husbands, fathers, and male relatives did. The wives of Republicans voted Republican, the daughters of socialists kept the radical faith of their parents. When asked by interviewers why they had not voted, women often responded with answers that revealed their own entrenched sexual prejudices. Some expressed no interest in politics. Others claimed that their husbands had failed to remind them to vote. A substantial number declared that politics should be left to men. American women voted more frequently in the years of depression and heated political controversy that came with Franklin Roosevelt and the New Deal after 1932, but this change reflected a more general upward surge in balloting by men and women who had not participated during the immediate postwar decade.

By 1928, the League of Women Voters reported that 145 women held seats in thirty-eight state legislatures. Both major parties had placed some women on their national and state committees. Two women served in the House of Representatives; two had been elected to governorships to succeed spouses who had earlier held the office. These figures hardly amounted to a gender revolution in American politics. Women could claim a few unique public policy triumphs after 1920, such as the Cable Act, which abolished the legal disabilities suffered by those who married male aliens. On other issues that directly touched their lives, however, women often remained divided. The Sheppard-Towner Act and the proposed Equal Rights Amendment were two notable examples of such discord.

THE POLITICS OF SHEPPARD-TOWNER

Many women reformers hailed the passage of the Sheppard-Towner Act in 1921 as a triumph for feminism and progressivism. And so it seemed, for the law placed the federal government and the states in the business of funding health care for pregnant women and their unborn children. In addition, it gave women a major role in the delivery of these health services through local clinics that they rather than male physicians controlled. Conservative opponents, fearing government intrusion into the family, took the opposite view, but the law's supporters successfully countered that Sheppard-Towner would strengthen, not weaken, home and hearth by lowering maternal and infant mortality rates. "Of all the activities in which I have shared during more than forty years of striving," said Florence Kelley, the *grande dame* of the settlement house movement, "none is . . . of such fundamental importance as the Sheppard-Towner Act." Declaring that women were "first, last and always mothers and will so continue," Charlotte Gilman, another leading feminist, supported the program, too.

Sheppard-Towner's focus on motherhood and childbearing made it attractive to many men and women in the progressive movement, but stirred some anxiety among other women reformers, who feared the law would perpetuate gender stereotypes and draw attention away from the importance of birth control. "No woman can call herself free who does not own and control her own body," declared Margaret Sanger, the queen of contraception. "No woman can call herself free until she can choose conscientiously whether she will or will not be a mother." Her own mother, recalled this pioneer of the birth control movement before the war, had died at forty-eight after bearing eleven children.

Denied a medical school education because of her family's lack of money, Margaret Higgins entered nursing, married a bright young architect, William Sanger, and bore him three children. In the pages of *Woman Rebel* and *Family Limitation* before the war, Sanger and her allies broadcast both their philosophy of birth control and explicit information about contraception. Women with money and social position had access to effective contraception and safe abortions. Poor women could usually secure neither. They were condemned to produce more unwanted, impoverished children who would fuel capitalist exploitation by keeping wages depressed.

For these views, Sanger was charged with violating Section 211 of the United States Penal Code, known as the Comstock Law, which banned "mailing, transporting or importing anything lewd, lascivious or obscene." Sanger fled to England to avoid prosecution. Abroad she met Havelock Ellis, the apostle of sexual liberation and expression, and learned about diaphragms from Dutch midwives. By uncoupling sex and procreation, Sanger now believed, contraception promised women both economic independence and erotic freedom.

In 1916, after she returned to the United States, Sanger and her sister went to jail for operating a birth control clinic in Brooklyn, where they dispensed contraceptive information to immigrant women for the minimal charge of 10 cents. The New York courts rejected her First Amendment defense, but altered the politics of birth control by ruling that licensed physicians could prescribe contraceptives in order to prevent or treat disease.

Sanger faced a hard choice: join forces with the conservative, male-dominated medical profession or continue direct-action tactics that gave women a central role in providing birth control through clinics run by midwives and nurses. The author of *Woman Rebel* opted for the first, legally secure alternative. She founded the eminently respectable American Birth Control League to unite physicians and middle-class women in the new campaign for sexual hygiene, and thus took much of the radical sting out of the movement. Male doctors, not women, now ran the birth control business.

Once the guardian of the poor and the working class, Sanger now linked the new birth control movement openly with militant eugenicists, who hoped to prevent the propagation of "unfit" and "defective" human beings, including those afflicted with diseases such as epilepsy or those who too often ran afoul of the law. Criminal traits, eugenicists assumed, were passed down from generation to generation. Influenced by these ideas, many states enforced compulsory sterilization laws during the twenties that fell mainly on impoverished people and racial minorities. Upholding such a law in 1927, Justice Holmes, speaking for eight members of the Supreme Court, including Brandeis, declared that "three generations of imbeciles are enough." Only Justice Butler, the lone Catholic on the bench, dissented.

Sanger also found herself drawn into conflict with supporters of Sheppard-Towner. Federal administrators and some women's rights advocates wished to keep the local clinics out of the birth control business in order to avoid sniping from moralists and religious groups. Sheppard-Towner clinics should stress health care for the living, they said, not family limitation. Grace Abbott, the devoted head of the Children's Bureau, argued that the law was intended "not to prevent children from coming into the world but to save the lives of babies and mothers." Sanger and other critics replied that this emphasis would guarantee a poor woman a healthy seventh child "when what she wants to know is how to avoid bringing into the world her eighth."

Conservative critics of Sheppard-Towner exploited these divisions among women to weaken the program steadily in Congress over the course of the decade. Physicians and the American Medical Association equated even modest federal expenditures with government reg-

Margaret Sanger.

ulation of their profession and communism. Twice reprieved during the Coolidge administration, Sheppard-Towner finally died when Congress cut off all federal funding in 1929.

EQUAL RIGHTS CRUSADE

While they did not actively oppose efforts such as Sheppard-Towner, the militant feminists in the National Women's Party had other, higher priorities. Led by Alice Paul and Rose Winslow, the NWP had given the suffrage campaign its most radical twist during the war. Carrying signs that equated Wilson with the Kaiser, they picketed the White House around the clock. Some chained themselves to its fence. Put in jail, they went on hunger strikes and had to be fed forcibly. The spectacle of government waging a war to make the world safe for democracy while dragging women off to prison and shoving pipes down their throats became a public relations fiasco for the administration and one that no doubt hastened passage of the suffrage amendment.

Beginning in 1923, Paul and her followers turned their attention to the far more controversial federal equal rights amendment. They denounced legislation that singled out women for special treatment as a badge of inferiority and a subtle trap designed by men to perpetuate gender differences and the exclusion of women from many fields. Their proposed constitutional amendment declared flatly that "men and women shall have equal rights throughout the United States and every place subject to its jurisdiction."

As members of the Women's Party saw it, the ERA represented the logical culmination of the fight begun at Seneca Falls and left unfinished by the Nineteenth Amendment. "There is not a single state in the union in which men and women live under equal protection of the law," said Doris Stevens of the NWP. "Woman is still conceived to be in subjugation to . . . [her] husband . . . or the male member of the family." Even with the suffrage amendment on the books, Paul added, "women . . . are still in every way subordinate to men before the law, in the professions, in the church, in industry, and in the home."

In the pages of their publication *Equal Rights,* the leaders of the Women's Party kept up a steady fire of criticism against sex discrimination sanctioned by common law, statute, and customs. They denounced such obvious manifestations of bias as the continued exclusion of women from juries. They also attacked more benign forms of legislation designed to protect the health and welfare of women in the workplace. To the chagrin of many old progressive leaders and women in the trade union movement, Paul and Stevens urged the abolition of all laws that restricted the hours women could work, the kinds of work they could perform, and the amount of remuneration they could receive.

Under the guise of protecting women, NWP leaders argued, sex-based statutes furthered the economic subordination of their sisters. Laws prohibiting women from working at night or on split shifts had forced the firing of female bookbinders and transit workers. Laws that restricted women from lifting heavy weights or working underground closed certain opportunities to them. When states fixed minimum wages for women in specified occupations, employers hired men at cheaper rates. Why shouldn't women be allowed to work in coal mines, bowling alleys, and pool halls—jobs all closed to them by various states with the justification of protecting feminine health, welfare, and morality?

To those like Florence Kelley and Jane Addams who had devoted much of their adult lives to securing protective legislation for women, the champions of the ERA were utopian fanatics who would leave working women at the mercy of unscrupulous employers in pursuit of a gender-blind social order. While they, too, deplored many forms of sex discrimination, the old progressives insisted that these barriers could be eliminated without giving up hard-won legislative achievements. They looked upon protective laws for women as the first stage in a long legal campaign to extend such protection to all workers, male and female. Doubtless a legislative compromise could have been devised, but the two camps continued to exchange verbal brickbats that accused each other of weakening the women's movement.

"WHITE-NOSED WOMEN WHO WEAR FURS IN SUMMER"

Members of the National Women's Party and the old progressives sparred over a number of issues, but they tended to agree on one thing: the younger, postwar generation of women seemed bent on dissipating their hard-won political inheritance through rampant self-indulgence and behavior designed to reinforce gender stereotypes. These reformers wanted American women to find fulfillment basically in the public sphere—running settlement houses, fighting corrupt politicians, battling against child labor, mounting suffrage campaigns. Confinement in the home denied full equality. Too much emphasis on homemaking, child-rearing, and sexual attractiveness subverted genuine feminism. The 1920s, to their displeasure, witnessed a noticeable flight by many American women, especially those in the college-educated urban middle class, from the public sphere to the private one, and a renewed emphasis on traditional feminine roles—capturing a mate, raising a family, and managing a household supplied with the latest consumer goods.

Before settling down, moreover, younger women of the post war generation appeared eager to abandon all social restraints on their behavior by taking to heart the idea that equality meant enjoying the pleasures customarily reserved for men. The *Ladies' Home Journal* called them "flappers." F. Scott Fitzgerald immortalized them in his early novels, which depicted them indulging in a seemingly endless round of drinking, smoking, and flirting. With their close-cropped bobbed hair and androgynous dress, many made a special effort to offend perceived notions of feminine decorum and modesty.

Salesclerks, secretaries, schoolteachers, and college students by day, young women flocked to urban speakeasies at night in skirts that stopped just below the knee, worn often with horizontal-striped sweaters and long, cascading necklaces. The more affluent among them appeared in a Callot beaded sheath or a Chanel two-piece jersey, sometimes worn without undergarments and with silk stockings rolled around garters at rouged knees. To these skimpy, provocative outfits might be added a pearl stud in one ear and a dangling paste gem in the other. This modern American woman, declared a Pope & Brally advertisement in 1926, "could be blown away by the gust of a summer breeze. . . . Scorning the elements, she has rapidly become more attractively male. She is fearless in her exposition, cultured in her symmetry and grace, and strangely enough, ethereally clad as she is, she catches more men than colds."

"Flappers," according to the *Journal* and other mass-circulation magazines, drank enormous quantities of bootlegged liquor, doubled the nation's consumption of cigarettes, ruined their postures with the "debutante slouch," danced all night to Paul Whiteman's music, and had numerous sexual liaisons. "She takes a man's point of view as her mother never could," observed the *New York Times*. "She will never make you a hatband or knit you a necktie, but she'll drive you from the station hot summer nights in her own little sports car." Amory Blaine,

For the June 1926 number, Held pictures the modern coed as an incongruous combination of ruffled innocence and hard-bitten sophistication.

John Held's 1926 magazine cover.

the hero of Fitzgerald's *This Side of Paradise*, "saw girls doing things that even in his memory would have been impossible. . . . But he never realized how widespread it was until he saw the cities between New York and Chicago as one vast juvenile intrigue."

As the *Times* and Fitzgerald hinted, American women experienced a sharp generational division over issues of manners and values. Many prewar feminists condemned the younger generation's social habits, especially their open sensuality and hedonism. "The behavior of women in this matter," wrote Charlotte Gilman, "is precisely that of any servile class set free. Indulgences previously enjoyed by the master and denied to the slave are eagerly seized upon." But, as Gilman concluded bitterly, "a generation of white-nosed women who wear furs in summer cannot lay claim to any real progress."

Popular magazines, newspapers, and aging feminists to the contrary, not all American women under thirty managed after 1920 to live the self-indulgent, carefree, emancipated existence of the "flappers" portrayed in *Vanity Fair*. The style attracted its share of young working-class girls, college students, and rich bohemians, but the shingle bob, puce berets, and Vuitton luggage were not found often among Polish-American housewives in Chicago, Japanese-American teenagers hoeing lettuce fields in California, or the daughters of black tenant farmers in Alabama. However exceptional as a social type, "flappers" managed simultaneously to challenge some prevailing notions about gender roles, while affirming others, especially those linked to beauty and sexuality.

THE CULT OF BEAUTY

Willa Cather, Amy Lowell, and Leonora Speyer all won Pulitzer Prizes in these years, Georgia O'Keeffe painted her famous *Radiator Building* and *Dark Abstraction*, Gertrude Ederle swam the English Channel and trimmed two hours off the men's record. The attention given to these feminine achievements paled, however, beside that lavished on motion picture stars such as Clara Bow, the Hollywood "It Girl." Her appeal, according to Elinor Glyn, was "the same as before but more of it showing" and "a little more available." Fitzgerald called Bow "the quintessence of what the term 'flapper' signifies. . . . pretty, impudent, superbly assured, as worldly-wise, briefly clad and 'hard-burled' as possible." Clara Bow had her own explanation for success: "It was easy for me t'cry," she told reporters. "All I hadda do was think of home."

Clara Bow in the film Call Her Savage.

Hollywood's image-makers began to offer their own models of American womanhood in competition with Mom, Aunt Sally, and the local schoolteacher. They were rather limited: the vamp (Theda Bara), the sex kitten (Clara Bow), the sexual sophisticate (Gloria Swanson and Greta Garbo), and the ingenue (Mary Pickford and Lillian Gish). And leading men of the silver screen reinforced these narrow feminine ideals. "I do not like women who know too much," Rudolph Valentino was said to have remarked.

The film sheik might have written the script for the hotel operators and merchants of Atlantic City who founded the "Miss America" beauty contest shortly after Harding's election. To the most pulchritudinous maiden in the land, they offered fame, cash, and a trophy. In a culture that touted competition as one of its highest virtues, it wasn't long before beauty contests such as Miss America became annual rituals rivaling the World Series and the Kentucky Derby. The requirements for victory were not demanding: attractive hair, a nice smile, and willingness to pose in a bathing suit. "Miss New York" or "Miss Ohio" was not even required in the initial pageants to recite poetry or play the flute. Contestants might have talent, noted one of the organizers, but "things would be better if they kept it to themselves."

The postwar decade did not see a marked expansion in the number of American women who worked in settlement houses or baked their own bread, but the number who patronized beauty parlors for manicures, permanent waves, and hair dyeing grew at an astonishing pace. So did the market for do-it-yourself beauty and hygiene aids: lipsticks, mascara, perfumes, deodorants, and mouthwashes. New York City, the nation's fashion hub, began the decade with 750 beauty parlors, most of them catering to the city's wealthy women; within five years the city boasted over three thousand such establishments, which pampered stenographers, telephone operators, salesgirls, and waitresses as well as the very rich. By 1930 the whole country claimed forty thousand such salons and the earnings of the cosmetics industry had grown from $17 million a year to over $200 million. According to one estimate, American women purchased on average one pound of face powder per year and dozens of lipsticks.

The cosmetics industry sold youth and beauty as the essence of femininity.

The cult of youthfulness, sensuality, and beauty made millionaires out of Coco Chanel, Charles Revson, Helena Rubinstein, and Elizabeth Arden. What their products could not cover up or accent, the plastic surgeons stood ready to modify. After her nose was reconstructed to the dismay of some adoring fans, the actress Fannie Brice assured "well-meaning friends, who have been incessantly telephoning me and expressing their condolences . . . that I am satisfied." For those who could not afford a face-lift, the Anita Nose Adjuster, which "shapes while you sleep," promised remarkable results.

The captains of cosmetology attempted to persuade American women of all social classes that they could catch the right man and live exciting, romantic lives with just the right blend of lotions, creams and hair rinses. The captains of industry assured them that once having caught that man, the effective management of their households depended less on fighting high utility rates or child labor than on the purchase of the most up-to-date home appliances. The old cult of domesticity became scientific and electrified. Toastmaster assured purchasers that its product would enhance both leisure and culture around the home. "You don't watch it, or think about it. You read, go out of the room, answer the phone, do anything you like. . . . No turning. No burning."

FROM SETTLEMENT HOUSE TO HOMEMAKING

The retreat from progressive feminism during the twenties touched even the leading women's colleges, pioneers in the struggle against separate sexual spheres. They too put new emphasis on dating, mating, and homemaking. From the moment of their founding in the late nineteenth century, institutions such as Smith, Vassar, and Bryn Mawr challenged many myths that had served to perpetuate sexual segregation and the subordination of women.

These schools offered their female students a broad liberal arts education that included the sciences. They encouraged their graduates to pursue advanced degrees and professional careers in medicine, law, architecture, and engineering. They contested the idea that women possessed a fixed, inherent nature—spiritual, intuitive, nurturing—that disabled them for many social and economic roles. And they made physical education a vital part of the college curriculum in an effort to topple the stereotype of the languid female who had to remain within the cloistered boundaries of the home. True, not every graduate of these elite schools became a militant feminist, but many did, and those who entered the settlement houses and other progressive institutions offered to Americans of their sex an enlarged definition of true womanhood.

"Practically all women . . . must look forward after leaving college to some form of public service," declared the president of Bryn Mawr before the war. Ten years later, with Coolidge in the White House and more college-educated women than ever before entering professions, the perspective of educational leaders and their institutions drew the focus away from public service to the domestic arena. At the inauguration of Skidmore's new president in 1925, the main speaker affirmed that "whatever else a woman may be, the highest purpose of her life always has been . . . to strengthen and beautify and sanctify the home." At the women's colleges before 1914, a student might take classes in Urban Social and Economic Conditions or Rural Social and Economic Conditions, courses in which the daughters from the best families learned about the harsh environment that confronted their poorer sisters in big cities and on the farm. Bryn Mawr students spent part of their holidays at a Long Branch, New Jersey, settlement house supported by the college.

By the middle of the 1920s, Vassar offered courses in Husband and Wife, Motherhood, and the Family as an Economic Unit. The college also founded a School of Euthenics whose purpose was to educate women "along the lines of their chief interest and responsibilities, motherhood and the home." Most of the Vassar women polled as early as 1923 believed that marriage was "the biggest of all careers." At Bryn Mawr, students complained about the arduous work at the Long Branch settlement house. It was not, one reported, "the ideal way of spending even part of a summer vacation." Progressive feminism did not wither up and die after the war, as evidenced by the activities of the Women's Party and by the increasing numbers of women who became professionals and who entered public service with the National Consumers' League, the Women's Trade Union League, or the federal Children's Bureau. But a good deal of its momentum had been lost, and much of the energy and enthusiasm of younger women had been channeled back into the sphere of self rather than society.

Mr. Freud

In 1909, the ambitious president of Clark University in Worcester, Massachusetts, assembled a distinguished group of lecturers for the school's twentieth anniversary. They included anthropologist Franz Boas, a brilliant critic of racial supremacy, and four scientists of the mind—Sandor Ferenczi, Ernest Jones, Carl Jung, and Sigmund Freud. Freud gave his Clark lecture in German, and visited New York City (where he saw his first motion picture), the Adirondacks, and Niagara Falls. After this brief tour, he pronounced the United States "a gigantic mistake" and went home to Vienna.

Few Americans rushed out to buy Freud's works. Except for a handful of experts in obscure organizations such as the American Psychoanalytical Association, scant attention was paid to the man or his revolutionary ideas about the human mind and its functioning until the 1920s. Then, especially among members of the educated middle class, so-called Freudian concepts became a widely marketed and consumed intellectual product. For many, Freud seemed to provide a justification for rebelling against all accepted social conventions, especially sexual ones. For still others, Freud's ideas offered a simple explanation for the personal and collective anxieties that afflicted American society in the postwar years.

For centuries, whether they conceived of human nature as basically good or inherently wicked, philosophers, theologians, physicians, and historians had attempted to explain behavior largely on the basis of rational calculation, fate, supernatural design, or environmental conditioning. Those inspired by religion tended toward the supernatural. Progressives opted for environmentalism, because it held out the promise of progress and redemption through reform of the social and economic structure. Freud questioned all of these notions when he posited a source of human motivation (sexual desire) rooted in the unconscious mind and capable of understanding only through intense psychiatric therapy.

Freud's perspective on the human condition was bleak indeed. The very emotional and physical bonds between men and women, parents and children that perpetuated the species and made possible the family and society were at the same time the greatest source of human aggression, suffering, and unhappiness. Even more scandalous, Freud claimed that young babes had powerful sexual desires. The repression and sublimation of this infant sexuality promoted civilization and progress in addition to anxiety, neurosis, and the more serious forms of mental disease.

Freud never sugar-coated his ideas. Many of his followers, especially in America, did just that by spreading them in a simplified form. On one level, even vulgar Freudianism promoted greater candor about one of society's most fundamental preoccupations—sex. But the crude version also led to the absurd conclusion that the founder of psychoanalysis had declared sex good and all inhibitions about sex bad. Even before the war, this naive reading of Freud had been extended by many intellectuals to a generalized attack on all manner of repression, social control, and self-restraint. In the twenties, vulgar Freudianism served to further commercialize sex and to bolster the consumer culture by ridiculing middle-class conceptions of modesty and self-control. Inhibition was denounced as the root cause of mental sickness. Self-expression and self-gratification were praised as the route to health and happiness.

In the era of taciturn Coolidge, terms such as "id," "superego," and "libido" entered popular discourse, along with "Freudian slip" and "Oedipus Complex." One of Freud's disciples advised parents, "Don't be afraid to turn your child loose. He wants . . . to get out from under the shadow of your soul." A cultural milestone of sorts was reached when the American Tobacco Company hired Freud's nephew the public relations expert Edward L. Bernays to advise the firm on how to sell its Lucky Strikes brand. Bernays retained the help of A. A. Brill from the New York Psychoanalytical Association, who cautioned against one ad in which a women offered a smoke to two men, because "the cigarette is a phallic symbol to be offered by a man to a woman." Bernays pronounced this insight "a brilliant piece of thinking" and "the first instance of [the] application of psychoanalysis to advertising."

The virtual legalization of birth control information and devices in many states—although under medical monopoly—permitted a substantial number of Americans to put into practice the radical idea that sex could be a source of pleasure detached from procreation. In Margaret Sanger's 1926 book *Happiness in Marriage*, erotic satisfaction replaced economic mobility as the primary benefit of birth control. "Never be ashamed of passion," Sanger wrote. "If you are strongly sexed, you are richly endowed." Using an automotive metaphor, she advised, "Do not be afraid to take the brakes off your heart, to surrender yourself to love. . . . Unclamp this emotion, let it have full, healthy, exercise." More prosaically the Berry Publishing Company of Pleasant Hill, Ohio, offered *How I Kept My Husband's Love*, a "fascinating little book . . . sent in plain wrapper" for only 10 cents. Margaret Mead's *Coming of Age in Samoa* became a huge best-seller in 1928, due in no small measure to its portrayal of an idyllic preindustrial culture in which the natives copulated freely without guilt.

In addition to Sanger, the leading advocate of a new sexual ethic during the twenties was another voice for the progressive past: Judge Ben Lindsey of Denver, pioneer of the juvenile justice system, who turned his considerable energy to the task of saving the institution of marriage and reversing the nation's climbing divorce rate. In numerous lectures and two books, *The Revolt of Modern Youth* (1925) and *Companionate Marriage* (1927), Lindsey argued that men and women should be encouraged to live together before marriage, enjoy sexual relations, and separate by mutual consent at any time without payment of alimony as long as children were not involved. The judge liked to shock his audiences by declaring, "I deny that sex is sin," but his goals remained quite traditional. Lindsey thundered against abortion, idealized the nuclear family, and hoped to strengthen it. His critics saw it otherwise. The Episcopal bishop of New York City called *Companionate Marriage* "one of the most filthy . . . pieces of propaganda ever published on behalf of lewdness, promiscuity, adultery, and unrestrained sexual gratification."

One should not exaggerate the degree to which sexual values and practice changed immediately following World War I. The notion of a pervasive "sexual revolution" sweeping the nation seems far off the mark. Not all middle-class women wrote away for Beery's little book in a plain wrapper. Even among the younger generation whose dress and conduct alarmed their elders, the ideas of Sanger and Lindsey about sexual liberation and companionate marriage did not go unchallenged.

More women than ever before, however, used birth control. According to the surveys conducted by Alfred Kinsey and his associates, only 7 to 8 percent of the women born between 1900 and 1919 reported that they had never practiced contraception. A decline in prostitution, a steady level of marriages, and a big jump in the divorce rate from one in ten to one in six (two-thirds of them initiated by the wife) were among the major consequences of the revolution in sexual attitudes and expectations that did occur. "Sex-love and happiness in marriage . . . do not just happen," Sanger told her readers. "Eternal vigilance is the price of marital happiness. . . . The nuptial relation must be kept romantic."

At about the time Sanger wrote, the nation's Episcopal bishops voted to strike the word "obey" from their marriage ceremony and novelist Fannie Hurst declared in a public interview that the present marriage structure was "drafty, it's leaky, the roof sags, the timbers shake, there's no modern plumbing, no hardwood floors, no steam heat. We don't feel comfortable in it. We've outgrown the edifice, but we don't dare get out of it." Neither the family nor the institution of marriage collapsed during these years, despite the repeated warnings of clergymen, psychologists, and other pundits. But as the affectionate and emotional dimensions of marriage assumed greater importance, especially in the urban middle class, both men and women felt new strains in their relationships.

For many American women, the vaunted sexual revolution of the twenties brought mixed blessings. To be sure, the old double standard of sexual conduct began to erode. Birth control reduced the risks of unwanted pregnancies. Divorce became a genuine option for those trapped in brutal, exploitative, or unfulfilled marriages. On the other hand, the rampant commercialization of sex, especially by Hollywood and Madison Avenue, reinforced gender stereotypes by emphasizing physical attractiveness as the most important feminine characteristic, a development that intensified women's passive role as both a consumer of beauty products and an object of consumption. The tension engendered by these contradictory messages continued long after the decade had passed into history.

8

Cult of Personalities

*A whole generation of females wanted to ride off into a
sandy paradise with him.*
—Bette Davis on Rudolph Valentino

*The greatest feat of a solitary man in the records of the
human race.*
—the *New York Evening World* on Lindbergh's flight

The era of assembly lines, large-scale bureaucracies, routinized labor,
and standardized products gave fresh urgency to the problem of the
survival of individualism in a world characterized increasingly by
impersonal organizations and social relationships. How did people
remain unique in such an environment? Where could a person find
heroism or adventure in a land where the frontier had given way to the
chain store and the automobile? Work had once provided much social
definition for men and women inside and outside the home, but now
prepared foods and ready-made clothing had altered even the lives of
women on the farm. How much creativity attached to putting fenders
on a Chevrolet, operating a cash register at Woolworth's, or typing
correspondence for a credit company? Personal consumption began to
fill this need for self-definition and expression.

In an age of mass consumption which emphasized the importance
of self-fulfillment, the products purchased—whether clothing, movies
or food—became as important to each person's identity as the more

traditional bonds of ethnicity, religion, and work. The mass media—
radio, motion pictures, magazines—answered part of this question by
helping to market a new product: celebrities, men and women who
both represented and transcended their culture, whose feats remained
out of the ordinary, yet whose lives somehow manifested the fears,
hopes, and anxieties of everyman and everywoman struggling for recognition in a cold universe. It was they who kept the myth of American
individualism alive and well in an age of collectivism. From politics to
sports, the selling of individual personalities became as important to
the maintenance of the social order as the selling of durable goods.
And the American appetite for vicariously participating in their lives
proved nearly inexhaustible.

Politicians, military leaders, captains of industry, inventors, and
explorers had long been icons of American individualism; now they
battled for public attention with a new array of social heroes who
included matinee idols, tennis players, and running backs of the Chicago Bears. Even President Coolidge, otherwise a traditionalist, was
forced to recognize the new ground rules of cultural influence, by which
the creation of a suitable public image had become a major component
of social and political life. Presiding over an era of rapid social change,
Coolidge posed regularly for the cameras in cowboy hat and chaps,
Indian headdress, and farmer's overalls, roles suggestive of some aspect
of the nation's vanishing rural past when life had been less frantic and
complex.

At decade's end, the president of the United States was clearly not
the nation's most striking political celebrity. That honor might have
gone either to the colorful mayor of New York City or the youthful,
flamboyant governor of Louisiana, both of whom reflected important
facets of the country's unsettled mood.

POLITICS AS SHOW BUSINESS

Before Ronald Reagan, movie actor–president, there was James J.
"Jimmy" Walker, the songwriter-mayor of the nation's largest city.
Reagan parlayed a series of B motion pictures, television programs,
and commercials into a potent political career. Walker did the same
with one hit tune, "Will You Love Me in December as You Do in
May," and a long series of other mediocre ones. During the twenties
he could capitalize, too, on the enormous popularity of singer-come-

dians such as Joe E. Lewis and Al Jolson, and the birth of talking motion pictures, which included *The Jazz Singer* and *Lights of New York*.

Armed with a law degree and the support of powerful Tammany Hall leaders, including his father and Charles Murphy, the dapper Walker won a seat in the state assembly and state senate. By the early twenties he had become floor leader of the Democratic Party in the upper house. In 1926, with the backing of the Tammany organization, Governor Al Smith, and a caravan of personalities from stage and screen, he was elected mayor, defeating one of William Randolph Hearst's protégés, Michael "Red" Hyland. To the strains of Cole Porter's "We'll Walk In with Walker," the lyricist of "There's Music in the Rustle of a Skirt" strutted into office, the first national political leader successfully to merge show business and politics.

As mayor, Walker personified the spirit of conspicuous, individualized consumerism. While Coolidge assured the country that it would emerge from years of self-indulgence with its values unchanged and its virtue intact, Jimmy Walker threw the party, blew up the balloons, and danced until dawn. His greatest legislative achievement in Albany had been a bill to legalize state boxing. Political leaders in New York City such as Robert Moses knew more than Walker about municipal finance and transportation. But none had a larger wardrobe or looked better in a tux. He was not the man to consult about the city's perpetual housing crisis, but Jimmy knew where the best speakeasies were located and could usually be found in one of them. He once squelched a rumor that he had been gunned down in such an establishment by calling reporters to his office and declaring: "Gentlemen, at this time of day I am seldom half-shot."

Except for filling city jobs and letting city contracts to his friends in Tammany Hall, Walker governed New York with a light hand. He seldom rose from bed before noon. He invariably arrived at public functions late. Once there, however, few could match his charm, repartee, and platitude-filled speeches. Accused of tolerating corruption in the city's courts, he described reformers as people "who ride through a sewer in a glass-bottomed boat." When someone at a Board of Estimate meeting shouted "liar" at him, Walker retorted, "Now that you have identified yourself, we shall proceed." He was one of the first American politicians to recognize that in a consumer society, politics had become another branch of marketing, that style often mattered more than substance, and that many voters simply wanted to be entertained.

Despite a divorce, remarriage to his former-actress mistress, and burgeoning rumors of illegal payoffs and mismanagement of the city's finances, Walker swept to an easy reelection victory in 1929. Asked to choose between an earnest reformer who echoed many themes of the progressive era, Fiorello H. La Guardia, and the playboy incumbent, New Yorkers did not hesitate to reconfirm the man who made them feel good rather than guilty. "He dresses snappy and talks snappy," observed one magazine. "Thus he becomes a symbol for some odd-million starved souls numbly seeking escape from reality. . . . He is five hundred years ahead of his time, or maybe only one hundred at the rate we're going."

Every Man a King

A year before New York City voters reelected Walker, the great planters, businessmen, and comfortable people of Louisiana, who had run the state for as long as anyone could recall, woke up to the shock of a new governor. He was Huey Pierce Long, Jr., then thirty-five years old, the seventh of nine children, reared in the notoriously radical parish of Winn, where residents had hated slavery, sided with the Union during the Civil War, and voted for Eugene Debs and the socialists. He became the first American tribune of the era of affluence and mass communications who attacked the concentration of wealth and built a political career around the idea of making "every man a king."

Huey Long kept up the Winn tradition of dissent and protest when he opened his legal practice there before the war. He fought against proposed legislation that sought to limit the amount of money workers could recover for industrial accidents. He successfully defended a man accused of violating the Espionage Act. In 1918 at the age of twenty-five, he captured a seat on Louisiana's Railroad Commission by barnstorming around the state in an automobile and promising the farmers protection from the predatory utilities. Writing in a New Orleans newspaper that year, Long noted that 2 percent of the people owned 70 percent of the wealth, "a problem . . . the good people of this country must consider."

For the first time since the Populist era of the 1890s, many of Louisiana's common people found a voice for their frustrations and resentments in the country lawyer from Winn. Long spoke for the sunbaked farmers who endured bad roads, few schools, and high railroad rates; for the mill hands and refinery workers who felt the lash of management and whose kids went to school in rags and without a decent pair of shoes. Pudgy and florid, he was an electrifying orator whose invective, sentimentality, and homespun tales easily moved crowds back and forth between anger and tears. His opponents, he said, were "thieves, bugs and lice," but speaking under the Evangeline Oak in Cajun country, he asked, "Where are the institutions to care for the sick and disabled? Evangeline wept bitter tears in her disappointment, but it lasted through only one lifetime. Your tears in this country, around this oak, have lasted for generations. Give me the chance to dry the eyes of those who still weep here!"

Long had a genuine desire to help the forgotten people of Louisiana and to curb the influence of landed wealth, oil companies, and utilities. In an age of conspicuous consumption before the economic roof fell in, his was one of the few voices calling for a redistribution of wealth. He also had an appetite for the personal power with which to do it. Long used his platform on the Public Service Commission after 1922 to pillory Standard Oil, telephone and telegraph companies, gas and electric utilities, and the railroads. And he used the commission in a bid to become governor in 1924, only a few months past his thirtieth birthday.

Long ran third in the Democratic primary that year, but to the astonishment of the state's old political establishment, he secured 31 percent of the total vote and ran ahead of the field in more parishes (twenty-eight) than any of his opponents. Four years later under the campaign banner of "Every Man a King, but No One Wears a Crown," he took the governorship by rolling up in the primaries the biggest victory margin in Louisiana history. "We'll show 'em who's boss," Long told cheering supporters. "You fellers stick by me. . . . We're just getting started."

His opponents pointed out that the thirty-five-year-old governor had not refused to represent corporations in his private legal practice, had recently built an expensive new home, and had also accepted campaign contributions from some of the very utilities he frequently excoriated. Long's supporters brushed aside these attacks and waited for him to deliver on his promises. They were not disappointed. In his first gubernatorial term, he rattled the state's political and economic foundations harder than anyone since Reconstruction. Using every means at his command—patronage, bluff, cajolery—he put his supporters in charge of every important state board and commission from law enforcement to vermin eradication. He pushed through the legislature laws to provide free textbooks to school districts and to build new roads

Huey Long, Louisiana's "Kingfish," drives home a point.

and hospitals in rural areas. And to the chagrin of the state's powerful energy companies, he shifted the tax burdens that paid for these new public services from real property to the oil and gas extracted from the ground.

At a time when American government on all levels was becoming more bureaucratic and distant from the average citizen, Long showed how personal charisma could move the levers of power. So vast became his influence in only one year that members of his entourage called him "Kingfish" after George "Kingfish" Stevens, the leader of the Mystic Knights of the Sea Lodge in the popular *Amos 'n' Andy* radio show. Once questioned about whether he could legally attend a meeting of the Highway Commission, Long recalled that he looked around "at the little fishes present" and declared, "I'm the Kingfish." Told by a legislator that the state's constitution did not permit the governor to take a certain action, he retorted, "I'm the constitution around here now."

When in early 1929 he proposed an additional "occupational license tax" on each barrel of oil refined in the state, Standard Oil and its minions in the legislature tried to impeach him. Long survived, but vowed further reforms and revenge on his political enemies. "I used to try to get things done by saying 'please,' " he said. "That didn't work and now I'm a dynamiter. I dynamite 'em out of my path."

Huey Long, using sound trucks and radio, fueled class resentment by calling for heavier taxes on the rich and more public services for the poor. He kept alive in one state questions of economic distribution that in 1924 had fizzled on the national level with the La Follette campaign. But even those who shared his goals began to question Long's methods. The lust for power, the drive to dominate every part of state government, the contempt for constitutional procedures—these bore an ominous similarity to political developments already taking countries like Italy down the road to dictatorship. Without any social or political restraints, the charismatic individual could become a tyrant. Jimmy Walker demonstrated how with limited intelligence and ambitions, one might fashion a comfortable political career powered by manipulation of public opinion and the media. Huey Long demonstrated how with more brains and energy, one could use these same forces to reach even loftier heights. The age of the electronic demagogue had dawned in America.

TRAMPS, VAMPS, AND SHEIKS

By the mid-twenties, thanks to Hollywood, the best-known figure in America, perhaps in the world, was not a president, a mayor, a governor, or a general, but a little tramp played on the silent screen by a refugee from English vaudeville, Charles Spencer Chaplin. The son of an alcoholic father who died when he was twelve and a mother who spent her life in and out of mental institutions, Chaplin knew the hard life; he had experienced at first hand in London before the war the exploitation and brutality that plagued individuals in an advanced capitalist society.

Sometimes penniless and out of work, Chaplin had slept in doorways and foraged for food scraps in garbage cans. Films, first in nickelodeons across the country and then in grand movie houses, made Chaplin a millionaire several times over. But from the first introduction of *The Tramp* in a one-reeler of 1915 through his later, feature-length productions such as *The Kid, City Lights,* and *The Gold Rush,* he never failed to provide biting commentary on the inequalities and cruelties that afflicted society's little people who lacked property, influence, and status. Puncturing the pompous and the powerful, he showed how the solitary individual might survive in the face of modern society's isolation and indifference.

A many-faceted man, Chaplin became America's greatest screen comic as well as one of the decade's severest social critics. Many of his comedy routines quickly became legends, such as the one in *City Lights* in which the little tramp, as a sanitation worker, struggles to clean up horse droppings only to face the greater task of a herd of mules and, finally, an elephant. In *The Rink*, as a waiter he manages to add up the customer's check by making an inventory of the stains on his necktie. But attired in baggy pants and derby hat, Chaplin's little tramp usually waged an often fruitless struggle against the social forces that assaulted and frustrated human dignity and dreams in modern society. He was a romantic, disappointed and betrayed by love; a generous good samaritan undone by more sinister people; a sensitive soul crushed by bad fortune. Many in the postwar era of social dislocation and moral ambiguity could identify with those roles.

Charlie Chaplin and Scraps.

Chaplin's little tramp, however, was not always the helpless victim, crushed by ruthless adversaries and impersonal forces. His creator's message could be more complicated. Sometimes the little tramp became his own worst enemy. As the product of an exploitative social system, the little tramp could exhibit callousness and selfishness. In *The Gold Rush*, for example, he is undone by his own greed when he throws away true love in the pursuit of wealth. In a memorable scene in *City Lights*, he bounds out of a swanky automobile in order to seize a dis- carded cigar butt before it can be picked up by a derelict. Chaplin used the newest form of media in the consumer society to question some of its most sacred dogmas and assumptions. Many Hollywood directors and actors admired Chaplin's art, but few risked imitating his brand of social criticism.

Most moguls of the movie industry had not read Freud, but sex had always been their most bankable commodity. Before and immediately after the war, motion picture fans could catch *Hot Romance, Women Who Give,* and *Virgin Paradise* along with *The Mark Of Zorro* and Mary Pickford's chaste *Pollyanna.* This preoccupation with pleasures of the flesh continued to flourish on the screen during the twenties, despite several notorious scandals, regular denunciations from the pulpit, the disapproval of many intellectuals, and the creation of a small bureau- cracy to ensure purity in films. If Hollywood did not invent the sexual revolution, neither did it slow its momentum or limit its market. And while openly promoting the ideal of individual sexual gratification, the industry could be ruthless with those who appeared to go too far in this direction.

In 1921, the district attorney of San Francisco filed manslaughter charges against three-hundred-pound Roscoe "Fatty" Arbuckle, a for- mer plumber's assistant turned actor. One of Hollywood's most famous stars, he was also reputed to be its highest-paid. With a script worthy of the silver screen at its most lurid, the prosecution held Arbuckle responsible for the death of sometime actress Virginia Rappe, who had died of a massive stomach infection and a ruptured bladder following a party in the actor's hotel suite.

The prosecution and the daily press turned the good-natured slap- stick comedian into the ultimate libertine, a sex-crazed monster, who ravaged Miss Rappe with a soda-pop bottle. Accounts of his liquor- soaked orgies grew more extravagant with each telling. "We are not trying Roscoe Arbuckle alone," intoned the judge, "we are trying our present-day morals . . . matters of . . . apprehension to every true lover of our American institutions." Arbuckle's lawyers countered by portraying their client as the good samaritan whose offer of financial aid to a pregnant actress, down on her luck, had been rebuffed in a hysterical frenzy that led to self-inflicted injuries. They charged the DA's office with attempted blackmail and the use of perjured testimony. The third jury not only acquitted the actor as the others had done, but reprimanded the prosecution for its conduct. Although he was acquitted, Arbuckle's career had been shattered.

Arbuckle's ordeal struck terror into studio bosses, who feared reprisals at the box office as the aroma of scandal and impending scandal thickened by the day. Not even Pollyanna escaped. Shortly before the Arbuckle trial, Mary Pickford, Hollywood's most virtuous role player, had announced she was divorcing her husband in order to marry her costar, Douglas Fairbanks. During the third Arbuckle trial, William Desmond Taylor, the director of *Huckleberry Finn*, was found shot to death on a studio lot. Although no one was charged with the slaying, newspapers linked Taylor romantically with literally hundreds of starlets, whose undergarments, carefully labeled, were said to be on display in his bedroom. Other reports placed him at the center of an extensive Hollywood narcotics ring that included famous actors such as Wallace Reid, who died suddenly after being admitted to a sanitarium. Eager to refurbish Hollywood's sullied image, the studios hired Will H. Hays of Indiana, former congressman, former chairman of the Republican National Committee, and Harding's postmaster general. For $100,000 a year, the diminutive Hays, who neither smoked nor drank, took on the task of elevating the moral tone of motion pictures and those who made them.

To their credit, Hays and his staff gave the Arbuckle case a thorough review and pronounced the actor blameless. The studios boycotted him anyway. Within a year, however, the Hays Office had drummed hundreds of others out of the industry, some on vague allegations of prostitution, drug addiction, homosexuality, or excessive heterosexual activity. With the exception of Rin Tin Tin, stars found a "morals clause" tacked onto their contracts that permitted the studios to fine or fire them for conduct deemed detrimental to the industry's welfare. Last, but not least, Hollywood adopted the official Hays Code, a lengthy list of dos and don'ts that instructed producers what to avoid on the screen. No kiss, for example, should last longer than seven feet of film. Members of the clergy "should not be used as comic characters or villains." Adultery was not to be explicitly treated, justified, or "presented attractively." Complete nudity was forbidden. Movies should not display sympathy with "murder, safecracking, arson, smuggling and so on in such detail as to tempt amateurs to try their hands." And the broadest rule of all: producers should eschew "low, disgusting, unpleasant though not necessarily evil subjects" and always follow "the dictates of good taste and regard for the sensibilities of the audience."

Civil libertarians looked with a skeptical eye on the Hays Code as a dangerous engine of self-censorship that threatened the artistic freedom of individual writers, directors, and actors. Moral zealots denounced it as a sham, a perspective probably closer to the actual truth. As one film critic noted at the time. Hays and his censors provided a "screen of righteous pronouncements [behind which] producers could do . . . approximately what they liked." The Hays Office might balk at Kit Carson, hero of the Boy Scouts, having a few drinks in the saloon, but all its lofty pronouncements about adultery and illicit sex did not stop the making of *Anna Christie, The Scarlet Letter, Flesh and the Devil, The Night of Love,* and *Up in Mabel's Room.* Producers and directors simply exercised more imagination and cunning with regard to copulation. The master of this technique was Cecil B. De Mille, who could cram more flesh and passion into a Biblical epic such as *King of Kings* (1927) than any filmmaker before or since.

Hollywood's biggest consumers were urban women, especially those from the working class or who labored in humdrum clerical and sales jobs. Looking for a little romance in lives otherwise filled with monotony, they lined up outside the courthouse each day in San Francisco to throw bouquets at Arbuckle and shout: "Fatty! Fatty! Fatty!" They packed theaters from coast to coast to see Rodolpho Alfonzo Raffaelo Pierre Filibert Guglielmi de Valentina d'Antonguolla, a.k.a. Rudolph Valentino, leap from his steed to embrace Agnes Ayres in *The Sheik.* She: "Why have you abducted me?" He: "Can't you guess?" Valentino was mobbed by females at the opening of *Son of the Sheik* in New York City. And when this thirty-one-year-old former janitor and headwaiter died suddenly of a gastric ulcer, appendicitis, and pleurisy in the summer on 1926, the line of sobbing women outside Campbell's Funeral Parlor in Manhattan stretched for eight blocks. Apparently unable to endure the thought of life without the hero of *The Four Horsemen of the Apocalypse,* several committed suicide in New York and London, one clutching his photograph.

SULTAN OF SWAT

Valentino's funeral, Arbuckle's trial, and any number of motion picture premiers vividly displayed the deep emotional bonds that bound together feminine consumers in this new marketplace of Hollywood fantasies. The intense, nearly religious loyalty invoked among movie fans by Fairbanks, Ronald Coleman, John Gilbert, Pola Negri, and Norma Talmadge exceeded the fealty shown by users of Quaker Oats and Ivory Soap. Its only counterpart was to be found among the largely masculine consumers who packed Yankee Stadium, the Polo Grounds, the Rose Bowl, or Forest Hills to participate in the rituals of professional and amateur sports. Journalist Ring Lardner, one of several gifted reporters who created a new genre of sports writing, described it as "an excess of anile idolatry."

What Coolidge was to a scandal-ridden Republican Party, George Herman "Babe" Ruth was to professional baseball, an emerging industry then at an important crossroads. A game rooted in the nation's rural past but played increasingly before large urban audiences who paid a great deal of money to see it, professional baseball had become big business even before the war. Most major league teams adopted the corporate form of organization, signed leading players to long-term contracts, and hired a bevy of lawyers and accountants to run their affairs.

And like other industries in their formative stages, ruthless competition among professional teams generated its share of exploitation and shady deals, especially when the players remained virtual slaves, capable of being bought and sold by the teams' owners like prize cattle. Players for the Chicago White Sox, including their greatest hitter, "Shoeless" Joe Jackson, rebelled against what they regarded as low pay and sweatshop conditions. They confessed to accepting gamblers' money to throw the 1919 World Series. The sports pages in 1920 bulged with the trial of the "Black Sox" and the appointment of federal judge Kenesaw Mountain Landis as baseball "czar," there to clean up the game which had become a major industry and a national disgrace.

Ruth did as much as anyone to repair baseball's sagging image. In the game's new corporate age, he reaffirmed the importance of the heroic individual player. He showed, too, how poor kids from the wrong side of the tracks could still strike it rich in the land of opportunity through big-time sports. This former denizen of a Baltimore orphanage, a pitcher-outfielder of uncommon ability, had been sold by the Boston Red Sox to the New York Yankees at the start of the 1920 season for $100,000 plus a $385,000 loan.

The Ruth trade was the best investment in baseball history, for in his first year with the Yankees the pug-faced, spindle-legged Ruth hit fifty-four home runs, which eclipsed the previous major league record by twenty-nine. More than a million fans, the first ever in one season,

The Bambino.

came to the Polo Grounds to watch him do it. The next year, he boosted his home run total to fifty-nine, drove in 170 runs, and batted .378. The Yankees won the American League pennant, but lost the World Series in eight games to the Giants. Two years later, the gate receipts having steadily mounted, the Yankees opened a grand new stadium in the Bronx, "the house that Ruth built." Despite a short right field fence made especially for him, the Bambino's home run total dipped to a mere forty-one, but he hit an amazing .398, and the Yankees defeated the Giants in six games. Probably the greatest legend in the game's history had begun to take shape.

Babe Ruth, a hot consumer item, was himself an avid consumer: flashy cars, sporty clothes, good food and drink, and pretty girls. The orphan boy also became one of the first national sports celebrities pursued by manufacturers for product endorsements, but he lost a lawsuit against the Curtiss Candy Company, which marketed a Baby Ruth bar in 1920 without his permission. The candy company argued that its caramel-and-peanut-filled delight had been named after Grover Cleveland's daughter, Ruth, the first child born to a president in the

White House. Although Cleveland and his daughter had left the White House in 1897 and Babe Ruth was already a household name, Curtiss's lawyers convinced a jury that the company had no intention of getting rich off the latter's fame.

By day, the Sultan of Swat signed balls for youngsters and terrorized opposing pitchers. At night, he hit the liveliest spots of whatever city he happened to be in, often in the company of other celebrities such as jazz musician Bix Beiderbecke. Ruth's escapades with liquor and women became so notorious that Commissioner Landis suspended him for forty days, the Yankees fined him $5,000, and his marriage broke down. But as long as he continued to hit home runs and the Yankees continued to win the American League title, these brushes with propriety only heightened Ruth's stature with the fans.

Ruth's very raffishness, combined with an absence of guile that bordered on naiveté, made him an almost perfect symbol of a big business that embraced the country's simple, rural past as well as its hedonistic urban present. Introduced to Harding prior to a game with the Washington Senators, he remarked, "Hot as hell, ain't it, Prez?" Once told that his salary exceeded the president's, the Bambino never missed a beat: "Well, I had a better year."

Indeed he had. The Yankees won the American League pennant three consecutive years from 1926 to 1928, and the World Series twice. Ruth clobbered forty-seven home runs in 1926 and forty-four in 1928. In 1927, on a team that also included Lou Gehrig (.378), Earle Coombs (.356), Bob Meusel (.336), and Tony Lazzeri (.309), he set a record never equaled: sixty home runs in a season of 154 games. In the 1926 World Series the Yankees lost, but he still hit three home runs. When they annihilated the Cardinals in 1928, four games to none, Ruth batted an incredible .625. A year later, he hit his five hundredth career home run.

GALLOPING GHOST

Babe Ruth and other gifted players—Lou Gehrig, Rogers Hornsby, Dazzy Vance, Walter Johnson, Grover Alexander—kept the myth of individualism alive in baseball's new corporate era of the 1920s, even as that sport faced vigorous competition from big-time college and professional football, the emerging symbol of industrial, ethnically diverse, urban America. 1925 was not Ruth's greatest year. His $52,000 salary bought too much booze and beef tenderloin and too many late nights.

He failed to win either the batting crown or the home run title, and the Yankees lost the pennant to the Senators. It was, however, a spectacular year for a deputy sheriff's son from Wheaton, Illinois—Harold Edward "Red" Grange. Grange played halfback for the University of Illinois football team, and it was he, not Ruth, who became that year the first athlete to appear on the cover of Henry Luce's *Time* magazine.

In his final college season, the young man whom sportswriter Grantland Rice dubbed the Galloping Ghost ran opposing teams ragged. Playing hapless Pennsylvania, he carried the ball for over 360 yards, almost doubling his usual average per game. Against Michigan, he scored a touchdown the first four times he touched the ball, scattering the Wolverines on runs of ninety-three, sixty-seven, fifty-six, and forty-four yards. The only thing more elusive in Illinois was Al Capone's tax return. Enraptured Illinois students carried Grange around the campus on their shoulders for two miles. The university retired his jersey. Pro football promoters and Hollywood studios dangled fat contracts before him. He signed first with C. C. "Cash and Carry" Pyle's touring all-stars for $80,000 and then joined the Chicago Bears, who paid him $12,000 a game. A crowd of 73,000 jammed the Polo Grounds to see him play the New York Giants, led by former Olympic champion Jim Thorpe.

Even without the Galloping Ghost, college and professional football would have become major consumer markets during the twenties as undergraduate enrollments soared across the country and more personal income became available for entertainment. Not every school had a Red Grange, but Cornell could boast of Edward Kaw, Michigan of Bennie Oosterban, Stanford of Ernie Nevers, and Minnesota of Bronko Nagurski. The center of gravity in the college sport shifted from the old-stock Americans of the Ivy League schools to second-generation Irish, Italians, and Slavs who played for universities, many of them public, in the Midwest and on the Pacific Coast.

A homely, gravel-voiced coach at Notre Dame, Knute Rockne, revolutionized the game by perfecting the forward pass offense and finding young men in the mining towns and steel mills of West Virginia and Pennsylvania who could throw, catch, and block for the Fighting Irish. In 1924, his upstart team, led by the "Four Horsemen of the Apocalypse" with funny-sounding names—Stuldreyer, Miller, Crowley, and Layden—upset heavily-favored Army, 13–7.

From the perspective of many in education, the Galloping Ghost and the Four Horsemen could not have come at a worse time. Administrators had long struggled to raise their institutions' academic stature by

Harold "Red" Grange, the "Galloping Ghost."

hiring better faculty and adding more books to the library. Now they faced clamorous alumni who demanded a bigger football stadium, a more famous coach, and a scholarship for the high school quarterback prospect from Gopher Prairie. Given the huge gate receipts, often enough to support other athletic programs, these demands were hard to resist. From Stanford to New Haven, schools erected huge new stadiums during the twenties and scrambled for the services of players and coaches much as public utility holding companies battled for control of operating plants.

As Grange's career at Illinois illustrated only too well, colleges and universities risked becoming mere subassembly plants for the larger professional football factories; high schools, in turn, became feeders of major universities. In 1929, probably not one American in a million knew who was president of Notre Dame or chancellor of the University of California, Berkeley, but virtually everyone knew who coached the Irish and that California's center, Roy Riegels, had run sixty yards the wrong way with a fumble before 101,000 screaming fans in the Rose Bowl on New Year's Day.

THE MANASSAS MAULER AND THE POET OF PUGILISM

Ruth and Grange were rich and famous, astronomically well paid for their time. But their compensation paled in comparison to the fortunes generated by the heavyweight title fights in the twenties, staged battles that pitted two men who exemplified many of the cultural tensions of their sport and their society—Jack Dempsey and Gene Tunney. When Dempsey and Tunney met in the ring for the first time in 1926 in a rain-soaked Philadelphia stadium, the gate hit $2 million. Dempsey, who had not defended his crown in three years, was still a four-to-one favorite. With good reason.

William Harrison "Jack" Dempsey was a throwback to the bare-knuckled era of prize fighting, when the sport often resembled a Saturday-night brawl in the local saloon, except that the decor and customers in the saloon were usually a cut above those attending the fights. Raised in Manassas, Colorado, he learned to slug it out with copper miners, cowboys, and construction hands. Jack Dempsey hit like a sledgehammer and absorbed punishment like a sponge. He was not a boxer, but an earthquake that left blood, flesh, and bone scattered in its wake. In 1919, this embodiment of the nation's raw, untamed industrial past took the heavyweight title from towering Jess Willard, who stood six foot five and weighed close to three hundred pounds. Dempsey knocked him down seven times in the first round. Willard, his face and body cut to ribbons, could not answer the bell for the fourth round.

Even when he shirked on training, which was often, Dempsey seemed invincible. He knocked out Bill Brennan in the twelfth and final round at Madison Square Garden. In 1921, before a live crowd that had paid $1.8 million to see the carnage and a huge East Coast radio audience, he took apart the French military hero Georges Carpentier. Two years later at the Polo Grounds, in what some regard as the most exciting two rounds ever fought, he survived two knockdowns in the first round—the second immortalized in George Bellows's famous painting—to KO "the Wild Bull of the Pampas," Luis Firpo, a game but ill-prepared Argentinean.

With the aid of his longtime promoter and sidekick, George "Tex" Rickard, the roughneck from Manassas became a millionaire, the toast of Broadway, wined and dined by movie stars, industrialists, and writers. Like bad boy Ruth, who hailed from the wrong side of the tracks, Dempsey was a bit of an outlaw, a hero to those who carried a lunch bucket to work, who toiled with their hands, and who dreamed of strik-

The Dempsey-Firpo fight.

ing it rich. They stood by the champ when newspapers published false rumors suggesting that he had dodged the draft in 1917.

James Joseph "Gene" Tunney, the man across the ring from Dempsey in Philadelphia, was every Irish mother's dream of a good son—tall, good-looking, honest, and brave. Although the Connecticut Tunneys had been only a few rungs above the Dempseys on the social ladder, those few rungs had made a difference. Gene read books, lots of them. His mother wanted him to wear a white collar to work. Like Hemingway's fictional Robert Cohen, he hoped to be rich and famous quickly. The way to do that, he discovered, was with his fists. He boxed as an amateur before 1917, and as a Marine in France during the war he rose to become light heavyweight champion of the American military forces. Tunney set out to become heavyweight champion of the world, a goal he pursued with the same single-minded devotion he lavished on reading the plays of Shakespeare. "I worship at his shrine," he said of the Bard.

By 1926, Tunney had won sixty professional fights and lost only once. He was not a brawler like Dempsey, who destroyed his opponents with a nonstop frontal assault. Tunney was a surgeon in the ring, a thinking man's fighter, quick and graceful, who set up his victims with a relent-less left jab and iced them with a powerful right. It was said that he trained seven days a week, fifty-two weeks a year. He ran mile after mile, often backward, to improve his foot speed and agility. While Dempsey downed a good meal at the Stork Club around midnight, Tunney went to bed before nine. Disciplined, organized, relentless, he was the Frederick Winslow Taylor of pugilism, boxing's own Harvard Business School.

The old fight crowd thought Tunney arrogant, aloof, stuck-up, a pretty boy. The new fight crowd of the twenties, more middle-class, affluent, and female, thought him magnificent. He was in the ring with Demp-sey, however, only because the champ and Tex Rickard feared meeting the number-one contender, Harry Wills, who was black. The Phila-delphia bout went the distance, but it was no contest from the opening bell. Before 125,000 fans, Tunney carved up Dempsey with his supe-rior speed and stamina. America had a new heavyweight champion.

A year later, with the gate reaching $2.6 million, they met again at Chicago's Soldier Field. The return bout was billed as the Battle of the Century. Among the 104,000 in attendance were more than a thou-sand reporters, ten governors, members of the United States Senate, and countless millionaires and movie stars. A radio audience estimated at over sixty million listened to Graham McNamee's blow-by-blow account from ringside. "Once, not so long ago," declared one skeptical newspaper, "utterly condemned by the law, it is now not only sanc-tioned by the law but even gladly attended by the highest officers of the law."

In the seventh round at Chicago, America came to a halt Dempsey decked the champion. Hoping to avoid a repetition of the Firpo fight, in which Dempsey had savagely pummeled the Argentinean before he could regain his feet, referee Dave Barry shoved the challenger into a neutral corner. When he returned to count over Tunney, five or six seconds had already passed. Dempsey's partisans said it was closer to ten or twelve seconds. Tunney staggered to his feet as Barry counted eight. He danced away from Dempsey for the remainder of the round, knocked him down in the eighth, and easily kept the title, despite pro-tests about Barry's "long count."

There would not be a third meeting. Dempsey, now a tired and bruised thirty-one, took his millions and opened a restaurant. Tunney defended his title once more, easily beating an obscure New Zealand black-smith. Then, richer by $1,742,282 for three years' work in the ring, he quit boxing forever, married into Connecticut society, and discussed

Troilus and Cressida with literature students at Yale. "Harvard, I trust, will counter by asking Babe Ruth to tell the boys at Cambridge just what Milton has meant to him," remarked one reporter, a Dempsey fan, no doubt.

BIG BILL

The exploits of Ruth, Grange, Dempsey, and Tunney filled newspapers and airwaves during the decade, but never exhausted the appetite of American consumers for sports heroes and heroines, who in baseball parks, stadiums, tennis courts, and swimming pools reaffirmed the myth of individualism in a corporate, collectivized society. Each year brought forth a profusion of new athletic triumphs and stars to tantalize an audience whose own physical activities became more and more routinized and sedentary.

William Tilden, Jr., a blue-blooded Philadelphia aristocrat, became the first American to win a tennis title at Wimbledon in 1920 and the oldest to do so a decade later at the age of twenty-seven. He won the United States Open seven times during the decade, five times back-to-back. Not even Barrymore or Tom Mix had a greater theatrical sense than Big Bill. Allowing even good opponents to steal a big lead, he always managed to snatch victory from the jaws of defeat. Down a couple of sets, he signaled the start of the real tennis match by stripping off his sweater and dousing his head with a pitcher of water. The crowds at Wimbledon, Newport, and Forest Hills went crazy as he stormed back to win.

In 1923, seventeen-year-old Helen Wills, nicknamed "Little Miss Poker Face" by reporters because of her methodical, machinelike play, won the women's singles title at the U.S. Open. Before the decade was done, she had captured that title and also Wimbledon three times in a row. Her 1926 match with Suzanne Lenglen at Cannes, which she narrowly lost, generated almost as much hoopla as the first Dempsey-Tunney fight.

The year Miss Wills won her first U.S. Open, a young, muscular Johnny Weismuller dived into a pool and swam the 200-yard freestyle in 1:59, the fastest time in history. In the 1924 Olympic Games in Paris, he demolished the competition in both the 100-meter and 400-meter freestyle events. Four years later at Amsterdam, he won a third gold medal by repeating his performance in the 400-meter. That year, having shattered an amazing sixty-seven swimming records in five years,

Weismuller retired from the water, signed a lucrative motion picture contract, and began his screen career as Tarzan of the Apes. By 1929 many roads on the American cultural map, whether in sports, politics, or business, wound west to Hollywood.

LONE EAGLE

The year 1927 brought stunning feats of American physical prowess and technological genius. The Bambino smashed sixty home runs. Tunney got off the canvas to retain his title. Much to the chagrin of white supremacists, an all-black baseball team, the Rens, split an exhibition series with the Brooklyn Dodgers. The Holland Tunnel opened, linking New York and New Jersey. Harvard professor Philip Drinker invented the iron lung. Arthur Compton won the Nobel Prize in physics for his discovery of wavelength change in diffused X-rays.

But it was also for many Americans a year of reflection and self-doubt about the state of their civilization. Sold under the counter, Nan Britton's memoir *The President's Daughter* told of her love affair with Warren Harding, including trysts in a White House closet and an illegitimate child. On the witness stand in a New York courtroom, Mrs. Ruth Brown Synder and her corset-salesman lover, Henry Judd Gray, accused each other of plotting and carrying out the murder of her husband, who had been found bludgeoned, strangled, and chloroformed. Chicago papers reported that in addition to $100 million from its liquor business, the Capone mob received $30 million in protection money, $25 million from gambling, and $10 million from what was called "rackets." Floods brought death and misery to residents of the Mississippi Valley. And then came Charles Augustus Lindbergh.

Lindbergh was neither the first nor the last aviator to capture the nation's imagination or headlines in the twenties. Six years earlier, dashing Brigader General William "Billy" Mitchell and his squadron of bombers had shown the awesome potential of air power off the coast of Virginia by sinking a number of old naval vessels, including the *Ostfriesland*, a captured German battleship. When the irrepressible Mitchell refused to heed his superiors' orders and continued to castigate both the Navy and the Army for their mismanagement and neglect of the air service, he was court-martialed, convicted of insubordination, and suspended for five years. One of the few moments Coolidge slipped in public esteem came when he upheld the conviction and sentence of the former leader of the Lafayette Escadrille.

Carl Rogers piloted a seaplane nonstop from San Francisco to Hawaii in 1925. Admiral Richard Byrd and Floyd Bennett flew over the North Pole a year later. In 1928, on the twenty-fifth anniversary of the Wright brothers' flight, Amelia Earhart became the first woman to fly alone across the Atlantic. "[Women] do get more glory than men for comparable feats," Miss Earhart observed. "But, also, women get more notoriety when they crash." All of these paled, however, before the public's adulation of Lindbergh during and after his 3,610-mile solo flight from New York to Paris in the spring of 1927. Except for the Armistice celebration of 1918 and V-J Day in 1945, nothing in American history is comparable. And the best explanation came at the time from Mary Mullet, writing in *American* magazine. Charles Lindbergh, she observed, "has shown us that we are not rotten at the core, but morally sound and sweet and good."

Indeed, extraordinary luck, bravery, and technological skill went into the creation of the nation's greatest postwar hero. For many, "Lindy's Luck" reaffirmed the blessing of Providence on the United States, the courageous and pioneering spirit of the American people, and their mastery of the world's newest frontier. By the time Lindbergh's single-engine plane, *The Spirit of St. Louis*, lifted off from Roosevelt Field in a driving rainstorm, the $25,000 Raymond Orteig prize for the first solo trip between Paris and New York had already claimed the lives of six expert flyers and injured three others. A few weeks earlier, Charles Nungesser and Francois Coli of France perished somewhere in the mid-Atlantic. The legendary Admiral Byrd had tried in a trimotor, but crashed and barely escaped with his life. Lindbergh's frail, fuel-heavy craft, carrying only its twenty-five-year-old pilot with his passport, razor, and six letters of introduction, narrowly missed the telephone wires at the end of Roosevelt's runway.

For the next thirty-three hours and twenty-nine minutes, most of it over water, the former congressman's son from Minnesota, a man who had flunked out of college, barnstormed, and flown airmail cargoes between St. Louis and Chicago, battled weather, hunger, and sleep. Indeed, fatigue was his greatest enemy, because Lindbergh had already spent over twenty-one hours in the air from California to New York shortly before taking off for Paris. He flew on guts and instinct, but also with the aid of a new earth inductor compass that permitted him to maintain a straight heading even in heavy fog and rain. After circling the Eiffel Tower, he set *The Spirit of St. Louis* down at Le Bourget airport. A crowd estimated at 100,000 engulfed the field. He climbed from the cockpit and announced, "I'm Charles A. Lindbergh."

Americans went mad for Lucky Lindy, the Lone Eagle. The normally staid *New York Times* carried a headline in type reserved for the beginning or end of wars: "LINDY DOES IT—TO PARIS IN 33 ½ HOURS." President Coolidge dispatched the cruiser *Memphis* to France to bring the young man and his plane back home. Each day, Americans deluged the White House with suggestions about how the nation should recognize Lindbergh's stunning achievement. Some urged Coolidge to name a star in the heavens after him, or declare May 21, the date of his flight, a new national holiday. He should share the 3-cent stamp with George Washington. The most practical advocated that he be forever exempt from federal income tax.

The Lone Eagle had to settle for a bit less in Washington. When the *Memphis* reached Chesapeake Bay, it was greeted by an escort of Navy destroyers, blimps, and airplanes. Artillery on the banks of the Potomac fired a twenty-one-gun salute, an honor accorded in the past only to heads of state. At the Washington Monument, against a backdrop of flags and banners, President Coolidge decorated Lindbergh with the Distinguished Flying Cross and gave him the rank of colonel in the Army reserves. The postmaster general later unveiled a new Lindbergh stamp—airmail, of course.

Several days later in New York, a flotilla of four hundred boats greeted Lindbergh in the city's harbor. Along the traditional Broadway parade route he was showered with confetti and ticker tape that sanitation workers later estimated at eighteen hundred tons. Mayor Walker presented him with the keys to the city and the state's Medal of Valor, the second of fifteen such awards he received in the next week. At New York's Commodore Hotel, Lindbergh was feted with the largest single dinner every served in Manhattan; the plates and cups alone numbered 36,000. L. Wolfe Gilbert, Abel Baer, and George M. Cohan wrote songs for him. A new dance, the Lindy, swept the nation. He became *Time* magazine's first "Man of the Year."

Lindbergh conquered the country not only because of what he had done, but because of how he did it and how he met fortune and fame. Unlike Admiral Byrd, for example, who invested his polar flight with grandiloquence appropriate to the Second Coming, Lindbergh spoke modestly about his achievement. He paid almost as much tribute to the plane and its builders as to his own heroic role. "Here were the imponderable processes and forces of the cosmos, harmonious and soundless," said Byrd. "The universe was a cosmos, not a chaos; man was as rightfully a part of that cosmos as were the day and night." The Lone Eagle spoke in more down-to-earth terms about diligence, hard

Charles A. Lindbergh.

work, persistence, concentration, and duty. Every aspect of the hero's life and values were scrutinized by the press. If Americans did not know before, they quickly learned that Lindbergh did not smoke, drink, or keep late hours. At times he seemed surprised by the adulation, almost embarrassed by the stir he had caused. The greatest American hero of the decade was painfully, obviously shy.

Millions of Americans, from the most seasoned statesmen to the youngest grade-school child, projected onto the six-foot-two-inch young man with the boyish face and the mop of tousled hair their most intense longings and fantasies. "Just like a child he simply smiled / while we were wild with fear," went the lyric from "Lucky Lindy." Speaking in New York, Charles Evans Hughes declared that Lindbergh "has lifted us into the freer and upper air that is his home. He has displaced everything that is petty, that is sordid, that is vulgar. What is money in the presence of Charles A. Lindbergh?"

Lindbergh showed the way to the future, yet he resembled a figure from the nation's simpler past, Daniel Boone or Davey Crockett in aviator's togs. Where older flyers with heavy corporate backing had failed, he had succeeded. Youth, innocence, and virtue seemed to triumph over power, organization, and Mammon. In a society of growing technological complexity, in which men and women often seemed victimized by machines and moved about by forces beyond their control, Lindbergh proved that human beings could still make a difference. In an age of inflated egos and hyperbole, he addressed his elders as "sir" or "madam" and invariably acknowledged his grasp of the situation with "check." Old-fashioned individualism, Yankee ingenuity, and common sense had been vindicated once again.

Lucky Lindy, however, finally cashed in too. Corporate sponsors paid well for endorsements. Aircraft manufacturers and infant airlines sought his advice and cachet. He fell in love with Anne Morrow, daughter of Dwight Morrow, a senior partner at J. P. Morgan. The Lindbergh-Morrow wedding in 1929 marked the close of the twenties as surely as the year's events on Wall Street. The fairy tale was ending. Prior to the ceremony, the bride's sister had been threatened with kidnapping. Even greater tragedy lay ahead for them as well as for a nation that in the spring of 1927 had found itself transported for a moment above all that was petty, sordid, vulgar, and fearful.

9

Lost Generation

> *For an old bitch gone in the teeth,*
> *For a botched civilization.*
> —Ezra Pound, *Hugh Selwyn Mauberley*

LIFE OF THE MIND

Briefly in the late twenties, the romance of Charles Lindbergh seduced
even American intellectuals. Gene Tunney might scoff that the Lone
Eagle "had a wonderful motor," but the hard-boiled Heywood Broun
was deadly serious when he wrote: "We came up out of slumps and
slouches. There was more brotherhood in being than I have ever seen
here since the Armistice." The mood couldn't be sustained. Three
months after Lucky Lindy's plane touched down at Le Bourget, the
Commonwealth of Massachusetts electrocuted two Italian anarchists,
Nicola Sacco and Bartolomeo Vanzetti. This, too, was a turning point,
a vivid reminder for the leaders of high culture why they remained
disenchanted with the America of Harding and Coolidge.

Looking back on the twenties from the vantage point of the Great
Depression, the novelist Willa Cather wrote: "The world broke in two
in 1922 or thereabouts." After World War 1, Gertrude Stein declared,
"we had the twentieth century." But, she quickly added, "the future
isn't important anymore." Amory Blaine, the hero of F. Scott Fitzgerald's 1920 novel *This Side of Paradise*, spoke for youth: "Here was a
new generation . . . grown up to find all Gods dead, all wars fought, all
faiths in man shaken." Few images are more deeply etched in our
historical imagination than those of American intellectuals and artists

of the 1920s. Miss Stein called them a "lost generation," men and women who struggled to define the relationship between their craft, their lives, and their society in the aftermath of the Great War. Among the words most often used to describe their behavior and attitudes are "disillusionment," "rebellion," and "alienation." They were disillusioned by the savagery of the war and the failure of peacemaking; they rebelled against the moral provincialism and boorishness of their own middle-class upbringing; they distrusted the institutions of mature capitalism and the nation's dominant commercial culture.

A generation is "lost," the library critic Frederick Hoffman wrote, when it believe itself to be cut off from the past and unconnected to the future. A great many American intellectuals and writers of the postwar era—Fitzgerald, Ezra Pound, T. S. Eliot, Ernest Hemingway, e. e. cummings, Malcolm Cowley, Joseph Wood Krutch—defined their situation in these terms. "Some generations are close to those that succeed them," Fitzgerald wrote, "between others the gulf is infinite and unbridgeable." Yet whatever their perceptions at the time, Fitzgerald's generation remained part of a longer cultural tradition and the impact of their ideas and methods grew ever larger as time passed. Despite their own posture, they were not the first generation of American intellectuals to be disillusioned by war, appalled by the suffering inflicted on men and women in an industrial society, or terrified by the loneliness of existence in an indifferent universe. Nonetheless, they explored these matters with uncommon sympathy, daring, and insight. The nation's first encounter with high mass consumption and affluence helped produce a literary renaissance unmatched since the generation of Emerson and Melville.

Those who pursued the life of the mind in America—whether in 1720 or 1920—had usually been alienated from the larger society. America's intellectuals often felt uncomfortable in an environment in which material pursuits dwarfed spiritual ones, practical knowledge was valued over speculative thought, and social reality often clashed sharply with lofty ideals. A deep strain of anti-intellectualism ran throughout American culture. Most citizens prized education and knowledge as vehicles of social mobility and instruments of progress, not as paths to self-awareness and social criticism. For most Americans, as Alexis de Tocqueville noted in the middle of the nineteenth century, "the pleasures of the mind" did not constitute "the principal charm of their lives."

The estrangement between American writers and their society became especially intense in the post–Civil War years of robber barons, racial oppression, and imperialism. Like Henry David Thoreau before him, Mark Twain showered ridicule on most of the culture's hallowed beliefs: white supremacy, the benefits of technology, the upward spiral of progress. William Dean Howells, Edith Wharton, Harold Frederic, Frank Norris, and Theodore Dreiser dissected the pernicious influences of wealth, archaic moral codes, and religious fanaticism. Henry James, echoing Nathaniel Hawthorne and James Fenimore Cooper, declared America wholly unfit for serious artistic endeavors: "No State . . . no sovereign, no court, no personal loyalty, no aristocracy, no church, no clergy, no army, no diplomatic service, no country gentlemen, no palaces, no castles, nor manors, nor old country-houses, nor parsonages . . . nor ivied ruins . . . no literature, no novels, no museums . . . no political society, no sporting class—no Epsom nor Ascot."

This was a harsh indictment, perhaps overharsh, but understandable coming from the intensely European Mr. James. In several ways, however, the prewar progressive era represented something of a rapprochement between certain intellectuals and American society. The economic system of corporate capitalism became ever more dependent on scientific, technical, and administrative competence for its growth and survival. Education and systematic knowledge began therefore to play a critical role in the organization and distribution of social status and political power. From the primary grades to graduate and professional schools, institutionalized learning exploded in America between 1890s and World War I. Education became for the first time an important industry and a ticket to success for the sons and daughters of the middle and the working class. They and their children created a burgeoning new market for the products of the mind and the spirit: books, magazines, periodicals, plays, musical productions, paintings, and sculpture.

Although a vast social and mental distance separated the bohemian poet of Washington Square from the chemical engineer at Du Pont, both shared membership in an expanding, self-conscious intellectual class that tasted new influence, prestige, and income before the war. The writings of many of them—Jacob Riis, Robert Hunter, John Reed, Upton Sinclair, Ray Stannard Baker—helped to shape public attitudes about immigration, poverty, business regulation, revolutions, and race relations. On a still more rarefied plain, Herbert Croly, Walter Lippmann, and John Dewey provided a dazzling set of philosophical and sociological justifications for the intellectuals' ascent to prominence.

Theodore Roosevelt, a Phi Beta Kappa from Harvard, a naturalist, and a historian, fraternized with intellectuals and appointed a few to government posts. One of their own, Woodrow Wilson, a Ph.D. and a university president, entered the White House in 1913. Not since the generation of the Founding Fathers had people of learning and cultivation ridden higher in American society. In the opinion of a few of them, notably Lippmann and Van Wyck Brooks, the literary critic, America stood on the threshold of a golden new era when artistic sensitivity and intellectual prowess would improve every important social institution from the classroom to the corporate boardroom. The poet Ezra Pound spoke in 1913 of the coming "American Risorgimento . . . an intellectual awakening. This will have its effect not only in the arts, but in all life, in politics, and in economics."

The carnage in Europe dashed most of these hopes. But even before the war, a sharp debate had erupted among American intellectuals over their newfound social role and influence. In works such as Lippmann's *Drift and Mastery* and Croly's *The Promise of American Life*, intellectuals were told that they had become indispensable to the efficient and enlightened management of the state, the economy, and the culture. They should therefore continue to extend their power through existing institutions. This same message came from John Dewey, the leader of progressive education, and the *New Republic* magazine, founded by Croly, Willard Straight, and Felix Frankfurter. On the left of the political spectrum, writing in journals such as *The Masses* or the *Liberator*, Reed, Max Eastman, Waldo Frank, and Randolph Bourne declared that capitalism and bureaucracy killed true intellectual freedom. Moreover, according to these writers, intellectuals who served the state, whether capitalist or revolutionary, compromised their objectivity and abandoned their most fundamental role as social critics.

America's declaration of war intensified the argument. Dewey and his allies endorsed Wilson's call to arms. Many of them joined the wartime bureaucracy in Washington. German militarism, they said, represented the greatest threat to the new age of rational politics. The "plastic juncture" of war, they argued, would permit a broad range of enlightened social reforms. Bourne and others rejected these assumptions. "The war will leave the country spiritually impoverished, because of the draining away of sentiment into the channels of war," the latter wrote, shortly before his death in 1918. "Those who have turned their thinking into war-channels have abdicated their leadership of this younger generation."

BOTCHED CIVILIZATION

By the early twenties, most in the younger generation had come to view World War I largely through Bourne's eyes. In their prosecution of the war, approach to peacemaking, and response to the Bolshevik Revolution, Wilson and the democratic nations had not exhibited greater rationality than the militaristic Germans. As Ernest Hemingway described the Italian retreat from Caporetto in *A Farewell to Arms*, the war annihilated all reason, virtue, and human compassion. Italians turned on Italians; soldiers murdered innocent civilians; the machinery of violence killed and maimed indiscriminately. All of the intellectual experts in Washington and in the delegation that accompanied Wilson to Paris could not prevent a reign of repression at home or a punitive peace abroad.

The battlefields of Europe had claimed, moreover, some of finest artistic talent of the younger generation. What had they died for? Pound, once optimistic about the capacity of art to civilize politics, expressed the rage of those left behind:

> Daring as never before, wastage as
> never before.
> Young blood and high blood,
> fair cheeks, and fine bodies;
>
> fortitude as never before
>
> frankness as never before,
> disillusions as never told in the old days,
> hysterias, trench confessions,
> laughter out of dead bellies.
>
> V
>
> There died a myriad,
> And of the best, among them
> For an old bitch gone in the teeth,
> For a botched civilization,

Like the trenches that now scarred the French countryside, the war left deep intellectual and emotional wounds that did not heal quickly in the twenties. The younger generation blamed its elders for the debacle. Pacifism sank deep roots in the intellectual community, because no national interest seemed worthy of the slaughter. Old precepts such as patriotism, honor, and fair play lost their authority. Language itself,

Poet Langston Hughes.

the common coin of politicians, diplomats, and novelists, had been debased and could not be trusted. The results of the war departed so dramatically from the intentions of those who began it that cause and effect seemed to have broken down entirely. Notions of time, both personal and historical, had been disrupted by the interminable conflict that engulfed the most civilized nations and that catapulted others from near-feudalism to socialism in the space of a few months.

With the exception of a handful of authors, American poets and prose writers saw the war as an unmitigated disaster. The extent of human suffering vastly outweighed the political and diplomatic changes that took place; few moral distinctions seemed worthy of mention among the belligerent nations; the high ideals ("self-determination," "peace without victory") articulated by leaders such as Wilson had been betrayed, often by the idealists themselves; and old-fashioned virtues such as courage, sacrifice, and heroism had little meaning in a world of routinized, impersonal death. "Now we spread roses / Over your tomb—" wrote the young black poet Langston Hughes:

> We who sent you
> To your doom.
> Now we make soft speeches
> And sob soft cries
> And throw soft flowers
> And utter soft lies.

Even Willa Cather, one of the least disaffected prewar novelists, passed a negative verdict on the legacy of the conflict. In *One of Ours*, the mother of a young American killed in France laments: "It seems as if the flood of meanness and greed had been held back just long enough for the boys to go over and then swept down and engulfed everything that was left at home."

Poet and ambulance driver Edward Estlin Cummings, clapped into a French prison camp for three months on suspicion of treason, expressed the war's sharp break with tradition in verse that dispensed with the usual conventions of punctuation, capitalization, and meter. In "Buffalo Bill's Defunct," written in 1920, e. e. cummings also said farewell to romantic American notions of military valor:

> Buffalo Bill's
> defunct
>   who used to
>   ride a watersmooth-silver
>   stallion
> and break onetwothreefourfive pigeonsjustlikethat
>   Jesus
> he was a handsome man
>   and what i want to know is
> how do you like your blueeyed boy
> Mister Death

The carnage left its mark on another ambulance driver, this one from Michigan, Ernest Hemingway. Wounded on the Italian front in the summer of 1918 and presumed to be dead, he wrote fiction deeply colored by those grim times. Hemingway's spare prose exhibited distrust of rhetorical excesses and hyperbole. His leading characters ridiculed abstract ideals and those who propound them. Instead, the Hemingway hero treasured everyday events and simple, concrete things—food, drink, sleep, fishing, making love. The war left in its wake the physically and spiritually crippled. Jake Barnes in *The Sun Also Rises* cannot consummate his love because of a wound suffered in combat. His inability to fulfill this natural, physical desire symbolizes the sterility of all the human relationships among the novel's expatriates. They are alienated from their past, incapable of lasting personal commitments in the present, and unable to conceive a future. In his 1925 short story "Soldier's Home," Hemingway wrote that Harold Krebs, a war veteran who could not adjust to civilian life, "did not want any consequences. He did not want any consequences ever again. He wanted to live along without consequences."

The old man of Hemingway's "A Clean, Well-Lighted Place" (1933) finds solace in the small café with its warmth and familiar faces. Beyond the café in the broader world there is "nada"—the void of nothingness. In *A Farewell to Arms*, Catherine Barkley asks Lieutenant Henry why he drove an ambulance for the Italian army:

> "It's very odd though," she said. "Why did you do it?"
> "I don't know," I said. "There isn't always an explanation for everything."
> "Oh, isn't there? I was brought up to think there was."

The Artist and Society

The war buried two other leading assumptions of many prewar intellectuals. The first was the notion that intellect and power, art and society could coexist peacefully. The second was a corollary of the first: that artists and intellectuals bore a special responsibility to promote social and moral improvement through their creative efforts. Prewar critics and writers often attacked the genteel tradition in literature for its failure to address important social problems, but they seldom doubted that literature could and should play an important role in shaping the country's social attitudes and political consciousness. As late as 1920, the prewar critic Van Wyck Brooks continued to urge American novelists "to [call] to life the innumerable impulses that make a society rich and significant. Let him create new heroes on the printed page." His was definitely a minority voice.

In the postwar decade many writers assumed, on the contrary, that an irreconcilable conflict existed between the true artist and society—especially American society—because it epitomized the sickness of modern industrial civilization. The expatriate critic Malcolm Cowley recalled that "the writers of our generation . . . did not hope to alter the course of events or even to build themselves an honored place in

society. . . . The younger generation had the brief vision of a world
adventurously controlled by men, guided by men in conflict, but the
vision died. Once more society became an engine whose course they
could not direct . . . nor did they much care."

One of the earliest and clearest statements of the new estrangement
appeared in a collection of essays entitled *Civilization in the United
States*, published in 1922 with the encouragement of Harold Stearns,
an editor of various little magazines. The contributors, including Stearns,
Lewis Mumford, H. L. Mencken, Van Wyck Brooks, and Robert Lovett, offered variations on an old theme played by Henry James: America did not have a civilization worthy of the name and what it did have
remained indifferent to or destructive of the artistic spirit. "We have
no heritage or tradition to which to cling," wrote Stearns, "except those
that have already withered in our hands and turned to dust." Mumford
criticized the sterile functionalism and chaos of the American city.
Mencken ridiculed the "incurable cowardice and venality" of American politicians. Lovett decried the banality of higher education. Stearns
and Brooks noted the absence of a viable literary tradition that left
each new generation adrift without mentors or models. Garet Garrett
skewered the greed and philistinism of businessmen. Alfred Kuttner
inventoried the collapse of family life, where husbands escaped into
commerce and adultery, wives into religious fanaticism.

Stearns and his contributors told the younger generation of American writers that it was absurd to think their efforts could change a
spiritually impoverished society or that they could fulfill their artistic
destinies in the United States. Coupled with a favorable exchange rate—
it was cheap to live abroad—and romantic notions of literary exile,
polemics such as Stearns's encouraged a further exodus of American
writers to Europe. Only there, declared Matthew Josephson, could
American writers find proper nourishment for their efforts. "The soil
of American perception is a poor, little barren artificial deposit. . . . We
poor aspirants must live in perpetual exile!" This perspective also gave
more ammunition to those who argued that the artist bore absolutely
no moral responsibility to society except to pursue his or her craft with
truth and diligence. Poets such as Pound and Eliot advanced a mild
version of "art for art's sake," but its most radical proponents launched
the Dadaist movement in the early years of the decade.

Art, said the Dadaists, remained separate from life, a private matter;
the artist was superior to other human beings. Any work of art that
could be readily understood by the masses was by definition second-
rate and unsophisticated. Dada exhibitions, designed to shock and offend

audiences, combined satire, violence, and pornography. In order to enter a celebrated Dadaist gallery in Cologne, guests passed through a public lavatory. Once inside, they were given hatchets and encouraged to attack the paintings and sculptures that displeased them. At the exit, a nubile young lady dressed in white for her first communion stood reciting obscene verse. The Dadaist poet Pierre Chapka-Bonnière offered the following memorable lines:

```
_____;_____:_____o_____O
!!! tsi _____:_____:_____I
_____et sam _____et sam _____sam _____saM
_____et sam _____et sam _____sam _____saM
? cha _____keink _____ tsi H
                            !rrroor_____O
_____atakak _____af _____af _____oh _____tzzi g
```

Dada, observed Cowley, represented the extreme of artistic individualism, because it denied "any psychic basis common to all humanity." Its aesthetic anarchy horrified most prewar literary radicals, such as Waldo Frank, who pronounced it unfit for the American critical scene: "A healthy reaction to our world must of course be contrary to dada; it must be ordered and serious and thorough."

Although it influenced surrealism, Dada never commanded a wide following among American authors in the postwar decade. But neither did the views of Brooks and Frank, who called for "a healthy reaction to our world" and "new heroes on the printed page." In much of the fiction of the twenties, society became the enemy of personal fulfillment, the nemesis of the authentic self. Felix Fay in Floyd Dell's *The Moon-Calf* (1920) and George Babbitt in Sinclair Lewis's *Babbitt,* for example, experience a new range of ideas and emotions when they break away from the conventional thinking and institutions of the American middle class. But even Babbitt's brief flirtation with bohemia, Lewis suggested, imprisoned his personality in yet another set of clichés and stereotypes. Whether conformist or rebel, real estate salesman or union demonstrator, George Babbitt could not escape from roles that society constructed and manipulated.

Heroism, if at all possible in the postwar American novel, took the form of small victories that preserved individual autonomy, dignity, and self-respect from otherwise hostile or indifferent social institutions. Hemingway's Jake Barnes and Lieutenant Henry were magnificent examples of heroic antiheroes. More often, a protagonist's pursuit

F. Scott Fitzgerald.

of a single dream—true love, respectability, wealth, power, moral purity—became so obsessive that it led to catastrophe, a fate that befell numerous fictional heroes, including Fitzgerald's Jay Gatsby, Theodore Dreiser's Clyde Griffiths in *An American Tragedy,* John Dos Passos's Charley Anderson in *USA,* and Quentin Compson in William Faulkner's *The Sound and the Fury.* In the memorable fiction of the decade, the range of human choice appeared tragically limited by history, social institutions, or psychological forces beyond the individual's control or understanding. Of Gatsby's fatal quest to possess Daisy Buchanan, Fitzgerald's narrator concluded:

> He [Gatsby] did not know that it was already behind him somewhere back in that vast obscurity beyond the city, where the dark fields of the republic rolled on under the night.
>
> Gatsby believed in the green light, the orgiastic future that year by year recedes before us. It eludes us then, but that's no matter—tomorrow we will run faster, stretch out our arms farther. . . . And one fine morning—
>
> So we beat on, boats against the current, borne back ceaselessly into the past.

NEW PESSIMISM

Most progressive intellectuals of the prewar era assumed that reason, clear thinking, and good ideas could transform social institutions for the better. Croly, Lippmann, and Brooks, for example, all sharply criticized the state of American politics and culture. But each held out the hope of improvement once the nation's values and institutional arrangements caught up with the ideas of its most advanced and creative minds. Such optimism disappeared from major works of social criticism that captured the imagination of American intellectuals in the postwar decade and defined their general outlook on society—*The Education of Henry Adams*, Joseph Wood Krutch's *The Modern Temper*, and Lippmann's *A Preface to Morals*.

Adams died during the war at the age of eighty. His now celebrated autobiography had been printed in a small limited edition of 1907. Yet in the twenties he became a posthumous member of the lost generation. Reprinted in 1918, Adams's reflections on his own odyssey through more than half a century of American life struck a responsive chord in the postwar generation of intellectuals. In a voice both mordant and resigned, the scion of one of the nation's founding political families advanced several propositions about the condition of Western civilization in general and America in particular. First, the exercise of political power in democratic society had become wholly divorced from intellectual and cultural sensibilities. Critical thinking was, in fact, a positive obstacle to political success. Intellectuals would remain marginal and isolated from the real sources of authority. Adams also questioned modern notions of social evolution and progress when considering that the culture produced leaders such as Grant and McKinley after Washington and Jefferson. Finally, science and technology, symbolized by the electric dynamo, had put extraordinary power into human hands. But without a force such as the religion that once bound medieval communities together, this new energy would fuel only individual greed and social disintegration. For Adams, the social and physical universe seemed headed in the same direction—toward disorder and entropy. "The movement from unity into multiplicity, between 1200 and 1900," he concluded, "was unbroken in sequence, and rapid in acceleration. . . . All the steam in the world could not, like the Virgin, build Chartres."

The myth of scientific "progress" also preoccupied Krutch, the Tennessee-born drama critic for the *Nation*, one of the remaining beacons of liberal journalism. As a consequence of modern science, especially physics, chemistry, and biology, Krutch wrote in 1929, human existence at least in the West was no longer nasty, brutish, and short. Life had become physically more comfortable and predictable. But along with these benefits had come a scientific explanation of the universe and of man's place there that reduced the meaning of life to a set of mathematical equations about the behavior of atoms, molecules, neurons, and synapses.

As a method of explanation, Krutch observed, science had routed magic, myth, and religion. Science had moved *Homo sapiens* from the center of the cosmology to the margins. It now appeared certain that the natural world would continue nicely without the species and that the universe was, in fact, totally indifferent to the fate of human beings. Man's most cherished idea—that the universe contained an inherent moral order capable of human understanding—had been shattered. "As that systematized and cumulative experience which is called science displaces one after another the myths which have been generated by need," wrote Krutch, "it grows more and more likely that he [man] must remain an ethical animal in a universe which contains no ethical element." The political and cultural implications of Krutch's ideas were devastating, because they suggested the impossibility of ascertaining values or distinguishing right from wrong by any scientific method. This left only subjective experience and naked power to mediate human conflicts in a cold, indifferent world.

At about the same time, Lippmann reached equally gloomy conclusions. Before the war he had placed his reformer's faith in the leadership of an intellectual elite who would utilize scientific management to promote progressive democracy. By mid-decade he was less sanguine about science, intellectual elites, and democracy. In *The Phantom Public* (1925), he lamented that democracy had never nurtured an educated public or educated leaders. Instead of seeking to make good citizens, it had been content to fashion good executives. "The result is a bewildered public and a mass of insufficiently trained officials. The responsible men have obtained their training not from the courses in civics' but in the law schools and law offices and in business. The public at large . . . has no coherent political training of any kind." He also deplored the "cult of the second best" and the "herd instinct" that he claimed "acquired the sanction of conscience in democracy."

Four years later in *A Preface to Morals*, Lippmann addressed what he called "the vast dissolution of ancient habits" in modern society that had left each citizen alone and adrift. Like the individual human being, society had progressed from childhood superstition to adult maturity, but the loss of certain illusions meant insecurity as well. With the help

Walter Lippmann.

of the scientific method and under the banner of freedom, social and intellectual reformers had succeeded all too well in weakening the sanctions of traditional institutions—the patriarchal family, religious faith, political authority—but they had been unable to fashion a set of arrangements or beliefs to replace them. On what basis, then, could people make decisions about personal or political life in modern societies? Echoing the Hemingway hero or heroine, Lippmann could only suggest that individuals display personal fortitude and fall back on their inner resources, a private code of behavior.

SAGE OF BALTIMORE

The mood of fatalism and resignation that permeated much of the serious fiction, poetry, and social criticism of the decade did not mean that American writers abandoned more conventional forms of social and intellectual protest. As the Stearns volume suggested early in the decade, the most popular target of the intellectuals remained the American middle class, especially the species found in the nation's small towns and villages. Some writers, notably Sherwood Anderson and Sinclair Lewis, treated this provincial middle class with mixed loathing, pity, and affection. Their fiercest adversary knew only the first of those feelings. He was Henry Louis Mencken of Baltimore, patron of Nietzsche, accomplished linguist, darling of the intellectuals, scourge of the masses. No American critic of the twenties threw a bigger or sharper harpoon dipped in sarcasm and vitriol.

Born in 1880 to German parents, H. L. Mencken began writing for the *Baltimore Morning Herald* at nineteen and later joined the *Baltimore Sun* as a columnist, a post he held for the remainder of his life. Four months after the outbreak of war, he also became coeditor with George Jean Nathan of *Smart Set*, a magazine that championed the naturalism of Dreiser and Frank Norris and also gave Americans their first opportunity to read James Joyce. In 1917, writing in the *New York Evening Mail*, Mencken pulled off one of the greatest hoaxes in the history of journalism when he wrote what readers took to be an authoritative version of the history of the bathtub in America. According to his sober account, later widely reprinted, the bathtub had been unknown in the land of the free until 1842 and opposition to it had not abated until Millard Fillmore ordered one installed in the White House. Mencken fabricated the entire story, of course, but its wide reception as truth convinced him that he had not underestimated the intelligence of the American people.

In 1924, Mencken began publishing the *American Mercury*, dedicated, as he put it, "to exposing the nonsensicality of all such hallucinations [as Marxism, Bryanism, Prohibition, etc.], particularly when they show a certain apparent plausibility." Mencken eschewed pessimism and despair. His was full-throated, uninhibited anger and sarcasm. Mark Twain's *Huckleberry Finn* had left a deep impression on him as a child. And like Twain, Mencken saw himself as the enemy of American hypocrisy, greed, religious intolerance, and political cant. Seldom lacking targets even before the war, he found them to be abundant in the era of Harding and Coolidge.

In the pages of the *Sun*, *Smart Set*, and the *Mercury* as well as in books such as *Notes on Democracy* (1926), Mencken carved up most of the decade's sacred cows. He reserved a special knife for politicians, farmers, members of the clergy, temperance reformers, Klansmen, and fanatics of whatever persuasion. Asked once by an outraged reader of the *Mercury,* "If you find so much to complain of in the United States, why do you live here?" the Sage of Baltimore replied, "Why do men go to Zoos?" Many of his other quips quickly became staples of American humor:

Puritanism: "The haunting fear that someone, somewhere, may be happy."

Conscience: "The inner voice which warns us that someone may be looking."

Religion: "Say what you will about the Ten Commandments, you must always come back to the pleasant fact that there are only ten of them."

Mencken seldom found anything positive to say about the nation's leaders, but Harding and Coolidge inspired him to new heights of ridicule. The Ohioan's prose, he wrote, "reminds me of a string of wet sponges; it reminds me of tattered washing on the line; it reminds me of stale bean-soup, of college yells, of dogs barking idiotically through endless nights. It is so bad that a sort of grandeur creeps into it. It drags itself out of the dark abysm (I was about to write abscess!) of pish, and crawls insanely up the top-most pinnacle of posh. It is rumble and bumble. It is flap and doodle. It is balder and dash." On Coolidge's election by the American voter in 1924 he observed: "It is as if a hungry man, set before a banquet prepared by master cooks and covering a table an acre in area, should turn his back upon the feast and stay his stomach by catching and eating flies."

Echoing the indictment of other intellectuals, Mencken pronounced America unfit for serious artistic endeavors. Capitalism, democracy, and religion had proved fatal to creative genius. Capitalism valued what would sell, not what was interesting. Democracy hated true individualism and tried to destroy it. Religion, especially what Mencken termed "Puritanism," justified repression and censorship in the name of morality. In 1926, Mencken personally took up the fight for artistic freedom in Boston, when the city banned the *Mercury* for publishing "Hatrack," an article about a prostitute who entertained both Protestant and Catholic clients. The former she did business with in Catholic cemeteries; the latter enjoyed her favors in Masonic ones. Mencken personally sold copies of the banned issue on the Boston Common and challenged the descendants of John Winthrop and the agents of the pope to do something about it. He was arrested, but not prosecuted because city fathers feared more publicity and a test of the law.

As the Boston incident illustrated, small towns and country folks whom Mencken stigmatized as "yokels" did not have a monopoly on prudery

H. L. Mencken, the Sage of Baltimore.

or censorship in the twenties. Nonetheless, the editor of the *Mercury* kept his biggest rhetorical guns trained throughout the decade on the territory west of the Appalachians and south of the Mason-Dixon Line. While Rotarians praised this region as the heart of the nation, Mencken equated it with other parts of the anatomy. In the arts as in politics, the nation's standards were set by those whom Mencken termed the "boo-boisie," the "massed morons," and the "hookworm carriers" who resided in this region of the country. The rank and file of Americans he dismissed as the "most timorous, sniveling, poltroonish, ignominious mob of serfs and goosesteppers ever gathered under one flag in Christendom since the end of the Middle Ages."

Mencken was a courageous man. He spoke out vigorously against shoddy thinking, censorship, and genuine threats, such as the Ku Klux Klan, to the nation's best traditions. Other writers and intellectuals lionized him as one who spoke their language, never pulled his punches, and fearlessly battled the enemies of artistic creativity and progress. They laughed when he impaled the "hookworm carriers" for their latest outrage against sophistication and enlightenment, be it prohibition or the Scopes trial. But Mencken's cleverness and wit often masked the shallowness of his own social vision and analysis. He failed to grasp the shock of change that tormented millions of Americans. He could be a demagogue while denouncing demagoguery. Parody and ridicule advanced the cause of social change only so far. Mencken could entertain the intellectuals and make them feel superior to the "massed morons." He could not give them something to believe in again. Two condemned men did that.

"Two Wops in a Jam"

In the winter and spring of 1919–20, the country remained in the grip of a Red Scare that made outcasts of political radicals. According to Attorney General Palmer and his federal agents, anarchists and followers of Lenin hoped to plunge the nation into social revolution. At the same time, a series of daring, violent robberies swept over the railroad yards and industrial towns of Rhode Island and Massachusetts. The most notorious took place on April 15, 1920, outside a shoe factory in South Braintree, where bandits stole the company's payroll and left the paymaster and his guard both dead on the sidewalk. Private detectives who investigated these crimes believed they had been carried out by professional criminals, perhaps the Joe Morelli gang of Providence. This plausible theory was rejected, however, by the Bridgewater police chief and high-ranking officers in the Massachusetts state police. They blamed the robbery and murder on political radicals—either communists or anarchists—and set out to find the culprits in the state's large immigrant community.

On the evening of May 5, 1920, police arrested Nicola Sacco, a shoemaker, and Bartolomeo Vanzetti, a fishmonger, on a Brockton trolley car. Both carried guns and ammunition. The two men were followers of the militant anarchist Luigi Galleani, who feared arrest and deportation for their political activities, which may have included bombings in the Boston area. Sacco and Vanzetti lied to their interrogators and soon found themselves charged with the South Braintree crime. They were tried in Dedham, Massachusetts, before judge Webster Thayer, a cadaverous old Yankee with a hearty dislike of radicals. He urged the jury to carry out their duties "like the true soldier . . . responded to that call in the spirit of supreme American loyalty. There is no better word in the English language than 'loyalty.' "

During the trial, Thayer and prosecutors made frequent reference to the defendants' political views and their flight to Mexico in 1917 to

avoid military service. Eyewitnesses from the robbery who could identify one or the other man were called to testify; eyewitnesses who
remained in doubt did not appear. Those who offered alibis for Sacco
and Vanzetti were dismissed on grounds of ethnic or political prejudice. The commonwealth's chief ballistics expert gave convoluted testimony linking a weapon like Sacco's with one of the murder bullets,
but not with his specific gun. The jury returned a guilty verdict. Thayer
sentenced them to die in the state's electric chair.

A reporter from New York sent to cover the Dedham trial in connection with a larger series about anarchism and the Red Scare told his
editor: "There's no story in it . . . just a couple of wops in a jam." He
was very wrong. Within a year, owing to the publicity generated by
Fred Moore, the pair's first lawyer, and by Carlo Tresca, the dashing
anarchist leader, Sacco and Vanzetti had become the most widely known
convicts in American history. Their legal and political appeals lasted
six years. In that time, the case polarized opinion in the state and the
nation as no event had since the debate over entering the war in 1917.

Moore and Tresca had little difficulty persuading communists and
anarchists that the shoemaker and the fishmonger were saintly workers about to be executed by capitalist reactionaries. They also raised
money and pricked consciences among liberals and Boston Brahmins
who became convinced that the defendants had been railroaded for
their political opinions and deserved a new trial. When Harvard law
professor Felix Frankfurter summarized all these doubts in the pages
of the conservative *Atlantic Monthly*, the cries of frame-up forced the
governor of Massachusetts to appoint a special commission to review
the entire case. Frankfurter pointed out that one juror had expressed a
belief in the defendants' guilt before the trial opened; that the commonwealth's ballistics expert had recanted his testimony prior to his
death; and that Judge Thayer's conduct during the trial had been "a
farrago of misquotations, misrepresentations, suppressions, and muti-
lations . . . infused by a spirit alien to judicial utterance."

All to no avail. The governor's commission, chaired by Harvard
president A. Lawrence Lowell, another doyen of the Yankee establishment, chastised Judge Thayer for being "indiscreet," but found the
trial otherwise spotless. It scoffed at evidence that the crime had been
committed by others, despite a confession from a former member of
the Morelli gang. With the executions scheduled for the night of August
23, 1927, Boston became a magnet for America's intellectuals, who
saw the two Italians as kindred spirits about to be killed by American
fear and bigotry. They idolized Vanzetti, who had mastered English,

Nicola Sacco (second from left) and Bartolomeo Vanzetti enter Norfolk County Court between two guards for trial in 1921.

spoke eloquently before Thayer at his sentencing, and wrote moving letters to his supporters. From the point of view of many who came to Boston to march and protest, the same malignant forces that led America into war, crushed the Boston police strike, imprisoned radicals without trial, and banned Mencken's *Mercury* were about to throw the switch on two innocent men.

The case generated despair among intellectuals, because it confirmed their worst nightmare about America. After the executions, many in the funeral cortege wore arm bands that proclaimed: "Remember—Justice Crucified—August 23, 1927." But the case also inspired a ray of hope, because it brought them together for the first time since the war in a common cause that was much larger than each individual. Facing death, Sacco and Vanzetti displayed genuine heroism, a mighty antidote to the decade's rampant pessimism. Walter Lippmann wrote editorials urging a new trial. The novelist Katherine Anne Porter and poet Edna St. Vincent Millay picketed and went to jail for Sacco and Vanzetti. "All right," declared John Dos Passos, hearing the two had been executed, "we are two nations." Malcolm Cowley immortalized them in verse:

> March on, oh dago Christs, whilst we
> march on to spread your name abroad
> like ashes in the winds of
> God.

More than half a century after their deaths, debate continues to rage over whether the two Italians were guilty and whether they received a fair trial. Defenders of the prosecution argue that higher courts and other judges, including Justice Holmes, did not find the proceedings so tainted as to justify a new trial; that at least one of the fatal bullets came from Sacco's gun; and that anarchists and communists fooled many well-intentioned intellectuals with clever propaganda.

Advocates for Sacco and Vanzetti have a stronger case, however. They point out that Massachusetts revised the standards of appellate review because of the controversy; that the single bullet from Sacco's gun proves he was framed, because it contradicts overwhelming eyewitness testimony about the number of fatal shots fired at South Braintree; and, finally, that the prosecution knowingly concealed exculpatory evidence concerning Vanzetti's revolver. About some things there is no doubt. The case defined political boundaries in America between left and right for many years to come. And the ordeal of the shoemaker and the fishmonger generated a renewed sense of purpose and fraternity among American intellectuals—a bond that would strengthen as the country faced a longer, more sustained social crisis.

10

Changing the Guard

> *Hoover says the tariff will be kept up. Smith says the tariff
> will not be lowered. Hoover is in favor of prosperity. Smith
> says he highly endorses prosperity. Hoover wants no votes
> merely on account of religion. Smith wants no votes solely
> on religious grounds. Both would accept Muhammed votes
> if offered. . . . If a man could tell the difference between the
> two parties, he could make a sucker out of Solomon.*
> —Will Rogers

UNAVAILABLE MAN

As he concluded a morning session with reporters on August 2, 1927,
at the summer White House in Rapid City, South Dakota, President
Collidge asked the group to return at noon for an additional statement.
Puzzled, but dutiful, the newsmen filed back into the president's office
at the local high school shortly after twelve o'clock. He told them to
form a single line and personally handed each one a small slip of paper
containing copies of a twelve-word statement he had composed a few
days earlier. It was vintage Coolidge: "I do not choose to run for President in nineteen twenty-eight." In a summer when the big news from
the Black Hills had been the relative merits of bait versus fly fishing
(Coolidge used worms), this was an astounding story.

Outside the farm belt, where his veto of the McNary-Haugen crop-
subsidy bill had produced great anger, Coolidge remained extremely
popular. The Republican nomination in 1928 and another four years
in a refurbished White House were his for the asking. Coolidge, however, stood fast. Reaffirming his position a few days later, he refused

CHOOSIN' TO RUN ISN'T AS RESTFUL AS THIS

Coolidge in 1928: Would he or wouldn't he?

thereafter to discuss it, even with other potential candidates, but his August bombshell generated intense speculation about the president's motives. Was this a clever ploy on Coolidge's part, a trial balloon to test the depths of support in the party and the nation? Did the president expect to be drafted for another term? Or, on the contrary, did he sense an impending economic disaster and hope to leave the ship in glory before it ran aground with a new captain?

Neither theory seems credible. When the inevitable displays of fealty came from key party leaders, Coolidge still did nothing to promote his own candidacy. And if he saw doom in the 1927 figures on rising bank failures, farm foreclosures, and stock prices combined with slowing auto sales and construction, the president had more foresight than most economists of his day. The best explanations for Coolidge's withdrawal, a few of which he mentioned to close friends at the time, were less dramatic but more plausible. He did not wish to subject his wife to the physical strain of another term in the White House. He had begun to worry about his own health. He believed the country was on a sound footing and that he had fulfilled the party's promise of prosperity and opportunity through common sense in Washington. Without a blueprint for the nation, except to reduce the size and scope of the federal government, Coolidge did not have an unfinished agenda. Finally, the dour little man from Plymouth Notch did not relish the presidency. Like the Puritan magistrates of old, he regarded it as one of those unpleasant but necessary burdens that upright citizens bore in order to protect the commonweal from the forces of darkness.

WONDER BOY

The president's noncandidacy touched off a flurry of political maneuvering by other Republicans, but in truth there was only one logical successor—the secretary of commerce, Herbert Hoover. Here was a man more revered in the country at large than in the Grand Old Party itself. Key leaders, starting with Coolidge and including Andrew Mellon and Senator William Vare of Pennsylvania, distrusted the Great Engineer. Hoover had, for one thing, often spoken favorably about Woodrow Wilson. Further, except for a student body election at Stanford University, Hoover had never run for or been elected to public office. Unlike others, he had not toiled very long in the party's vineyards. His shyness the Republican powers took to be either aloofness or arrogance. Behind his back they called him, contemptuously, Wonder Boy or Sir Herbert. "That man has offered me unsolicited advice for six years, all of it bad," snapped Coolidge, when asked privately about Hoover's qualifications.

Among the general public by 1928, Hoover was a trusted household name. Inside the party, doubts remained. The isolationist wing of the GOP, represented by Senators Borah and Johnson, viewed Hoover nervously because of his past identification with Wilson and his vocal support for the League of Nations. Old progressives such as Senator Norris thought him too cozy with the great capitalists. In fact, the traditional Republican business elites in banking and manufacturing, symbolized by Mellon, did not consider Hoover sound on a great many public issues. He favored public works spending in times of economic decline. He opposed labor injunctions. They much preferred the bedrock conservatism of a Coolidge.

But Hoover, like George Bush in 1988, had an impressive-looking résumé, one studded with many nonpartisan achievements in business and philanthropy. More important, for nearly eight years as secretary of commerce he had shrewdly and methodically built a potent political organization outside the usual party channels. By 1928, thanks to this effort, Herbert Hoover had become probably as well known as the president of the United States. At the controls of Hoover's campaign machine sat George Akerson, his press secretary, who hired a talented group of experts in public relations and mass communications to sell the secretary of commerce to the nation just as one sold other products. Akerson recruited Bruce Barton, already a legend on Madison Avenue; Henry Sell, a newspaperman who specialized in opinion polling; and Will Irwin, a Stanford classmate and prewar muckraker, who wrote a flattering biography of the Great Engineer and who proved to be equally adept at political-film making.

What Hoover lacked in support among party professionals, he and Akerson more than made up for by utilizing the old and new tools of mass persuasion—newspapers, magazines, radio, and motion pictures. Hoover's campaign exploited all of the technological possibilities of image-building through radio and film. For someone considered retiring and reticent, Secretary Hoover had an uncanny ability to pop up everywhere between 1921 and 1928 in newsreels and still photographs, most often as the wizard of progress or the angel of mercy. When Congress created a new aeronautics branch in his department in 1926, Hoover posed with the dashing pilots. His face became the first one transmitted by the miracle of television in 1927. But disasters, such as the terrible Mississippi Valley flood of 1927, became Hoover's forte. They showed the Great Engineer and Great Humanitarian in action, surveying the damage, exhorting the rescuers, comforting the afflicted, organizing relief efforts. The only rest Herbert Hoover got, quipped Will Rogers, was between calamities. Irwin wove yards of film footage together in 1928 for a stirring campaign documentary, appropriately entitled *Master of Emergencies*.

In campaign techniques as well as substance, Hoover could easily claim to be a progressive, certainly the most progressive Republican candidate since Charles Evans Hughes in 1916. Although he lost some primaries to favorite-son candidates, Hoover and his well-oiled, well-financed organization rolled into Kansas City in June 1928 with a huge lead among the 1,089 delegates to the Republican national convention. Many from farm states carried placards proclaiming "Anyone but Hoover." George Peek and other supporters of the McNary-Haugen legislation mounted a last-minute effort on behalf of Governor Frank Lowden of Illinois, but it fizzled along with their attempt to include in the party's platform a specific endorsement of their controversial farm relief plan. Even leaders of the old guard such as Mellon and Chief Justice Taft, who hoped until the last minute that Coolidge would run again, jumped on Hoover's bandwagon before the balloting began. The man described as "the minister of mercy to the hungry and the poor" captured 837 votes on the first ballot, more than enough to make his nomination unanimous.

The Hoover forces sprang into action and produced a party platform
that sang the praises of President Coolidge and the economic prosperity fostered by his policies. Vowing to continue them, it endorsed the
protective tariff, economy in government, and sound money. Those
who believed in temperance received reassurance that the GOP would
not abandon efforts to enforce national prohibition. Labor was told
that judges had sometimes issued injunctions too freely and that cor-
rective measures might be called for. Having rebuffed supporters of
McNary-Haugen, Hoover and his allies extended an olive branch to
agriculture. The platform rejected the idea that government should
seek to manage farm production through taxation and price supports,
but promised new legislation to create a federal farm board with authority
to assist in the formation of cooperatives that in turn would "control
[farm] surpluses through orderly marketing."

Two months later, before a crowd of seventy thousand in Stanford's
football stadium and a nationwide radio audience estimated in the
millions, Hoover formally accepted the party's nomination. One hand
jammed in his pants pocket, head bowed over his text, and speaking in
a dry monotone, candidate Hoover restated the generalities of the platform, and uttered words that would haunt him for the rest of his life:
"We in America today are nearer to the final triumph over poverty than
ever before in the history of any land. The poorhouse is vanishing from
among us. We have not yet reached the goal, but given a chance to go
forward with the policies of the last eight years, we shall soon with the
help of God be in sight of the day when poverty will be banished from
this nation." In the summer of 1928, Hoover's forecast seemed little
more than the usual campaign hyperbole, no more ludicrous than the
GOP's 1928 slogan of "a chicken in every pot and two cars in every
garage." Within two years, both would be recalled with derision as
examples of a fundamental political betrayal.

SIDEWALKS OF NEW YORK

Near the conclusion of his Stanford speech, Hoover made a plea for
religious toleration. This was both a heartfelt wish from one whose
Quaker ancestors had endured terrible persecution and a calculated
political gesture at the start of the presidential campaign. By the time
he delivered the speech, Hoover knew that his Democratic opponent
would be "the Happy Warrior," New York's four-term governor Alfred
Emanuel Smith. Al Smith was as urban as the Brooklyn Bridge near

which he had grown up, as Irish as the Blarney Stone, and as Catholic as St. Patrick's Cathedral. He was also an outspoken opponent of national prohibition. Al Smith wore a brown derby hat and sometimes a checkered vest. He said Lou Gehrig was the Yankee's "foist" base-man and that Babe Ruth often played "hoit." In 1928, all of these characteristics endeared him to New Yorkers, but made him either a curiosity or an object of suspicion to large numbers of Americans beyond the Empire State.

The Southern wing of his own party greeted Smith's nomination at the national convention in Houston with sullen resignation. The death of William Jennings Bryan and the virtual eclipse of William McAdoo had left the supporters of prohibition and Protestant cultural hegemony without a major national leader. Democrats from all regions of the country longed to avoid a repeat of the 1924 convention, which had stigmatized their party as a quarrelsome mob of children who could agree upon neither a platform nor a candidate. Party leaders from the big cities believed Smith had earned the right to head the ticket and that another rebuff to their hero would constitute blatant political robbery. Southern and Western Democrats feared, finally, that the urban machines would take a walk if Smith was denied the nomination again. After one ballot and a single fistfight on the floor, the most placid Democratic convention in decades chose Smith and named as his vice-presidential running mate the senior United States senator from Arkansas, Joe Robinson, a loyal supporter of prohibition. The Democrats in Houston, quipped Will Rogers, had behaved like Republicans. But another wag observed that the ticket of Smith and Robinson was like trying to carry fire and water in the same bucket.

Many scholars see the Hoover-Smith contest as the last epic cultural battle of the twenties, one pitting religious, ethnic, and geographic opposites. Irish Catholic versus native-stock Protestant. City versus country. Wet versus dry. The truth of this perspective should not obscure the fact that the two candidates had much in common. Each represented important sources of prewar progressivism: the urban working class in Smith's case and enlightened corporate management in Hoover's. To the discomfort of many leaders in both parties, the Republicans and Democrats in 1928 put forward the most reform-minded candidates since Wilson and Hughes battled for the White House in 1916. Both Hoover and Smith had risen from childhoods of tragedy and poverty. Hoover, the second of three children, lost both parents before he was ten. His blacksmith father left an estate of $1,500. The Hoover children were shuffled around from relative to relative until finally taken in by an uncle in Oregon. There Hoover worked as an office boy before enrolling at the newly opened Stanford University in 1891. Smith's father died when Al was fifteen, an event that forced him to abandon school in the ninth grade and to support his mother and four siblings by working as a bookkeeper in a Fulton Street fish market commission house.

Herbert Hoover became a world-renowned mining engineer whose managerial skills took him to four continents, where he ran vast enterprises and became very rich. Smith displayed equal talent in his profession: politics. He ran successfully for the New York state assembly in 1902 and was later elected sheriff of New York County and president of New York City's board of aldermen before winning the statehouse for the first time in 1918. Except for the Harding landslide in 1920, he won the governorship every two years thereafter. Although a protégé of the notorious Tammany Hall organization, which savored of corruption, Smith often pitched his own political tent outside the Wigwam. In Albany he surrounded himself with savvy reformers and good-government types such as Belle Moskowitz, Judge Joseph Proskauer, and Yale-educated Robert Moses, whose ambitious plans for state parks and highways gained the governor's enthusiastic support. Smith streamlined and strengthened the executive branch by pushing through the legislature measures that consolidated governmental functions into a few major departments and gave the governor authority to control their budgets. When it came to efficient administration of governmental affairs, Smith took a backseat to no one, including Herbert Hoover, who utilized many of the same techniques in the Commerce Department. Observing him before the war in New York's constitutional convention, Elihu Root called Smith "the best informed [member] on the business of the State."

Al Smith's progressivism had a heart as well as a head. It sprang from his own experiences on the Lower East Side and from Tammany's constituents, mostly members of the working class and lower middle class who struggled daily for economic security, one step ahead of poverty. Hoover had always observed workers from afar, bossing them in China, Russia, Egypt, the Transvaal, and Ceylon. Al Smith mingled regularly with New York's common people and depended on them for votes. Practical politics and compassion led him to support state laws to improve factory inspection, to limit the hours of work, to fix minimum wages, and to compensate workers injured on the job. By 1928, he also backed state ownership and operation of hydroelectric facilities. Despite a checkered record on civil rights and liberties, Smith became the darling of liberal intellectuals on the *New Republic*. They noted that he spoke out against the purge of socialists from the state legislature during the Red Scare, but they ignored his long opposition to women's suffrage and his support for New York's so-called Padlock Act, which imposed censorship on theatrical productions deemed obscene by the courts.

PRIDE AND PREJUDICE

In 1928, the public record of neither candidate mattered a great deal. If American politics is normally 60 percent emotion and 40 percent rational calculation, the ratios in 1928 leaped to 80–20. Only two issues absorbed public attention in the campaign from July to November, although neither proved decisive: Al Smith's Catholicism and his stand on prohibition. Hoover, who limited his campaign to seven rambling, fact-filled addresses over the radio, never had to mention either one. Others inflicted the fatal wounds—leaders of the Methodists and Southern Baptists, and Al Smith himself.

In their Houston platform, the Democrats had blasted the Republicans for lax enforcement of prohibition and blamed them for spawning criminal activity. Even so, the party promised to uphold the Constitution and the laws, including, presumably, the Volstead Act. Shortly before the convention adjourned, however, candidate Smith released a telegram to the delegates advocating "fundamental changes in the present provisions of national prohibition." Seasoned politicians blanched. Many Southerners called it a stab in the back. The governor compounded his problems in August when he called flatly for state control of liquor and vowed to lead a nationwide campaign to repeal the Eighteenth Amendment. This was good, orthodox states' rights philosophy that Southern Democrats might applaud in another context. On the issue of prohibition, however, it placed Smith in opposition to his own party's national platform and the sensibilities of millions of voters whose support he needed in his uphill battle against Hoover.

The Houston telegram and the August declaration proved two things: Smith was no hypocrite and he often failed to understand the texture of political life beyond his home state. As H. L. Mencken once observed, the governor's universe "begins at Coney Island and ends at Buffalo." Smith had now reignited old stories about his open defiance of prohibition and his own fondness for drink. In 1923, opponents reminded voters, Smith had endorsed a New York law that repealed all statewide enforcement of the Volstead Act. He never denied serving alcohol on social occasions at the governor's mansion, which lead William Allen White to say: "He must be either violating the law or knowing that someone else does. If this is true he is not a fit man to be either Governor or President." When the Anti-Saloon League came out for Hoover, it could be dismissed as the prejudice of small-town bigots. When the *grande dame* of progressivism, Jane Addams, did the same, however, it represented a serious blow to Smith's credibility with reformers.

In his choice of a national chairman for the Democratic Party, Smith again shot himself in the foot on the prohibition issue. He tapped John J. Raskob, whose portfolio of corporate offices included high posts at E. I. du Pont de Nemours and General Motors. Raskob also headed the Association Against the Prohibition Amendment, a Du Pont–financed organization that churned out propaganda on behalf of the wet forces. These corporate barons feared prohibition as a precedent for more government regulation of private enterprise. Cynics also noted that the Du Ponts and other wealthy benefactors of the association hoped to lighten their own tax burdens through the legalization of taxable liquor. To the shock of those who hoped that Smith would focus his campaign on economic themes such as the plight of agriculture or public power, Raskob described prohibition as a "damnable affliction" and called it the "chief issue" against Hoover.

Raskob proved to be a liability in other respects as well. His corporate ties alienated progressives, who urged Smith to attack the Republicans as the party of big business and social privilege. And Raskob's Catholicism—including a papal knighthood in the Order of Saint Gregory the Great—became another reminder to voters of Smith's own beliefs. Al Smith was not simply a good Catholic. He was a proud, sometimes defiant one who never attempted to hide his or his wife's devotion to the faith. Smith had written a forceful article on the importance of the separation of church and state for the *Atlantic Monthly* in 1924. As governor he had signed a new, liberal divorce statute that the Catholic church opposed. But these actions were offset by other symbolic gestures. In the governor's mansion in Albany, guests could view a portrait of Pope Pius XI, signed "To my beloved son, Alfred E. Smith." And at a New York City reception for eight cardinals in 1926, the governor knelt before them and kissed the ring of the papal legate. In a society where anti-Catholicism had deep, strong roots reaching back a century or more, Smith's behavior gave more ammunition to fanatics who warned of papal conspiracies to stamp out political and religious liberty.

Smith and his inner circle of advisers also blundered with respect to general campaign strategy. They might have fought Hoover from the left, seeking to build on the protest vote cast four years earlier for La Follette and Wheeler. Since that November, despite a rising stock market and the general aura of well-being, conditions in several sectors of the economy, notably agriculture, had worsened. By calling aggressively for farm relief, aid to depressed industries, and public power, Smith could have portrayed Hoover as the rich man's candidate, who ignored the cries of prosperity's orphans.

Instead, Smith ran an ideologically conservative campaign by attempting to reassure voters that he could manage prosperity as well as Hoover and would not derail the gravy train with wild schemes to redistribute wealth. Smith hoped Raskob's appointment would build confidence with business leaders and encourage corporate campaign contributions. It worked. The governor surrounded himself with other millionaires—Jesse Jones, James W. Gerard, Herbert H. Lehman— and raised $7 million from them and their friends. Smith rarely attacked the protective tariff, long a staple of antibusiness rhetoric in the Democratic Party. He remained silent on Mellon's tax packages, which

Governor Al Smith, the "Happy Warrior," on the campaign trail in 1928.

subsidized millionaries while soaking wage earners. He endorsed the principles of the McNary-Haugen bill, but remained vague on a specific mechanism for boosting farm prices. He threw away his advantage on the public power issue by endorsing private distribution of such energy, which placed him very close to Hoover, who backed a similar formula for Boulder Dam. Smith sounded a lot like Grover Cleveland or John W. Davis when he declared that "government should interfere as little as possible with business" and demanded a "fearless application of Jeffersonian principles" to the nation's problems. Many old progressives such as Felix Frankfurter, Clarence Darrow, and John Dewey came out for the governor, but the radical Women's Party endorsed Hoover, as did a large majority of the workers polled by Lillian Wald.

By refusing to wage the struggle on socioeconomic and class issues, Smith allowed prohibition and Catholicism to become the dominant themes of a campaign that reached new depths of hysteria and scurrility. Not all of it was generated by Hoover partisans. Southern Democrats, for example, circulated a doctored photograph showing Hoover dancing with Mary Booze, a black Republican official. They alleged that in addition to desegregating the Commerce Department, he had slept with black women during the Mississippi River relief effort. But the racial innuendoes hurled by both sides paled in comparison with the attacks mounted against Smith's religion and his stand on prohibition.

—The *Fellowship Forum*, a fundamentalist publication, ran cartoons that featured Smith driving a beer truck with the caption: "Make America 100 percent Catholic, Drunk, and Illiterate."

—Billy Sunday described Smith's supporters as "the damnable whiskey politicians, the bootleggers, crooks, pimps and businessmen who deal with them."

—John Roach Straton, minister of the Calvary Baptist Church in New York City, called Smith "the nominee of the worst forces of hell."

—Arriving in Oklahoma City for a speaking engagement, Smith faced a burning cross erected by the local Klavern of the Ku Klux Klan. There, too, the head of the city's largest Baptist church warned his flock: "If you vote for Al Smith, you're voting against Christ and you'll all be damned." These sentiments were echoed by Bishop James Cannon, Jr., spiritual leader of the Methodist Episcopal Church in the South; Arthur J. Barton, chief of the Southern Baptist Convention; and Alfred C. Dieffenbach, spokesman for the liberal Unitarians.

Smith's supporters, led by H. L. Mencken, seldom invoked the flames of hell, but they fired back with attacks suggesting that anyone who opposed the New Yorker probably belonged to the Klan, advocated the lynching of Catholics, and never got past the sixth grade. "The majority of rural Americans, with the best blood all drained to the cities, are probably hopelessly uneducable," declared Mencken. America's cities would have to throw off "the hegemony of these morons . . . get rid of campmeeting rule," and defeat "those sorry betrayers of intelligence who, like Hoover . . . flatter and fawn over the hookworm carriers in order to further their own fortunes."

REALIGNMENT

On November 6, Hoover rolled to an overwhelming victory. He garnered 21.4 million popular votes (58 percent of those cast) to 15 million for Smith, and 265,000 for socialist Norman Thomas and other minor party candidates. In the electoral college, Hoover's margin was even more crushing. He carried forty of the forty-eight states, including New York, for 444 votes to Smith's 87. Five states of the Old Confederacy, which had never given a majority to the party of Lincoln, lined up behind Hoover. The victor's coattails were long enough, moreover, to give Republicans big majorities in both houses of Congress. In the wake of another Republican sweep, seasoned political observers began to talk seriously about the extinction of the Democrats. The party of Jefferson and Jackson had held the White House in only eight of the past thirty-two years. They had won in 1912 because of the Republican split and in 1916 because of impending war. The Democrats, according to this theory, might soon become as obsolete as the Federalists or the Whigs.

Like Mark Twain's death, however, reports of the Democrats' demise seemed premature. Even in defeat, Smith polled more popular votes than Davis had in 1924 and more than any Democratic presidential candidate in history. Of even greater significance was the source of Smith's support. Since 1896, the nation's largest cities, heavily immigrant and Catholic, had voted Republican in presidential elections. Harding in 1920 and Coolidge in 1924 carried the twelve most populous cities by 1.3 million votes. In 1928, however, these same cities plus 122 northern counties with substantial immigrant and Catholic populations returned a majority for Smith. The shift to Smith and the Democrats by Italian-Americans and French Canadians was especially notable; so, too, the heavy turnout by Catholic women and first-time voters, both of whom gave majorities to the New Yorker. Republican gains among white Southerners in 1928 proved temporary in comparison to these dramatic shifts in the Northern urban electorate, soon to be accelerated by the economic calamity of the Great Depression.

Smith's own urban, immigrant, Catholic background contributed powerfully to these realignments. The venomous attacks on his religion by Protestant leaders encouraged many big-city Catholics to go to the polls in self-defense and retaliation. On the other hand, Smith's religion cost him millions of votes in the Bible belt. In the end, however, the Happy Warrior's defeat probably sprang less from ethno-religious prejudices, which may have negated one another, than from other ingredients. Hoover had become a household name across the country. From the perspective of many voters, his national and international experience also made him more qualified than the governor of New York to run the nation. In 1928, Hoover appeared presidential and Smith did not.

Finally, Smith ran against prosperity. In areas of the country where hard times had already hit, especially the farm belt, Smith picked up impressive support, even among Protestants. He carried Iowa, for example, and bettered significantly the Democrats' 1920 and 1924 totals in states such as Ohio, Illinois, Wisconsin, and the Dakotas. Those who felt the economic pinch in 1924 had voted for La Follette. In 1928, they backed Smith. But these pockets of discontent were not enough in the climate of economic well-being that continued to bathe the country. No Democrat alive, Protestant or Catholic, could have defeated the Great Engineer in the fall of 1928. As Mencken observed ruefully: "I incline to believe that Hoover could have beaten Thomas Jefferson quite as decisively as he beat Al. He could have knocked off Grover Cleveland even more dramatically. . . . His victory was a triumph of technique, of sound political engineering."

Fate treated Al Smith with both cruelty and kindness. The White House would forever elude the Happy Warrior, a man surely as qualified for the post as three-quarters of those who ever held it. Franklin Roosevelt, who narrowly won the governorship of New York on election day in 1928, would reap the fruits of the voter realignment that Smith's campaign set in motion. But fate also spared Al Smith the agony and humiliation of trying to master the whirlwind of economic misfortune about to smash the nation and its new leader.

11

Götterdämmerung

> *If a man saves $15 a week and invests in good common*
> *stocks . . . at the end of 20 years, he will have at least*
> *$80,000 and . . . $400 a month. He will be rich. And*
> *because income can do that, I am firm in my belief that*
> *anyone not only can be rich, but ought to be rich.*
> —John T. Raskob, capitalist
>
> *[There is just] a little distress selling on the Stock*
> *Exchange.*
> —Financier Thomas Lamont

OCTOBER 1929

Certain dates remain stamped forever on the memories of entire generations: December 7, 1941, the day the Japanese bombed Pearl Harbor; November 22, 1963, the day President Kennedy was shot. For those who lived through the end of the twenties and into the Great Depression that followed, October 24 and October 29, 1929, were such days. On those dates, "Black Thursday" and "Black Tuesday," panic gripped the New York Stock Exchange as the value of corporate securities bought and sold there fell like autumn leaves in Central Park during a hurricane. This was the Great Crash, the death of the bull market of the twenties, the curtain call for flush times. Nothing remotely comparable would occur in American financial history; the stock market collapse of 1987 and its consequences were but a ripple compared to October 1929.

The collapse of the stock market did not "cause" the terrible economic depression that followed. Most economic historians point to other, long-term difficulties in the nation's economic system, especially the failure of purchasing power to keep pace with rising productivity in the case of farmers and most industrial workers. Many industries that employed large numbers of workers, notably coal, textiles, and railroads, had become less profitable and were suffering depression even before the panic on Wall Street. The Great Crash, however, exposed their ailments and those of jerry-built corporate structures, too. The collapse of stock prices also had serious consequences for the financial structure, because many commercial banks that had made loans to investors on the promise of rising values were now left holding depreciated assets. A serious credit squeeze or liquidity crisis quickly developed. To these tangible impacts of the market collapse must be added the huge psychological blow of falling prices.

For two years before October 24, the stock market had soared upward, the value of common stocks reaching stratospheric levels. At the end of 1927 the *Times* industrial index stood at 245. A year later it hit 331. By September 1929 the figure was 452, an appreciation of about 85 percent in twenty months. On the morning of October 24, however, terror struck the New York exchange as sellers unloaded huge batches of securities for which there were no buyers. Stock prices plummeted. By noon, with the report of transactions already running hours behind, the market had taken a $9 billion loss. By the end of trading, close to thirteen million shares had changed hands, a record that lasted only four days. Even blue-chip securities took a beating. General Motors, which had sold at 60 two days before, fell to 53. Standard Oil was down almost ten points, from 77 to 68; United States Steel declined six points; AT&T lost eighteen. Only an afternoon buying effort by a syndicate of prominent bankers headed by J. P. Morgan & Company prevented an even bigger sell-off of securities.

The syndicate's purchases, estimated at $20 to $30 million, combined with the shock and confusion of that day, steadied the market for several days. On the 29th, however, nothing halted the avalanche of sales. In the first half hour, over three million shares changed hands. The ticker again ran over two hours late. When the final bell sounded, the volume had reached 16,410,000 shares. It was, according to John Kenneth Galbraith, a connoisseur of this financial disaster, "the most devastating day in the history of the New York stock market, and it may have been the most devastating day in the history of markets." The average price of industrial securities listed by the *New York Times* fell 43 points, wiping out the gains of an entire year. Speculative issues such the Blue Ridge Corporation and the Goldman Sachs Trading

Corporation lost nearly half their value that day. Again, the blue chips sank like stones. General Electric and AT&T lost 28 points, Allied Chemical 35. The governors of the exchange huddled briefly at midday, considered closing the institution down, but finally determined that such a move would only inspire greater panic.

Those caught in the maelstrom would not soon forget it. "October 29, 1929—I remember that day very intimately," recalled Sidney J. Weinberg of Goldman Sachs, then a young investment banker. "I stayed in the office a week without going home. "The [ticker] tape was running, I've forgotten how long that night. It must have been ten, eleven o'clock before we got the final report. It was like a thunderclap. Everybody was stunned. Nobody knew what it was all about. The Street had general confusion." Long after the events, bankers, stockbrokers, their customers, and ordinary people would repeat stories to their children and grandchildren about those October days, some true, some apocryphal:

—The trading floor of the exchange, normally only unruly, degenerated into anarchy as brokers literally fought one another to place selling orders. Fistfights broke out. Shirts and suits were ripped. Men lost shoes, spectacles, false teeth, and even a wooden leg in the melee.

—When no buyers could be found for the common stock of the White Sewing Machine Company, which had plunged in value from 48 to 11, a cunning messenger boy bid $1 per share and became a major stockholder.

—Exploding firecrackers in the center of Chicago's financial district triggered rumors that Al Capone had dispatched gunmen to rub out the brokers he held responsible for the decline in his portfolio.

—Millions of investors had purchased their shares on credit, borrowing from brokers and using the securities as collateral for the loan, a technique known as margin trading. The collapse of stock prices wiped out their collateral and brought demands from brokers for additional cash on pain of selling out the customer's entire account. In a vain effort to hold their vanishing investments, people raided their savings, then hocked jewelry, china, even clothing. A policeman reported finding a caged parrot, abandoned in a Wall Street alley by either a disoriented broker or customer, whose only words were "More margin! More margin! More margin!"

—Reports of ruined investors committing suicide were greatly exaggerated, but when the stock of the Union Cigar Company fell almost 100 points in one day, its president eluded a waiter's grasp and leaped

One loser in the market seeks to raise more cash in 1929.

to his death from a ledge of Manhattan's Beverly Hotel. In Kansas City, a man who failed to raise more cash to save his heavily margined account shot himself, gasping: "Tell the boys I can't pay." Comedian Eddie Cantor, himself a victim of the October panic, brought roars of laughter with the joke about the man who asked for a hotel room and was queried by the clerk: "Sir, will this be for sleeping or for jumping?"

Most Americans in the fall of 1929 had little idea that they were about to enter a prolonged economic slump. This stock market panic, they assumed, resembled earlier ones that wiped out many speculators, but from which the country soon recovered. All too soon many realized that what had happened to the New York Stock Exchange was no laughing matter. In the next few weeks, stock prices held, even rose once or twice, but their general direction was downward. "Financial storm definitely passed," Bernard Baruch told his British friend Winston Churchill. But despite such soothing words from financiers, businessmen, even President Hoover, the patient slowly, inexorably slipped away. The longest and biggest speculative orgy in the nation's history was over, and its impact on the country's banking system, consumption patterns, and mental state was just beginning to be felt by the end of the year. People then and now asked, how did it happen? What did it mean? In retrospect, the warning lights, some specific to the stock market, others reflecting a national addiction to speculation and get-rich-quick schemes, had been flashing for years.

PONZI'S PROSPERITY

Early in 1920, the Old Colony Foreign Exchange Company of Boston made an astonishing offer to readers of the city's newspapers. For every $10 invested with the firm for ninety days, it promised $15 back, or a 50 percent return. Potential customers were told that Old Colony intended to buy International Postal Union money orders in some foreign currencies and later redeem them in others, reaping profits from the daily and often substantial fluctuations in exchange rates from country to country. Old Colony assured the curious that its activities were perfectly legal and that all who entrusted their funds to the firm would become very rich, very soon. At first the dollars only dribbled in from cautious Bostonians, but as Old Colony honored its pledge, paying out 50 percent interest on ninety-day deposits, investors jammed its offices, thrusting wads of money into the hands of the company's president, a suave forty-two-year-old gentleman by the name of Charles Ponzi. By July 4, 1920, according to some estimates, Ponzi's company was raking in a cool $1 million each week.

From Beacon Hill to the North End, Old Colony and its president became instant celebrities, toasted for their financial acumen even by some of Boston's staid businessmen, who made substantial investments. Among Boston's poorer Italian-Americans, Ponzi was mentioned in the same breath with Columbus, Michelangelo, and Marconi. He played the role of tycoon to the hilt by purchasing a mansion, elegant automobiles, expensive suits, and even a controlling interest in one of Boston's most venerable banks, Hanover Trust Company. So dazzling was the light reflected from Ponzi's surface that few investors bothered to peek under the hood, where they would have found a few questionable parts. President Ponzi of Old Colony Foreign Exchange and Hanover Trust was a former vegetable peddler with considerable experience in both forgery and smuggling. His capital resources in 1919 had amounted to $150.

The booming business at Old Colony also attracted attention by midsummer of 1920 from enterprising local reporters and the district

Charles Ponzi, swindler.

attorney. They discovered an intriguing fact. Ponzi had taken in millions, claiming to invest these huge sums in International Postal Union money orders, but in all of 1919 less than $60,000 of these financial instruments had been printed. Clearly, Ponzi had been putting considerable sums of money elsewhere. When allegations of fraud began to pop up, Ponzi ridiculed them. He announced ambitious plans to expand his operations and even offered to pay investors a 50 percent return on money left with him for forty-five days. Once again clients flooded his offices eager to invest, and Old Colony continued to meet its obligations, forking over $300,000 on a single day.

For Ponzi and those who put their money into his hands, the end came in August 1920. Court orders closed the Old Colony offices while state and federal investigators combed through the firm's records. The reporters had been right. It was quickly discovered that Old Colony's assets amounted to zero, while its liabilities exceeded $2 million. At Ponzi's subsequent trial for grand larceny and mail fraud, further depressing facts came to light: he had taken in $15 million in less than a year, and tiny amounts had been invested in international money orders, but only $200,000 could be physically located.

In short, Charles Ponzi had been taking in money through the front door, paying some of it out almost immediately to those who presented ninety-day notes, and stealing the remainder. As long as the flow of new funds steadily increased, Ponzi and a few of his lucky clients could become very rich. The vast majority lost everything. The judge who sentenced him to prison remarked that Ponzi's cunning placed him a few notches above the ordinary pickpocket or burglar, but he offered choice observations as well on the responsibility of those who eagerly sought him out, hoping to reap a 50 percent return on their money. They, he suggested, in addition to being very credulous could have been prosecuted for violating the state's usury laws.

FLORIDA, 1925

While out on bail appealing his conviction in Massachusetts, Charles Ponzi found employment in Florida selling real estate. Not even Hollywood could have concocted a more perfect story line to capture the trajectory of the decade's speculative mania. Much the same blend of avarice, gullibility, and fantasy that led fifty thousand people to follow Ponzi in Boston also fueled the great Florida land boom a few years later. The players, however, now numbered in the tens of thousands and the stakes were vastly greater. So was the wreckage when the bubble burst.

Beginning in 1513 with the Spanish explorer Ponce de León, outsiders always had grandiose plans for Florida, whether it entailed civilizing the native Indians or exterminating them, locating the fountain of youth, erecting great cotton plantations like those in the upper South, or looting the state's many natural resources. In the late nineteenth century the railroad provided new urban markets in the Northeast for the products of Florida's rich fields and forests. But until the eve of World War I, the state remained a colonial backwater, an exporter of cheap raw materials, where dreams of fabulous wealth always encountered the harsh reality of blistering heat, mosquitoes, and mangrove swamps. Southern Florida, both east and west coasts, had few inhabitants. Tampa marked the most southern outpost on the Gulf side. Miami with 5,400 souls in 1910 was the largest city south of Jacksonville on the Atlantic. In between were alligators and the remnants of the Seminole Indians who had escaped Andrew Jackson's soldiers a hundred years earlier.

Prior to the twenties, the notion of marketing Florida's greatest resources—sunshine and salt water—had occurred only to a few wealthy robber barons like Henry M. Flagler of Standard Oil and the Florida East Coast Railroad and Henry B. Plant of the Southern Express Company and the Atlantic Coast Line. To woo their rich friends from New York, Boston, Philadelphia, and Chicago for a winter vacation in the sun, they built elegant hotels such as Flagler's Ponce de León at St. Augustine and Plant's Belleair on Tampa Bay. They put up lavish homes in a place called Palm Beach, but always on the assumption they were creating an upper-class haven secure from the unwashed masses and the riffraff.

The automobile changed that. So did the ambitions of other millionaires such as Carl Fisher, George Merrick, T. Coleman Du Pont, D. P. Davis, and John Ringling, all of whom saw the possibilities of becoming even wealthier by selling a piece of the rich man's winter paradise to the newly prosperous and chilly middle-class denizens of Hartford, Pittsburgh, Columbus, and Iowa City. By 1920–21, a steady stream of Fords, Maxwells, and Chevys poured into Florida from the Northeast and the Midwest, their occupants clutching copies of the *St. Petersburg Times* or the *Miami Daily News*, which touted the state's climate, beaches, business opportunities, and rising land values.

Chambers of commerce, tourist bureaus, and real estate firms from one end of Florida to the other churned out tons of pamphlets and brochures—often festooned with bathing beauties and palm trees—that waxed eloquent about Coral Cables, Fort Lauderdale, and Sarasota. "Go to Florida—where the whispering breeze springs fresh from the lap of the Caribbean and woos with elusive cadence like unto a mother's lullaby." These and other odes found their way into mailboxes from Maine to Minnesota, swelling further the tide of migrants and new residents, who by 1925 were pumping billions into Florida's tourist economy and sending land prices sky-high. Between 1920 and 1925, Florida's population grew from 968,000 to over 1.2 million; Miami's from less than 30,000 to 130,000. The strain on public and private facilities became such that the railroads refused to haul all but essential food and medical supplies for a period in 1925.

What the newcomers found when they arrived were development plans worthy of the pharaohs or Venetian princes. Across Biscayne Bay from the city of Miami proper, Carl Fisher sank a portion of his auto headlight fortune into creating Miami Beach by scooping up the bay bottom, filling in the swampland, and broadening the ancient barrier key. He built a new bridge from the mainland, carved out a golf course, dredged more bay to create artificial islands, and sold oceanfront lots for hotels and mansions. His two elephants, Carl and Rosie, posed for photographers, pulled up mangrove stumps, and gave children a ride.

Farther south, George Edgar Merrick, a Congregational minister's son, conjured up what he called "America's most beautiful suburb," Coral Gables, complete with gondolas on dredged canals and streets named Caligula, Esteban, and Corniche. From a platform in the middle of the municipal swimming pool, William Jennings Bryan did not curse the money changers of Wall Street but extolled the wonders of Merrick's city, which grew from nothing to two thousand houses in a few years.

"Here," said the advertisements, "Mother Nature . . . broke her mold and threw away her palette and easel." The here was Fort Lauderdale, once a military post, by 1924 a subdivision built by Charles G. Rodes on canals and finger islands similar to Miami Beach. Not to be outdone in the scramble for prestige and customers, D. P. Davis, the hot-dog tycoon of Jacksonville, created his own island subdivision in the middle of Tampa Bay on the Gulf Coast. John Ringling, master of the three-ring circus, unleashed his dredging equipment on Sarasota Bay, where it, too, brought forth a string of islands and choice building lots. Ringling's staff sold parcels from a downtown hotel as trapeze artists swung from the rafters and clowns sprayed one another with seltzer bottles in the lobby.

Du Pont attempted to turn Boca Raton into a newer, swankier version of Palm Beach, complete with electric-powered gondolas plying its lagoons and canals. South of Forth Myers on the edge of Florida's famous swamp, home normally to alligators and water moccasins, the king of Coney Island, Barron Collier, moved ahead with yet another tropical Shangri-la, which he christened Everglades. "The raw land is being laid out as if for an exposition," observed one reporter. "Surveyors' theodolites are seen everywhere. . . . The available supply of wood is used up for lot-stakes. Yet, houses . . . pop out like the measles—they weren't there yesterday." If Everglades proved unattractive, buyers in pursuit of rising land values could always pick up a piece of Hollywood-by-the-Sea, between Miami and Fort Lauderdale; Amphibious Acres, near Miami; Indrio, "America's most beautiful home town"; or Manhattan Estates, described as "three-fourths of a mile from the prosperous and fast-growing city of Nettie."

BUST

Nettie, according to maps of the time, did not exist. But this did not discourage people from buying a lot at Manhattan Estates or elsewhere as Florida's land boom reached dizzying heights in 1925. Railroads put on extra cars to accommodate the traffic. Hotels that usually closed in the late spring because of the oppressive summer heat remained booked solid through the fall. According to one estimate, Florida had more real estate lots up for sale that year than there were families in the entire United States. The thought of actually building a house there became irrelevant to purchasers, who sought quick appreciation, not long-term investment. Salesmen made it easy with options or binders that permitted buyers to own a piece of paradise for as little as 10 percent down and modest monthly payments. With property values shooting up by the month, the week, even the day, who could resist?

In the Miami area, where a single edition of the *Daily News* in 1925 topped five hundred pages, most crammed with real estate ads, tales of feverish speculation and fabulous wealth abounded. Prime business lots sold for $5,000 a front foot. Those on Biscayne Bay commanded $15,000 to $20,000. A woman who purchased a parcel for $25 at the turn of the century sold it for $150,000 in 1925. A man who sold a lot for $2,500 in 1923 claimed he bought it back for $35,000 at the peak of the boom. Binders changed hands, sometimes as often as five times a day, each price higher than the last. At a local hotel, a New York reporter overheard an excited telephone conversation: "Momma! Momma! Is that you, Momma? This is Moe! I bought ten t'ousand acres today. Yes, ten t'ousand. Vat? Vat you say? Vy—Momma! How should I tell you where that land iss? I don't know myself!" A few years later, the Marx Brothers captured the madness in their first film, *Cocoanuts*, when real estate broker Groucho announces: "Now folks, everybody this way for the grand swindle! Buy a lot, you can have any kind of house you want, you can get stucco—oh boy, can you get stucco!"

When the Florida land market began to falter and then collapsed in 1925 and 1926, a large number of people, as Groucho said, got stucco. Like the Ponzi episode before it, the Florida land boom could be sustained only with a steady infusion of new money, representing new buyers willing and able to pay ever higher prices that allowed earlier ones to sell out at a profit. The escalator slowed for a number of reasons. Builders could not meet construction deadlines when critical supplies were caught in the railroad embargo. Major capitalists such as Du Pont bailed out of projects, dampening the enthusiasm of other developers. The Internal Revenue Service announced that it planned to tax short-term binder profits as income. These developments sent real estate prices into a tailspin, even before a bigger gust blew them down in 1926.

In the era before the weather service named hurricanes, the residents of south Florida could not be certain whether the one that slammed into them on September 18, 1926, was male or female. Whatever the gender, it packed winds in excess of 120 miles per hour, uprooted trees, tossed automobiles around like toys, and deposited yachts on the streets of Miami. Where partially built subdivisions stood the day before, only heaps of kindling and tile remained. It killed four hundred people and left fifty thousand homeless, including those in the hapless town of Moore Haven, now sinking under the waters of Lake Okechobee. No glossy pamphlets graced by fetching bathing beauties on sun-drenched beaches could soon erase these pictures of destruction.

The bloom was definitely off the Florida boom. What had been a flood of eager buyers in 1925 dwindled to a trickle by 1927. Even tourism fell off. Those who managed to hold on to their Coral Gables property for at least another twenty years would do very well indeed. But in the meantime, thousands of investors were wiped out, left holding options on land for which taxes and payments far exceeded the market value. All across southern Florida from coast to coast, the map was dotted with half-finished subdivisions, some little more than a graveyard of faded lot flags wafting in the breeze. Miami bank clearings, which hit the sum of $1,066,528,000 right before the erosion of land prices, had skidded to $260 million by 1927 and fell to $143 million a year later. From the perspective of most Floridians and those trapped in the wreckage of its land boom, the great crash had already taken place years before the stock market plummeted.

The Bull Market

The shattered palm trees had barely been removed from the streets of Fort Lauderdale when the decades' last and biggest speculative fever began on Wall Street. The same passion for quick riches that drove the Ponzi craze and the Florida land mania now fueled the rise of stock prices on the New York Stock Exchange. Instead of sinking their money into International Postal Union money orders or subdivision lots, Americans bought the securities offered for sale by the nation's business corporations.

At first slowly in 1926 and 1927, then with heart-pounding speed in 1928 and 1929, stock prices soared upward. The number of shares listed on the New York Stock Exchange rose from under 500,000 in 1925 to 757,000 in 1928 and hit 1,127,000 on the eve of the crash. The industrial averages, which stood at 159 in 1925, zoomed to 300 in 1928 and then added another 81 points between January and October 1929. The market value of all shares listed on the New York Stock Exchange almost doubled between 1925 and 1929, from $34 billion to $64 billion. The price of a coveted seat on the exchange went from a mere $76,000 in 1923 to $625,000 in mid-1929. Only the foolish, it seemed, were not buying a piece of American Can, New York Air Brake, RCA, Eastman Kodak, General Securities, or Insull Utilities Investments.

The great bull market of the twenties surged forward, powered by profound structural changes in the financial and corporate world coupled with large doses of economic fact and fiction. Until World War I, most Americans who managed to get through a month with some cash surplus tucked it away in a savings account. Only the very rich invested in the limited number of public and private securities offered for sale by government entities, railroads, public utilities, and industrial corporations. From 1917 to 1919, however, the United States government created a new market of middle-class investors by selling $27 billion in Liberty Bonds and Victory Bonds to finance the war against Germany. Few decisions did more to create the stock market boom of the next decade. Over 22 million Americans from all walks of life, responding to the patriotic calls of the U.S. Treasury, bought war bonds and received their first initiation into the mysteries of the securities market. By the mid-twenties, many formerly novice consumers considered themselves seasoned investors who knew the significance of price-earnings ratios and the difference between debentures and preferred stock.

Prior to the war, only railroads and a handful of industrial corporations attempted to raise capital by selling securities to the public. Most American business corporations financed their long- and short-term needs with bank loans. The small number of investment banking and brokerage firms who sold corporate securities formed a close-knit fraternity, one dominated by a few venerable houses such as J. P. Morgan; Kuhn, Loeb; Kidder, Peabody; and Dillon, Read. The spectacular success of the government's wartime bond program encouraged more and more corporations to seek public financing in the next decade. Corporations also began paying dividends with new shares of stock, thereby saving their cash for future expansion. By 1929, excluding people who owned multiple shares, there were probably 1.5 to 2 million stockholders in American corporations. On the New York Stock Exchange alone, one of twenty-nine exchanges where the buying and selling of securities took place, shoppers could chose from over twelve hundred issues in 1929. These included many securities issued by high-flying investment trusts such as International Securities Corporation or the Goldman Sachs Trading Corporation, which attracted buyers by offering professional management of a diversified investment portfolio.

The growth of this paper economy brought forth a parade of new investment firms to market its wares. By selling their own securities, corporations gained greater autonomy from commercial banks. The investment bankers and their syndicates reaped bonanzas in commissions and brokerage fees. In the consumer society, stocks and bonds were hawked like automobiles and toothpaste, often by salesmen with only a few weeks of training. "What counted for us," recalled writer Matthew Josephson, who became a securities salesman during the boom, "was the business of keeping our customers trading in and out . . . so that win or lose we gathered our broker's fees at fifteen dollars for each hundred shares."

By cutting both personal and corporate income taxes during the decade, Treasury Secretary Mellon and Congress also stoked the market's rise. Wealthy individuals and corporations had substantially more money to spend and invest. Since capital gains were taxed at the same rate whether one earned $10 or $10 million in profits, this provision made it very attractive for investors to shift their funds from fixed-interest obligations such as bonds to common stocks, whose value appreciated rapidly in a bull market. Owing less to Uncle Sam in taxes between 1922 and 1929, corporations reported higher net incomes and rising earnings per share, which also made their securities more attractive to investors. And finally, there was the magic of margin trading— buying securities on credit with a loan from your broker. No device had greater seductive power, because it promised a high return with a minimum cash investment.

The rapid expansion of installment purchase plans for many consumer goods after 1920 encouraged many people to think of brokers' loans as just another way to buy today and pay later, only the benefits could be much greater. With a cash down payment of $100, brokers noted, one could buy on installments a new Chevrolet or Dodge that in two years would be worth far less than the original purchase price because of depreciation. The same $100 down, combined with a broker's loan of $900 secured by the securities, would permit an investor to purchase a hundred shares of Commercial Solvents, selling at $10 a share. Assuming the stock rose to $20 a share in six months, which was not at all untypical in the surging market of 1928–29, the lucky buyer stood to make a 1,000 percent profit, less interest payments on the original loan and commission fees for the purchase and sale. When stocks such as Piggly-Wiggly rose 52 points in one day, General Motors 75 points in two months, and Wright Aeronautical 220 points in nineteen months, the lure of brokers' loans became irresistible. In the halcyon days of the great bull market, few investors stopped to consider what might happen if stocks fell at the same rate.

Between 1926 and the fall of 1929, money poured into New York both to purchase securities and, more crucially, to sustain the frenzied demand for brokers' loans, whose rate of interest climbed from 5 percent in the former year to 20 percent before the market crashed. Commercial bank loans to brokers reached a peak of $2.9 billion in December 1926, then fell to $2.5 billion in 1928 and to $1.8 billion in early October 1929 as the Federal Reserve Board raised its discount rate in an effort to discourage member institutions from making such speculative loans.

The central bank's attempt to discourage commercial bank loans to brokers did not dampen margin trading. Nonbanking lenders, principally corporations, pumped even more money into brokers' loans. Between 1926 and October 1929, brokers' loans from nonbanking sources rose from $1.3 billion to $6.6 billion. Bethlehem Steel Corporation and Electric Bond and Share headed the list of firms that preferred market speculation to investing in new plant and equipment. Each had sunk $157 million into the brokers' loan market by the fall of 1929. Among the other big corporate plungers were Standard Oil of New Jersey ($97 million) and Chrysler Corporation ($60 million).

There were sound reasons for stock prices to rise after 1926, including the steady growth in GNP and per capita income, rising productivity, and higher corporate profits. But the magnitude of the increases that took place, especially in 1928 and 1929, remained out of all proportion to these rational indicators. Fantasy, not facts, ruled the market. Although it had not paid a single dividend, for example, the stock of the Radio Corporation of America zoomed from 85 to 420 in the course of 1928. Montgomery Ward, another of the decade's glamour stocks, shot up in that same period from 117 to 440, and Du Pont from 310 to 525. In the frantic summer of 1929, according to one estimate, the securities of Insull's vast utilities empire appreciated at a rate of $7,000 a minute during one fifty-day period.

In addition to the influence of margin trading, the stratospheric rise in many issues resulted from the manipulations of floor traders on the exchange who operated pools designed to inflate prices artificially. William Durant, the sometime head of the General Motors Corporation, operated the most famous "bull pool" of the day. By selling shares back and forth to each other, experienced pool leaders such as Durant, Arthur Cutten, and George Breen could create the illusion of intense market activity in a particular issue. Once the unwary outsiders began to buy, driving the price still higher, the pool operators sold out at a handsome profit. Such a pool launched the boom in RCA stock. Another fleeced the lambs in Kolster Radio, whose stock went from 70 to 95 in 1929, despite zero earnings for the year. After the pool leaders bailed out, Kolster tumbled to 3.

While at the mercy of inside traders, even the most diligent investor had difficulty securing reliable financial information about the companies whose stock he wished to buy or sell. The New York Stock Exchange, eager to attract business, imposed minimal disclosure requirements on its listed companies. Other exchanges such as the New York Curb demanded even less. Investment bankers, lawyers, and accountants who prepared financial statements as well as brochures for prospective customers wanted a quick sale of stock, not a careful inventory of a company's assets and liabilities. With the seal of approval of the prestigious banking firm of Lee, Higginson and accountants at Ernst & Ernst and Price-Waterhouse, the International Match Company sold American investors nearly $150 million worth of securities before 1929. That company's president, Swedish tycoon Ivar Kreuger, ran little more than an upgraded Ponzi operation through which he stole hundreds of millions of dollars from the public.

As the bull market roared along, America did not lack for skeptics, who warned of the disaster lurking in excessive securities floated by investment trusts, bloated margin accounts, pool manipulations, and dubious financial reports. Early in 1929, both Moody's Investment Service and the Harvard Economic Society warned that stock prices had reached unreasonable levels and that a readjustment could be expected. Stronger words came that spring from Paul Warburg, the legendary chief of Kuhn, Loeb. In his opinion, brokers' loans had already reached "a saturation point" and unless "the orgy of unrestrained speculation" stopped, it would plunge the country into a depression. At the National Business Conference in September, economist Roger Babson predicted that "sooner or later a crash is coming, and it may be terrific." He painted a black picture of the nation if stock prices fell even 60 points on average: "Factories will shut down . . . men will be thrown out of work . . . the vicious circle will get in full swing and the result will be a serious business depression."

Storm warnings coupled with efforts to stem speculation in the market came as well from the Federal Reserve System beginning in 1928.

Benjamin Strong, the head of the New York District Bank and a long-time advocate of cheap money to promote European monetary stability and business expansion at home, became sufficiently concerned with the volume of brokers' loans from commercial banks that he urged a boost in interest rates to discourage such borrowing. Prior to Strong's death in October 1928, the Federal Reserve hiked the rate it charged member banks (the discount rate) from 3.5 percent to 4.5 percent. In December, it tightened the screws again by raising the rate to 5 percent. Federal Reserve Board governor Roy A. Young, a Minneapolis banker, condemned market speculation in February 1929 and threatened sanctions against member banks that continued to finance brokers' loans. Two months before the market crashed, the Federal Reserve lifted the discount rate another notch to 6 percent.

A wave of optimistic forecasts and acts of outright defiance swamped these alarms about market speculation. Queried about the rising volume of brokers' loans, President Coolidge described them as a "natural expansion of business." Other economists dismissed Babson as a pessimist. Yale's renowned Irving Fisher declared that stock prices "have reached what looks like a permanently high plateau." Charles Dice of Ohio State added that the surge in stock prices reflected simply "the tremendous changes that were in progress." Other leaders of Wall Street heaped ridicule on Warburg, who, they alleged, was "sandbagging American prosperity" and trying to drive down prices to cover his own speculations.

In what proved to be the single most irresponsible decision of 1929, Charles A. Mitchell, president of the powerful National City Bank and a director of the Federal Reserve District Bank, announced on March 26 that if money became tight as a result of the Federal Reserve's higher discount rate, his bank stood ready to pump an additional $25 million into the brokers' loan market. Furthermore, Mitchell added, his bank would continue to borrow from the Fed and use the money any way it saw fit: "We feel that we have an obligation which is paramount to any Federal Reserve warning, or anything else, to avert any dangerous crisis in the money market." Mitchell came under fire in Congress for sabotaging Federal Reserve policy, but neither the national legislature nor the banking agency pushed for new legislation to make such defiance impossible in the future. The dominant view among economists and financial writers at the time seemed to be that Roy Young and the Federal Reserve spoke for an "unenlightened and militant provincialism," while Charles Mitchell and those like him represented the wave of the future.

AMID THE RUINS

A month or so after the October storm hit Wall Street, Charles Mitchell no longer appeared so powerful or so wise. Along with other titans of the Street, he had attempted to halt the market's plunge on Black Thursday with a $20 million buying pool. It was like bailing Niagara Falls with a bucket. The stock of his own National City Bank lost close to half its value during the crash. AT&T fell from 310 to 193; General Electric from 403 to 168; United States Steel from 261 to 150. Even a $50 million purchase by the Rockefellers of Standard Oil stock failed to stop its slide from 83 to 48. By slashing the discount rate to 4.5 percent in November, the Federal Reserve Bank in New York tried to revive the market and prevent an even greater disaster. Banks that had been left holding depreciated securities as collateral on now-defaulted brokers' loans could at least borrow some cash on easier terms.

But for the remainder of 1929, despite the Federal Reserve's easy-money policy, stock prices on Wall Street and elsewhere continued their downward trend two days out of every three. It was becoming more difficult to believe the words of optimism flowing from New York and Washington:

—Irving Fisher said the decline represented only the "shaking out of the lunatic fringe."
—President Hoover declared that "the fundamental business of the country is sound."
—Andrew Mellon saw "nothing in the present situation that is either menacing or warrants pessimism."
—Charles Schwab believed that "never before has American business been as firmly entrenched in prosperity as it is today."

Then and later, people asked two fundamental questions about the Great Crash of 1929. What triggered the debacle? Did the stock market panic lead inevitably to the Great Depression that followed? To the first question, some students of the American economy point to a series of events in the summer and fall of 1929 that led to panic on Wall Street. Both new car sales and building construction declined, which led many to fear a major slowdown in the economy. In England the financial empire of Clarence Hatry, the Samuel Insull of coin-operated vending machines, collapsed, and with it confidence in other enterprises financed heavily with debt. In financial circles word spread that many smart speculators, including Durant, Bernard Baruch, and Joseph P. Kennedy, had already cashed in their chips and expected a decline

Variety *headline says it all.*

in the market. And finally, the Federal Reserve's modest credit restrictions suggested that tougher measures might be forthcoming to limit margin trading.

Individually and collectively, these factors may explain why many investors became especially nervous in October and why they stampeded at the first sign of trouble. But they also ignore a larger issue: the stock market was bound to collapse at some time as surely as Ponzi's scheme or the Florida land boom. In order to make a profit in a bull market, buyers must become sellers at ever-higher prices, but this process depends on a constant infusion of new players with new money who believe that they, too, will later make a capital gain. A relatively small number of investors, perhaps 1,500,000 with active accounts and less than 600,000 margin traders, sustained the bull market of the late twenties. The Billy Durants of the world drove it onward, not housewives who tapped coookie jars or taxi drivers who cashed in their life insurance. Those with considerable means fueled the boom. And given the poor distribution of national income by 1929, there were not enough of them to keep it rising forever.

While only a few people, therefore, suffered a direct loss, it was nonetheless a substantial one, and the indirect consequences for the economy were even greater. The stock market debacle dealt Americans both a financial and an emotional body blow. It did more than expose many of the structural flaws in the economy. As a result of the crash, investors lost billions in the space of a few months, which dampened both capital formation and personal consumption. Banks and corporations, having made large commitments to brokers' loans, now held depreciated paper assets that could not be turned into ready cash. Faced with frightened depositors, the banks called in other loans and refused to make new ones, thereby cutting off the flow of normal credit.

Major corporate employers began to trim dividends, to defer new spending, to trim inventories, and to lay off workers. Within one year, domestic investment as a share of GNP fell from 15.2 percent to 11.2 percent. The gross national product itself declined from $87.8 billion to $75.7 billion; employees' salaries were reduced by more than $4 billion, and unemployment mounted from 1.5 million Americans to 4.3 million. The slide into economic chaos had begun, and the Great Crash had played something more than a minor role.

PART TWO

1

The Trials of Herbert Hoover

A severe depression like that of 1920–21 is outside the range of possibility.
—Harvard Economic Society, *Weekly Letter*

Any lack of confidence in the economic future of the basic strength of business in the United States is foolish.
—Herbert Hoover

SCAPEGOAT

In the 1980s broadway musical *Annie,* based on the famous comic strip about a little orphaned girl, her dog, Sandy, and her wealthy benefactor, Oliver "Daddy" Warbucks, an early scene takes place under a New York City bridge. Homeless people huddle around trash-can fires to cook their food and keep warm. The year is 1932. They sing one of the play's most memorable numbers: "We'd Like to Thank You, Herbert Hoover":

> Today we're living in a shanty,
> Today we're scrounging for a meal,
> Today I'm stealing coal for fires,
> Who knew I could steal?
>
> I used to winter in the tropics,
> I spent my summers at the shore,
> I used to throw away the papers,
> I don't any more.

We'd like to thank you, Herbert Hoover,
For really showing us the way!
We'd like to thank you, Herbert Hoover,
You made us what we are today!
. . .

In every pot he said "a chicken,"
But Herbert Hoover he forgot!
Not only don't we have the chicken,
We ain't got the pot!
. . .

Come down and share some Christmas dinner,
Be sure to bring the missus, too,
We've got no turkey for our stuffing,
Why don't we stuff you.

We'd like to thank you, Herbert Hoover,
For really showing us the way.
You dirty rat, you Bureaucrat,
You made us what we are today.

Nearly fifty years after his presidency and twenty after his death, Herbert Clark Hoover remained in popular song and story the person most Americans held responsible for the economic calamity that struck the nation after 1929. Few of our political leaders have been more ridiculed and vilified during their tenure in office. By 1931, new words and usages based on his name had entered the country's cultural vocabulary:

—"Hooverville": a temporary bivouac of homeless, unemployed citizens.
—"Hoover blankets": the newspapers used by people to keep warm at night while sleeping in parks or doorways.
—"Hoover flags": empty pants pockets, turned inside out as a sign of poverty.
—"Hoover wagons": any motor vehicle pulled by horses or mules.
—In the heat of the 1932 presidential election, hitchhikers displayed signs reading "If you don't give me a ride, I'll vote for Hoover."
—Stock speculator Bernard E. Smith claimed that he made a fortune in the market between 1930 and 1932 by selling short every time the president made an optimistic pronouncement about economic recovery.

Such opinions still rule the popular conception of Hoover and the Great Depression; but in a half century of reassessment, many historians take a softer view. Unlike Harding or Coolidge, who enjoyed public esteem while in office but far less favor with later generations, Hoover's reputation has grown with the passing of time. Most scholars now reject the idea of his culpability for the economic collapse of 1929–32. They stress his innovations as well as his serious limitations as a leader. Seldom did a person enter the White House with stronger credentials or brighter promise and leave it under a darker cloud of reproach. Could Americans have selected anyone to pilot them through an economic depression during the 1920s, they would have probably chosen the Great Engineer from Iowa.

As president, for example, he signed into law a path-breaking labor law, the Norris–La Guardia Act, that curbed the use of injunctions during strikes. Yet he stubbornly refused to support direct federal relief to the victims of the Depression, many of them industrial workers. He named the greatest state jurist of his age, Benjamin Cardozo, to the Supreme Court of the United States. But he also attempted to place on that same Court the Honorable John J. Parker of North Carolina, a staunch enemy of organized labor, whose nomination was turned down by the Senate. He appointed a distinguished task force of experts who wrote an impressive analysis of the nation's many domestic problems entitled *Recent Social Trends.* But he often blamed Europeans for the Depression and ignored the many serious defects in America's economic system.

Hoover remained convinced of his own rectitude and usually treated most professional politicians in both parties with contempt. This proved to be a near fatal flaw at a time when the economic crisis required maximum cooperation between president and Congress. Although a trained engineer and businessman, accustomed to looking facts squarely in the eye, Hoover finally shrank from the grim reality of the Depression. He retreated near the end into a fantasy world, where soothing words were used to paper over the accumulating evidence of disaster. When his policies of self-help and voluntary cooperation failed again and again, he stubbornly refused to change course. His words began to depreciate as rapidly as the assets of rural banks, and he lost the most precious and elusive political capital in a democracy: trust and credibility.

Hoover had the double misfortune of occupying the White House at the beginning of the Depression and prior to FDR, one of history's most charismatic leaders. Shy, taciturn, ill at ease with crowds and politicians, Hoover would always suffer by comparison with the dashing, aristocratic Roosevelt. An introvert and a bit of a prig, he marched

*Herbert Hoover, a riddle in 1929 and for later histori-
ans.*

always to an inner drumbeat, even when it led him to political calamity. Roosevelt, on the other hand, was a debonair, charming extrovert,
who relished most social occasions and thrived in the political arena.
Less bookish and intellectual than Hoover, he drew his energy and
inspiration largely from people, whose emotions and interests he read
and played like a master conductor leading a symphony orchestra.
Roosevelt, not Hoover, became the hero of the Depression drama, the
commander in chief of a generation tested first by economic privation
and then by war. Symbolically and institutionally, FDR fashioned the
modern presidency, but in doing so he drew not only on the legacy of
his cousin Theodore and Woodrow Wilson, but also on the failed
example of Herbert Hoover. An astute William Allen White made this
same point in 1933: "So history stands hesitant, waiting for time to tell
whether Herbert Hoover by pointing the way to social recovery is the

first of the new Presidents, or whether he is the last of the old." In fact, he was both.

THE PROPHET OF VOLUNTARY COOPERATION

The most apt historical comparisons are not between Hoover and FDR, but between Hoover and earlier presidents who faced financial panics and economic depressions: Martin Van Buren in the 1830s, U. S. Grant in 1873, Grover Cleveland in the early 1890s, Theodore Roosevelt in 1907, and Harding in 1921. Judged against their standard of performance, Hoover was a dynamo of energy, a president who mobilized as never before the powers of his office and the national government to combat the spreading plague of economic collapse.

Treasury Secretary Andrew Mellon set forth the orthodox view about depressions in the wake of the stock market collapse: "Liquidate labor, liquidate stocks, liquidate farmers, liquidate real estate." Hoover spurned this advice. While perhaps appropriate to an economy of self-sufficient farmers in the eighteenth century, Mellon's callous prescription could bring only human suffering and political chaos in the interdependent capitalist society of 1929. "The economic fatalist believes that these crises are inevitable and bound to be recurrent," Hoover said. "I would remind these pessimists that exactly the same thing was once said of typhoid, cholera, and smallpox. . . . That should be our attitude toward these economic pestilences. They are not dispensations of Providence."

When the crisis hit, Hoover took action, but always within a narrow intellectual universe. His press secretary once observed that "the number of times he reversed himself or modified an important position could be counted on the fingers of one hand." Rexford Tugwell, a member of Roosevelt's "brain trust," captured the very essence of Hoover when he remarked, "We all thought he was an engineer, but, in fact, he was a moral philosopher." Engineers are task-oriented, concerned with achieving practical results. To build a bridge or dig a mine they focus first on the quality of the materials or the machinery to be employed, not on the character of the people who will build or use it. Hoover, however, worried about character.

The foundation of American civilization, Hoover believed, rested on the moral fiber of its citizens. Examining his own life and projecting it on the larger society, he equated sound morals with self-reliance and initiative. As he had conquered adversity, rising from childhood poverty to success and wealth, so might others. "The spread of government," he once wrote, "destroys initiative and thus destroys character. Character is made in the community as well as in the individual by assuming responsibilities, not by escaping them." No effort to fight the Depression, he believed, should subvert the character of Americans by violating the fundamental principles of their social and political life: individualism, self-reliance, and voluntarism.

These core concepts tapped a venerable tradition in American political thought. For nearly two centuries Americans had emphasized free will, personal autonomy, and consent, while rejecting forms of domination that arose either from the exercise of private power or official, state power. Americans, by and large, feared dependency and hated coercion. Of course, the ideal often conflicted with reality. Because of class, race, gender, or religion, some Americans had far less opportunity to choose than others. The exercise of one person's individualism or autonomy could mean the domination or exploitation of others. Certain tendencies were repressed sternly by a disapproving social consensus—for example, polygamy, homosexuality, anarchism, and communism. At some point, even voluntarism became coercion, else the principle of majority rule could not have worked in American political life. The ideals of individualism, autonomy, consent, and voluntary cooperation fueled the destruction of slavery and the campaign against monopoly, but they also prevented the adoption of minimum wage legislation, effective unionization in most industries, and the abolition of child labor.

Hoover seldom explored these contradictions. But he did set himself apart from those who touted laissez-faire, unrestricted competition, and the survival of the fittest. As secretary of commerce, he labored mightily to implement his conception of voluntary cooperation and to define the appropriate boundaries of governmental action. He endorsed a major role for government in regulating radio broadcasting and aviation. These industries resembled traditional public utilities, and unchecked competition threatened the economy, human safety, and the profits of initial investors. But for most sectors of the economy, he rejected direct government controls in favor of voluntarism. Private trade associations, he believed, could rationalize and humanize competition and raise productivity by promoting uniform standards for various industries. Hoover balked, however, when these associations tried to use the government to restrict output, allocate markets, or surreptitiously fix prices, because he feared the capture of state power by special interests and classes. Of course, unrestricted competition spawned as much human misery in the coalfields or textile mills, where Hoover opposed direct government controls, as in radio or aviation, where he endorsed it, but these inconsistencies did not lead the Great Engineer to reconsider his general theories. Self-help and voluntary cooperation failed to bring stability or prosperity to many industries during the 1920s. Despite this legacy of failure, Hoover sought to extend these principles to the nation's suffering agricultural producers in one of the first major policy decisions of his administration prior to the stock market crash.

Poverty of Abundance

Redeeming a campaign pledge made in agricultural states, Hoover called the new Congress into special session in April 1929 to address the special problems of rural producers. From this session sprang both more tariff protection (which farmers did not need) and what the president called "a great instrumentality clothed with sufficient authority and resources to assist farmers." At the threshold, Hoover told congressional leaders he would veto any new tax on producers such as the equalization fee of the old McNary-Haugen bill. Nor would he support mandatory production controls, because they entailed government coercion. And he opposed any export subsidies to encourage the dumping of American farm surpluses abroad. Those subsidies cost too much and would alienate European allies.

Given these presidential strictures, the "great instrumentality" that Congress brought forth was the Federal Farm Board, the centerpiece of the Agricultural Marketing Act of 1929. Although the Farm Board was clothed with greater powers than any other agricultural agency in American history, its mandate depended mainly on the voluntary cooperation of farmers. Congress gave the nine-person board a budget of $500 million and authorized it to help farmers help themselves in several ways. First, it could make loans to existing agricultural cooperatives and finance the organization of new ones. On the production side, co-ops could use their buying power to reduce the farmer's bill for fertilizers, pesticides, and equipment. On the selling side, farmers could use these co-ops to reduce the profits of middlemen and prevent sharp price declines that resulted when crops came on the market all at once.

Congress also authorized the Farm Board to loan money to so-called crop stabilization corporations organized by cooperatives as part of their effort to promote "orderly marketing." With these loans, the stabilization corporations could buy, sell, store, and process various crops such as wheat and cotton. Because the law did not set a limit with respect to either quantity or price, the stabilization corporations could attempt to boost farm prices by making purchases above the market as long as the Farm Board lent them money. On a practical level, the Farm Board's financial support of cooperatives and stabilization corporations put the United States government directly into the business of competing with private enterprise and seeking to fix farm prices. Hoover supported it because anything less would bring down the wrath of the farm bloc and the competition would be carried out by private associations and corporations. This distinction seemed artificial to many people who advocated a larger role for the government, but for Hoover it defined a rigid boundary between economic tyranny and economic freedom.

What seemed to Hoover and others to be a bold expansion of federal aid to agriculture in the summer of 1929 proved woefully inadequate within a year. The Agricultural Marketing Act proposed a domestic solution to an international crisis. By early 1930, as waves of grain from the United States, Argentina, Canada, and the Soviet Union swamped the international market and sent wheat prices down to 85 and then 80 cents a bushel, the stabilization corporations became the only institutions supported by the Farm Board with the hope of salvaging the situation. Farmers from Iowa to the Dakotas who had borrowed money with wheat at 90 cents or $1 a bushel faced bankruptcy and foreclosure. The country banks that had made mortgage and crop loans stared at insolvency. Drawing on Farm Board funds, the Grain Stabilization Corporation, organized in February 1930, began buying surplus wheat from cooperatives and trading in futures, hoping in this way to halt the decline.

But the grain buyers proved no more successful at reversing the disintegrating market than Richard Whitney and his allies had been on Wall Street during the panic of 1929. The Grain Stabilization Corporation bought wheat in Chicago for 80 cents a bushel in January 1931, although the world price had by then plummeted below 60 cents. By summer, when it ceased to make more purchases, the corporation had become the owner of nearly 300 million bushels of wheat for which it had paid on average 82 cents. The world price was then under 40 cents and still headed down. In short, the Farm Board and the corporation had saved American farmers millions of dollars, but, in the words of one observer, they had also found "a first-class way of throwing good money in to a bottomless pit."

Within a year or so, as more farmers went broke and with them rural banks and local merchants, mandatory crop controls received a hearing in Washington. Congressional committees investigating the failure of the Farm Board in 1932 heard from Professor M. L. Wilson of Montana State, who outlined a "domestic allotment plan" that he and other agricultural economists such as John D. Black of Harvard had worked on for several years. Wilson and Black proposed to pay farmers a subsidy if they reduced acreage, an idea put into legislative form by Senator Elmer Thomas of Oklahoma. Most of Thomas's congressional colleagues thought the scheme too radical. And because it clearly violated his cherished ideal of voluntarism, Hoover helped to kill the measure by threatening a veto. In the farm belt, meanwhile, fear, frustration, and anger rose steadily as the index of wheat, corn, and cotton went down. "We farmers have been the underdogs too long," a dairyman told a reporter from a national magazine. "We have been humbugged by the politicians, cheated by the railroads . . . and now we are going to get justice or know the reason why."

THE ZENITH OF PROTECTIONISM

Apart from its futile price support activities, Hoover's Farm Board could not be blamed for making economic conditions much worse in the countryside between 1929 and 1932. The same could not be said for the other legislative accomplishment of the special congressional session in 1929, the infamous Hawley-Smoot tariff, signed into law on June 17, 1930. This tariff raised American import duties to stratospheric levels and made it even more difficult for foreign nations to earn dollars that would pay off their World War I loans. A dreary example of national selfishness, the new tariff encouraged other nations to retaliate with protectionist measures of their own. As the stock market crash helped to dry up the springs of international credit, the Hawley-Smoot tariff choked off international trade and compounded economic misery from Boise to Berlin, from San Diego to Singapore.

Hoover, Congressman Willis Hawley of Oregon, and Senator Borah hoped to restrict any tariff revision in 1929 to the agricultural sector. Instead, they opened the floodgates to a general tariff overhaul. Despite the efforts of Borah and Reed Smoot of Utah to maintain the measure's dominant agricultural flavor, they and Hoover were no match for Senator Joseph Grundy, a former president of the Pennsylvania Manufacturers Association. Grundy put together a powerful coalition of protectionist groups from the Northeast and West who rewrote the bill to give manufacturers even greater aid than the farmers. When Grundy and his allies had wrapped up their work, the rates on many items stood 50 and 100 percent above the Fordney-McCumber schedules. Even the average ad valorem rates had soared from 33 percent to 40 percent. With biting sarcasm, an editorialist in the farm belt praised Senator Grundy for giving help to all the farmers who grew cement, shoes, umbrellas, oil, bricks, and pocketknives. "In fact there is nothing the Grundyites will not do for the farmer except to give him what he wants. All they wish to do is to tax him out of house and home— perhaps on the theory that the only way to solve the farm problem is to exterminate the farmer."

The final Hawley-Smoot bill passed the Senate with only two votes to spare, which set the stage for possible intervention by the White House. Hoover could have threatened a veto unless the Grundyites gave greater concessions to agriculture and moderated their outrageously high demands for nonfarm products. The prestigious American Economics Association, representing over a thousand of the leading scholars in the profession, urged the president to reject the bill on numerous grounds. Hoover could have utilized any one of them. Despite such prescient advice, the president signed Hawley-Smoot into law with a statement that sugar-coated its protectionist features and pledged modifications through the Tariff Commission. This proved to be a huge policy blunder; for the first time the American people learned that what Herbert Hoover often said to be true did not square with the facts.

MORE VOLUNTARISM

Both the Agricultural Marketing Act and the Hawley-Smoot tariff were soon tested and found wanting in the furnace of economic decline. But neither represented Hoover's immediate response to the stock market panic. In the face of the uncertainty that rippled across the county in its wake, the president went against the grain. He took immediate, decisive, and, in retrospect, intelligent action. Darkening economic skies, according to the orthodox view, dictated retrenchment. Hoover sought to mobilize the country behind a program of economic expansion.

First, he called the nation's leading businessmen and elected officials to the White House for a series of meetings at which he urged them to continue as if the panic had not occurred. Since private corporations combined with state and local governments contributed the lion's share of investment in the economy, this plan of action made very good sense indeed.

From the captains of industry Hoover secured pledges that they would not reduce wage levels, lay off employees, engage in price cutting, or lower production. The National Business Survey Conference, led by Julius Barnes of the United States Chamber of Commerce, endorsed the president's plan and urged homeowners to spend money for "the extra sunporch, new fixtures for the bathroom, or a new floor in the cellar."

From the nation's mayors and governors, who controlled the bulk of public expenditures, Hoover secured similar pledges of aid. They would not reduce expenditures for planned public works such as roads, schools, libraries, and parks. For his part, the president promised to maintain and expand major federal construction projects for rivers and harbors, public buildings, highways, and dams. He applauded Federal Reserve Board decisions to lower interest rates. And he proposed an immediate reduction in federal personal and corporate income taxes in order to stimulate more investment and consumer spending. Hoover kept his initial promises.

The president and his corporate allies asked Americans to alter deeply ingrained patterns of behavior about how to act during moments of economic crisis and uncertainty. Although reliable statistics were hard to come by in 1930, the numbers of Americans out of work seemed to be growing. They had nothing to spend on "the extra sunporch, new fixtures for the bathroom, or a new floor in the cellar." They were lucky to have food on the table. Workers believed resolutely that the only way to weather such a crisis was by means of austerity—cutting back on expenditures, not enlarging them; saving money, not spending it. In flush times they had been willing to follow the prophets of the new profligacy. Fearing more unemployment, they repaired to the time-tested wisdom of their parents' generation: be cautious, retrench.

Businessmen cracked first, despite the persuasive efforts of the National Business Survey Conference. Concerned about a total collapse of sales, they cut production and sold off inventories. While not trimming wage levels at first, they laid off workers. Now without income, these unemployed fulfilled the grim expectation of reduced consumer spending. Corporate investment in new plant and equipment also fell off sharply from 1929 to 1931. From 15 percent of the gross national product before the crash, it had dipped to 7 percent two years later.

By the spring of 1931, wage cuts had become epidemic in key industries such as textiles and coal mining. At summer's end, United States Steel, followed by Bethlehem Steel, General Motors, and United States Rubber, announced general wage cuts between 10 and 20 percent. The gross national product had fallen almost 30 percent in two years, and unemployment stood at nearly 16 percent of the labor force. A newspaper in upstate New York reported the discovery by police of a young couple in a remote snowbound cottage. Out of work and without food for three days, they had nearly starved to death. The *New York Times* reported that 100,000 Americans had applied for work in the Soviet Union.

Promises by local pubic officials to maintain expenditures depreciated quickly once business activity declined, tax revenues shrank, and budgets became tight. Soon overwhelmed by demands for immediate relief to the unemployed, local governments from Maine to California shelved plans to refurbish city hall or build a new library. They began to lay off public employees, too. Hoover and Congress fulfilled federal spending plans, but the tax cut, touted as a powerful antidepression measure, proved to be a dud. Secretary Mellon's prior reductions had left little to trim. On a $5,000 income, for example, the reduction amounted to only $11.25. A taxpayer earning $10,000 saw his bill from Uncle Sam lowered by $55, but there were too few individuals in this bracket or even paying the income tax to make a difference. Despite the spending and the tax cuts, the United States government still had a small budget surplus at the end of the 1930 fiscal year.

Undaunted by the inability of the Farm Board or the National Business Survey Conference to generate much economic cooperation, Hoover mounted two additional efforts in banking and unemployment relief to fight by voluntary means the spreading economic and social crisis. Bankers faced a situation both simple and terrifying: too many of them, rural and urban, had made loans that went sour, especially in the stock market and real estate. While they legally held title to securities and land as collateral, banks could neither collect on the defaulted loans nor turn this collateral into cash. Who wanted to buy 10,000 shares of common stock whose market value had fallen almost to zero? Who would buy a Kansas farm with wheat selling at 30 cents a bushel?

Under intense pressure from Hoover, the nation's great bankers organized the National Credit Corporation, which opened for business in October 1931. With a capital fund of $500 million contributed by some of the country's major financial institutions, the NCC was a perfect expression of Hoover's philosophy. Bankers, not government, would help other bankers weather the storm. The NCC would use its resources to break the liquidity crisis by purchasing the dubious assets held by banks on the verge of insolvency and some of those already closed. Fear would be checked. Depositors would be reassured. Bankers generally would gain confidence and make new loans. "It is a movement of national assurance and of unity of action in an American way," declared Hoover. The National Credit Corporation, declared *Business Week*, "puts private leadership and the philosophy that sponsors it to the supreme test. The public is bound to judge the soundness of this philosophy by the results achieved."

The results proved dismal. Voluntary cooperation failed Hoover again. Testifying before Congress at the end of 1931, the head of the New York Federal Reserve Bank confessed that the National Credit Corporation had expended only a tiny fraction of its funds, about $10 million to be exact, while the banking crisis continued to get worse. Sober, cautious, judicious bankers all, the managers at the NCC proved reluctant to use the $500 million to take over most of the dubious assets offered to them by other bankers. They feared for the liquidity of the National Credit Corporation! That year, total bank failures hit 2,293, the highest of the Depression era. In his own *Memoirs*, Hoover passed a scathing judgment on the banker-run NCC. It became, he said, "ultraconservative, then fearful, and finally died."

By the time voluntarism failed among the bankers, it appeared unavailing as well in the most critical area of all: providing basic relief—food and shelter—to millions without work. With little or no savings to fall back upon, working-class and middle-class families who had earlier tasted the fruits of high mass consumption faced unpaid mortgages and bills, foreclosure, bankruptcy, and destitution. From the president's perspective, the nation's private charities and disaster relief organizations such as the Red Cross, the Salvation Army, Community Chest, the YMCA, and Travelers' Aid offered the first line of defense against the calamities of unemployment.

Hoover promptly created the President's Emergency Committee for Employment, later renamed the President's Organization of Unemployment Relief, to assist these private and state relief efforts. He appointed distinguished philanthropists and businessmen such as Colonel Arthur Woods of the Rockefeller Foundation and Walter S. Gifford of AT&T to lead these organizations. Both committees began to gather and spread information on local relief activities across the country and to urge still greater voluntary efforts. The president himself gave substantial donations to charity.

But Hoover adamantly opposed a larger role for the federal government, especially direct employment or relief payments to those without jobs. Such federal intervention, he alleged, would discourage private giving, undermine voluntarism, and destroy self-reliance by creating a class of dependent citizens. "The humanism of our system demands the protection of the suffering and the unfortunate," Hoover declared. "It places that prime responsibility upon the individual for the welfare of his neighbor, but it insists also that in necessity the local community, the State government, and in the last resort, the National government shall give protection to them."

Hoover's approach to relief received a stern test when the severe drought of 1930–31 added to the staggering woes of farmers from the Mississippi River to the Rocky Mountains. In states such as Arkansas, where temperatures soared above 100 degrees for over a month, crops withered in the field; livestock died from starvation; Red Cross workers distributed food and clothing in virtually every county. Hoover pressured the railroads to deliver feed grains into the region below normal rates. His Federal Farm Board offered farmers with sufficient collateral loans to assist in these purchases.

The president balked at more aid, however. When Congress pushed for an additional $60 million in loans to help drought victims buy fuel, feed, fertilizers, and food, Hoover raised strong objections to the last item. Feeding farmers, he argued, would put the federal government into the business of providing direct relief, similar to the hated British dole. With reluctance, the president finally accepted legislative language that permitted drought loans for fuel, feed, fertilizer, and something called "rehabilitation," which, the secretary of agriculture soon ruled, might include food. Congress proved stingy, too. The final sum appropriated for these loans, $47 million, was pathetically small in comparison to the need of the farmers. Only those with some resources could qualify for the loans, and Hoover's opposition to the food provision became another self-inflicted political wound.

Woods and Gifford, misled by haphazard information from around the country, regularly offered upbeat commentary on the national relief situation. Hoover echoed their optimism. "The country as a whole," said Woods, "has responded most heartily to the emergency. Evidence is pouring in that communities are organizing to meet their own problems." Down to the smallest village and hamlet, he added, "there has been a recrudescence of that community spirit hitherto reserved for wartime emergencies." But accumulating evidence also suggested that the tide of joblessness had overwhelmed the heroic efforts of private charities as well as state and local governments, which faced shrinking tax revenues and constitutional limits on borrowing.

By the winter of 1931, for example, Illinois labor experts estimated that 40 percent of the men and women seeking work in Chicago could not find it. Their combined lost wages amounted to $2 million a day, while the Chicago funds available from all relief organizations, private and public, totaled about $100,000 a day. Chicago therefore provided relief only to the destitute and set its payments at $2.40 per week for an adult and $1.50 per week for a child. President Hoover, meanwhile, quoting the head of the Public Health Services, affirmed that despite mounting unemployment figures and rising relief demands, "our people have been protected from hunger and cold." That statement drew fire from physicians, social workers, and state public health workers in dozens of cities. They pointed to hospital statistics that indicated a growing number of deaths attributed to starvation and illnesses associated with malnutrition. The head of the Federation of Jewish Charities in Philadelphia reported hundreds of families "reduced for actual subsistence to something of the status of a stray cat prowling for food."

New Departures

The failures of the banking community to solve voluntarily the liquidity crisis through the National Credit Corporation generated near-panic among Hoover's senior financial advisers by the end of 1931. Both Eugene Meyer, a Hoover appointee to the Federal Reserve Board, and Ogden Mills, the president's new Treasury secretary, predicted more disastrous bank failures and total economic chaos unless the federal government now intervened directly. They proposed the creation of an agency similar to the War Finance Corporation of World War I, which had been authorized by Congress to help fund enterprises deemed essential to the war effort. Hoover, also a veteran of the wartime federal bureaucracy, had been thinking along these same lines.

These ideas gave birth to the administration's first significant departure from voluntary cooperation—the Reconstruction Finance Corporation, approved by Congress in January 1932 with authorization to lend up to $2 billion of the taxpayers' money to rescue commercial banks, savings banks, trust companies, credit unions, and insurance companies. After approval of the Interstate Commerce Commission, the new agency could also lend funds to railroads on the verge of insolvency. With passage of the RFC statute, Hoover both confessed the inadequacy of voluntarism and launched the boldest antidepression measure ever undertaken by the national government.

In the face of complaints that the administration's first dose of direct federal aid targeted financial institutions and corporations instead of people out of work, Hoover declared that the RFC was "not created for the aid of big industries or big banks." Secretary Mills said he looked upon the new agency as "an insurance measure more than anything else," a psychological stimulus that would restore confidence in financial institutions and make massive federal loans unnecessary. Hoover and later apologists for the RFC in 1932–33 argued that the agency had done its best to help the little people in the financial and business world. They pointed to statistics showing that 90 percent of the loans authorized by the RFC went to small and medium-sized banks and that over 70 percent of such authorizations had been made to help institutions in cities or towns with fewer than five thousand inhabitants.

Critics of the RFC read the agency's statistics differently. They focused on the size of the loans, not on the absolute number. By this measure, for instance, 7 percent of the borrowers, usually the largest banks, got over half the money lent by the agency in its first two years. Of the first $61 million committed by the RFC, $41 million went to just three institutions, and one—former vice president Charles Dawes's own Central Republic National Bank and Trust Company—tapped the agency for a total of $90 million after the Chicago financier resigned from the RFC and went back home in a vain attempt to prevent its reorganization.

RFC loans to railroads and public utilities presented a similar picture. Again, the largest dollar amounts went to the biggest companies. While some experts noted that it made very little economic sense to saddle debt-ridden enterprises such as the railroads with additional loan obligations—even from benevolent Uncle Sam—the chief complaint against the RFC centered on the issue of equity and social justice, not economic efficiency. The administration claimed that saving the largest firms from insolvency saved more jobs and prevented further economic chaos.

But by the summer of 1932, the Hoover administration had great difficulty explaining why the federal government should directly assist faltering corporations but not destitute workers and their families. An angry spokesman for North Dakota farmers announced to Congress: "The same people who have cried, 'Socialism' against us Bolsheviks out on the farm, have gone to the United States Government and asked for the most socialist program that has ever been put over in the history

Eugene Meyer, head of the RFC.

of this Government. We feel that, without any blush of shame, we can come and ask for the same thing."

Senators Robert La Follette, Jr., of Wisconsin and Edward Costigan of Colorado along with Congressman James Lewis of Illinois emerged as champions of direct federal aid to the unemployed. Their bill, introduced almost simultaneously with the initial RFC measure in late 1931, proposed the creation of a Federal Emergency Relief Board authorized to spend $375 million to assist the states in their efforts to provide food, clothing, and shelter to the jobless.

Hoover quickly denounced the La Follette–Costigan–Lewis bill as extravagant and destructive of the constitutional balance between the states and the federal government. Other congressional leaders sided with the president. Although the Republicans' advantage in the Senate and House had been cut substantially in the elections of 1930, the Southern Democrats, who now held the balance of power in Congress, were not prepared to support so bold an initiative. They too feared runaway federal spending and national intervention; such policies might disturb the racial status quo in their region. When finally put to a vote in February 1932, the bill fell fourteen votes short in the Senate.

By the summer of 1932, however, the case for some federal aid to the unemployed had become almost irresistible. By then, the RFC's generosity to banks and utilities was generally known. Hoover finally endorsed a bill sponsored by Senator Robert Wagner of New York and

House majority leader Henry T. Rainey that authorized the RFC to loan up to $1.5 billion to states for the purpose of financing local public works. The president and congressional leaders made certain, however, that this so-called Emergency Relief and Construction Act would not degenerate into a direct federal relief program.

In order to be even eligible for RFC loans under the new Emergency Relief and Construction Act, state governments had to take a virtual pauper's oath by declaring that they had reached the end of their constitutional tether with respect to borrowing and taxation. In addition, only "self-liquidating" public works, those that would produce revenues to pay off the federal loan, could be funded. This provision sharply limited types of construction and the kinds of workers—generally the more skilled—who would be hired under the program. The federal government thus entered the relief business, indirectly and with great reluctance. Hoover and congressional leaders had been driven there by necessity, not moral conviction. The governor of New York, Franklin Roosevelt, although opposed like Hoover to the dole, told his con-

"While Washington Makes Up Its Mind . . ." (caption). On the issue of relief to the unemployed, Congress also remained confused and divided.

stituents plainly in 1931 that government aid to the jobless "must be extended . . . not as a matter of charity, but as a matter of social duty." In 1932, however, his remained a minority voice among the nation's political leaders.

The creation of the Reconstruction Finance Corporation and approval of the Emergency Relief and Construction Act represented the limits of Herbert Hoover's willingness to utilize directly the fiscal and legal resources of the national government to combat the Depression. Both proved pathetically inadequate. The agency's modest lending activities in 1932–33 could not halt the slide into economic darkness. Yet very few leaders in either major party advocated more radical measures. La Follette and Costigan could not get a direct relief bill through even one house of Congress. And had Hoover abandoned voluntary cooperation earlier and sanctioned creation of the RFC in 1931, it is not likely that RFC loans to the banks, railroads, utilities, and states would have turned the tide. The economic collapse now outran political initiatives. Hoover did take two final actions in 1932 that sealed his fate, however: he raised people's taxes and he drove World War I veterans from the nation's capital.

Budgets and Bonuses

By the spring and summer of 1932, nothing meant more to Hoover than balancing the federal budget. The president and his key advisers believed that unless the government practiced fiscal responsibility by paying its own bills each year, all of their antidepression measures would be eroded by a general loss of confidence. A balanced budget, he declared, was "the most essential factor to economic recovery"; it was "the foundation of all public and private financial stability." But by early 1932 the federal red ink mounted to over $2 billion as antidepression spending rose while fewer tax dollars came into the Treasury because of falling personal and corporate income. Further borrowing by the government, the president said, would only increase the deficit and make it harder for corporations to raise capital. The fact that private borrowing remained stagnant and that a tax increase would further dampen consumer spending did not weaken Hoover's resolve. His was not the only voice urging fiscal restraint. Democrats and liberal Republicans in Congress wanted larger public works spending, but virtually all of the Democratic Party leadership criticized the growing deficit and urged the president to balance the budget.

Act Hoover did. On June 6, 1932, he signed into law the largest peacetime tax hike in American history. Liberal Democrats in the House, led by New York's Fiorello La Guardia, scuttled the president's request for an increase in the general sales tax by arguing that it would hit hardest those least able to pay. In addition to new levies on income, the bill raised excise taxes on luxuries such as yachts and jewelry and imposed a new gift tax on the wealthy as well.

But whatever its equitable features, the Revenue Act of 1932 was a wholly counterproductive measure. In a time of soaring unemployment, business failures, and waning consumer demand, the tax increase demonstrated the power of symbolism over substance. The administration and a majority of senators and representatives preferred building confidence with bankers and businessmen by budget balancing to filling empty stomachs with public works jobs and relief payments. During the final showdown in the House, speaker John Garner of Texas, his voice choked with emotion, left his chair and pleaded with his colleagues from the well of the chamber to keep faith with the American people by displaying fiscal responsibility. Those in favor of a balanced budget should stand up and be counted, said the speaker. No member of the House stayed seated.

Two weeks after the Revenue Act became law, the United States Senate engaged in another act of fiscal responsibility. It refused to advance the payment to World War I veterans of their "adjusted compensation certificates," or bonuses, scheduled for disbursement in 1945. Nearly twenty-thousand veterans, calling themselves the Bonus Expeditionary Force (and also called the Bonus Army or Bonus Marchers), had assembled in the Capitol plaza during the Senate debate. The veterans received the news of their legislative defeat stoically. Then, following the advice of their leader, Sergeant Walter S. Waters of Portland, they marched back to their tar-paper shacks and tents on the other side of the Anacostia River. Their decorum and calm contrasted sharply with the fury of law enforcement and military forces soon unleashed against them.

Congress first passed a veteran's bonus bill, over Coolidge's veto, in 1925. Based on years of service, it provided a Treasury-paid endowment for each veteran, payable in full at the end of twenty-five years. In 1931, responding to further demands from the nation's former servicemen, Congress adopted additional legislation permitting veterans to borrow up to 50 percent of the value of their certificates. Hoover predictably vetoed the bill because it would, he said, "provide an enormous sum of money to a vast majority who are able to care for themselves." Congress overrode him.

A year later, the veterans came back for more. With many of their number now unemployed, they demanded immediate payment of the entire bonus. On grounds of equity and economics, they had a good case. The federal government had begun to spend public funds to assist farmers, banks, utilities, and railroads. And like the public works projects funded by the RFC, the bonus money would increase consumer spending. Led by Representative Wright Patman of Texas, the House passed the bonus bill, but barely a third of the Senate could be persuaded to vote for it.

Hoover meanwhile refused to meet with the veterans or their representatives throughout their stay in Washington, although as president he found time to greet a heavyweight wrestling champion and delegates from various fraternal organizations. How long after the Senate vote the Bonus Army would have remained in Washington, camped in vacant federal buildings and on Anacostia Flats, is difficult to say. They had fashioned a sophisticated social organization complete with a newspaper and committees that handled everything from cooking to sanitation.

At the same time, the Senate vote and the adjournment of Congress on July 16 deflated the hopes of a great many who had waited patiently outside the Capitol. At Hoover's request, Congress appropriated $100,000 to assist those who wanted to go home. The money advanced was to be deducted from the final bonus. Even on these Scrooge-like terms, perhaps a quarter of the veterans had already left Washington when Secretary of War Patrick Hurley and Treasury Secretary Mills made an announcement—the government would begin to clear several vacant buildings of Bonus Marchers in order to rehabilitate the structures. Many questioned the urgent necessity for these removals, especially the superintendent of the District of Columbia police, Brigader General Pelham D. Glassford, who had cultivated friendly and civilized relations with the veterans and helped to keep the demonstrations peaceful. It is virtually certain that Hurley hoped to provoke an incident; further, he would not have acted without the knowledge of the president.

The showdown came on July 28, when police attempted to carry out Hurley's orders by removing veterans from two buildings. Until then, the communist-led faction in the Bonus Army had been more strident than influential. When force replaced patience, the communists' influence rose. The police retreated from one building under a barrage of bricks and garbage. In the second assault, an officer tripped, accidentally discharged his revolver, and triggered a burst of gunfire by other policemen who mistakenly thought themselves under attack. When the smoke had cleared, two veterans lay dead.

Later that afternoon, Hoover ordered federal troops under General Douglas MacArthur into the streets of the nation's capital to restore order. Despite pleas to the president from Glassford and several senators not to send the soldiers across the river to the main Bonus Army camp, MacArthur marched on to Anacostia with his cavalry, six machine-gun-laden tanks, and infantry with bayonets at the ready. Men, women, and children fled in panic before the soldiers, who fired off tear-gas bombs and burned down the BEF's tents and shanties. By nightfall, one infant had died from the gas attack. The remnants of the Bonus Army fled into the Maryland countryside, many nursing wounds and bruises. Plumes of acrid smoke drifted over Capitol Hill.

Although MacArthur had not followed the orders of his commander in chief when assaulting the veterans, Hoover and his advisers attempted to diffuse criticism of the administration by heaping blame on the protesters. The president claimed that the Bonus Army threatened the very existence of the government of the United States, a point of view shared by MacArthur, who equated his former comrades in arms with foreign invaders occupying the nation's capital. A War Department official branded them a "mob of tramps and hoodlums, with a generous sprinkling of Communist agitators." Secretary of War Hurley claimed MacArthur's soldiers treated the BEF with "unparalleled humanity and kindness."

Americans who viewed news photographs and reports in the following days thought otherwise. Whatever their opinion about the bonus, they found it hard to believe that the men, women, and children gassed and manhandled by the military constituted a revolutionary menace or were pawns of the Communist Party. "If the Army must be called out to make war on unarmed citizens," wrote one newspaper, "this is no longer America." At the Veterans of Foreign Wars convention in Sacramento, California, the members condemned "the unhumanitarian and un-American manner" in which the administration had dealt with their fellows. General Glassford, speaking around the country, accused Hoover of pushing the panic button and manufacturing the incidents that led to tragedy. "The peacetime army of our present commander in chief," he said to large crowds, "drove from the National Capital at

Police from the District of Columbia battle members of the Bonus Army at Anacostia Flats, 1932.

the point of the bayonet the disarmed, disavowed and destitute army of Woodrow Wilson."

In mishandling the Bonus Army, Hoover made his last and greatest political blunder. His belief in voluntary cooperation, his constitutional scruples, his fiscal conservatism—these might be forgiven, but not sending tanks and cavalry against unarmed civilians. That smacked too much of newsreels from Italy, Germany, or China. In symbol and substance, events beyond America's shores began to close in on Herbert Hoover, too.

BITTER MEMORIES

In 1930 as unemployment mounted, banks closed, and soup kitchens opened, Americans flocked to movie theaters across the country to relive the horror and confusion of World War I. The film that most touched them in this first year of the Great Depression was *All Quiet on the Western Front*, a haunting rendition of Erich Maria Remarque's 1929 novel. Directed by Lewis Milestone, *All Quiet on the Western Front* held unforgettable images of gas attacks, rotting corpses, and hungry

rats. Such suffering evoked sympathy for the film's two main characters, German infantrymen played by Lew Ayres and Louis Wolheim,
and left a vivid sense of the war's complete futility.

As their own domestic economic order began to erode and its crum-
bling touched the world, many Americans saw in this film a grim
reminder of the dangers of idealism, the folly of involvement in foreign
quarrels, and the imperative to steer an independent course in international affairs. These assumptions were tested and found wanting by
some Republican leaders in the next few years, but no alternative seemed
more palatable to most Americans, who daily grew more anxious about
their own security and welfare.

As with the domestic economy he inherited on March 4, 1929, Hoover attempted to pick up the pieces of Coolidge's floundering foreign
policy. This was especially the case with disarmament, an issue over
which the previous administration had stumbled badly at Geneva. Two
weeks before the Wall Street crash, however, the Quaker who abhorred
war and budget deficits met at his mountain retreat in the Virginia
mountains with the new British prime minister, Ramsay MacDonald.
The first leader of the Labour Party to head his majesty's government,
MacDonald had opposed England's entry into the Great War and hoped
to shift the country's priorities from military to social spending. Soon,
both he and Hoover would be destroyed politically by the economic
crisis, but now they made history. The prime minister and the president quickly agreed to a formula permitting each naval power to tailor
cruiser construction to its own military needs while still imposing a
ceiling on total tonnage. With their two nations at least in accord, the
Americans and the British invited the other great powers to London in
early 1930 for another round of naval talks.

The care and diligence that Hoover and his secretary of state, Henry
Stimson, lavished on the London conference brought tangible results:
a six-year treaty signed by the United States, Britain, and Japan. It set
cruiser, destroyer, and submarine tonnage ratios almost identical to
those put in place earlier at the Washington Conference. The London
pact also included a provision outlawing submarine attacks without
warning, a principal American grievance during World War I.

Although limited and filled with loopholes, the treaty hammered out
at London represented the high tide of disarmament sentiment in the
post-Versailles era. There would not be others. In Japan, for example,
an angry debate erupted over provisions of the London treaty. Conservatives and military leaders, growing stronger in the cabinet, denounced
the pact because England and the United States retained a 30 percent

naval superiority. Not long after its approval in Tokyo, assassins murdered one of the treaty's leading supporters, Prime Minister Yuko Hamagachi. Two years later, when Hoover proposed scrapping a third of all arms to a new League-sponsored conference in Geneva, only silence greeted his plan. By January 1933, Germany's new government, headed by Adolf Hitler, openly advocated rearmament.

THINGS FALL APART

On the eve of the Great Crash, the Republicans who had managed America's foreign relations since 1920 could claim that with a small commitment of the nation's resources, time, and energy they had fashioned a new world order of peace, disarmament, and prosperity, especially in Western Europe. Fueled by private American investments and loans, the German economy revived, which permitted successive Weimar governments to meet their reparations payments to England and France. The Allies, in turn, continued to pay their American creditors. In a series of treaties signed at Locarno, Italy, in 1925, the Germans, French, and Belgians agreed to respect the borders established at Versailles. They agreed also to maintain a demilitarized zone west of the Rhine, and to settle all disputes peacefully. England and Italy guaranteed what observers called "the spirit of Locarno." Germany soon joined the League of Nations and signed the Kellogg-Briand Pact. The last foreign troops began to leave German soil a few months after the U.S. stock market collapsed. By the fall of 1929, virtually every great power except the United States had extended diplomatic recognition to the Bolsheviks in Russia. They too had taken the pledge renouncing war as an instrument of policy.

The fragility of this international goodwill and harmony became quickly evident once the bubble of economic prosperity burst in the United States. The liquidity crisis that gripped America's banks in the wake of the market debacle choked off foreign and domestic loans. The drying up of American credit, coupled with the rising tariff walls of the Hawley-Smoot Act, dealt a heavy blow to the world's economies, which depended on a steady flow of capital from New York and access to North American markets. Contrary to Hoover's interpretation, the Depression began in America and spread elsewhere. The value of international trade fell by almost $500 million from 1929 to 1930, and a year later it had declined by nearly $1.2 billion. At the same time, world production plummeted by about 25 percent, throwing workers into unemployment lines from Liverpool to Vienna.

Cut off from American credit and markets, the German government sought to remedy its mounting economic problems in 1931 by negotiating a common market or customs union with Austria. But this plan, rekindling fears of German hegemony in Europe, drew a heated response from the French, who claimed that it violated the Versailles Treaty. When the Germans backed down, economic anxieties rose throughout Central Europe and triggered a run on numerous banks, including Austria's very large Creditanstalt, which collapsed in early June. Now tottering on the edge of bankruptcy, the Weimar government announced a suspension of its reparations payments and the possibility of defaulting on all its loans, too. Bankers everywhere trembled at the news.

The German crisis forced Hoover to take decisive action on what Stimson always referred to as "the damned debts." The president feared a chain reaction—France might resort to military action as in the past; a German default would further undermine America's banks; the Allies might stop debt service and trigger retaliation in Congress. On June 21, therefore, the president declared that the United States would defer the collection of all intergovernmental debts for eighteen months if other nations agreed to do the same. Hoover's "moratorium" was probably the most decisive and popular action of his final years in office. But since it only recognized the inevitable, the moratorium did virtually nothing to arrest the collapse of the world economy.

The debt moratorium did not prevent the downward plunge in England. Unemployment there soon reached 25 percent and brought both the end of MacDonald's Labour government and the abandonment of the gold standard. This last act, by making British goods cheaper on the international market, also threatened a bitter trade war. In Germany, the economic chaos pumped new life into Hitler's National Socialist Party, whose numbers in the Reichstag grew from twelve in 1928 to 107 by 1930. The former World War I corporal blamed his nation's misery on the Versailles Treaty, communists, international bankers, chain stores, and, above all, the Jews. From Munich to Hamburg, many Germans cheered his message of revenge and hate. By the summer of 1932, the Nazis, although still short of a majority, constituted the largest bloc in the German parliament with 230 seats.

RISING SUN

The official demise of the post-Versailles world came first in Asia, however, not in Europe. Two days after the Labour government resigned in London, Japanese soldiers blew up their own railway tracks near the Manchurian town of Mukden. Since trains continued to move over the South Manchurian Railway, confirming the fabrication, the damage was not serious, but Japanese military leaders on the scene blamed the Chinese for the incident. Japan proceeded to send over ten thousand troops against Mukden and other towns in a band stretching almost one-hundred miles south and west of the railroad. On October 8, 1931, having crushed Chinese resistance on the ground, Japanese planes bombed Chinchow, 130 miles from the South Manchurian Railway. Clearly, the Japanese military, present in Manchuria since the turn of the century, meant to conquer the entire region for the Empire of the Rising Sun.

For over thirty years, Japan had enjoyed extensive economic and legal privileges in the three eastern provinces of Manchuria, including ownership of the South Manchurian Railway and the Antung-Mukden Railway, which connected Manchuria to Japan's major colony in Korea. Japan regarded Korea as her Cuba and Manchuria as her Central America. Other powers, busy exploiting their own leaseholds and privileges in China, seldom questioned Japanese behavior in either place. No nation dared to challenge Japan's formidable Kwantung Army.

That army, moreover, not the civilian government in Tokyo, called the tune in Manchuria. It did so, however, to a score made popular by many Japanese politicians, businessmen, and intellectuals, who argued that Japan ought to shake off the inferior military and economic status imposed by the Western powers and drive the white imperialists out of Asia. Japanese nationalists pointed to the disarmament treaties and America's anti-Asian immigration laws as examples of Western arrogance and racism; these affronts could be checked only when Japan took its rightful place as the most important power in East Asia.

The deepening world depression, which closed foreign markets and restricted trade, also made an expanded Manchurian empire attractive to Japan's leaders in 1931. New agricultural lands would ease population problems at home and secure important food supplies; Manchuria's rich deposits of iron ore and coal would fuel the nation's industrial development. Finally, the Kwantung Army leaders feared the further growth of Chinese nationalism and military strength under an ambitious new leader, General Chiang Kai-shek.

Chiang, married to the daughter of China's great revolutionary leader, Sun Yat-sen, had already begun to consolidate his power over various warlords and the communists. He vowed to restore China's sovereignty by ending foreign exploitation. In 1929 Chiang's regime had mounted a reckless military campaign against the Soviet Union in northern Manchuria, where it sought to wrest control from the Russians of the Chinese Eastern Railway. The general's regime in Nanking had also launched a nationwide boycott of all Japanese cotton goods. Chiang posed no military threat to Japanese interests in 1931, but the Kwantung Army leaders came to believe that only a preemptive strike could secure their future.

The Hoover administration held few cards in Asia. On the one hand, it had displayed little sympathy for the resurgence of Chinese nationalism; on the other, it had been curtly rebuffed by the Russians when it urged a cease fire in the Eastern Railway conflict. Still, the boldness of Japan's Manchurian offensive demanded some response from a nation that professed to believe in the Open Door, the Washington Conference's Nine-Power Treaty, the Kellogg-Briand Pact, and protecting its own stake in East Asia. What to do? Clearly, the United States lacked a credible military presence in the area. America's troop strength in the Philippines was minuscule. Great Britain, racked by an internal economic and political crisis, was unlikely to act with much conviction. Close cooperation with the League of Nations would call down the wrath of isolationists in Congress. The president and his secretary of state commanded, therefore, largely an arsenal of words.

The Manchurian crisis brought to the surface of policy formation a sharp personality clash between Hoover and Stimson; a conflict long suppressed by the absence of serious issues and the usual veneer of political etiquette. A seasoned lawyer who prized rigorous analysis and crisp answers, Stimson loathed Hoover's philosophical musings and his penchant for gathering piles of information. Attending cabinet meetings with the president, he once noted sourly, was "like sitting in a bath of ink."

Even before Japanese troops marched across Manchuria, the former artillery commander and secretary of war confided to his diary a conversation with Elihu Root: "I told him [Root] frankly that I thought the President being a Quaker and an engineer did not understand the psychology of combat the way Mr. Root and I did." As the confrontation with Tokyo heated up, Stimson complained that Hoover "has not got the slightest element of even the fairest kind of bluff." According to William Castle, a Hoover partisan in the State Department, the president thought his secretary "more of a warrior than a diplomat," and that Stimson "would have had us in a war with Japan before this if he had his way."

Hoover's caution sprang from sources other than Quaker pacifism. Like Castle and others, he admired Japan's economic progress. Japan's action, he hinted to the cabinet, might have been justified by the failure of the Chinese to maintain law and order and by the military's genuine fear of communist infiltration from the Soviet Union. Sanctions by the League of Nations, he believed, would not be supported by other great powers, especially England and France. Alone, the United States could do little; public denunciations or threats against Japan might make matters even worse.

In the end, compared to the dovish Hoover, Stimson emerged as a hawk against Tokyo, but his initial strategy had been one of caution, too. Until almost the end of December 1931, Stimson believed that the civilian politicians in Japan would curb the appetite of generals in Manchuria. Nursing this vain hope and not wishing "to play into the hands of . . . nationalist agitators," he therefore opposed creation of a League of Nations fact-finding commission that ultimately demolished Japan's claims to have acted in self-defense. When the Scripps-Howard newspapers beat the drums for vigorous action against Japan, Stimson gave Roy Howard a sharp lecture on "the folly of taking an aggressive step" without a long-range plan to back it up.

By January 1932, Stimson had lost his illusion about the balance of power in Japan and embraced Hoover's suggestion to send notes to Japan and China that reaffirmed the old principles set forth by Bryan in 1915: the United States would not recognize any territorial changes created in violation of her existing treaty rights. This so-called Stimson-Hoover Doctrine made pointed reference to both the Nine-Power Treaty of 1922 and, of course, the Kellogg-Briand Pact. For the president, the affirmation of moral and legal rights against Japan was sufficient.

For Stimson, however, the note represented only the beginning. He wished to keep the Japanese government guessing about America's next move by utilizing bluff, public opinion, and even the prospect of economic sanctions in cooperation with the League. Stimson's resolve hardened two weeks after the dispatch of his notes when Japanese planes and seventy-thousand soldiers attacked Shanghai, seven-hundred miles south of Mukden. The Japanese intended only to bloody Chiang's nose and to discourage any Chinese counterattack. From America's perspective, however, the Shanghai offensive appeared part of a conspiracy to subdue all of China.

In late February, Stimson raised the ante when he released the text of a letter to Senator Borah suggesting that continued Japanese violations of the Nine-Power Treaty and the Open Door would leave the United States with little choice but to reconsider the naval treaties and fortify its Pacific bases, especially Guam and the Philippines. These stakes were too high for Hoover, however. He kept his distance from the Borah letter, denounced the idea of a privately organized economic boycott of Japan, and forced Stimson to delete passages from a speech to be delivered in New York in which the secretary suggested that the United States would back any League sanctions against Japan with an embargo of its own.

Even before the president shortened Stimson's leash, the Kwantung Army had installed its own governors in the Manchurian provinces, renamed them the republic of Manchukuo, and proclaimed its independence from Chinese authority. And one year after Stimson's letter to Borah, on February 24, 1933, Japanese delegates permanently walked out of the League of Nations in Geneva, and compared that body's criticism of its Manchurian campaign with the crucifixion of Christ.

Eight years later, as Japanese bombs rained death and destruction at Pearl Harbor, Stimson emerged for some as a farsighted statesman, a man whose tough-minded strategy in 1931–32 could have prevented a larger, bloodier war in Asia; Hoover was lumped with the appeasers, someone whose timidity had encouraged more aggression in the thirties. Forty years later, as American troops left a hopeless war in Vietnam, Hoover became the prophet of peace who wisely shunned a land war in Asia, Stimson the bellicose militarist too willing to sacrifice American youth to the dreams of empire. Thus time often rearranges historical interpretations and reputations. In this case, however, both perspectives are distorted.

Stimson never contemplated direct American military action against Japan in 1931–32, for one very good reason: the United States would have to fight alone, and it was ill prepared to do so. Given this fundamental premise, Hoover correctly questioned the usefulness of the secretary's strategy, which rested on pure illusion and bluff. On the other hand, Japan in 1931–32 represented a far greater threat to American interests in Asia and to the general peace of the region than Vietnamese communists in the 1960s. Blinded by his admiration for Japan's economic prowess and by his loathing for communism, Hoover could

Secretary of State Henry L. Stimson.

not confront that reality or the obvious death of the Kellogg-Briand world.

Finally, neither Stimson nor Hoover had an answer to a pungent Japanese observation. Yosuke Matsuoka, Japan's spokesman at the League of Nations, noted bitterly that his country had learned the game of conquest and empire by watching the Europeans and Americans carve up weaker nations in Asia and Latin America. In the summer of 1932, however, the eyes of most Depression-battered Americans focused not on Geneva, where the League was slowly dying, or on Nanking, Shanghai, or Berlin. They had turned to Chicago, where Republicans and Democrats assembled to choose the next president.

2

The Making of the President, 1932

A kind of amiable Boy Scout.
—Walter Lippmann on FDR

—My friends, my policy is as radical as American liberty.
—Franklin D. Roosevelt

BREAKING TRADITION

Many in the crowd at Chicago's Midway Airport on the afternoon of July 2, 1932, breathed easier when they caught sight of the silver Ford Trimotor approaching the runway. The plane was nearly three hours late from Albany, New York. It had refueled in Buffalo and Cleveland and been buffeted by squalls and fierce headwinds that slowed its progress and churned the stomachs of its passengers. Now as the plane touched down and taxied to a stop, the crowd cheered and surged forward to meet its principal occupant, who emerged smiling and buoyant after the nine-hour ordeal: the fifty-year-old governor of New York, Franklin Delano Roosevelt, since ten o'clock the night before the Democratic Party's nominee and very likely the next president of the United States.

"Let it from now on be the task of our Party to break foolish traditions," a beaming Roosevelt told the Democrats later that evening in Chicago Stadium. The American people wanted two things, he said: "Work and security—these are more than words. They are more than facts. They are the spiritual values, the true goal toward which our efforts of reconstruction should lead." He closed with words reminiscent of Theodore Roosevelt's Bull Moose movement two decades earlier: "I pledge you, I pledge myself, to a new deal for the American people. . . . This is more than a political campaign; it is a call to arms. Give me your help, not to win votes alone, but to win in this crusade to restore American to its own greatness."

Roosevelt's decision to fly to Chicago was bold, unprecedented, and a bit risky. One of his key advisers, Louis Howe, opposed it—he feared the plane might crash and give the nomination to the party' vice-presidential candidate, John Garner of Texas. In a day when air travel remained primitive, uncomfortable, and dangerous, FDR defied the odds. He also ignored another tradition, which said that a nominee did not accept the party's mantle at the convention. Herbert Hoover had broken partially with that in 1928, when he delivered his acceptance speech to a large rally at Stanford Stadium, two months after his nomination. FDR now went a step further. The third summer of the Depression, he reasoned, was no ordinary time. With nearly a quarter of the labor force idle, factories shut down, banks continuing to fail, farmers on the verge of revolt, and the national government adrift, Roosevelt believed that the emotional state of the nation and his own political future demanded innovation. It was not the last time he would ignore convention and do the unexpected. He would soon rattle the country's political foundations as well.

The words "new deal" captured the headlines the next morning and entered the political culture. But in his famous acceptance speech, FDR also advocated some very traditional nostrums for getting the country out of its economic predicament. He pledged to cut taxes and to balance the budget. "Government—Federal and state and local—costs too much," Roosevelt told the Democrats. "We must abolish useless offices. We must eliminate unnecessary functions of Government—functions in fact that are not definitely essential to the continuance of Government." Calvin Coolidge and generations of later conservatives could have endorsed those goals with enthusiasm. The plane trip, the speech—together they were vintage Roosevelt: unusual, daring, eloquent, yet flecked with canniness and caution. The speech, written with the aid of several advisers who held conflicting views about political strategy and public policy, contained both radical and conservative elements. So did the man delivering it.

"A Prominent and Democratic Fellow"

The candidate chosen by the Democrats to lead the nation out of the economic wilderness had never known material hardship. Unlike Hoover, a self-made millionaire, Franklin Roosevelt's family had been well off for generations. Unlike Hoover, too, he enjoyed the consistent warmth and affection of doting parents. His father, James Roosevelt, was the very embodiment of the Victorian country gentleman, a man who never allowed his business affairs (chiefly railroads and coal mining) to interfere with the enjoyment of the family's estate at Hyde Park on the Hudson. James did not dissipate the Roosevelt inheritance, but neither did he swell it through a single-minded devotion to money-making like his neighbors the Vanderbilts.

A vestryman and warden of St. James Episcopal Church in Hyde Park, a town selectman, and a member of the board of the local state hospital, James Roosevelt taught his son the importance of *noblesse oblige*—those blessed with wealth and good fortune had a duty to serve the community and help the less fortunate. He also instilled in Franklin a love for country life, horsemanship, and sailing in the Bay of Fundy near the island of Campobello, where he built a summer home. In 1880, four years after the death of his first wife, the fifty-two-year-old James Roosevelt married twenty-six-year-old Sara Delano, the strikingly beautiful daughter of another member of the Dutchess County gentry. Their child Franklin arrived two years later.

Franklin Roosevelt's mother stepped straight from the pages of an Edith Wharton novel. Well-bred, imperious, sharp-tongued, cultured but not intellectual, Sarah Delano remained absolutely secure in the knowledge that people of her class ran the country's affairs and set its moral tone. Some years later, when her son the president hosted the flamboyant Huey Long at a Hyde Park dinner, his mother was overheard to say at the table: "Who is that awful man sitting next to Franklin?" Franklin, her only child, was the sun of Sara's life. Until her death in 1941 she tried her best to run his life, too. From this regal, smothering woman, Franklin Roosevelt acquired his own unshakable self-confidence and serenity, and, no doubt, those streaks of aloofness, cruelty, and arrogance that sometimes left deep wounds on others.

At Hyde Park, the center of his emotional life for sixty-three years, Roosevelt enjoyed a protected, comfortable childhood; this was a world of manicured lawns, ponies, ice skating, sailing, and private tutors for English, French, and German. One of his playmates once asked Franklin if he had a tutor for tree climbing, too.

In the summer of 1896, as Bryan and McKinley battled for the White

House, young Franklin entered the exclusive Groton School near Boston. He arrived with his parents in a private railroad car, an entrance overshadowing even the arrival of wealthier classmates named Morgan, Whitney, and Thayer. "It is hard to leave my darling boy," Sara confided to her diary. "James and I both feel this parting very much."

At Groton, it was the old virtues that mattered—good manners, patriotism, sportsmanship, Christianity, and respect for learning. Here the male offspring of wealthy Anglo-Saxon families from the Northeast, Roosevelt among them, fell under the influence of the school's rector, Endicott Peabody. "You know he would be an awful bully if he weren't such a terrible Christian," Averell Harriman later observed of Groton's leader. Somewhat less charitably, novelist Louis Auchincloss wrote of Peabody: "A man who considers that Theodore Roosevelt was America's greatest statesman and 'In Memoriam' England's finest poem is well equipped to train young men for the steam room of the Racquet Club."

In fact, Peabody helped train generations of socially prominent young men who spent more time in the public arena than in the steam room, including diplomats Harriman, Dean Acheson, and Sumner Welles,

Franklin Roosevelt, age two, with his first dog, Budgy, and pet donkey.

Senator Bronson Cutting, and FDR's wartime attorney general, Francis Biddle. Groton's motto, *Cui servire est regnare* ("To serve Him is to rule"), captured Peabody's philosophy of education: heavy on Christian ethics and morality, light on the academics. In the pulpit and on the playing fields, Peabody admonished his charges daily concerning the difference between right and wrong. He told them that God kept a record of unclean thoughts and idleness, that the rich had a duty to aid the poor and that the essence of manliness was to fight hard, always do your best; if you didn't win, at least be a good sport about it. Roosevelt always said that Groton and Peabody were among the most important influences in his life. That may have been an understatement.

The same could not be said of Harvard, which FDR entered in 1900. Its aging president, Charles W. Eliot, had built a distinguished university whose faculty luminaries included William James, George Santayana, George Kittredge, and Frederick Jackson Turner, but there is no evidence that Roosevelt dined heavily on their intellectual fare. In four years he eked out a C average. Lacking also great athletic skills, Roosevelt invested most of his time in the undergraduate newspaper, the *Crimson*, where as editor in chief he beat the drums on behalf of bigger budgets for the department of athletics. Out of deference to his cousin Ted, the president of the United States, he joined the local Republican Club, although the Hudson River Roosevelts had always been Democrats.

Franklin's good looks, charm, and name did not, surprisingly, provide an entrée into the exclusive Porcellian society, rejection that he took very hard, but Roosevelt never lacked for social invitations from mothers and aunts who hoped to land the president's distant cousin for one of their daughters or nieces. "Last week I dined at the Quincys', the Amorys' & the Thayers'," he wrote his mother. "I have been up every night till all hours, but am doing a little studying, a little riding & a few party calls. It is dreadfully hard to be a student, a society whirler, a 'prominent & democratic fellow,' & a fiancé all at the same time."

TESTING TIME

This reminder that her son was someone's fiancé in 1905 no doubt rankled Sara Roosevelt, who had moved to Boston following her husband's death to be closer to Franklin during his last year at Harvard.

No woman would have been good enough in his mother's eyes, but the one FDR chose seemed especially inappropriate: his distant cousin Anna Eleanor Roosevelt, the gangly, rather plain-looking daughter of Theodore Roosevelt's younger brother, Elliott.

Where FDR's childhood had been one of indulgence and affection, Eleanor's had been marked by tragedy and emotional cruelty. Her father suffered from severe bouts of alcoholism until his death when she was ten. Her mother, a strikingly beautiful woman, never forgave her for being female and physically unattractive. Mrs. Elliott Roosevelt often called her daughter "Granny." "Eleanor, I hardly know what's to happen to you," she remarked. "You're so plain that you really have nothing to do except be good." Her mother's death, two years before her father's, placed her under the care of a grandmother and governess, neither of whom provided more than harsh discipline and criticism.

Eleanor Roosevelt learned that wealth and station were no substitute for love and compassion. Deprived of the latter in her youth, she identified throughout the remainder of her life with those who also suffered emotional or material neglect. Attendance at the Allenswood School near London, run by a progressive Frenchwoman, Mlle. Souvestre, began her liberation from the social and ethnic prejudices of her class; so, ironically, did her marriage to FDR at nineteen, although for the next eleven years she seldom escaped the burdens of motherhood (giving birth to six children, one of whom died) or the domination of her husband's mother. Her husband's infidelity during the war and his life-threatening illness shortly thereafter became Eleanor's emancipation proclamation, his own Gethsemane, and the basis for a new partnership between them. It became a partnership based on realism and respect rather than fantasy and subservience.

Although he earned a law degree from Columbia, passed the bar exam, and took a position with the Wall Street firm of Carter, Ledyard, and Milburn, Roosevelt's eyes remained fixed on politics, not the courtroom. As early as 1907, he told young associates in the firm that he planned to follow in the footsteps of cousin Ted, who had given away the bride at his wedding. First he would win a seat in the New York state assembly; then he would run the Navy Department in Washington; next become governor of the Empire State. From there, it would be a logical jump to the White House. FDR nearly got it right. Instead of the state assembly, he had to settle for the upper house of the Albany legislature, where he gained a reputation as an anti-Tammany, good-government reformer before moving on to Washington during the Wilson years as Josephus Daniels's assistant in the Navy Department.

Eleanor and Franklin at Hyde Park, 1906.

Despite TR's example, FDR did not expect to make a run for the vice presidency, long regarded as the graveyard of political careers. But he did and emerged even so with an enhanced reputation from the Cox ticket's 1920 debacle. Along the way, he made valuable connections inside the Democratic Party, which positioned him well for another try at high office in New York or Washington. In fact, Roosevelt became the only defeated vice presidential candidate ever to enter the White House. However, two events almost changed the course of his history and America's.

While managing the Navy brass, settling labor disputes, and negotiating multimillion-dollar contracts, Assistant Secretary Roosevelt found time during the Great War to fall in love with Eleanor's social secretary—Lucy Mercer, the beautiful daughter of a socially prominent but impecunious Maryland family that traced its American roots back to a signer of the Declaration of Independence. This was not a grammar-school crush. Roosevelt was very serious. When Eleanor discovered some of Lucy's letters to her husband in 1918, she gave him a choice: the marriage could continue if he stopped seeing the other woman or they could divorce. Roosevelt wanted the latter. Sara Roosevelt made that choice more difficult for her wayward son: divorce Eleanor, disgrace the family, and she would cut him off financially. Lucy Mercer gave him no choice at all. A devout Catholic, she shrank finally from the prospect of marrying a divorced man whose ex-wife remained alive.

Because young Franklin Roosevelt had seldom failed to get what he wanted in life, Lucy Mercer's refusal to marry him was surely a bitter disappointment. He and Eleanor stayed together, but FDR would never again be the center of his wife's universe. His political career remained intact, assisted and encouraged by her efforts, but she would also use his success to build a separate world of friendships and activities. And this world sustained her through future disappointments and betrayals. FDR's promise to break entirely with Lucy Mercer proved empty. Although unwilling for reasons of faith to marry a divorced man, she apparently had no difficulty renewing their dormant relationship after her own spouse died in the early 1940s. It was she, not Eleanor, who was with FDR when he died at Warm Springs, Georgia.

Lucy Mercer wounded his ego, and their affair almost destroyed his marriage. Poliomyelitis nearly killed him in August 1921. Stricken while at Campobello Island after a grueling few days of sailing, fishing, jogging, and swimming, he was initially misdiagnosed by a local physician. By the time Dr. Robert W. Lovett, a polio specialist, arrived from Boston, FDR had become paralyzed from the waist down. He could not sit up in bed without help and had virtually lost control of bodily functions. Polio, a very painful disease, hit FDR with full force, espe-

Assistant Secretary of the Navy Franklin Roosevelt reviews fleet during World War I. Eleanor Roosevelt is second from left.

cially during a harrowing train ride back to New York City for further treatment in mid-September. Lovett and other doctors by then knew the grim truth: Roosevelt would not walk again on his own. If the patient reached a similar conclusion, he never let on, but remained ever optimistic about his recovery, even as weeks and months passed without noticeable improvement in the mobility of his lower body. "He has such courage," wrote Dr. George Draper, another specialist, "such ambition . . . that it will take all the skill which we can muster to lead him successfully to a recognition of what he really faces without utterly crushing him."

Spiritually, Roosevelt revived. His legs were another matter. By 1923, Lovett and the other doctors agreed that he would be paralyzed from the waist down, although his upper body, including bowel, bladder, and sexual functions, remained normal. "I cannot help feeling," Lovett wrote, "that he has almost reached the limit of his possibilities." A physically graceful and energetic man, one who had climbed the rigging of ships as assistant secretary of the Navy, now had to rely on a wheelchair, heavy metal leg braces, crutches, and the support of others when leaving automobiles and trains. Faced with this daunting physical handicap, Roosevelt could have chosen the life of a wealthy, pampered invalid. His mother preferred this role for her son in the hope of renewing FDR's dependency. Instead, propelled by his own ambition and encouraged by Eleanor, his secretary Missy LeHand, and press adviser Louis Howe, FDR resolved to continue a life of public service.

Roosevelt's biographers and historians of the New Deal continue to debate the impact of polio on the future president's character and career. Some agree with Frances Perkins, FDR's secretary of labor, who claimed that the ordeal worked a spiritual metamorphosis, changing a callow playboy into a more serious, reflective person. Others, noting that basic structural changes in personality seldom occur after adolescence, question this radical transformation theory, but suggest that the crisis probably strengthened many of Roosevelt's positive traits: his enormous self-confidence and optimism, for example, received their sternest possible test and emerged unscathed. And this optimism, often communicated to the American people during the greatest social crisis of their time, became Roosevelt's most precious political asset. His withered legs also gave the aristocratic Roosevelt something in common with those many Americans who saw themselves as outcasts or marginal people because of physical handicaps, economic deprivation, or racial and religious prejudice. He too, despite family, wealth, and education, was now part of a minority group. As one scholar shrewdly noted, crutches became FDR's log cabin.

POLITICAL REBIRTH

An indifferent lawyer, Roosevelt abandoned efforts to make a living at the bar, much to the relief of his partners Grenville Emmett and Langdon Marvin. He maintained a formal practice with his former Harvard Law School classmate D. Basil "Doc" O'Connor, another trusted political confidant. Like millions of others attracted by the bustling business environment of the Coolidge era, FDR tried to strike it rich in several ventures—notably vending machines—but succeeded only in losing money. As the unpaid president of the American Construction Council, a trade association for builders, he also mirrored the attitudes of the time by often speaking out against government regulation of the industry. Roosevelt derived his principal income, however, from the sale of Fidelity and Deposit surety bonds to labor unions, banks, brokerage firms, and city governments, a job that utilized his past political ties and cemented new ones. At the same time, FDR poured most of his financial and emotional resources into the rehabilitation of a decaying resort in Warm Springs, Georgia, where along with a small group of other polio victims he sought a miracle cure in its soothing waters. Above all, he awaited the moment of political resurrection.

That moment came in 1924, when Al Smith tapped FDR to make the key nominating speech for him at the Democratic National Convention in Madison Square Garden. Its memorable description of Smith as the "Happy Warrior," words provided by one of the governor's advisers, had been resisted by Roosevelt until the bitter end. But the rousing speech, preceded by a dramatic walk to the convention lectern on crutches, proved to be the inspirational peak of a convention that ended in bitter acrimony and the nomination of the lackluster Wall Street lawyer John W. Davis.

Four years later, facing an uphill battle against Hoover, the Smith forces asked two more favors from Roosevelt: nominate their candidate again in Houston and run for governor of New York to help the national ticket in the Empire State. "It's undoubtedly a good name to carry the ticket with," said Smith's ally Robert Moses, "but of course, he [Roosevelt] isn't quite bright." Roosevelt agreed to the first request—he would nominate Smith again—but turned thumbs down on the governorship race, a decision strongly backed by his advisers. They all predicted a Hoover landslide over Smith in New York, a similar defeat for Roosevelt, and a sharp blow to their man's future political fortunes. But Smith would not be denied. He put intense pressure on FDR and turned him around. Like the "Happy Warrior" speech, this decision too proved to be a blessing in disguise. Hoover crushed Smith in the New York vote, but Roosevelt eked out a narrow victory over his Republican opponent, Richard Ottinger. Earlier than planned and against his own wishes, FDR had become governor of the nation's largest state; this victory automatically made him a leading contender for the party's presidential nomination four years later. With the collapse of prosperity after 1929, that nomination suddenly meant something.

GOVERNOR ROOSEVELT

As New York's first Depression-era governor, Roosevelt compiled a solid but hardly radical record of reform. "It is hopeless for the Democrats," he observed after Davis's 1924 defeat, "to try and wear the livery of the conservative." Faithful to this idea and to his TR-Wilson progressive roots, he steered the ship of state slightly to the left of center. He did his best to keep the number of purely political appointees to a minimum and named able people to public office, including Frances Perkins as industrial commissioner and Henry Morgenthau, Jr., to head the state's department of agricultural affairs. As his chief legal counsel he hired Samuel Rosenman, a Polish Jew from Texas, then in his early thirties, who possessed a rich knowledge of the state legislature, a sure political touch, and a gift for writing fine speeches. To the state's public service commission, long subservient to the private power companies, he named Milo Maltbie, a champion of lower rates and public power. When New York began to tackle the problems of providing relief to the unemployed in 1931, Roosevelt turned to Jesse Straus, chief of Macy's, to run the Temporary Emergency Relief Administration; Straus in turn recruited Harry L. Hopkins, the tall, chain-smoking son of an Iowa harness maker, who had ministered to the needy at the New York Tuberculosis and Health Association.

To the disgust of many reformers, Governor Roosevelt did his best not to attack the Tammany Hall leaders who ran New York City, even when the stench of corruption arising from Mayor Jimmy Walker's city hall became all but unbearable. Not wishing to antagonize any major faction in the national party, he let others stalk the Tammany tiger. Only when Walker had been seriously wounded did he move in for the kill and some of the glory. On the other hand, Governor Roosevelt helped to bring New York's penal system out of the dark ages by building new prisons, revising the state's harsh sentencing laws, and exercising his pardoning authority humanely. Among the nation's governors, he took the lead in advocating state-controlled unemployment insurance financed jointly by employees, employers, and the government. Against strong opposition in the legislature, he secured the creation of a five-person Power Authority to study the development of publicly owned hydroelectric facilities on the vast St. Lawrence River. Ever sensitive to the needs of the state's farmers, he lowered their taxes and improved their highways.

Roosevelt's critics noted that he did not speak out against speculation on Wall Street before the Great Crash and that his response to the spreading banking crisis in New York after 1930 was halfhearted and disorganized. He did, however, compile a solid record on conservation and in the face of rising unemployment and destitution became a pioneer in public relief efforts. He opened National Guard armories to the homeless. Of even greater significance, New York's Temporary Emergency Relief Administration, financed through a sharp increase in the state income tax, began spending $20 million for work relief in the winter of 1931. Roosevelt's TERA was the first state-run relief effort in the nation. The beneficiaries of America's recent economic progress, FDR declared, now had an obligation "in relieving those who under the same industrial and economic order are the losers and sufferers."

FRONT RUNNER

Roosevelt's easy reelection victory in 1930 and his aggressive antidepression measures made him the front-runner for the party's presidential nomination two years later. To bolster Howe's efforts in this arena, he recruited James A. Farley, the savvy political boss of Rockland County, a Catholic and a dry, who cultivated the support of both big-city politicians and Southerners. And to strengthen the governor's policy-making and speech-writing staff, Rosenman put FDR in touch with three Columbia University professors, who became the nucleus of what reporters soon called "the brain trust." Raymond Moley, a pipe-smoking, balding Ohioan, had imbibed the economic radicalism of Henry George in his youth and become one of the nation's leading authorities on penology and the criminal justice system. He headed the group. Rexford Tugwell was a brilliant agricultural economist with devastating charm and good looks. Adolf A. Berle, a Congregational minister's son, had graduated from both Harvard College and the Harvard Law School by the time he was twenty-one. Moley, Tugwell, and

Berle began to ply the governor with ideas on everything from farm relief to corporate regulation. In addition, FDR began to utilize on a regular basis the fertile mind of Harvard law professor Felix Frankfurter, another colleague from the Wilson era, who knew virtually every liberal intellectual and academician in the land.

Roosevelt had put together a first-class campaign organization by early 1932, but his candidacy also attracted powerful opposition inside the Democratic Party. For the first time in a decade the Democratic nominee would likely win in November. Al Smith headed the list of contenders. The Happy Warrior and his handpicked national chairman, John Raskob, wielded considerable power over both the party's machinery and emotions. Smith believed that he had earned another run at the White House. He also nursed growing resentment against his successor in Albany, who had ousted several Smith loyalists from their state posts and kept the Happy Warrior at arm's distance. Growing more and more infatuated with business leaders like Raskob, Smith came to feel that Roosevelt could not be trusted to defend economic orthodoxy in the face of the growing crisis.

Raskob, the front man for a tiny group of business tycoons who paid the party's bills and made it their toy, feared Roosevelt for the same reasons. The national chairman also hoped to turn the 1932 election into another crusade against prohibition in order to boost Smith's candidacy, deflect class conflict, and shift the tax burden away from his patrons at Du Pont and General Motors. Smith still remained the darling of big-city politicians. Even in New York, he could count on half of the state's delegates. And he locked up most of those in the New England states as well. When Roosevelt made the mistake of challenging him head to head in the Massachusetts primary, Smith trounced his onetime ally.

In the West and the South, Roosevelt faced another formidable challenge from the speaker of the House of Representatives, John "Cactus Jack" Garner, a hard-drinking, tough-talking Texan who had inherited much of William Jennings Bryan's following, despite his lack of progressive credentials and his penchant for good bourbon. In addition to his own base of support in Dixie, Garner could count on the political muscle of Smith's old nemesis, California's William Gibbs McAdoo, and the bankroll of McAdoo's friend, the newspaper mogul William Randolph Hearst. Garner dealt FDR's fortunes another blow when he won the California primary. In a year when political hopes sprang eternal, Roosevelt also had to contend with a large contingent of favorite-son candidates and dark horses. These included the governors of

Maryland and Oklahoma, Albert Ritchie and William "Alfalfa Bill" Murray, as well as FDR's old ally at the War Department, attorney Newton D. Baker, the former progressive reformer from Ohio, whose newfound corporate clients made him a clone of John W. Davis.

Despite setbacks in Massachusetts and California, however, FDR swept most of the Democratic primaries held that year. He could claim a popular mandate in addition to support from party professionals. FDR's political machine, guided by Howe, Farley, and Rosenman, cornered a majority of the 1,154 delegate votes before the Democrats assembled in Chicago. In a bid to steal some of Smith's thunder and curry favor with Chicago's influential mayor, Anton "Pushcart Tony" Cermak, a vigorous supporter of the right to drink, Roosevelt came out in favor of repeal of the Eighteenth Amendment with an option for strict state controls. He also announced that membership in the League of Nations no longer seemed appropriate, thereby repudiating his 1920 campaign rhetoric and attempting to silence the rabid isolationists. The attention given to these issues by candidate Roosevelt in the middle of the worst economic calamity in American history provided dismal testimony to the low level of political consciousness in his party and the difficulty of securing its nomination. In 1932, a majority of the delegates did not put a candidate over the top. It required two-thirds, which gave a veto to the South and encouraged Roosevelt's enemies to think they could stop him.

If Roosevelt didn't win early, they reasoned, his delegate lines would begin to crack and open the way for a compromise candidate, probably Baker or one of the other governors. "Together we can bust this feller [Roosevelt]," Smith told McAdoo at a peacemaking luncheon arranged by the rich and pompous financier Bernard Baruch. Like Raskob, Baruch wanted a more conventional candidate than FDR. "If we go to the fifth ballot, we've got him licked. . . . We can [then] sit around a table and get together on a candidate." The Baruch-Smith-McAdoo strategy nearly succeeded. Roosevelt's commanding 666½ votes on the first ballot still fell 104 short of the needed two-thirds. On the second and third ballots he inched ahead to 677 and 682, but with the vote count of his leading opponents also remaining steady, many Roosevelt delegates became restive; some feared a reprise of the 1924 marathon.

On the fourth ballot, however, McAdoo announced California's switch to Roosevelt. That sealed FDR's victory. Baruch was stunned. Smith loyalists cried foul. The Happy Warrior, furious about the outcome, fled Chicago before FDR's coronation. From that moment forward, assorted people took credit for Roosevelt's convention triumph and, they added, for changing the course of history, too. There was not a single kingmaker, however, but several. Farley kept the shaky delegates together over three ballots and massaged Garner's key Texas leader, Congressman Sam Rayburn, who delivered most of his delegation when the speaker gave up the fight. Without a last-minute rescue operation by Huey Long, moreover, the Roosevelt coalition might have come apart on the third ballot before California's switch. The Kingfish, arms flailing, soaked by sweat, pummeled the Mississippi delegates with sarcasm, threats, and promises until they agreed to support Roosevelt for another round. The margin was a single vote.

Behind Garner's change of heart lurked several factors, but especially his own fear of another deadlocked convention that could help only Hoover and the last-minute defection of his chief financial backer, Hearst. After the inconclusive third ballot, Joseph P. Kennedy, one of FDR's leading supporters in the business community, told the newspaper tycoon, "I think if Roosevelt cracks on the next ballot, it'll be Baker." The thought of Baker, an avowed League supporter and unreconstructed Wilsonian, in the White House was too much for the newspaper baron, who passed the word to McAdoo and other Garner supporters. Hearst didn't like or trust Roosevelt, but he detested Baker more.

Although McAdoo had not been a central figure in these negotiations, he sweetened the deal for himself with guarantees from the Roosevelt camp—he would obtain some patronage in California, a voice in selecting the next cabinet, and the vice presidency for Garner. The Garner concession was odd, because the speaker himself regarded the vice presidency as "not worth a pitcher of warm spit." He agreed to run with FDR only to promote party unity. "Hell," he told Rayburn, "I'll do anything to see the Democrats win one more national election." To a reporter who expressed some astonishment at his decision, Garner took another puff on his cigar and said, "I'm a little older than you are, son. And politics is funny."

The Electable Progressive

And, finally, there was the candidate himself. A solid majority of the delegates came to Chicago pledged to Roosevelt. They thought he could win in November, and they believed rightly that he stood for change inside their party and out. In this judgment the political pros often showed more insight than some political pundits. Many of Roosevelt's preconvention opponents had tried to portray him as a weak, indecisive dilettante who was attempting to win the White House on charm alone. Baruch called him "wishy-washy." Walter Lippmann, editor of the *New York World* and one of the intellectuals' favorite journalists, told Newton Baker that FDR "doesn't happen to have a very good mind, [and] he never really comes to grips with a problem which has any large dimensions." He dismissed New York's governor as a "kind of amiable Boy Scout." Later in a famous column, Lippmann came out for Baker and heaped more scorn on Roosevelt as "a pleasant man, who, without any important qualifications for the office, would very much like to be President."

An amiable Boy Scout, however, would not have stirred the anxiety and opposition Roosevelt did among the party's old guard and its genuine conservatives such as Raskob and Baruch. Nor would he have attracted support from Huey Long and Burton K. Wheeler. When Roosevelt called for new government programs to help "the forgotten man" in a nationwide radio address prior to the convention, it touched off a storm of indignation from Smith and other pro-business Democrats. They accused FDR of stirring up class hatred and warfare. "I will take off my coat and fight to the end," declared Smith, "any candidate who persists in a demagogical appeal to the masses of the working people of the country to destroy themselves." In a speech at Georgia's Oglethorpe University in May, Roosevelt made his plea for "bold, persistent experimentation" to fight the Depression. He denounced "that small group of men whose chief outlook upon the social welfare is tinctured by the fact that they can make huge profits from the lending of money and the marketing of securities," and he vowed to bring about "a wiser, more equitable distribution of the national income." Roosevelt was not only the Democrats' most electable candidate in 1932, he was also one of their most progressive candidates.

As Roosevelt carried that progressive vision into the fall campaign against Hoover, he came to rely more and more on the ideas of brain trusters like Tugwell, Berle, and Moley, who had crafted the "forgotten man" speech. Some historians, however, have made much of the fact that during the Roosevelt-Hoover race, FDR frequently attacked the incumbent's "extravagant government spending" and pledged greater frugality, including a 25 percent cut in the federal budget. In September 1932 before the Commonwealth Club in San Francisco, candidate Roosevelt also declared that government should assume the function of economic regulation "only as a last resort, to be tried only when private initiative . . . has finally failed." FDR said a few other things during the campaign that later proved embarrassing. He described the gold clause in most securities contracts as a sacred covenant that government should respect. He made fun of the Farm Board's proposal that farmers voluntarily "plow up every third row of cotton and . . . shoot every tenth dairy cow." Roosevelt, on the basis of this evidence, seemed as conservative as his Republican opponent, another defender of the status quo, an opinion shared by many intellectuals, who voted for either the Communist Party candidate, William Z. Foster, or socialist Norman Thomas.

But even Roosevelt's most orthodox campaign speeches, designed to reassure the right wing of his own party and capture the frightened middle class, usually contained liberal caveats. His Pittsburgh address on federal fiscal policy, for example, pledged a balanced budget, but ended with another vow: "If starvation and dire need on the part of any of our citizens make necessary the appropriation of additional funds which would keep the budget out of balance, I shall not hesitate to tell the American people the full truth and ask them to authorize the expenditure of that additional amount."

His audience at the Commonwealth Club heard him defend big business on grounds of efficiency, but also denounce "economic oligarchy" and "princes of property" who had become the despots of the twentieth century. "Judge me by the enemies I have made," he told Oregonians, outlining his program for public power and utility regulation. "Judge me by the selfish purposes of these utility leaders who have talked of radicalism while they were selling watered stock to the people and using our schools to deceive the coming generation. My friends, my policy is as radical as American liberty."

Lippmann had declared Roosevelt to be "no crusader . . . no tribune of the people . . . no enemy of entrenched privilege." In some abstract sense, this was probably true, but the Depression-battered Americans who gave him the greatest landslide since Lincoln in 1864 (472 electoral votes to 59 for Hoover and 57 percent of the popular vote) did more than cast their ballots against the failed policies of his Republican opponent. They voted for change. How much, no one, not even the president-elect and his advisers, could foretell. But this much was certain: the Roosevelt empowered on November 8, 1932, although not a deep, profound thinker, knew where to find intellectual talent and was seldom intimidated by it; he was a cripple, but also a person of unconquerable will and optimism; he possessed deep-rooted beliefs—in fairness, charity, duty, patriotism, hard work—but they were not such as to inhibit what he had called "bold, persistent experimentation" by

Candidate Roosevelt gets an earful from one voter.

government. In the sad winter of 1932, these were impressive qualities for a national leader.

MIRACLE IN MIAMI

Before he exercised that leadership,, however, the man who seemed to lead a charmed life had to dodge yet other bullets, these fired by a real assassin. Two weeks before his March inauguration, Roosevelt interrupted a Florida fishing trip to speak to a throng of American Legionnaires gathered at evening in a Miami park. As he spoke from the backseat of an open car, the president-elect was greeted by an old nemesis, Chicago's Mayor Cermak, there to shake hands and make his peace with the new leader of the Democrats. "I don't like the son of a bitch," Cermak had protested a few days earlier, when urged to show solidarity with Roosevelt. Suddenly, five shots rang out in the

Chicago mayor Anton Cermak, killed by assassin firing at FDR.

park, fired by an Italian bricklayer, Joseph Zangara, who hated capitalism and hoped to kill the man pledged to save it. Although only about ten yards from the gunman, Roosevelt was not hit, but "Pushcart Tony" took one of the bullets intended for FDR and died later in a Miami hospital. In the past—in 1865, 1881, and 1901—assassins had altered the course of American history. They would do so again. That March evening in 1933, however, luck rode in FDR's car and with the American people.

3

Launching the New Deal

The air suddenly changed, the wind blew through the cor-
ridors, a lot of old air blew out the windows. You suddenly
felt, "By God, the air is fresh, it's moving, life is resuming."
—RFC attorney Milton Katz

NADIR

After hearing Roosevelt deliver his inaugural address on March 4, 1933,
the actress Lillian Gish said FDR seemed "to have been dipped in
phosphorus," so luminous were his words in contrast to the gray, blus-
tery weather. The president's firm, rich voice exuded resolution and
confidence when he declared that "this great nation will endure as it
has endured, will revive and will prosper." The only thing Americans
had to fear, he said, was fear itself, "nameless, unreasoning, unjusti-
fied terror which paralyzes needed efforts to convert retreat into
advance." He would ask Congress, he told the crowd before the Capitol, for "broad executive power to wage a war against the emergency,
as great as the power that would be given to me if we were invaded by
a foreign foe."

It was a great address—more powerful in delivery than in substance,
but even when heard a half century later it still retains its capacity to
inspire an audience. Roosevelt knew, however, that the nation required
more than eloquence and optimism. In the fourth winter of the Great
Depression, America faced staggering problems, none greater than those
stalking the nation's banks on March 4.

Raymond Moley recalled one customer at his hometown bank in

Ohio who told the teller: "If my money's here, I don't want it. If it's not, I want it." In the nation's capital, where the potentates of the two major parties assembled for Roosevelt's inauguration, hotels informed their guests that because of "unsettled banking conditions throughout the country, checks on out-of-town banks cannot be accepted." Political power seemed to be about all Americans could transfer or exchange on March 4, 1933. "The bankers are descending on Washington. They seem utterly hopeless and defeated," a visitor remarked to Justice Brandeis. "Well," responded the old progressive, "aren't they known as the Napoleons of finance?"

Credit, the lubricant of capitalism, had virtually dried up. In the week before Roosevelt's inauguration, terrified Europeans withdrew nearly $1 billion in gold from New York City banks alone. Americans everywhere hoarded currency. Even as FDR took the oath of office, over five thousand banks were already closed, including all of those in New York and Illinois, which had been shut down earlier in the day by order of the states' governors. A de facto banking holiday already existed throughout the United States when Roosevelt officially proclaimed one on March 6 and called Congress into special session a week later to deal with the financial crisis. That Congress, led as never before by the president, stayed in session for a hundred days. And when it left town, the relationship between Americans and their national government would never again be quite the same.

SAVING CAPITALISM

How FDR, his advisers, and Congress dealt with the banking crisis in 1933 prefigured much of the legislation of the Hundred Days and the controversies that have swirled around the New Deal ever since. The banking holiday proclamation Roosevelt issued on March 6, based on the old Trading with the Enemy Act from World War I, had been written by Walter Wyatt of the Federal Reserve Board staff. FDR had refused to endorse virtually the same proclamation in the final days of the Hoover regime, when the outgoing president attempted to secure his successor's cooperation to prevent a deepening of the banking crisis.

The Emergency Banking Act of 1933, signed into law barely eight hours after Congress received a copy of the bill on March 9, had been drafted largely by Wyatt and other Hoover advisers, chiefly Ogden Mills, Francis Awalt, and Arthur Ballantine. To the shock of conservatives, it officially took the United States off the gold standard by forbidding the export of the metal except under license from the Treasury Department. It required those who held gold to turn it in at Federal Reserve banks for $20.67 an ounce and made the dollar no longer redeemable in gold.

The new banking law also gave to a public official, the comptroller of the currency, sweeping powers to reorganize all national banks threatened with insolvency, including the authority to adjust equitably the interests of stockholders and depositors. It also offered manifold benefits to those banks allowed to reopen after government inspection. To strengthen the banks' capital position the law authorized the Reconstruction Finance Corporation to buy their preferred stock and assume many of their debts. To ease the liquidity squeeze, Federal Reserve banks might accept for discount a wider range of their members' less profitable assets.

Between March 11 and 15, when nearly 70 percent of the banks that had still functioned before the holiday reopened for business, auditors and accountants from the RFC, the comptroller's office, the Treasury Department, and the Federal Reserve fanned out across the nation to implement the emergency legislation. They quickly separated the solvent national banks from the less fortunate ones. Those with unimpaired capital and sufficient liquid assets received a license to reopen. The rest were placed in the hands of conservators and the RFC to be refinanced and reorganized prior to doing business again.

"It was a very heady experience to sit down and represent the government on a transaction involving some large bank like the Detroit National and watch $15 or $20 million pass across the table to brace up the bank," recalled Frank Watson, then a young RFC attorney fresh from the Harvard Law School. "Soon most of us were working on our tenth, twelfth, or fifteenth bank reorganization." Struggling through the books of one Southern institution, Watson and a federal bank examiner encountered the manager, who offered him $20 to speed up the autopsy. "We said that was typical of the Democrats to offer little people $20 bribes whereas the Republicans would have offered large bribes to big people."

On the evening of March 14, FDR gave his first "fireside chat" over the radio, patiently explaining to the American public what the banking experts had been doing for a week and reassuring depositors that any bank open for business on the next day carried the government's stamp of approval. By March 15, deposits exceeded withdrawals. At the end of the first week, customers had returned over $600 million in hoarded currency to the banks; by the end of March, nearly $1 billion had flowed back into the system. "I can only describe the change as physical, virtually physical," recalled former RFC attorney Milton Katz. "The air suddenly changed, the wind blew through the corridors. . . . You suddenly felt, 'By God, the air is fresh, it's moving, life is resuming.' " American capitalism, Raymond Moley noted somewhat later, "was saved in eight days."

To make certain that the revived patient received some long-term rehabilitation, Roosevelt signed more permanent banking legislation into law during June. Cosponsored by Congressman Henry Steagall of Alabama and Senator Carter Glass of Virginia, one of the original architects of the Federal Reserve System, this Banking Act of 1933 contained a number of important structural reforms. Except for underwriting state and local government securities, the Glass-Steagall Act prohibited commercial banks from engaging in investment banking, a practice that had encouraged speculation in the previous decade. The act also raised the capital requirements of national banks. Their officers were given two years to divest themselves of all personal loans from their own institutions.

Most important of all, the Glass-Steagall measure transferred the authority over open market operations (the buying and selling of government securities) from the privately managed Federal Reserve banks to the publicly appointed Federal Reserve Board in Washington. And, despite Roosevelt's initial opposition, the law included a momentous amendment offered by Republican senator Arthur Vandenberg of Michigan—a state hit very hard by bank failures—that insured national bank deposits up to $2,500. The insurance fund, subsidized by the federal government and the banks, was to be administered by a new agency, the Federal Deposit Insurance Corporation (FDIC).

When Moley declared that the New Deal's initial banking measures had saved capitalism, he intended it as a compliment. When others scrutinized the emergency and permanent banking legislation passed in 1933, however, they were more critical. Hoover and his supporters pointed out that virtually all of the measures taken during the banking holiday could have been adopted earlier if only Roosevelt had cooperated before March 4. Such action might have saved individual depositors and a number of the eleven hundred banks that never reopened after 1933. Roosevelt, they claimed, rejected cooperation because he wanted the crisis to worsen so that he could reap all the political benefits from adopting their rescue plans after his inauguration.

At the other end of the political spectrum, many denounced Roosevelt's willingness to utilize the ideas of his opponent's advisers and his failure to propose more radical structural changes in the banking system. They cried betrayal. In his inaugural address, FDR had blasted "unscrupulous money changers" who had "fled from their high seats in the temple of our civilization" and vowed to pursue social policies "more noble than mere monetary profit." The "money changers" may have fled the temple on March 4, grumbled one congressman from the farm belt, but "they were all back on the 9th."

Both the emergency law and the Glass-Steagall Act, critics argued, had been written largely by bankers for bankers and they had reaped the greatest benefits, including lavish government financial subsidies, liquidation of their weaker brethren, and authorization for branch banking by national institutions in those states permitting it. This provision, combined with the enhanced authority of the Federal Reserve Board over open market activities and the requirement that state banks join the Federal Reserve System if they wished to enjoy the protection of the FDIC, gave more power to the larger commercial banks at the expense of their smaller competitors. Instead of throwing the banks a number of life preservers, skeptics continued, FDR should have pushed for either nationalization of these credit institutions or expansion of the federal postal savings system, in which Americans had already deposited millions of dollars since 1929. In March 1933, given the demoralization of the bankers and the panic in the country at large, more fundamental changes seemed possible.

These complaints, however, ignored a number of restraints on FDR's freedom of action. Hoover urged cooperation on a banking holiday prior to March 4 as part of a larger package that he hoped would limit Roosevelt's options on both fiscal and monetary issues. When FDR offered to support the banking holiday alone, Hoover spurned the offer. Second, those who talked boldly about nationalizing the nation's banks never presented a blueprint for doing it. Speed was of the essence if one hoped to restart the country's credit machinery. Even routine banking operations required trained personnel. Where to find them? The comptroller, the Treasury Department, and the Federal Reserve had barely enough people to audit the banks, yet alone run them. The employees of the postal savings system had no experience with checking accounts or making commercial loans. As would soon become clear in other New Deal programs, the government of the United States in 1933 simply lacked the experience and manpower to undertake large-scale regulatory efforts without the active participation of the private sector.

The banks could be expected to fight nationalization, especially in the courts. The legal and financial costs of expropriation, assuming the Constitution and its Just Compensation Clause remained in force, would have been considerable. Roosevelt had vowed economy in government, not expansion. And finally, Roosevelt did not believe he had been given a mandate to do other than save capitalism. When Senators Robert La Follette, Jr., and Edward Costigan urged genuine nationalization on the president, he quickly replied: "That isn't necessary at all. I've just had every assurance of cooperation from the bankers."

THE HUNDRED DAYS

Roosevelt's call to the 73rd Congress had not been limited to the banking crisis, but no one could have predicted on March 9 the blizzard of other legislation that came from Capitol Hill before the exhausted senators and congressmen adjourned in early June:

—The Economy Act fulfilled Roosevelt's campaign pledge to reduce government spending by trimming government salaries in Congress and the executive branch (FDR himself took a voluntary cut). It consolidated a few departmental functions and lowered non-service-related disability payments to World War I veterans. The measure saved about $243 million initially, but Congress wiped that out a year later with salary increases for government employees and voted a bonus to veterans in 1935.

—The Beer Tax Act authorized the manufacture and sale of beverages containing not more than 3.2 percent alcohol as the Twenty-first Amendment, repealing the Eighteenth, moved toward ratification in the state legislatures.

—The Wagner-Peyser Act created a United States Employment Service in the Department of Labor and made federal grants available to the states on a matching basis when they created similar local public employment offices.

—The Civilian Conservation Corps Reforestation Relief Act provided government jobs for young men from relief families between the ages of seventeen and twenty-four in camps run by the U.S. Army. For $30 a month, CCC recruits planted trees (eventually over two billion), fought forest fires, repaired reservoirs, and refurbished national historic sites and parks. Within two years, the agency employed over half a million men in 2,500 camps.

—The Emergency Railroad Transportation Act attempted to shore up an industry devastated by decades of financial mismanagement, falling revenues, and new competition (especially from motor trucks) by creating a national railroad czar with authority to encourage greater cooperation among the individual companies and affected labor unions.

—The Federal Emergency Relief Act, realizing the dreams of Senators Wagner, La Follette, and Costigan, liberalized significantly the relief program inherited from Hoover by authorizing $500 million in direct grants, not loans, to the states for the purposes of assisting the nearly fifteen million people out of work. Roosevelt named Harry Hopkins to run the program. In November, the president gave Hopkins an even bigger job when he created the Civil Works Administration to assist millions of the unemployed through the harsh winter months. Although not technically a part of the Hundred Days, the CWA became one of the most innovative New Deal programs. With only $400 million to work with, Hopkins performed a near miracle by hiring over 4.2 million workers in four months and paying them minimum wages instead of relief checks. They laid eleven million feet of sewer pipes, sent fifty thousand teachers into rural school districts, and built over four hundred airports and 255,000 miles of roads.

—The Securities Act required corporations and investment bankers who wished to market stocks and bonds in the future to file comprehensive statements of disclosure with the Federal Trade Commission and provided criminal and civil penalties for those who failed to do so and for those whose statements were false or misleading.

—The Home Owners' Refinancing Act, sponsored by Senate majority leader Joe Robinson of Arkansas, rescued individual homeowners from foreclosure and prevented a further collapse of mortgage lending institutions by putting the federal government into the business of refinancing these loans through the Home Owners' Loan Corporation. The HOLC, equipped with funds from the Reconstruction Finance Corporation and the power to market its own bonds, could also issue cash advances for the payment of real estate taxes and home repairs. By the mid-1930s the HOLC had refinanced nearly 20 percent of the urban homes in the country.

—The Emergency Farm Mortgage Act authorized the Federal Land Banks to refinance farm mortgages with the proceeds of up to $2 billion worth of tax-exempt government bonds. The act also made available money from the RFC to assist farmers in redeeming lands already foreclosed.

—The Farm Credit Act and FDR's executive order creating the Farm Credit Administration, managed by Henry Morgenthau, Jr., brought under one roof four major agricultural credit programs, including the Federal Land Banks and the Federal Intermediate Credit Banks. Within eighteen months, Morgenthau and his assistants had helped to refinance more than 20 percent of all the nation's farm mortgages and prevented thousands of country banks from going broke.

—The Tennessee Valley Authority Act created a federal agency to plan and develop multiple uses for one of the nation's great rivers and watersheds, including navigation, flood control, reforestation, fertilizer production, and hydroelectric power.

And finally, Congress authorized two unprecedented programs, one for agriculture and one for industry, that became the centerpieces of the New Deal's initial recovery program:

—The Agricultural Adjustment Act (AAA) put into effect the Voluntary Domestic Allotment Plan of Professors John Black and M. L. Wilson. It authorized the secretary of agriculture to enter into marketing agreements with farmers raising wheat, cotton, corn, hogs, tobacco, rice, and milk. In exchange for reducing their production, the participating farmers would receive a government benefit payment financed by a tax on processing companies. The law also contained an amendment by Senators Elmer Thomas of Oklahoma and Burton K. Wheeler of Montana giving the president broad discretion to devalue the dollar by as much as 50 percent and inflate the money supply by issuing $3 billion in paper money or purchasing and coining silver.

—The National Industrial Recovery Act (NIRA) suspended the antitrust laws and permitted the nation's trades and industries to draft codes of fair competition that were to include labor standards such as minimum wages. The NIRA outlawed the use of anti-union yellow-dog contracts and guaranteed employees the right to form unions and to bargain collectively. It also established a Public Works Administration with a $3.3 billion budget to build highways, federal buildings, and military facilities.

This in a nutshell was the Hundred Days. From home mortgages to raising hogs, from reforestation to codes of fair competition—never had the government of the United States become so deeply involved in the day-to-day economic and social arrangements of the American people. Rex Tugwell called it "a renaissance spring," a "time of rebirth after a dark age." Even Walter Lippmann, who had dismissed FDR as a political lightweight a year before, applauded. "At the end of February," he wrote, "we were a congeries of disorderly panic-stricken mobs and factions. In the hundred days from March to June we became an organized nation confident of our power to provide for our own security and to control our own destiny."

While radical critics of the New Deal soon complained that these efforts were weak palliatives designed to shore up a dying economic order, a far larger number of citizens looked upon them as unprecedented forms of government intervention that threatened tyranny. Some later historians, seeking a way to organize the sprawling and diverse programs of the Roosevelt administration, put the label of "First New Deal" on this burst of legislative activity during the Hundred Days. From this perspective, FDR and his key advisers, especially the "brain trust" of Moley, Tugwell, and Berle, hoped to jettison the ideals and practice of a market economy in favor of national planning and centralized management by the federal government.

In the spring of 1932, it is noted, Moley presented FDR with a legislative blueprint that included large-scale relief and public works programs, the segregation of investment from commercial banking, securities regulation, and government ownership of major hydroelec-

"The Galloping Snail" (caption). FDR takes command of Congress during the Hundred Days.

tric sites. Berle believed that the regime of laissez-faire capitalism was dead, that giant corporations, operated by professional managers, defined the new social reality, and that the federal government was the only agency capable of promoting cooperation among such large economic units. Tugwell, a longtime supporter of the Black-Wilson plan for controlling agricultural production, argued that rationality and fairness could be brought to the American economic order only as a result of top-down planning by the government with respect to investment, production, pricing, and income levels.

Except in the fevered imagination of New Deal critics on the right, who portrayed Roosevelt as a captive of subversive professors, it is difficult to discern the influence of the "brain trust" or coherent ideas about national planning in most of the measures adopted during the Hundred Days. The voluntary cooperation of the Hoover years had been abandoned in favor of a larger government role, but vital programs such as the AAA and the NRA would not have functioned without the active support and self-regulation of private-interest groups. Indeed, the New Deal would be criticized in some quarters for giving too much power to them.

Key measures of the Hundred Days, especially banking, relief, and mortgage assistance, arose from the immediate need to deal with near-terminal conditions. They would have taken the form they did with or without Moley, Berle, and Tugwell. Furthermore, some of the new statutes had legislative histories reaching back decades to the progressive era. The Wagner-Peyser Act, for example, traced its roots to a 1918 proposal for a federal-state system of public labor exchanges. The idea had been kept alive in the twenties through the efforts of Republican senator William Kenyon and Republican congressman John Nolan. The Tennessee Valley Authority owed its existence largely to Senator George Norris, the crusty progressive Republican from Nebraska, who kept the vital properties at Muscle Shoals in northern Alabama out of the hands of private developers during the Coolidge-Hoover years.

Other powerful members of the House and Senate—speaker John Rainey of Illinois, Sam Rayburn of Texas, Joe Robinson, Robert Wagner, Elmer Thomas, and Burton Wheeler—played pivotal roles in shaping the legislation of the Hundred Days. So did government bureaucrats from agencies such as the Federal Reserve and the Federal Trade Commission as well as lobbyists representing bankers, businessmen, farmers, and labor. An equally decisive influence was wielded by some administration advisers who looked with disapproval on schemes of national planning and centralization.

The Securities Act and its 1934 companion regulating the stock exchanges, for instance, bore the imprint of the fertile mind of Felix Frankfurter and several of his protégés, Benjamin V. Cohen, James Landis, and Thomas G. "Tommy the Cork" Corcoran. Frankfurter and his "happy hot dogs" all subscribed more or less to the antidepression views of Justice Brandeis, who detested bigness in either business or government. While endorsing large public works expenditures and heavy taxes on the rich, the "people's lawyer" placed his faith ultimately in innovations coming from state and local governments.

In short, the great legislative achievements of the Hundred Days, like most of the New Deal, bore the stamp of many authors, arose from no master plan, and did not fit neatly into a single ideological box. What often drew the clashing, discordant views into temporary harmony was the basic, standard lubricant of American politics, compromise—liberally applied by one of the profession's master players, Franklin Roosevelt.

Felix Frankfurter

This is not to say that FDR, his advisers, and most of the Democratic leadership in Congress did not have a general theory about the causes and cures of the Great Depression which guided their legislative course in 1933–34. The nation had been brought to disaster, they believed, because of abuses of power by small groups of bankers, businessmen, and speculators and by a maldistribution of income that flowed from misguided Republican policies that enriched the few at the expense of the many. The antidote, likewise, could be found in laws such as the Banking Act and the Securities Act that attempted to root out these abuses and in efforts to better adjust production and consumption, especially by raising the purchasing power of America's forgotten men and women. The fortunes of the Triple A and the National Industrial Recovery Act demonstrated how difficult this latter task could be.

SOMETHING FOR AGRICULTURE

Roosevelt may have been the ringmaster of the Hundred Days, but he and the New Dealers had to share the arena with a number of cunning political animals in the Congress—none more dangerous than South Carolina's profane, tobacco-chewing senior senator, Ellison Durant "Cotton Ed" Smith, chairman of the powerful Committee on Agriculture. FDR's secretary of agriculture, Henry Wallace, had recruited some of the smartest economists and lawyers in the country to fashion the administration's farm program. In the nation's great wheat, hog, and cotton belts from the Dakotas to the Carolinas, farmers and their suppliers and bankers stared at foreclosures and bankruptcies. Some talked strikes and revolution. Cotton Ed, however, was in no hurry to move new programs through his committee, especially legislation written by a bunch of professors with names like Mordecai Ezekiel.

When Leon Keyserling, a native of South Carolina and a 1931 graduate of the Harvard Law School, strolled into the legal division of the Department of Agriculture in March 1933, the first thing he was asked by his future boss, Jerome Frank, was "What do you know?" When Keyserling, whose father was one of South Carolina's biggest cotton ginner and dealers, responded, "I know Cotton Ed Smith," Frank hustled the young attorney into a taxi and took him up to Capitol Hill to see the senator. Cotton Ed emerged from the short meeting and threw his arm around Frank. "My boy," he drawled, "you're gonna get your law and you're gonna be confirmed, too." The Senate soon passed the Agricultural Adjustment Act. Frank became general counsel to the AAA and a center of controversy with respect to its treatment of sharecroppers and tenant farmers. Keyserling quickly moved on to become Senator Wagner's chief legislative assistant, his career as an agricultural lobbyist having been short but spectacular.

Despite the initial hesitation of Cotton Ed Smith, the New Deal and the 73rd Congress probably spent more time and money on agriculture than on any other sector of the ailing American economy. This is hardly surprising, given the sheer number of rural producers who faced destitution, their sizable representation in Congress, the political sophistication of a few of their organizations, such as the Farm Bureau, and the inclinations of FDR himself, who associated farming with wholesomeness and virtue. But in fact, unless something could be done immediately to boost the income of millions of farmers, no economic recovery would be possible. Its framers intended the Agricultural Adjustment Act to do just that.

The measure Cotton Ed Smith finally endorsed and Roosevelt signed into law on May 12, 1933, proposed to gain the old objective of "parity" for farmers by boosting the price received for their commodities to the level where they could buy manufactured goods of equivalent value based on index years of 1909–14 (or 1919–29 in the case of cotton). Higher prices were to be achieved by encouraging farmers to reduce their output and adopt production quotas in exchange for cash payments from the Agricultural Adjustment Administration. Corn and hog producers, for example, would receive 30 cents a bushel for corn not raised and $5 a head for pigs not produced. Congress appropriated $100 million to start up the benefit program and proposed to finance it almost entirely from a new tax on processing companies. They, in turn, would pass along the increased costs to consumers. Securing economic justice for farmers by curbing production and raising their commodity prices proved very elusive. So did the task of establishing some equity among farmers, rich and poor, and between farmers and those who ultimately paid the bill for food and fiber.

The Triple A faced two gigantic problems from the beginning: an agency boss, George N. Peek, a veteran of the McNary-Haugen wars of the 1920s, who did not believe in the program; and potentially ruinous surpluses in hogs and cotton as a result of the legislative delay in passing the law. Peek detested the domestic allotment plan, tried to scuttle it in Congress, and hoped to revive some version of McNary-Haugen whereby American farmers would be guaranteed a high domestic price and encouraged to unload their surpluses abroad with additional subsidies from the government. A paradise for some farmers, it promised untold burdens for the American taxpayer.

Peek also hated the "plague of young lawyers" hired for the Triple A by Tugwell and Frank. They didn't have dirt under their fingers, many had funny urban accents, and they wanted to change the world. He dismissed them as "young men with their hair ablaze" who "all claimed to be friends of somebody or other and mostly of Felix Frankfurter and Jerome Frank. They floated airily into offices, took desks, asked for papers and found no end of things to be busy about. I never found out why they came, what they did or why they left." But Peek had influential friends in Congress and when he failed to get the cabinet post in agriculture, Roosevelt felt obliged to give him something else. He and his co-administrator, Charles J. Brand, another supporter of the McNary-Haugen scheme, quarreled incessantly with Wallace, Wilson, and Frank. They both quit before the year was out.

The bumper crops of hogs and cotton in 1933 represented a bigger threat to the AAA's success than the agency's internal wars. If they came on the market in addition to the existing surpluses, any immediate hope of raising prices seemed doomed. Without much hesitation, therefore, Secretary Wallace ordered the plowing under of ten million acres of growing cotton and the slaughter of six million baby pigs and 200,000 sows.

Over 100 million pounds of pork soon reached hungry people through the Federal Surplus Relief Corporation, organized by Wallace, Hopkins, and Interior Secretary Harold Ickes, but these acts of destruction in the countryside dramatized for many the moral obscenity of capitalism. "That we should have idle and hungry and ill-clad millions on the one hand, and so much food and wool and cotton upon the other that we don't know what to do with it, this is an utterly idiotic situation . . . which makes a laughingstock of our genius as a people," declared one disillusioned farm spokesman. Such destruction was not a noble policy in "any sane society," Wallace conceded, but he quickly pointed out that the alternatives would bring more suffering to the farmers and that the wholesale collapse of the agricultural economy between 1929 and 1933 had been an equivalent moral disaster.

THE MYTH OF GRASS-ROOTS DEMOCRACY

In one of the great organizational feats in the nation's history, AAA officials and county agents from the land grant colleges crisscrossed the country to sign up farmers for the agency's domestic allotment programs. By the spring of 1934, they had formed over four thousand local committees with more than 100,000 farmer members to carry out the Triple A's production control efforts. By then, more than three million individual farmers had agreed to participate. In the South, for example, this translated into the writing of 1,030,433 individual contracts through which cotton farmers agreed to take ten million acres out of production and produce 4.4 million fewer bales. By one estimate, nearly three-quarters of the South's total cotton acreage came under the program during the first year. Checks from the federal government began to reach the cotton producers at the end of 1934. By then, too, the AAA's basic program had been expanded by Congress to include the producers of barley, cattle, peanuts, rye, flax, grain sorghum, sugar beets, and sugar cane, all of whom clamored for government assistance.

Despite the enthusiasm of participating farmers, parity for agriculture did not come easily under the Triple A. Only the worst drought in 70 years kept wheat and corn production down in 1934–35. Elsewhere, surpluses continued to mount as local committees miscalculated or fudged on quotas and as other farmers cheated on their contracts or simply refused to participate. The situation became so unstable in cotton and tobacco that producers cried out for more punitive controls, which Congress legislated in 1934 by imposing a heavy tax on those who violated their quotas.

In an allied effort to raise prices, the Commodity Credit Corporation, a subsidiary of the ubiquitous Reconstruction Finance Corporation, helped farmers keep their surpluses off the market by making loans somewhat below parity prices and taking the crops as collateral. In years when production dipped, it was assumed, the farmers would sell their crops at a good price and pay back the CCC. By the end of the decade, however, while prices had moved ahead by inches, the Commodity Credit Corporation had become the world's largest holder of dozens of farm commodities ranging from cowhides and dates to turpentine and figs.

The New Deal's AAA pumped $4.5 million into the pockets of American farmers through direct benefit payments between 1934 and 1940. The Commodity Credit Corporation extended $1.5 billion in crop loans. Together with mortgage assistance and various other loans programs, these efforts doubled net farm income over the course of the Depression decade from $2 billion to $4.6 billion. Yet at the decade's end, farm income reached only 80 percent of parity and per capita farm income remained less than 40 percent of that received by non-farmers. The New Deal clearly put the brakes on agriculture's downward slide, but failed to reverse the general imbalance between country and city. Among farmers, moreover, the Triple A compounded existing differences in wealth and power. It brought more disaster to the rural poor.

In terms of the capacity of the federal government to execute a complex nationwide program, the Triple A proved a huge success, thanks largely to the presence of trained personnel in the extension service and the long tradition of federal involvement with agriculture on the local level. Peek, Wallace, Wilson, and other leaders of the Triple A praised the agency for starting "a new epoch, in which Democracy, embracing the economic as well as the political field, becomes for the first time a reality." The AAA represented the finest traditions of "grassroots democracy," they argued, because farmers did most of the planning through local committees run by other farmers. They pointed to high rates of voluntary participation (95 percent of the flue-cured-tobacco growers, for instance) and whopping majorities in referenda to continue domestic allotment as examples of popular support for AAA and democratic control of the New Deal's farm program.

A substantial number of farmers thought otherwise, however. They noted that handpicked representatives of the extension service, the land grant colleges, and the Farm Bureau Federation, all of whom favored the interests of the wealthiest commercial farmers, dominated the county committees that fixed quotas. According to critics such as John Simpson of the National Farmers' Union and Milo Reno of the Farmers' Holiday Association, the Triple A benefited the big landowners and the well-to-do growers while discriminating against small and medium-sized operators. By basing subsidies on the size of farms rather than on need, they pointed out, the Triple A would encourage further economic concentration in the countryside and set the national government on the mistaken path of storing huge surpluses year after year.

THE OTHER COUNTRYSIDE

In Southern agriculture, racism compounded class oppression. Oligarchies of white landlords ran the county committees, while the sharecroppers and tenants (many of them blacks) who operated more than 700,000 farms in the cotton belt had no voice in the Triple A. When the landlords signed their acreage reduction contracts, they did not renew long-standing agreements with tens of thousands of tenants on lands taken out of production. When they received their govern-

ment benefit checks, they didn't share a penny with their sharecroppers. "I had I reckon four renters and I didn't make anything," said
one typical Oklahoma farmer. "I bought tractors on the money the
government give me and got shet o' my renters." Homeless, destitute,
the now landless tenants swelled the ranks of unemployed migrants
desperately seeking relief in Southern cities or cities to the north. Some,
however, stayed to fight the power structure.

"The landlord is always betwixt us, beatin' us and starvin' us and
makin' us fight each other," declared a black tenant farmer in Poinsett
County, Arkansas, to an audience that included men and women of
both races. "There ain't but one way for us to get him where he can't
help himself and that's for us to get together and stay together." In
Arkansas and Alabama, tenants, croppers, and farm laborers took bold
and dangerous steps to protect themselves in 1934. They organized the
Alabama Sharecroppers Union and the Southern Tenant Farmers Union
in an attempt to stem the tide of evictions and form organizations with
sufficient power to bring their landlords to the bargaining table.

Organizers from the Communist Party and Norman Thomas, the
presidential candidate of the Socialist Party, came to the Arkansas
croppers' aid with strike funds and fiery speeches. So did Jerome Frank
and other of the young, idealistic lawyers in the Triple A, who had
been locked also in a bitter struggle with the processing companies
over their refusal to open company records to government auditors.
Frank and his staff went so far as to issue an interpretation of the
cotton reduction contracts that made it illegal for landlords to displace
existing tenants while they received government payments.

Southern landlords, backed by local law enforcement officials and
vigilantes, struck back with fury. Tenants and croppers who dared to
join the Southern Tenant Farmers Union saw their credit cut off by
local merchants and their homes burned down. Mobs kidnapped union
organizers, beat them, and threatened them with death. Union meetings were attacked and routed. "We don't need no Gawd-damn Yankee bastard to tell us what to do with our niggers," one opponent shouted
at Thomas, who was driven from a speaker's platform and from the
town.

In Washington, Frank and his allies also faced determined, if less
violent, opposition inside the Triple A. The new head of the agency,
Chester Davis, demanded that Wallace fire the entire bunch, a purge
finally endorsed by the secretary and FDR himself. When Norman
Thomas protested the reign of terror in the South, FDR admonished
him: "I know the South, and there is arising a new generation of lead-

*The New Deal's Agricultural Adjustment Act did little to help Southern ten-
ant farmers and sharecroppers.*

ers in the South and we've got to be patient." When a Senator expressed
alarm at the removal of Frank and the other liberals, FDR told him:
"All I can tell you is that I am sorry and have the highest respect for all
parties concerned."

Roosevelt's decision to support the status quo in agriculture arose
predictably from his own insouciance about issues of race and civil
liberties and from his fear that powerful Southern conservatives in
Congress would block important New Deal programs. Others shared
his caution. Even Senator La Follette, about to embark on a long inquiry
into violations of civil liberties, stayed away from rural violence in the
South for fear of antagonizing majority leader Robinson and seeing his
committee's appropriation cut. The protests in the South, the Triple A
purge, and an outbreak of strikes by farm workers in California's lettuce fields forced FDR, however, to pay some attention to the plight of
agriculture's dispossessed men and women.

In 1935, with funds from Hopkins's relief program and the Interior
Department, Roosevelt created the Resettlement Administration. He
placed Tugwell in charge of it, and encouraged the new agency's efforts

to provide financial assistance and social services to displaced tenants and migratory farm workers. A year later, he asked Wallace to head a special committee to study farm tenancy. Its report, documenting the horrors of rural poverty and exploitation, hastened the passage of additional legislation, the Bankhead-Jones Farm Tenancy Act of 1937, which folded the activities of the Resettlement Administration into the new Farm Security Administration (FSA).

Tugwell's RA and its successor, bringing government aid to some of the country's poorest inhabitants, were among the most humane of all New Deal efforts to treat the symptoms of the Depression. The RA and the FSA helped over four thousand displaced tenant farmers become landowners, organized collective farms in four states, built three suburban greenbelt communities for the urban and rural poor, and operated sanitary camps where migrant farm workers found decent housing and medical treatment. But Congress, with Southern racists and big agricultural interests holding the purse stings, feared Tugwell's agency and kept it on starvation rations. Had they been given the funds, Tugwell and his assistants, for example, could have relocated perhaps half a million tenant families. Instead, the money went elsewhere. For every federal dollar spent by RA and FSA on the rural poor, probably ten dollars went to more prosperous farmers through the AAA and the Commodity Credit Corporation.

BALANCE SHEET

The basic farm programs of the New Deal, especially the Triple A, did not lack for critics on the right, who denounced it as "regimentation" and an effort to "sovietize" the American farmer. In 1936, a majority of justices on the Supreme Court seemed to agree when they declared the AAA unconstitutional on the grounds that the federal government had no business attempting to regulate local economic activities such as farming or forcing processing companies to make involuntary contributions to the welfare of agricultural producers. Congress subsequently passed the Soil Conservation and Domestic Allotment Act of 1938 and a second Agricultural Adjustment Act in 1938 that continued the essentials of the program with general appropriations from the Treasury. These two laws fixed the course of American agricultural policy for almost fifty years.

From Roosevelt's left, his policies of planned scarcity for agriculture drew even more devastating criticism from those who argued that they were run in an undemocratic manner, enriched the already well-to-do, swelled the relief rolls with displaced tenants, and did little to raise total purchasing power. These skeptics, who included representatives of the Farmers' Union as well as Justice Brandeis, pointed out that the producers with the largest incomes and acreage reaped virtually all of the benefits. Except for those of the tiny Resettlement Administration, few benefits flowed to the rural poor. Taking money out of the pockets of processing companies and consumers to pay some farmers higher prices redistributed income, but did little to boost total demand in the economy. Similar controversy soon engulfed the New Deal's other instrument of recovery, the National Recovery Administration.

SOMETHING FOR BUSINESS, SOMETHING FOR LABOR

Like the Triple A, the National Industrial Recovery Act emerged as the administration's response to an immediate crisis, although its roots reached back to the industrial mobilization of World War I and the trade association movement of the twenties. The immediate crisis was both economic and political. In key industries, unless something could be done to prevent further price cutting, the erosion of profits, and additional unemployment, the patient would only grow sicker.

Senator Hugo Black of Alabama and William Connery, chairman of the House Labor Committee, offered a dramatic solution. The Black-Connery bill, eagerly endorsed by the leadership of the American Federation of Labor, which threatened a general strike unless Congress acted favorably, made it illegal for employers to ship any products in interstate commerce from mine or factories where the employees worked more than thirty hours in a five-day week. This plan would improve working conditions, Black argued, and by forcing firms to hire more employees it would also raise purchasing power and end the Depression.

The Black-Connery bill presented Roosevelt with a sudden and serious political problem. Businessmen, of course, viewed the thirty-hour plan with abhorrence. Many economists thought it simpleminded. Most lawyers believed the courts would never uphold it, given current constitutional theories. But the Senate passed it, by a vote of 53–30, and Connery's committee was disposed to do likewise when FDR secured a temporary delay to allow a cabinet committee, headed by Frances Perkins, to study the measure and offer amendments. Perkins and her group focused on labor standards and curbing cutthroat competition.

While the president gave one mandate to Perkins, he also told Moley, Tugwell, and John Dickinson from the Commerce Department to overhaul the Black bill or come up with their own set of proposals for industrial recovery. Tugwell advocated a strong hand for the government in planning, including a voice in new investment decisions, but trade association representatives and advocates of business self-regulation largely dominated the Dickinson committee. In the office of Senator Wagner, meanwhile, still a third group of draftsmen hoped to attach public works spending and additional guarantees for labor to whatever legislation finally emerged. Administration supporters kept the Black-Connery bill bottled up in the House Rules Committee as Roosevelt finally locked these competing factions into a room and told them to weave their ideas together.

Compared to the hybrid National Industrial Recovery Act that Congress finally passed and Roosevelt signed into law on June 16, Senator Black's bill had been a model of simplicity. For the trade associations and proponents of business self-government such as Bernard Baruch and Gerard Swope of General Electric, the NIRA suspended the hated antitrust laws for two years and called for the creation of codes of fair competition to eliminate price cutting and overproduction. Although Tugwell's plan for investment controls did not survive, the advocates of industrial planning secured provisions authorizing the president to impose codes in situations where industries failed voluntarily to adopt them and giving him the power to restrict imports and interstate oil shipments. Through the efforts of Wagner and Perkins, the codes were required to contain a floor under wages, a ceiling on hours, a ban on yellow-dog contracts, and in Section 7a of the law a guarantee of labor's right to organize and bargain collectively. Despite the vehement objections of fiscal conservatives such as budget director Lewis Douglas, the law also authorized $3.3 billion in public works expenditures.

An intense battle between the Perkins-Wagner forces and Douglas over public works highlighted the chaotic circumstances that attended the NIRA's birth. Bowing to his budget director's argument that $3.3 billion would violate the spirit of the recently adopted Economy Act, FDR agreed to drop it. Several hours later, his arm twisted by Perkins, Roosevelt agreed to restore the money. The final version of the bill was printed and sent to Congress before Douglas knew what happened on Monday morning. Watching the conflict unfold and end, Perkins's twenty-five-year-old legal adviser Charles Wyzanski expressed astonishment. "I've studied law. I've studied political science," he told the secretary of labor. "I never could have conceived that important matters were settled like this."

THE BLUE EAGLE: TAKEOFF

Jerry-built, riddled with compromises, festooned with some benefits for virtually every constituency, the NIRA could, depending upon your point of view, be hailed as a great victory for business self-regulation, for government planning, for industrial democracy, or for priming the pump. Within two years, however, it disappointed most of its original supporters as well as those who thought it a bad idea in the first place. Heralded as an example of business, labor, and government cooperation; of Americans all pulling together for economic recovery, the NIRA soon became a source of disillusionment and even more bitter political strife because of its conflicting goals and interests.

The NIRA suffered from both personal and institutional problems. To head the National Recovery Administration, Roosevelt chose General Hugh Samuel Johnson, known as "Iron Pants," a West Point graduate who had run the draft during World War I and played a key role in the War Industries Board. Johnson was allied politically with Baruch and George Peek, his business associate at the Moline Plow Company. "He stimulated a large part of the population," recalled one NRA attorney, "and terrorized another part." Perkins called him "an erratic person . . . with strokes of genius." Even Baruch, his patron, warned Perkins about the general: "He's dangerous and unstable. He gets nervous and sometimes goes away for days without notice. I'm fond of him, but do tell the President to be careful."

A chain-smoker, a chain-talker, and fond of alcohol, Johnson had few rivals in the New Deal when it came to energy or invective. "It will be red fire at first and dead cats afterwards," he told reporters on the day of his appointment. "This is just like mounting the guillotine on the infinitesimal gamble that the ax won't work." His critics, soon legion, he dismissed as those "in whose veins there must flow something more than a trace of rodent blood." All he wanted out of life, the general once declared, "was to be down between Brownsville and Matamoras where the owls f———d the chickens."

Himself a businessman, Johnson envisioned industrial self-government as the cornerstone of the NRA. Given sufficient encouragement, he believed, businessmen would voluntarily adopt codes of fair competition that saved their industries from ruinous competition and raised their profits while giving their employees a minimum wage of $12 for a forty-hour week. He would provide the encouragement—loud, unceasing, flamboyant—by barnstorming across the country in an airplane to mobilize industries behind the codes, making speeches until he was hoarse, and presiding over spectacular NRA parades and demonstrations. Those businessmen who signed the blanket code could say proudly "We Do Our Part" and display the NRA's Blue Eagle symbol. By the end of September, against a background of hoopla unrivaled since the Liberty Loan drives of World War I, over five hundred codes of fair competition had been written and approved by Johnson and the White House.

THE BLUE EAGLE: CRASH LANDING

The general and the NRA soon came under fire, however, for allowing businessmen too great a voice in drafting the codes and for giving them an even bigger role in running the NRA's compliance machinery, the various code authorities. Many small entrepreneurs accused the NRA of fostering monopoly through code provisions and sanctions beneficial to their larger competitors. Consumers complained that the codes restricted output and encouraged higher prices before pay envelopes grew any thicker.

Union leaders and workers, inspired by Section 7a to organize, berated the agency for failing to enforce the wages and hours provisions in the codes adequately and for undermining genuine collective bargaining by allowing employers to support company unions. These and other grievances filled the air by 1934 at congressional hearings and before the NRA's own review board, chaired by the outspoken criminal lawyer Clarence Darrow. There was considerable truth to these charges, but much hyperbole, too.

The confusion at the NRA again dramatized the problems of limited state capacity that hampered the New Deal when it attempted to implement a new program. Like the administrators of the Triple A, Johnson faced the staggering task of attempting to develop a nationwide program within a short period of time. But unlike the Triple A, which could call upon the seasoned personnel in the agricultural extension service and land grant colleges, Johnson had no corps of skilled bureaucrats who stood ready to spearhead the federal government's industrial recovery efforts. Financing and training such a corps of government workers would have taken precious months.

In the face of this administrative bottleneck, Johnson and his staff relied on those experts already at hand who were best organized and informed in 1933 to draw up the codes and enforce them. This meant, by and large, businessmen and trade association members from the industries themselves. Those who caught the first train to Washington often had their way with the handful of NRA administrators, whether they represented large companies or small ones. In short, the primitive level of government expertise accounted for business domination of the NRA, not a conspiracy by big capitalists.

Except for a few zealots like Swope, most big capitalists looked with suspicion on the Blue Eagle from the beginning. Henry Ford said he wouldn't have "that Roosevelt buzzard on my cars," even after General Motors and Chrysler signed the automobile code. In those sectors of the economy in which a handful of firms already had power to control prices—steel, aluminum, automobiles, chemicals, electrical equipment—the large corporations had no need for NRA. They tolerated it, "did their part" for reasons of public relations, and grew increasingly restive as their workers took advantage of Section 7a and signed up for union membership.

Johnson and the NRA drew their most fervent support not from the titans of capitalism, but from industries such as textiles and coal mining, where competition among hundreds of small operators had produced excess capacity and price cutting for decades. In a few industries, ironically, the largest firms claimed bitterly that their tiny opponents had written the codes and ran the authorities to the detriment of consumers. This appears to have been the case with respect to used cars and furniture manufacturing.

Johnson's biggest mistake appears not to have been his reliance on businessmen—he had little choice in that matter, given the minuscule size and experience of the federal bureaucracy—but his frantic efforts to extend the codes and the Blue Eagle symbol to virtually every industry in the land. Common sense dictated codes of fair competition for autos, steel, the garment trades, lumber, coal, and shipbuilding, which employed millions of workers. Common sense ruled out codes for those producing nose rings for hogs, shoulder pads for women's dresses, and dog food, but Johnson wanted them to fly the Blue Eagle, too. The NRA code for the burlesque industry went so far as to fix the number of strippers permitted in each show. Efforts of this sort subjected the NRA to ridicule and charges of government dictatorship, but the bigger impact was on Johnson. First, he drove himself to near physical collapse by flying around the country and negotiating codes nonstop. Then, as criticism of the NRA began to mount, he took more and more refuge in drink.

While small businessmen complained that the Blue Eagle strangled them with red tape and favored monopolists, labor leaders and workers protested that employers sabotaged their rights under Section 7a. Across the nation, from the coalfields of Kentucky to the waterfront of Seattle, workers flocked to union banners in numbers unknown since the great organizing drives of World War I, when the federal government had also protected them. In a single month, for example, the membership of John L. Lewis's once-struggling United Mine Workers shot up by 100,000. Another 50,000 poured into the hastily built unions of the rubber tire industry. "The president wants you to unionize," declared organizers. "It is unpatriotic to refuse to unionize. Here is your union. Never mind about the dues now. Just join up." Companies responded by firing employees who signed union cards, hiring thugs to bust up union meetings, and bringing in strikebreakers when pickets began to march. Violence and bloodshed erupted in 1934 as over a million and a half workers walked off their jobs in 1,856 separate strikes. The worst disorders took place among the truckers in Minneapolis, the miners in Harlan County, Kentucky, the textile operators in Gastonia, and the longshoremen in San Francisco, where a general strike paralyzed the entire city.

Johnson attempted to deal with this threat to the NRA's recovery efforts by creating labor advisory boards to mediate disputes in strike-plagued industries and finally by forming a distinguished National Labor Board to interpret and apply Section 7a uniformly across the country. Chaired by Senator Wagner, the NLB included three influential labor leaders—Lewis, William Green of the AFL, and Leo Wolman of the Amalgamated Clothing Workers—as well as three captains of industry—Swope, Louis Kirstein, and Walter Teagle, chairman of Standard Oil. To the shock and horror of employers, the board adopted what it called the "Reading Formula" for enforcing Section 7a and resolving strikes. Its key provisions called for the reinstatement of strikers, a secret ballot election to determine who would represent the workers, and rule by the majority. "This is America," declared Swope, "and that's the way we do things here."

But most employers in 1934 didn't share Swope's vision of America. Henry Ford said he would never accept the Reading Formula, a sentiment shared by others, who continued to ignore the board and to place their faith in strikebreakers, tear gas, and guns. Roosevelt didn't

The NRA inspires demands for a union.

help matters when he refused to endorse the Reading Formula as the basis for a settlement in the automobile industry. Instead, he accepted a scheme for proportional representation that included the companies' own captive unions. This was a typical Roosevelt solution—giving something to everybody—but it undermined the authority of his own National Labor Board and helped weaken the NRA with key labor leaders. Disillusioned, many workers condemned the Blue Eagle as pro-business, and Senator Wagner vowed to push new legislation to protect labor's rights outside the NRA's tottering structure.

During his tenure as NRA chief and later, after FDR eased him out of the agency, Johnson complained bitterly that his recovery efforts had been frustrated by the president's refusal to give him control over spending the $3.3 billion in public works money authorized in the initial legislation. Instead, FDR put Interior Secretary Ickes in charge of the fund and what became the Public Works Administration (PWA). While his code-writing efforts prevented a further deterioration in the economy, Johnson argued, Ickes spent money so cautiously that little new stimulus was given to recovery.

In retrospect, Roosevelt probably made the right decision about the public works component of NRA. Johnson was all sail and no ballast. Trusting him with $3.3 billion, as Perkins and others warned would have been like trusting an infant with a flamethrower. "Honest Harold" Ickes spent only $2.8 billion of the original appropriation, and most of that on projects already underway through other federal agencies. He probably lavished too much time scrutinizing every construction contract and defending against graft, but what Ickes did build— 34,000 projects, including Grand Coulee Dam in Washington State, the Golden Gate Bridge in San Francisco, and the Queens Tunnel in New York—became permanent monuments to the nation's infrastructure. It is unlikely Johnson could have done as well.

Autopsy

Even before the Supreme Court declared the NRA unconstitutional on May 27, 1935, the agency had become a political orphan, denounced by scores of businessmen, labor leaders, economists, and critics inside the administration. The verdict of most historians has hardly been more friendly. Johnson and the Blue Eagle, it is often said, tried to promote

FDR with cabinet secretaries Harold Ickes and Henry A. Wallace.

recovery with smoke and mirrors. What the American economy needed in 1933–34 was a large stimulus, not the trickle of spending provided by Ickes and the policy of scarcity embodied in the codes of fair competition.

As an engine of recovery, the NRA indeed sputtered and died, because the temptation for businessmen to boost prices before wages proved almost irresistible. But the NRA was hardly a total failure. It did contain a commitment to higher, decent labor standards. The cotton textile code, for example, sounded the death knell for child labor in Southern mills, a goal long sought by progressives and Northern textile interests, which resented the region's wage differential. If not exactly the working man's Magna Charta, Section 7a unleashed new hopes and prospects for organized labor. The NRA's Consumers' Advisory Board and its Research Planning Division, potential counterweights to the initial influence of trade associations, had begun to gather strength and expertise in 1934 and early 1935, which is one reason most businessmen did not lament the agency's judicial demise.

In little more than a year, the New Deal had reversed the economy's long slide since 1930 by breaking the liquidity crisis, pumping new capital into ailing banks, rescuing homeowners from foreclosure, offering direct relief to the unemployed, and providing new organizational incentives to farmers, businessmen, and industrial workers. For many, the immediate terrors of further liquidation and destitution had been lifted. Pessimism had been checked. It was far too early to say that real economic recovery had begun, but recovery of a different sort had been set in motion, aided by the New Deal's enthusiasm and experimental programs. Across the country, from union halls to city halls, political debate revived and flourished, energized in part by Washington. FDR and the New Dealers had helped to set in motion forces that wished to stop it from going any further and others that demanded more fundamental changes.

4

Critics Left, Critics Right

Boys—this is our hour! We've got to get everything we want—a works program, social security, wages and hours, everything—now or never.
—Harry Hopkins, 1934

I can take him [FDR]. He's a phony. . . . He's scared of me. I can outpromise him, and he knows it. People will believe me and they won't believe him.
—Huey Long, 1934

RISING EXPECTATIONS

Hope often fuels social revolt. Historians have long noted that revolutions occur when times are getting better, not worse; when economic misery and oppression begin to loosen their grip; when people sense new opportunities for social improvement and no longer accept the status quo as inevitable. Such was the American experience in the Great Depression, especially as the initial programs of Roosevelt's New Deal took hold and began to lift the pall of gloom and doubt that hung over the nation in the winter of 1932–33.

This is not to suggest that Americans passively accepted their economic fate prior to FDR's inauguration. Frequent outbursts of popular anger and rebellion led some to believe that the country faced genuine revolution on the eve of the Hundred Days. "I never heard such cynicism about democracy as in that period," recalled Norman Thomas. "Whatever else you may say about Mr. Roosevelt and his New Deal, it is incontrovertible that, if he had not done about as much as he did,

America would have been in for very serious social unrest." Farmers rose to the defense of their neighbors threatened with foreclosure by disrupting auctions and greeting sheriffs and other officials with pitchforks and shotguns. Other rural rebels blockaded highways in an attempt to prevent milk and produce from reaching the market. Striking coal miners beat up company guards in Harlan County, Kentucky.

The cities saw similar outbursts of spontaneous protest. Cuban cigar makers in Tampa went on strike when their employers banned the tradition of readers on the factory floor, who had enlightened workers from the pages of Cervantes and Zola as well as the *Socialist Call.* In many urban communities, groups of tenants banded together to resist the eviction of families unable to pay the rent. Landlords who defied these community norms faced jeering crowds of men, women, and children. Often as not, they carted the victims' furniture back to the vacant apartment and dared the landlord to try it again. Friendly police officers did not always intervene to rescue the landlord from his tenants' wrath. Organizers for the Communist Party skillfully channeled the anger of the unemployed and those on relief into raucous protests against further layoffs and cuts in public assistance.

Since the eighteenth century, Americans had seldom been stoic in the face of economic downturns. The early 1930s were no exception. But what had been scattered episodes of protest against particular acts of injustice in 1932–33 turned into larger and more sustained rebellion against the status quo between 1934 and 1936. The successes of the early New Deal unleashed fresh hopes. Its failures generated new frustrations. The rhetoric of the New Dealers and programs of the Hundred Days raised the level of critical debate about the country's economic predicament and at the same time encouraged some people to think about even more radical solutions.

Government spending played a crucial role in lifting morale and expectation. Some farmers pocketed their first benefit checks and felt reborn. "I think we'd just pack up and move out and leave our stock to starve if the government hadn't stepped in," one cattle rancher told a reporter. "This gives us new hope to try again." Over Roosevelt's veto, Congress insisted that veterans get their World War I cash bonus. The unemployed spent new relief money or went to work for Hopkins's CWA, Ickes's PWA, or the Civilian Conservation Corps. Social workers noted that a government job restored dignity and purpose to the lives of individuals and families. "The mere fact of his having responsibility and a pattern of routine for existence completely changed the man," one observed. "He went around whistling. His wife was happier."

Suddenly, many people on the verge of destitution had money to spend again, which dampened protest in some cases, but intensified it elsewhere as the gap between those with something and those with very little grew wider. When the efforts of the Hundred Days, especially NRA and AAA, failed to deliver recovery, the milk of optimism turned sour quickly. Workers, inspired by the language of NRA's Section 7a to organize, became especially bitter and militant when the New Deal appeared to abandon them.

Midway through his first term, therefore, Roosevelt found his program under attack from newly energized political forces that demanded more sweeping alterations in the nation's social and economic arrangements. Almost simultaneously, the New Deal came under fire from many of those only recently saved from catastrophe, who now believed that the administration had already gone too far and that the mobilization of more radical groups threatened outright revolution, complete with a wholesale redistribution of power and property. Buffeted by those who called for greater change and deserted by many conservatives, Roosevelt brought his boat about and headed downwind, as always, slightly to the left of the mainstream. There followed a second burst of national reform in 1935 that surpassed the Hundred Days and a stunning reelection triumph for FDR a year later.

March, Left: Congress and the States

In 1932, a disillusioned electorate gave the Democrats control of both houses of Congress for the first time since the Wilson era. They increased the party's majority in the lower chamber to 310–117 over the Republicans and gave them a 60–35 advantage in the Senate. Two years later, defying historical tradition, which dictated that the president's party lost seats in an off-year election, the Democrats gained an astonishing nine seats in both the House and Senate. Combined with ten Farmer-Laborites in the House, the Republican contingent in that chamber had been reduced to 103. No party had ever held such a wide margin in the Senate. Most political pundits pronounced the results a ringing endorsement of FDR and the New Deal. William Allen White said the President had been "all but crowned by the people." Other journalists, viewing the carnage inflicted on the GOP, predicted that

Republicans would soon take their place in museums next to the mastodons and dodo birds.

The geographical distribution and ideological leanings of these new Democrats proved more important that their absolute numbers. They came predominantly from the cities and their environs in the Northeast, the Midwest, and the Far West. While some of their constituents were small shopkeepers and middle-class professionals who had usually voted Republican, an even larger number wore blue collars, carried lunch pails to work, and could still read a foreign-language newspaper. In 1932 they and their families had voted for Roosevelt hoping to salvage what remained of their dignity. Now, repairing a highway for the CWA, buying groceries with a relief check, or joining a labor union under the NRA, they had become Democrats out of self-interest and conviction. And the representatives and senators they elected in 1934, such as Harry S Truman from Kansas City, had promised them more government assistance, not less.

A more liberal Congress assembled in 1935 than the one that approved the measures of the Hundred Days. It was inclined to favor the interests of the cities, their emerging ethnic majorities, and the budding labor movement. Coming from areas with high levels of unemployment and many relief recipients, the newest congressmen brought greater class consciousness and a willingness to think in terms of redistributing wealth from the haves to the have-nots. The traditional Southern leadership in the Congress and the party sensed this momentous shift in the balance of power and worried about how to control it. Congressional liberals such as Robert Wagner, however, welcomed the shift as an opportunity to push forward with bolder plans to aid labor, the cities, and the poor.

Roosevelt's most progressive advisers—Hopkins, Ickes, Tugwell, Mrs. Roosevelt, Wallace, and Frankfurter—also saw the new Congress as an ally in their battle with the administration's fiscal conservatives. In the spring of 1934, for instance, Roosevelt had ordered Hopkins to shut down the innovative CWA program. It had put millions to work during the desperate winter months with jobs planned and run directly by the federal government, but also had infuriated state and local politicians, who complained that they had little voice in what was built and who got the jobs. Roosevelt preferred work relief to the dole, but he told Hopkins to scale back his plans for the coming year in any event. Emboldened by the 1934 election returns, however, Hopkins and his key assistants advocated a major expansion of public works to replace CWA, confident that if FDR went along they had the votes in

Congress. Hopkins saw opportunity elsewhere, too: "Boys—this is our hour! We've got to get everything we want—a works program, social security, wages and hours, everything—now or never. Get your minds at work on developing a complete ticket to provide security for all the folks of this country up and down and across the board."

Election returns from the states in 1934 also led New Dealers like Hopkins to believe that local political winds had shifted in their direction and might blow them down unless they picked up the pace of reform. Again, Republican causalities had been heavy. Among the governorships, only seven remained in GOP hands after November. Even more impressive than the Democratic gains, however, had been the strong showing of independent candidates, who sounded rhetorically far more radical than the man in the White House. Voters in Minnesota returned Farmer-Laborite Floyd Olson to the governor's mansion for a third term on a platform that called for state ownership of mines, utilities, transportation facilities, and other productive assets. Pennslyvanians gave another vote of confidence to the old progressive warrior Gifford Pinchot, the dean of the conservation movement and a zealous foe of big business.

Scorning both parties, Philip La Follette and Robert La Follette, Jr., recaptured the Wisconsin governorship and the state's U.S. Senate seat on a Progressive Party ticket that backed most of the New Deal, but also called for collective bargaining, unemployment insurance, and old-age pensions. The strong showing in California by the muckraking novelist and radical Upton Sinclair terrified conservatives, too. He won the Democratic primary election for governor on a program called EPIC (End Poverty in California), which went beyond demands for a redistribution of wealth. Sinclair harkened back to an older nineteenth-century reform tradition that advocated placing control over productive resources in the hands of workers. EPIC promised to the state's unemployed the operation of idle factories and farms.

Roosevelt hinted to several advisers that he saw nothing terribly dangerous about Sinclair's platform, but regular California Democrats did everything possible to sabotage the EPIC crusade. So did others close to the president. In a much-quoted editorial that appeared in *Today* magazine, Moley ridiculed EPIC as "back to barter, back to nature," and warned voters that the author of *The Jungle* had "no experience in practical administration." Even in the face of FDR's active neutrality and a vicious smear campaign orchestrated by motion picture mogul Louis B. Mayer, Sinclair received over 870,000 popular votes while losing to Republican Frank Merriam. In order to beat Sinclair and ward off EPIC's appeal, however, his Republican opponent came out for several progressive measures.

The congressional elections, the stunning success of Olson and the La Follettes, the near miss by Sinclair—all indicated a growing if somewhat inchoate demand for more radical forms of economic experimentation than those so far advanced by FDR. Nor was it lost upon Roosevelt's political advisers that between 1928 and 1932, the presidential vote for Socialist Party candidate Norman Thomas had increased threefold to over 800,000 and for the Communist Party's William Z. Foster from 21,000 to 102,000. Who could tell what might happen in 1936 if recovery stalled and died? Neither Olson nor the La Follettes harbored thoughts of mounting a broad, nationwide crusade against the inadequacies of Roosevelt's New Deal. Such was not the case, however, with respect to Louisiana's junior United States senator, a popular radio priest from Detroit, or a doctor and part-time real estate salesman from Long Beach, California.

SHARE THE WEALTH

In the roiling political waters of 1934, few trolled with more enthusiasm than the Kingfish, Huey Long, who hoped to export his brand of Southern populism to the entire nation. During the late 1920s, Governor Long had built a formidable political empire in Louisiana through a program that taxed corporations and the rich in order to bring social services to the poor and, of course, oil the Kingfish's own machine. Now in harder times and from the floor of the United States Senate he found many people beyond Louisiana who listened when he skewered the wealthy and the powerful. The Depression had been caused by a maldistribution of wealth, Long affirmed, and its cure could come only through redistribution from the top of the income pyramid to the bottom. Roosevelt and many New Dealers often said much the same thing, but Huey Long said it loudly, poignantly, sarcastically, and repeatedly.

Smart, ambitious, cunning, and absolutely ruthless, the Kingfish campaigned tirelessly on Roosevelt's behalf in 1932, but his love affair with the New Deal and its Senate allies remained short and tempestuous. When the Senate Banking and Currency Committee exposed the misdeeds of investment bankers and stockbrokers as a prelude to securities regulation, the Kingfish scoffed at the inquiry. "First we prod them, kick them, poke them, and make sure they're dead," he said. "Then, once we're sure of that, we all shout together, 'Let's go after them,' and we do."

He seldom missed an opportunity to jab the Senate's conservative leaders, especially Southern nabobs like Joe Robinson and Carter Glass. He ultimately voted for the NRA, but not before denouncing it as a sham. "Every fault of socialism is to be found in this bill, without one of its virtues," he fumed. "Every crime of monarchy is in here, without one of the things that would give it credit." When Roosevelt vetoed the veterans' bonus legislation, Long took the lead in denouncing the president for coldhearted indifference to the plight of impoverished ex-soldiers.

In February 1934, Long announced the creation of a nationwide Share Our Wealth Society, whose central platform guaranteed to every American family a "homestead allowance" of $5,000 and a minimum annual income of $2,500. The plan would be financed, Long declared, by steeply graduated income and inheritance taxes such that no personal fortune would exceed $5 million and no individual could keep as earnings more than $1.8 million in a year. Robin Hood with a vengeance.

Long's critics quickly pointed out that the Kingfish needed a refresher course in arithmetic. In order to give each American family $2,500 per year, no family could retain more than $3,000, and to finance the $5,000 homestead allowance, the cap on inheritance would have to be $7,000 instead of $5 million. But few of those who flocked into the Share Our Wealth clubs in 1934 and 1935 bothered with long division. Like the title of his 1933 book *Every Man a King*, Long offered to many an enticing vision of economic justice and personal prosperity.

The Kingfish, said some of his opponents, advocated socialism or communism. Others, including FDR, regarded Long as the harbinger of American fascism, noting his taste for absolute personal power and his not infrequent use of political violence in Louisiana. But Long's economic and political ideas were, like the man himself, *sui generis*. His redistribution scheme flatly rejected collectivism or state ownership of the means of production. Nor could Share Our Wealth be called corporatist in the mold of European fascists. Long himself seldom engaged in crude anti-Semitism or racism.

At his core, the Kingfish remained an old-fashioned economic individualist who took as his model of success the druggist on Main Street and the corner grocer. Like Upton Sinclair in California, Long advocated a producer-oriented utopia in which Americans ran their own business instead of working for somebody else. This had broad appeal in a society in which independent proprietorship seemed doomed to extinction in the face of giant corporations, chain stores, and factory labor. Long usually denounced big business and harshly attacked the

Senator Huey Long, the New Deal's most formidable critic.

New Deal for encouraging big government and bureaucracy. But his own tax program, ironically, would have required an administrative apparatus of enormous size.

Long seldom recognized these contradictions. Neither did his followers—the druggists, grocers, barbers, gas station operators, farmers, and skilled workers—who joined Share Our Wealth clubs from coast to coast and swelled its coffers with their tiny donations. Roosevelt might comfort and inspire them, but the Kingfish gave voice to their deep resentments and fears. They saw in Long a David fighting the Goliaths of industry, finance, and government, someone who would humble the rich, crush the monopolists, limit the size of government, and restore the little people to the independence and power stolen from them by corporations and politicians in Washington.

By early 1935, Long's ambitions for national power could not be ignored. Share Our Wealth clubs had sprouted up from the Deep South to the Pacific Coast, numbering perhaps 27,000 chapters with over eight million members. Millions also tuned in on the NBC radio network in March when he replied to an earlier attack by General Johnson. A crowd estimated at over ten thousand packed the Iowa State Fairgrounds a month later to hear the Kingfish blast the New Deal for destroying crops, evicting tenant farmers, and giving more aid to bankers than to those on relief. Roosevelt hit back, not only through anti-Long speeches by subordinates like Johnson and Ickes, but by cutting off all federal patronage to the senator and sending a swarm of Treasury agents into Louisiana to search for evidence of income tax evasion.

But Long easily won the battle of invective against "Prince Franklin" and his spokesmen, whom he labeled the "chinchbug of Chicago" (Ickes), "Lord Corn-Wallace, the "honorable lord destroyer" (Wallace), and the "Nabob of New York" (Jim Farley). No one seriously believed that this "engagingly boyish figure, jovial and impudent, Tom Sawyer in a toga" could wrest the Democratic nomination from FDR in 1936, but Long's popularity was such that a third-party candidacy might be enough to tip the election to the Republicans. One poll gave him about 12 percent of the popular vote and enough support to carry eight or nine states. The Kingfish's thoughts moved along those lines, and he seemed to relish the prospect of a head-to-head fight with the president. "I can take him [FDR]," Long bragged to a friend. "He's a phony. . . . He's scared of me. I can outpromise him, and he knows it. People will believe me and they won't believe him. . . . He's living on an inherited income. I got nothin', so I don't have to bother about that."

"Golden Hour of the Little Flower"

Even as a solo act, Huey Long challenged FDR's top billing on the nation's political stage. By 1934, however, the Kingfish had a supporting cast of other characters whose antidepression nostrums likewise threatened to siphon off support from the president and the New Deal. The most charismatic and unpredictable was a forty-three-year-old Catholic priest from the Detroit suburb of Royal Oak, Father Charles Edward Coughlin. Three years before the stock market crash, Coughlin persuaded a local radio station to give him airtime in order to raise funds for his Shrine of the Little Flower, then on the brink of insolvency. The former Basilian priest soon became a smash hit, and by 1930 when CBS offered him a nationwide forum on Sunday nights, Coughlin's *The Golden Hour of the Little Flower* reached an audience of between thirty and forty million listeners. Funds flowed in to his parish at the rate of $5 million a year, and the staff of his Radio League for the Little Flower opened an average of eighty-thousand letters a week.

In addition to homilies on the gospel, the owl-faced bespectacled Coughlin soon offered the faithful a large dose of social and economic analysis which warned of the evils of communism and investigated the causes and cure of the depression. The former he blamed on a shortage of money deliberately engineered by the bankers of Wall Street and London, who because they worshiped "the pagan god of gold" exploited the nation's hardworking producers. As a remedy, which he advocated tirelessly in a style that combined slashing sarcasm with sweet reason, Coughlin argued inflation of the money supply by reducing the gold content of the dollar and recoining silver. "Silver is the key to world prosperity," said the radio priest, "silver that was damned by the Morgans." As a demonstration of his confidence in this panacea, the Little Flower's financial adviser accumulated large holdings of silver futures. The priest also advocated the abolition of the banker-dominated Federal Reserve System and its replacement by a publicly owned central bank.

Coughlin's scathing attacks on British financiers cemented his already large following among working-class Irish Catholics. His passionate advocacy of inflation endeared him to many debt-ridden farmers and businessmen, who saw cheap money as the instrument of their own salvation and the engine of recovery. Like Long, he came out for FDR in 1932, telling his radio audience that it was a choice between "Roosevelt or ruin." During most of 1933 he continued to shower praise on FDR. "The New Deal is Christ's Deal," he told his audience. He assured them that the angel Gabriel, not Lucifer, hovered over the White House. But Coughlin's ego was too large and FDR's commitment to inflation too mild for the alliance to last very long. The radio priest found little to praise in the banking reforms of the Hundred Days. And although Roosevelt took the country off gold and devalued the dollar by about 25 percent, he never implemented fully the sweeping inflationary schemes authorized by the Thomas Amendment to the Agricultural Adjustment Act.

Coughlin's enthusiasm for FDR began to cool in late 1934. The New Deal, he declared, was both a communist conspiracy and a Wall Street plot intended to keep the common people enslaved. FDR presided over "government of bankers, by the bankers and for the bankers." Near the end of 1934 the priest announced the formation of the National Union for Social Justice, intended, he told his radio listeners, to elect candidates who supported true monetary reform, the end of Wall Street's control over the banking system, and redistribution of the nation's wealth. It would not be long before a nasty note of anti-Semitism also began to creep into Coughlin's speeches and the pages of his magazine *Social Justice*, which started publication in 1936. By then, too, he focused more and more criticism upon particular New Dealers, especially Jews such as Morgenthau and Frankfurter.

The administration sought to discredit Coughlin by exposing his silver speculations and later unleashed both General Johnson and Ickes against him. Johnson linked Long, the "Louisiana dictator," and Coughlin, "this political padre," as "pied pipers" who menaced the country with their demagogic appeals. The secretary of the interior dismissed the radio priest as someone whose "rich but undisciplined imagination has reduced politics, sociology, and banking to charming poetry which he distills mellifluously into the ether for the enchantment of mankind." But Roosevelt also displayed some vacillation in dealing with Coughlin, owing in part to his clerical garb and large following among traditional big-city Democrats. FDR hoped as well to keep Coughlin out of Long's camp. He employed various Catholic

Father Charles E. Coughlin attacks the New Deal.

emissaries (Jim Farley, Detroit mayor Frank Murphy, and Joseph P. Kennedy) in an effort to retain Coughlin's loyalty and attempted to flatter the radio priest by inviting him to Hyde Park for lunch.

Neither the carrot nor the stick seemed to work with Coughlin, however, who continued his attacks against the New Deal and seemed to regard himself as someone capable of delivering the country from the Reds and the money changers. Despite the warning of Johnson and others about a Long-Coughlin alliance, the two men eyed each other suspiciously. Long, who ridiculed the priest in private as "just a political Kate Smith," dismissed his monetary ideas as half-baked alternatives to genuine economic redistribution. Coughlin thought Share Our Wealth too close to communism. But as Roosevelt knew, politics sometimes produced strange bedfellows.

PIED PIPER OF PENSIONS

Whatever their ideological differences, both Long and Coughlin appealed to people who had absorbed the brunt of the Depression and felt ignored by the initial programs of the New Deal. Few groups fell more readily into both categories than the nation's elderly, especially those who had not worked in years, had watched their savings vanish in the banking panic, and could no longer count on assistance from hard-pressed families and relatives. Social workers from coast to coast told mournful tales of aging men and women evicted from homes and apartments, forced to accept relief, and, when that ran out, reduced to scrounging in garbage cans for food. Even the old folks who managed to save their homes and who scraped by because of tiny private or state pensions did not know when the money might vanish. Many of these found a potential savior in Dr. Francis Townsend and his Old Age Revolving Pensions, Limited.

Beginning with a letter in his hometown newspaper in Long Beach, California, Townsend between 1933 and 1935 put forward a plan of utmost simplicity and attractiveness to the nation's older citizens. All persons over sixty years of age would receive a government pension of $200 a month upon condition that they retire from work and spend the whole amount within thirty days. The pensions were to be financed by a 2 percent tax on business transactions. Although skeptics immediately pointed out that the tax was likely to dampen recovery, Townsend argued that the benefits of his revolving pension plan would quickly outweigh the costs. The elderly would no longer compete with younger workers for scarce jobs, they would not become a burden on their families, and their spending would lift the economy out of the Depression. Old people had "more buying experience than those of younger years," Townsend said, and "they could become a research, educational, and corrective force in both a material and spiritual way."

A scheme more calculated to stir wild enthusiasm among the seven to eight million Americans over the age of sixty is difficult to imagine. And the man who proposed it looked as though he had just stepped from a Norman Rockwell painting. Tall, white-haired, mild-mannered, Dr. Townsend oozed sincerity. His speeches effectively combined religious and patriotic themes typical of revivalist preachers on the Southern California evangelical circuit. At a time when only twenty-eight states had any kind of old-age pensions ranging from $8 to $30 a month, Townsend's $200 a month represented heaven on earth to many elderly citizens.

It was also a fool's paradise. In order to fund Townsend's plan, the so-called transaction tax would have too be raised far above 2 percent, with some estimates about the actual increase in prices reaching as high as 80 or 90 percent. In one year, Townsend's plan would have required payments to the elderly amounting to one half of the nation's income. But he promised his listeners what in fact they deserved: security in their old age, independence, and dignity. They opened their hearts and pocket books to the doctor from Long Beach.

By 1935, over half a million old people had joined three thousand vocal Townsend clubs that the founder and his assistants had located strategically in congressional districts around the country. Townsend himself received thousands of letters of support each day, while Townsendites flooded local, state, and national politicians with demands to enact their leader's program. Enthusiasm for the Old Age Revolving Pension Plan became so great in California that even Sinclair's conservative Republican opponent for governor jumped on the bandwagon. Three months after a bill modeled on the doctor's plan was introduced in the House of Representatives in January 1935, the Townsend clubs secured twenty million signatures calling for its immediate passage. The doctor and his chief administrative aide, real estate promoter Robert Clements, found a ready market for the organization's wares, too, which included Townsend buttons, tire covers, license plates, songs, and a newspaper, the *Townsend National Weekly*. The latter raked in $200,000 a year through advertising remedies for every malady from baldness to rheumatism.

Long, Coughlin, and Townsend tapped different sources of discontent with the New Deal and offered clashing solutions to their follow-ers, but the message they sent to Roosevelt and his supporters was clear enough: unless the president did something to counter their rising influence, he risked loosing substantial political support. This was the pessimistic conclusion of one of Hopkins's astute field investigators, who reported to her boss from New Jersey in late 1934 that among relief clients and the unemployed, confidence in the president had plummeted sharply. "They say to you," she reported, " 'How does he [FDR] expect us to live . . . does he know what food costs, what rents are, how can we keep clothes on the children. . . ?' "

LIBERTY LEAGUERS

While the followers of Olson, Sinclair, Long, Coughlin, and Town-send believed that the New Deal had not done enough to redistribute wealth, restore independent proprietorship, or protect the little people from the ravages of the Depression, a substantial number of business-men and politicians argued that Roosevelt had already gone too far. From their perspective, he had already begun to turn class against class and had extended government controls over the economy far beyond what the Constitution permitted. Some, regarding even Hoover as a dangerous innovator, looked upon the first years of the New Deal as the equivalent of Bolshevism. A large number of these conservative critics came together in the American Liberty League, an organization formed in the summer of 1934 and pledged "to defend and uphold the Constitution . . . to foster the right to work, earn, save and acquire property and to preserve the ownership and lawful use of property."

The league drew support from a few of FDR's old enemies inside the Democratic Party—Al Smith, Jowett Shouse, and John Raskob. "I am for gold dollars as against baloney dollars. I am for experience against experiment," Smith said in denunciation of the New Deal's monetary policy. Before a cheering throng of tuxedo-attired business-men at the Mayflower Hotel, the former governor blasted the New Deal and declared that "there can only be one capital—Washington or Moscow." The American Liberty League's financial benefactors read like a who's who of corporate America: Irénée Du Pont, Edward F. Hutton of General Foods, Alfred Sloan of General Motors, J. Howard Pew of Sun Oil, and Nathan Miller of United States Steel. And its legal advisers, headed by John W. Davis and James M. Beck, came from some of Wall Street's leading firms.

Throughout his presidency, Roosevelt enjoyed considerable support from influential businessmen and financiers. The idea that corporate leaders formed a united bloc against the New Deal is largely a myth. But those who backed FDR—bankers Winthrop Aldrich and Averell Harriman, movie tycoon Jack Warner, Standard Oil's Walter Teagle, IBM's Thomas Watson, AT&T's Walter Gifford, and department store magnate Edward A. Filene—represented newer, high-technology service and entertainment industries that did not feel threatened immediately by a large, militant blue-collar labor force. In more traditional manufacturing sectors, especially steel, automobiles, and textiles, fear of organized labor and the New Deal ran deep almost from the beginning. This was also true of the small to medium-sized firms that formed the backbone of the National Association of Manufacturers and the American Chamber of Commerce.

The rising chorus of business protests against the administration in 1934 and 1935 miffed Roosevelt, despite the continued support he received from key capitalists. He had rescued the bankers from insolvency and exempted trade associations from the detested antitrust laws, but still came under attack. Big business seemed ungrateful for other favors, too. His monetary policies reduced the debt burdens of railroads and other public utilities. He surrounded himself with conservative fiscal advisers, trimmed ordinary government spending, and vetoed the veterans' bonus. He had appointed businessmen like Joseph P. Kennedy to new regulatory agencies like the Securities and Exchange Commission over the protests of many progressives.

And what, Roosevelt began to ask, did he get in return from many businessmen except fulminations against the NRA, complaints that he was bankrupting the country, and constant innuendoes that he wished to establish a dictatorship over business and industry? Probably the last straw for Roosevelt came in late April 1935, when the incoming president of the Chamber of Commerce told the organization's cheering delegates that "businessmen are tired of hearing promises to do constructive things, which turn out to be only attempts to Sovietize America."

Roosevelt hit back. In all the speeches that came out of the Chamber of Commerce gathering and other recent business meetings, he told reporters, not one "took the human side, the old-age side, the unemployment side." As large numbers of businessmen jumped off the right

"Come along. We're going to the Trans-Lux to hiss Roosevelt" (caption).

Peter Arno's cartoon captured the attitude of many of the wealthy, who regarded FDR as a traitor to his own class.

side of FDR's ship, it began to list inevitably to the left, even without encouragement from Huey Long and others. His own advisers, busy since late 1933, quickly put the final touches on proposals for social security, taxation, and further banking reforms.

JUDICIAL VETOES

As many of the nation's businessmen intensified their attacks on FDR and the New Deal, they found a sympathetic ear among many federal judges, now called upon to weigh the constitutionality of the legislative and executive actions of the Hundred Days. In choosing to fight the

New Deal on legal grounds by invoking the Constitution, conservative opponents such as those in the American Liberty League made a shrewd decision. Ordinary Americans, many out of work, were not likely to be moved in defense of wealth and privilege. Far better to wrap oneself in the Constitution and portray the New Dealers as dangerous radicals who would subvert the country's fundamental law.

The administration and Congress had rushed through many laws without careful study. Given this haste, some New Deal statutes probably contained serious flaws. Roosevelt had also allowed Attorney General Homer Cummings and Postmaster General Farley to staff the Department of Justice with political hacks and lawyers not of the highest intellectual caliber. And finally, Republican presidents from Harding to Hoover had packed the federal courts with jurists who normally cast a skeptical eye on legislation that touched the rights of property and contract or that appeared to upset the traditional balance between federal and state jurisdiction. Playing before the judicial branch, New Deal opponents held mainly trumps.

The lower federal bench did not disappoint the administration's enemies. By early 1935, according to one estimate, federal judges had issued hundreds of injunctions staying the enforcement on constitutional grounds of virtually every New Deal measure. Overworked and outmanned administration lawyers labored around the clock simply to stay abreast of this crushing caseload. Fearing even more judicial roadblocks, they delayed enforcement of other laws. The real test would come, however, when cases came before the nine justices of the Supreme Court of the United States, where, most agreed, the outcome was very much in doubt.

Four justices—Sutherland, McReynolds, Butler, and Van Devanter—continued to anchor the Court's conservative wing as they had under Chief Justice Taft in the 1920s. All but McReynolds owed their appointment to Republican presidents. Known as "the Four Horsemen of the Apocalypse," they looked upon the Constitution as a document of limitations and a charter of free enterprise, intended to protect hardworking businessmen from meddlesome government regulation and spoliation by radical legislative majorities. When the Constitution spoke of liberty, they took it to mean liberty in the marketplace, but not necessarily the liberty to speak or print what one pleased about politics and society. They believed that the Constitution prohibited laws that fixed wages or prices or sought to abolish child labor, but imposed few obstacles to laws that punished those who displayed the red flag of communism or published articles highly critical of public officials.

Three justices—Harlan Stone, Brandeis, and Cardozo—preached the gospel of "judicial restraint" with respect to government's power to regulate economic affairs under the Constitution. And they displayed more sensitivity to questions of civil liberties. Maneuvering back and forth between these two factions were two Hoover appointees, Chief Justice Charles Evans Hughes and Owen Roberts. Their votes could tip the outcome of any close case. As a junior justice before World War I, Hughes, whose impressive countenance and white beard suggested that he had recently come down from Mount Olympus, had written some far-reaching opinions sustaining government regulation. Like Brandeis, he cared a great deal about civil liberties, too. But Hughes also loathed discord on his Court, disliked 5–4 decisions that suggested judicial confusion over basic Constitutional questions, and remained apprehensive about the pace of change. Roberts, a mediocre lawyer and a middle-of-the-road Republican, shared many of these anxieties and was prone to follow his chief's lead.

This unstable mixture of personalities and ideology had produced jurisprudential confusion on the Court of considerable magnitude by 1935. With Hughes leading the way, usually over the opposition of the Four Horsemen, the justices had handed down several courageous decisions protecting civil liberties, including one that invalidated a Minnesota gag law against scandalous newspapers and another that ordered a new trial for impoverished black teenagers condemned to death in Alabama without adequate legal counsel.

With respect to the Depression and economic regulation, however, the Court followed a more tortured course. Hughes and Roberts voted with the conservatives in 1932, for example, when the Court struck down an Oklahoma law that attempted to stabilize the state's chaotic ice industry by limiting the number of new firms allowed to enter the business. This law, said the majority, unconstitutionally deprived persons of their economic liberty. Two years later, however, Hughes and Roberts joined the progressives to sustain two innovative state laws, one giving Minnesota homeowners a moratorium on their mortgage payments, the other permitting New York State to fix minimum prices for milk sold at retail.

The Minnesota and New York cases outraged conservatives and heartened liberals, who saw them as indicators of judicial restraint toward economic experimentation and important precedents for the New Deal. Somewhat less encouraging had been the majority's grudging support of the administration's monetary policies in two cases that challenged

Congress's power to suspend gold payments on private contracts and the public debt. In these Gold Clause opinions the chief justice rebuked FDR and Congress, but did not join the Four Horsemen, who saw the laws as the harbinger of a general confiscation of wealth by the New Deal. "This is Nero at his worst," fumed Justice McReynolds from the bench. "The Constitution as we know it is gone!"

But shortly before and after the Gold Clause decisions, the Court handed the New Deal two defeats that suggested a more inflexible approach to constitutional interpretation and open hostility to certain economic reform sponsored by the federal government. First, by an 8–1 vote, with only Cardozo dissenting, the justices declared unconstitutional Section 9c, the "hot oil" provisions of the National Industrial Recovery Act, which had given the President authority to prohibit interstate shipments of petroleum produced in excess of state quotas. While conceding ample precedent for Congress's authority to assist the states by utilizing its powers over interstate commerce, the justices found the "hot oil" provisions invalid because the legislature had delegated too much undefined rule-making power to the executive branch. This was the first time the Court had ever struck down a federal statute on grounds of improper delegation.

Second, and even more portentous, five justices, led by Roberts, held that Congress had no authority to require the nation's interstate railroads to adopt a mandatory pension plan for their employees. Since the Court had sustained virtually every exercise of Congress's power over the railroads for nearly half a century, including the fixing of rates, the hours of labor, safety standards, and the liability for injuries, this decision struck even some conservative critics of the New Deal as unprincipled and misguided. Chief Justice Hughes wrote an impassioned dissent suggesting as much. Three weeks later, however, on May 27, 1935, Hughes himself led the attack against the New Deal. It was "Black Monday."

On that day, as New Dealers watched grimly from the audience, the Court struck down two more federal laws, including the administration's centerpiece, the National Industrial Recovery Act. The justices also sharply limited the president's power to remove hostile members of the various independent regulatory agencies. First, speaking through Justice Brandeis, the justices buried the Frazier-Lemke Emergency Farm Mortage Act on the grounds that it deprived creditors of their property without due process of law. Next, virtually overruling a recent opinion by the late Chief Justice Taft, they also declared that the president's authority to remove executive officials without the consent of Congress did not extend to a member of the Federal Trade Commission, in this case the notoriously pro-business William Humphrey.

And, finally, without dissent in *Schechter Poultry Corp.* v. *United States*, the Court gave the constitutional ax to the troubled NRA by finding it defective both because Congress had again delegated too much to the president and because Congress's power to regulate interstate commerce did not extend to the slaughtering of kosher chickens. This last leg of Hughes's opinion in *Schechter*, coupled with Roberts's narrow reading of the commerce power in the *Railroad Retirement Board* case, seemed especially ominous from Roosevelt's perspective. It immediately threw a cloud of doubt over every past and future act of Congress that rested on the Commerce Clause in the Constitution.

The former Columbia University law student now in the White House spoke to reporters four days after "Black Monday." FDR vented his displeasure with the court's interpretation of the commerce clause. He

The death of the NRA at the hands of the Supreme Court as seen by the New Dealers.

compared *Schechter* to the infamous *Dred Scott* decision that had endorsed slavery and discredited the Supreme Court. He asked in view of Hughes's opinion whether "the United States Government . . . [has] control over any national economic problem," and suggested that the chief justice had invoked a definition of the commerce power that had not been in vogue since the late nineteenth century. "We have been relegated," the president concluded, "to the horse-and-buggy definition of interstate commerce."

While the restrictive interpretation of the commerce power put forward by the chief justice, Roberts, and the Four Horsemen presented the most direct threat to the New Deal, Roosevelt and his advisers knew that their troubles with the Supreme Court ran even deeper. On issues such as legislative delegation and removal they had also lost the support of liberal justices. "Where was Ben Cardozo?" FDR asked after surveying the damage of May 27. "And what about old Isaiah [Brandeis]?"

Brandeis, of course, had watched the unfolding of the New Deal in 1933–34 with mounting fear and loathing. In his judgment, both the NRA and the AAA were misguided attempts at managing scarcity and creating a planned economy. The Depression should be fought with more public works spending, heavier taxes on the rich, and all-out war on concentrations of economic power. He thought Roosevelt naive to expect real cooperation from big business, but also feared the president's appetite for greater executive power.

As he left the bench and removed his judicial robes on May 27, the usually reticent Brandeis took Tommy Corcoran and Ben Cohen aside and delivered an unprecedent rebuke to the president, who, he said "has been living in a fool's paradise." The whole direction of the New Deal was wrong, Brandeis scolded, and future programs would have to be redesigned. "This is the end of this business of centralization," he concluded with some heat, "and I want you to go back and tell the president that we're not going to let this government centralize everything. It's come to an end."

Stung by the results of "Black Monday" and the reported tongue-lashing by old Isaiah, Roosevelt soon realized that the justices had probably done him a major favor. The much-maligned NRA, still embroiled in controversy, had now been officially executed by the Court, which spared the president a nasty fight over its renewal. The administration's dismal record before the justices also hastened a house-cleaning at the Department of Justice and the recruitment of more talented attorneys to handle future litigation.

Justice Louis D. Brandeis.

But most important of all, the hail of judicial vetoes, combined with rising hostility from sectors of big business, grumblings from conservative Democrats, and the threat posed by Senator Long, left Franklin Roosevelt with fewer political options. His most dependable allies now appeared to be on the left of the political spectrum among the old progressives like La Follette or the freshly elected urban Democrats, many of whom spoke for labor and the poor. A new political coalition was taking shape at the same time that new legislative proposals, many in the works since the spring of 1933, came forth from the administration and Congress. Together these produced a different New Deal, one more class-conscious than the first and much less interested in maintaining a broad consensus that had begun to dissolve.

5

High Tide

. . . the most comprehensive program of reform ever achieved in this country in any administration.
—Walter Lippmann

I should like to have it said of my first administration that in it the forces of selfishness and lust for power met their match. I should like to have it said of my second administration that in it these forces met their master.
—Franklin Roosevelt

THE SECOND HUNDRED DAYS

The Supreme Court gave FDR an important nudge away from the consensus-oriented policy of the NRA, but an even sharper push had been administered ten days earlier when a group of progressive senators headed by La Follette, Norris, Costigan, and Wheeler met with the president and several of his most liberal advisers at the White House. The evening meeting had been arranged by Frankfurter and David K. Niles, a former La Follette aide who was soon to become Hopkins's chief assistant in the Works Progress Administration. The exchange of views was remarkably blunt. Why, the president asked, were progressives so critical of his administration when he had supported so much of their agenda, including banking reforms, TVA, federal relief, and securities regulation? Why, retorted some of the senators present, did the president try to curry favor with big businessmen and make common cause with some of the worst reactionaries in Congress, including Pat Harrison and Joe Robinson? Why did conservatives seem to have the upper hand in the White House? Why was it so difficult for them to see the president, except on occasions like this?

Wheeler and La Follette told the president that he could never appease the capitalists without losing the country to the likes of Long, Coughlin, and Townsend. He should immediately throw his support behind important legislation then stalled in Congress, especially Senator Wagner's labor relations and social security bills and Wheeler's measure designed to break up the giant public utility holding companies. The president's endorsement of these bills would go a long way toward securing their passage and would reaffirm his alliance with the nation's genuine progressive forces. For his part, Roosevelt agreed that some businessmen and financiers, now allied in the American Liberty League, had let him down, and he promised a new burst of leadership in the days ahead.

FDR's first display of new leadership, a veto of the veterans' bonus bill on May 22, was not exactly what the senators had in mind. Making an unusual personal appearance before the legislators to emphasize the gravity of his action, he appealed for fiscal austerity and once again displayed the depth of his devotion to a balanced budget. But during the first week of June as Congress prepared to adjourn for the summer, Roosevelt called its leaders to the White House and gave them a list of "must" legislation that he expected on his desk for signature before they left town. They were incredulous. It couldn't be done. Some of the measures, social security and the labor bill, had only recently gone through hearings. All were incredibly complex and controversial. But Roosevelt was deadly serious. And a few days later he upped the ante by asking Congress for new tax legislation as well in a message that criticized the present system for benefiting only the rich and promoting an "unjust concentration of wealth and economic power."

When the weary legislators finally left Washington two months later, FDR had all of his "must " legislation and what Walter Lippmann called "the most comprehensive program of reform ever achieved in this country in any administration." The Hundred Days may have saved capitalism, but eighty-eight days in 1935 literally changed the face of America for the next half century.

Many ingredients produced this new wave of New Deal reforms—swollen Democratic majorities in Congress, the specter of Huey Long and the Townsend movement, the decisions of the Supreme Court, defections in the business community, astute bill-writing by Cohen, Corcoran, and Frankfurter, and the tenacity and courage of particular legislators like Robert Wagner. Still there could be no doubting the central role played by the president of the United States. Over three months FDR used all of his considerable charm and political skills to cajole, threaten, reward, punish, and manipulate his allies and enemies in Congress. Ruefully commenting on FDR's talents with the legislature that had gone far to steal his own thunder, Long observed: "Hoover is a hoot owl and Roosevelt is a scrootch owl. A hoot owl bangs into the nest and knocks the hen clean off and catches her while she's falling. But a scrootch owl slips into the roost and scrootches up to the hen and talks softly to her. And the hen just falls in love with him, and the next thing you know there ain't no hen."

Banking and Spending

On August 23, 1935, Roosevelt signed into law the most far-reaching revisions in the nation's banking laws since the creation of the Federal Reserve System in 1914. The administration's bill produced one of the sharpest conflicts between the New Deal and big business during the decade, but when the smoke had lifted, control of the nation's monetary policy had been shifted decisively from Wall Street to Washington. The principal architect of this fundamental change was a forty-five-year-old former Mormon missionary from Utah, Marriner Stoddard Eccles. Without a college degree, Eccles had built his family's considerable fortune into one that included thirteen major corporations and a string of banks, none of which failed during the worst years of panic after 1929. In 1933, Eccles astonished members of the Senate Finance Committee with his pungent criticism of bankers and his straightforward cure for the Depression, which, he said, arose from underconsumption and a shortfall in investment. "Seeking individual salvation," he said, "we were contributing to collective ruin." He urged more government spending to compensate for both, a solution that anticipated the ideas put forth with more analytical rigor a few years later by British economist John Maynard Keynes.

Eccles's impeccable capitalist credentials and his vigorous support for more government spending made him a natural ally for those like Hopkins and Wallace who wanted Roosevelt to adopt a more aggressive fiscal policy. His superb command of commercial banking matters and his anti–Wall Street bias endeared him also to Henry Morgenthau, Jr., and others in the Treasury Department, who urged FDR to give the Utah banker a vacant seat on the Federal Reserve Board in 1934. Eccles took the job on the condition that the administration would support some fundamental changes in the existing Federal Reserve System. His ideas formed the basis of key provisions in the proposed Banking Act of 1935, which gave the revamped board of governors (seven members appointed by the president and confirmed by the Senate) enhanced power over the regional Federal Reserve banks, including a veto over the selection of their officers and direct control over reserve requirements, discount rates, and all open market operations.

New Dealers expected the centralizing features of Eccles's plan to stir up furious opposition from some bankers and old Federal Reserve patrons such as Senator Glass of Virginia. The administration therefore attempted to sweeten the measure by lowering the assessments levied for the new Federal Deposit Insurance Corporation and giving national bank officers more time to liquidate old personal loans from their own institutions, a reform mandated in 1933. Despite these concessions, many of the nation's largest banks and Senator Glass did their best to sabotage Eccles's reforms, which they correctly perceived as an effort to curb the influence of member banks and especially the role of the New York Reserve Bank, which had dominated open market operations in the past. In the end, the main features of the Eccles plan survived, thanks in part to the support of anti-Morgan, non–New York bankers such as Amadeo Peter Giannini of California's Bank of America, who much preferred regulation from Washington to regulation from Wall Street.

The original Federal Reserve Act in 1914 had given the United States the foundation for a true national banking system generations after other industrialized countries had realized that goal. But authority within the structure had gravitated to the regional reserve banks—especially New York's—following World War I and left the board appointed by the president as a largely advisory, ceremonial body. Roosevelt's reforms now strengthened the board and its publicly appointed governors at the expense of the banker-dominated regional institutions. From the perspective of some New York banks like J. P. Morgan & Company that had dominated the local reserve district and hence the entire system, the new legislation seemed dangerously radical and hostile to their interests. But other financiers, including Winthrop Aldrich of the Rockefeller-backed Chase National bank, saw in the reforms an effective tool for national credit management, a way to curb the power of their rivals, and an opportunity in the long run for bankers to gain an important, permanent foothold in the new Washington power structure.

The Banking Act of 1935 and Eccles's appointment as chairman of the new board of governors gave the New Deal a golden opportunity to test his and Keynes's ideas about deficit spending. The Utah financier had advocated keeping interest rates down in order to faciliate heavy borrowing by the federal government to combat the Depression. Unfortunately for the spenders, however, FDR never warmed to Eccles personally, remained unimpressed by Keynes even after a personal meeting with the economic wizard arranged by Frankfurter, and seldom gave up hope that the federal budget would soon be in balance. The president who signed the Economy Act and twice vetoed the veterans' bonus bill was no big spender, until driven there by absolute necessity.

DEATH SENTENCE

The Banking Act promised greater centralization in the management of the nation's credit, but Roosevelt hastened in 1935 to demolish concentrations of private power in the hands of behemoth public utility holding companies. Insull and other promoters had assembled these financial giants in the previous decade in order to achieve greater operating efficiency, provide cheaper power, and milk local utility companies by selling them management, engineering, and financial services. In FDR's gallery of rogues, the holding company barons ranked next to the floor traders who manipulated stock prices and the bankers who looted their own institutions. He regarded them as an irresponsible group of promoters whose avarice and lust for power threatened the entire economic system. "I am against private socialism of concentrated private power as thoroughly as I am against governmental socialism," he told Congress. "The one is equally as dangerous as the other; and the destruction of private socialism is utterly essential to avoid governmental socialism."

FDR endorsed a measure written largely by Corcoran and Cohen to give the Federal Power Commission and the new SEC extensive regulatory powers over these companies. But in addition, despite Cohen's objections, he insisted that the proposed law contain a mandatory "death sentence" to require the complete elimination of any holding company that could not justify its existence on grounds of economic efficiency and geographic integration after January 1, 1940. Sponsored by Senator Wheeler and Texas congressman Sam Rayburn, this bill produced a legislative battle that made the struggle over banking reform seem tame by comparison.

Utility executives, led by Wendell Willkie of the giant Common-wealth and Southern Corporation, regarded the Wheeler-Rayburn bill as a declaration of war more threatening than TVA, which they were also fighting on several fronts. Armed with a war chest of millions of dollars, their public relations firms bombarded Congress and the public with pamphlets, letters, and advertisements designed to discredit the legislation and the president, who was alleged to support the bill because he suffered from a mental breakdown. The "death sentence," they claimed, would return the utility industry to the era of the water-wheel and bring financial destitution to innocent widows and orphans who had invested in holding companies. Their lobbyists swarmed over Capitol Hill, buying votes and threatening legislators with the eco-nomic collapse of their regions in the event the measure became law.

The utilities' free spending and outrageous tactics produced some equally dubious behavior from the president's allies in Congress. Sen-ator Black, a fierce enemy of big business, hauled numerous executives and their hirelings before his special committee on lobbying. Utilizing dragnet subpoenas, Black forced them to produce all of their corre-spondence during a certain time period, a technique that drew sharp protest from, among others, the American Civil Liberties Union. Black's sledgehammer tactics revealed, for example, that Western Union and officials of Associated Gas and Electric had manufactured a thousand phony telegrams from residents of Warren, Pennsylvania, which turned up on the desk of one harassed local congressman. Defenders of the Fourth Amendment still denounced the senator's methods as an inva-sion of privacy and an abuse of congressional power.

Even Black's fireworks could not save the controversial "death sen-tence" in the House, where frightened Democrats, led by J. J. O'Con-nor of New York and George Huddleston of Alabama, voted to strike it from the final bill. For nearly a month, through the steamy Wash-ington summer, House and Senate conferees attempted to reach a compromise. Roosevelt and the Senate members continued to insist on a provision that would give the SEC final authority to dissolve holding companies, and angry House members insisted that Cohen and other White House lawyers be barred from all conference sessions.

Frankfurter helped to break the deadlock by writing a "death sen-tence" provision that gave a little to both sides. It authorized the SEC to simplify existing holding companies, but permitted them to retain two geographically related systems unless the agency found such an arrangement contrary to the most efficient operation. Frankfurter had retained the "death sentence," but shifted the burden of proof on dissolution to the government. Diehard opponents in the House still voted against this compromise, but they could not stop final passage. After much grumbling, FDR signed it into law. He chided Frankfurter that the law professor sounded more and more like John W. Davis, one of the utilities' chief attorneys.

For all the sound and fury that accompanied its birth, the Public Utility Holding Company Act produced neither the economic calamity predicted by its opponents nor the restoration of competitive enterprise desired by some of its supporters. The utilities fought the law in the courts for years, refusing even to register with the SEC and the Federal Power Commission. But once the courts upheld the statute and the two agencies began to enforce the law during and after World War II, it proved highly useful to the industry as a whole. The reorganization plans finally worked out by experts from the FPC, the SEC, and the industry created more compact and efficient holding company systems that redounded to the benefit of consumers and investors. Denounced by many businessmen as an example of the New Deal's radicalism, the holding company legislation probably did more good for capitalism than the supposedly pro-business NRA.

Taxing the Rich

When FDR sent his 1935 tax proposal to Congress, friends and foes alike soon dubbed it a "soak-the-rich" revenue plan. Newspaper baron William Randolph Hearst instructed all of his editors to refer to it henceforth as Roosevelt's "soak-the-successful" scheme and to the entire New Deal as "the raw deal." An elderly Republican from Kansas wrote the president that his tax message "furnishes the convincing assurances that the New Deal . . . means to go to the root of the evils that plague the nation." Reading FDR's words, Huey Long paraded through the Senate chamber saying, "Amen."

On paper, the plan drafted by Morgenthau's Treasury staff breathed fire. It called for the creation of a graduated tax on corporate income, an excess profits tax on these same corporations, and a levy on intercorporate dividends. In addition, the bill provided for a federal inheritance tax to supplement the existing estate tax, a hike in the maximum income tax rate from 59 to 79 percent, and a constitutional amendment that would permit the federal government to tax the interest earned by those who invested in state and municipal bonds, long a lucrative tax shelter for the very wealthy. Anticipating the response of some congressional leaders such as the chairman of the Senate Finance Committee, FDR remarked, "Pat Harrison is going to be so surprised he'll have kittens on the spot."

The Revenue Act of 1935 tied up both houses of Congress for about ten weeks and produced volumes of turgid and angry debate about tax equity and confiscating wealth. In the end, Harrison and the conservative Democrats won most of the key battles. The graduated corporate income tax and the intercorporate dividend tax survived, but in mutilated form. The highest levy on personal incomes over $50,000 was cut back to 75 percent. Neither the inheritance tax nor the proposed constitutional amendments survived, however. Hearst continued to denounce the measure as "essentially communism," while Long, branding FDR "a liar and a fake," accused the president of not fighting harder for real tax reform.

In Roosevelt's defense it can be said that the new law restored some progressive features to the federal income tax and represented a philosophical shift away from the tax-cutting, pro-wealth ideas of Andrew Mellon and the Republicans. A year later, moreover, the administration persuaded Congress to close many of the loopholes from the Mellon era and to impose a new undistributed profits tax on corporations that declined to pay out dividends to their shareholders. This measure, many New Dealers hoped, would stimulate new private investment and hence economic recovery by transferring funds from stagnant corporate treasuries to more venturesome entrepreneurs. But because of technical defects in drafting the undistributed profits tax, it imposed a greater burden on medium-sized firms than on General Motors or General Electric. Within a year, Congress abolished it, without much protest from the administration.

Roosevelt pursued mixed motives on the tax front and achieved mixed results. In pushing the Revenue Act of 1935, he hoped principally to display fiscal responsibility by raising the money to close a growing budget deficit. Injecting greater equity into the tax laws and outflanking Huey Long seem to have been secondary concerns. For Long or FDR, targeting the rich was good politics but poor finance, when only 1 percent of all American families earned above $10,000. A tax increase aimed at them might achieve equity, but it could not raise much revenue. Imposing even heavier levies on Hearst, the Du Ponts, and the Rockefellers would not ultimately bring the budget into balance.

Some progressives such as La Follette recognized the need for taxing more than the very rich. They urged Roosevelt to eliminate many of the exemptions for the middle class, but the administration, eager to maintain its electoral edge, declined for both political and economic reasons. Hefty tax increases might have solved FDR's budget problems, but further dried up purchasing power. This was especially true if one factored in the administration's soon-to-be-collected payroll taxes for social security and the equally regressive tax policies pursued by the individual states throughout the decade. Most balanced their budgets with sales taxes and property levies.

Even after the New Deal restored some progressive features to the income rates and closed loopholes, the distribution of national income did not change significantly during the 1930s. The middle class reaped most of the resulting redistribution, and the rich managed to remain rich under the New Deal. According to one estimate, the wealthiest 1 percent of the population actually saw its share of personal income increase from 28.3 percent to 30.6 percent over the course of the decade. This was not much improvement on the Harding-Coolidge-Hoover era. But New Deal tax policy, despite these serious failings, did set the stage for a more aggressive use of the federal income tax to help pay for World War II. Then, briefly, the burdens actually fell on the wealthy more than ever before or since.

JOBS, JOBS, JOBS

A restructured banking system, a simplification of holding companies, and a modest attempt at tax reform all raised the spirits of progressives, but did little to succor those who most needed the help and protection of the federal government. Three final measures in the spring and summer of 1935 looked in that direction: creation of the Works Progress Administration, adoption of social security, and passage of the National Labor Relations Act.

On April 8, Congress approved the Emergency Relief Appropriation Act, which authorized the single largest expenditure to that time in the nation's history—$4.8 billion. Of that sum, Congress allocated about $1.4 billion to a new federal relief agency, the Works Progress Administration, headed by Hopkins. Very soon, the WPA became one of the New Deal's most innovative and controversial attempts to provide jobs rather than a dole to the unemployed. "Give a man a dole and you save his body and destroy his spirit," Hopkins believed, echoing FDR. "Give him a job and pay him an assured wage, and you save both the body and the spirit."

From its creation until its official demise in 1943, the WPA spent over $11 billion on work relief and ultimately employed eight million Americans, about one-fifth of the nation's entire workforce. At its peak in 1936–37, more than three million workers a month received checks from the WPA. In seven years, they built 2,500 hospitals, 5,900 schools, 350 airports, 570,000 miles of rural roads, and 8,000 parks. In addition to these traditional blue-collar jobs, Hopkins launched "Federal Project One," which utilized about forty-thousand creative artists for the Federal Writers' Project as well as efforts in theater, the arts, and music. WPA writers, for example, produced state and regional guidebooks and pioneering volumes in oral history, including narratives by former slaves. Musicians gave concerts, composed new pieces, and taught schoolchildren to play instruments. Federal actors and playwrights brought dramas and musicals to people in forty states, many of whom had never before seen a live theatrical production.

Hopkins added a National Youth Administration to the WPA's major activities in 1935. Through this agency, the New Dealers hoped to meet the special needs of college-age and high school youths and blunt a dangerous politicization of this age cohort such as was then taking place under fascist regimes in Europe. Hopkins's most able assistant, Aubrey Williams, ran the NYA with imagination and guts. The NYA provided work-study jobs to help over half a million college student stay in school and gave part-time work to four million high school students and other unemployed young people. Williams allocated special NYA funds to black students, whose jobless rate remained double that of whites. He placed the famous educator Mary McLeod Bethune at the head of the NYA's Division of Negro Affairs.

Almost from the beginning, conservatives reserved special venom for the WPA and its satellite programs. Hopkins's agency, they said, diverted needed labor from the private sector by coddling workers with high wages and easy jobs. From their perspective, WPA stood for "We Poke Along." Hopkins's agency not only encouraged idleness, critics complained, but engaged in partisan politics by giving local Democratic Party organizations a major voice in who was hired and fired at its major projects. Finally, opponents of WPA denounced "Project One," especially the Federal Theatre, as a propaganda arm of the administration because it produced pro–New Deal dramas and left-wing polemics that encouraged class hatred. In 1939, Congressman Martin Dies of Texas, chairman of the House Committee on Un-American Activities, singled out the WPA–Federal Theatre *Sing for your Supper* as pro-communist, which led its producers to respond with a musical number, "Leaning on a Shovel":

When you look at things today
Like Boulder Dam and TVA
And all those playgrounds where kids can play
We did it—by leaning on a shovel!

We didn't lift a finger
To build the parks
That you see in every city.
At home we always linger
And read Karl Marx
If you don't believe us—ask the Dies Committee.

Miles of roads and highways, too,
And schools and buildings bright and new—
Although it may seem odd to you
We did it—by leaning on a shovel!

Conservative critics of the WPA vastly exaggerated its power and influence. At no time did the WPA receive enough money from Congress to provide jobs for more than a third of those who remained unemployed throughout the decade. Because of the precariousness of funding, the typical WPA worker could count on employment for about a year. The agency's wages, $100 a month for a skilled engineer, $60 for an unskilled laborer, and $21 in some areas of the South, seldom discouraged employment in the private sector, except in cases where workers faced the most exploitative alternatives.

Some Southern farmers, for example, bemoaned the fact that black field hands preferred to work for the WPA at its lowest wage rather than pick cotton. In some parts of the country, wealthy matrons complained about the shortage of servants in the same terms. Many WPA jobs—surveying historic sites, composing books in Braille, caring for small children, painting murals—simply did not compete with employment opportunities in the private sector during the 1930s. Furthermore, had the private sector offered more Americans employment, the WPA would have gone out of existence long before 1943. Congress, not the administration, first politicized the WPA by insisting that all of its employees earning more than $5,000 a year receive Senate confirmation.

The Works Progress Administration also had detractors on the other side of the political spectrum, whose criticisms seemed more on target. Senate liberals, led by La Follette, wanted an initial appropriation for WPA closer to $10 billion in 1935, but neither FDR nor most congressmen would tolerate such an astronomical sum. In retrospect, La

Works Progress Administration (WPA) poster.

Follette's figure was realistic in terms of the unemployment problem. Angered by irregular funding, broken promises, and autocratic administrators, many WPA employees conducted strikes and sit-ins against the agency through the Workers' Alliance. Leaders of this organization alleged that Hopkins and his subordinates regarded WPA jobs as temporary palliatives, not genuine alternatives to private employment. There was much truth in that observation. Blacks, Mexican-Americans, and women also complained that the agency made too many accommodations with local political elites, which often discriminated against them. Hopkins, Williams, and a few local administrators like Lyndon Johnson of the Texas NYA did their best to combat racism, but they were the exceptions, not the rule.

Despite its fiscal and political woes, the WPA constituted a major watershed in American public life. It advanced the idea of government responsibility for public works and relief in times of economic distress far beyond anything imagined by Hoover or FDR in 1932. WPA's bridges, roads, sewer systems, and parks constituted a permanent addition to the nation's wealth. For some of its most needy employees, such as the 2,600 women in Mississippi who earned perhaps $20 a month on sewing projects, the WPA meant that fewer American families went to bed hungry. In allocating public funds to the arts, finally, the WPA laid the foundation for more ambitious federal programs in the 1960s and 1970s, including the National Endowment for the Humanities and the National Endowment for the Arts.

Promoting the General Welfare, Somewhat

Always strapped for funds, Hopkins could never provide steady work for all the able-bodied people who sought it. His agency could do nothing for those who remained unemployed or who, because of age, sickness, or physical disability, had no prospects of supporting themselves—the elderly, the blind, the crippled, and dependent children in single-parent, female-headed households. In 1935, only one state, Wisconsin, had a functioning system of unemployment insurance. The few private pension plans initiated in the 1920s became casualties of the Depression. Public pension plans usually covered only law enforcement personnel, firemen, and teachers. State-funded old-age assistance reached fewer than 500,000 of the nearly 6.6 million elderly in need. Half the states did not offer public assistance even to the destitute blind or dependent children, which left them to the care of penurious local governments.

Roosevelt had endorsed unemployment insurance as governor of New York and signed into law that state's old-age assistance law, which helped localities pay for the support of needy residents over sixty-five. Labor unions, headed by the AFL, once a stronghold of voluntarism, called for expanded unemployment insurance. The Townsend clubs and groups such as the American Association for Old-Age Security, founded in 1929 by Abraham Epstein, pushed for federal pensions or a comprehensive federal insurance program for the elderly. The General Welfare Clause of the Constitution, FDR concluded in 1934, made it "our plain duty to provide for that security upon which welfare depends." But faced with a welter of conflicting proposals in the House and Senate over who should be covered, who should pay the bill, and who should run the programs, he created in the early days of the New Deal a Committee on Economic Security, chaired by Secretary of Labor Perkins, to make comprehensive recommendations to Congress.

The report of Perkins's committee became the basis for a bill introduced by Senator Wagner and Congressman David Lewis of Maryland in early January 1935 and the core of the final Social Security Act that FDR signed into law on August 14. The Wagner-Lewis social security law represented both a major milestone in American public policy and, as a later historian observed, "an astonishingly inept and conservative piece of legislation." While in broad outline the measure established the principle of what FDR once called "cradle to grave" security, the extent of coverage, the methods of finance, the level of benefits, and the structure of administrative control created an American welfare system of bewildering complexity and inequality.

In Perkins's committee, Congress, and the administration, the issues of social security triggered a furious debate over the fundamentals of American federalism. Nationalists like Wallace and Tugwell advocated a broad federal role with respect to both the financing and administration of unemployment insurance and old-age insurance. The localists—Morgenthau, Frankfurter, and most members of Congress—wanted to preserve a larger role for the states and for fiscal and political reasons did not wish to place the entire cost on the federal treasury. On most issues, Roosevelt threw his support to the localists.

The Tugwell group, supported by Epstein's organization and many labor leaders, argued that both unemployment insurance and old-age pensions should be paid for by general federal revenues with uniform benefits fixed by the national government. This method of finance might actually redistribute income from rich to poor. And if the federal government helped the states with grants to assist the blind, the disabled, and dependent children, the Tugwell-Epstein group argued, it should also prescribe minimum levels of aid for these categories and monitor the competence of state personnel who ran the programs.

In the final legislative showdown, the nationalists secured only federal old-age pensions in a program to be financed by regressive payroll taxes levied on both employers and workers. Congress mandated this same method to finance unemployment insurance. And the states would control unemployment benefits through a provision whereby 90 percent of a federal payroll tax on employers would be offset if they contributed to a state unemployment compensation system. Since employers would pass along their taxes to consumers, Perkins and Tugwell pointed out, these payroll deductions imposed the main burden for most of the social security program on the workers themselves.

Roosevelt conceded the regressive features of social security financing, but he vehemently opposed using general tax revenues to underwrite the program. If social security remained self-financing and based on individual contributions, he argued, this would guarantee its long-term survival in the face of future political attacks. "We put those payroll contributions there so as to give the contributors a legal, moral, and political right to collect their pensions and their unemployment benefits," he later explained. "With those taxes in there, no damn politician can ever scrap my social security program."

Politically astute but economically backward, the regressive payroll taxes became a drag on economic recovery as early as 1936. The original social security law contained other glaring defects, too. Its federal-state unemployment insurance scheme created a crazy quilt of benefits and eligibility requirements, with some states, notably in the South and West, paying much less than those in the Northeast. A similar lack of national standards characterized the assistance programs to the blind, disabled, and families with dependent children (AFDC) after Congress voted down a provision to require each state receiving federal grants to offer "reasonable subsistence compatible with decency and health."

In 1939, therefore, a poor child in Massachusetts received $61 a month, while Mississippi granted the same child only $8, although both states received the same amount per child from the federal government. Most New Dealers and members of Congress assumed that AFDC would remain a token part of the entire social security program by providing financial aid to a few widows and their small children. They did not anticipate the massive migration of poor black Americans from the South to the North before and after World War II, an exodus hastened by the New Deal's Triple A and the stingy public assistance programs south of the Mason-Dixon Line. The emphasis upon local control of AFDC, however, meant that taxpayers in the North subsidized the social dislocations generated by the New Deal's agricultural programs. Finally, social security excluded entirely both agricultural workers and domestic servants from unemployment compensation and old-age insurance.

Small wonder that Roosevelt's social security program did not entirely deflate the Townsend movement or other efforts to redistribute wealth in the 1930s. When the first pension checks went out from the Social Security Administration in 1940, recipients pocketed a maximum of

$85 a month. Across the country in that same year, the typical unemployed worker, assuming he was eligible under state law, could expect a maximum benefit of $15 a week for four months.

Conservative Republicans and a substantial number of Southern Democrats, nonetheless, denounced social security as tyranical and extravagant, a breeder of sloth and indolence among American workers. Congressman James Wadsworth of New York said the law had created "a power so vast, so powerful as to threaten the integrity of our institutions and to pull the pillars of the temple down upon the heads of our descendants." The editor of the *Jackson Daily News* affirmed that "the average Mississippian can't imagine himself chipping in to pay pensions for able-bodied Negroes to sit around in idleness on front galleries . . . while cotton and corn crops are crying for workers." Among the Americans who refused to apply for a social security card was Herbert Hoover, who declared he was constitutionally opposed to being "numberified." The agency gave this apostle of individualism a number anyway.

LABOR'S MAGNA CHARTA

Roosevelt's fingerprints could be found all over the Social Security Act, especially its financial provisions. He remained largely a spectator, however, to passage of Senator Wagner's National Labor Relations Act, arguably the most important and revolutionary federal law put on the statute books in the 1930s. It cemented a long and fruitful alliance between FDR's party and a newly energized labor movement. The law also channeled working-class energy away from a lingering emphasis on issues about production to ones that focused on wages, hours, and fringe benefits in an economic system managed by capitalists. The Wagner Act redounded to Roosevelt's great political benefit, but he and leading members of the administration such as Secretary Perkins came to its aid reluctantly, almost as an afterthought.

Disillusioned with the toothless Labor Board established under the NRA, Wagner and his chief assistant, Leon Keyserling, had written a bill that abandoned all pretense to neutrality between workers and their employers. Wagner's bill aggressively supported labor. It prohibited companies from engaging in a wide range of "unfair labor practices" such as firing union members or financing company unions. It also created an independent, three-person National Labor Relations Board to enforce these prohibitions through the federal courts. Even more menacing from the point of view of employers, Wagner's bill empowered the NLRB to conduct secret-ballot elections among employees to determine if they wanted union representation; the union chosen by the majority would represent all workers; and the companies would be required to bargain "in good faith" with the union so chosen.

Business leaders, spearheaded by the American Chamber of Commerce and the National Association of Manufacturers, denounced the legislation as un-American and the death knell of free enterprise. They could count on the support of key Senate leaders such as Robinson and Harrison, who feared the growth of union strength in the low-wage South. They could also count on the support of some journalists, including Lippmann, who said the Wagner bill put a "preposterous . . . burden upon moral men" and should be scrapped. But because Wagner had enough votes to get the bill out of committee, Robinson and Harrison dragged him to the White House for a full-scale debate before Roosevelt, in which they hoped to kill the measure.

At the very least, the Senate barons wanted FDR to pressure the New Yorker to delay the whole matter for another year. Robinson and Harrison sensed correctly that FDR did not care deeply about either collective bargaining or the structure of industrial relations. For all his humanitarian compassion and distrust of businessmen, Roosevelt remained at heart a paternalist like his father when it came to labor. The question of majority rule or proportional representation in the auto industry mattered about as much to him in 1935 as who became Sultan of Swat or the emir of Kuwait.

The Senate leaders argued the standard National Association of Manufacturers line: Wagner's bill trod too deeply on the prerogatives of management; it would terrify businessmen and discourage recovery; it was probably unconstitutional. Wagner answered his critics brilliantly. The failure to secure labor's legitimate rights under the NRA, he told Roosevelt, had "driven a dagger close to the heart of the recovery program" by fomenting industrial conflict. Since 1933, average working hours had actually gone up, while wages had fallen. On the other hand, the net profits of over one thousand leading corporations had soared 64 percent. If this imbalance between profits and wages continued, the country would remain mired forever in depression. His bill would go a long way to prevent that calamity.

Roosevelt, not eager to offend either the Southern leadership in the Senate or the progressives who backed Wagner, said he would remain neutral, but urged a final vote as soon as possible. Two days before the Senate vote, in response to a reporter's question about the Wagner bill, the president said he had not "given it any thought one way or the other." Only after Wagner's resounding victory in the Senate and the Supreme Court's death blow to the NRA did Roosevelt finally join the parade of supporters, but it would have passed the House easily without his imprimatur.

Passage of the Wagner Act could not have come at a more crucial moment for the New Deal or the nation, because the labor movement soon erupted into full-scale civil war and conflicts between workers and their employers reached a similar level of intensity. The Wagner Act had little to do with fomenting these epic struggles, but the NLRB's machinery helped to channel them toward resolution in 1937–38. American workers won their own victories in the late thirties, but the National Labor Relations Act sealed them with the force of public law for the first time in the nation's history.

THE CIO AND THE WAGNER ACT

Three months after FDR signed the Wagner Act, United Mine Workers president John L. Lewis and his supporters walked out of the annual AFL convention at Atlantic City. They had failed to persuade a majority of the AFL delegates to suspend their particular craft union jurisdictions in order to organize more effectively the millions of workers in industries such as autos, steel, rubber, textiles, and aluminum. The flamboyant Lewis, perhaps the most spellbinding orator of the era, believed the AFL's dogmatic insistence upon craft autonomy had little relevance to the unskilled workers in the mass-production industries and would serve only to hold back successful unionization. Unless existing union leaders changed tactics, Lewis feared, they would be either run over by rank-and-file militancy or crushed by management. "Heed this cry from Macedonia," he thundered, "that comes from the hearts of men."

William Green and the AFL leaders refused to listen to Lewis, but he had the support of other talented unionists such as David Dubinsky of the International Ladies Garment Workers Union and Sidney Hillman of the Amalgamated Clothing Workers, who also believed in industrial unionism. They joined Lewis's walkout at Atlantic City and within weeks announced the creation of the Committee for Industrial Organization (CIO) to help organize workers in steel, autos, textiles, and rubber. By the spring of 1936, fueled with funds from the dissident unions, the CIO mounted aggressive and successful organizing campaigns that were underway in the mass-production industries. In August, the AFL officially expelled ten of its unions that had defected to Lewis and the CIO.

A more important event took place almost simultaneously at the Akron plant of the Goodyear Rubber Company, where workers went on strike for recognition of their union. Much to the surprise of their leaders and the company, instead of leaving the factory to picket, they sat down on the production floor and refused to leave until management met their demands for union recognition. The "sit-down" strike was born. It soon proved successful with the autoworkers in Flint, Michigan, and from there spread like wildfire across the mass-production industries.

With industrial workers actually occupying factories, most employers and a fair number of journalists regarded the sit-down strikes as the dawn of genuine revolution in America, a vision also endorsed by some communist organizers, who played key roles in many of the confrontations. The goals of most strikers, however, remained more limited. They wanted employers to recognize their union. They wanted more in their pay envelope each week and a larger say about working conditions on the floor, but only a few seriously contemplated assuming the functions of management. In short, the typical autoworker or steelworker wanted a larger slice of the economic pie, a greater claim on the consumer society; not a radical reorganization of corporate power or productive relations.

The sit-down strike proved to be a powerful weapon to achieve these modest but important benefits. How did one dislodge these strikers? Employers who did not blink at using force to break up a picket line and crush strikers outside the factory gate thought twice about unleashing security forces inside their own plants, where valuable machinery might be destroyed. Legally, it was not even clear that these workers had committed a trespass upon private property. By remaining peaceful, they threw the onus of violence upon their opponents and gathered sympathy from many local political leaders, such as Detroit's mayor, Frank Murphy, who refused to side with the auto companies.

More rapidly than anyone including Lewis and the CIO leadership had imagined, the structure of industrial relations and national political power had been transformed—not by FDR, not by Senator Wagner, and not by the law that bore his name, but by millions of workers sitting down and standing up for their rights. Lewis was correct on one point. "No tin-hat brigade of goose-stepping vigilantes or Bible-babbling mob of blackguarding corporation scoundrels," he declared, "will prevent the onward march of labor." By early 1937, General Motors had agreed to bargain exclusively with the United Automobile Workers Union; U.S. Steel, long the symbol of corporate hostility to organized labor, also bowed to the demands of the Steel Workers Organizing Committee. Violence and death greeted workers who struck against the four "Little Steel" companies that same year, but now backed by the National Labor Relations Board, the steelworkers finally gained union recognition in these last outposts of resistance, too.

Despite the fears of some corporate leaders, the passage of the Wagner Act and the coming of industrial unionism through the CIO did not sound the death knell of capitalism or seriously dilute the powers of management. The most painful adjustment for big businessmen proved to be the formal bargaining session, in which for the first time they had to sit down at the same table with union leaders whose ancestors did not trace their roots back to the *Mayflower*. More often their parents had come in steerage from Dublin, Minsk, Prague, Krakow, or Genoa. Big business soon discovered, however, it could live in peace with these new partners, who cared more about wage levels than the prerogatives of management. The CIO unions proved useful, too, in

Coal miners and company guard clash near Pittsburgh.

reducing worker turnover, absenteeism, and the number of wildcat strikes. The courts held the pro-labor NLRB in check by denying it the power to impose a final contract settlement on even the most stiff-necked anti-union companies. Organized labor would play a key role in the New Deal's welfare state, a larger role than labor had ever played before in the nation's public policies—but it remained nonetheless a subordinate role.

RENDEZVOUS WITH DESTINY

Entering the White House in 1933, Roosevelt had hoped to govern through consensus, to lead a grand coalition of businessmen and farmers, bankers and laborers, Northerners and Southerners, Catholics and Protestants, out of the storm of depression into the sunshine of prosperity. In the summer of 1936, as he stood before the Democratic faithful at Philadelphia's Franklin Field to accept renomination, the economic clouds had parted somewhat, but Franklin Roosevelt was no longer a symbol of national unity or the architect of common purpose. Through events and circumstances not always of his own choosing, he had become instead the leader of the have-nots against the haves, of the outsiders against the insiders, and of all those believed, as he told the delegates, that "against economic tyranny . . . the American citizen could appeal only to the organized power of Government." Listening to the Philadelphia acceptance speech, written largely by Moley, Corcoran, and Rosenman, Ickes thought it the greatest he had ever heard, especially when FDR denounced "economic royalists," vowed to replace "the palace of privilege" with "a temple . . . of faith and hope and charity," and told his audience they had "a rendezvous with destiny."

Many of his initial allies in the business, financial, and legal communities had abandoned him and taken refuge in organizations such as the American Liberty League, from where they denounced the New Deal as communistic and unconstitutional. For them, 1935 and 1936 marked the beginning of revolution in America. Roosevelt had encouraged it by radical legislation such as the holding company and tax law and it had culminated in sit-down strikes in which workers actually took over private property. Among Southern Democrats, too, anxiety mounted that the president had now surrounded himself with subversive advisers and curried too much favor with organized labor. Soon, they feared, the programs of the New Deal might upset the region's racial status quo, too.

On the other hand, millions of Americans had come in four years to regard Roosevelt as a savior and patron who had rescued them from economic disaster and taken their side against those who abused and exploited them. "You have saved my life," wrote a woman who had kept her home through the HOLC. A Kansas farmer compared the president to "Moses . . . come to alleviate us of our suffering." Black migrants to Chicago, thrown off their farms as a result of the Triple A and finding some work with the WPA, hung photographs of FDR next to those of Lincoln and Jesus Christ. The president of Bethlehem Steel, Charles M. Schwab, asked the superintendent of his large Pennsylvania farm to survey the political sentiments among 130 employees. All but two declared for FDR. "I will say one thing for this administration," quipped Will Rogers. "It is the only time when the fellow with money is worrying more than the one without it." Asked why he would be voting for Roosevelt in 1936, a North Caroline textile worker said flatly, "Because he knows my boss is a son of a bitch."

The 1936 election became a referendum on Roosevelt and the New Deal, and FDR relished his new role as tribune of the common people. To those who criticized his budget deficits, the president replied in Pittsburgh: "When Americans suffered, we refused to pass by on the other side. Humanity came first." His opponents, he told a cheering audience in Madison Square Garden, had brought America "nine crazy years at the ticker and three long years in the breadlines." Now the forces of greed and reaction were mobilizing against him. "They are unanimous in their hatred of me," he said, "and I welcome their hatred. I should like to have it said of my first administration that in it the forces of selfishness and lust for power met their match. I should like to have it said of my second administration that in it these forces met their master."

To do battle with the new master of American politics and save the nation from further economic experimentation, the Republicans in 1936 tapped Alfred M. Landon, the two-time governor of Kansas, whom some journalists had labeled the "Kansas Coolidge" because of his fiscal conservatism. The characterization did Landon a great disservice. The former independent oil producer had supported Theodore Roosevelt's revolt against the GOP regulars in 1912. He had fought against the influence of the Klan in Kansas politics and once introduced Socialist Party leader Norman Thomas to a Topeka audience. Because of his influence at the convention, the GOP platform lashed the New Deal for its inefficiency, free spending, and coercion, but also vowed to help the elderly and the unemployed and to protect the rights of labor. Landon, in short, was no George Babbitt, but a decent, reasonably progressive Midwestern businessman. Under even ordinary circumstances, however, this moon-faced, bespectacled man with a typical Kansas twang in his voice did not inspire fanatical enthusiasm. Matched against FDR, he was positively bland.

Landon ran a sensible, middle-of-the-road campaign until mid-October, when most opinion polls began to show him falling far behind the president. He then succumbed to the influence of his principal adviser, John Hamilton, a rock-ribbed conservative, who urged more slashing attacks on FDR and the programs of the New Deal. Landon called social security a "a cruel hoax," a program that was "unjust, unworkable, stupidly drafted and wastefully financed." Hamilton and the Hearst press, now bitterly opposed to Roosevelt, even suggested that the Social Security Administration would soon launch a new program requiring those who enrolled to wear metal identification tags around their necks. Landon's attack on social security sealed his fate. The head of the new agency, John Gilbert Winant, a former Republican governor of New Hampshire and himself an old Bull Moose supporter, resigned from the government to campaign for Roosevelt, defend the program, and ridicule Landon.

The legislative victories of 1935, especially social security, tax reform, and the Wagner Act, had stolen thunder from Long, Coughlin, and Townsend, and reduced the threat of a third-party challenge to Roosevelt. That threat withered completely on September 8, 1935, when a young physician, Carl Weiss, blaming Long for his father-in-law's failed political career, shot the Kingfish as he strolled through the halls of the Louisiana capitol building. Long's bodyguards immediately opened fire and emptied their revolvers into the assassin. The Kingfish did not survive Weiss's gunshot wound and the careless surgery that followed. He died within two days.

Leadership of the Share Our Wealth movement soon passed to one of Long's assistants, an unstable egomaniac, Gerald L. K. Smith, ex-Klansman and sometime fundamentalist preacher. In the summer of 1936, Smith helped Coughlin and Townsend organize the National Union Party with North Dakota congressman William "Liberty Bell" Lemke as its presidential candidate. By mid-July, Coughlin seemed to be the candidate as he crisscrossed the country denouncing "Franklin Double-crossing Roosevelt" as America's "great betrayer and liar."

Lemke's campaign suffered from a number of defects, anyone of which might have proved fatal. Although a Yale Law School graduate, the ill-clad, unshaven congressman usually looked like a skid row bum.

His platform of currency inflation and farm relief did not have wide appeal outside the Midwest. Smith, Coughlin, and Townsend tried to dominate most Union Party rallies, but they proved niggardly when it came to giving the party financial support. On election day, with Townsend having recently defected to Landon, Lemke polled a disappointing 882,479 votes.

Landon did better, securing over 16 million of the 44 million votes cast, about a million more than Hoover had received four years earlier. Roosevelt made history by winning over 27 million votes and carrying every state except Maine and Vermont. His popular vote margin was the biggest in American history, and not since 1820 in an era of weak party competition had a candidate achieved a larger percentage of electoral votes, 523 to 8. Across the nation in other races, the Republican casualties were equally gruesome. Their numbers had been further reduced in the House and Senate and they had lost twenty-six of the thirty-three contests for governor. On election night, when the outcome was no longer in doubt, the liberal journalist Dorothy Thompson

FDR and his New Deal progeny.

proposed a toast to the president from her table at the St. Regis Hotel in New York City. Only her guests lifted their glasses. Virtually all of the other well-dressed, well-heeled patrons, Republicans no doubt, sat in grim silence.

Roosevelt had won his referendum and secured a greater mandate than in 1932, but how he might use it was not entirely clear. His opponents on the right had been thrashed decisively. With Lemke's poor showing and the minuscule vote for both the socialists and the communists (Thomas won only 187,000 votes; Earl Browder a little over 80,000 for the latter), the challenge from the left had been diffused as well. The *Economist* of London pointed out, "On the whole, the poor won the election from the well-to-do." Yet with millions still out of work or subsisting on various government programs, the Depression had hardly been conquered and the Supreme Court had recently ruled out a large number of solutions. Perhaps the most prescient observation also came from the *Economist:* "President Roosevelt," it predicted, "is more enviable today than he is likely to be a year hence."

6

Deadlock

Very confidentially, I may give you an awful shock in about two weeks.
—FDR to Felix Frankfurter

That's that.
—FDR, signing the Fair Labor Standards Act in 1938

COURTING DISASTER

For American presidents, the road to political disaster has often begun with a big reelection mandate. That fate befell George Washington and Thomas Jefferson. Later it struck Lyndon Johnson, destroyed by the Vietnam War; Richard Nixon, brought down by Watergate; and Ronald Reagan, crippled by the Iran-Contra affair. Franklin Roosevelt was no exception. His crushing victory in 1936 did not become a prelude to further triumph. Instead, it was the final taste of victory before storms battered the president and his administration in their second term. When the wreckage was at last surveyed, the damage proved considerable: FDR's liberal coalition had been seriously strained, conservative opponents had gained new strength, and the momentum for further social and economic innovations by the New Deal had been slowed considerably. Shadowed increasingly by terrible events abroad, America again bid adieu to domestic reform.

Many of Roosevelt's wounds were self-inflicted, and none more so than his first postelection decision to remove the constitutional road-blocks placed in his way by the Supreme Court. FDR's Judicial Procedures Reform Act of 1937, soon branded as the "court-packing" bill, became the single biggest blunder of his political career. FDR did not act without great provocation, but his method of retaliation against the Court proved both premature and politically maladroit. While the justices' reckless behavior generated torrents of criticism even from some conservative Republicans, the president and his advisers sorely miscalculated the depth of popular veneration for both the Constitution and the Court as an institution.

From Roosevelt's perspective, the Court had declared war on the New Deal. Rather than lowering constitutional barriers to legislative action, Chief Justice Hughes and five of his brethren had erected even higher ones during the months before the 1936 election. The fragile unity of the *Schechter* case had given way to bitter conflict inside the Court as the conservative majority forged new and radical legal chains restricting both national and state efforts to cope with the Depression. Appalled by these developments, the Court's three liberals—Stone, Brandeis, and Cardozo—now caucused together to plan their strategy before the regular Saturday conferences in which votes were cast and opinions assigned. One of Stone's law clerks glimpsed the depth of hard feelings when he suggested to the justice's chauffeur, Edward, that they give a ride to Justice McReynolds, who seemed unable to locate a cab on Connecticut Avenue. The chauffeur politely demurred. When Stone returned to his car and learned of the incident, he bluntly told the clerk: "Well . . . it's perfectly clear that Edward has a lot more sense than you have."

Compounding the constitutional restrictions already fixed in *Schechter*, Hughes and the majority literally cut the heart out of congressional power by striking down both the Agricultural Adjustment Act and the Guffey-Snyder Bituminous Coal Conservation Act. While Congress could levy taxes and spend money to promote the general welfare, wrote Justice Roberts in the Triple A case, this power could not be used to destroy individual liberty or invade the sovereign authority of the states. He invalidated the taxing provisions of the AAA, therefore, because they coerced farmers into joining the program and attempted to regulate agricultural production, a local economic activity within the states' jurisdiction. Likewise, the majority killed the federal government's attempt to stabilize the bituminous coal industry by restricting production and fixing wages. Such federal regulation could not pass constitutional muster because coal mining too rested on local production and fell under the states' jurisdiction.

The majority brushed aside arguments that most of the nation's wheat,

Chief Justice Charles Evans Hughes (right) and Justice Benjamin N. Cardozo.

cotton, tobacco, corn, and coal moved across state lines and ignored
ample precedents that supported the government's case. Some of these
precedents had been written by Hughes himself before World War I.
The decisions did provoke passionate and telling dissents from Stone
and Cardozo, joined by Brandeis, who accused the majority of tram-
pling on existing law and attempting to erect a judicial dictatorship
over the country's economic affairs. Stone denounced Roberts's interpretation of the Tenth Amendment as "a tortured construction of the
Constitution" and warned that "courts are not the only agency of government that must be assumed to have capacity to govern." By its narrow interpretation of the Commerce Clause, Cardozo wrote in the *Carter
Coal* case, the majority had stripped Congress of authority given to it
by the framers of the Constitution and set itself on a collision course
with the other branches of government.

Hughes, Roberts, and the Four Horsemen moved against the New
Deal on two other fronts as well. In the first test of the Securities Act
and the administrative powers of the SEC, they upheld the right of a
registrant to withdraw his registration statement before the expiration
of a twenty-day "cooling-off period" and thus evade the commission's
order to stop selling the securities. Sutherland's opinion for the major-

ity compared the SEC to the Star Chamber of Tudor and Stuart kings, which provoked the normally mild Cardozo to complain about the majority's "denunciatory fervor" since later historians "may find hyperbole in the sanguinary simile." Declining to rule on the ultimate constitutionality of the Tennessee Valley Authority, Hughes wrote an opinion that sanctioned the right of minority shareholders in public utilities to sue those corporate officers who cooperated with the agency's power programs. This decision opened up an entirely new avenue of legal challenges to the New Deal.

Having emasculated the federal government in defense of states' rights, the majority proceeded to show its hostility to local regulatory efforts, too. First, it struck down a section of Vermont's new income tax law by invoking the obscure "privileges and immunities" clause of the Fourteenth Amendment, a provision adopted originally to protect blacks from racial discrimination. Until the Vermont case, the clause had never been used to nullify a state's economic policy. Next, reviving the hoary doctrine of "liberty of contract," it overturned New York's attempt to fix minimum wages for certain categories of poorly paid workers. Coupled with the earlier *Carter Coal* decision, this ruling meant that neither the federal government nor the states now had constitutional power to do much at all about substandard working conditions.

The New York decision provoked a cry of outrage even from former president Hoover, who protested that the Supreme Court had stripped the states of their legitimate powers. The Republican Party platform in 1936 went so far as to call for a constitutional amendment to nullify the Court's ruling. Viewing the legal graveyard at the end of 1936, Frankfurter denounced the majority's "unreason and folly" that crippled both Washington and the states. "This fateful term is over," he wrote to Justice Stone, "but its ghosts will walk for many a day." A despondent Cardozo, fearing for the judiciary's reputation and safety in the wake of such sharply divided and partisan judgments, confided to a friend, "We are no longer a court."

"An Awful Shock"

Based on the Court's performance in 1936, many New Dealers, including the president, expected even worse calamities in the coming judicial term. Other reform measures would be on the justices' docket, and given the majority's views on taxation, spending, and interstate commerce, the outlook was not promising for the Social Security Act

Justice Harlan F. Stone.

and the Wagner Act. Even TVA and the new holding company law appeared in jeopardy.

What could Roosevelt do in the face of a judical threat to the remaining programs of the New Deal? Some, including Frankfurter, had advocated amending the Constitution: give Congress explicit authority over things such as wages, hours, and labor relations; require a unanimous vote of the justices to invalidate acts of Congress; or permit Congress to repass laws struck down by the Court in the same way it could override a presidential veto. But amending the Constitution was a long, tedious process. It could take years. Roosevelt observed that with $10 million to spend he could stop the ratification of any amendment by the states.

Stanley Reed, the solicitor general whose office had taken a regular beating before the Court, thought the judicial roadblock could be broken by pushing legislation already before Congress. It would permit federal judges to retire at full salary. Such had been the law prior to

FDR's Economy Act of 1933, which had cut their retirement income in half. No less an opponent of the New Deal than Justice McReynolds leaked word that two of his brethren—Van Devanter and Sutherland— wanted to step down if their retirement income could be restored under the old formula. How easy, direct, and uncontroversial. Roosevelt would quickly have two vacancies to fill with loyal New Dealers. Combined with the votes of Stone, Cardozo, and Brandeis, the administration would have a new majority for liberal construction of the Constitution.

Roosevelt choose a legislative solution to his problem, but it proved to be far more explosive than the retirement plan and ultimately more costly to his administration and the nation. "Very confidentially," he wrote to Frankfurter in January, "I may give you an awful shock in about two weeks. Even if you do not agree, suspend judgment and I will tell you the story." On the morning of February 5, 1937, he called congressional leaders and members of the cabinet to the White House, where he read them a message embodying proposed legislation to be introduced at noon that same day. The White House distributed copies almost simultaneously to the press corps. In brief, FDR's Judicial Procedures Reform Act, drafted under a shroud of secrecy by Attorney General Homer Cummings, provided that if a federal judge who had served at least ten years did not resign six months after his seventieth birthday, the president could nominate another new judge to that court. The president could name up to six new justices to the Supreme Court and forty-four to the lower federal courts.

Expanding or contracting the size of the Supreme Court by statute was clearly constitutional and not unprecedented. Congress fixed the original number at six in 1789, reduced it to five in 1801, expanded it to ten during the Civil War, trimmed it back to eight in 1866, and finally settled on nine three years later, where it had remained ever since. In jest, Huey Long had once observed to Ray Moley that if Congress desired, it could swell the size of the Supreme Court to that of the United States Army! In 1913, James McReynolds, then Wilson's attorney general, had proposed adding new blood to the Court through a similar plan of expansion. This ironic piece of information delighted the president when Cummings showed him McReynolds's original memorandum. With huge Democratic majorities in both houses of Congress, as *Time* magazine soon noted, "if he [FDR] chose to whip it through, the necessary votes were already in his pocket." What Democratic legislator could resist, especially if the Court continued to overturn New Deal legislation?

But what if the Court suddenly changed course? Roosevelt had not

counted on that. The President and the small group of advisers who
devised the plan also failed to assess the possible consequences of their
secrecy and public reaction to the first explanations put forward as justification for the measure. The problem with the Judicial Procedures
Reform Act was not its constitutionality, but its utter deviousness. Aside
from Cummings, no member of the cabinet had been taken into the
president's confidence before February 5. Cummings had consulted
Princeton's distinguished legal scholar Edward Corwin, but not the
best legal brains in the administration—Rosenman, Frankfurter, Cohen,
Corcoran. Usually deferential to Congress, Roosevelt failed to lay any
groundwork with his legislative leaders on Capitol Hill. Taken by surprise, they listened impassively as the president read them his message.

Roosevelt sought to justify the legislation on the grounds that the
overworked justices could not keep up with their caseload. He noted
that during a recent term they had declined to hear nearly 90 percent
of the petitions for review presented to them. Although some maintained "full mental and physical vigor," FDR explained, others "not so
fortunate are often unable to perceive their own infirmities. They seem
to be tenacious of the appearance of adequacy."

FDR could not have chosen a less informed or more politically inept
justification. Congress had given the Supreme Court complete discretion over its docket during the Taft years in order to permit the justices
to concentrate on the most important cases. They declined to hear
appeals not because they were overworked, but because they were
selective. By correlating age with mental competence, moreover, FDR
touched a raw nerve with Chief Justice Hughes, then seventy-five, and
with the Court's oldest member, Brandeis, eighty, who had often supported the New Deal. Roosevelt's argument would not win friends among
the party elders in Congress, some of whom were already eligible for
social security.

Several days later, primed by Frankfurter and others, Roosevelt offered
a more candid and thoughtful explanation for the Judicial Procedures
Reform Act in a nationwide "fireside chat." Wisely, he played down
the age theme and frankly accused the justices of waging a calculated
political war against his administration and the will of the American
people. Echoing Lincoln's response to the *Dred Scott* decision, he said,
"We cannot yield our constitutional destiny to the personal judgment
of a few men who, fearful of the future, would deny us the necessary
means of dealing with the present." FDR attempted belatedly to recap-

*FDR springs his court-packing plan on the country and
some members of the cabinet.*

ture the ideological high ground by casting the struggle as one between
democracy and oligarchy, but the damage had already been done.

The president's plan drew an immediate negative response from
Republican leaders and the conservative press, as predicted, but the
private reaction of administration loyalists forecast troubled seas ahead.
House speaker William Bankhead and majority leader Sam Rayburn
seethed with anger because they had been kept in the dark about the
proposal. Hatton Summers, the crusty chairman of the House Judiciary Committee, said bluntly after hearing FDR's message: "Boys, here's
where I cash in my chips." A stunned Frankfurter told the president
and others that the justices had provoked the confrontation, and he
offered to give FDR more ammunition for the battle. On the other
hand, he could not bring himself to endorse Roosevelt's specific remedy. Attorney Milton Katz, working at the SEC, told Corcoran and
Cohen he would write speeches criticizing the Court, but not speeches
supporting the "court-packing" plan. When Corcoran made the rounds
of Senate offices in an initial effort to line up support for the bill, he
encountered a furious Burton K. Wheeler, who announced, "Well,
Tommy, he [FDR] isn't going to get it!"

"Switch in Time"

Roosevelt discovered how formidable an opponent Senator Wheeler could be two weeks after the Senate Judiciary Committee opened hearings on his controversial plan. Wheeler presented the committee with a letter from Chief Justice Hughes that point by point demolished the president's arguments. The justices remained fully abreast of their work, Hughes wrote. Furthermore, expanding the size of the court would make matters worse by increasing the number of memoranda to be read and the number of views to be heard during conference.

Although Roosevelt didn't know it, Brandeis had been the real architect of Hughes's extraordinary document. Believing that the president had been swept away by a lust for power, the aging progressive arranged for the chief justice and Wheeler to meet secretly. Brandeis added his signature to Hughes's letter and persuaded Van Devanter to do the same. He thus secured an ideological cross section of the Court's members against Roosevelt's plan. Cardozo and Stone, who had not been consulted by Brandeis, believed the letter and Hughes's intervention about as offensive to the Court's dignity and independence as all the scheming in the White House. But they remained silent. The Hughes-Brandeis-McReynolds letter represented the beginning of the end for the Judicial Procedures Reform Act.

One week after Hughes's letter, on March 29, 1937, the chief justice and four other justices drove a second nail into the coffin of the court-packing bill. To everyone's amazement, they sustained for the first time a minimum wage law, a measure from the state of Washington almost identical to the New York statute invalidated six months earlier. Justice Roberts, who had provided the fifth vote to invalidate the New York law, now sided with Stone, Brandeis, Cardozo, and Hughes to make the new majority. On April 12, that same majority also surprised the country by upholding in sweeping terms the controversial collective bargaining provisions of the Wagner Act.

Outside and inside the Court, observers greeted the sudden about-face by Roberts and Hughes with a combination of shock and dismay. Most attributed the outcome to the court-packing plan and pure political expediency on the part of the chief justice and his junior colleague. "In order to reach the result which was reached in these cases," Justice Stone told his son, "it was necessary for six members of the Court either to be overruled or to take back some things they subscribed to in the Guffey Coal Act case." Reading the *Labor Board* opinion, Frankfurter told FDR that "after today I feel like finding some honest profession to enter," while Charles Wyzanski, who had argued the case before the justices, quipped that "the President's castor oil seems to work."

Roosevelt's court-packing plan, in fact, had nothing to do with Justice Roberts's famous vote in the minimum wage case, his "switch in time that saved nine." Although the justices did not issue their opinions until March, the decisive vote had been taken in December, long before FDR unveiled his surprise package—but not long after his landslide reelection victory. Roberts and his admirers later maintained that political considerations had absolutely nothing to do with his change of heart on the minimum wage issue. In the earlier New York case, the justice affirmed, he had been prepared to overrule the notorious "liberty of contract" doctrine from the 1925 *Adkins* case, but the lawyers for the state had not framed their arguments properly. Six months later, when the Washington law squarely presented the choice of overturning *Adkins*, he quickly sided with the majority.

Roberts's defense fails to account for one stubborn fact. New York's lawyers had asked the justices for a rehearing on their case, and they specifically requested a reconsideration of the *Adkins* doctrine. Roberts, who later claimed to be eager to dispose of *Adkins*, voted against a rehearing. This was before Roosevelt's decisive reelection in November. By focusing on the Washington case, the defenders of Roberts and Hughes also tend to ignore their intellectual flip-flops on the commerce clause in the six months between the Guffey Coal decision and the Wagner Act case. The Judicial Procedures Reform Act cannot explain Justice Roberts's "switch" in the minimum wage case. But when combined with the November election returns, it provided a powerful incentive for Roberts and Hughes to rethink their constitutional principles.

Hughes and Roberts, both loyal Republicans who distrusted many of the New Deal's innovations, had played a high-stakes political game against the president in 1935–36. Voting with the Four Horsemen on crucial issues, they hoped to mobilize popular opposition against the administration by portraying it as dangerously radical, a threat to established constitutional norms. When the voters rejected this interpretation and gave FDR an overwhelming mandate, the chief justice and Roberts had little choice but to temper their opposition, especially after February, when most observers predicted a quick presidential victory on the court-packing bill. "I may not know much law," FDR's cousin Ted once remarked, "but I do know that one can put the fear of God in judges."

Burial in the Senate

Whatever the later verdict of historians about the behavior of Roberts and Hughes in the minimum wage and Wagner Act cases, the court's sudden change of heart doomed FDR's court-packing bill. Support for the Judicial Procedures Reform Act melted away in the Senate. It turned into a route against the president, when Justice Van Devanter became the first justice to take advantage of the new retirement law (passed in early March) by announcing that he would step down on May 18. Two weeks later, speaking through Justice Cardozo, the Court put the seal of constitutional approval on the Social Security Act by a 5–4 vote, with Hughes and Roberts again siding with the majority. The Senate Judiciary Committee had shortly before voted against the bill, 10–8, with six Democrats deserting the President. All administration hopes for the measure vanished on July 14, when majority leader Robinson, who continued to lead the fight on the Senate floor, succumbed to heart failure in his Washington apartment. By 70–20, the full Senate finally ended FDR's agony by voting to send the bill back to committee a week after Robinson's funeral.

Anytime after Van Devanter's announced retirement, FDR might have sought a face-saving compromise in Congress. It would have spared him a humiliating defeat and salvaged some of his political capital. The Court had capitulated. Soon he could make his first appointment, perhaps two, thereby firming up a majority on the court for the New Deal. Two days before the final Senate action, Vice President Garner told him bluntly he was beaten. Governor Herbert Lehman, his successor in New York and another bellwether liberal, had come out against the plan. Still Roosevelt refused to back down and insisted on a vote.

The president defended his position by saying that Hughes and Roberts might shift again; the margin of safety on the Court for his programs would remain too thin. But the patience of many of the president's supporters had worn thin as well. Not a few of them thought he had lost touch with political reality, blinded by a belief in his own invincibility and by a stubborn desire to further humiliate the justices. In 1936 most voters rejected the idea that FDR and the New Deal had tampered unreasonably with the nation's constitutional foundations. A year

Congressional Democrats revolt against FDR's "court-packing."

later, in the aftermath of the court-packing fiasco, they could not be so certain.

Most historians say that with respect to the Supreme Court, FDR lost the immediate battle, but won the longer war. Beginning in 1937, the Hughes Court upheld the legislation of the Second Hundred Days. In 1938 the justices ruled without dissent in the *Carolene Products* case that on questions of economic policy, they would normally uphold the judgment of Congress, while utilizing higher standards of judicial review for issues of voting rights, civil rights, and civil liberties. From that date until the mid-1970s, they did not invalidate another act of the national legislature touching economic arrangements. They exhibited similar deference to the regulations adopted by the states. Between 1937 and 1943, the "old" Court passed away and the New Deal Court came into existence as Roosevelt filled nine vacancies, more than any president since Washington.

And yet in a larger sense, the president's opponents, Hughes, Brandeis, and Wheeler, could claim victory. By defending the Court from a blatant political attack, they preserved judicial independence and judicial review. The post-1937 Supreme Court retreated from its heavy-handed attempt to control the country's economic destiny, but it still retained the considerable power of statutory interpretation. Instead of making economic policy wholesale, it continued to do a brisk retail business by fixing the boundaries of administrative power in the burgeoning federal bureaucracy.

In addition, judicial review took on new life as the post-1937 Court, influenced in part by the *Carolene Products* decision, shifted its attention away from issues of political economy to the defense of civil liberties and civil rights. Instead of overturning minimum wage laws, the late Hughes Court began to curb the states' efforts to throttle political speech, convict defendants without due process of law, and enforce racial segregation, all issues that moved to the very top of the judicial agenda in the next half century. A Supreme Court humiliated by the Judicial Procedures Reform Act in 1937 probably would not have had the prestige and confidence to hand down *Brown* v. *Board of Education* in 1954.

ROOSEVELT'S RECESSION

In the middle of June, as the court-packing bill moved inexorably toward burial in the Senate, FDR made his second fateful decision of 1937. He ordered substantial cuts in the government's work relief and other programs in an attempt to trim the expected federal deficit and balance the budget. The president hoped in this way to avoid higher interest charges that were certain to occur because the Federal Reserve Board, fearing an outbreak of inflation, had tightened reserve requirements over the previous six months, thus shrinking the money supply. At about the same time, the second year of social security taxes hit both employers and employees. On October 19, in a terrifying reprise of 1929, stock prices collapsed suddenly in New York as investors dumped seventeen million shares. America entered the "Roosevelt recession." By the time the dark clouds lifted in the summer of 1938, the American people had been put through another economic ringer, Roosevelt's credibility had suffered more damaging blows, and the New Deal had embarked on yet another policy course that threw the political landscape into still greater confusion.

The economic misery inflicted on millions of Americans by the Roosevelt recession from the fall of 1937 through the summer of 1938 was every bit as serious as what they suffered in the early years of the

Depression. Employment in manufacturing fell 23 percent, the national income plummeted by 13 percent, and the production of durable goods such as automobiles and appliances went down by 50 percent, the same percent decline suffered by common stock prices. Instead of contracting, the work relief rolls of the Works Progress Administration grew by 500 percent. Social workers in major cities reported growing numbers of children with malnutrition and destitute families again scrounging for scraps of food in trash containers outside restaurants. In his second inaugural address a few months earlier, Roosevelt said he saw "one-third of a nation ill-housed, ill-clad, ill-nourished" and pledged to eradicate this blight from the land. By the winter of 1937 the fulfillment of that promise seemed as remote as in 1932.

As the grim statistics of economic decline accumulated, the search for explanations and scapegoats began both outside the administration and inside. As one might have predicted, a great many businessmen and their allies in the press blamed the radical reforms of the New Deal for undermining confidence among investors and employers. They singled out for special criticism the tax revisions of 1935–36, the holding company and stock exchange legislation, and the Wagner Act. That law, they said, encouraged the outburst of sit-down strikes, sabotaged production, and undermined the authority of management. A few critics even threw in the court-packing battle for good measure. This perspective found support among some of FDR's advisers, notably Morgenthau, RFC chief Jesse Jones, and Commerce Secretary Daniel Roper, who urged the president to stay on course with his budget reductions and reassure the business community by putting on the shelf any additional social reforms.

Certain reforms of the New Deal no doubt terrified capitalists accustomed to a more consistent pro-business policy from Washington, but the fundamental causes of the recession flowed from the New Deal's restrictive fiscal and monetary policies, which conservatives applauded. Government spending on the order of $4.1 billion in 1936 had kept the economy moving ahead as farmers, veterans, and WPA employees spent their subsidies, bonus certificates, and payroll checks from Uncle Sam. This stimulation also generated exaggerated fears of inflation among experts on the Federal Reserve Board, including its usually expansive chairman, Marriner Eccles, who pushed for curbing the money supply. FDR did not enter a demurrer to these decisions and also supported spending reductions to narrow the budget deficit. He behaved exactly as Hoover had in 1932. In short, the Roosevelt recession flowed in large measure from FDR's propensity to follow deflationary, orthodox fiscal policies instead of more stimulating ones.

As criticism from the business and financial community became more vituperative, Roosevelt boiled inside, but also seemed uncertain about what to do about the economy's slide. One adviser found him growing "very dictatorial and very disagreable" as the crisis intensified. At a cabinet meeting in November he lashed out at those around the table and declared he was "sick and tired of being told . . . by everybody . . . what's the matter with the country and nobody suggests what I should do." Vice President Garner thought the President looked scared for the first time in his administration, and several commentators compared his indecision to Hoover's.

Another round of debate now raged inside the administration that mirrored the conflict between spenders and budget balancers from the year before. Roosevelt, not eager to be blamed for the economic woes he had helped to create, listened with growing enthusiasm to the expansionists—Hopkins, Ickes, Corcoran, Leon Henderson, and Robert Jackson. They argued that the recession arose fundamentally from a dearth of private investment deliberately created by bankers and businessmen who wished to kill the New Deal, from the policies of monopolistic corporations that rigged prices, and from the continued income gap between rich and poor. They recommended a large dose of new government spending to combat the "strike" by organized capital and aggressive enforcement of the antitrust laws to restore price competition.

Still tied emotionally to the fiscal conservatives, FDR had a difficult time accepting more budget deficits, but when the economy continued to falter in early 1938, he had little choice but to cast his lot with Hopkins, Ickes, and the other spenders. Their antibusiness rhetoric also allowed FDR to vent his frustrations against an ever-popular target of the public's wrath. In April he asked Congress for $3 billion in additional spending for WPA, PWA, and other federal programs. Faced with elections in the fall, Congress quickly upped the ante to $3.75 billion. Morgenthau and other fiscal conservatives who lost the policy debate expressed horror at the new spending plans. "They had just stampeded him [FDR]," the Treasury secretary lamented. "He was completely stampeded. They stampeded him like cattle."

The resurgence of federal spending in 1938–39 did not break the back of unemployment, which remained at around ten million, but it did prevent the Roosevelt recession from becoming much worse. The economy continued to limp along until larger injections of defense spending came after 1940. Without much enthusiasm, FDR had become a Keynesian by necessity rather than conviction, although the efficacy of deficit spending as an antidepression remedy would not be fully demonstrated until the war years.

The president showed much greater enthusiasm for the renewal of trust-busting in April 1938 when he called on Congress to both raise spending and investigate the extent of monopoly power in the economy. He hiked the budget of the Antitrust Division in the Department of Justice and recruited a new assistant attorney general, Thurman Arnold, to crack down on violators. Arnold, the former mayor of Laramie, Wyoming, and an iconoclastic law professor at Yale, seemed a curious choice for the chief job of trust buster. He had recently published *The Folklore of Capitalism,* which ridiculed the Sherman Act as an empty political and cultural ritual. The congressional inquiry itself, known as the Temporary National Economic Committee, produced volumes of expert testimony and many turgid reports, but very little in the way of concrete recommendations.

Arnold, to the surprise of many, attempted to enforce the antitrust laws with considerable zeal against both corporations and labor unions that engaged in anticompetitive activities. His suits against powerful trade unions, notably the carpenters and joiners in the AFL, set off howls of protest from even the federation's enemies in the CIO, who protested that the antitrust laws were never intended to curb union abuses. A series of Supreme Court rulings brought Arnold's campaign to a stop; so did the imperatives of defense mobilization, and FDR's waning enthusiasm for pummeling big business after Pearl Harbor.

Roosevelt's response to the economic collapse of 1937–38 brought the New Deal almost full circle. Having begun with the Economy Act, he finally supported deliberate budget deficits. Having proposed to cure the Depression by suspending the antitrust laws in the NRA, he concluded with a crusade to invigorate them. From the perspective of his critics, then and now, this trajectory indicated massive confusion and ignorance that prolonged the nation's economic difficulties. From the perspective of his admirers, it revealed a healthy evolution on FDR's part from conservatism to real progressivism and a pragmatic adjustment to the ever-shifting sands of American politics. One thing was certain, however. Coming on the heels of the court-packing defeat, the Roosevelt recession had further weakened the president and eroded the momentum for domestic reform.

THE FAILURE OF EXECUTIVE REORGANIZATION

The court-packing battle destroyed FDR's reputation for political sagacity, estranged him from old allies like Senator Wheeler and revived old enemies, who now vowed to fight the New Deal on other fronts as well. The onset of the recession in 1937 added to his political woes. Among the immediate casualties was the president's bold plan to restructure the executive branch in the interests of greater efficiency and to enhance the ability of the White House to implement a coherent set of public policies. Unfortunately, this worthwhile effort ran afoul of intense bureaucratic infighting, the desire of congressmen to preserve their existing influence with executive agencies, and mounting fears that Roosevelt was once again attempting to grasp too much power. When the rhetoric died down and the results were tallied, FDR and the New Deal had suffered another important political setback.

Fighting waste, mismanagement, and corruption through governmental reorganization at the local, state, and federal level had been high on the agenda of progressives since the turn of the century. The key to effective and virtuous government, many reformers believed, was choosing "good men" and rearranging the lines of official authority in a systematic and rational fashion. Following Al Smith's example, FDR had helped to streamline New York's state administration. After four years of unparalleled governmental expansion under the New Deal, Roosevelt and others believed the time had come to put the federal executive branch in like order by consolidating agencies and bureaus with similar functions, expanding the merit system for employment, and giving the president greater authority over his subordinates. Like the Economy Act of 1933, reorganizing the executive branch would also help to counter critics who accused the administration of incompetence and extravagance.

Roosevelt gave the task of devising a reorganization plan to three of the most able experts on public administration in the country, Louis Brownlow, director of the Public Administration Clearing House in Chicago; Charles E. Merriam, a founder of the Social Science Research Council; and Luther Gulick, head of the Institute for Public Administration in New York City. The report of their President's Committee on Administrative Management recommended sweeping changes, including the creation of six new executive assistants to the president and a permanent National Resources Planning Board in the White House. A single administrator would replace the Civil Service Commission and would run a federal bureaucracy with more merit categories and higher salaries. The number of executive departments would grow from ten to twelve, including a new Department of Welfare; various agencies and bureaus such as the Forest Service and the Public Health Service would be reassigned to departments according to their functions; the Bureau of the Budget would be placed directly under the president's control; and the independent regulatory agencies such as the ICC and the SEC would be made responsible to the executive departments.

When FDR submitted the Brownlow Report to Congress in January 1937 with his strong endorsement for quick approval, the chances of its passage were probably 50 percent. After his court-packing plan went to Capitol Hill a month later, the odds dropped almost to zero. Critics immediately linked the two measures as part of a presidential plot to draw all of the powers of government into the hands of one man in the White House. With the collapse of democratic regimes throughout Europe, these attacks had enormous popular appeal. The president's reorganization bill, declared anti–New Dealer Senator Josiah Bailey of North Carolina, would give him "all the powers of a dictator." Others accused the White House of submitting a plan designed by radical professors who hoped to pack.the government with subversives and "social desperados" from the CIO. The proposed new Department of Welfare became a special target of conservatives, who alleged it would be run by Hopkins and the big relief spenders.

Defections inside the executive branch matched rising hostility in Congress. Officials of the Veterans Administration, backed by battalions of their constituents, protested the agency's merger into the Welfare Department, as did the bureaucrats at the Public Health Service. The reorganization plan would have realized one of Harold Ickes's fondest dreams by creating a Department of Conservation and shifting the Forest Service from the Department of Agriculture to his jurisdiction, but the foresters and their allies fought bitterly against this move, as did Henry Wallace. Leaders of the Bureau of Indian Affairs claimed the measure would dilute the influence of real experts in their agency and threaten its existence altogether. These frightened administrators found sympathetic ears on various committees and subcommittees in Congress, where the members had forged comfortable and profitable relationships with many executive agencies going back decades and resented any changes that might reduce their own power.

By pulling out all the political stops, FDR and the Senate leadership managed to push the bill through the upper house in March 1938, but with only seven votes to spare. In the House, however, the debate raged for six weeks before opponents prevailed on a motion to send the bill back to committee, which effectively killed it. The 204–196 tally indicated massive defections among House Democrats against the president, who suffered a more humiliating defeat than in the court-packing debacle. One elated Republican hailed the reorganization vote as "the biggest political event which has taken place since 1932."

A year later, Congress gave Roosevelt a watered-down version of his initial reorganization plan that authorized the president to hire six new executive assistants, but retained little else from the Brownlow recommendations. Congress eliminated the civil service reforms and rejected the creation of new departments. The final version of the Reorganization Act of 1939 spared from realignment virtually all existing bureaus and the independent regulatory agencies. As probably the last New Deal measure passed by Congress, its toothlessness indicated the extent to which FDR had lost his political magic on the domestic scene and the growing strength of anti-administration forces in Congress.

FAREWELL TO REFORM

A year before the weakened Reorganization Act became law, Congress sent to Roosevelt the only significant domestic reform of his entire second term: the Fair Labor Standards Act, which fixed minimum wages and maximum hours and prohibited the employment of children under the age of sixteen. The FLSA enshrined in federal law goals progressives had struggled for since the turn of the century. But it had been stalled by the court-packing fight, sustained numerous debilitating amendments in Congress, and finally passed only because of the strong support of both the AFL and the CIO, and some Northern business groups who wished to eliminate the South's competitive advantage in labor costs.

Intended to protect basic labor standards in the wake of the death of NRA, the wages and hours legislation introduced by Senator Black and Congressman William Connery in the spring of 1937 immediately took a legislative backseat to the fierce battle over the Court. It also generated stout opposition from many Southern Democrats, who hoped to preserve their region's low wage differential, and from the chairman of the House Ways and Means Committee, John O'Connor of New York. An inveterate opponent of the New Deal, O'Connor had fought against the "death sentence" in the Public Utility Holding Company Act and also led the charge against reorganization of the executive branch. By the time the original Fair Labor Standards measure came to a final vote in Congress, it contained so many exemptions and loopholes that one legislator in jest offered an amendment instructing the secretary of labor to report in ninety days "whether anyone is subject to this bill."

Although a landmark of social legislation, the Fair Labor Standards Act did not become the death rattle of free enterprise, as forecast by some of its opponents. Congress set the minimum wage at 25 cents an hour for 1938, with increases scheduled to take it to 40 cents by 1945. The law fixed the standard work week at forty-four hours for the first year, with a reduction to forty hours by 1940. Employers were required to pay time and a half for all overtime. Even at these less than munificent levels, the Fair Labor Standards Act boosted immediately the wages of nearly half a million workers and shortened the work week for over a million. But the law also left the question of wage differentials to administrative discretion and excluded from protection some of the nation's most vulnerable and exploited workers, including domestic servants, retail clerks, streetcar operators, all agricultural laborers, and fishermen. "That's that," Roosevelt said, as he put his signature on the wages and hours bill after the long legislative battle. He didn't realize it at the time, but the New Deal was over.

FAILED PURGE, CONSERVATIVE RESURGENCE

Stung by the defeat of both his court-packing and executive reorganization plans, Roosevelt and those close to him pointed their fingers at the culprits in Congress, especially conservative Democrats, mostly in the South, who had deserted the administration on both occasions. The president wanted revenge. Roosevelt and some of his advisers also nursed the fond hope of restructuring the two major parties along strict ideological lines, with liberals in command of the Democratic Party and conservatives joining the GOP. They thought they saw such an opportunity in the Democratic primaries and the general election of 1938. At the end of June, Roosevelt delivered a blistering, highly political "fireside chat" in which he compared his opponents inside the party to the Copperheads of the Civil War era who tried to sabotage the war effort in the North and pursued "peace at any price." He made it clear he would take sides in the coming party primaries.

The White House rolled out its heavy political artillery against five incumbent Democratic senators: Millard Tydings of Maryland, Walter George of Georgia, Cotton Ed Smith of South Carolina, Frederick Van Nuys of Indiana, and Guy Gillette of Iowa. While presidential surrogates such as Hopkins blasted Van Nuys and Gillette, FDR personally went hunting for George, Smith, and Tydings. In Maryland, he denounced Tydings as a hypocrite who spoke on behalf of the downtrodden, but voted the other way. With Senator George in the audience, he told a gathering of Georgia Democrats that their leader did not "deep down in his heart" support the objectives of the party. And in South Carolina the president portrayed Cotton Ed as someone who didn't care if many of the state's workers earned only 50 cents a day.

When Democrats cast their primary ballots, however, the "purge" failed and FDR took another political drubbing. Tydings, George, Smith, Van Nuys, and Gillette all swept to victory. Roosevelt may have tipped the balance against a conservative Democrat in only a single

Political defeats in 1937 did not dampen FDR's spirits.

race—New York, where his old nemesis Representative O'Connor went down to defeat. While pro–New Dealers such as Claude Pepper, Lester Hill, and Alben Barkley also withstood conservative challenges, there would not be a realignment inside the Democratic Party in 1938 or for some years thereafter.

In the November general elections, with the recession underway, the Democrats took a major beating as voters held them responsible for the return of hard times. The Republicans gained eight Senate seats and nearly doubled their numbers in the House from 88 to 170. That gain swelled the ranks of a conservative coalition of Southern Democrats and members of the GOP who had already brought the New Deal to a virtual standstill. And as Roosevelt turned his attention more and more toward events in Europe and Asia after 1938, this coalition would likewise limit the administration's initiatives abroad. "Dr. Win the War" might soon replace "Dr. New Deal," as FDR later remarked, but a deadlock between president and Congress had developed on the domestic front that would not soon be broken.

7

New Deals, Old Deals

> *Mr. Roosevelt may have given the wrong answers to many*
> *of his problems. But he is at least the first President of*
> *modern America who has asked the right questions.*
> —*The Economist*

THE RIDDLE OF RECOVERY

In one conspicuous way, Franklin Roosevelt and the New Deal failed
the American people: in six years of effort, economic prosperity had
not returned and the Depression lingered. Nearly ten million citizens,
over 17 percent of the labor force, remained out of work in 1939, a
figure that would not diminish until American factories began to turn
out tanks, guns, destroyers, and warplanes in the following years. A
much larger percentage remained in 1939 as in 1936 "ill-housed, ill-
clothed, ill-nourished." Then and now, conservative critics of the New
Deal offered a simple explanation for this greatest of all its shortcomings. Too much government regulation, too much reform, and too much
radical rhetoric from the president and the administration had destroyed
the confidence of businessmen, undermined the incentive to invest,
and thereby prolonged the country's economic misery.

As an explanation for the long duration of the Depression in America, however, this one is too simplistic and one-dimensional. It slights
the fundamental political context in which all decisions about economic affairs are made in a democratic society. Even in the frantic
days of 1933, Roosevelt was never a dictator. Without substantial
concessions to farmers, the unemployed, and laboring men and women,

no administration could have long survived at the ballot box after 1932. Hoover's fate made that point clear.

Had the New Deal desired a serious rapprochement with conservative businessmen, this would have entailed abandonment of farm subsidies, WPA, social security, the Wagner Act, wages and hours legislation, securities regulation, and most tax reform. Politically, therefore, recovery without a significant dose of structural reform and economic redistribution was a practical impossibility. In addition, it would have left the system more vulnerable to another storm similar to 1929–32.

Faced with a frightened, demoralized, and resentful business community that remained reluctant to generate sufficient investment to boost the economy, the New Deal might have compensated for the deficit with a bold spending program of its own. But Roosevelt's fiscal conservatism ultimately frustrated the implementation of a genuine Keynesian policy. The president vacillated back and forth between fiscal expansion and contraction. Even in 1938 he regarded the renewed spending program as a temporary expedient, another brief aberration before the restoration of a balanced budget.

On the whole, the New Deal pursued a regressive fiscal policy throughout the decade, and neither state nor local governments took up much of the slack. They too practiced fiscal austerity by frequently raising taxes to balance their budgets. A federal spending program of considerable magnitude would have been necessary to reverse this national trend. The countries that pursued the most aggressive fiscal expansion in the 1930s—Germany and Sweden, for example—defeated unemployment and the Depression long before the United States, England, or France.

But even a consistent and aggressive federal policy of countercyclical spending would not have cured another serious structural problem in the American economy that prolonged the depression. By the late 1920s, the center of gravity in the nation's economy had already begun to shift away from agriculture and traditional heavy industries such as railroads, mining, and metals production to newer consumer-oriented and service industries such as home appliances, retail sales, banking, insurance, and entertainment. While the nation's agricultural and traditional manufacturing sectors faced intensified competition throughout the world, shrinking markets, and falling rates of profit, the newer sectors were poised for significant new growth.

The financial collapse of 1929–32 disrupted and delayed this structural transformation, which would not become visible until the postwar

FDR's critics said he spent too much or not enough.

decades. During the thirties, most American workers remained stranded in jobs in which investment would have been declining and unemployment rising even without a serious liquidity crisis. These were also sectors of the economy, especially agriculture, that retained enormous political influence in state legislatures and Congress, which permitted them to secure the lion's share of government assistance even though these dollars might have been better invested elsewhere. America's traditional manufacturing industries continued to languish until defense orders came along after 1940, but the newer high-technology, service, and consumer-oriented sectors revived much sooner. While textiles and coal withered, motion pictures and radio sales boomed. In terms of total employment and investment, however, industries such as motion pictures remained too small relative to the entire economy to spark a general recovery.

Democratizing Consumption

While Roosevelt and the New Dealers could not claim to have restored the golden days of economic prosperity, they could be justifiably proud of putting questions of economic justice back on the agenda of public policy. The Republican administrations of the 1920s had not always been shy about using the power of the federal government to shape economic affairs, but when the government intervened, as it did with tax cuts and tariff protection, it usually did so on behalf of the rich and powerful. Economic conservatives raised high the banner of economic liberty before and after 1933, but it was a hollow liberty for millions of producers and workers, given only the freedom to sell their cotton below the price of production or to work long hours for subsistence wages. The maldistribution of national income that accompanied the prosperity of the 1920s threatened to undermine economic growth. It also constituted a moral affront to a society dedicated to life, liberty, and the pursuit of happiness.

The New Deal did not eradicate poverty or economic inequality and some of its programs even enriched those who were reasonably well off, but it did begin to deploy the resources of the national government on behalf of those who had received very little succor in the past. By fashioning a basic welfare state, it provided Americans with a level of security that some European societies had known for decades. It guaranteed millions of industrial workers for the first time the liberty to join a union and to bargain collectively. It put a floor under wages and a ceiling over hours, and it created a modest safety net for those who were thrown out of work, disabled, or retired. It saved the homes and farms of middle-income Americans from foreclosure. Through TVA and the Rural Electrification Administration, it brought jobs, electric power, and hope to some of the nation's most depressed rural areas. To the old lexicon of American rights—freedom of religion, speech, press, voting—the New Deal suggested new ones that were the affirmative responsibility of government—freedom from economic deprivation and exploitation.

The New Deal also helped to change forever the basic debate about the meaning of economic opportunity and justice in an urban, industrial economy shaped by giant corporations, big labor unions, and a permanent government bureaucracy. Beginning in the eighteenth century, generations of American reformers had held aloft the banner of "producerism" as the ultimate test of the good society. Only those who controlled their own productive resources—the farmer, the artisan, the self-employed businessman—could be truly free and independent citizens. This vision of a producers' commonwealth fired Jefferson's faith in yeoman farmers, fueled the Jacksonians' attack on monopoly, inspired the antislavery movement, shaped the mentality of many trade unionists, helped pass the Sherman Antitrust Act, and guided large numbers of progressives such as Brandeis. In the thirties, although Roosevelt sometimes spoke in these terms, the leading popular exponents of a producers' commonwealth were Upton Sinclair and Huey Long.

The success of the New Deal sealed the fate of "producerism" as a dominant reform ideology in America. In its place came a new emphasis on "consumerism," a guarantee that government would attempt to provide citizens with equal access to goods and services rather than direct control of productive resources. For all its criticism of big business, including Thurman Arnold's antitrust crusade, the New Deal accepted large-scale corporate enterprise as a permanent and desirable feature of American life. With few exceptions, the leaders of organized labor who backed the New Deal—Lewis, Hillman, Philip Murray, Walter Reuther—wanted a larger slice of the pie baked by big business, not an entirely new recipe that might have given workers more control over production.

In an economic world already characterized before the thirties by assembly lines, wage labor, hired managers, corporate farms, and bureaucracy, could the New Deal have really restored a producers' commonwealth of independent proprietorship? Was there an alternative to democratic consumerism? Probably not. But as later critics of the New Deal would argue and as Roosevelt himself observed during the debate over financing social security, the government benefits bestowed by one generation might be taken away or substantially reduced by another. In a regime of consumerism, in which most citizens worked for salaries and wages, productive assets remained in the hands of a few, not the many.

POLITICAL REALIGNMENT

Roosevelt and the New Deal consummated a realignment of the nation's major political parties that began with the Smith-Hoover election of 1928. Just as McKinley's victory at the end of the depression of the 1890s had ushered in almost four decades of Republican supremacy in national politics, FDR's electoral triumph began a Democratic

reign that lasted until 1952. Moreover, the political coalition that Roosevelt helped to build continued to elect American presidents as late as
Jimmy Carter in 1976 and permitted the Democrats to control both
houses of Congress with even greater consistency over the next half
century.

To the lily-white South, a bastion of the Democrats since the time of
Jefferson and Jackson, the party in the 1930s added millions of industrial workers and their families, who constituted critical voting blocs in
big cities stretching from New England to the Pacific Coast. The
Depression and the New Deal also shook loose from their traditional
Republican moorings a large number of farmers and middle-class professionals, whose livelihoods and dignity had been saved by assorted
farm programs, mortgage assistance, educational benefits, and WPA
jobs. Men and women who voted for the first time between 1932 and
1940, such as Ronald Wilson Reagan, cast their votes overwhelmingly
for FDR and the Democrats, a pattern they did not break until the
Eisenhower years. The biggest switch of all came with the old and new
black migrants to Northern cities. As late as 1932, they still gave a
majority of their ballots to Hoover and the party of Abraham Lincoln.
By 1936, blacks voted in large numbers for FDR, and four years later
their attachment to his coalition in the North had become unmistaka-
ble and unshakable.

OUTSIDERS AS INSIDERS

The New Deal broke the monopoly long held over American government and public policy by those who happened to be rich, white, male,
Anglo-Saxon, Protestant, and members of the business community.
Secure in his own social and economic position, FDR enjoyed the
company of men and women from diverse backgrounds. Pursuing at
times unorthodox programs, he could not count on the support of the
nation's traditional ruling elites, most of whom despised "that man in
the White House" and regarded him as "a traitor to his class." To a
remarkable extent, therefore, FDR forged a coalition of economic, ethnic, and cultural minorities, a collection of outsiders driven to some
extent by their common experience of alienation from the old Establishment.

Roosevelt gave legitimacy, status, and power as never before to both
Irish Catholics and Jews, who had tasted the lash of discrimination in
business, law, and other professions. Among his most astute political

advisers were Jim Farley, who aspired to be president, and Ed Flynn, the renegade Tammany Hall leader. To these he added by 1935 Tom Corcoran, whose charm was exceeded only by his cunning at cutting legislative deals and who lightened the president's evenings with his bawdy humor, passable tenor voice, and mastery of the accordion.

In Charles Fahy, a Notre Dame graduate known as "Whispering Charlie" because of his soft voice and Southern manners, FDR found another brilliant legal mind; Fahy's skill piloted the National Labor Relations Act through the courts and its early administrative battles with the business community. And who but Roosevelt would have named Joseph P. Kennedy, the upstart Wall Street speculator and motion picture tycoon, to the chairmanship of the SEC and later tapped him to be the first Roman Catholic ambassador to Great Britain? This second assignment proved to be a serious error on Roosevelt's part when Kennedy turned soft on Nazi Germany, but they both must have relished the discomfort Kennedy's appointment caused among Boston Brahmins.

Jewish lawyers such as Frankfurter and Rosenman had counseled Roosevelt on appointments, drafted laws, and written speeches before the New Deal. With the extraordinary burst of legislation, administration, and litigation generated by the New Deal, the need for able lawyers in Washington grew at an astonishing pace. It increased on Wall Street, too, as a result of the New Deal, but because of anti-Semitism many of the brightest young attorneys found the doors there shut tight against them. Wall Street's bigotry proved to be FDR's gain as the New Deal became, as one scholar has noted, "a lawyer's deal," which drew on the skills of this profession as never before in the nation's history.

Not all the lawyers who came to Washington to work for the New Deal were Jews (e.g., Adlai Stevenson, Thomas Emerson, and Alger Hiss), not all of the Jews were dedicated liberals (e.g., Donald Richberg), and not all of them were impoverished (e.g., Ben Cohen and Jerome Frank). But many of them had been alienated from the elite bar, and virtually all had a social conscience that distinguished them from their peers in the great corporate law firms. A substantial number had studied with Frankfurter at Harvard and clerked for Holmes, Brandeis, or Cardozo. They were an impressive group, and they used the opportunities opened by the New Deal to start dazzling legal careers at the bar, on the bench, and in the academy—Joseph L. Rauh, Jr., one of the foremost civil rights and civil liberties lawyers of his generation; Charles Wyzanski, later chief judge of the U.S. district court for Massachusetts; Paul Freund, one of the leading constitutional scholars of the postwar era; and Abe Fortas, an associate justice of the Supreme Court of the United States.

In addition to Irish Catholics and Jews, of course, the New Deal attracted and recruited a broad array of other outsiders, people from different minority groups or those who didn't quite fit the traditional mold of their class, profession, or region. There was Eccles, the Mormon banker-entrepreneur from Utah, who espoused deficit spending; Hallie Flanagan, a graduate of Grinnell College, the first woman to receive a Guggenheim Fellowship, who founded the Experimental Theatre at Vassar College and was later hired by Hopkins to run the controversial Federal Theatre of WPA; Gardner "Pat" Jackson, heir to a great railroad and land fortune in Colorado, who covered Washington for the *Montreal Star* and joined the Triple A, where he became a passionate defender of sharecroppers and tenant farmers; and gentle John Collier, who had lived among the Pueblo Indians in New Mexico, founded the American Indian Defense Association in the 1920s, and struggled against great odds to bring a New Deal to Native Americans as the commissioner of Indian affairs.

Among the New Deal's ablest lawyers were three iconoclasts, William O. Douglas, Robert Houghwout Jackson, and Thurman Arnold. From Yakima, Washington, felled by polio in his youth and once a denizen of hobo camps, Bill Douglas had practiced law on Wall Street and taught at Yale Law School before joining the staff of the SEC and becoming a regular at FDR's poker parties. Jackson, reared in Jamestown, New York, and a graduate of the obscure Albany Law School, became general counsel to the Bureau of Internal Revenue, solicitor general, and attorney general, and, like Douglas, was a Roosevelt appointee to the Supreme Court of the United States. Part small-town attorney, part bon vivant, Jackson relished a good fight and a good turn of phrase. Arnold, a Westerner from Laramie, Wyoming, earned a Phi Beta Kappa key at Princeton, served in the field artillery in World War I, raised sheep, taught law, and wrote one of the decade's most pungent and witty books, *The Folklore of Capitalism*, which skewered many national icons, including the antitrust laws that he later enforced with vigor.

And finally there were many of the Southerners from America's poorest and most backward area, who in their zeal for economic justice often cut across the grain of their region's political and racial norms. Aubrey Williams, Hopkins's tireless deputy of relief, fought bravely against racial discrimination in the WPA and the National Youth Administration. Hugo Black, a biting critic of big business, became

FDR's first appointment to the Supreme Court despite revelations of his past membership in the Klan. On questions of race he lived to prove his detractors wrong. Lyndon Baines Johnson of Texas, elected to Congress in the waning years of the New Deal, made certain that his poor constituents received a share of the electricity generated by the Rural Electrification Administration and that even Mexicans garnered a slice of NYA benefits in his state.

The Wagner Act and the National Labor Relations Board, offering legal protection as never before to union organizing efforts and collective bargaining, opened up entire new careers of power and influence to the sons and daughters of immigrants and minorities, including the three Reuther brothers, Walter, Roy, and Victor, who helped found the United Automobile Workers Union; Harry Bridges, the militant leader of the West Coast longshoremen; Mike Quill of the transport workers; and A. Philip Randolph, the guiding spirit of the Brotherhood of Sleeping Car Porters.

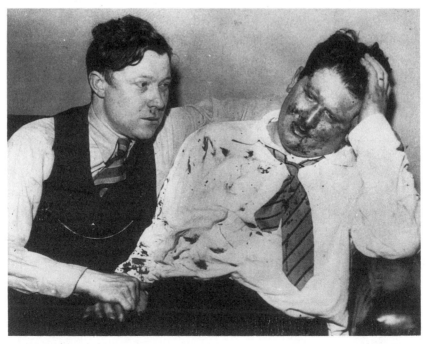

Richard T. Frankenstein (right), organizer for United Auto Workers, is comforted by Walter Reuther after receiving a savage beating outside Ford Moto. Company plant in Dearborn, Michigan, 1937.

BLACK AMERICANS

In 1935, as Roosevelt battled Congress over taxes, holding companies, and collective bargaining, a young black man from Cleveland,
running and jumping in the gray and crimson of Ohio State University,
turned in the greatest single performance by an athlete in the history
of American track and field. At the Big Ten championships at Ann
Arbor, Jesse Owens broke or equaled four world records in the 100-
and 220-yard dash; the broad jump, and the 220-yard high hurdles. If
one included his times in the 100 and 200 meters as well, the man they
called the "Ebony Antelope" had set six world records that day, all
within the space of about 45 minutes.

A year later at the Berlin Olympics, with Adolf Hitler and Nazi dig-
nitaries in attendance, Owens and other black athletes from America
blasted notions of Aryan supremacy. The Ebony Antelope won four
gold medals at Berlin. He and Mack Robinson, a Californian whose
little brother would one day make history by becoming the first black
to play baseball in the major leagues, ran one-two in the 200 meters.
Nine of the ten American blacks who competed at Berlin won gold
medals, which prompted the Führer to leave the stadium before the
official awards ceremony.

In the same year that Owens swept the Olympics, Germany's premier heavyweight boxer, Max Schmeling, won a twelve-round victory
for Hitler's master race over the son of an Alabama sharecropper, Joseph
Louis Barrow. It was Joe Louis's first defeat in the ring. He would not
lose again until 1950. "He fought like an amateur," Schmeling crowed.
"This is no man who could ever be champion." In 1937, however, Joe
Louis became the youngest man to hold the heavyweight title when he
registered a technical knockout in the eight round against the reigning
champion, James J. Braddock. And a year later, in one of boxing's
most devastating displays of power, the "Brown Bomber" sent a battered Schmeling down for the count in the first round. Joe Louis, said
one writer, had become "the first American to KO a Nazi."

Whether Louis or Owens was the first American to whip the best of
Hitler's athletes is a moot point, but not the fact of their skin color. The
Negro baseball league of the 1930s housed players such as Josh Gibson, Satchel Paige, and Judy Johnson who performed feats as impressive as those turned in by Ruth and Gehrig, but few white Americans
paid attention to the all-black Homestead Grays or the Pittsburgh
Crawfords. Owens and Louis garnered more attention, but even when

Heavyweight champion Joe Louis leaves Max Schmeling on the canvas in first round at Yankee Stadium, 1938.

they defeated white opponents from nations regarded as hostile to the United States, they were never fully accepted as America's champions because of their race. Aryan supremacy took a beating in Berlin in 1936 and when Schmeling hit the deck, but it continued to flourish in Owens's and Louis's own land.

New Yorkers, for example, gave the Ebony Antelope a ticker-tape parade, but the White House never acknowledge his triumphs in a speech or a letter. When the Amateur Athletic Union handed out its famous Sullivan Award to America's best athlete in 1935 and 1936, the honor went to a white golfer and a white decathlon champion, who had won a single gold medal at Berlin. Richard Wright, the novelist, declared that in Louis's triumph "blacks took strength, and in that moment all fear, all obstacles were wiped out, drowned," but white sportswriters referred to the new champ as "a jungle killer," a "slightly sullen Negro youth" whose "hulking body might have been lolling in a cabin doorway in Alabama, listening to somebody inside making mouth music." Aware of the racial phobias that stalked and destroyed an earlier black champion, Louis avoided confrontations outside the ring and kept secret his romantic affairs with several white women.

The year that Owens set six world records in the Big Ten champion-ships, that league excluded blacks from its basketball teams. "This is an indoor sport," one reporter noted, "and the taboos are strong . . . against any contact between half-clad, perspiring bodies, even on the floor of a gym." In 1935, too, white mobs lynched nearly two dozen blacks in the United States. Harlem erupted that year in the worst racial rioting since 1919. While Owens won four gold medals in Berlin, the citizens of Owensboro, Kentucky, held one of the country's last public hangings. The condemned was a young black man, Rainey Bethea, convicted of killing a white woman. According to one newspaper account, twenty-thousand attended the execution and attempted to strip the corpse for souvenirs. In the era of the Depression and the New Deal, Ameri-can blacks experienced new triumphs and bitter frustrations in a nation still mired in segregation and discrimination.

The New Deal did much in one decade to challenge the social status quo, but with respect to black Americans critics complained that it did not do nearly enough to attack historic patterns of bigotry and discrim-ination. The New Deal's NLRB required the Pullman Company to sit down at the bargaining table with Randolph's all-black labor union in 1938, but as president, Roosevelt did not attempt to alter the two most obvious forms of oppression afflicting the majority of black citizens in the South: segregation and disenfranchisement, which relegated them to inferior public facilities and stripped them of any voice in the region's politics.

Even in the face of several savage incidents of white violence against blacks, FDR still refused to use his political influence to break Senate filibusters against new federal antilynching legislation. As long as Southerners like Pat Harrison and Joe Robinson ran the Senate, he said, he could not put other New Deal legislation at risk by opposing them. "I did not choose the tools with which I must work," he told Walter White of the National Association for the Advancement of Col-ored People, who unsuccessfully pleaded with him to intervene. Attor-ney General Cummings ruled in 1934 that existing federal statutes, especially the Lindbergh Law, which made kidnapping with transport across state lines a capital offense, did not apply because lynchings were motivated by racial hatred, not a desire for financial gain!

Black Americans could list other grievances against the administra-tion. They dubbed the NRA "Negro Run-Around" because the codes forced the shutdown of many small black-run businesses and the layoff of black employees. The Triple A proved to be an economic disaster for nearly a million black sharecroppers and tenants, who were excluded from a voice in local committees and a proportionate share of its benefits. Both the Civilian Conservation Corps and the Tennessee Valley Authority adopted the traditional patterns of racial segregation. Eleanor Roosevelt's favorite subsistence homestead community, Arthurdale in West Virginia, turned away black applicants and reserved admission to families of "white native stock."

A few courageous individuals took initiatives that leavened the New Deal's otherwise bleak record on racial discrimination and held out hope for the future. Before his death in 1936, Louis Howe battled for equal treatment for blacks in the CCC, and these efforts permitted a small number to serve in integrated camps. Outside the South, where they faced intractable odds, both Hopkins and Ickes fought to guarantee blacks a fair share of jobs under WPA and PWA, with Hopkins having the greater success because his programs hired more unskilled workers and did not have to deal with racist trade unions in the AFL. The New Deal found administrative posts for over a hundred Afro-Americans, who were soon called a "Black Cabinet" by the Washington press corps and whose token appearance called down the wrath of white Southerners on the president. When the Daughters of the American Revolution refused to allow the black contralto Marian Anderson to sing before an integrated audience at Constitutional Hall in 1939, Ickes arranged for her to sing at the Lincoln Memorial before 75,000, including Mrs. Roosevelt and many other New Dealers.

Even FDR worked quietly to promote racial justice. At the Democrats' 1936 convention, which finally abolished the ancient two-thirds rule for nomination, the party seated blacks for the first time as convention delegates, and one gave a seconding speech on behalf of the president. The defeat of the two-thirds rule was itself a significant breakthrough for the opponents of racism in the party, because it finally broke the South's veto over presidential candidates. By 1940, the party's national platform called for an end to racial discrimination in all government programs.

In 1937, much to the horror of racial bigots, Roosevelt appointed the first black federal judge to the bench, William Hastie, a product of the Harvard Law School and a former attorney for the NAACP. He also encouraged his newest attorney general, Frank Murphy of Michigan, to create a Civil Rights Division in the Department of Justice in 1939. Utilizing old Reconstruction-era federal laws that had long been ignored, Murphy and his successors in the department commenced legal challenges to discriminatory voting practices in the South. These would

Eleanor Roosevelt addresses National Conference on Negro Youth in 1939. Seated is Mary Bethune.

bear fruit during the early 1940s in Supreme Court rulings that out-lawed all-white primary elections. FDR's Supreme Court appointees, with two exceptions, were strong opponents of segregation and disen-franchisement.

Civil rights and racial justice never headed the list of the New Deal's priorities, but the administration's efforts signaled a shift in elite atti-tudes that would bear fruit in the future, especially when coupled with growing black impatience and militancy. Encouraged by several deci-sions of the Hughes Court in the late thirties, the civil rights lawyers in the Justice Department began to target segregation and voting rights in Southern states for renewed legal action. When Randolph, head of the Brotherhood of Sleeping Car Porters, threatened a massive march on Washington in 1940 to protest racial discrimination in the burgeon-ing defense plants, FDR had little choice but to issue an executive order banning such behavior and creating a Fair Employment Prac-tices Committee to oversee enforcement. Slowly, the Depression and the New Deal helped fashion positive changes in the lives of black Americans.

Women

In 1942, Katharine Hepburn captivated film audiences with her portrayal of a spirited politician in MGM's *Woman of the Year*. Self-assured, independent, highly intelligent, and a professional, Hepburn's role was one of a number on and off the screen in the thirties that suggested that American women were continuing to make great breakthroughs on the road to social equality. The nation's First Lady, Eleanor Roosevelt, spoke and acted like none of her predecessors in the White House, engaging in a wide range of political and social causes. She defied racial segregation at the 1938 Conference of Human Welfare in Birmingham, Alabama, by taking a seat in the "colored" section and refusing to move to the "white" side.

Until her mysterious disappearance over the Pacific in 1937, Amelia Earhart, known as Lady Lindy, captured more headlines than any aviator since Lindbergh when she flew solo across the Atlantic and set a coast-to-coast speed record for women. Men as well as women eagerly devoured the rich journalistic fare served up throughout the decade by the irreverent Dorothy Thompson, Freda Kirchwey, editor of the *Nation*, and Meridel Le Sueur, who kept radical fires burning on the pages of *New Masses* and the *Daily Worker*. On the screen, led by Hepburn, other self-reliant and strong-willed women—Joan Crawford, Mae West, Bette Davis, Marlene Dietrich, Vivien Leigh—replaced the sex kittens and ingenues of the previous decade. But there was another side as well to the experience of American women during the Depression and the New Deal. If black Americans tasted success and failure over the course of the decade, the same proved true for American women.

In certain fundamental respects the Depression and the New Deal proved to be a major setback for the historic causes of sexual equality and feminism. Women continued to work in rising numbers outside the domestic sphere, but the kinds of jobs they held and the remuneration they received remained static or deteriorated. Many popular images of the female role during the decade stressed her independence, power, and rising professionalism, but the reality for most women was quite different. Even in the traditional areas of marriage and childbearing, the Depression decade brought more frustration than fulfillment to women as both rates dropped in response to economic hardship.

With male breadwinners thrown out of work in unprecedented numbers and their families placed under severe economic strain, it is not surprising that both married and single women continued the post–

World War I trend of entering the job market outside the home. In 1930 approximately 22 percent of all American workers had been female; this figure rose slightly to 25 percent at the end of the decade. During the thirties as well, the percentage of married women who held jobs rose from 11.7 to 15.3, an indication of the vital role their earnings played in the struggle for economic survival.

These gross employment figures, however, hid a more profound set of truths. The tidal wave of unemployment that swept the nation hit women especially hard. Most of their limited gains from the twenties, especially in the professions, vanished. Between 1930 and 1940, the percentage of women in the professions declined from 14.2 to 12.3, with significant drops in areas such as medicine, law, and higher education. Even more alarming from the perspective of feminists, the proportion of women who filled seats in colleges and universities as a stepping-stone to professional careers also fell from nearly 44 percent of total enrollment to 40.2 percent. By 1940, only one woman job holder in ten could be classified as a professional; the remaining nine were clustered in clerical, sales, manufacturing, and domestic service. Not surprisingly, these women workers earned on the average about half of the yearly income of working men—$525 to $1,027.

The deteriorating economic status of American women arose in part from conscious government policies designed to favor the employment of men in a time of dwindling economic opportunities. Married women came under especially sharp attack. A section of FDR's Economy Act in 1933 barred members of the same family from federal employment. Through this so-called nepotism rule, three-quarters of those who lost their jobs in the early days of the New Deal were women. Despite protests from the League of Women Voters and others, most states passed other laws during the decade to exclude married women—called "undeserving parasites" by one state legislator—from public employment. Even the Women's Bureau in Frances Perkins's Department of Labor espoused a national policy of putting the needs of married men first.

In traditional "female occupations" such as teaching, nursing, and social work, married and single women faced heightened pressure to make room for male breadwinners. At one time or another between 1931 and 1940, probably a majority of the nation's local school boards passed regulations that restricted the hiring of married women, except in cases of dire want. By the end of the decade, therefore, men had increased their share of the teaching ranks in public schools from 19 percent to nearly 25 percent. On the eve of World War II, they constituted 40 percent of the enrollment in teacher-training programs, an increase of nearly 10 percent since the Great Crash.

New Deal agencies and programs were riddled with sex discrimination. The CCC, barring women entirely, was not a "she-she-she," as critics pointed out. Most NRA codes permitted employers to pay women less than men, even in the same jobs. The WPA tolerated similar wage differentials, although feminists noted that women who toiled in government-sponsored canning and sewing projects hardly toiled less hard than men putting up playground equipment or writing state guidebooks. The Social Security Act provided no protection for the millions of women who worked as domestics or who labored as housewives; the Fair Labor Standards Act did not begin to address these inequities either.

Against this backdrop of retreat and stagnation, however, must be placed some of the gains made by American women as a result of the New Deal. As a consequence of FDR's own commitments and the constant vigilance of his wife, no administration in history to that time accorded women greater access to the official levers of political influence and power. In addition to Secretary Perkins, who left her mark on assorted legislative achievements of the New Deal, the administration attracted a broad array of women to serve in a variety of posts, ranging from ministers abroad to subcabinet administrators.

Grace Abbott, a veteran of Hull House, served on the NRA's Consumers' Advisory Board and the Committee on Economic Security, which shaped the Social Security Act. Dorothea Lange's haunting photographic record documented the plight of the rural poor for the Farm Security Administration and the Bureau of Agricultural Economics. Jane Margueretta Hoey, raised in a Tammany Hall political family and later head of New York City's child welfare program, came to Washington with other social workers and established the Bureau of Public Assistance in the Social Security Administration. Hallie Flanagan kept the Federal Theatre vibrantly alive for four years against the efforts of cultural and fiscal conservatives to destroy it. Florence Allen became one of FDR's first appointments to the federal circuit court of appeals in 1934, and Daisy Harriman, named minister to Norway in 1937, broke through another gender barrier.

By far the most influential women in the administration were Mrs. Roosevelt, Perkins, Molly Dewson, head of the Women's Division of the Democratic Party, and the extraordinary cadre of reporters headed by Lorena Hickok, Martha Gellhorn, Hazel Reavis, and Ernestine Ball, who became Harry Hopkins's eyes and ears as they crisscrossed the country filing reports on the relief program, WPA, and the fight against poverty. When a "woman's issue" demanded the president's attention, it was usually Eleanor who made certain that its most active advocate sat next to the president at lunch or dinner. It was Eleanor who spoke out on controversial issues of racial and sexual discrimination, thereby deflecting criticism from FDR. And most of Hickok's moving and critical accounts of the administration programs and the plight of the poor found their way into the White House through the efforts of the First Lady.

Probably the single greatest breakthrough of the New Deal for women's rights against intense resistance came through the efforts of John Collier, commissioner of Indian affairs, who attempted to bring some measure of gender equality to the reservations under the Indian Reorganization Act of 1934. The native constitutions written after passage of that statute gave women the right to vote in tribal elections and hold office. By the end of the decade, Indian women occupied tribal posts among the Assiniboine, Gros Ventres, Oneidas, and Blackfeet. Collier insisted that the Bureau of Indian Affairs and the Agricultural Extension Service offer educational programs to improve the skills of native women in agriculture and animal husbandry as well as in nursing and secretarial work. He lobbied successfully to place Indian women in jobs on and off the reservations with the CCC and the WPA.

By supporting the right of workers to unionize and bargain collectively, the New Deal also provided some assistance to women wage earners, especially those in the garment industry and textile production, in which nearly 40 percent of the employees were female. As workers, wives, daughters, and sisters, women had played a vital role in many of the successful CIO strikes of the late 1930s. They joined picket lines, handed out literature, prepared food, nursed the injured, and endured tear gas attacks along with men.

Women did not share equally, however, in the fruits of labor's early victories. Union-negotiated contracts permitted employers to pay women less than men in the same job classification. Sex and racial segregation remained the norm in most unions, where the top officials and organizers were invariably men. By one estimate, perhaps fourteen out of fifteen women wage earners—field hands, domestics, pieceworkers, and clerks—remained outside any union organization. And neither the reactionary AFL nor the struggling CIO devoted much effort to including them.

Inside the women's movement, finally, the struggle continued throughout the thirties between those who insisted on preserving special legal protection for female workers and those who demanded adoption of an equal rights amendment to the Constitution. The latter were regularly denounced by their trade union opponents as "leisure-class women" filled with resentment for "not having been born men." The New Deal's Fair Labor Standards Act in 1938 tended to weaken the argument of the protectionists by mandating wages and hours limitations for both men and women, but the Women's Party still faced an uphill battle with the ERA. House and Senate committees endorsed it in 1936 and 1938. The Republican Party and its presidential candidate Wendell Willkie backed the measure two years later. Congress as a whole still declined to act.

"It is true that the millennium in race relations did not arrive under Roosevelt," declared an official of the NAACP. "But cynics and scoffers to the contrary, the great body of Negro citizens made progress." Those who wanted a New Deal for American women or Native Americans or farmers or labor could have said much the same thing at the end of the decade. Indeed, the NAACP statement probably summed up the whole of the New Deal. Roosevelt "had no answers that were good for a hundred years," wrote *New York Post* columnist Samuel Grafton at the end of World War II. "But in a six-month crisis he always had a six month answer." The editors of the *Economist* put it somewhat differently: "Mr. Roosevelt may have given the wrong answers to many of his problems," they wrote. "But he is at least the first President of modern America who has asked the right questions."

8

Best of Times, Worst of Times

> *The Depression affected people in two different ways. The great majority reacted by thinking money is the most important thing in the world. Get yours. And get it for your children. Nothing else matters. Not having that stark terror come at you again. . . . And there was a small number of people who felt the whole system was lousy. You have to change it.*
> —Virginia Durr

SCENES FROM THE DEPRESSION

Many of America's greatest musicians, composers, and lyricists produced some of their finest work during the Great Depression—George Gershwin, Duke Ellington, Benny Goodman, Lionel Hampton, Cole Porter, Jerome Kern. The Great Depression forced Americans to defer marriage and put off having children as never before, but even it could not kill flirting, romance, passion, and sentimentality. At decade's end, Irving Berlin wrote probably the most widely known song ever composed by an American—"White Christmas." But in 1932, lyricist E. Y. "Yip" Harburg composed what most people recall as the decade's most representative song: "Brother, Can You Spare a Dime?"

> Once in khaki suits,
> Gee, we looked swell,
> Full of that Yankee Doodle-de-dum.
> Half a million boots went sloggin' through Hell,
> I was the kid with the drum.

> Say, don't you remember, they called me Al—
> It was Al all the time.
> Say, don't you remember I'm your pal—
> Brother, can you spare a dime.

Harburg's lyrics touched the nation's soul at a time when Army troops drove hundreds of World War I veterans, some perhaps named Al, from the streets of Washington, D.C., and burned down their make-shift homes. They evoked memories of dreams dashed and promises broken; of once-prosperous, dignified citizens reduced to selling apples or panhandling on street corners.

When author Studs Terkel interviewed Harburg in the late 1960s for his oral history of the Great Depression, *Hard Times*, the lyricist remained full of anger at the social injustice and cruelty inflicted on people like Al during the depression: "This is the man who says: I built the railroads. I built that tower. I fought your wars. I was the kid with the drum. Why the hell should I be standing in line now? What happened to all this wealth I created?" But in more personal terms, Harburg also recalled those desperate early years of the 1930s as a time of liberation and self-fulfillment: "Someone who lost money found that his life was gone. When I lost my possessions, I found my creativity. I felt I was being born for the first time. So for me the world became beautiful."

Harburg's experience was not unique. It reminds us that a far-reaching, shattering social crisis like the Great Depression or the Civil War touches the people who live through it in profoundly different ways. Even for those born long after the decade, certain images of the Great Depression in America remain fixed in the mind. We have seen them many times in old newsreels, documentary films, and photographs. They are overwhelmingly images of human tragedy, despair, anger, and sadness.

—The wife of a migrant farm worker, her face etched with weariness, stares anxiously into the distance. She cradles a baby in a soiled and ragged blanket, while two older children hide their faces from the camera.
—A long line of men in heavy dark coats, their hats and caps pulled down against the cold, stand passively on the sidewalk outside a soup kitchen in Manhattan waiting for a meal.
—A small, wood-frame shack somewhere in Oklahoma lies buried beneath drifts of dry soil, only a portion of its roof and metal chimney visible against the ominous black sky.

Dorothea Lange captured one face of the Great Depression.

—As plumes of tear gas float overhead, a line of police and security guards, wielding nightsticks, surge forward to attack striking workers, who fight back with their picket signs. Armed with baseball bats, strikers smash the headlights and windows of automobiles as strikebreakers attempt to enter a factory gate.

But other images of the Great Depression can be recalled, too, and these tell us that amid the era's economic misery and blighted hopes there flourished moments of human compassion, heroism, and creativity as impressive as any in the nation's history.

—Beginning in Harlem and soon spreading to other black communities in the North, residents organized house-rent parties where for 15 cents on a Thursday or Saturday night participants enjoyed chitterlings, pig's feet, corn liquor, music, and dancing while the host raised enough cash to pay the landlord on Monday morning.
—Following the death of two infants from whooping cough in the Jane

Addams Public Housing Project in Chicago, the women tenants organized to fight the epidemic and found a doctor willing to give inoculations to all the remaining children under the age of six.

—When Dorothy Day and other Catholic radicals opened a soup kitchen to feed striking seamen in New York City in 1937, their poverty-stricken Italian neighbors, eager to share what little they had with the workers, contributed pots of spaghetti, leftover furniture, and spare clothing.

—With money from the federal government after 1933, hundreds of communities built their first sewage or water purification plant, public library, and high school gymnasium.

—Architect Frank Lloyd Wright completed many of his most magnificent structures, including Falling Water in Bear Run, Pennsylvania, Taliesen West near Scottsdale, Arizona, and the Johnson Wax Building in Racine, Wisconsin.

—Edward Hopper painted *Cape Cod Evening* and *Gas;* José Orozco finished the largest mural in the world, three thousand square feet, at Dartmouth College; Lillian Hellman wrote *The Children's Hour* and Katherine Anne Porter finished *Pale Horse, Pale Rider;* George Balanchine and Lincoln Kirstein organized the American Ballet Theatre.

The Great Depression, in seems, drove some Americans apart and simultaneously brought others together in a common cause. It stirred conflict as well as cooperation; rage and resignation; selfishness and altruism. For some it confirmed the rottenness of capitalism, the futility of democratic government, and the need for revolution. For others it suggested the importance of holding tight to traditional values and institutions, not rocking the boat. Because of the material deprivation it brought to their lives, most Americans who lived through the Great Depression recalled it as the worst of times. But for others it would remain the best of times, an era unlike any other, when people reached out to help others, when idealism replaced selfishness, and when the government in Washington took the side of the underdogs to battle injustice and poverty. "There is no longer I," announced the writer Dorothy Parker in a moment of high enthusiasm. "There is WE. The day of the individual is dead."

THE QUESTION OF VALUES

Dorothy Parker's observation raises a profound issue that scholars continue to debate about the era: did the Great Depression transform the basic values of the American people? The question is often framed in terms of the conflict between individualism and community. Did the economic collapse and the hardship it inflicted upon millions produce a major revision in popular attitudes concerning self-reliance, material success, and the virtues of competition? Was there a new emphasis upon the welfare of the whole, the desirability of collective solutions to social problems, and the virtues of cooperation? And if such a shift in beliefs and behavior took place during the 1930s, was it a transitory change easily abandoned when the economic skies brightened, or was it something more durable and permanent?

Beyond the statements of Dorothy Parker and others, small pieces of evidence and larger ones suggest a decisive tilt in the thirties toward a more communitarian ethic that stressed the importance of the group and the necessity for defining justice and happiness, economic or otherwise, in more than individualistic terms. While hard times spawned divorce and desertion in families, for example, it also brought solidarity to them as never before. To make ends meet and in the face of social and legal pressures, wives went back to work or entered the labor force for the first time. Young adults deferred college or marriage both from economic necessity and in order to help the family financially through the crisis.

The success of the infant CIO unions in the mass-production industries, especially during the sit-down strikes, rested upon self-interest, but more importantly upon bonds of community that led men and women to risk their lives and make great sacrifices on behalf of the United Automobile Workers or the United Steel Workers. The social and economic reforms of the New Deal also encouraged a new emphasis upon individuals as parts of a larger whole and stressed the importance of group entitlements. This was the meaning of collective bargaining under the Wagner Act. The New Deal thought of farmers as members of a commodity group, a cooperative, or a grazing district. Social security defined for the first time what it meant to be part of a social constituency called "the elderly" or in a "family with dependent children." By adding to America's stock of schools, libraries, bridges, and highways and by expanding the concept of "public works," the PWA and the WPA encouraged people to think about their stake in the country's common goods that remained distinct from objects of individual consumption.

Two of the decades most popular and acclaimed films, *Mr. Smith Goes to Washington* (1939) and *The Grapes of Wrath* (1940), vividly emphasized these communitarian themes. Frank Capra's melodrama pitted an idealistic citizen-legislator, Jefferson Smith (Jimmy Stewart), against a corrupt political boss, James Taylor. A small-town Boy Scout leader brimming with integrity, Smith is named by the governor to fill the unexpired term of a recently deceased United States senator. He sponsors legislation to create a national summer camp for boys on a piece of land near his hometown, but the land is also coveted by Boss Taylor and his cronies, who wish to build a useless dam on the property at taxpayers' expense in order to enrich themselves. Resisting bribes and turning back attacks on his reputation, Smith carries out a two-day filibuster to block Taylor's selfish scheme. Bone-tired, he tells the other senators:

> Those boys'll be sitting at these desks someday. Yes—it seemed a pretty good idea—boys coming together—all nationalities and ways of living— finding out what makes different people tick the way they do. 'Cause I wouldn't give you a red cent for all your fine rules, without there was some plain everyday, common kindness under 'em—and a little looking-out for the next fella. Yes—pretty important, all that. Just happens to be blood and bone and sinew of this democracy. . . .
>
> No sir! If anybody here thinks I'm going back to those boys and say to 'em: 'Forget it, fellas. Everything I've told you about the land you live in is a lotta hooey. It isn't your country—it belongs to the James Taylors—!' No, sir, anybody that thinks that has got another think coming!

In director John Ford's screen version of John Steinbeck's novel, the Joad family travels from the dust bowl to California in search of the American dream of owning their own land again. These dispossessed tenants come to the realization that in order to secure justice for their own family, they must join a larger social movement dedicated to bettering the lives of all people like themselves. In Ford's climactic scene, young Tom Joad (Henry Fonda), unfairly accused of killing a labor camp official and sought by the police, bids farewell to his mother:

> Well, maybe it's like Casey says, a fella ain't got a soul of his own, but on'y a piece of a soul—the one big soul that belongs to ever'body—and then . . . Then it don't matter. There I'll be all aroun' in the dark. I'll be everywhere—wherever you look. Whenever there's a fight so hungry people can eat . . . I'll be there. Wherever there's a guy beatin' up a guy, I'll be there. I'll be in the way kids laugh when they're hungry an' they know supper's ready. An' when our people eat the stuff they raise, an' live in the houses they build, why, I'll be there too. . . .

But over and against these numerous examples of a heightened communitarianism in the thirties must be placed the fact that genuine

Henry Fonda and Jane Darwell as Tom and Ma Joad in film version of The Grapes of Wrath.

schemes for the collectivization of production or consumption, such as EPIC or the platform of the Socialist Party, did not command broad popular support. Most commercial farmers wanted parity and co-ops in order to boost their personal incomes, not to limit private ownership. Displaced tenants and sharecroppers like the Joads hungered for their own land, where "our people eat the stuff they raise, an' live in houses they build." Union leaders and the rank and file of industrial workers wanted to curb the arbitrary power of shop foremen and management, but their vision of industrial democracy usually stopped short of demanding a reorganization of production priorities. Higher wages, shorter hours, and improved benefits were seen largely in the context of promoting the welfare of individual workers and their families.

Those traditional American values of individualism, self-reliance, private ownership, and consumption never disappeared during the decade. They quickly resurfaced with a vengeance after World War II, when Americans went on a spending binge for new homes, automobiles, and durable goods that dwarfed the boom of the 1920s. Economic necessity only dampened such values in the Great Depression and tempered them with a renewed emphasis upon other long-standing and traditional American values, such as fairness, equal opportunity, and justice. In a country as large and diverse as the United States, social values and behavior remained ever in tension and conflict, even during a time that resembled war in terms of its broad and penetrating impact upon the nation and individual lives.

Successes and Failures

Social contradictions abounded in the 1930s, as they would during later years of economic decline. While hungry men, women, and children stood in line outside soup kitchens or foraged in garbage cans for a meal, the exclusive Rainbow Room at Rockefeller Center in New York City never lacked for wealthy patrons, who dined on filet mignon and a French Bordeaux. For every investor ruined in the Wall Street panic, there was another who picked up a bargain by buying stocks cheap, holding on to them, and reaping a fortune after 1940.

The Great Depression brought suffering to millions thrown out of work, and fortune to a few who exploited the new opportunities created by economic dislocation. While advertising agencies with clients in traditional manufacturing industries went broke, the firm of William Benton and Chester Bowles raked in a fortune marketing Pepsodent toothpaste and Maxwell House coffee over the radio. Gas stations multiplied as Americans like the Joads took to the highways in search of jobs and new opportunities. An enterprising restaurant owner in Camden, New Jersey, viewing the increase in auto traffic, opened the first "drive-in" to sell food to those just passing through. And because migratory people living out of automobiles needed somewhere to wash their clothes, a Fort Worth, Texas, businessman leased a vacant store and installed coin-operated washing machines—America's first public laundromat. To fill his idle hours as an unemployed draftsman, Alfred Butts created the game of Scrabble.

The people of the United States had known hard times, poverty, unemployment, and social-economic conflict before the 1930s, and they would experience these calamities again after the Great Depression. Jacob Riis had exposed *How the Other Half Lives* at the turn of the century. In 1932–33, farmers were alive who recalled not only the lean years after World War I, but the economic collapse of the 1890s that brought forth the Populist movement. The IWW had passed into history and Eugene Debs had been dead for a decade, but more than a few struggling industrial workers in the thirties remembered the great Lawrence, Massachusetts, textile strike in 1912 and even the Pullman boycott in 1895. In the 1960s, books such as Michael Harrington's *The Other America* and the civil rights movement once again seared the nation's conscience about poverty and social injustice. Homelessness, farm foreclosures, and the collapse of financial institutions reached epidemic proportions in the late 1980s and early 1990s.

But the Great Depression was different, both quantitatively and qualitatively, from the social and economic upheavals that battered the United States before or later. Put simply, it lasted much longer and it cut a wider swath through the social structure. It brought fear, uncertainty, and destitution to substantial portions of the white middle class that had begun to taste moderate affluence in the previous decade. In a 1934 survey of residents of Columbus, Ohio, who ranged from waitresses and bank tellers to detectives and professors, a local newspaper found that most listed "money" as their chief requirement for happiness and either "poverty" or "loss of job" as their greatest anxiety. The Great Depression altered some long-developing social trends. And it left scars, upon both the physical environment and the mental landscapes of the men, women, and children who endured it. For those between the ages of five and forty-five when the stock market crashed, the Great Depression was the transforming event of a lifetime, one that rivaled even the trauma of another world war.

FAMILIES IN CRISIS

For nearly a century, Americans had moved steadily from country to city, driven by economic hardship and boredom, lured by the prospect of greater opportunity. The Great Depression did not stop this migration entirely, but it slowed the momentum. The population of several large cities, all growing steadily since the late nineteenth century, fell over the course of the decade. Plagued by falling prices, drought, dust storms, and locusts, life on the farm was hardly a paradise in the 1930s. The programs of the New Deal forced millions of poor farmers off the land, especially in the South. Yet millions of other Americans moved back to the countryside during the decade, many returning to live with grandparents and other relatives. The dream of individual proprietorship that never died with the Joads took on fresh urgency for others. Farmers, they assumed, seldom went hungry.

As a substitute for the farm, home gardens sprouted up everywhere, in backyards, in vacant lots. Cities such as Detroit and private corporations such as United States Steel and the Pennsylvania Railroad made plots of land available to workers for cultivation. So did Henry Ford, but he charged his employees 50 cents to have theirs plowed. Asked if they would farm a small tract of land if the government gave it to them, a surprising number of residents of Columbus, Ohio, said yes, including a hotel clerk, a detective, a geologist, and an advertising man. An unemployed college professor responded, however, "Not unless I had to."

For even longer, beginning in the colonial era, the American population had continued to grow through both natural increase and foreign immigration as material conditions showed steady improvement. However jagged the economy's performance, however unequal the fruits of growth, America seemed by comparison with most other nations a place of plenty, a land of boundless opportunity where tomorrow would almost inevitably be better than today or yesterday. The Great Depression cut the ground from under those conditions and assumptions.

Immigration from abroad, already subject to sharp limitations under the laws of the 1920s, fell off even more in the face of shrinking economic incentives and rising nativism. Hoover had told the State Department to enforce strictly the ban against issuing visas to persons "likely to become a public charge," and Roosevelt, not eager to confront Congress on the immigration issue, kept that policy in place throughout the decade. Even in the face of Germany's mounting campaign of anti-Semitism, the United States barred most Jewish refugees. In California, federal immigration officials and local law enforcement agencies forcibly deported hundreds of thousands of resident Mexicans who they claimed had entered the country illegally. In 1931, for the first time in the country's history, more people left the United States than entered. Officials in the Soviet Union reported a year later that over three hundred Americans a day were applying for jobs in the communist nation.

The birthrate among native-born whites in the middle and upper classes had been falling in the United States since the end of the nineteenth century, which generated fears of "race suicide" among the social elite. The Great Depression witnessed a sharper decline in births across all social classes and ethnic groups. Without a steady job or the prospect of one, men and women deferred marriage. According to one estimate, nearly one million couples did not go to the altar because of the economic crisis. Married couples also put off having children when wives came under intense social pressure not to seek employment and to abandon even the jobs they had. By eroding the possibilities of marriage, childbirth, and domesticity for many women, the Depression accomplished brutally what decades of radical feminist ideology had been unable to do. Not surprisingly, the years after World War II brought an upsurge in family formation and an unprecedented "baby boom" as well.

The divorce rate, already on the rise since the turn of the century, continued to inch upward as families came under the combined strains of soaring unemployment, shrinking resources, and declining male self-esteem. As the number of abandoned wives and children increased along with the transient population of boys and men between the ages of twelve and twenty-five, social workers predicted a bleak future for the American family. Not a few social workers heard the following refrain: "My husband went north about three months ago to try his luck. The first month he wrote pretty regularly. . . . For five weeks we have had no word from him. . . . Don't know where he is or what he is up to."

Working in one Pennsylvania community, a young psychiatrist observed the severe emotional wounds inflicted on miners who remained unemployed for several years. "They hung around street corners and in groups. They gave each other solace. They were loath to go home because they were indicted, as if it were their fault for being unemployed. . . . These men suffered from depression. They felt despised, they were ashamed of themselves. They cringed, they comforted one another. They avoided home." The former editor of a farm journal, unemployed for the first time at the age of fifty-five, wondered when others would first recognize that he, too, had joined the ranks of the jobless: "You wear the same suit, more carefully brushed and pressed than ever before to conceal your poverty." Women, too, felt the anguish and humiliation of joblessness. "If, with all the advantages I've had, I can't make a living, then I'm just no good, I guess," an unemployed schoolteacher told her social worker.

Benefiting from abundant land and resources, the nuclear family of parents and children had been the middle-class American norm for generations, but the economic collapse of the thirties changed that, too. Depending upon who remained employed and able to pay the rent or mortgage, parents moved back to live with their children and grandchildren or vice versa. They were often joined now in the same household by uncles, aunts, and other blood relatives who had fallen on hard times. The extended family, regarded as typical among impoverished,

slum-dwelling immigrants, spread to many middle-class neighborhoods.

With traditional sex roles, marriage, and family arrangements facing
new pressures, it is not surprising that some of the decade's most popular radio soap operas and motion pictures idealized romantic love and
portrayed the family as fundamentally a place of warmth and security,
presided over by wise fathers, suffused with motherly love, and enlivened by the antics of mischievous but otherwise healthy children.

Daytime radio listeners avidly followed *Stella Dallas*, "the true-to-
life story of mother love and sacrifice, in which Stella Dallas saw her
own beloved daughter, Laurel, marry into wealth and society"; *Mary
Noble, Backstage Wife*, the tale of "an Iowa stenographer who fell in
love with and married Broadway matinee idol Larry Noble"; *The
Romance of Helen Trent*, about a woman who learned "that romance
can live in life at thirty-five and after"; or *Our Gal Sunday*, "the story
of an orphan girl . . . who in young womanhood married England'
richest, most handsome lord, Lord Henry Brinthrope." At decade's end
millions gathered around their Philco or Stromberg-Carlson sets in the
evening to hear Mrs. Aldrich call, "Henry! Hen-ry Aldrich!" And Henry
always answered, "Coming, Mother!"

In 1937, despite the New Deal, the "American Way" still eluded many.

Between 1936 and 1940, MGM made a small fortune at the box office and brought fame to Mickey Rooney and Judy Garland with *The Hardy Family,* a series of nine movies about a small-town judge and the trials and tribulations of his son. Poverty, industrial violence, and crime never intruded upon Judge Hardy or his brood around their ample dinner table, but there was seldom a problem of youthful adolescence, ranging from courtship to the family automobile, that the judge could not solve. Three of the decade's biggest attractions on the stage, in bookstores, and on the screen, Margaret Mitchell's *Gone with the Wind,* John Steinbeck's *The Grapes of Wrath,* and Thornton Wilder's *Our Town,* all focused upon families, their encounters with social and individual tragedies, and their capacity to survive them. Is it any wonder that many members of the Depression-era generation after 1945 made haste to the suburbs and to the single-family home where they raised 3.2 children?

SIN AND SEX

Economic misery, delayed marriages, and the disruption of family life did not, however, diminish the American appetite for sex or the capacity of the popular culture to provide it. If anything, Americans generally became more preoccupied and sophisticated about these matters during the Great Depression than they were in the previous, "liberated" decade of the 1920s. Sex became more democratic, too, as experimentation spread from the bohemia of intellectuals, artists, and musicians to the middle class and beyond, much to the chagrin of moral guardians, who saw in these changes another manifestation of the era's dangerous radicalism.

Henry Luce's *Fortune* magazine, the voice of enlightened capitalism during the decade, announced in 1936 that according to its survey of the sexual behavior of college students, "the campus takes it more casually than it did ten years ago. . . . It is news that it is no longer news." The magazine reported that almost 67 percent of the students surveyed favored birth control. A year later, *Fortune* shocked the country with a poll indicating that half of the men and one-quarter of the women on campus had engaged in premarital sexual relations. Two-thirds of the women said they probably would do so "for true love." The birthrate may have dropped between the Great Crash and Pearl Harbor, but all evidence points to soaring contraceptive sales (Sears, Roebuck offered them by catalog in 1934, and North Carolina opened the first state-run birth control clinic in 1938), more abortions than before, and an increase in venereal disease. When reporting on Dr. Thomas Parran's crusade against syphilis in the New York City area, newspapers broke convention by actually naming the disease.

Early in the decade, moviegoers could not fail to notice that Constance Bennett gave birth to several children out of wedlock in films such as *Common Clay* and *Born to Love,* but the real revolution arrived with Brooklyn-born Mae West, a blond bombshell who wore dresses that accented her voluptuous figure, sported big diamond rings, ate steaks rare, and lifted weights to keep in shape. A group of Milwaukee gynecologists might praise her as "a boon to motherhood" because of her somewhat plump dimensions, but West's sexual interests were far from procreative. They were recreative—aggressively so. In her first film, *Night After Night* (1932), she responded to "Goodness, what beautiful diamonds" with the memorable "Goodness had nothing to do with it." A year later in *She Done Him Wrong,* saloonkeeper West fell for Cary Grant, an undercover cop who sought to put her out of business. "Why don't you come up sometime and see me?" she asked this officer of the law. "Maybe Wednesday, it's amateur night." Raising innuendo to new heights, she also asked one of her leading men, "Is that a gun in your pocket, big boy, or are you just glad to see me?"

Highbrow critics such as Joseph Wood Krutch branded her work "simple-minded, lurid, and crude," but by mid-decade West's popularity at the box office earned her one of the biggest salaries in Hollywood. And she refused to tone down her routines, such as the famous 1937 radio skit on Adam and Eve with Edgar Bergen that religious leaders denounced as blasphemous:

Snake: "Wait a minute. It won't work. Adam'll never eat that forbidden apple."

Eve: "Oh, yes, he will—when I'm through with it."

Snake: "Nonsense. He won't."

Eve: "He will if I feed it to him like women are gonna feed men for the rest of time."

Snake: "What's that?"

Eve: "Applesauce."

West's innuendos and frankness led over a hundred radio stations to ban her name from the airwaves by the end of the decade. In addition she became one of the most visible targets for the Catholic Legion of Decency and other purity crusaders who pressured Hollywood into adopting a stricter code of censorship in 1934 that banned on the screen long kisses, nudity (even for babies), cohabitation, and "the sympa-

Mae West.

thetic treatment of wrongdoing." While the Hays Office made a bow
to respectability, however, Hollywood bestowed five of its Academy
Awards that year upon Frank Capra's *It Happened One Night*, wherein
Clark Gable and Claudette Colbert shared a motel room with only a
bedsheet between them and "the King" removed his shirt to reveal
only a bare chest. At about that same time, the city fathers in Atlantic
City, New Jersey, prohibited men from wearing bathing suits without
tops and fined over forty who ignored the ordinance.

In the battle of the flesh, however, Gable and the forces of liberation
appear to have won. Retailers noted a sharp drop in the sale of men's
undershirts for the remainder of 1934. Women's swimsuit manufacturers also reported a brisk business in their backless creation made of
linen and Lastex yarn that when wet did not leave much to the imagination. And the decade would soon bring the introduction of strapless
evening dresses, the bare midriff and South Sea sarong in summer,
uplift bras, and falsies.

Those who believed that the country was about to drown in a sea of libidinous impulses also tried to manage its reading tastes in the decade, but again without much success. Despite the legal efforts of the New York City Society for the Prevention of Vice, a New York court refused to ban as obscene Erskine Caldwell's *God's Little Acre*, a steamy novel about greed and lust among Southern hillbillies. Random House publisher Bennett Cerf also won a major victory against censorship when U.S. district court judge William Woolsey lifted the government's prohibition against printing James Joyce's *Ulysses*, complete with Molly Bloom's long reverie about her past sexual encounters. Woolsey assured the public that Joyce employed four-letter words for artistic reasons, not for mere titillation, and that while many passages in the sprawling novel were "emetic," it was "nowhere aphrodisic [sic]."

Most Americans gained their titillation during the decade not from Joyce, but from mass publications of considerably less literary distinction that catered to the public's appetite for sex, violence, and exposing the private peccadilloes of the rich and famous. Neither local vice crusades nor the Legion of Decency had much success raising the moral tone of the corner newsstand. Beginning in 1933, *Esquire* magazine attracted a growing male audience with hard-boiled fiction and numerous illustrations of fetching young women in scanty dress. Bernarr Macfadden's *True Confessions* had a circulation in excess of seven million by mid-decade, a figure exceeded only by the combined sales of the numerous motion picture fan magazines such as *Photoplay* that kept their readers up to date on the latest Hollywood gossip and scandals. An issue seldom passed without *Photoplay* exploring the wicked ways of the silver screen's many unmarried couples, including Gable and Carole Lombard, George Raft and Virginia Pine, and Charlie Chaplin and Paulette Goddard.

The hard economic times of the decade engendered class conflict, disrupted normal family life, and put many private dreams on hold. They forced Americans for a while to think more communally, to see themselves in one social boat buffeted by a common storm, and to consider the fate of the other person. But hard times in addition encouraged Americans to look longingly to the recent more prosperous past when getting and spending and living like the kings and queens of Hollywood had seemed within the grasp of all. That powerful fantasy, too, stayed alive despite the Depression.

9

Ordeal of the Intellectuals

> *Money-making and . . . a money-making society . . . are*
> *not enough to satisfy humanity—neither is a social system*
> *like our own where everyone is out for himself and the*
> *devil take the hindmost.*
> —Edmund Wilson
>
> *The good artist is a deadly enemy of society.*
> —James Agee

LOOKING BACKWARD

The Depression brought economic misery to American intellectuals as
well as to farmers and textile workers. Publishers cut back on the books
they produced. Advances got smaller. Newspapers and magazines pared
their editorial force. Colleges and universities laid off faculty. Yet a fair
number of the nation's most creative spirits greeted the crisis with
euphoria. Somewhat like Henry Ford or Andrew Mellon, they believed
the Depression would be "a wholesome thing in general" because it
could "purge the rottenness from the [economic] system."

American intellectuals brooded less about the sexual revolution during the 1930s than about the long-anticipated one in the nation's economic and political arrangements. Their collective left-wing sympathies
have been somewhat exaggerated by scholars who regard the era as
"the Red Decade," but there is little doubt that a substantial number
saw themselves as the vanguard of a major political and cultural transformation generated by the economic crisis.

Many American intellectuals greeted the stock market crash and the

ensuing economic collapse of the Hoover years as a harbinger of progress. Such a debacle, the argument went, exposed the bankruptcy of
industrial capitalism, the shallowness of the country's individualistic
ethic and business civilization, the futility of traditional political organizations, and the opportunity to make a fresh start. "The breakdown
in which we are living is the breakdown of the particular romance known
as business," declared John Dewey, the king of American philosophers
and American liberals in 1932. "It is the revelation that the elated
excitement of the romantic adventure has to be paid for with an equal
depression." But while members of the business elite such as Ford and
Mellon expected a rebirth of capitalism once the speculators had been
ruined and labor chastised, the intellectuals hoped for the creation of
a wholly different social order.

But what kind of order? Since the late nineteenth century a substantial number of American intellectuals, headed by Henry Adams, had
looked to the past for inspiration and solace. Rejecting machine civilization, science, urbanization, and an economic system that pitted individual against individual in an endless war, they idealized the Middle
Ages as an organic community built on fixed but harmonious social
relations and infused with a passionate religious faith. Amid the economic ruin brought on by capitalism, technology, and individualism,
an antimodernism exemplified by the poet T. S. Eliot and the literary
critics Irving Babbitt and Paul Elmer More continued to attract intellectual followers in the early thirties who usually referred to themselves
as royalists, Catholics, and classicists.

Eliot, the elegant aesthete who ridiculed both fascism and communism as "the natural idea for the thoughtless person," made common
intellectual cause with a group of Southern novelists, poets, and historians centered at Vanderbilt University who in 1930 published *I'll
Take My Stand*, a manifesto on behalf of agrarianism and regionalism
that held up the civilization of the Old South (including slavery) as an
ideal against which to measure the chaos and emptiness of modern
American life. John Crowe Ransom, Allen Tate, Robert Penn Warren,
and other "Southern Agrarians" contrasted the neighborliness, harmony, and wholeness of country life with the impersonal social relations and exploitation that characterized factory production and urban
existence. "The evil of industrial economics," wrote Donald Davidson,
"was that it squeezed all human motives into one narrow channel and
then looked for humanitarian means to repair the injury. The virtue of
the Southern agrarian tradition was that it mixed up a great many

motives with the economic motive, thus enriching it and reducing it to a proper subordination."

THE COMMUNIST PARTY

Other American intellectuals, less enamored with Aristotle, the medieval world, monarchy, or the antebellum South as models for the ideal community, found much to admire in the simple life of other contemporary, premodern peoples, the peasants of Latin America and Asia or the South Sea islanders. But by far the largest number of American intellectuals did not retreat into an antimodern past or idealize the peasant villages of the Yucatan. They regarded the breakdown of American capitalism as an opportunity to harness the machine to the fulfillment of human needs by finally separating industrial technology from the profit motive. They believed it was possible to create a society of abundance with communitarian values, a planned society that would remain basically democratic.

"Money-making and . . . a money-making society . . . are not enough to satisfy humanity—neither is a social system like our own where everyone is out for himself and the devil take the hindmost," announced the literary critic Edmund Wilson, who urged American writers to "take Communism away from the Communists," but soon urged them to vote for the Communist Party ticket in 1932 as the only real alternative to the traditional bourgeois parties of Hoover and Roosevelt. The editor of the *New Republic* called for "a genuine economic liberty by planning and organizing industry for the general welfare." Lewis Mumford believed Americans had the opportunity to "go beyond the machine," and to institute a true "collective economy" in which production and consumption would be balanced, thereby restoring order and integrity to communities and individuals fragmented by the dog-eat-dog system of capitalism.

In the short run, especially during the darkest days of the Depression, a considerable number of American writers and intellectuals turned to the Communist Party as Marxism gained new prestige. It seemed to offer an intellectual framework for analyzing the crisis and a practical way of organizing discontent against the status quo. Karl Marx had predicted widespread revolt as productive resources fell into fewer and fewer hands and the working class became more and more impoverished. The Bonus Marchers, militant farmers in the countryside, and the formation of councils among the unemployed seemed to herald the coming of revolution.

From the perspective of many disillusioned intellectuals in the early thirties, the Soviet Union, about to inaugurate a new Five-Year Plan, seemed to promise a sensible, planned economy without the unemployment and mass misery of capitalism in the West. In the spring of 1932, fifty-two famous writers, philosophers, scientists, and other intellectuals endorsed Wilson's "Culture and Crisis" manifesto, which called upon "all honest professional workers" to vote for the Communist Party ticket of William Z. Foster and James W. Ford. The nation, according to Wilson, had been plunged into economic crisis by "grabbers, advertisers, traders, speculators, salesmen, the much-adulated immensely stupid and irresponsible 'business men.' " The Democrats and Republicans were "hopelessly corrupt" and incapable of solving America's fundamental problems. Those who signed Wilson's call to arms included Sherwood Anderson, Erskine Caldwell, Malcolm Cowley, Countee Cullen, John Dos Passos, Langston Hughes, Grace Lumpkin, Sidney Hook, and Lincoln Steffens.

Despite the Communist Party's crushing defeat in 1932, enthusiasm among intellectuals ran high. They saw themselves as members of a revolutionary vanguard who were steering the locomotive of history toward a new utopia of equality and justice. They had joined the only organization that truly fought on behalf of the working class. Roosevelt's New Deal, especially the NRA, was dismissed as American fascism. "My own plan is to work very closely with the communists in the future," playwright John Howard Lawson told John Dos Passos, "to get into some strike activity, and to accept a good deal of discipline in doing so. It seems to me the only course open to people like ourselves."

But the marriage between the CP and what Wilson called "the engineers of ideas" or the "brain workers" proved to be a stormy and disappointing one for the remainder of the decade. To the dismay of many intellectuals, party officials spent as much time and energy fighting their natural allies on the left (the Trotskyists, the Lovestonites, and the Socialists) as they did attacking the capitalists and reactionaries. Instead of adapting Marxism to American conditions, moreover, the CP leaders usually tailored their ideology and strategy to the needs of Soviet foreign policy as defined by Joseph Stalin.

As the Soviet dictator became more alarmed by the power of Hitler's Germany after 1933, he demanded that national communist parties abroad abandon their revolutionary struggle against bourgeois liberals and join "popular front" organizations to fight fascism. By 1936, in response to the new order from Moscow, the American CP had embraced Roosevelt and the New Deal and elevated Jefferson and Lincoln to sainthood next to Marx and Lenin. The CP, in short, left American intellectuals stranded by the mid-thirties without a revolutionary party. Further intellectual betrayals followed, when Stalin engineered the starvation of millions of peasants during the Five-Year Plan, purged his party rivals through rigged show trials, and finally signed a non-aggression pact with the devil himself, Hitler. By then, 1939, many of those who had joined the CP or become "fellow travelers" in its various front organizations had abandoned ship. "One of the worst drawbacks of being a Stalinist at the present time," lamented a chastened Edmund Wilson, "is that you have to defend so many falsehoods."

In defense of the American Communist Party during the thirties it should be noted that its lawyers, especially those in the International Labor Defense Fund, defended clients in civil liberties and criminal cases initially scorned by the respectable bar. Without the efforts of the ILD, the Scottsboro boys, young black teenagers charged with the rape of two white women in Alabama, would have been unjustly put to death for a crime they did not commit. Its labor organizers played an absolutely crucial role in the many struggles for union recognition and collective bargaining in the period 1936 to 1938, a fact noted by John L. Lewis, who once observed in a moment of candor that the CIO would not have succeeded without its communist organizers. Lewis and other CIO leaders, however, soon tired of their communist supporters and purged many of them from top leadership posts.

WRITING FOR THE REVOLUTION

On the other hand, the Communist Party's impact upon the nation's artistic and intellectual life in the thirties was far less salutary. Its chief cultural commissars, writers Mike Gold, Granville Hicks, and Joseph Freeman, and its main organs of opinion, *The New Masses* and the John Reed clubs, insisted that writers who joined the revolution had to view the world exclusively through the lens of the class struggle. Members of the working class were to be encouraged to write their own literature that scorned middle-class pretensions and conventions. "Who are we afraid of?" Gold asked. "Of the critics? Afraid that they will say *The New Masses* prints terribly ungrammatical stuff? Hell, brother, the newsstands abound with neat packages of grammatical offal." Upon pain of ostracism, novelists, playwrights, and poets were to focus their attention upon capitalist oppression and the travails of labor. They were to create a "proletarian literature" inspiring workers to resist exploitation and portraying them in a heroic light.

Communist Party critics like Gold and Hicks favored literary realism and plain, unvarnished prose to works that relied too much on symbolism and long, convoluted sentences. They condemned an excessive preoccupation with sex or the internal moral dramas of individual characters as bourgeois decadence. "Every poem, every novel and drama," Gold declared, "must have a social theme, or it is merely confectionery." Bourgeois writers would concentrate on "their spiritual drunkards and superrefined Parisian émigrés," he continued, while the true revolutionary writers focused on the "suffering of the hungry, persecuted and heroic millions." By this standard, Theodore Dreiser and Dashiell Hammett (both CP members) were lionized as great creative artists, while James Joyce, William Faulkner, T. S. Eliot, and F. Scott Fitzgerald were relegated to the ash heap of literary reaction, along with Hawthorne, Poe, Melville, Henry James, and Mark Twain. Gold, for instance, dismissed Marcel Proust as the "master-masturbator of . . . bourgeois literature."

Even literary works that examined important social issues often ran afoul of the party's gospel when they displayed ambivalence about the working class or the CP's efforts to lead the revolution. John Steinbeck's 1936 novel *In Dubious Battle,* which took as its theme a strike by agricultural workers in California, came under attack because it portrayed the party's organizers as cynical opportunitists and the workers as easily manipulated and prone to acts of irrational violence. By decade's end, the party's literary orthodoxy had been rejected by some of its most faithful early supporters, including the gifted black novelist Richard Wright. His 1940 masterpiece *Native Son* refused to idealize a CP attorney who defends a black man accused of murder or to attribute the tragic fate of the hero solely to the social and economic forces of capitalist exploitation.

The left-leaning *Partisan Review* asked some American authors in 1939, "Do you find, in retrospect, that your writing reveals any allegiance to any group, class, organization, region, religion, or system of thought, or do you conceive of it as mainly the expression of yourself as an individual?" Some responses:

—James T. Farrell: "I want my writing to have allegiance to what I think is true."
—Gertrude Stein: "I am not interested."

—Katherine Anne Porter: "My whole attempt has been to discover and understand human motives, human feelings, to make a distillation of what human relations and experiences my mind has been able to absorb. I have never known an uninteresting human being, and I have never known two alike; there are broad classifications and deep similarities, but I am interested in the thumb print."

FREE SPIRITS, CONSERVATIVE VISIONS

As Wright's example demonstrated and the *Partisan Review* survey suggested, the attempt by the Communist Party to corral American writers and to contain their creative energies within a single ideological framework largely floundered on the latter's stubborn intellectual independence. All but the most devoted party hacks refused to sacrifice their particular artistic insights to the dictates of Marxist slogans. And many of the decade's towering literary achievements eschewed a revolutionary vision entirely. This was especially true with regard to Steinbeck's *Grapes of Wrath*, the quintessential novel of the Great Depression, to virtually all of the works of William Faulkner, and to James Agee and Walker Evans's magnificent exploration of rural poverty *Let Us Now Praise Famous Men*.

In his haunting story of the Joad family's forced migration from the Oklahoma dust bowl to California's lush Salinas Valley, Steinbeck fictionalized the real-life calamity of millions of farmers uprooted from their traditional homes by the combined forces of technology, nature, greed, and ignorance. Once proudly independent on the land, the Joads have become bewildered vagabonds who travel along Route 66 in search of a new beginning on land in the West. Instead, they and others like them fall prey to new forms of exploitation and misery in California's vast agricultural industry, where the only spark of hope comes in the form of government-managed labor camps and the migrants' own efforts at collective resistance.

No writer penned a more devastating indictment of the waste and cruelty produced by the Depression or paid a larger tribute to the capacity of ordinary human beings to cope with its manifold misfortunes and disasters. Steinbeck's book outraged California's social establishment, but it touched the nation's soul in 1939, as did John Ford's screen version a year later. But although *The Grapes of Wrath* offered unsparing criticism of the American social order, its overall message was not a revolutionary one. Like the Southern Agrarians and Franklin Roosevelt himself, Steinbeck romanticized the rural past as the ultimate source of spiritual wholeness in an America corrupted by machines, cities, and technological progress. The Joad family gradually discovers that their predicament is shared by many others. They join the collective struggle for social justice, but remain attached to the ideals of independent proprietorship as the foundation of hope for the future.

In his two major novels published during the decade, *Light in August* (1932) and *Absalom, Absalom!* (1936), Faulkner the Southerner did not romanticize the nation's agrarian heritage, but suggested how difficult it was for human beings to strike off the chains of the past and to know the truth about the present. While practitioners of proletarian fiction postulated a simple reality of class conflict and a plastic future molded by heroic revolutionaries, Faulkner reminded his readers of the heavy burdens of history and the dangers of fanaticism. All of his central characters are crippled by ancient cultural and psychological wounds they barely understand and seldom transcend. Each remains a prisoner of a particular version of past events that distorts present reality and ultimately leaves them either incapable of action or doomed to make the wrong choices—for themselves and for others. Little wonder that a radical critic such as Hicks dismissed Faulkner as a writer who evaded "the central issues" of his time and failed to forge "a new art that shall be a weapon in the battle for a new and superior world."

The editors of *Fortune* magazine sent writer James Agee and photographer Walker Evans to the South in 1936 to document the life of poor white tenant farmers. The magazine expected Agee and Evans to produce a narrative and photographic record that would confirm the reigning stereotype of both liberals and radicals, who perceived the South's tenant farmers as ignorant and wretched victims of an exploitative social system or, as Agee later wrote with irony, "social integers in a criminal economy." What Agee and Evans produced was not to their editors' liking. *Fortune* refused to publish it. When *Let Us Now Praise Famous Men* finally appeared in 1941, it sold about six hundred copies, but outraged and confounded critics on both the right and the left.

Evans's photographs captured the poverty of the Gudger, Woods, and Ricketts families—the small, dark interiors of their wooden shacks, their meager furnishings, shabby clothing, and emaciated features—but his lens recorded another side of their existence as well, especially the pride and dignity they displayed in what they had and who they were. In many of the individual portraits and group photographs, the family members wore their finest shirts, overalls, and dresses to pro-

Novelist William Faulkner.

duce scenes of decorum and self-esteem every bit as impressive as those presented by the great society families of Boston or Philadelphia. Evans's photographs also recorded the striking individuality in each person's clothing and in each tenant family's home, where no pieces of furniture, no cooking and eating utensils, and no wall decorations were exactly alike.

Agee's astonishing narrative, part exhaustive description, part stream of consciousness, lyrical, angry, often blurring past and present, reinforced the dominant theme of Evans's photographs: these were real, unique human beings, each one a "single, unrepeatable, holy individual" who yet remained part of a complex regional subculture and a larger American nation. "All that each person is, and experiences, and shall never experience, in body and mind," Agee wrote, "all these things are differing expressions of himself and of one root, and are identical; and not one of these things nor one of these persons is ever quite to be duplicated, nor replaced, nor has it ever quite had precedent; but each is a new and incommunicably tender life, wounded in every breath, and almost as hardly killed as easily wounded: sustaining, for a while, without defense, the enormous assaults of the universe."

Tossing aside the pose of reportorial objectivity and detachment as well, Agee wove his own feelings and struggles into the text. He and Evans considered themselves outsiders and "spies" whose prying camera and inquiries threatened the dignity of the tenants. "These I will write of are human beings, living in this world, innocent of such twistings as these which are taking place over their heads; and that they were dwelt among, investigated . . . revered, and loved by other quite monstrously alien human beings, in the employment of still others still more alien." He even confessed to erotic impulses toward one of the women.

Agee wrote of the white tenant families as "an undefended and appallingly damaged group of human beings," but he refused to sentimentalize them as noble savages or heroic rural proletarians. He believed their prejudices, hatreds, and cruelties could freeze the blood of an urban intellectual. In their ignorance and innocence the tenants were tragically ill-equipped to deal with the moral and technical problems of a modern society, but this same lack of consciousness mercifully spared them from the emotional afflictions of his middle-class

Georgia tenant family from James Agee's and Walker Evans's Let Us Now Praise Famous Men.

friends and neighbors in Manhattan. Agee doubted, finally, that well-intentioned radicals and reformers, whether socialists, communists, or New Dealers, would ever truly understand the tenant farmers or be capable of helping them except on terms that violated their individuality and further dehumanized them.

The Triumph of Consumer Culture: Radio

Despite the heroic efforts of the Communist Party and its intellectual commissars, a genuine proletarian literature and culture did not take deep root in America during the Great Depression. Nor did a revolutionary literature and culture predicted by many noncommunist radicals. From John Dos Passos, James Agee, and John Steinbeck on the left to William Faulkner and Thornton Wilder on the right, American writers remained individualistic and idiosyncratic. The least communal of all the nation's social groups, they refused to cut their artistic cloth to patterns designed by either *The New Masses* or *Fortune*.

Nor, despite the New Deal's Federal Theatre and Federal Writers' Project, did the country sustain an extensive public culture that was simultaneously democratic, participatory, and respectful of the nation's enormous diversity. Federal arts programs under the WPA were always modestly funded, were attacked in Congress, and often were forced to choose between supporting new creative activities or bringing standard classics to audiences that had never before seen Shakespeare or Marlowe. The Federal Theatre developed an experimental theater, a Negro youth theater, a Yiddish vaudeville unit, and a German unit, and performed controversial contemporary dramas such as *Battle Hymn* and *It Can't Happen Here*, about an imagined fascist coup in America, but congressional budget cuts forced the cancellation of its most imaginative social drama, *The Cradle Will Rock* in 1937.

With its series of state guidebooks and topical Life in America series, the Federal Writers' Project enjoyed modest success in recording and preserving regional history and folklore, but it too remained woefully underfunded and subject to constant torment from conservative congressmen who regarded its efforts as trivial and a waste of the taxpayers' money.

In the absence of a revolutionary or public alternative, the fledgling consumer culture of the 1920s continued its conquest of America even in the face of massive unemployment and grinding poverty. Its principal vehicles were radio and motion pictures, now enlivened by sound, which brought standardized tastes, habits, and values to the American people as the New Deal simultaneously attempted to impose nation-wide standards with respect to labor-management relations, securities regulation, old-age pensions, and minimum wages. The private consumer culture conquered more thoroughly than New Deal culture.

By 1937, virtually 80 percent of the population could pull up a chair in front of the radio in the late afternoon or early evening to hear the president of the United States, *Dr. Christian, Amos 'n Andy, Information Please, The Green Hornet,* or *Fibber McGee and Molly.* New Deal programs such as TVA and the Rural Electrification Administration brought electricity and *One Man's Family* even to remote towns and villages in the South and Southwest. According to one survey, Americans listened to radio on the average of four and half hours per day by the end of the decade. They could tune in *Major Bowes and His Original Amateur Hour,* on which "the wheel of fortune goes 'round and 'round and where she stops nobody knows," or hear Joe Kelly ask the Quiz Kids: "What would I be carrying home if I bought an antimacassar, a dinghy, a sarong, and an apteryx?"

Radio and the common culture.

Along with *Portia Faces Life* and *Truth or Consequences*, of course, came a torrent of new products and brands to stimulate the appetite of those with money to spend and those who soon hoped to have money to spend: canned orange juice and canned beer, vitamin pills, air-conditioned automobiles, nylon stockings, electric carving knives. The nation's advertisers had to adjust their slogans to a world characterized by unemployment, class conflict, ideological division, big government, and assorted tyrannies, but they proved worthy of the occasion:

—"If you ask me, doctor, the only thing that will build him up is a Hart Schaffner & Marx suit!"

—"The U.S. government has helped farmers raise finer tobacco—and the better grades go to LUCKIES!"

—"Good servants need good masters." (Hartford Boiler Co.)

—"Be one of the crowd—and be moderate, too!" (Martini and Rossi Vermouth)

Advertisers and manufacturers attempted to turn the depths of the Depression to their advantage.

—"How to please a dictator." (Dictaphone)

—"Just what does the word *fascist* mean, Henry?" (Webster's New International Dictionary)

Radio in the thirties helped to nationalize the country's speech and slang as listeners heard Charlie McCarthy tell Edgar Bergen, "I'll clip ya! So help me, I'll mow ya down." Or comedian Joe Penner say, "You *nasty* man." And brand names from Pepperidge Farms to the Jolly Green Giant, usually advertised over the radio or in mass-circulation magazines such as *Life*, brought a degree of standardization as pervasive as social security numbers.

The Triumph of Consumer Culture: Hollywood

By 1939, American families spent an all-time high $25 a year at motion picture box offices, which translated into roughly one film per week per family. Faced with an appalling economic and social disaster, some Hollywood studios and producers did not shrink from creating films that explored some of America's most wrenching problems. Notable in this regard were Mervyn LeRoy's *I Am a Fugitive from a Chain Gang*, a 1932 production which told the story of how an ex-serviceman, unable to find work, falls in with the wrong crowd, becomes involved in a robbery, and is forced to endure the brutal conditions on a chain gang; *Black Legion* (1936), about a factory worker lured into the Ku Klux Klan; *Make Way for Tomorrow* (1937), the tale of an elderly couple's harrowing financial woes and their struggle to survive; and, of course, John Ford's production of Steinbeck's *The Grapes of Wrath*.

Other American films of the Depression era examined the relationship between poverty and crime (*Dead End*, 1937; *Angels with Dirty Faces*, 1938); the evils of mob violence (*Fury*, 1936); the monotony of industrial civilization (*Modern Times*, 1936); the perils of political corruption (*Mr. Smith Goes to Washington*, 1939); and the importance of community and social solidarity (*Stagecoach*, 1939). But poverty, exploitation, social injustice, and community were hardly the dominant themes emanating from Hollywood and luring fans to the local box office in the era of Roosevelt and the New Deal.

A year after directing *I Am a Fugitive from a Chain Gang*, for example, LeRoy brought forth *Gold Diggers of 1933*, the first in a long series of dazzling musical extravaganzas choreographed over the next four years by Busby Berkeley and featuring Joan Blondell, Ruby Keeler, Dick

Powell, Rudy Vallee, and Ginger Rogers. With its electrically wired chorus girls singing "In the Shadows Let Me Come and Sing to You" and other numbers of "innocent vulgarity," *Gold Diggers* epitomized much of the decade's escapist fare. "Even those of us who were children at the time did not mistake *Gold Diggers* for art," recalled one critic, "and certainly no one took it for life." In this same category one would have to place three-quarters of the films produced by Hollywood during the era. William Dieterle's powerful *The Life of Emile Zola*, about the French writer who defended Captain Dreyfus, won the Academy Award for Best Picture in 1937, but the more usual winners avoided social controversy and complexity: *You Can't Take It with You, The Great Ziegfeld, It Happened One Night*, and *Cavalcade*.

The most powerful and imaginative American film of the period, although not released until 1941, won only a single Academy Award, for script writing, and was a flop at the box office as well: Orson Welles's *Citizen Kane*, a motion picture based loosely on the life and times of newspaper tycoon William Randolph Hearst, who attempted through money and political pressure to block its distribution. *Citizen Kane* had little appeal to those who wished to avoid the Depression's problems

Orson Welles (center) and Joseph Cotten (left) in Citizen Kane.

by watching tuxedo-clad Fred Astaire twirl Ginger Rogers across the highly polished dance floor of a posh country club. Nor did it pander to those radicals who believed that the era's difficulties could be solved by invoking a few simple slogans that pilloried the rich and powerful.

Welles examined the life of the late Charles Foster Kane by having a reporter interview those who knew him, feared him, loved and despised him. The collective portrait that emerged of the publisher was diverse and subtle: a man with a social conscience who seldom missed an opportunity to make himself richer. Charles Foster Kane could be generous and cruel, self-deprecating and egotistical; a democrat and a tyrant. The truth about Kane, Welles suggested, was manifold and ever-shifting, a product of the point of view of each observer. Welles did for the cinema what Faulkner did for the novel and Agee for the documentary: suggest to audiences how complicated social reality could be.

But the message that most Americans wanted to hear in the 1930s was a simpler one conveyed by Hollywood in films that often focused on the life-styles of the rich and celebrated: good times would return in America, bringing with them a restoration of the age of high mass consumption. In this Hollywood marched in step with Washington, for FDR's New Deal, despite its many innovations and humane spirit, was no challenge to the consumption ethic, but rather a pledge to make getting and spending more democratic and accessible to all.

10

Over There, Again

*We shall continue to observe a true neutrality in the dis-
putes of others. . . . to work for peace and to take the profits out of war; to guard against being drawn, by political
commitments, international banking, or private trading,
into any war which may develop anywhere.*
—Democratic Party national platform, 1936

*There are worse things than war. Cowardice . . . treachery
. . . simple selfishness.*
—Ernest Hemingway

LESSONS OF HISTORY

"Those who do not remember the past," wrote George Santayana, "are
doomed to repeat it." Santayana's aphorism is one of the most famous
penned by an American, but what the distinguished Harvard philosopher did not add is equally important: people do not always agree about
the past; they read their history in very different ways and therefore
often draw radically different conclusions about the lessons it teaches.
There are few more dramatic illustrations of this than how Americans
of the 1930s came to view their nation's participation in World War I
and how these perceptions shaped their response to the many crises
that finally brought them into the century's second great conflagration.

For some Americans the lesson of 1914–18 seemed inescapable: the
world had grown interdependent; no country the size of the United
States could long remain untouched by a military conflict that engulfed
the major nations of Europe. Traditional ideas of neutrality were a
dangerous illusion. A few leaders, principally Theodore Roosevelt and

Henry Cabot Lodge, had advocated a formal Anglo-American alliance as the centerpiece of a system of international relations managed by the great powers on the basis of spheres of influence. For Woodrow Wilson and his followers, however, such American internationalism smacked too much of the wicked alliances and balance-of-power arrangements that had brought on the Great War. The true path to national security, in their judgment, lay in some kind of international organization capable of resolving peacefully disputes among the great powers or employing collective sanctions against any nation that waged an aggressive war. Americans with these views had rallied behind Wilson's war aims in 1917 and remained staunch supporters of the rejected League of Nations throughout the twenties and thirties. With the former president they believed that "the great creators of the government . . . thought of America as a light to the world, as created to lead the world in the assertion of the right of peoples and the rights of free nations."

But a far larger number of Americans looked back on the war experience through a different set of lenses. Ranging from extreme hemispheric nationalists to outright pacifists, these isolationists viewed American intervention in 1917 as a ghastly mistake, a decision that brought only death, economic dislocation, and the erosion of civil liberties to the American people and a dictated, vengeful peace settlement in Europe. Wilson's neutrality had been a sham from the beginning, because it permitted Americans to lend money to the British and French, to trade in munitions, and to travel into war zones where their safety became an issue of national rights. The League of Nations was little more than a victors' device for perpetuating the status quo, a cunning plot to suck the United States into endless foreign wars that were none of her business. In the future, the United States should pursue genuine neutrality when conflicts erupted abroad, never fight unless attacked, and pursue her own independent destiny, especially in the Western Hemisphere. President Harding once summed up these sentiments by observing, "We seek no part in directing the destinies of the world."

THE NATIONALIST AS INTERNATIONALIST

The man who pledged a new deal for the American people in 1932 and who told them a few months later they had "nothing to fear but fear itself" devoted one sentence in his stirring inaugural address to foreign relations. "In the field of world policy," Franklin Roosevelt told the nation, "I would dedicate this Nation to the policy of the good neighbor—the neighbor who resolutely respects himself and, because he does so, respects the rights of others." The outgoing Hoover regime had already articulated such a policy for Latin America. In addition, this vapid generality illuminated neither FDR's thinking about diplomacy nor his foreign policy plans. Subordinates and heads of state alike were left in the dark.

The generality no doubt masked Roosevelt's own uncertainty in 1933. He brought to the White House a congeries of conflicting attitudes about America and the world. At Groton, Roosevelt had once spoken out against annexation of Hawaii and in favor of independence for the Philippines, two bouts of youthful idealism. The more mature Roosevelt had been an ardent nationalist who admired the robust "big stick" diplomacy of his cousin Ted, supported a large naval building program as assistant secretary, and boasted of the success of American intervention into Haiti and Santo Domingo. He thought Wilson too slow in responding to German provocations and beat the drums for war long before April 1917. But Roosevelt was no narrow, provincial nationalist in the mold of Hiram Johnson or William Borah. His nationalism was tempered by extensive foreign travel, personal friendships with many influential Europeans, and a sophisticated understanding of events abroad and their impact on the United States. FDR, it might be said, remained a Wilsonian of the heart, but a disciple of TR in his head.

Although critical of Wilson's caution during the neutrality crisis, Roosevelt became an ardent supporter of the Fourteen Points and the League of Nations, the centerpieces of his futile campaign for the vice presidency in 1920. When criticized during that election about all the votes Great Britain would wield in the proposed world organization because of her colonies, Roosevelt made a revealing response. "Does anybody suppose that the votes of Cuba, Haiti, San Domingo, Panama, Nicaragua and the other Central American States would be cast differently from the vote of the United States?" he asked. "We are in a very true sense the big brother of these little republics." Beneath his internationalist garb, in other words, there still beat the heart of a genuine nationalist, who had come to accept the fact that beyond the Western Hemisphere, the United States might best project its influence through an organization such as the League of Nations.

Like the League, however, Roosevelt went down to defeat in 1920. "They'll vote for you," one of his advisers told him before the debacle, "but they won't vote for Cox and the League." FDR absorbed the message well. In 1923, writing a proposal for the Edward W. Bok Peace Prize Committee, he suggested scrapping the existing League of Nations for a new Society of Nations that would be run by four countries—the United States, Britain, France, and Japan. But instead of the controversial Article 10 in the League Covenant, which pledged collective action "to respect and preserve as against external aggression the territorial integrity and existing political independence of all members," Roosevelt's "continuing permanent society" would be obliged only to meet and confer in such circumstances. The great powers ought to run any international association of nations, Roosevelt suggested, but the organization itself should not automatically resist aggressors or, above all, cramp the independence of these same great powers.

During the 1932 campaign, candidate Roosevelt dismayed League supporters and thrilled isolationists by declaring American membership in that organization to be a dead issue. The League, he told the New York Grange, had departed from Wilson's original vision and no longer merited even American cooperation. With isolationist sentiments rising ever higher in the face of mounting domestic problems, he was not willing to allow the ghost of his Wilsonian past to spoil the election. The evolution of FDR's stand on the League said a great deal about his conception of the presidency and foreign relations. He would strive constantly not to repeat Wilson's errors in 1918–19 or his own in 1920 by ignoring public opinion and the domestic political context in which decisions were to be made. Ever the astute politician, he would seldom advance very far ahead of popular prejudices and often allowed them to overcome his better judgment. In short, American politics would largely drive Franklin Roosevelt's foreign policy, not events abroad, until conflict in the North Atlantic and the western Pacific threatened to wipe out the national independence and autonomy of action that he and others so prized.

PUNISHING THE DEFAULTERS

Roosevelt put domestic recovery and national self-interest above international cooperation in a series of decisions he made between 1933 and 1935 about war debts, disarmament, and currency stabilization. These actions, plus his encouragement of drastic new neutrality legislation and Senate rejection of the World Court, also showed he had lost much of the initiative on foreign affairs to Congress and had little appetite for confronting militant isolationists who might trigger a legislative brawl that would disrupt the New Deal's other legislative efforts.

With Hoover's debt moratorium scheduled to expire in December 1932, the principal European nations met in Lausanne, Switzerland, during the summer to hammer out a long-term settlement. England and France agreed to cancel about 90 percent of Germany's remaining reparations bill, if Allied creditors (meaning the United States) would make a corresponding cut in their war debts. Hoover urged FDR to use his influence with congressional Democrats to back the plan, but the president-elect, sensing little enthusiasm on Capitol Hill for it, kept silent. A year later, Roosevelt went further when he endorsed Senator Hiram Johnson's measure that made it illegal to market within the country any foreign securities by governments that defaulted on war debts owed to the United States. Only pressure from the administration prevented the Johnson Act from including defaults on private bank loans as well.

Given the liquidity crisis and the general collapse of confidence in all securities, the draconian provisions of the Johnson Act were probably of little real consequence to foreign borrowing, but the law became a powerful symbol of national selfishness unrivaled since the Hawley-Smoot tariff and a dreadful example to set for others. The only nation that faithfully continued to pay its war debt to the United States, Finland, found that its probity did not guarantee a corresponding degree of American support in times of international crisis. When the Soviet Union invaded Finland and seized some of its territory in 1939, members of Congress and the Roosevelt administration denounced the attack and offered condolences to the Finns, but little more.

DEBACLE IN GENEVA

In Geneva, with an American observer present, another group of European diplomats and League of Nations experts had attempted to draw up a general disarmament agreement in 1932. Prior to FDR's inauguration, however, they had remained deadlocked among German demands for arms parity, French insistence on absolute security guarantees against renewed German aggression, the Soviet Union's call for unlimited disarmament, and British and American efforts to limit the treaty to "offensive" weapons. In an attempt to break the stalemate, Roosevelt dispatched veteran negotiator Norman H. Davis, a devout Wilsonian and international financier, to the disarmament conference table with a plan that contained as its centerpiece an American pledge to cooperate with League economic sanctions against any nation branded as an aggressor by the organization. "The overwhelming majority of peoples feel obliged to retain excessive armaments," FDR wrote to fifty-two nations, "because they fear some act of aggression against them and not because they themselves seek to be aggressors."

Europe was on the threshold of ominous developments. Sanctioned by the Nazi Party, a nationwide boycott of Jewish businesses and professions had begun in Germany. Acting under the broad powers of the Enabling Act, Chancellor Adolf Hitler had appointed new Reich governors for each German state and armed them with the authority to disband local assemblies and fire local officials, including judges. On May 1, Hitler's government banned all trade unions. A week later, Nazi students in Berlin burned over twenty thousand books, including the works of Thomas Mann, Albert Einstein, and Sigmund Freud. Rumors flew that Hitler would soon announce Germany's intention to rearm in defiance of the Versailles Treaty. "Hitler is a madman," Roosevelt told the French ambassador, "and his counselors, some of whom I personally know, are even madder than he is."

With FDR's encouragement, a resolution giving the president authority to embargo arms shipments to a League-designated aggressor passed the House. But it soon ran into a barrage of protest from isolationists on the Senate Foreign Relations Committee. Senators Johnson and Borah insisted that the arms embargo apply to both sides in any conflict, a solution that completely undermined the Davis proposal at Geneva. Rather than fight, FDR first announced that he agreed with Johnson's blanket embargo approach and then under pressure from his own State Department allowed the entire measure to die in committee. With it passed the last opportunity for some kind of collective disarmament agreement.

ECONOMIC NATIONALISM TRIUMPHANT

Having abandoned the disarmament field at the first whiff of isolationist fire, Roosevelt simultaneously pulled the plug on the World Monetary and Economic Conference in London, which he had earlier called of "vital importance to mankind." In addition to each nation's individual recovery efforts, the president noted, the London meeting should seek the stabilization of currencies "by wise and considered international action." Roosevelt raised hopes further when he chose another old Wilsonian, Secretary of State Cordell Hull, to lead the American delegation. The former Tennessee congressman ranked low tariffs and free trade right next to patriotism and motherhood; neither goal could be achieved, however, without some broad agreement among the leading industrial nations on exchange rates. Hull probably sensed disaster even before his boat docked in England, when Roosevelt cabled him that any reciprocal trade bill would have to be put off for at least a year because of the legislative logjam in Congress.

The London Conference bogged down at the end of June 1933. The French, who remained on the gold standard, insisted on a quick return to fixed exchange rates, while the British and Americans feared the deflationary consequences of such a move. Roosevelt dispatched archnationalist Ray Moley to London with a soothing statement that the United States would cooperate with attempts to work out a reasonable settlement among the gold-bloc nations. The London conferees actually came up with such a plan, a vague statement that pledged monetary stability "as quickly as possible," vowed to restore gold "as the international measure of value," but still gave each country absolute freedom to choose when and how to implement these goals.

The declaration, in other words, committed Roosevelt and the United States to nothing apart from pious hopes. In no way would it have limited FDR's desire to raise American prices and spur exports by devaluing the dollar. Even Moley, champion of national planning, urged acceptance of the declaration in the interests of international goodwill. Roosevelt nonetheless turned it down with a blistering "bombshell message" to the conference that lectured the delegates for wasting their time on "purely artificial and temporary experiments." Those economists and politicians who like Keynes favored bold monetary and fiscal experimentation hailed Roosevelt's message as the death blow to the icon of gold and a declaration of independence from the rule of international bankers. Others, concerned with symbolism as well as substance, believed it sent the wrong message abroad by confirming that the United States intended to go it alone in a world of intensified economic nationalism.

The High Tide of Isolationism

With the White House humming such nationalistic tunes, it is not surprising that isolationists in Congress soon picked up the tempo. Supported by well-organized pacifist groups such as the Women's

International League for Peace and Freedom and influential senators such as George Norris, the Senate created a special committee in late 1934 to investigate the role of American munitions makers in the international arms trade. Republican Gerald P. Nye of North Dakota, a zealous critic of virtually every New Deal domestic program, chaired the committee, which was also packed with other stalwart opponents of international entanglements, including Michigan's Arthur Vandenberg and Missouri's Bennett Champ Clark. Nye's headline-grabbing inquiry exposed the stupendous profits earned by firms such as Du Pont and Remington Arms during and after World War I. Unfolded were unsavory methods, including bribes, used to drum up business around the world, and the incestuous ties between these private companies and the armed services.

The Nye Committee's revelations, appearing simultaneously with *Fortune* magazine's "Arms and the Men," and books such as *Merchants of Death, Iron, Blood and Profits,* and Walter Millis's *Road to War: America, 1914–1917,* underlined the notion that American participation in the Great War had been a horrible mistake. Such exposure also encouraged the simple thesis that this participation had resulted from a nefarious conspiracy among the arms manufacturers and bankers. Privately, Roosevelt deplored the rhetorical excesses of Nye and his colleagues. Politically, he had little choice but to call on Congress to pass legislation to take "the profit out of war."

Before Congress acted on this suggestion, however, it severed the last symbolic link to the League of Nations by again rejecting American membership on the World Court, although the spurned protocol had been so watered down as to give that body virtually no jurisdiction over the United States. The 1934 elections had given Roosevelt more than a two-thirds majority in the Senate, but despite this edge, the combined forces of Johnson, Borah, Hearst, and Father Coughlin proved too much for the administration. Hearst's papers warned against the "entangling alliance" of the World Court. The Detroit cleric Coughlin urged his radio listeners to deluge the Senate with mail protesting the abandonment of "our national sovereignty to the World Court." He claimed that the protocol's chief sponsors were the same international bankers who had caused the Depression.

Western Union delivered between forty thousand and fifty thousand anti–World Court telegrams to the Senate before the crucial vote in January 1935. With seven senators conspicuously absent from the chamber, the World Court protocol failed to muster two-thirds support, 52–36. "As to the thirty-six Senators who placed themselves on record against the principle of the World Court," an angry Roosevelt told majority leader Robinson, "I am inclined to think that if they ever get to Heaven they will be doing a great deal of apologizing for a very long time—that is if God is against war—and I think He is." On the World Court vote the Wilsonians suffered their worst defeat since the failure of the Versailles Treaty. Roosevelt also took his worst legislative trouncing prior to the court-packing battle in 1937. But an even more significant setback soon took place, and FDR was partially to blame.

The Neutrality Acts

Meeting with members of the Nye Committee in mid-March, the president astonished the senators by urging them to draw up and submit new neutrality legislation. This legislation would not only "take the profit out of war," but also insulate the United States from future conflicts. Wilson's critics had probably been right in 1914, Roosevelt noted, when they insisted on prohibiting travel by Americans on all belligerent ships in time of war. Perhaps restrictions should also be placed on American loans to warring nations. Several weeks later, taking the president at his word, Senator Nye introduced in the Senate what became the basis for the first of three Neutrality Acts passed by Congress between 1935 and 1937. To the utter dismay of FDR, Hull, and the State Department, the Nye package not only banned travel and loans, but also required the president to impose a mandatory arms embargo on any nation engaged in any conflict. It thereby stripped the president of his discretion to assist the victims of obvious aggression.

Before the first Neutrality Act passed, Congress dropped the ban on loans and gave the president discretionary authority to warn citizens about travel on belligerent vessels. But the mandatory arms embargo stuck, along with a new government commission whose permission was now required before munitions could be exported to any foreign country whether at war or not. A year later, Congress extended these original provisions and imposed additional ones: the mandatory arms embargo would be automatically applied to any third country that joined an existing conflict; private loans by American citizens to governments at war were prohibited. The final piece of neutrality legislation, in May 1937, extended the arms embargo even to civil wars, made the travel ban mandatory, and gave the president authority to place all trade with nations at war on a "cash-and-carry" basis that would keep American merchant ships out of harm's way. "I would just as soon close every port in the United States, including Houston and Galveston," said one Texas congressman, "if it would save the life of one human being."

Roosevelt strongly objected to the mandatory features of the neutrality legislation. He especially opposed those sections that limited his ability to distinguish aggressor nations from their victims. But having through words and deeds encouraged the isolationist forces in Congress and sensitive to their enormous political muscle, he had little choice but to sign the three laws. They sharply reduced his diplomatic options. At the same time, he warned the nation that the mandatory, impartial arms embargo "might have exactly the opposite effect from that which was intended. In other words, the inflexible provisions might drag us into war instead of keeping us out." Looking to the past, Congress sought to perfect neutrality legislation that would avoid the entanglements of 1914–1917 and save America from the horrors of another war. But as it did so, the world created after the Great War began to crumble:

—On October 3, 1935, less than two months after the first Neutrality Act became law, Italian dictator Benito Mussolini, whom Roosevelt had described in 1934 as "the admirable Italian gentlemen," ordered his troops into Ethiopia, whose forces had to confront the Italian artillery, machine guns, and poison gas with spears and bows and arrows.

—On March 7, 1936, one week after FDR signed the second Neutrality Act, Hitler informed the other nations of Western Europe that Germany would no longer be bound by the terms of the Locarno Treaty and German forces occupied the Rhineland in defiance of the Versailles Treaty.

—Four months after that, in July 1936, civil war erupted in Spain between the established Republican government and disaffected military forces led by General Francisco Franco. Soon Italy and Germany joined in the effort to crush the Spanish Republic.

—Roosevelt had no sooner signed the third Neutrality Act in May 1937 than renewed fighting broke out between Japanese and Chinese forces at the Marco Polo Bridge near Beijing, China. By the end of the year, the Japanese military controlled virtually all of north China and her major port cities from Nanking to Canton after inflicting massive casualties on Chinese civilians in those cities.

—In October 1936, Germany and Italy settled the differences between them and signed protocols soon branded the Rome-Berlin Axis. That year Japan signed an Anti-Comintern Pact with Germany, directed

"Come on in, I'll treat you right . . ." (caption). Isolationists warned Americans about repeating the follies of World War I.

at communism, and Italy added its signature a year later. Although these agreements never materialized into working military alliances, they certainly conveyed the impression to Americans of a growing worldwide conspiracy among dictatorial regimes.

THE RUSSIANS AND RECIPROCITY

During Roosevelt's first term, internationalists faced an uphill battle. They could claim a few modest gains that had important consequences for the future. On November 16, 1933, reversing sixteen years of policy commencing with Wilson, the Roosevelt administration extended formal diplomatic recognition to the Soviet Socialist Republics. Among those pushing hardest for a rapprochement with the communist regime now headed by Joseph Stalin were American capitalists, eager to tap a vast potential market of eager Soviet consumers. Roosevelt had long believed that "if I could only, myself, talk to some one man representing the Russians, I could straighten out this whole question." He was less concerned with American exports than with using the Soviets as a counterweight to Japan's ambitions in China.

In exchange for American recognition, the Soviet government agreed to grant religious liberty and judicial protection to American residents. It would, further, commence serious negotiations about prerevolutionary debts owed to Americans, and curb its anticapitalist propaganda machine in the United States. Like the vast Russian market, the second and third of these promises proved illusory, but Roosevelt's initiative would pay high dividends once Hitler turned on Stalin in 1941. Unfortunately, it also fueled conservative paranoia about the pro-communist tendencies of the New Deal.

Rebuffed by FDR on tariff reform in 1933, Cordell Hull realized a lifelong ambition a year later when Congress approved and Roosevelt signed the Reciprocal Trade Agreements Act. This measure gave the president broad authority over three years to slash American import duties by as much as 50 percent in exchange for corresponding reductions by foreign nations. As a further incentive to broad international tariff reductions, the law also encouraged the inclusion of "most favored nation" provisions in new trade agreements. If one country cut its duties on an American import, for instance, the United States would be obliged to reduce its own duties on that same product coming from any nation that did not discriminate against American trade.

Hull the Southerner had long regarded high tariffs such as Hawley-Smoot as the tool of monopoly capital that preyed on agricultural producers who needed wider foreign markets. Hull the Wilsonian regarded freer trade as a precondition for world peace. Those who traded with one another, he believed, would be less likely to fight one another. By 1939 the secretary had assiduously negotiated over twenty reciprocal trade agreements, the majority with Latin American nations and Canada. Hull's treaties drew these countries ever closer into America's economic orbit and left other trade rivals to complain that reciprocity amounted to little more than Uncle Sam's quest for international domination. Whether Hull's reciprocity agreements actually increased American exports during the Depression is debatable. Whether they reduced international rivalries is even more doubtful. That they positioned the United States well for the postwar economic era, however, is almost certain.

Good Neighbor, Almost

The nations of Latin America and the Caribbean, long accustomed to Yankee meddling in their internal affairs, had been promised a new era of restraint by Hoover and FDR. And they did secure a measure of relief, owing to America's preoccupation with her own domestic problems, the desire of the United States to stimulate more trade with the region, and the need to counter a growing fascist threat with something other than guns and harsh rhetoric. As FDR vowed, the United States became a Good Neighbor, almost. At the Seventh International Conference of American States in Montevideo, Uruguay, in December 1933, Hull signed a Convention on the Rights and Duties of States affirming that "no state has the right to intervene in the internal or external affairs of another." A year later, having trained a local constabulary to maintain order, the last U.S. Marines pulled out of Haiti, under Roosevelt's orders.

But Cuba proved an exception. Even as Hull signed the historic Montevideo pact, American naval vessels remained anchored off Havana. Their very presence supported the high-pressure tactics of Ambassador Sumner Welles, who sought the graceful exit of besieged dictator Gerardo Machado and the avoidance of a revolutionary regime led by intellectuals, workers, and peasants. The Navy never fired a shot. No Marines stormed onto Cuban beaches. But the State Department would not recognize any Cuban regime without Welles's approval, and he turned thumbs down on university professor Grau San Martin as the new Cuban president. Welles gave his blessing to the military's favorite, Carlos Mendieta. Without American backing, Grau's provisional government collapsed. Mendieta became president, American loans flowed back into the island, and the United States renounced the hated Platt Amendment of 1903 that had served as the basis for prior interventions into Cuba. In return, the Mendieta government allowed the United States to maintain its naval base at Guantanamo Bay until *both* nations agreed to its termination.

Welles's bloodless coup in Havana demonstrated how difficult it was to alter the old habits of American imperialism in the hemisphere. The Good Neighbor Policy received a sterner test in Mexico a few years later, however. Finally, the Roosevelt administration lived up to the ideals of Montevideo and a later 1936 protocol signed by Hull in Buenos Aires that prohibited intervention "directly or indirectly, and for whatever reason."

The Mexican response to the Great Depression had been the election in 1934 of perhaps the greatest president in the republic's history, Lázaro Cárdenas, whose agenda of social and economic reforms resembled Roosevelt's New Deal. Cárdenas pushed for speedy implementation of provisions in Mexico's 1917 constitution requiring the expropriation (with compensation) of foreign-owned agricultural and mining properties. He defended traditional Indian rights and restored lands seized from them by Mexican farmers. He encouraged collective organization among peasants and industrial workers, including the large number of employees who labored for foreign-owned oil companies. When British and American firms defied an arbitration award by the Mexican government that favored the oil workers, Cárdenas nationalized the companies in March 1938.

The audacity of Cárdenas's move stunned Whitehall and Washington. The British broke off diplomatic relations. American oil firms demanded economic and military retaliation. So did the Hearst press, whose boss had suffered the loss of Mexican grazing lands as a result of Cárdenas's reforms. Leaders of the American Catholic Church urged stern measures against a regime they accused of persecution and confiscation. In the White House sat a man who in 1917 as assistant secretary of the Navy had accused Wilson of coddling the Mexicans during the occupation of Veracruz.

But 1938 was not 1917. Now, German troops had marched into Austria, Hitler made fresh demands on Czechoslovakia, Nazi agents swarmed over Latin America, and Japan stood poised for new military advances in Asia. The oil companies received a chilly reception from key administration leaders, especially Interior Secretary Ickes. Other influential businessmen and bankers warned that American pressure on the Mexican government would exacerbate their own problems with the regime. The American ambassador in Mexico City, FDR's old Navy boss Josephus Daniels, urged similar restraint and patient negotiations. These voices prevailed. The Mexican oil crises soon vanished from the nation's consciousness, buried beneath the greater catastrophes of Europe and Asia. The oil barons, who at one point demanded $260 million in compensation, had to settle with the Mexican government as best they could. They came away with only $24 million after the war.

THE FASCIST ASSAULT

In the spring of 1937, as German and Italian military aid poured into Spain to assist the fascist assault on the Spanish Republic, New York's outspoken, liberal mayor, Fiorello La Guardia, made a suggestion—the city's World's Fair should open an exhibit called "The Chamber of Horrors" that featured a brown-shirted, mustachioed dictator eager to plunge the world into another round of bloodletting. The German-language press branded La Guardia a Jewish communist warmonger. Berlin filed a formal protest with the State Department, and Hull apologized on behalf of the United States. At a cabinet meeting a few days later, however, Roosevelt turned to his secretary of state and said: "What would you say if I should say that I agree completely with La Guardia?" He then lightly tapped his fingers on his wrist and added, "We will chastise him like that."

Those who backed the Neutrality Acts believed they would keep the United States out of war. As Roosevelt had warned in 1936, however, their mandatory provisions, permitting no distinction between aggressors and the victims of aggression, might eventually create circumstances that would bring conflict right to the nation's own doorstep. This possibility grew more and more likely as Roosevelt's first term ended. And while the momentum of the domestic New Deal nearly came to a halt in 1937 with the court-packing fight and the recession, nothing, it seemed, could slow down the Italian, German, and Japanese military juggernauts abroad.

In the hope of inspiring League economic sanctions against Italy following its brutal invasion of Ethiopia, FDR invoked the arms embargo of the Neutrality Act and warned Americans that they traded with the two countries at their own risk. Roosevelt aimed his policy directly at Italy, since it had access to American markets while the government of Emperor Haile Selassie did not. After the council of the League condemned Italy and moved for the first time in its history to impose economic sanctions against an aggressor, Hull and Roosevelt indicated that the United States would not undermine these policies. The League, however, led by Britain and France, refused to put oil on the embargo list despite the pleas of Haile Selassie. Mussolini's army therefore rolled on through the African nation with the aid of petroleum from League members and the United States.

Disgusted by the League's cowardice on oil, the State Department threatened to publish the names of American firms that continued to sell large amounts of such strategic materials to Italy. This reduced somewhat the volume of trade between the United States and Il Duce's regime. The Roosevelt-Hull response to the destruction of Ethiopian sovereignty was hardly bold, but it contrasted favorably with that of the British and French governments, who proposed an end to the fighting by granting Italy sixty thousand acres of Ethiopia and virtual economic hegemony over the country. When details of this plan appeared in the press, it forced the resignation of the British foreign secretary, Sir Samuel Hoare. Within a few months, Italy had completed its conquest anyway, without the assistance of Ethiopia's so-called friends.

As the Italian army tightened the noose around the Ethiopian capital of Addis Ababa, Hitler sent German troops into the Rhineland in defiance of the Versailles Treaty. His generals believed the move suicidal in view of British and French military superiority in 1936, but the Nazi leader gambled that Germany's old adversaries, preoccupied with the crisis in Africa, would not respond. He reasoned further that loathing for war ran very high in both countries. He could exploit the growing feeling abroad that the Versailles Treaty had been unfair and that modest "adjustments" would secure lasting peace in Europe. He was right on all counts. Britain and France, capable of derailing Hitler before he grew stronger, did nothing. Despite Soviet pleas, the league declined to impose sanctions as well.

Spanish Agony

If the United States could not be blamed directly for the debacles in Ethiopia or the Rhineland, neither were its hands entirely clean. When the British government recognized the Italian conquest in 1938 in exchange for Mussolini's promise to pull back his forces in Spain, FDR praised the treaty. No one in the administration publicly condemned the Rhineland invasion. In the case of Spain, however, the Roosevelt administration bore a major share of the responsibility for the collapse of the republic, the failure to confront fascist aggression there, and the eventual coming of another general war in Europe.

Neither the 1935 nor the 1936 Neutrality Act applied to civil wars, but Roosevelt applied the arms embargo to both sides when hostilities erupted in the summer of 1936, and he urged Congress to close this loophole in 1937. The legislators quickly complied with the final Neutrality Act. Loathing the communist and anarchist influences in the Spanish government and fearful of igniting a broader conflict, the French and British governments also called for nonintervention and cut off military aid to the regime. Although paying lip service to the nonintervention policy, Hitler and Mussolini showed no such restraint. German planes helped to rain death on Spanish cities such as Madrid and Barcelona. Italian soldiers, over fifty thousand of them, fought next to Franco's Falangists.

The United States therefore found itself in the position of denying needed military equipment to an elected government it had recognized since 1931 and in effect condoning its destruction. Hull complained to Roosevelt that the Spanish government had put guns in the hands of what he called "irresponsible members of left-wing political organizations," as if the Loyalists had a choice when faced with German and Italian machine guns and artillery. One of Hull's closest advisers displayed as much distaste for the Spanish radicals as the British and French. He called the Loyalists "a lot of hoodlums." Inside and outside the administration, however, liberals condemned the administration's policy. They saw the fight in Spain as one pitting peasants, workers, and intellectuals against landlords, goose-stepping generals, big business, and the Catholic Church. The New Deal had taken the wrong side.

American supporters of the Spanish Republic organized parades and demonstrations on behalf of the regime. They raised money for medical and relief supplies and cheered when a New Jersey businessman, Robert Cuse, tried to break the embargo by shipping airplane parts and engines to the Loyalists. Representative John Toussaint Bernard of Minnesota condemned Congress for legislating the blanket embargo because it assisted the fascists "in the rape of Spain." Almost three thousand young Americans volunteered to fight on the Loyalist side in the famous Abraham Lincoln Brigade organized by the Communist Party, although not all of them were members of the CP. "Spain is no political allegory," the poet Archibald MacLeish told the American Writers' Congress, "Spain is not . . . a dramatic spectacle in which the conflict of our time is acted out. These actors are not actors. They truly die. These cities are not stage sets. They burn with fire. . . . And in that war, that Spanish war on Spanish earth, we, writers who contend for freedom, are ourselves, and whether we so wish or not, engaged." Hemingway told the same audience: "We must realize that these murders are the gestures of a bully, the great bully of fascism. There is only one way to quell a bully and that is to thrash him."

It availed little. Bernard cast the only dissenting vote against the embargo in the House. Despite the mobilization of intellectuals like MacLeish and Hemingway, most Americans wanted no part of the conflict in Spain that in two years killed over half a million people

Uncle Sam watched Spain's agony.

before Franco imposed his fascist-style government on the country. The Spanish Republic succumbed both to outside aggression and internal sabotage as Soviet-backed troops killed anarchists as well as Falangists. Stalin, some argued, did not relish a fascist victory in Spain, but he was not eager for the independent left to triumph there either if it meant the establishment of a competitive revolutionary regime. Roosevelt never wavered in his embargo policy. Many attributed his passivity to fear of alienating the party's large and vocal Catholic constituency, which accused the Loyalists like the Cárdenas government in Mexico of looting the church and persecuting its clergy. When Hull declined at one point to issue passports to Americans who wished to go to Spain as ambulance drivers, Harold Ickes noted in his diary: "This makes me ashamed."

"QUARANTINE THE AGGRESSORS"

Roosevelt had been quick to invoke the neutrality legislation in the Spanish crisis and condemned businessmen like Robert Cuse as unpatriotic when they attempted to aid the Loyalists. He did not, however, find that a state of war existed between China and Japan in 1937, even as the Japanese blockaded the Chinese coast and bombed its major cities. This policy did permit Chinese nationalists continued access to American arms and money, but produced a number of unfortunate consequences. It gave the impression that the administration had a double standard, one for conservative regimes that came under siege and another for left-wing governments, which could expect little help.

Critics of FDR's double standard pointed out that Chinese strongman Chiang Kai-shek had not shown much devotion to democracy. He had dealt ruthlessly with his internal enemies, especially the communists. He and his supporters had lined their own pockets with American aid money. In addition, the administration's China policy suggested a special animus toward the Japanese and their expansionist plans in Asia. Roosevelt's China policy, in short, nurtured the later myth that the President sought to provoke Japan as part of his cunning scheme to maneuver the United States into war through the Asian back door.

But finally, by failing to invoke the neutrality laws, Roosevelt encouraged Chiang to believe that the United States would provide even greater assistance in his struggle against the invaders. This was wholly illusory in 1937–38. Like the League of Nations, the United States condemned Japan for violating both the Nine-Power Treaty on China and the Kellogg-Briand Pact and endorsed a conference in Brussels to discuss the deteriorating situation in Asia. But Brussels produced nothing. The Japanese never sent a representative. Neither the United States nor Britain was prepared to go beyond moral condemnation. Chiang had meanwhile spurned a Japanese settlement, which only infuriated Toyko and encouraged further escalation of the Japanese offensive around Shanghai and Nanking.

On December 12, 1937, showing a resolve to tolerate no interference in the China war, Japanese planes attacked an American gunboat, the *Panay*, and its convoy of oil tankers in the Yangtze River. The *Panay* sank and three Americans were killed when Japanese pilots continued to strafe their lifeboats. Roosevelt had no doubt the attack was deliberate. His aging secretary of the Navy, Claude Swanson, thought the *Panay* incident justified war, but most members of Congress and the press wanted to know why the administration placed American servicemen in such dangerous circumstances. Roosevelt had to be content with a Japanese apology, a $2.2 million indemnity, and promises from Toyko of no further incidents involving American vessels.

Japan's actions in China prompt outrage, but little aid.

Even before the *Panay* went down, however, Roosevelt felt obliged to say something in public about the renewed fighting in China, the violence in Spain, the Italian conquest of Ethiopia, and Hitler's blood-less coup in the Rhineland. He was less direct than La Guardia. On October 5, he chose Chicago, the heartland of the isolationists, to say: "When an epidemic of physical disease starts to spread, the commu-nity approves and joins in quarantine of the patients in order to protect the health of the community against the spread of the disease." What Roosevelt meant by "quarantine" is not entirely clear. At most, he probably contemplated an economic embargo. At a press conference the next day he turned aside a question about aligning the United States with any group of nations by declaring, "What do you mean, 'align-ing'? You mean a treaty? . . . There are a lot of methods in the world that have never been tried yet." Was FDR trying to lead public opinion in a new direction or merely testing the waters himself?

Public reaction to the speech remained as confused as Roosevelt's remarks. Leading urban newspapers such as the *New York Times* and the *Washington Post* endorsed his call. But a public opinion poll also indicated that given a choice between Congress and the president on the issue of keeping America out of war, only 31 percent backed the president. Some isolationists, noting that Roosevelt proposed nothing specific, greeted the "quarantine" address as an endorsement of continued neutrality in a world teetering on the brink of further conflicts. A far larger number denounced the president for proposing to inject the United States into conflicts from Spain to China. Congressman Hamilton Fish from FDR's Hyde Park district said the president ought to be impeached. Several magazines claimed he was beating the drums for war.

If Roosevelt had a major plan to reorient American foreign policy in the fall of 1937, he kept it to himself and it has remained a well-guarded secret ever since. He did favor Sumner Welles's idea of a major address to the Washington diplomatic corps that would have appealed for a world conference to attack the issues of arms control, trade barriers, and neutral rights. Prime Minister Neville Chamberlain, about to embark on a strategy to satisfy the Italians and Germans with concessions, thought little of Roosevelt's scheme, however. Without England's support the president believed it useless to go ahead. He never spoke to the diplomats.

While Roosevelt seemed without direction in the wake of the "quarantine" speech and the *Panay* incident, Congress showed no ambivalence. The House of Representatives nearly gave a vote of approval to Congressman Louis Ludlow's constitutional amendment that would have required a popular referendum before Congress could declare war. The amendment had been buried in the House Judiciary Committee since Ludlow introduced it in 1935, but by the end of 1937, especially after the sinking of the *Panay*, he had secured the necessary 219 signatures to force a vote by the full House. Ludlow lost, but it was close, 209–188. Only intense lobbying by Roosevelt, his key political advisers, and the entire Democratic leadership in the House prevented consideration of this fundamental restructuring of the Constitution.

Roosevelt's "quarantine" speech soon passed from the front pages. With the demise of Welles's plan and the narrow defeat of the Ludlow amendment, the isolationists continued to ride high in the United States. In Europe, the initiative passed to Chamberlain and his policy of appeasement.

Epilogue: The Road to War

> *This decision [to aid Britain] is the end of any attempts at appeasement . . . the end of compromise with tyranny and the forces of oppression.*
> —FDR after signing the Lend-Lease Act

THE COLLAPSE OF APPEASEMENT

In his diary during the final days of August 1939, the head of the State Department's European division, Jay Pierrepont Moffat, wrote: "These last two days have given me the feeling of sitting in a house where somebody is dying upstairs. There is relatively little to do and yet the suspense continues unabated." Four days later, on September 1, German tanks, spearheading an invasion force of over a million men, rolled into Poland while German pilots, seasoned in Spain, reduced much of Warsaw to rubble. The Poles surrendered within a week, but on September 3, Britain and France, choosing finally to honor their treaty obligations, had declared war on Hitler's Reich. From the narrow defeat of the Ludlow amendment in early 1938 to the German invasion of Poland eighteen months later, the government of the United States had been little more than a spectator to Europe's unfolding tragedy.

—With German troops marshaled on Austria's borders in March 1938, the Austrian government gave the reins of power to one of the country's leading Nazis, who quickly invited in Hitler's forces to preserve law and order. The unification of the two nations, prohibited by the Versailles Treaty, was officially completed a month later in a plebiscite conducted under the shadow of Hitler's guns. The Führer told the world that as in the case of the Rhineland, he was only reuniting Germans in pursuit of the self-determination so lauded by Woodrow Wilson. Neville Chamberlain told the House of Commons much the same thing.

—Hitler next turned his ambitions toward the three million ethnic Germans living in the Sudeten region of Czechoslovakia, the last bastion of democratic government in Central Europe, a nation possessed of a well-trained and well-equipped army and formally allied with France and the Soviet Union. Pressured by the French and British, the Czechs offered greater autonomy to the Sudeten minority in September 1938, but Hitler raised the ante by demanding outright cession of the territory with a deadline of early October.

—Discounting Soviet vows to stand by the Czechs militarily and their own intelligence reports that indicated a probable coup against the Führer if war came, the British and French capitulated again. At the notorious Munich Conference, attended by Hitler, Chamberlain, Premier Edouard Daladier of France, and Mussolini at the end of September, the Czechs were forced to give up the Sudetenland—which left them militarily defenseless—in return for Germany's promises that it would make no further territorial demands in Europe. Munich, Chamberlain told his people, brought "peace with honor" and "peace for our time." Hitler, he told Ambassador Kennedy, resembled a boa constrictor "that had eaten a good deal and was trying to digest the meal before taking on anything else."

—On November 7, 1938, in retaliation for the shooting of a German diplomat in Paris by a young Jew, the German government unleashed a reign of terror against its Jews, "Crystal Night," so named from all the broken windows left when mobs burned and looted synagogues, homes, and shops. Hundreds died in the rioting.

—On March 15, 1939, breaking his word to Chamberlain, Hitler sent his army into Bohemia-Moravia, the Czech portion of Czechoslovakia. With Czechoslovakia erased from the map, he now demanded from Warsaw the port of Danzig and the Polish Corridor. Almost simultaneously, Mussolini invaded Albania.

—Stalin, weakened by the purge of his best generals and sensing correctly that the British and French hoped to turn the German war machine against him, tried to buy time and territory. He astonished the world on August 23, 1939, by signing a nonagression pact with Hitler. The Soviets thus bought themselves time to prepare for Hitler's panzers; the Germans gained a respite from a two-front war. Secret protocols of this agreement gave each party a slice of Poland and the Baltic states in the event of a general war—which arrived two weeks later.

Chamberlain, Daladier, and other spokesmen for appeasement in England and France had allowed Hitler to steal the military advantage in Europe. Prior to September 1, they also believed, mistakenly, that the Führer and his Nazi regime were simply traditional instruments of German national self-interest who would be satisfied once the most obvious territorial defects of the Versailles settlement had been corrected. The invasion of Poland destroyed that illusion in Europe, but it gave fresh ammunition to American isolationists and pro-Germans. No European country could defeat Hitler, they argued; the democracies were bankrupt, and the United States should avoid being dragged into the conflict by hysterical Jews.

Joseph P. Kennedy, the American ambassador in London, spoke for many of them when he said the United States "would be very foolish

"The Harvest" (caption). Daniel Fitzpatrick expressed the outrage of many in the wake of Hitler's triumph at Munich.

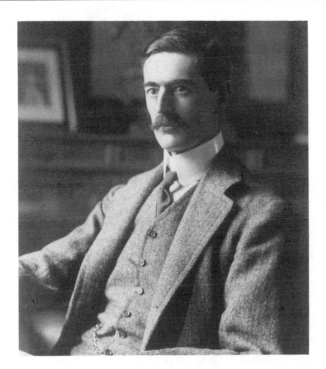

Neville Chamberlain, architect of appeasement.

to try and mix in." One of FDR's original brain trusters, Adolf Berle, now in the State Department, thought Hitler "the only instrument capable of reestablishing a race and economic unit which can . . . leave Europe in balance," a view shared by Charles A. Lindbergh, who pronounced the German leader "undoubtedly a great man." William C. Bullitt, the former American ambassador to the Soviet Union, who had once described his Russian counterpart as "a wretched little kike," advised Roosevelt to instruct the FBI "to keep an especially vigilant eye on the Jewish refugees from Germany," while another State Department veteran referred to Nazi anti-Semitism as "a purely domestic matter and none of our concern."

The president of the United States, tied down by isolationist chains that he had often helped to forge, watched these tragic events unfold with a mixture of revulsion and resignation. He continued to send mixed signals to his own advisers, the British, the French, and Adolf Hitler. Hearing that Chamberlain had agreed to meet the German leader at Munich, FDR cabled the prime minister: "Good man." He informed Hitler that the United States "will assume no obligations in the conduct of the present negotiations," and following the conference he told Chamberlain that "there exists today the greatest opportunity in years for the establishment of a new order based on justice and on law." Privately, Roosevelt thought the results at Munich had been a moral and political calamity; publicly, he took no steps to reverse it.

At the same time, Roosevelt listened sympathetically to other of his advisers who loathed Hitler and the Nazis. Ickes, Morgenthau, and Frankfurter all warned him of the Führer's insatiable appetite for conquest and the violent prejudices against religious and ethnic minorities that helped to fuel it. When the results of Munich became known, the president compared the British and French to Judas Iscariot and told the British ambassador that American public opinion would have a hard time accepting the sacrifices required of the Czechs. In the aftermath of Crystal Night, he recalled the American ambassador in Berlin and told journalists he "could scarcely believe that such things could occur in a twentieth-century civilization." Unlike Wilson in 1914, FDR told a radio audience on September 3, "I cannot ask that every American remain neutral in thought. . . . Even a neutral cannot be asked to close his mind or his conscience." Few mistook his meaning. In the fall of 1939, FDR had neither the authority not the desire to fight Hitler, but morally he remained light-years away from the mentality of the Kennedys, Berles, Lindberghs, and Bullitts.

RETHINKING NEUTRALITY

While the fall of Poland dealt a death blow to appeasement in Europe, it also opened the first crack in the American wall of isolationism. On September 8, Roosevelt told reporters that he would call Congress into special session to consider repeal of the arms embargo provisions of the neutrality law. Two weeks later in a major address to Congress, he asked for legislation permitting nations to buy arms from the United States so long as they carried them away in their own vessels. This "cash-and-carry" principle, the president declared, was in the tradition of true neutrality from which the nation had erroneously departed in 1935. He did not seek to modify the existing ban on loans or travel by Americans on belligerent ships, but the proposal called down the fury of the isolationists nonetheless. Borah, Nye, Wheeler, and La Follette led the charge in Congress against what they called Roosevelt's scheme "to send the boys of American mothers to fight on the battlefield of Europe." Former president Hoover, Lindbergh, and Norman Thomas fought the plan, too.

The administration countered by enlisting prominent Republicans, including Governor Landon and Frank Knox, the president's opponents in 1936; Hoover's secretary of state, Henry Stimson; and the celebrated newspaper editor William Allen White, who organized a Non-Partisan Committee for Peace Through Revision of the Neutrality Act. Even Al Smith dropped his anti–New Deal rhetoric long enough to make a radio speech backing Roosevelt's plan. At the end of October the repeal bill passed the Senate handily and the House by a sixty-two-vote margin, although many members probably shared the reservations of Senator Vandenberg: "I do not believe that we can become an arsenal for one belligerent without becoming a target for another."

BLITZKRIEG

Roosevelt and his supporters won the repeal fight by invoking the traditional rights of neutrals, appealing to the economic self-interest of groups who stood to benefit from the war trade, and by arguing that the surest way to keep America at peace was to help England and France defeat Hitler. No one doubted that Germany's adversaries would reap the greatest benefits from "cash-and-carry," because of Britain's ability to keep open the sea lanes with her superior naval power. But in late 1939, Roosevelt did not regard repeal of the arms embargo as part of a master plan to maneuver the United States into war. Neither he nor anyone else then anticipated the speed with which Hitler's forces would bring fresh disaster to Western Europe in the spring and summer of 1940:

—On April 9, German Troops occupied Denmark and Norway "to defend their true neutrality."
—Claiming that England and France were about to invade them, Hitler sent his forces into Belgium, Holland, and Luxembourg on May 10.
—On May 14, the day the Dutch surrendered, German tanks cut through the Ardennes Forest and outflanked the "impregnable" Maginot Line along the Franco-German border. Other panzers smashed the French army at Sedan and drove toward the English Channel, where they pinned down English and French troops in the town of Dunkirk.

Adolf Hitler addresses Nazi youth at Nuremberg Stadium.

Beginning on May 26, with the aid of over eight hundred private craft of every size and shape, the British managed to evacuate nearly 350,000 soldiers from the besieged town, thereby averting an even greater military calamity.

—France surrendered on June 21, 1940, only six weeks after the first German tank crossed the Dutch border.

—In August, backed by nearly two thousand bombers and eleven hundred fighter planes, Hitler began Operation Eagle to destroy the British air force in the skies and British morale on the ground as a prelude to an invasion of the island. "I've seen some horrible sights in this city during these days and nights," reported American radio commentator Edward R. Murrow from London in September, "but not once have I heard man, woman, or child suggest that Britain should throw in her hand. These people are angry. How much they can stand I don't know."

FAREWELL TO NEUTRALITY

Hitler's assault on Poland destroyed the illusions of most Europeans about the intentions of the Nazi regime. Newsreels of the British retreat at Dunkirk and of the Führer riding up the Champs Élysées shattered America's. Saddened by the spectacle, songwriter Oscar Hammerstein wrote his mournful "The Last Time I Saw Paris." A frightened Congress quickly appropriated more money for national defense. Roosevelt had asked for 2 billion in early January, but even before the French surrender, the House and Senate had boosted that figure with FDR's approval to over $4.5 billion. During the historic debate, critics pointed out that the United States could not protect the Panama Canal, that the size of the nation's army placed it nineteenth in the world, and that Italy's air force had greater firepower. The administration asked for and received another $5 billion, which brought the total defense appropriation for 1940 to over $10.5 billion. That spending stimulated the economy. By 1941 the Depression was officially over.

So was the era of American neutrality and isolationism, although its burial would not be made official until Roosevelt signed the Lend-Lease Act on March 11, 1941. The six months between passage of the Defense Appropriation Act of 1940 in September and Lend-Lease witnessed one of the great sea changes in the history of American foreign relations, punctuated by a presidential election and political warfare between president and Congress as brutal as any since the creation of the republic. Apart from the Hundred Days, Roosevelt never faced a series of more difficult or important decisions; they would shape the destiny of America and the world for decades to come.

The first concerned atomic energy. A month prior to the German invasion of Poland, New York banker and economist Alexander Sachs brought Roosevelt a letter written by Albert Einstein and Hungarian émigré physicist Leo Szilard which warned that German scientists had already accomplished nuclear fission and that "extremely powerful bombs of a new type may thus be constructed." Roosevelt passed the Einstein-Szilard letter along to his staff with the note "this requires action," and although top Army brass dismissed the idea as preposterous, Szilard and his associates wheedled several thousand dollars out of the War Department to begin experiments. At the moment of the fall of France, an official Advisory Committee on Uranium had been meeting for several months in Washington. A joint British-American research effort commenced in the summer of 1940. By the end of 1940 a major contract had been given to Columbia University to develop the ideas of Szilard and Enrico Fermi, a refugee from Mussolini's regime. The Manhattan Project, with unpredictable consequences for the entire human race, had begun.

Quickly shrouded in secrecy, Roosevelt's executive decision to pursue the development of nuclear fission did not provoke a spirited public debate. It was otherwise with his decision to provide the English with the chance to buy surplus U.S. military equipment and to give Great Britain fifty overage American destroyers. In exchange for the destroyers, the British government, now headed by Winston Churchill, agreed to transfer to the United States naval bases on British possessions in the Western Hemisphere and never to surrender its fleet to Germany. Opponents of the proposed swap said it would be difficult to imagine a less neutral action by the United States. Supporters pointed out that if Hitler crippled the British navy and thereby cut England's economic lifeline across the Atlantic, the Battle of Britain would soon be over. America would be the Third Reich's next target.

Replenishing the British fleet with surplus American destroyers could be regarded as a purely defensive act, however, intended to bolster England's war effort and to give the United States time to secure its Fortress America against any German attack. From May, when Churchill made his plea, until late August, Roosevelt hesitated. He feared that isolationists would raise an outcry in Congress, that public opinion would not tolerate the aid to Britain, and that the Republicans would exploit the issue in the fall campaign. The nation's laws also seemed against him, because Congress had specifically prohibited the transfer of any American warship unless the chief of naval operations certified it was "not essential to the defense of the United States."

William Allen White, now leading a nationwide Committee to Defend America by Aiding the Allies—it included both rabid interventionists and old-fashioned nationalists—lectured FDR that he would never lead the American people "unless you catch up with them." White's committee, mobilizing the likes of World War I hero General John J. Pershing, mounted an intensive publicity campaign on behalf of the destroyer deal. The exchange, they argued, would actually keep the U.S. out of war. He persuaded Republican candidate Wendell Willkie to endorse the swap, while lawyers for the committee came up with the arguments that allowed the chief of naval operations to certify the exchange on the grounds that the British bases made a net addition to American national defense.

Churchill, choking on the territorial transfer, proved a bigger obstacle than some of the isolationists in Congress. "I told Winston," Roosevelt reported, "those places are nothing but a headache to you. . . . They cost the British Treasury five million pounds—nearly twenty-five million dollars—every year. They are nothing but a headache." The prime minister later complained that the president of the United States had gotten the best of the deal after his admirals told him the American ships were "the worst destroyers . . . ever seen, poor seaboats with appalling armaments and accommodations." The destroyers may not have saved Britain in 1940, but they symbolized as dramatic a shift in American policy as the first peacetime draft, approved also by Congress in September 1940, the same month Germany and Japan signed a formal ten-year military and economic alliance.

THE NONDEBATE

Roosevelt and his allies had thrown the isolationists on the defensive by outvoting them on the arms embargo, defense spending, and the draft. The president and White's committee had outmaneuvered them, too, on the destroyers-for-bases agreement, which 70 percent of the American people soon endorsed in one opinion poll. Only one thing could save the isolationist cause—an election. They hoped to turn the 1940 presidential race into a referendum on the future of American foreign policy. With Roosevelt's intentions unclear until the Democratic convention opened in early July, they banked on the Republicans' nominating either Michigan senator Arthur Vandenberg, Ohio senator Robert Taft, or youthful New York district attorney Thomas Dewey. All of these potential candidates had expressed skepticism to one degree or another about American aid to the beleaguered Allies. A major surprise greeted them in Philadelphia, however, when an enthusiastic band of amateurs stole the nomination for Wendell Lewis Willkie, a former utility executive, the darling of Henry Luce and many progressive businessmen who read *Fortune* magazine.

Willkie had waged a long battle against both TVA and PWA on behalf of his utility companies, but he had voted for FDR in 1932, remained a registered Democrat until 1938, and earned the respect of New Dealers such as Ben Cohen. Bright, eloquent, and tireless, the Indiana native was destined to be Roosevelt's most formidable political opponent. To the chagrin of the isolationists, however, he proved to be an outspoken internationalist; he called for aid to England short of war, endorsed the destroyer-for-bases agreement, and later pushed for Lend-Lease. He also wrote *One World*, a piece of vintage Wilsonianism that sold millions of copies after Pearl Harbor.

Willkie's candidacy effectively eliminated a serious foreign policy debate from the 1940 campaign once FDR came down off the fence and orchestrated a convention "draft" for an unprecedented third term.

Republican presidential candidate Wendell Willkie campaigns in Elwood, Indiana, 1940.

"I do not want to run," he told Morgenthau early in the year, "unless between now and the convention things get very, very much worse in Europe." Hitler's tank commanders cast the decisive vote. Following the fall of France, FDR reached out for moderate Republicans and outflanked Willkie by luring two GOP veterans into his cabinet, Frank Knox as secretary of the navy and Henry Stimson for the War Department. Roosevelt also faced the realization that the leading contenders should he drop out—Vice President Garner, Postmaster General Jim Farley, and Hull—seemed to be either politicians he hated (Garner), those who had no experience in foreign affairs (Garner and Farley), or those who did not share his liberalism on domestic issues (Garner, Farley, and Hull).

The campaign degenerated quickly into a nasty brawl and a contest over who could make the more extravagant promises about keeping the nation out of war while fighting Hitler by aiding the British. After backing Roosevelt's horse trade with Churchill, Willkie turned around and denounced Roosevelt for not seeking the approval of Congress. It was, he said, "the most dictatorial and arbitrary act of any president in the history of the United States." By returning FDR to the White House, the Republican candidate told a Baltimore audience, "you may expect we will be at war."

Democratic Party propagandists tossed around equally wild accusations. They tried to link Willkie with the German-American Bund and Mussolini's black-shirted legions. His father was described as a drunkard, and Willkie himself was branded as a union-busting capitalist who opposed civil rights for Negroes. "You can't say that everyone who is opposed to Roosevelt is pro-Nazi," the president remarked in September, "but you *can* say with truth that everyone who is pro-Hitler in this country is also pro-Willkie." The Democratic platform had declared that America would not fight unless attacked; in Boston near the end of the campaign, FDR distinguished that proviso from the conflict abroad. "Your boys," he pledged, "are not going to be sent into any foreign war."

With the solid backing of organized labor and Northern blacks, Roosevelt won an impressive victory in the electoral college, 449 to 82, and commanded 54.8 percent of the popular vote, 27,244,160 to Willkie's 22,305,198. For FDR, the landslide could not compare with 1936, but

FDR tells Rochester audience America will not fight in a foreign war.

then Willkie's numbers would not be bettered by a Republican until Eisenhower ran in 1952.

H.R. 1776

The great debate over American foreign policy that did not materialize during the fall election soon erupted. On December 17, Roosevelt met reporters in the White House and explained to them the dire military and financial conditions facing Great Britain. German submarines continued to take a heavy toll on her merchant fleet and navy. More critically, she would run out of hard currency within six months, according to Churchill, and not be able to make further purchases in the United States under the cash-and-carry provisions of the revised Neutrality Act. Since England's defense remained America's security from war, Roosevelt proposed "eliminat[ing] the dollar sign" by leasing war materials to her. If your neighbor's house caught fire and he had no garden hose, he told the reporters, the prudent thing to do in order to prevent the fire from spreading was to lend him your hose. In one of his most persuasive fireside chats two weeks later, FDR reaffirmed that aid to England was America's insurance policy against war. He saw America as "the great arsenal of democracy."

The legislation sent by the administration to Congress in early January, symbolically numbered H.R. 1776, made a grant of power to the president unprecedented in American history. It authorized him "to sell, transfer title to, exchange, lease, lend, or otherwise dispose of" any defense material to any government that he judged "vital to the defense of the United States." A specific appropriation measure, authorizing the expenditure of $7 billion for Lend-Lease, moved through Congress almost simultaneously. In the wake of France's defeat and the air battle raging over Britain, Roosevelt and his allies in Congress banked on a decisive shift in public sentiment. They were right.

Faced with opinion polls that clearly backed the White House and dwindling support in Congress, isolationists put on a last-ditch stand to rally the country and defeat Lend-Lease. The America First Committee, organized in the summer of 1940 by the heir to the Quaker Oats fortune and including on its roster of supporters Charles Lindbergh, Eddie Rickenbacker, Henry Ford, Alice Roosevelt, and Lillian Gish, denounced the plan as a cunning plot to draw the nation into war. Lindbergh, shocking many of his supporters, singled out American Jews as the "principal war agitators" who favored H.R. 1776 and manipulated America through their control of Hollywood, radio, and the press.

The Lend-Lease fight produced some strange alliances. The communists, arguing that Churchill was no better than Hitler, lined up with the Lone Eagle. So did many liberal isolationists, including one of the country's greatest living historians, Charles A. Beard. Sensing defeat even so, an angry Senator Wheeler compared Lend-Lease to the Triple A. It would, he said, "plow under every fourth American boy." Roosevelt never forgave him. "That really is the rottenest thing that has been said in public life in my generation," he told reporters for the record.

With the support of Willkie, other moderate Republicans, and most Southern Democrats, however, the result in the House and Senate was never in doubt. But the administration had to accept some restrictive amendments that limited Lend-Lease appropriations to six months. Roosevelt signed the historic measure on March 11. America took a fateful step with Lend-Lease. "This decision," Roosevelt declared, "is the end of any attempts at appeasement . . . the end of compromise with tyranny and the forces of oppression." Hitler took an equally fateful decision three months later, when along a nine-hundred-mile front from the Baltic to the Black Sea he invaded the Soviet Union. He predicted victory in six weeks.

A great many Americans, including Senator Harry Truman of Missouri, outraged by the earlier Nazi-Soviet pact and Stalin's attack on Finland, thought it would be a good idea for the United States to give aid to whichever dictator appeared to be losing, thereby helping to kill as many fascists and communists as possible. Roosevelt rejected such ideas and did not hesitate long in making the Russians eligible for Lend-Lease. He agreed with Churchill, who remarked that "if Hitler invaded Hell, I would at least make favorable reference to the Devil in the House of Commons."

Lend-Lease contained provisions forbidding American naval vessels from convoying merchant ships and barring any American vessel from entering a combat zone in violation of earlier neutrality legislation. Notwithstanding, by summer American destroyers were sailing the Atlantic on "neutrality patrols" to alert British ships to the menace of German submarines. Three were attacked between September 4 and October 30, including the *Reuben James*, with the loss of ninety-six officers and men. The Gallup Poll revealed that 12 percent of the American public backed an immediate declaration of war on Germany, while 60 percent wanted to continue aid to Britain, even at the risk of conflict. As fall turned to the winter of 1941 in the North Atlantic, it seemed they would soon have their wish.

THE OTHER WAR

Mirroring the sentiments of the people he had led for nearly a decade, the president of the United States in 1941 prepared to go forward with aid to Great Britain and the Soviet Union even if it meant a shooting war with Hitler's submarines in the North Atlantic. That much can be stated with certainty about his policies, but it remains a far cry from saying that he desired war in 1941 with Germany or thought it inevitable. At times he appeared to believe that sufficient material aid to Churchill and later to Stalin would turn the tide against the Third Reich without a large-scale American military commitment beyond naval convoys and armed merchant ships. But the other war across the Pacific altered these calculations.

Since the *Panay* incident, Roosevelt and his advisers had pursued two parallel but ultimately contradictory policies with respect to Japan. On the one hand they would negotiate with Japan both in the hope of a peaceful resolution to the war in China and in order to buy more time to strengthen the pitifully weak American military presence in the Pacific. But they were also determined to employ economic sanctions against Japan in an effort to loosen her grip on China and discourage her military advance against the remaining outposts of European colonialism in East Asia. In the end, the sanctions outpaced the negotiations and left Japan's military-dominated government with little choice but to wage an offensive war against the United States if it hoped to achieve the nation's imperial ambitions in the region.

Roosevelt and Hull have been harshly criticized by some historians for the choices they made with respect to Japan between September 1939 and December 1941. These critics hold that the United States could have reached a *modus vivendi* with Japan's rulers to avoid an immediate two-front war and all of its horrible consequences. Some still accuse Roosevelt of willfully driving the Japanese into a corner with the intention of provoking an armed attack. Both conclusions are dubious.

Armed struggle between Japan and the United States was not inevitable after 1939, but highly probable given the history of their relations, the manifold domestic pressures in both nations, and the disintegrating international situation produced by war in Europe. The leaders of both nations would have had to overcome a legacy of racial bigotry and chauvinism that produced stereotypes of frightening proportions. Roosevelt himself regarded the Japanese as physically and mentally inferior to whites, and as ruthless barbarians who displayed little regard for human life. The Japanese, in turn, viewed the Americans as rapacious, violent agents of Western imperialism. They were "white devils" who along with the British, French, and Dutch had oppressed Asians for centuries and looted their countries.

Viewing other Asians as inferior, too, the Japanese sought to replace European hegemony with their own Greater East Asia Co-Prosperity Sphere. Chinese, Koreans, Vietnamese, Filipinos, and Indonesians would serve Tokyo rather than London, Paris, or Washington. Once Hitler had swept through the Netherlands and France and begun his assault on England, the Japanese could hardly resist a temptation to pluck a few prizes for themselves—the Dutch East Indies, French Indochina, and British Malaya and Burma with their rich stores of petroleum, rubber, and other raw materials. From the American perspective, Japanese suzerainty over these colonies would deal another material and morale blow to those fighting Hitler in Europe and menace her own economic stake in Asia, too.

And then there was China. In the end, it proved the biggest obstacle of all. Both Japan and the United States had long looked upon the country with a mixture of contempt, paternalism, and commercial interest. For nearly a half century, the United States had pledged its solemn word to the territorial integrity and independence of China, but had made only token investments there of either capital or military resources. In comparison, Japan had made a substantial economic commitment in China following her conquest of Manchuria. By 1940–41 she had deployed close to two million soldiers on the mainland. To demand of the Japanese government, as the United States continued to do through the fall and early winter of 1941, that it pull these troops out of China was to demand the impossible. The Japanese military leaders in the cabinet would not have allowed it. Further, such a disengagement would have meant the reintegration of troops into Japan's domestic society. On the other hand, neither Roosevelt not any American leader after Munich could throw in the China card as part of a settlement with Japan. To do so would invite charges of appeasement and a huge political firestorm.

Far from being a hawk on the matter of economic sanctions against Japan, Roosevelt held out for a long time against the pleas of three powerful cabinet members, Ickes, Morgenthau, and Stimson, that he

War in Europe and Asia presents FDR and the New Dealers with some hard choices.

use sanctions both to punish Japan's aggression in China and to discourage her from moving against the Dutch East Indies and Indochina. England and France were fading factors in the Far East. With the creation of a puppet, pro-Nazi Vichy regime in France and the beginning of German air attacks on England, the Japanese demanded that both countries shut down supply routes from Indochina and Burma into China. To the chagrin of the Americans who hoped to keep Chinese resistance alive, Vichy and London complied. Acting under provisions of the National Defense Act of 1940, which empowered the president to prohibit the export of any materials he deemed vital to the national defense, Roosevelt retaliated against Japan by cutting off trade in forty critical materials in the summer of 1940, but he left both scrap iron and petroleum untouched.

For the next twelve months, a furious battle raged inside the administration. Hull wanted the United States to proceed cautiously on extending the embargo. Ickes, Morgenthau, and Stimson argued passionately that fuel oil propelled the Japanese navy and high-octane gasoline lifted her airplanes, and that over 90 percent of these products came from the United States of America. Morgenthau scorned those in the State Department who, he said, believed "Japan is going to come over and kiss our big toe and say 'We love you, darling.'" Ickes was furious with Roosevelt's inaction on scrap iron and oil. "Oh, hell," he remarked, "it ought to have been done . . . first. . . . The way they piddle around here!"

Anti-Japanese sentiment in the country supported the administration hawks. FDR might have exploited it, but he sided with the State Department, fearful that an embargo on oil would encourage a Japanese attack on the Dutch East Indies, expand the war in the Pacific, and make more difficult the defeat of Hitler. "I simply have not got enough Navy to go around," an angry Roosevelt told his secretary of the interior, "and every little episode in the Pacific means fewer ships in the Atlantic."

Between the summer of 1940 and the summer of 1941, therefore, Roosevelt allowed the Japanese to purchase and store four million barrels of aviation fuel and ten million barrels of fuel oil. Only when the Japanese occupied Indochina in July 1941 and seemed poised to strike from there at the Dutch East Indies did FDR finally freeze Japan's assets in the United States. That turned off the American petroleum spigot. Even then, he worried that the decision would "tip the delicate scales and cause Japan to decide to attack Russia or to attack the Dutch East Indies," either of which he regarded as a serious setback in the struggle against Hitler.

Roosevelt read correctly Japan's response to the freeze, but he was wrong about its precise location. The Japanese military had already decided to avoid conflict with the Soviet Union in favor of a strike to the south against the Netherlands Indies, but the success of that enterprise would also depend on neutralizing the British at Singapore as well as the American forces in the Philippines and its Pacific fleet in Hawaii. At a fateful meeting with the emperor on November 5, 1941, Japan's military and civilian rulers agreed that unless a settlement could be reached with the United States within twenty days, conflict was inevitable. "Rather than await extinction," Prime Minister Tojo told his cabinet, "it were better to face death by breaking through the encircling ring and find a way for existence." Two days later, Japan's leaders even fixed a date for war with the United States—December 8, Tokyo time—if negotiations failed to yield results.

Secretary of State Cordell Hull (center) escorts Japanese representatives Nomura (left) and Kurusu to the White House.

Japan's terms for a settlement were not promising. The United States would have to resume trade in oil while accepting the status quo in China. In the winter of 1941, no American president could realistically make that deal. When Hull and Roosevelt turned it down, the Japanese government decided on war. It was December 1. Under radio silence, a flotilla of Japanese surface vessels and submarines was then already en route to Hawaii. On board the aircraft carrier *Akagi*, officers and pilots studied maps of Oahu and a mock-up of the American naval base at Pearl Harbor.

Suggestions for Additional Reading and Notes on Sources

On the assumption that most people who read this book will wish to deepen their general understanding of particular historical controversies and events rather than conduct independent research, I have refrained in this bibliography from listing relevant manuscript collections housed at the Library of Congress, the National Archives, and presidential libraries at West Branch, Iowa, and Hyde Park, New York. I have also not noted the many newspapers and periodicals that I consulted, such as the *New York Times*, the *Wall Street Journal*, the *American Mercury*, *Fortune*, the *Ladies' Home Journal*, the *New Republic*, the *Saturday Evening Post*, and the *Nation*.

PART ONE

1. Republican Restoration

A number of works that survey the postwar decade have achieved the status of classics and should be read by any serious student of the period. These include Frederick Lewis Allen's *Only Yesterday: An Informal History of the 1920s* (New York, 1931); Arthur M. Schlesinger, Jr., *The Crisis of the Old Order* (New York, 1957); William E. Leuchtenburg, *The Perils of Prosperity, 1914–1932* (Chicago, 1958); John D. Hicks, *Republican Ascendancy, 1921–1933* (New York, 1960); and Arthur S. Link, "What Happened to the Progressive Movement in the 1920s?" *American Historical Review* 64 (1959), 833–51. Still useful for their insight into how historians have viewed the era are Henry F. May, "Shifting Perspectives on the 1920's," *Mississippi Valley Historical Review* 43 (1956), 405–27; and Burl Noggle, "The Twenties: A New Historiographical Frontier," *Journal of American History* 53 (1966), 299–314.

The best accounts of the impact of World War I upon American society and the progressive movement are David Kennedy, *Over Here: The First World War and American Society* (New York, 1980); and chapters 10 and 11 in John Milton Cooper, Jr., *Pivotal Decades: The United States, 1900-1920* (New York, 1990). For the tragic end of the Wilson administration see Gene Smith, *When the Cheering Stopped: The Last Years of Woodrow Wilson* (New York, 1964). The presidential election of 1920 is detailed in Wesley M. Bagby, *The Road to Normalcy: The Presidential Campaign and Election of 1920* (Baltimore, 1962).

The suppression of civil liberties during and immediately after the conflict is treated in Paul L. Murphy, *World War I and the Origins of Civil Liberties* (New York, 1970); Harry N. Scheiber, *The Wilson Administration and Civil Liberties, 1917–1921* (Ithaca, N.Y., 1960); Robert K. Murray, *Red Scare: A Study in National Hysteria, 1919–1920* (Minneapolis, 1955); Michal Belknap, "The Mechanics of Repression: J. Edgar Hoover, the Bureau of Investigation and the Radicals, 1917–1925," *Crime and Social Justice* 7 (1977); and two works by Stanley Coben, *A. Mitchell Palmer* (New York, 1962) and "A Study in Nativism: The American Red Scare of 1919–20," *Political Science Quarterly* 79 (1964), 52–75.

On the racial violence of the immediate postwar period see Lee E. Williams, *Anatomy of Four Race Riots: Racial Conflict in Knoxville, Elaine, Tulsa, and Chicago, 1919–1921* (Hattiesburg, Miss., 1972); and William M. Tuttle, *Race Riot: Chicago in the Red Summer of 1919* (New York, 1970). Two of the most important labor strikes are analyzed in Robert L. Friedheim, *The Seattle General Strike* (Seattle, 1964); Francis Russell, *A City in Terror: 1919, the Boston Police Strike* (New York, 1975); and Jonathan R. White, "A Triumph of Bureaucracy: The Boston Police Strike and the Ideological Origins of the American Police Structure" (Ph.D. dissertation, University Microfilms, 1982).

The best biography of Warren G. Harding remains Francis Russell, *The Shadow of Blooming Grove* (New York, 1968), but it should be supplemented with Randolph C. Downes, *The Rise of Warren Gamaliel Harding, 1865–1920* (Columbus, Ohio, 1970); and Charles L. Mee, *The Ohio Gang: The World of Warren G. Harding* (New York: 1981). Robert K. Murray has written two excellent studies of the administration's overall approach to public policy: *The Harding Era: Warren G. Harding and His Administration* (Minneapolis, 1969) and *The Politics of Normalcy: Governmental Theory and Practice in the Harding-Collidge Era* (New York, 1973). A useful perspective is also provided by Eugene P. Trani and David L. Wilson, *The Presidency of Warren G. Harding* (Lawrence, Kan., 1977). For the Teapot Dome affair, two scholars have separated fact from fiction: J. Leonard Bates, *The Origins of Teapot Dome: Progressives, Parties, and Petroleum, 1909–1921* (Urbana, Ill., 1963); and Burl Noggle, *Teapot Dome: Oil and Politics in the 1920s* (Baton Rouge, 1962).

On leading figures in Harding's administration see especially Betty Glad, *Charles Evans Hughes and the Illusion of Innocence: A Study in American Diplomacy* (Urbana, Ill., 1966); Donald Winters, *Henry Cantwell Wallace* (Urbana, Ill., 1970); Harvey O'Connor, *Mellon's Millions: The Biography of a Fortune* (New York, 1933); Ellis W. Hawley, ed., *Herbert Hoover as Secretary of Commerce, 1921–1928: Studies in New Era Thought and Practice* (Iowa City, 1981); and Gary D. Best, *The Politics of American Individualism: Herbert Hoover in Transition, 1918–1921* (Westport, Conn., 1975). The Supreme Court under William Howard Taft is dissected in Paul Murphy, *The Constitution in Crisis Times* (New York, 1972); and S. J. Konefsky, *The Legacy of Holmes and Brandeis: A Study in the Influence of Ideas* (New York, 1956).

On foreign relations in the immediate postwar period see Selig Adler, *The Uncertain Giant, 1921–1941: American Foreign Policy Between the Wars* (New York, 1965); and the now-classic essay by William A. Williams "The Legend of Isolationism in the 1920s," *Science and Society* 18 (1954), 1–20. On Secretary of State Hughes see Glad, *Charles Evans Hughes;* Nelson E. Woodward, "Postwar Reconstruction and International Order:

A Study of the Diplomacy of Charles Evans Hughes, 1923–1925" (Ph.D. dissertation, 1970); and Thomas Buckley, *The United States and the Washington Conference, 1921–1922* (Knoxville, Tenn., 1970). See also Kenneth J. Grieb, *The Latin American Policy of Warren G. Harding* (Fort Worth, Tex., 1976).

Specific social and economic policies of the Harding years can be traced in Frank W. Taussig, *The Tariff History of the United States* (8th ed., New York, 1931); Abraham Berglund, "The Tariff Act of 1922," *American Economic Review* 14 (1923), 13–33; John F. Witte, *The Politics and Development of the Federal Income Tax* (Madison, Wis., 1985); and Harold Wolozin, *American Fiscal and Monetary Policy* (Chicago, 1970). On the Sheppard-Towner Act see Shelia M. Rothman, *Woman's Proper Place: A History of Changing Ideals and Practices, 1870 to the Present* (New York, 1978), chapter 4; and Joseph B. Chepaitis, "The First Federal Social Welfare Measure: The Sheppard-Towner Maternity and Infancy Act, 1918–1932" (Ph.D. dissertation, 1968).

2. The Great Boom

Although published nearly a half century ago, George Soule's *Prosperity Decade: From War to Depression, 1917–1929* (New York, 1947) is still the best survey of broad postwar economic developments. It can be usefully supplemented by Stanley Lebergott, *The American Economy: Income, Wealth and Want* (Princeton, N.J., 1976).

On consumer culture the best place to start is with Susan Strasser, *Satisfaction Guaranteed: The Making of the American Mass Market* (New York, 1989); Richard Wightman Fox and T. J. Jackson Lears, eds., *The Culture of Consumption: Critical Essays in American History, 1880–1980* (New York, 1983); Stuart Ewen, *Captains of Consciousness: Advertising and the Social Roots of the Consumer Culture* (New York, 1976); and Peter d'Alroy Jones, *The Consumer Society: A History of American Capitalism* (Baltimore, 1965). An important contemporary statement is found in Stuart Chase, *The Economy of Abundance* (New York, 1934). Some of the social and intellectual consequences are examined in Daniel Horowitz, *The Morality of Spending: Attitudes Toward the Consumer Society in America, 1875–1940* (Baltimore, 1985); and Ronald Edsforth, *Class Conflict and Cultural Consensus: The Making of a Mass Consumer Society in Flint, Michigan* (New Brunswick, N.J., 1987). A recent critique is found in Michael Schudson, "Delectable Materialism: Were the Critics of Consumer Culture Wrong All Along?" *The American Prospect* 5 (1991), 26–35.

The impact of technology on economic productivity is examined in John H. Lorant, "Technological Change in American Manufacturing During the 1920's," *Journal of Economic History* 27 (1967), 243–46. On business corporations and economic innovation see the two path-breaking books by Alfred D. Chandler: *Strategy and Structure: Chapters in the History of the Industrial Enterprise* (Cambridge, Mass., 1962) and *The Visible Hand: The Managerial Revolution in American Business* (Cambridge, Mass., 1977). There are excellent studies of particular industries and firms. See, for example, Kenneth W. Bilby, *The General: David Sarnoff and the Rise of the Communications Industry* (New York, 1986); Robert Sobel, *RCA* (New York, 1986); Alfred D. Chandler and Stephen Salsbury, *Pierre S. Du Pont and the Making of the Modern Corporation* (New York, 1971); Marquis James, *The Texaco Story: The First Fifty Years, 1902–1952* (New York, 1953); John F. Magee, *Arthur D. Little, Inc.: At the Moving Frontier* (New York, 1986); Forrest McDonald, *Insull* (Chicago, 1962); and Harold L. Platt, *The Electric City: Energy and the Growth of the Chicago Area, 1880–1930* (Chicago, 1991).

The popular and scholarly literature on the American automobile industry and especially on Henry Ford and his company is voluminous. A good place to start is with James J. Flink, *The Car Culture* (Cambridge, Mass., 1975). Three key figures wrote firsthand accounts. See Henry Ford, *My Life and Work* (New York, 1922); Walter Chrysler, *Life of an American Workman* (New York, 1950); and Alfred P. Sloan, *My Years with General Motors* (New York, 1963). On the Ford Motor Company and its founder, the best single volume is Keith Sward, *The Legend of Henry Ford* (New York, 1948), which can be supplemented with Peter Collier and David Horowitz, *The Fords: An American Epic* (New York, 1987); Robert Lacey, *Ford: The Men and the Machine* (Boston, 1986); Reynold M. Wik, *Henry Ford and Grass-Roots America* (Ann Arbor, Mich., 1972); and Albert Lee, *Henry Ford and the Jews* (New York, 1980).

The early days of General Motors are traced in Sloan's autobiography and also in Lawrence R. Gustin, *Billy Durant: Creator of General Motors* (Grand Rapids, Mich., 1973); and Bernard A. Weisberger, *The Dream Maker: William C. Durant, Founder of General Motors* (Boston, 1979). A readable account of the Chrysler Corporation is found in Richard M. Langworth, *The Complete History of Chrysler Corporation, 1924–1985* (New York, 1985).

3. Puritan in Babylon

Donald R. McCoy has written a good recent study of Coolidge and his administration based on official presidential papers, *Calvin Coolidge: The Quiet President* (New York, 1967), but one should not fail to read what William Allen White penned over a half century ago in *A Puritan In Babylon: The Story of Calvin Coolidge* (New York, 1938). I also relied upon Robert K Murray, *The Politics of Normalcy*; Thomas B. Silver, *Coolidge and the Historians* (Durham, N.C., 1982); John McKee, *Coolidge Wit and Wisdom* (New York, 1933); Robert H. Ferrell and Howard H. Quint, eds., *The Talkative President: The Off-the-Record Press Conferences of Calvin Coolidge* (New York, 1964); Jules Abels, *In the Time of Silent Cal* (New York, 1969); and Coolidge's own *The Autobiography of Calvin Coolidge* (New York, 1929).

Murray's *The Politics of Normalcy* and McCoy's *Calvin Coolidge* contain good accounts of the domestic policies of the Coolidge years. On specific issues I also found helpful Preston J. Hubbard, *The Origins of the TVA: The Muscle Shoals Controversy, 1920-1932* (Nashville, Tenn., 1961); Lester V. Chandler, *Benjamin Strong: Central Banker* (Washington, D.C., 1958); and Carl McFarland, *Judicial Control of the Federal Trade Commission and the Interstate Commerce Commission, 1920–1930* (Cambridge, Mass., 1933).

An excellent account of the tangled war debts controversy can be found in William G. Pullen, *World War Debts and United States Foreign Policy, 1919–1929* (New York, 1987). See also Melvin Leffler, "The Origins of Republican War Debts Policy, 1921-1923: A Case Study in the Applicability of the Open Door Interpretation," *Journal of American History* 59 (1972), 585–601; and Richard H. Meyer, *Bankers' Diplomacy: Monetary Stabilization in the Twenties* (New York, 1970). On Frank Kellogg and the Peace of Paris see Lewis E. Ellis, *Frank B. Kellogg and American Foreign Relations, 1925–1929* (New Brunswick, N.J., 1961); Robert H. Ferrell, *Peace in Their Time: The Origins of the Kellogg-Briand Pact* (New Haven, Conn., 1952); and John C. Vinson, *William E. Borah and the Outlawry of War* (Athens, Ga., 1957).

On the United States and Nicaragua in the Coolidge era see Neill Macaulay, *The Sandino Affair* (Chicago, 1967); Godfrey Hodgson, *The Colonel: The Life and Wars of Henry Stimson, 1867–1950* (New York, 1990); Elting E. Morison, *Turmoil and Tradition: A Study of the Life and Times of Henry L. Stimson* (Boston, 1960); and Lejeune Cummins, "The Sandino Insurrection, 1927–1934" (Ph.D. dissertation, 1951). On the Good Neighbor Policy generally see Bryce Wood, *The Making of the Good Neighbor Policy* (New York, 1961). U.S.–Mexican relations are traced in Harold Nicolson, *Dwight Morrow* (New York, 1935); Wayne O. Gibson, "Ambassador Morrow and His Influence on the Calles Administration" (Ph.D. dissertation, 1952); and Christopher J. McMullen, "Calles and the Diplomacy of Revolution: Mexican-American Relations, 1924–1928" (Ph.D. dissertation, 1980).

The ordeal of the Democratic Party in 1924 and the presidential election of that year is treated in depth by David Burner, *The Politics of Provincialism: The Democratic Party in Transition, 1918–1932* (New York, 1967). Also useful are William H. Harbaugh, *Lawyer's Lawyer: The Life of John W. Davis* (New York, 1973); and Lawrence W. Levine, *Defender of the Faith: William Jennings Bryan, the Last Decade, 1915–1925* (New York, 1965).

4. Winners and Losers

On economic inequality and the distribution of income in the postwar period see Jeffrey Williamson and Peter Lindert, *American Inequality: A Macroeconomic History* (New York, 1981); Gabriel Kolko, *Wealth and Power in America* (New York, 1962); Charles Holt, "Who Benefited from the Prosperity of the Twenties?" *Explorations in Economic History* 14 (1977), 277–89; Gene Smiley, "Did Incomes for Most of the Population Fall From 1923 Through 1929?" *Journal of Economic History* 42 (1983), 209–16; and Robert Lampman, *The Share of Top Wealth-Holders in National Wealth, 1922–1956* (Princeton, N.J., 1962).

The rise of Hollywood and the motion picture industry is told in Neal Gabler, *An Empire of Their Own: How the Jews Invented Hollywood* (New York, 1988); Scott A. Berg, *Goldwyn: A Biography* (New York, 1989); Michael Freedland, *The Warner Brothers* (New York, 1983); Bosley Crowther, *Hollywood Rajah: The Life and Times of Louis B. Mayer* (New York, 1960); and David Robinson, *Hollywood in the Twenties* (London, 1968).

America's advertising industry has undergone provocative examination in Roland Marchand, *Advertising the American Dream: Making Way for Modernity, 1920–1940* (Berkeley, Calif., 1985); and Michael Schudson, *Advertising the Uneasy Persuasion: Its Dubious Impact on American Society* (New York, 1984). On Bruce Barton see the essay by T. J. Jackson Lears in Fox and Lears, *The Culture of Consumption;* as well as Bruce Barton, *More Power to You* (New York, 1922), *The Man Nobody Knows: A Discovery of Jesus* (Indianapolis, 1925), and *The Man of Galilee: Twelve Scenes from the Life of Christ* (New York, 1928).

The social and economic controversy over chain stores can be traced in Godfrey M. Lebhar, *Chain Stores in America, 1859–1950* (New York, 1952); Charles Daughters, *Wells of Discontent: A Study of the Economic, Social, and Political Aspects of the Chain Store* (New York, 1937); Theodore N. Beckman, *The Chain Store Problem: A Critical Analysis* (New York, 1938); and Stanley S. Kresge, *The S. S. Kresge Story* (Racine, Wis., 1979).

On the crisis in postwar agriculture see Clarence A. Wiley, *Agriculture and the Business Cycle Since 1920* (Madison, Wis., 1930); H. Thomas Johnson, "Postwar Optimism and the Rural Financial Crisis of the 1920s," *Explorations in Economic History* 11 (Winter 1973–74), 173–92; and Donald L. Winters, "Henry Cantwell Wallace and the Farm Crisis of the Early Twenties" (Ph.D. dissertation, 1966). On the Farm Bureau Federation and the McNary-Haugen plan see Gilbert Fite, *George N. Peek and the Fight for*

Farm Parity (Norman, Okla., 1954); Wesley McCune, *The Farm Bloc* (Garden City, N.Y., 1943); Grant McConnell, *The Decline of Agrarian Democracy* (Berkeley, Calif., 1953); and Steve Neal, *McNary of Oregon: A Political Biography* (Portland, Ore., 1985). Class conflict in the countryside is examined in David Montejano, *Race, Labor Repression, and Capitalist Agriculture: Notes from South Texas, 1920–1930* (Berkeley, Calif., 1977).

The social welfare programs of American business corporations are examined in Stuart D. Brandes, *American Welfare Capitalism, 1880–1940* (Chicago, 1976); and David Brody, "The Rise and Decline of Welfare Capitalism," in John Braeman, Robert H. Bremner, and David Brody, eds., *Change and Continuity in Twentieth Century America: The 1920s* (Columbus, Ohio, 1968). The best studies of Frederick W. Taylor and the impact of scientific management are Samuel Haber, *Efficiency and Uplift: Scientific Management in the Progressive Era, 1890–1920* (Chicago, 1964); Daniel Nelson, *Frederick W. Taylor and the Rise of Scientific Management* (Madison, Wis., 1980); and Bernard Doray, *From Taylorism to Fordism: A Rational Madness* (London, 1988).

The most comprehensive study of organized labor and the working class in the years before the Great Depression remains Irving Bernstein, *The Lean Years: A History of the American Worker, 1920–1933* (Boston, 1960), but it should be read along with David Montgomery, *The Fall of the House of Labor: The Workplace, the State, and the American Labor Activism, 1865–1925* (New York, 1987); and Mark Perlman, "Labor in Eclipse," in Braeman, Bremner, and Brody, eds., *Change and Continuity in Twentieth Century America: The 1920s.* For the American Federation of Labor in the post-Gompers era see also Craig Phelan, *William Green: Biography of a Labor Leader* (Albany, N.Y., 1989); and Melvyn Dubofsky and Warren Van Tine, *John L. Lewis: A Biography* (New York, 1977).

5. Wets, Drys, and Immigrants

The literature on the prohibition movement and the Volstead Act is extensive. I found most useful John J. Rumbarger, *Profits, Power, and Prohibition: Alcohol Reform and the Industrializing of America, 1800–1930* (Albany, N.Y., 1989); Jack S. Blocker, *American Temperance Movements: Cycles of Reform* (Boston, 1989); Joseph R. Gusfield, *Symbolic Crusade: Status Politics and the American Temperance Movement* (Urbana, Ill., 1963); Norman H. Clark, *Deliver Us from Evil: An Interpretation of American Prohibition* (New York, 1976); and Thomas Coffey, *The Long Thirst: Prohibition in America, 1920–1933* (New York, 1975). On the relationship of prohibition and the underworld see Evert S. Allen, *The Black Ships: Rumrunners of Prohibition* (Boston, 1979); Kenneth Allsop, *The Bootleggers: The Story of Chicago's Prohibition Era* (London, 1968); and John Kobler, *Capone: The Life and World of Al Capone* (New York, 1971).

The final triumph of immigration restriction in the 1920s and its consequences for the United States still awaits historical inquiry, but the place to begin is with John Higham's *Strangers in the Land: Patterns of American Nativism, 1860–1925* (New Brunswick, N.J., 1955). An important source is *Hearings: Restriction of Immigration,* House Committee on Immigration and Naturalization, 68 Cong., 1 Sess. (Washington, D.C., 1924). I also found helpful Michael C. LeMay, *From Open Door to Dutch Door: An Analysis of U.S. Immigration Policy Since 1820* (New York, 1987); and Kitty Calavita, *U.S. Immigration Law and the Control of Labor, 1820–1924* (London and Orlando, Fla., 1984). Contemporary debate is also found in Roy L. Garis, *Immigration Restriction: A Study of the Opposition to and Regulation of Immigration into the United States* (New York, 1927);

and Madison Grant, *The Passing of the Great Race; or the Racial Basis of European History* (New York, 1921).

6. One Nation, Divisible

The resurgence of the Ku Klux Klan in the early twentieth century has attracted a host of talented scholars. Among the more important book-length studies are Kenneth T. Jackson, *The Ku Klux Klan in the City, 1915–1930* (New York, 1967); and David M. Chalmers, *Hooded Americanism: The First Century of the Ku Klux Klan, 1865–1965* (Garden City, N.Y., 1965). Studies of the Klan's regional influence abound. Especially informative are two articles by David Horowitz, "Social Morality and Personal Revitalization: Oregon's Ku Klux Klan in the 1920s," *Oregon Historical Quarterly* 90 (Winter 1989), 365–84; and "The Klansman as Outsider: Ethnocultural Solidarity and Anti-Elitism in the Oregon Ku Klux Klan of the 1920s," *Pacific Northwest Quarterly* 80 (January 1989), 12–20. See also Charles C. Alexander, *The Ku Klux Klan in the Southwest* (Lexington, Ky., 1965); William D. Jenkins, *Steel Valley Klan: The Ku Klux Klan in Ohio's Mohoning Valley* (Kent, Ohio, 1990); Larry Gerlach, *Blazing Crosses in Zion: The Ku Klux Klan in Utah* (Logan, Utah, 1982); and Leonard J. Moore, "White Protestant Nationalism in the 1920s: The Ku Klux Klan in Indiana" (Ph.D. dissertation, 1985). The rise and fall of D. C. Stephenson is chronicled by M. William Lutholtz, *Grand Dragon: D. C. Stephenson and the Ku Klux Klan in Indiana* (West Lafayette, Ind., 1991). On Klan women see the pioneering work of Kim Blee, "Women in the 1920s Ku Klux Klan Movement," *Feminist Studies* 17 (Spring 1991), 57–77. Hugo Black and the Stephenson trial are treated in Virginia Van der Veer Hamilton, *Hugo Black: The Alabama Years* (Baton Rouge, 1972).

There is a rich literature on the Harlem Renaissance. Two insightful interpretations are David L. Lewis, *When Harlem Was in Vogue* (New York, 1981); and Nathan I. Huggins, *Harlem Renaissance* (New York, 1971). I also found useful Cary D. Wintz, *Black Culture and the Harlem Renaissance* (Houston, 1988); Houston Baker, *Modernism and the Harlem Renaissance* (Chicago, 1987); Tony Martin, *Literary Garveyism: Garvey, Black Arts, and the Harlem Renaissance* (Dover, Mass., 1983); and Martin B. Duberman, *Paul Robeson: A Biography* (New York, 1989). Important contemporary accounts can be found in Ara W. Bontemps, *The Harlem Renaissance Remembered* (New York, 1972); and Langston Hughes, *The Big Sea: An Autobiography* (New York, 1986).

Marcus Garvey and the Universal Negro Improvement Association received an initial full-length treatment in Edmund Cronon, *Black Moses: The Story of Marcus Garvey and the Universal Negro Improvement Association* (Madison, Wis., 1955), but this work should be supplemented with Tony Martin, *Race First: The Ideological and Organizational Struggles of Marcus Garvey and the Universal Negro Improvement Association* (Westport, Conn., 1976); Judith Stein, *The World of Marcus Garvey: Race and Class in Modern Society* (Baton Rouge, 1986); and Jeannette Smith-Irvin, ed., *Footsoldiers of the Universal Negro Improvement Association: Their Own Words* (Trenton, N.J., 1989). On the role of the federal government in the destruction of the UNIA see Theodore Kornweibel, ed., *Federal Surveillance of Afro-Americans, 1917–1925* (Frederick, Md., 1986).

Leslie H. Allen has compiled a documentary history of the Scopes trial, *Bryan and Darrow at Dayton: The Record and Documents of the "Bible-Evolution Trial"* (New York, 1967). The best narrative account remains Ray Ginger, *Six Days or Forever? Tennessee v. John Thomas Scopes* (Boston, 1958). See also Willard H. Smith, *The Social and Religious Thought of William Jennings Bryan* (Lawrence, Kan., 1975); Arthur Weinberg,

Clarence Darrow: A Sentimental Rebel (New York, 1980); and Garry Wills, *Under God: Religion and American Politics* (New York, 1991).

There are two recent excellent studies of fundamentalism during the period: Bruce B. Lawrence, *Defenders of God: The Fundamentalist Revolt Against the Modern Age* (San Francisco, 1989); and George M. Marsden, *Fundamentalism and American Culture: The Shaping of Twentieth Century Evangelicalism, 1870–1925* (New York, 1980). An earlier wide-ranging survey is Norman Furniss, *The Fundamentalist Controversy, 1918–1931* (New York, 1954). Other insights can be gleaned from Willard B. Gatewood, ed., *Controversy in the Twenties: Fundamentalism, Modernism, and Evolution* (Nashville, 1969). On Billy Sunday see William G. McLoughlin, *Billy Sunday Was His Real Name* (Chicago, 1955). On Aimee Semple McPherson see Robert Bahr, *Least of All Saints: The Story of Aimee Semple McPherson* (Englewood Cliffs, N.J., 1979); and Robert V. P. Steele, *Storming Heaven: The Lives and Turmoils of Minnie Kennedy and Aimee Semple McPherson* (New York, 1970).

7. Fortunes of Feminism

The past two decades have seen an explosion in historical writing about American women, with some of the best focused on the first half of the twentieth century. Students might begin with the following: Nancy Woloch, *Women and the American Experience* (New York, 1984), especially chapters 13–16; William H. Chafe, *The American Woman: Her Changing Social, Economic, and Political Roles, 1920–1970* (New York, 1972), especially part one; Glenda Riley, *Inventing the American Woman: A Perspective on Women's History* (Arlington Heights, Ill., 1986), chapters 7–8; and Nancy F. Cott, *The Grounding of Modern Feminism* (New Haven, Conn., 1987). I also found very useful Elaine Showalter, ed., *These Modern Women: Autobiographical Essays from the Twenties* (New York, 1989).

On the twentieth-century suffrage campaign see Aileen S. Kraditor, *The Ideas of the Woman Suffrage Movement, 1890–1920* (New York, 1965); Sally Hunter Graham, "Woodrow Wilson, Alice Paul, and the Woman Suffrage Movement," *Political Science Quarterly* 98 (Winter 1983–84), 665–80; Sharon H. Strom, "Leadership and Tactics in the American Woman Suffrage Movement: A New Perspective from Massachusetts," *Journal of American History* 63 (September 1975), 296–315; Jane Lewis, ed., *Before the Vote Was Won: Arguments for and Against Women's Suffrage* (New York, 1987). For a history of the League of Women Voters see Louise M. Young, *In the Public Interest: The League of Women Voters, 1920–1970* (New York, 1989).

On women and the postwar economy see Alice Kessler-Harris, *Out to Work: A History of Wage-earning Women in the United States* (New York, 1982); Maurine Weiner Greenwald, *Women, War, and Work: The Impact of World War I on Women Workers in the United States* (Westport, Conn., 1980); Philip S. Foner, *Women and the American Labor Movement: From World War I to the Present* (New York, 1980); Leslie W. Tentler, *Wage-earning Women: Industrial Work and Family Life in the United States, 1900–1930* (New York, 1979); Winifred D. Wandersee, *Women's Work and Family Values, 1920–1940* (Cambridge, Mass., 1981); and Patricia M. Hummer, *The Decade of Elusive Promise: Professional Women in the United States, 1920–1930* (Ann Arbor, Mich., 1979).

On Sheppard-Towner see Shelia Rothman, *Woman's Proper Place*, chapter 4; and Joseph B. Chepaitis, "The First Federal Social Welfare Measure: The Sheppard-Towner Maternity and Infancy Act, 1918–1932" (Ph.D. dissertation, 1972). On the Equal Rights Amendment and the Women's Party see Susan D. Becker, *The Origins of the Equal*

Rights Amendment: American Feminism Between the Wars (Westport, Conn., 1981); Peter Geidel, "The National Woman's Party and the Origins of the Equal Rights Amendment, 1920–1923," *Historian* 42 (August 1980), 557–82; and Christine A. Lunardini, *From Equal Suffrage to Equal Rights: Alice Paul and the National Woman's Party, 1910–1928* (New York, 1986). The life and work of Margaret Sanger and the birth control movement in America are discussed in David M. Kennedy, *Birth Control in America: The Career of Margaret Sanger* (New Haven, Conn., 1970); Linda Gordon, *Woman's Body, Woman's Right: A Social History of Birth Control in America* (New York, 1976); and Margaret Sanger, *An Autobiography* (New York, 1938).

Changing images of femininity and the commercialization of beauty are examined in Lois Banner, *American Beauty* (New York, 1983); and Billie Melman, *Women and the Popular Imagination in the Twenties: Flappers and Nymphs* (London, 1988). See also Kathy Peiss, "Mass-Culture and Social Divisions: The Case of the American Cosmetic Industry," *Movement Social,* (July–September 1990), 7–30; and Joseph Hansen, *Cosmetics, Fashion, and the Exploitation of Women* (New York, 1986). On the images of American women projected by Hollywood see Marjorie Rosen, *Popcorn Venus: Women, Movies and the American Dream* (New York, 1973); and Molly Haskell, *From Reverence to Rape: The Treatment of Women in the Movies* (New York, 1974).

The impact of Freud on American life and thought is traced in Hendrik M. Ruitenbeek, *Freud and America* (New York, 1966). See also Juliet Mitchell, *Psychoanalysis and Feminism* (New York, 1974). On marriage and divorce see Elaine Tyler May, *Great Expectations: Marriage and Divorce in Post-Victorian America* (Chicago, 1981).

8. Cult of Personalities

On the social construction of fame and celebrities see Richard Schickel, *Common Fame: The Culture of Celebrity* (London, 1985), and *Intimate Strangers: The Culture of Celebrity* (Garden City, N.Y., 1985); as well as Leo Braudy, *The Frenzy of Renown: Fame and Its History* (New York, 1986).

The career of James J. Walker is the focus of Gene Fowler, *Beau James: The Life and Times of Jimmy Walker* (New York, 1949); and George Walsh, *Gentleman Jimmy Walker: Mayor of the Jazz Age* (New York, 1974). On Huey Long the place to begin is with T. Harry Williams's biography, *Huey Long* (New York, 1969); and Allan P. Sindler, *Huey Long's Louisiana: State Politics, 1920–1952* (Baltimore, 1956). But Alan Brinkley has written the best single study of Long and American political culture in *Voices of Protest: Huey Long, Father Coughlin, and the Great Depression* (New York, 1982). For a more contemporary, scathing portrait see Harnett T. Kane, *Huey Long's Louisiana Hayride: The American Rehearsal for Dictatorship, 1928–1940* (New York, 1941).

On the mass media in the 1920s and 1930s see C. L. Covert and J. D. Stevens, eds., *Mass Media Between the Wars: Perceptions of Cultural Tension, 1918–1941* (Syracuse, N.Y., 1984). A superb study of the American cinema and social change is Lary May, *Screening Out the Past: The Birth of Mass Culture and the Motion Picture Industry* (New York, 1980). The literature on Chaplin is extensive. I found most helpful Charles J. Maland, *Chaplin and American Culture: The Evolution of a Star Image* (Princeton, N.J., 1989); Maurice Bessy, *Charlie Chaplin* (New York, 1985); David Robinson, *Chaplin: His Life and Art* (New York, 1985); Harry M. Geduld, *Chapliniana: A Commentary on Charlie Chaplin's 81 Movies* (Bloomington, Ind., 1987); and Isabel Quigly, *Charlie Chaplin: Early Comedies* (London, 1968). On the controversial Arbuckle trial see Leo Guild, *The Fatty Arbuckle Case* (New York, 1962); and Andy Edmonds, *Frame-Up! The Untold Story of Roscoe "Fatty" Arbuckle* (New York, 1991). There is not a modern, scholarly treatment of Will Hays, his office, and his code. But see Raymond Moley, *The Hays Office* (Indianapolis and New York, 1945); Will H. Hays, *Memoirs* (Garden City, N.Y., 1955); and Richard S. Randall, *Censorship of the Movies: The Social and Political Control of a Mass Medium* (Madison, Wis., 1968). On Valentino see Alexander Walker, *Rudolph Valentino* (New York, 1976); and Norman Mackenzie, *The Magic of Rudolph Valentino* (London, 1974).

The rise of big-time professional baseball is treated in Steven A. Reiss, *Touching Base: Professional Baseball and American Culture in the Progressive Era* (Westport, Conn., 1980). Eliot Asinof has written an excellent account of the White Sox and the 1919 World Series, *Eight Men Out: The Black Sox and the 1919 World Series* (New York, 1986). On Babe Ruth see Marshall Smelser, *The Life that Ruth Built: A Biography* (New York, 1975); Robert Smith, *Babe Ruth's America* (New York, 1974); and Ken Sobol, *Babe Ruth and the American Dream* (New York, 1974).

College football awaits scholarly investigation, but I found useful Tom Perrin, *Football: A College History* (Jefferson, N.C., 1987); Tim Cohane, *Great College Football Coaches of the Twenties and Thirties* (New Rochelle, N.Y., 1973); Reed Harris, *King Football: The Vulgarization of the American College* (New York, 1932); and Harold E. Grange, *The Red Grange Story* (New York, 1953).

Elliott J. Gorn has written an insightful study of the social transformation of boxing, *The Manly Art: Bare-Knuckle Prize Fighting in America* (Ithaca, N.Y., 1986). On the heavyweight title and the career of Jack Dempsey see Nat Fleischer, *The Heavyweight Championship: An Informal History of Heavyweight Boxing from 1719 to the Present Day* (New York, 1961), and *Jack Dempsey* (New Rochelle, N.Y., 1972). See also Randy Roberts, *Jack Dempsey: The Manassa Mauler* (Baton Rouge, 1979).

There are two excellent books on William Tilden: Frank Deford, *Big Bill Tilden: The Triumph and the Tragedy* (New York, 1976); and Arthur Voss, *Tilden and Tennis in the Twenties* (Troy, N.Y., 1985).

Over thirty years ago, John W. Ward wrote what remains the classic study of Lindbergh's flight and its impact on American life: "The Meaning of Lindbergh's Flight," *American Quarterly* 10 (1958), 3–16. But see also Kenneth S. Davis, *The Hero: Charles A. Lindbergh and the American Dream* (Garden City, N.Y., 1959); Walter S. Ross, *The Last Hero: Charles A. Lindbergh* (New York, 1968); and Brendan Gill, *Lindbergh Alone* (New York, 1977).

9. Lost Generation

On the general topic of intellectuals and American culture in the late nineteenth and early twentieth centuries see especially T. J. Jackson Lears, *No Place of Grace: Antimodernism and the Transformation of American Culture, 1880–1920* (New York, 1981); James B. Gilbert, *Work Without Salvation: America's Intellectuals and Industrial Alienation, 1880–1910* (Baltimore, 1977); Henry F. May, *The Discontent of the Intellectuals: A Problem of the Twenties* (Chicago, 1963); Christopher Lasch, *The New Radicalism in America (1889–1963): The Intellectual as a Social Type* (New York, 1965); Peter J. Conn, *The Divided Mind: Ideology and Imagination in America, 1898–1917* (New York, 1983); and Jack P. Diggins, *The American Left in the Twentieth Century* (New York, 1973).

The impact of World War I on European and American writers has been superbly analyzed in Paul Fussell, *The Great War and Modern Memory* (New York, 1975). See also Tim Cross, ed., *Lost Voices of World War I: An International Anthology of Writers, Poets and Playwrights* (London, 1988); the essay on Randolph Bourne in Lasch, *The New Radicalism in America*; and Randolph S. Bourne, *War and the Intellectuals: Essays, 1915–1919* (New York, 1964).

No one has yet written a better study of postwar literary trends than Frederick J. Hoffman, *The Twenties: American Writing in the Postwar Decade* (New York, 1949), which may be read along with Maxwell Geismar, *The Last of the Provincials: The American Novel, 1915–1925: H. L. Mencken, Sinclair Lewis, Willa Cather, Sherwood Anderson, and F. Scott Fitzgerald* (London, 1947); Malcolm Cowley, *After the Genteel Tradition: American Writers, 1910–1930* (Carbondale, Ill., 1964); Cowley, *The Second Flowering: Works and Days of the Lost Generation* (New York, 1973); and Cowley's memoir, *Exile's Return* (New York, 1934). Not to be missed as well are two books by Edmund Wilson, *The American Earthquake* (New York, 1958) and *The Shores of Light: A Literary Chronicle of the Twenties and Thirties* (New York, 1952). From the extensive scholarship on Hemingway and Fitzgerald I found most helpful Michael S. Reynolds, *Hemingway's First War: The Making of A Farewell to Arms* (Princeton, N.J., 1976); and Malcolm Cowley, *Fitzgerald and the Jazz Age* (New York, 1966).

The place to begin with Henry Adams is with *The Education of Henry Adams* (Washington, D.C., 1907); R. P. Blackmur, *Henry Adams* (New York, 1980); and David R. Contosta, *Henry Adams and the American Experiment* (Boston, 1980). For Joseph Wood Krutch see his *The Modern Temper: A Study and a Confession* (New York, 1929); and John D. Margolis, *Joseph Wood Krutch: A Writer's Life* (Knoxville, Tenn. 1980). On Lippmann see his *A Preface to Morals* (Boston, 1929); Larry L. Adams, *Walter Lippmann* (Boston, 1977); and Ronald Steel, *Walter Lippmann and the American Century* (Boston, 1980).

A good sample of Mencken's writing can be found in Edward L. Galligan, ed., *A Choice of Days: Essays from Happy Days, Newspaper Days, and Heathen Days* (New York, 1980); and William H. Nolte, ed., *H. L. Mencken's Smart Set Criticism* (Ithaca, N.Y., 1968). See also Charles A. Fecher, ed., *The Diary of H. L. Mencken* (New York, 1989). On the range of Mencken's interests and his impact on the nation's intellectual life in the 1920s see Vincent Fitzpatrick, *H. L. Mencken* (New York, 1989); Douglas C. Stenerson, ed., *Critical Essays on H. L. Mencken* (Boston, 1987); Charles Scruggs, *The Sage in Harlem: H. L. Mencken and the Black Writers of the 1920s* (Baltimore, 1984); and Fred C. Hobson, *Serpent in Eden: H. L. Mencken and the South* (Chapel Hill, N.C., 1974).

The case of Sacco and Vanzetti has generated more controversy than any other single criminal trial in American history. The brief for the Commonwealth of Massachusetts is set forth in Francis Russell, *Sacco and Vanzetti: The Case Resolved* (New York, 1986). The most compelling arguments on behalf of the two defendants are presented in two books by Herbert B. Ehrmann, *The Untried Case: The Sacco-Vanzetti and the Morelli Gang* (New York, 1933) and *The Case That Will Not Die: Commonwealth vs. Sacco and Vanzetti* (Boston, 1959), as well as in William Young and David E. Kaiser, *Postmortem: New Evidence in the Case of Sacco and Vanzetti* (Amherst, Mass., 1985). Important accounts are also found in Katherine Anne Porter, *The Never-ending Wrong* (Boston, 1977); John Dos Passos, *Facing the Chair: The Story of the Americanization of Two Foreign-born Workmen* (Boston, 1927); and Felix Frankfurter, *The Case of Sacco and Vanzetti: A Critical Analysis for Lawyers and Laymen* (Boston, 1927). I also found useful David Felix, *Protest: Sacco-Vanzetti and the Intellectuals* (Bloomington, Ind., 1965); and Paul Avrich, *Sacco and Vanzetti: The Anarchist Background* (Princeton, N.J., 1991).

10. Changing the Guard

The best general account of the 1928 presidential election can be found in David Burner, *The Politics of Provincialism: The Democratic Party in Transition, 1918–1932* (New York, 1967); and John D. Hicks, *Republican Ascendency, 1921–1933* (New York, 1960). These should be read along with Richard Hofstadter's penetrating essay "Could a Protestant Have Beaten Hoover in 1928?" *Reporter* 22 (March 17, 1960), 23–34; Paul A. Carter, "The Campaign of 1928 Reexamined: A Study in Political Folklore," *Wisconsin Magazine of History* 46 (Summer 1963), 259–68; and Samuel Lubell's classic study *The Future of American Politics* (New York, 1952).

The influence of ethnocultural voting patterns and especially anti-Catholicism in 1928 is reaffirmed in Ruth C. Silva, *Rum, Religion, and Votes: 1928 Reexamined* (University Park, Pa., 1962); and Allan J. Lichtman, *Prejudice and the Old Politics: The Presidential Election of 1928* (Chapel Hill, N.C., 1979). On the question of political realignment and the Lubell thesis see Arthur M. Schlesinger, Jr., and Fred L. Israel, eds., *History of American Presidential Elections, 1789–1968*, vol. 3 (New York, 1971); and especially Kenneth Allen, "Components of Electoral Evolution: Realignment in the United States, 1912–1940" (Ph.D. dissertation, 1988).

Al Smith's political career and gubernatorial years are examined in Oscar Handlin, *Al Smith and His America* (Boston, 1958); and Paula Eldot, *Governor Alfred E. Smith: The Politician as Reformer* (New York, 1983). His campaign speeches have been collected in *Campaign Addresses of Governor Alfred E. Smith* (Washington, D.C., 1929). On Hoover see Kent Schofield, "The Public Image of Herbert Hoover in the 1928 Campaign," *Mid-America* 51 (October 1969), 34–46; and Herbert Hoover, *The New Day: Campaign Speeches of Herbert Hoover, 1928* (Palo Alto, Calif., 1928).

11. Götterdämmerung

The most readable and lively account of the stock market collapse and its consequences remains John K. Galbraith, *The Great Crash* (Boston, 1955), but it should be supplemented with Barrie A. Wigmore, *The Crash and Its Aftermath: A History of Securities Markets in the United States, 1929–1933* (Westport, Conn., 1985); Harold Bierman, *The Great Myths of 1929 and the Lessons to be Learned* (New York, 1991); and Edward N. White, "The Stock Market Boom and Crash of 1929 Revisited," *Journal of Economic Perspectives* 4 (Spring 1990), 67–83.

Less technical but very entertaining are Gordon Thomas, *The Day the Bubble Burst: A Social History of the Wall Street Crash of 1929* (Garden City, N.Y., 1979); William K. Klingaman, *1929: The Year of the Great Crash* (New York, 1989); Warren Sloat, *1929: America Before the Crash* (New York, 1979); and Robert Sobel, *Panic on Wall Street: A Classic History of America's Financial Disasters with a New Exploration of the Crash of 1987* (New York, 1988).

The relationship of the market crash to the disintegration of the nation's banking system has generated a substantial literature, with most of it focused on the activities of the Federal Reserve Board after 1929 and whether its monetary policies "caused" the Great Depression. The classic monetarist argument can be found in Milton Friedman and Anna J. Schwartz, *A Monetary History of the United States* (Princeton, N.J., 1965), especially pp. 299–545. A rejoinder is presented in Peter Temin, *Did Monetary Forces Cause the Great Depression?* (New York, 1976). See also Benjamin Bernanke, "Non-Monetary Effects of the Financial Crisis in the Propagation of the Great Depression,"

American Economic Review 73 (1983), 257–76; Allan H. Meltzer, "Monetary and Other Explanations of the Start of the Great Depression," *Journal of Monetary Economics* 2 (1976), 455–71; and Eugene N. White, "A Reinterpretation of the Banking Crisis of 1930," *Journal of Economic History* 44 (1984), 119–38.

The Ponzi affair is discussed in Robert Sobel, *The Great Bull Market: Wall Street in the 1920s* (New York, 1968); Donald H.Dunn, *Ponzi! The Boston Swindler* (New York, 1975); and Isadore Barmash, *Great Business Disasters: Swindlers, Bunglers, and Frauds in American Industry* (Chicago, 1972). There is no first-rate history of land speculation and economic development in Florida during the 1920s, but see Theyre H. Weigall, *Boom in Florida* (London, 1931).

PART TWO

1. The Trials of Herbert Hoover

There are a number of excellent biographical studies of Herbert Hoover. I found most helpful George H. Nash, *The Life of Herbert Hoover: The Engineer, 1874–1914* (New York, 1983) and *The Life of Herbert Hoover: The Humanitarian, 1914–1917* (New York, 1988); David Burner, *Herbert Hoover: A Public Life* (New York, 1979); and Richard N. Smith, *An Uncommon Man: The Triumph of Herbert Hoover* (New York, 1984). These can be read with Hoover's own *The Memoirs of Herbert Hoover*, 3 vols. (New York, 1951–52).

Shorter interpretive books and essays that offer important insights into Hoover's philosophy and behavior are Joan Hoff Wilson, *Herbert Hoover: Forgotten Progressive* (Boston, 1975); Richard Hofstadter, "Herbert Hoover and the Crisis of American Individualism," in *The American Political Tradition and the Men Who Made It* (New York, 1948), pp. 281–314; Carl Degler, "The Ordeal of Herbert Hoover," *Yale Review* 52 (1963), 563–83; David Burner and Thomas R. West, "A Technocrat's Morality: Conservatism and Hoover the Engineer," in Stanley Elkins and Eric McKitrick, eds., *The Hofstader Aegis: A Memorial* (New York, 1974), pp. 235–56; William A. Williams, *Some Presidents: Wilson to Nixon* (New York, 1972), chapter 2; and Lee Nash, ed., *Understanding Herbert Hoover: Ten Perspectives* (Stanford, Calif., 1987). For a historiographical assessment of recent scholarly trends see Mark M. Dodge, ed., *Herbert Hoover and the Historians* (West Branch, Iowa, 1989); and Robert H. Zieger, "Herbert Hoover: A Reinterpretation," *American Historical Review* 81 (1976), 800–10. For criticism of much revisionist writing on Hoover see Arthur M. Schlesinger, Jr., "Hoover Makes a Comeback," *New York Review of Books* 8 (March 1979), 10.

The best general studies of Hoover's response to the economic crisis of 1929–33 are Albert U. Romasco, *The Poverty of Abundance: Hoover, the Nation, the Depression* (New York, 1965); Jordan A. Schwarz, *The Interregnum of Despair: Hoover, Congress, and the Depression* (Urbana, Ill., 1970); William J. Barber, *From New Era to New Deal: Herbert Hoover, the Economists, and American Economic Policy, 1921–1933* (New York, 1985); Martin L. Fausold and George T. Mazuzan, eds., *The Hoover Presidency: A Reappraisal* (Albany, N.Y., 1974); and Arthur M. Schlesinger, Jr., *The Crisis of the Old Order, 1919–1933* (Boston, 1957).

On the Hoover administration and the commercial banking system see Richard Stauffer, "The Bank Failures of 1930–1931," *Journal of Money, Credit and Banking* 13 (1981), 109–13; Susan Estabrook Kennedy, *The Banking Crisis of 1933* (Lexington, Ky., 1973), especially chapters 2–6; and James S. Olson, "The End of Voluntarism: Herbert Hoover and the National Credit Corporation," *Annals of Iowa* 41 (1972), 104–13. On agricultural policy and the Federal Farm Board see Martin L. Fausold, "President Hoover's Farm Policies, 1929–1933," *Agricultural History* 51 (1977), 362–77; David E. Hamilton, "From New Era to New Deal: American Farm Policy Between the Wars," in Lawrence Gelfand and Robert Neymeyer, eds., *Agricultural Distress and the Midwest: Past and Present* (Iowa City, Iowa, 1986), pp. 19–54; and Bernard M. Klass, "The Federal Farm Board and the Antecedents of the Agricultural Adjustment Act, 1929–1933," in Carl E. Krog and William R. Tanner, eds., *Herbert Hoover and the Republican Era: A Reconsideration* (Lanham, Md., 1984), pp. 191–219.

On the Hoover years and unemployment relief see Udo Sautter, "Government and Unemployment: The Use of Public Works Before the New Deal," *Journal of American History* 73 (1986), 59–86. On the tariff see Richard J. Snyder, "Hoover and the Hawley-Smoot Tariff: A View of Executive Leadership," *Annals of Iowa* 41 (1973), 1173–89. On the Reconstruction Finance Corporation see Gerald D. Nash, "Herbert Hoover and the Origins of the Reconstruction Finance Corporation," *Mississippi Valley Historical Review* 46 (1959), 455–68; and James S. Olson, *Herbert Hoover and the Reconstruction Finance Corporation, 1931–1933* (Ames, Iowa, 1977). There are three useful works on the Bonus March: Roger Daniels, *The Bonus March: An Episode of the Great Depression* (Westport, Conn., 1971); Donald J. Lisio, *The President and Protest: Hoover, Conspiracy, and the Bonus Riot* (Columbia, Mo., 1974); and Louis Liebovich, *Press Reaction to the Bonus March of 1932: A Reevaluation of the Impact of an American Tragedy* (Columbia, S.C., 1990).

Among the many excellent studies of Hoover's foreign policies I found most helpful Ethan L. Ellis, *Republican Foreign Policy, 1921–1933* (New Brunswick, N.J., 1968); Joan Hoff Wilson, *American Business and Foreign Policy, 1920–1933* (Lexington, Ky., 1971); Alexander DeConde, "Herbert Hoover and Foreign Policy: A Retrospective Assessment," in *Herbert Hoover Reassessed: Essays Commemorating the Fiftieth Anniversary of the Inauguration of Our Thirty-first President* (Washington, D.C., 1981), pp. 313–34; Selig Adler, "Hoover's Foreign Policy and the New Left," in Fausold and Mazusan, eds., *The Hoover Presidency*, pp. 153–63; Norman A. Graebner, "Hoover, Roosevelt and the Japanese," in Dorothy Borg and Shumpei Okamoto, eds., *Pearl Harbor as History: Japanese-American Relations, 1931–1941* (New York, 1973), pp. 25–52; Armin Rappaport, *Henry L. Stimson and Japan, 1931–1933* (Chicago, 1963); Frank Costigliola, *Awkward Dominion: American Economic, Political, and Cultural Relations with Europe, 1919–1933* (Ithaca, N.Y., 1984), Benjamin D. Rhodes, "Herbert Hoover and the War Debts, 1919–1933," *Prologue* 6 (1974), 130–44; and Earl R. Curry, *Hoover's Dominican Diplomacy and the Origins of the Good Neighbor Policy* (New York, 1979).

2. The Making of the President, 1932

There are a number of distinguished biographical studies of Franklin Roosevelt. I relied especially upon two volumes by Geoffrey C. Ward, *Before the Trumpet: Young Franklin Roosevelt, 1882–1905* (New York, 1985) and *A First-Class Temperament: The Emergence of Franklin Roosevelt* (New York, 1989), as well as two volumes by Frank Freidel, *Franklin D. Roosevelt: The Apprenticeship* (Boston, 1952) and *Franklin D. Roosevelt: The Ordeal* (Boston, 1954); Kenneth S. Davis, *FDR: The Beckoning of Destiny, 1882–1928* (New York, 1972); Nathan Miller, *FDR: An Intimate History* (Garden City,

N.Y., 1983); and James MacGregor Burns, *Roosevelt: The Lion and The Fox* (New York, 1956).

The definitive book on Eleanor Roosevelt and FDR is Joseph P. Lash, *Eleanor and Franklin* (New York, 1971), but see also James Roosevelt, *My Parents: A Different View* (Chicago, 1976); Elliott Roosevelt and James Brough, *Mother R: Eleanor Roosevelt's Untold Story* (New York, 1977); and Eleanor Roosevelt's own *This I Remember* (New York, 1949). Other aspects of their relationship are discussed in Alfred B. Rollins, Jr., *Roosevelt and Howe* (New York, 1972); James Roosevelt with Sidney Shalett, *Affectionately, F.D.R.: A Son's Story of a Lonely Man* (New York, 1959); Joseph P. Lash, *Love, Eleanor: Eleanor Roosevelt and Her Friends* (New York, 1982); and Doris Faber, *The Life of Lorena Hickok, E.R.'s Friend* (New York, 1980).

Roosevelt's gubernatorial years and his campaign for the presidency are treated in Frank Freidel, *Franklin D. Roosevelt: The Triumph* (Boston, 1956); Kenneth S. Davis, *FDR: The New York Years, 1928–1933* (New York, 1974); Arthur M. Schlesinger, Jr., *The Crisis of the Old Order* (Boston, 1957); and Elliot A. Rosen, *Hoover, Roosevelt and the Brains Trust: From Depression to New Deal* (New York, 1977). See also Samuel I. Rosenman, ed., *The Public Papers and Addresses of Franklin D. Roosevelt* (New York, 1938–50), especially vols. 1 and 2.

3. Launching the New Deal

In every chapter dealing with the impact of the Great Depression on American society, including both the Hoover and Roosevelt years, I relied upon collections of reminiscences and contemporary accounts about the 1930s. The most important works in this genre are Studs Terkel, *Hard Times: An Oral History of the Great Depression* (New York, 1970); Ann Banks, ed., *First-Person America* (New York, 1980); Richard Lowitt and Maurine Beasley, *One Third of a Nation: Lorena Hickok's Reports on the Great Depression* (Champaign, Ill., 1981); John H. Bauman and Thomas H. Coode, *In the Eye of the Great Depression: New Deal Reporters and the Agony of the American People* (DeKalb, Ill., 1988); Robert S. McElvaine, ed., *Down and Out in the Great Depression: Letters from the "Forgotten Man"* (Chapel Hill, N.C., 1983); Tom E. Terrill and Jerrold Hirsch, eds., *Such as Us: Southern Voices of the Thirties* (Chapel Hill, N.C., 1978); Alice and Staughton Lynd, *Rank and File: Personal Histories by Working-Class Organizers* (Boston, 1973); and Katie Louchheim, ed., *The Making of the New Deal: The Insiders Speak* (Cambridge, Mass., 1983).

Franklin Roosevelt and the New Deal continue to stir passionate feelings among historians comparable to the lively debates that swirled around them fifty years ago. The best one-volume study from a sympathetic but not uncritical liberal perspective remains William E. Leuchtenburg, *Franklin D. Roosevelt and the New Deal, 1932–1940* (New York, 1963), which should be read with his important article "The New Deal and the Analogue of War," in John Braeman, Robert Bremner, and Ron Walters, eds., *Change and Continuity in Twentieth-Century America* (Columbus, Ohio, 1964); and the two magisterial volumes by Arthur M. Schlesinger, Jr., *The Coming of the New Deal* (Boston, 1959) and *The Politics of Upheaval* (Boston, 1960).

The New Deal's defects from the point of view of the left are examined by Barton J. Bernstein, "The New Deal: The Conservative Achievements of Liberal Reform," in Barton J. Bernstein, ed., *Towards a New Past: Dissenting Essays in American History* (New York, 1968); Paul Conkin, *The New Deal* (New York, 1968); and Howard Zinn's introduction to *New Deal Thought* (Indianapolis, 1966). Economist Milton Friedman offered a blunt conservative critique in *Free to Choose: A Personal Statement* (New York, 1980). A cogent rebuttal to the New Deal's "New Left" critics in the 1960s can be found in Jerold S. Auerbach, "New Deal, Old Deal, or Raw Deal: Some Thoughts on New Left Historiography," *Journal of Southern History* 35 (1969), 18–30. Several recent studies stress the institutional constraints on the New Deal rather than its ideological limitations. See especially Theda Skocpol, "Political Response to Capitalist Crisis: Neo-Marxist Theories of the State and the Case of the New Deal," *Politics and Society* 10 (1980), 155–201; and Theda Skocpol and Kenneth Feingold, "State Capacity and Economic Intervention in the early New Deal," *Political Science Quarterly* 97 (1982), 255–79.

Several broad surveys successfully incorporate most of the recent literature on the New Deal and reach judicious conclusions about its achievements and failures. They are Robert S. McElvaine, *The Great Depression: America 1929–1941* (New York, 1984); Anthony J. Badger, *The New Deal: The Depression Years, 1933–40* (New York, 1989); and Steve Fraser and Gary Gerstle, eds., *The Rise and Fall of the New Deal Order, 1930–1980* (Princeton, N.J., 1989). An important analysis of the Great Depression in the United States, with a strong comparative flavor, is John A. Garraty, *The Great Depression* (San Diego, 1986).

On the Hundred Days, in addition to the books cited above, one should not ignore Frank Freidel, *Franklin D. Roosevelt: Launching the New Deal* (Boston, 1973); Raymond Moley, *After Seven Years: A Political Analysis of the New Deal* (New York, 1939); Bernard Sternsher, *Rexford Tugwell and the New Deal* (New Brunswick, N.J., 1964); and Kenneth S. Davis, *FDR: The New Deal Years, 1933–1937* (New York, 1979).

The New Deal's banking reforms are examined in detail by Susan Estabrook Kennedy, *The Banking Crisis of 1933* (Lexington, Ky., 1973); and Helen M. Burns, *The American Banking Community and New Deal Banking Reforms, 1933–1935* (Westport, Conn., 1974).

The broad impact of the Depression on American agriculture is treated by Gilbert C. Fite, *American Farmers: The New Majority* (Bloomington, Ind., 1981), especially chapter 2; and *Cotton Fields No More: Southern Agriculture, 1865–1980* (Lexington, Ky., 1984). The literature on the New Deal's agricultural programs, particularly the Triple A, is extensive. Among the more important works are William D. Rowley, *M.L. Wilson and the Campaign for the Domestic Allotment* (Lincoln, Neb., 1971); Van L. Perkins, *Crisis in Agriculture: The Agricultural Adjustment Administration and the New Deal, 1933* (Berkeley, Calif., 1969); Richard S. Kirkendall, *Social Scientists and Farm Politics in the Age of Roosevelt* (Columbia, Mo., 1967); Richard S. Kirkendall, "The New Deal and Agriculture," in John Braeman, Robert Bremner, and David Brody, eds., *The New Deal: The National Level* (Columbus, Ohio, 1975); Anthony Badger, *Prosperity Road: The New Deal, Tobacco, and North Carolina* (Chapel Hill, N.C., 1980); and Christiana M. Campbell, *The Farm Bureau and the New Deal: A Study in the Making of National Farm Policy, 1933–1940* (Urbana, Ill., 1962).

On the New Deal, the rural poor, and class conflict in the countryside see Paul L. Metz, *New Deal Policy and Southern Rural Poverty* (Baton Rouge, 1978); Donald Grubbs, *Cry from the Cotton: The Southern Tenant Farmers Union and the New Deal* (Chapel Hill, N.C., 1971); Pete Daniel, "The New Deal, Southern Agriculture and Economic Change," in James C. Cobb and Michael V. Namaroto, eds., *The New Deal and the South* (Jackson, Miss., 1984), pp. 37–61; Cletus E. Daniel, *Bitter Harvest: A History of California Farmworkers, 1870–1941* (Ithaca, N.Y., 1981); Donald Worster, *Dust Bowl: The Southern Plains in the 1930s* (New York, 1979); and Donald S. Holley, *Uncle Sam's*

Farmers: The New Deal Communities in the Lower Mississippi Valley (Urbana, Ill., 1975).

Early New Deal industrial policy and the NRA have likewise generated a rich historical literature. The place to begin is with Ellis W. Hawley, *The New Deal and the Problem of Monopoly* (Princeton, N.J., 1966); Hawley, "The New Deal and Business," in Braeman, Bremner, and Brody, eds., *The New Deal: The National Level*, pp. 50–82; Bernard Bellush, *The Failure of the NRA* (New York, 1975); Albert U. Romasco, *The Politics of Recovery: Roosevelt's New Deal* (New York, 1983); and Edward Berkowitz and Kim McQuaid, *Creating the Welfare State: The Political Economy of Twentieth Century Reform* (New York, 1980), especially pp. 78–86. See also Sidney Fine, *The Automobile Under the Blue Eagle: Labor, Management and the Automobile Manufacturing Code* (Ann Arbor, Mich., 1963); Leverett L. Lyon et al., *The National Recovery Administration: An Analysis and Appraisal* (New York, 1972); and Hugh S. Johnson, *The Blue Eagle from Egg to Earth* (Garden City, N.Y., 1935). James S. Olson has written the first comprehensive study of the New Deal's most successful long-term program to aid the private sector, *Saving Capitalism: The Reconstruction Finance Corporation and the New Deal* (Princeton, N.J., 1988).

On labor and the NRA see especially Robert H. Zieger, *American Workers, American Unions, 1920–1985* (Baltimore, 1985), pp. 26–61; David Brody, *Workers in Industrial America: Essays on the Twentieth Century Struggle* (New York, 1980), pp. 82–172; Fine, *The Automobile Under the Blue Eagle*, pp. 142–409; and James P. Johnson, *The Politics of Soft Coal: The Bituminous Industry from World War I Through the New Deal* (Urbana, Ill., 1979), pp. 166–93.

4. Critics Left, Critics Right

There is no general study of local economic and political responses to the Great Depression, but a plethora of works that focus upon social protests in various geographic regions by many social groups. Anthony Badger has summarized much of the recent research in "The New Deal and the Localities," in Rhodri Jeffrey-Jones and Bruce Collins, eds., *The Growth of Federal Power in American History* (Edinburgh, 1983), pp. 102–15. See also Jo Ann E. Argersinger, *Toward a New Deal in Baltimore: People and Government in the Great Depression* (Chapel Hill, N.C., 1988); John L. Shover, *Cornbelt Rebellion: The Farmers' Holiday Association* (Urbana, Ill., 1965); John W. Hevener, *Which Side Are You On? The Harlan County Coal Miners, 1931–39* (Urbana, Ill., 1978); Roger Keeran, *The Communist Party and the Auto Workers' Union* (Bloomington, Ind., 1980); Donald McCoy, *Angry Voices: Left-of-Center Politics in the New Deal Era* (Lawrence, Kan., 1958); Mark Naison, *Communists in Harlem During the Depression* (Urbana, Ill., 1983); Gary Gerstle, "The Mobilization of the Working-Class Community: The Independent Textile Union in Woonsocket, 1931–1947," *Radical History Review* 17 (1978), 161–72; Frances Fox Piven and Richard A. Cloward, *Poor People's Movements: Why They Succeed, How They Fail* (New York, 1977).

On the changing social-economic base of the Democratic Party and the growing influence of its Northern urban wing see John M. Allswang, *The New Deal and American Politics: A Study in Political Change* (New York, 1978); Gerald H. Gamm, *The Making of New Deal Democrats: Voting Behavior and Realignment in Boston, 1920–1940* (Chicago, 1989); Kristi Andersen, *The Creation of a Democratic Majority, 1928–1936* (Chicago, 1979); Mark I. Gelfand, *A Nation of Cities: The Federal Government and Urban America, 1933–1965* (New York, 1975); Bruce Stave, *The New Deal and the Last Hurrah: Pittsburgh Machine Politics* (Pittsburgh, 1970); and Joseph J. Huthmacher, *Senator Rob-*

ert F. Wagner and the Rise of Urban Liberalism (New York, 1971).

On state-level reform movements see John E. Miller, *Governor Philip La Follette, the Wisconsin Progressives and the New Deal* (Columbia, Mo., 1982); Millard L. Gieske, *Minnesota Farmer-Laborism: The Third Party Alternative* (Minneapolis, 1979); George H. Mayer, *The Political Career of Floyd B. Olson* (Minneapolis, 1951); Charles E. Larsen, "The EPIC Campaign of 1934," *Pacific Historical Review* 27 (Fall 1958), 127–47; and Upton Sinclair, *I, Candidate for Governor: And How I Got Licked* (Pasadena, Calif., 1934).

Alan Brinkley has written the best study of Huey Long and Father Coughlin, *Voices of Protest: Huey Long, Father Coughlin, and the Great Depression* (New York, 1982). Additional insight can be gleaned, however, from David H. Bennett, *Demagogues in the Depression: American Radicals and the Union Party, 1932–1936* (New Brunswick, N.J., 1969); and Charles J. Tull, *Father Coughlin and the New Deal* (Syracuse, N.Y., 1965). Bennett also provides an excellent account of Francis Townsend's movement, which can be supplemented with Jackson K. Putnam, *Old Age Politics in California: From Richardson to Reagan* (Stanford, Calif., 1970); and Abraham Holtzmann, *The Townsend Movement: A Political Study* (New York, 1963).

Conservative, pro-business opposition to the New Deal is assessed in George Wolfskill and James A. Hudson's study of the Liberty League, *All But the People: Franklin D. Roosevelt and His Critics, 1933–1939* (New York, 1969). Right-wing protest from a different source is treated in Leo Ribuffo, *The Old Christian Right: The Protestant Far Right from the Great Depression to the Cold War* (Philadelphia, 1983); and Raymond Swing, *Forerunners of American Fascism* (New York, 1935).

On the New Deal and the federal judiciary from 1933 to 1936 see Paul L. Murphy, *The Constitution in Crisis Times, 1918–1969* (New York, 1972), pp. 98–169; Peter H. Irons, *The New Deal Lawyers* (Princeton, 1982); and Michael E. Parrish, "The Hughes Court, the Great Depression, and the Historians," *The Historian* 40 (1975), 286–308. Richard A. Maidment has offered a defense of judicial behavior in "The New Deal Court Revisited," in Stephen W. Baskerville and Ralph Willett, eds., *Nothing Else to Fear: New Perspectives on America in the Thirties* (Manchester, U.K., 1985).

5. High Tide

A good overview of the second Hundred Days can be found in Arthur M. Schlesinger, *The Politics of Upheaval* (Boston, 1960), although most scholars now reject his sharp dichotomy between a "first" and a "second" New Deal in 1933–1936. On this debate see William H. Wilson, "The Two New Deals: A Valid Concept?" *The Historian* 28 (1966), 268–88; Anthony Badger, *The New Deal: The Depression Years* (New York, 1989), pp. 94–98; and Robert S. McElvaine, *The Great Depression: America, 1919–41* (New York, 1984), pp. 250–63.

On the Banking Act of 1935 and the emergence of Marriner Eccles, see Helen M. Burns, *The American Banking Community and New Deal Banking Reforms, 1933–1935* (Westport, Conn., 1974); John Morton Blum, *From the Morgenthau Diaries: Years of Crisis, 1928–1938* (Boston, 1959), pp. 297–358; and Eccles's own *Beckoning Frontiers: Public and Personal Recollections* (New York, 1951). Mark Leff has written a searching study of the New Deal's efforts to reform the nation's revenue laws, *The Limits of Symbolic Reform: The New Deal and Taxation, 1933–1939* (Cambridge, Mass., 1984). See also the classic studies by Herbert Stein, *The Fiscal Revolution in America* (Chicago,

1969), 6–168; and E. Cary Brown, "Fiscal Policy in the Thirties: A Reappraisal," *American Economic Review* 46 (1956), 857–79.

On the creation of the Securities and Exchange Commission and passage of the Public Utilities Holding Company Act see my two books *Securities Regulation and the New Deal* (New Haven, 1970) and *Felix Frankfurter and His Times: The Reform Years* (New York, 1982). Also Donald A. Ritchie, *James M. Landis: Dean of the Regulators* (Cambridge, Mass., 1980); and Philip J. Funigiello, *Toward a National Power Policy: The New Deal and the Electric Utility Industry, 1933–1941* (Pittsburgh, 1973).

No one has yet written a full-length study of either the Federal Emergency Relief Administration or the Works Progress Administration. But see two pioneering works by James T. Patterson, *America's Struggle Against Poverty, 1900–1980* (Cambridge, Mass., 1981) and *The Welfare State in America, 1930–1980* (British Association for American Studies, 1981); and William R. Brock, *Welfare, Democracy, and the New Deal* (Cambridge, Mass., 1988). There is, however, a first-rate account of the New Deal's initial work relief effort, Bonnie F. Schwartz's *The Civil Works Administration, 1933–1934: The Business of Emergency Employment in the New Deal* (Princeton, N.J., 1984), a good assessment of Harry Hopkins, and legions of books and articles that examine the impact of these New Deal programs at the state and local level. On Hopkins see George McJimsey, *Harry Hopkins* (Cambridge, Mass., 1987); and Searle F. Charles, *Minister of Relief: Harry Hopkins and the Depression* (Syracuse, N.Y., 1963). On FERA and the localities see Richard Lowitt and Maurice Beasley, eds., *One Third of a Nation: Lorena Hickok Reports on the Great Depression* (Urbana, Ill., 1981); James T. Patterson, *The New Deal and the States: Federalism in Transition* (Princeton, N.J., 1969); Robert E. Burton, "The New Deal in Oregon," and David J. Maurer, "Relief Problems and Politics in Ohio," both in John A. Braeman, Robert H. Bremner, and David Brody, eds., *The New Deal: The State and Local Levels* (Columbus, Ohio, 1975).

On the WPA and its various satellite programs see Donald S. Howard, *WPA and Federal Relief Policy* (New York, 1943); Barbara Blumberg, *The New Deal and the Unemployed: The View from New York City* (Lewisburg, Pa., 1977); William W. Bremner, "Along the American Way: The New Deal's Work Relief Program for the Unemployed," *Journal of American History* 42 (1975), 636–52; Jane DeHart Mathews, *The Federal Theatre, 1935–1939: Plays, Relief and Politics* (Princeton, N.J., 1967); Monte N. Penkower, *The Federal Writers' Project: A Study in Government Patronage of the Arts* (Urbana, Ill., 1977); Richard D. McKinzie, *The New Deal for Artists* (Princeton, N.J., 1973); Roy Rosenzweig and Bruce Melosh, "Government and the Arts: Voices from the New Deal Era," *Journal of American History* 77 (1990), 596–608; Jerre Mangione, *The Dream and the Deal: The Federal Writers' Project, 1935–1943* (New York, 1972); and John A. Salmond, *A Southern Rebel: The Life and Times of Aubrey Willis Williams, 1890–1965* (Chapel Hill, N.C., 1983).

The origins of social insurance in the United States, the passage of the 1935 law, and its early administration under the New Deal have all received extensive historical treatment. Among the most important works are Roy Lubove, *The Struggle for Social Security, 1900–1935* (Cambridge, Mass., 1968); William Graebner, *A History of Retirement: The Meaning and Function of an American Institution, 1885–1978* (New Haven, Conn., 1980); Edwin E. Witte, *The Development of the Social Security Act* (Madison, Wis., 1963); and Jerry Cates, *Insuring Inequality: Administrative Leadership in Social Security, 1935–1954* (Ann Arbor, Mich., 1982).

The struggles of American workers during the decade, the rise of the CIO, and the impact of the Wagner Act have produced a rich crop of historical writing, only a small fraction of which can be mentioned here. The place to begin is with Irving Bernstein, *The Turbulent Years: A History of the American Worker, 1933–1941* (Boston, 1969); Steve Fraser, "The 'Labor Question,' " in Steve Fraser and Gary Gerstle, *The Rise and Fall of the New Deal Order, 1930–1980* (Princeton, N.J., 1989), pp. 55–84; David Brody, "The Emergence of Mass Production Unionism" and "Reinterpreting the Labor History of the 1930s," in *Workers in Industrial America: Essays on the Twentieth Century Struggle* (New York, 1980); Bernard Sternsher, "Great Depression Labor Historiography in the 1970s: Middle Range Questions, Ethno-cultures and Levels of Generalization," *Reviews in American History* 11 (1983), 300–19; and Robert H. Zieger, *American Workers, American Unions, 1920–1985* (Baltimore, 1985).

The story of the Wagner Act is told in Joseph J. Huthmacher, *Senator Robert F. Wagner and the Rise of Urban Liberalism* (New York, 1971); and James A. Gross, *The Making of the National Labor Relations Board, 1933–1937* (Albany, N.Y., 1974). For a view more critical of the administration see Christopher L. Tomlins, *The State and the Unions: Labor Relations, Law and the Organized Labor Movement in America, 1880–1960* (Cambridge, Mass. 1985); and Rhonda F. Levine, *Class Struggle and the New Deal: Industrial Labor, Industrial Capital, and the State* (Lawrence, Kan., 1988). On John L. Lewis, the CIO, and the sit-down strikes see Melvyn Dubofsky and Warren Van Tine, *John L. Lewis: A Biography* (New York, 1977); Daniel Nelson, "Origins of the Sit-Down Era: Worker Militancy and Innovation, 1934–1938," *Labor History* 23 (1982), 198–225; Sidney Fine, *Sit-Down: The General Motors Strike of 1936–37* (Ann Arbor, Mich., 1969); and John Barnard, *Walter Reuther and the Rise of the Auto Workers* (Boston, 1983). The impact of the New Deal upon class relations in another key industry is told by James A. Hodges, *New Deal Labor Policy and the Southern Cotton Textile Industry, 1933–1941* (Knoxville, Tenn., 1986).

Roosevelt's 1936 campaign and reelection are covered in Schlesinger, *The Politics of Upheaval*; David Burner, *The Politics of Provincialism: The Democratic Party in Transition, 1928–1936* (New York, 1968); Kristi Andersen, *The Creation of a Democratic Majority, 1928–1936* (Chicago, 1979); and Donald R. McCoy, *Landon of Kansas* (Lawrence, Kan., 1966).

6. Deadlock

The Supreme Court's offensive against the New Deal and various state reform efforts is analyzed in my own "The Hughes Court, the Great Depression, and the Historians," *Historian* 40 (1975), 286–308. A more sympathetic perspective on Chief Justice Hughes and his colleagues can be found in Richard A. Maidment, "The New Deal Court Revisited," in Stephen W. Baskerville and Ralph Willett, eds., *Nothing Else to Fear: New Perspectives on America in the Thirties* (Manchester, U.K., 1985); and John Knox, "Some Comments on Chief Justice Hughes," *Yearbook of the Supreme Court Historical Society*, 1984.

William Leuchtenburg has written two articles that provide the best account of the court-packing scheme and its demise. See "The Origins of Franklin D. Roosevelt's 'Court-Packing' Plan," *Supreme Court Review*, 1966, pp. 352–99; and "Franklin D. Roosevelt's Supreme Court 'Packing' Plan," in Harold M. Hollingsworth, ed., *Essays on the New Deal* (Austin, Tex., 1969), pp. 69–115. A lively journalistic account can be found in Joseph Alsop and Turner Catledge, *The 168 Days* (Garden City, N.Y., 1938). See also Theresa A. Niedziela, "Franklin D. Roosevelt and the Supreme Court," *Presidential Studies*

Quarterly 6 (Fall 1976), 87–98. The opposition among FDR's progressive allies in the Congress is recounted in Ronald Feinman, *The Twilight of Progressivism: The Western Republican Senators and the New Deal* (Baltimore, 1981); Otis Graham, *Encore for Reform: The Old Progressives and the New Deal* (New York, 1967); and Richard A. Mulder, *The Insurgent Progressives in the United States Senate and the New Deal, 1933–39* (New York, 1979).

The causes and consequences of the "Roosevelt recession" in 1937 are analyzed in Mark Leff, *The Limits of Symbolic Reform: The New Deal and Taxation* (Cambridge, Mass., 1984), pp. 209–20. On the tug-of-war between fiscal conservatives and spenders see Dean L. May, *From New Deal to New Economics: An American Liberal Response to the Recession of 1937* (New York, 1981); and Robert M. Collins, *The Business Response to Keynes, 1924–1964* (New York, 1981), pp. 53–112.

The relationship between Keynes and the New Deal is explored by Stephen W. Baskerville, "Frankfurter, Keynes, and the Fight for Public Works," *Maryland History* 9 (1978), 1–16; John K. Galbraith, "How Keynes Came to America," in *Economics, Peace and Laughter* (Boston, 1971); and Richard P. Adelstein, " 'The Nation as an Economic Unit': Keynes, Roosevelt, and the Managerial Ideal," *Journal of American History* 78 (June 1991), 160–87.

The failure of FDR's executive reorganization plan and the rise of the conservative coalition in Congress has been the subject of several excellent studies. On the first see Richard Polenberg, *Reorganizing Roosevelt's Government: The Controversy over Executive Reorganization* (Cambridge, Mass., 1966); and Barry D. Karl, *Executive Reorganization and Reform in the New Deal* (Chicago, 1963). On the resurgence of conservatism see James T. Patterson, *Congressional Conservatism and the New Deal: The Growth of the Conservative Coalition in Congress, 1933–1939* (Lexington, Ky., 1967); and David L. Porter, *Congress and the Waning of the New Deal* (Port Washington, N.Y., 1980).

7. New Deals, Old Deals

On the broad issue of economic recovery during the 1930s see Albert U. Romasco, *The Politics of Recovery: Roosevelt's New Deal* (New York, 1983); Theodore Rosenof, *Dogma, Depression and the New Deal: The Debate of Political Leaders over Economic Recovery* (Port Washington, N.Y., 1975); and John A. Garraty, *The Great Depression* (San Diego, 1986), especially pp. 128–160. The persistence of unemployment is treated in Ben Bernanke, "Employment, Hours and Earnings in the Depression: An Analysis of Eight Manufacturing Industries," *American Economic Review* 76 (March 1986), 267–98. See also John A. Garraty, *Unemployment in History: Economic Thought and Public Policy* (New York, 1978).

On the political consequences of the New Deal and the forging of the new Democratic Party see John M. Allswang, *The New Deal and American Politics: A Study in Political Change* (New York, 1978); Samuel Lubell, *The Future of American Politics*, 3rd ed. (New York, 1965); Christopher G. Wye, "The New Deal and the Negro Community: Toward a Broader Conceptualization," *Journal of American History* 41 (1972), 621–39; and Gerald H. Gamm, *The Making of New Deal Democrats: Voting Behavior and Realignment in Boston, 1920–1940* (Chicago, 1989).

There are many excellent studies, collections of letters, and autobiographies of leading New Dealers. Those I found most useful included Joseph P. Lash, *Dealers and Dreamers: A New Look at the New Deal* (New York, 1988); Nelson L. Dawson, *Louis D. Brandeis, Felix Frankfurter and the New Deal* (Hamden, Conn., 1980); Michael E. Parrish, *Felix*

Frankfurter and His Times: The Reform Years (New York, 1982); Peter Irons, *The New Deal Lawyers* (Princeton, N.J., 1982); T. H. Watkins, *Righteous Pilgrim: The Life and Times of Harold L. Ickes, 1874–1952* (New York, 1990); Graham J. White and John Maze, *Harold Ickes of the New Deal: His Private Life and Public Career* (Cambridge, Mass., 1985); Harold Ickes, *The Secret Diaries of Harold L. Ickes,* 2 vols. (New York, 1953); Gene Gressley, *Voltaire and the Cowboy: The Letters of Thurman Arnold* (Boulder, Colo., 1977); Wilson D. Miscumble, "Thurman Arnold Goes to Washington: A Look at Anti-Trust Policy in the Later New Deal," *Business History Review* 56 (1982), 1–15; Kenneth R. Philp, *John Collier's Crusade for Indian Reform, 1920–1954* (Tucson, Ariz., 1977); John A. Salmond, *A Southern Rebel: The Life and Times of Aubrey Willis Williams, 1890–1965* (Chapel Hill, N.C., 1983); Susan Ware, *Partner and I: Molly Dewson, Feminism, and New Deal Politics* (New Haven, Conn., 1987); Robert A. Caro, *The Years of Lyndon Johnson* (New York, 1982); William O. Douglas, *Go East, Young Man: The Early Years* (New York, 1974); Robert E. Sherwood, *Roosevelt and Hopkins: An Intimate History* (New York, 1948); Joanne Bentley, *Hallie Flanagan: A Life in the American Theatre* (New York, 1988); Hallie Flanagan, *Arena* (New York, 1940); George Martin, *Madam Secretary: Frances Perkins* (Boston, 1976); Doris Faber, *The Life of Lorena Hickok: E.R.'s Friend* (New York, 1980); Carl E. Rollyson, *Nothing Ever Happens to the Brave: The Story of Martha Gellhorn* (New York, 1990); Martha Gellhorn, *The Trouble I've Seen* (New York, 1936).

There is a substantial and growing literature on American blacks during the Great Depression and the impact of the New Deal upon their lives. I found three books especially helpful: Raymond Wolters, *Negroes and the Great Depression: The Problem of Economic Recovery* (Westport, Conn., 1970); John B. Kirby, *Black Americans in the Roosevelt Era: Liberalism and Race* (Knoxville, Tenn., 1980); and Harvard Sitkoff, *A New Deal for Blacks: The Emergence of Civil Rights as a National Issue: The Depression Decade* (New York, 1978). On the role of blacks in the New Deal political coalition see Christopher R. Reed, "Black Chicago Political Realignment During the Great Depression and the New Deal," *Illinois Historical Journal* 78 (Winter 1985), 113–29; and Nancy Weiss, *Farewell to the Party of Lincoln: Black Politics in the Age of FDR* (Princeton, N.J., 1983). On grassroots protest see William Muraskin, "Black Nationalism and the Rise of Labor-Union Consciousness: The Harlem Boycott of 1934," *Labor History* (Summer 1972), pp. 117–32; Mark Naison, *Communists in Harlem During the Depression* (Urbana, Ill., 1983); and Nell Irwin Painter, *The Narrative of Hosea Hudson: His Life as a Negro Communist in the South* (Cambridge, Mass., 1979).

On black employment, families, and communities see in addition to Wolters, *Negroes and the Great Depression,* Wye, "The New Deal and the Negro Community: Toward a Broader Conceptualization"; as well as Lois R. Hembold, "Beyond the Family Economy: Black and White Working-Class Women During the Great Depression," *Feminist Studies* 13 (Fall 1987), 13–32; Beverly W. Jones, "Race, Sex, and Class: Black Female Tobacco Workers in Durham, North Carolina, 1920–1940, and the Development of the Female Consciousness," *Feminist Studies* 10 (Fall 1984), 176–87; and Kathryn L. Morgan, *Children of Strangers: The Stories of a Black Family* (Philadelphia, 1980). On the New Deal and racial violence in the South see Robert L. Zangrando, *The NAACP Crusade Against Lynching, 1909–1950* (Philadelphia, 1980).

On the career of Jesse Owens see William J. Baker, *Jesse Owens: An American Life* (New York, 1986). On Joe Louis see Chris Mead, *Champion—Joe Louis: Black Hero in White America* (New York, 1985); and Gerald Astor, ". . . And a Credit to His Race": The Hard Life and Times of Joseph Louis Barrow* (New York, 1974). Jervis Anderson has written an excellent biography, *A. Philip Randolph: A Biographical Portrait* (New York, 1973); and there are two good studies of his role in the labor movement and civil rights: William H. Harris, *Keeping the Faith: A. Philip Randolph, Milton P. Webster, and the Brotherhood of Sleeping Car Porters, 1925–37* (Urbana, Ill., 1977); and Paula F. Pfeffer, *A. Philip Randolph: Pioneer of the Civil Rights Movement* (Baton Rouge, 1990).

The historical literature on women, the Great Depression, and the New Deal is likewise very rich. Excellent overviews are provided by Alice Kessler-Harris, *Out of Work: A History of Wage-Earning Women in the United States* (New York, 1982), especially pp. 259–271; Lois Scharf, *To Work and to Wed: Female Employment, Feminism, and the Great Depression* (Westport, Conn., 1980); Winifred D. Wandersee, *Women's Work and Family Values, 1920–1940* (Cambridge, Mass., 1981); and three volumes by Susan Ware: *Beyond Suffrage: Women in the New Deal* (Cambridge, Mass., 1981), *American Women in the 1930s: Holding Their Own* (Boston, 1982), and *Partner and I: Molly Dewson, Feminism, and New Deal Politics* (New Haven, Conn., 1987).

I also found very helpful Sharon Hartman Strom, "Challenging Woman's Place: Feminism, the Left, and Industrial Unionism in the 1930s," *Feminists Studies* 9 (Summer 1983); Winifred D. Wandersee, "The Economics of Middle-Income Family Life: Working Women During the Great Depression," *Journal of American History* 65 (June 1978), 60–74; Maureen Honey, "Images of Women in *The Saturday Evening Post*, 1931–1936," *Journal of Popular Culture* 10 (Fall 1976), 352–58; Kathryn Weibel, *Mirror Mirror: Images of Women Reflected in Popular Culture* (New York, 1977); Jeanne Westin, *Making Do: How Women Survived the Depression* (Chicago, 1976); and Alison Bernstein, "A Mixed Record: The Political Enfranchisement of American Indian Women during the Indian New Deal," *Journal of the West* 23 (July 1984), 13–20.

I also found the following biographies and autobiographies quite useful: Joseph P. Lash, *Eleanor and Franklin* (New York, 1971); Eleanor Roosevelt, *This I Remember* (New York, 1949); Joseph P. Lash, *Love, Eleanor: Eleanor Roosevelt and Her Friends* (New York, 1982); Doris Faber, *The Life of Lorena Hickok: E. R.'s Friend* (New York, 1980); Eloise Greenfield, *Mary McLeod Bethune* (New York, 1977); Sara Alpern, *Freda Kirchwey: A Woman of the Nation* (Cambridge, Mass., 1987); Lela B. Costin, *Two Sisters for Social Justice: A Biography of Grace and Edith Abbott* (Urbana, Ill. 1983); Leslie Frewin, *The Late Mrs. Dorothy Parker* (New York, 1986); and Robert Coles, *Dorothy Day: A Radical Devotion* (Reading, Mass., 1987).

8. Best of Times, Worst of Times

In addition to the reminiscences and contemporary accounts noted earlier for chapter 3, I profited greatly from the insightful discussion about American values and the 1930s in Robert S. McElvaine, *The Great Depression: America, 1929–1941* (New York, 1984), pp. 196–223; Warren I. Susman's pathbreaking essays *Culture as History: The Transformation of American Society in the Twentieth Century* (New York, 1984); the now classic study by Robert S. and Helen M. Lynd *Middletown in Transition: A Study in Cultural Conflicts* (New York, 1937); Catherine L. Covert and John D. Stevens, eds., *Mass Media Between the Wars: Perceptions of Cultural Tension, 1918–1941* (Syracuse, N.Y., 1984); Frederick L. Allen, *Since Yesterday* (New York, 1940); Daniel Aaron and Robert Bendiner, eds., *The Strenuous Decade* (New York, 1970); Charles R. Hearn, *The American Dream in the Great Depression* (Westport, Conn., 1977); and Hadley Cantril and Mildred Strunk, eds., *Public Opinion, 1935–1946* (Princeton, N.J., 1951).

A number of books examine the Depression's impact upon American films and vice versa: Lewis Jacobs, *The Rise of the American Film* (New York, 1939); John Baxter, *Hollywood in the Thirties* (New York, 1968); Andrew Bergman, *We're in the Money: Depression America and Its Films* (New York, 1971); Robert Sklar, *Movie-Made America: A Social History of American Movies* (New York, 1975); and Nick Roddick, *A New Deal in Entertainment: Warner Brothers in the 1930s* (London, 1983).

9. Ordeal of the Intellectuals

Richard Pells has written the best one-volume survey of intellectual and cultural trends during the 1930s: *Radical Visions and American Dreams: Culture and Social Thought in the Depression Years* (New York, 1973), which can be read along with Douglas Tallack, *Twentieth-Century America: The Intellectual and Cultural Context* (London, 1991), especially pp. 145–212; and Paul Buhle, *Popular Culture in America* (Minneapolis, 1987). I also found two other surveys helpful: Robert Crunden, *From Self to Society, 1919–1941* (Englewood Cliffs, N.J., 1972); and R. Alan Lawson, *The Failure of Independent Liberalism, 1930–1941* (New York, 1971). The best survey of literary trends remains Alfred Kazin, *On Native Grounds: An Interpretation of Modern American Prose Literature* (New York, 1942).

On the Southern Agrarians see 12 Southerners, *I'll Take My Stand* (New York, 1930); Herbert Agar and Allen Tate, eds., *Who Owns America?* (Boston, 1936); and Richard H. King, *The Southern Renaissance: The Cultural Awakening of the American South, 1930–1955* (New York, 1980).

On the Communist Party and the decade's intellectual and literary life the place to begin is with Daniel Aaron, *Writers on the Left* (New York, 1961). Paul Buhle gives additional insight into the CP and the era in *Marxism in the United States: Remapping the History of the American Left* (New York, 1987). See also Harvey Klehr, *The Heyday of American Communism: The Depression Decade* (New York, 1984); Vivian Gornick, *The Romance of American Communism* (New York, 1977); and Theodore Draper, "American Communism Revisited," *New York Review of Books* 9 and 23 (May, June 1985). On the Popular Front and the anticommunist left see Frank Warren, *Liberals and Communism* (Bloomington, Ind., 1966); Alan M. Wald, *The New York Intellectuals: The Rise and Decline of the Anti-Stalinist Left from the 1930s to the 1980s* (Chapel Hill, N.C., 1987); James B. Gilbert, *Writers and Partisans: A History of Literary Radicalism in America* (New York, 1968); and Norman H. Pearson, "The Nazi-Soviet Pact and the End of the Dream," in Daniel Aaron, ed., *America in Crisis* (New York, 1952), pp. 327–48.

Among the large crop of memoirs, essays, and reminiscences from the era I found the following to be especially valuable: Malcolm Cowley, *The Dream of the Golden Mountains: Remembering the 1930s* (New York, 1980); Alfred Kazin, *Starting Out in the 1930s* (Boston, 1965); Matthew Josephson, *Infidel in the Temple* (New York, 1967); Edmund Wilson, *The American Jitters* (New York, 1932) and *Travels in Two Democracies* (New York, 1936); Louis Adamic, *My America* (New York, 1938); Harold Clurman, *The Fervent Years* (New York, 1945); and William Phillips, "What Happened in the 1930s," *Commentary* 34 (September 1962), 204–12.

In addition to the books on Hollywood and the 1930s noted in chapter 8, I relied here upon Robert B. Ray, *A Certain Tendency of the Hollywood Cinema, 1930–1980* (Princeton, N.J., 1985); Raymond Carney, *American Vision: The Films of Frank Capra* (Cambridge, Mass., 1988); and Peter Bogdanovich, *John Ford* (Berkeley, Calif., 1978).

On James Agee, Walker Evans, and the documentary genre see William Stott, *Documentary Expression and Thirties America* (New York, 1973); Lawrence Bergreen, *James*

Agee: A Life (New York, 1984); Ross Spears and Jude Cassidy, eds., *Agee: His Life Remembered* (New York, 1985); J. A. Ward, *American Silences: The Realism of James Agee, Walker Evans, and Edward Hopper* (Baton Rouge, 1985); and Walker Evans, *Walker Evans at Work* (New York, 1982). On Welles and the making of *Citizen Kane* see Ronald Gottesman, ed., *Focus on Citizen Kane* (Englewood Cliffs, N.J., 1971); and Pauline Kael's essay "Raising Kane," *New Yorker*, February 20, 1971, pp. 43–89, and February 27, 1971, pp. 44–81; Frank Brady, *Citizen Welles: A Biography of Orson Welles* (New York, 1989); and Peter Cowie, *A Ribbon of Dreams: The Cinema of Orson Welles* (New Brunswick, 1973).

10. Over There, Again and Epilogue

There are several notable attempts to survey the foreign relations of the United States during the 1930s. The most impressive is by Robert Dallek, *Franklin D. Roosevelt and American Foreign Policy* (New York, 1979). This should be supplemented with Robert Divine, *Illusion of Neutrality* (Chicago, 1962) and *The Reluctant Belligerent* (New York, 1965); William L. Langer and Everett S. Gleason, *The Challenge to Isolation* (New York, 1952); Lloyd C. Gardner, *Economic Aspects of New Deal Diplomacy* (Madison, Wis., 1964); Robert H. Ferrell, *American Diplomacy in the Great Depression* (New Haven, Conn., 1957); and Leonard P. Liggio and James J. Martin, eds., *Watershed of Empire: Essays on New Deal Foreign Policy* (Colorado Springs, Colo., 1976).

Key memoirs, diaries, and collections of letters include George W. Baer, ed., *A Question of Trust: The Origins of U.S.–Soviet Diplomatic Relations: The Memoirs of Loy W. Henderson* (Stanford, Calif., 1986); Beatrice B. Berle and Travis B. Jacobs, eds., *Navigating the Rapids, 1918–1971: From the Papers of Adolf A. Berle* (New York, 1973); Orville H. Bullitt, ed., *For the President, Personal and Secret: Correspondence Between Franklin D. Roosevelt and William C. Bullitt* (Boston, 1972); Nancy H. Hooker, ed., *The Moffat Papers: Selections from the Diplomatic Journals of J. Pierrepont Moffat, 1919–1943* (Cambridge, Mass., 1956); Cordell Hull, *The Memoirs of Cordell Hull*, 2 vols. (New York, 1948); George F. Kennan, *Memoirs, 1925–1950* (Boston, 1967); and Warren F. Kimball, ed., *Churchill and Roosevelt: The Complete Correspondence*, 3 vols. (Princeton, N.J. 1984).

On the collapse of the London Economic Conference and FDR's nationalism see Arthur M. Schlesinger, Jr., *The Coming of the New Deal* (Boston, 1959); and Jennette P. Nichols, "Roosevelt's Monetary Diplomacy in 1933," *American Historical Review* 56 (January 1951), 295–317. On the failure of the Geneva conference see Hugh R. Wilson, Jr., *Disarmament and the Cold War in the Thirties* (New York, 1963). On the battle over the World Court in the post–World War I era see Michael Dunne, *The United States and the World Court, 1920–1935* (New York, 1988). The evolution of the decade's neutrality legislation and the triumph of isolationism is traced in Wayne S. Cole, *Roosevelt and the Isolationists, 1932–45* (Lincoln, Neb., 1983); and Langer and Gleason, *The Challenge to Isolation*, pp. 13–51. See also John E. Wiltz, *In Search of Peace: The Senate Munitions Inquiry, 1934* (Baton Rouge, 1963).

U.S.–Soviet relations in the early Roosevelt years are covered in Robert P. Browder, *The Origins of Soviet-American Diplomacy* (Princeton, N.J., 1953); and Donald G. Bishop, *The Roosevelt-Litvinov Agreements: The American View* (Syracuse, N.Y. 1965). Cordell Hull's long battle for reciprocity can be viewed through his own *Memoirs* as well as William R. Allen, "Cordell Hull and the Defense of the Trade Agreements Program, 1934–1940," in Alexander DeConde, ed., *Isolation and Security* (Durham, N.C., 1957). The myth and reality of the Good Neighbor Policy are treated by Dick Steward, *Trade and Hemisphere: The Good Neighbor Policy and Reciprocal Trade* (Columbia, Mo., 1975); Bryce Wood, *The Making of the Good Neighbor Policy* (New York, 1961) and *Dismantling the Good Neighbor Policy* (Austin, Tex., 1985); Irwin Gellman, *Good Neighbor Diplomacy: United States Policies in Latin America, 1933–1945* (Baltimore and London, 1979); Gerald K. Haines, "Under Eagle's Wing: The Franklin Roosevelt Administration Forges an American Hemisphere," *Diplomatic History* 1 (Fall 1977), 373–88; and Walter LaFeber, *Inevitable Revolutions: The United States in Central America* (New York, 1984).

On the Spanish Civil War and America's response see Hugh Thomas, *The Spanish Civil War* (New York, 1961); Allen Guttman, *The Wound in the Heart: America and the Spanish Civil War* (New York, 1962); Arthur H. Landis, *Death in the Olive Groves: American Volunteers in the Spanish Civil War, 1936–1939* (New York, 1989); and Stanley Weintraub, *The Last Great Cause: The Intellectuals and the Spanish Civil War* (New York, 1968).

On the coming of World War II in Europe see Martin Gilbert, *Britain and Germany Between the Wars* (London, 1964); Patrick J. Hearden, *Roosevelt Confronts Hitler: America's Entry into World War II* (New York, 1987); Waldo Heinrichs, *Threshold of War: Franklin D. Roosevelt and American Entry into World War II* (New York, 1988); William L. Langer and Everett S. Gleason, *The Undeclared War, 1940–1941* (New York, 1953); Anthony Read and David Fisher, *The Deadly Embrace: Hitler, Stalin, and the Nazi-Soviet Pact, 1939–1941* (New York, 1988); David Reynolds, *The Creation of the Anglo-American Alliance, 1937–1941: A Study in Competitive Cooperation* (London, 1982); William Rock, *Chamberlain and Roosevelt* (Columbus, Ohio, 1988); Alan Dobson, *U.S. Wartime Aid to Britain, 1940–1946* (London, 1986); and Donald Cameron Watt, *How War Came: The Immediate Origins of the Second World War, 1938–1939* (New York, 1989).

On the U.S.–Japanese confrontation in Asia see James B. Crowley, "A New Deal for Japan and Asia: One Road to Pearl Harbor," in James B. Crowley, ed., *Modern East Asia: Essays in Interpretation* (New York, 1970); Jonathan G. Utley, *Going to War with Japan, 1937–1941* (Knoxville, Tenn., 1985); Dorothy Borg, *The United States and the Far Eastern Crisis of 1933–1938* (Cambridge, Mass., 1964); Michael Schaller, *The U.S. Crusade in China, 1938–1945* (New York, 1979); Christopher Thorne, *The Issue of War: States, Societies, and the Far Eastern Conflict of 1941–1945* (New York, 1985); Akira Iriye, *Power and Culture: The Japanese-American War, 1941–1945* (Cambridge, Mass., 1981); Herbert Feis, *The Road to Pearl Harbor: The Coming of the War Between the United States and Japan* (Princeton, N.J., 1953); and Roberta Wolstetter, *Pearl Harbor: Warning and Decision* (Stanford, Calif., 1962).

Credits

PHOTOGRAPH CREDITS

In all cases, the publisher has made every effort to contact all copyright holders. Should there be any oversight, we would be happy to update our information.

P. 9, Library of Congress; p. 17, Library of Congress; p. 19, Library of Congress; p. 21, Library of Congress; p. 32, Library of Congress; p. 36, Library of Congress; p. 40, Library of Congress; p. 42, AP/Wide World Photos; p. 44, Library of Congress; p. 50, Library of Congress; p. 55, National Archive; p. 59, Library of Congress; p. 63, National Archive; p. 68, Library of Congress; p. 73, National Archive; p. 77, Library of Congress; p. 79, Library of Congress; p. 84, Library of Congress; p. 101, The Bettmann Archive; p. 103, Library of Congress; p. 107, Chicago Historical Society; p. 118, National Archive; p. 123, Library of Congress; p. 125, Warder Collection; p. 128, The Bettmann Archive; p. 130, The Bettmann Archive; p. 132, Library of Congress; p. 133, The Bettmann Archive; p. 139, Library of Congress; p. 145, The Bettmann Archive; p. 148, Courtesy Henry T. Rockwell; p. 150, The Bettmann Archive; p. 151, Library of Congress; p. 163, The Bettmann Archive; p. 165, Library of Congress; p. 170, Library of Congress; p. 173, Culver Pictures, Inc.; p. 175, Library of Congress; p. 181, Library of Congress; p. 188, Springer/Bettmann Film Archive; p. 193, Library of Congress; p. 196, Library of Congress; p. 199, The Bettmann Archive; p. 202, Library of Congress; p. 205, Library of Congress; p. 213, The Bettmann Archive; p. 220, The Bettmann Archive; p. 222; The Bettmann Archive, p. 234, The Bettmann Archive; p. 242, National Archive; p. 255, Library of Congress; p. 256, National Archive; p. 261, N.Y. Daily News; p. 269, Warder Collection; p. 273, Franklin D. Roosevelt Library Collection; p. 276, Franklin D. Roosevelt Library Collection; p. 277, Franklin D. Roosevelt Library Collection; p. 287, The Bettmann Archive; p. 288, The Bettmann Archive; p. 297, National Archive; p. 299, Library of Congress; p. 306, Library of Congress; p. 314, Library of Congress; p. 315, Library of Congress; p. 324, Culver Pictures, Inc.; p. 327, AP/Wide World Photos; p. 332, National Archive; p. 336, National Archive; p. 338, Library of Congress; p. 350, Library of Congress; p. 358, Library of

Congress; p. 362, Library of Congress; p. 366, Collection of the Supreme Court of the United States; p. 368, Library of Congress; p. 371, National Archive; p. 375, Library of Congress; p. 384, The Bettmann Archive; p. 388, Library of Congress; p. 394, The Bettmann Archive; p. 396, AP/Wide World Photos; p. 399, United Press International; p. 407, Library of Congress; p. 411, The Bettmann Archive; p. 416, Margaret Bourke-White, Life Magazine © 1937 Time Inc; p. 419, Library of Congress; p. 429, Warder Collection; p. 430, Library of Congress; p. 432, Library of Congress; p. 433, Library of Congress; p. 435, Museum of Modern Art Film Stills Archive; p. 447, National Archive; p. 454, Library of Congress; p. 456, Library of Congress; p. 460, National Archive, p. 461, Library of Congress; p. 464, The Bettmann Archive; p. 468, AP/Wide World Photos; p. 469, AP/Wide World Photos; p. 474, Library of Congress; p. 476, AP/Wide World Photos.

TEXT CREDITS

Acknowledgment is made for permission to quote from the following works: *Hugh Selwyn Mauberley* excerpt is reprinted from *Personae*. © 1926 by Ezra Pound. Reprinted by permission of New Directions Publishing Corporation.
"Poem to a Dead Soldier" by Langston Hughes. Reproduced with permission from Harold Ober Associates Incorporated. Copyright © 1973 by Faith Berry.
"Buffalo Bill's" is reprinted from *Tulips & Chimneys* by E. E. Cummings, Edited by George James Firmage, by permission of Liveright Publishing Corporation. Copyright 1923, 1925 and renewed 1951 by E. E. Cummings. Copyright © 1973, 1976 by the Trustees for the E. E. Cummings Trust. Copyright © 1973, 1976 by George James Firmage.
"We'd Like to Thank You Herbert Hoover" from "Annie." Lyric by Martin Charnin. Music by Charles Strouse. © 1977 Edwin H. Morris & Company, a Division of MPL Communications, Inc. and Charles Strouse. All rights reserved. Reprinted by permission.
"Brother, Can You Spare a Dime?" Lyric by E. Y. Harburg, music by Jay Gorney. Copyright 1932 by Harms, Inc.

Index

Page numbers in *italics* refer to illustrations.